# MAGIC AND MAGICIANS IN THE GRECO-ROMAN WORLD

This absorbing work assembles an extraordinary range of evidence for the existence of sorcerers and sorceresses in the ancient world, and addresses the question of their identities and social origins.

From Greece in the fifth century BC, through Rome and Italy, to the Christian Roman Empire as far as the late seventh century AD, Professor Dickie shows the development of the concept of magic and the social and legal constraints placed on those seen as magicians.

The book provides a fascinating insight into the inaccessible margins of Greco-Roman life, exploring a world of wandering holy men and women, conjurors and wonder-workers, prostitutes, procuresses, charioteers and theatrical performers.

Compelling for its clarity and detail, this study is an indispensable resource for the study of ancient magic and society.

**Matthew W. Dickie** teaches at the University of Illinois at Chicago. He has written on envy and the Evil Eye, on the learned magician, on ancient erotic magic, and on the interpretation of ancient magical texts.

# MAGIC AND MAGICIANS IN THE GRECO-ROMAN WORLD

*Matthew W. Dickie*

Routledge
Taylor & Francis Group

LONDON AND NEW YORK

First published in hardback 2001 by Routledge

First published in paperback 2003
by Routledge
2 Park Square, Milton Park, Abingdon, Oxon, OX14 4RN

Simultaneously published in the USA and canada
by Routledge
270 Madison Ave, New York NY 10016

*Routledge is an imprint of the Taylor & Francis Group*

Transferred to Digital Printing 2006

Typeset in Baskerville by
RefineCatch Ltd, Bungay, Suffolk

*British Library Cataloguing in Publication data*
A catalogue record for this book is available from the British Library

*Library of Congress Cataloging in Publication data*

ISBN 0–415–31129–2

**Publisher's Note**

The publisher has gone to great lengths to ensure the quality
of this reprint but points out that some imperfections in the original
may be apparent

# CONTENTS

# PREFACE

This book had its origins in a footnote on the drunken old women mentioned by Athanasius and John Chrysostom who were summoned to houses to cure the sick by incantations and amulets. The footnote became an article on drunken old women as sorceresses in Classical and Late Antiquity. That expanded into an article on sorceresses in general. At that point I realized that sorceresses could not be treated satisfactorily on their own but needed to be looked at alongside male magic-workers. That meant a book, not an article. I hope that what began as an attempt to satisfy my own curiosity about a subject on which virtually nothing had been written will be of some use to others. Since the compass of the book is fairly wide, extending as it does from the fifth century BC to the seventh century AD, there will no doubt be references that I have missed. I thank my wife for her forbearance in putting up with a project that took rather longer to complete than had been expected and that was delayed by its author's natural indolence and the ease with which he could be distracted from his task. I should also like to record a particular debt to David Jordan, who has offered unstinting help and support in my stumbling efforts to understand ancient magic.

# ABBREVIATIONS

The abbreviations for classical authors are those given in the *Oxford Classical Dictionary*, 3rd edition (eds) Simon Hornblower and Anthony Spawforth, for Late Greek authors those found in *A Patristic Greek Lexicon*, (ed.) G.W.H. Lampe and for Late Latin authors those in *A Glossary of Later Latin to 600 AD*, (ed.) A. Souter. Besides these, the following abbreviations are used:

| | |
|---|---|
| *ACO* | *Acta conciliorum oecumenicorum*, (ed.) E. Schwartz, Berlin 1927–40 |
| *CCSL* | *Corpus Scriptorum Series Latina*, Turnholt |
| *CSEL* | *Corpus Scriptorum Ecclesiasticorum Latinorum*, Vienna |
| *DTAud* | Auguste Audollent, *Defixionum tabellae quotquot innotuerunt tam in graecis Orientis quam in totius Occidentis partibus praeter atticas in Corpore inscriptionum atticarum editas*, Paris, 1904 |
| *DTWü* | *IG* III (3) = *Appendix continens defixionum tabellas in attica regione repertas*, (ed.) Richard Wünsch, Berlin, 1897 |
| *GCS* | *Die Griechischen christlichen Schriftsteller der ersten drei Jahrhunderte*, Berlin |
| *KAR* | E. Ebeling, *Keilinschrifttexte aus Assur religiösen Inhalts*, Leipzig 1915, 1923 |
| Lauchert | F. Lauchert *Die Kanones der wichtigsten altkirchlichen Concilien nebst den apostolischen Kanones*, Freiburg i. B. and Leipzig, 1896 |
| *LSAM* | F. Sokolowski, *Lois sacrées de l'Asie Mineure*, Paris, 1955 |
| *PG* | *Patrologia Graeca*, (ed.) J.P. Migne, Paris, 1857–66 |
| *PGM* | *Papyri graecae magicae: Die griechischen Zauberpapyri*, (ed.) K. Preisendanz, rev. edn by A. Henrichs I-II, Stuttgart, 1973 |
| *PL* | *Patrologia Latina*, (ed.) J.P. Migne, Paris, 1844–64 |
| *PO* | *Patrologia Orientalis*, (eds) R. Graffan, F. Nau *et al.*, Paris, 1907 |
| *POxy* | *Oxyrhynchus Papyri*, London, 1898– |
| *RAC* | *Reallexikon für Antike und Christentum*, Stuttgart, 1941– |
| *RE* | *Realencyclopädie der klassischen Altertumswissenschaft*, (eds) A. Pauly, G. Wissowa and W. Kroll, Stuttgart, 1893–1980 |
| *SC* | *Sources chrétiennes* |
| *SEG* | *Supplementum Epigraphicum Graecum*, Leiden, 1923– |
| *SIG³* | *Sylloge Inscriptionum Graecarum*, 3rd edition, (ed.) W. Dittenberger, Leipzig, 1915–24 |
| *SupplMag* | *Supplementum Magicum* I–II, (eds) Robert W. Daniel and Franco Maltomini, *Abhandlungen der rheinisch-westfälischen Akademie der Wissenschaften, Sonderreihe Papyrologica Coloniensia* XVI, 1–2, Opladen, 1990 |

# INTRODUCTION

Much has been written on the techniques of magic-working in antiquity. Great advances have been made in the understanding of the way in which spells written on lead, papyrus or a sherd of pottery were composed, what kinds of formulae were employed in them, what symbols were inscribed on magical amulets and what manner of devices were worn to ward off evil forces. The belief systems that informed the practices of the more sophisticated and educated sorcerers of the ancient world have been studied, in particular their debt to Platonism and its strange offspring, Neopythagoreanism and Gnosticism. But little attention has been paid to the men and women who were believed by their contemporaries to be expert in magic or who themselves professed expertise.[1] There has been no study of who it was to whom men and women went for help, if they wanted to put a spell on someone, to have a spell taken off, to nullify the effects of an ominous dream or to have a child cured of some inexplicable illness by incantations and amulets. Nor has there been any comprehensive treatment of the educated men who in their fascination with magic made collections of magical lore or who engaged in magical rituals either to effect a union with the divine or with the more mundane goal of altering the course of nature. Nor yet again has the magic-working of the holy men who wandered from community to community been investigated.

This is somewhat surprising in the light of the current interest on the part of many historians in recapturing the lives and beliefs of the more humble inhabitants of the ancient world. It is even more surprising that the figure of the female magician has not attracted more attention from those who are interested in the history of women or in representations of the female in antiquity. Witches and sorcerers, who for the most part did not belong to the more elevated levels of society, would seem to be an obvious topic of research for those concerned with the down-trodden and the oppressed. What can be reconstructed of their lives is not especially edifying, but an examination of the careers of magicians and wise women does give us an entry to areas of life in Classical Antiquity and the Late Roman world to which it is otherwise hard to gain access. It also forces on our attention aspects of life to which we would

1

not in the normal course of events have directed our gaze. My predilection is for that kind of social history that tries to recapture something of the texture of past societies in all of their richness and diversity. The ancient historian does not have the archival resources that the historian of late eighteenth-century France can draw upon to illustrate the minutiae of low life. There are no police records preserved from antiquity. There is, accordingly, a limit to how complete a picture can be drawn of life in any period of Greco-Roman antiquity, but just because the picture can never be complete that is no reason for our ignoring aspects of it and for attempting only to write political or military history, or if we lose faith in these enterprises, for confining ourselves to recreating the ideology of some ancient social group.

There is, so far as I know, neither in the historical nor in the ethnographic literature a model for the sort of study undertaken here. Ethnographic studies do deal with witches and sorcerers and their place in the community, but they tend to concentrate their attention on a village or at most a few villages in societies that bear little resemblance to the societies of the Greek and Roman worlds. Such studies afford little help or guidance, however intrinsically interesting they may be, for someone trying to understand how witches and sorcerers fitted into the fabric of ancient society. With a few exceptions historians of Late Mediaeval and Early Modern Europe have little to say about who exactly it was to whom men and women resorted to have magic performed for them.[2] There is one main reason why most historians are not at all interested in the identity of those practising magic: the focus of their attention is on explaining why in some areas of Europe there was a high incidence of persons brought to trial for witchcraft and on the larger social forces that gave rise to prosecutions in these places and not in others. Because so many of the charges brought in witchcraft-trials and the confessions extracted are so patently fantastic, it is easy to lose sight of the fact that magic was practised and that there were those who pretended to an expertise in it. It is true that the real magic-workers in a community, the cunning folk in England and in France the *devins* and *devineresses*, may play a part in accounts of judicial prosecutions for witchcraft, either because of their rôle in witch-hunting or because the white magic they practised had led to the accusation that they also engaged in black magic, but they have not generally been thought worthy of a treatment in their own right.[3] Modern history, accordingly, offers little by way of a model for the study of the identity of sorcerers and sorceresses.

That said, it has to be admitted that there are historians who take the accusations of witchcraft made in Late Mediaeval and Early Modern Europe seriously and believe that what the judicial investigations uncovered were groups of men and women who did engage in witchcraft or something like it. These scholars are not primarily interested in the identity of those accused of witchcraft but in trying to show that what is taken to be witchcraft by outsiders is an ancient ritual practised from time immemorial.[4] Of the scholars who believe that there was an underlying reality to the prosecution of witches the best known is Margaret Murray, whose real field of expertise was Egyptology. In the 1920s she published a book, heavily influenced by Sir James Fraser's *The Golden Bough*, in which she argued that in Early Modern Europe groups of women were to be found engaging in a fertility-cult of great antiquity and that it was their existence that spawned the notion of covens of witches.[5] Murray based her case primarily on the records of Scottish judicial investigations of the sixteenth and seventeenth centuries and argued that the confessions given by those under indictment were not put into their mouths by the examining authorities but were accurate accounts of the meetings that they had attended. Murray's thesis won a surprising degree of acceptance, but has now been laid to rest, principally by Norman Cohn.[6] His detailed analysis of the way in which Murray built her case by suppressing the fantastic elements in the confessions extracted from the women makes it difficult to believe that there was any reality to the confessions.

A form of Murray's thesis has recently resurfaced in a new guise: Carlo Ginzburg has argued in his book on the Witches' Sabbath in Late Mediaeval and Early Modern Europe that there were groups of persons who came together to arouse themselves to an ecstatic state in which they believed they took leave of their bodies and made long journeys; he further maintains that these groups had their roots in the very ancient past in the shamanistic cults of Northern Asia.[7] Ginzburg complains in the introduction to the book that no attempt has been made by those historians who have written about the persecution of witches in that period to examine the world-picture of the men and women who were the subject of the persecutions.[8] Ginzburg would exempt himself from those strictures, since he has sought to recover the actual beliefs of some of those prosecuted.[9] That the bizarre stories recorded in the transcripts of the trials which Ginzburg has brought to the light of day are the authentic voice of the defendants and not the normal stereotyped confession created by the prompting of the inquisitor seems likely. It remains unclear what their further significance is, but it is exceedingly unlikely that the confessions describe shamanistic practices which have their roots in Eurasian pre-history.

So far as is known, magicians and sorceresses were seldom figures of great moment in the political life of ancient communities and virtually never wielded direct political power. It is, nonetheless, important to keep in mind that since they very often functioned as diviners, they came into contact with the rich and the mighty, who summoned or went to them to ask what the future might bring. The predictions they gave will in some cases have had an influence on the course of events. The examples of Mrs Reagan and her astrologer and of Mrs Clinton and the lady with leanings towards the occult with whom she communed are instructive here. The only known occasion on which a magician may be said to have exercised direct political power was Eunus, the Syrian holy man-cum-magician who led an uprising of slaves in

Sicily in the 130s BC and actually had coins minted with his portrait on them. Although their political significance may not have been great, magicians and sorceresses were nonetheless very much part of the fabric of most ancient communities and played a significant rôle in the domestic lives of many people, rich and poor, male and female. Finally, sorcerers in particular are of interest because, while they are almost certainly always present in cities of any size, they very often do not belong to the community. They represent a type of person not easily classified in the terms that are normally used to describe the different categories of person living within an ancient city, such as citizen, slave, resident alien. These are categories that we have inherited on the one hand from the Athenians and on the other from Roman Law. Not everyone present in an ancient city necessarily fitted easily into it. Vagabond is not a legal category, but many ancient magic workers are better described as vagabonds than as non-resident aliens or foreigners. They very often wandered from community to community, staying in a place until their credit was exhausted and they had to move on elsewhere. Their existence serves to remind us of the large floating element that existed within the population of many ancient cities. The origins and precise legal status of many magic-workers were necessarily obscure, even when they were more or less permanently domiciled in a city.

Witches and sorcerers also cut across social categories in the sense that they may have dealings with persons from very different backgrounds. They do not on the whole belong to the higher reaches of society, although in the Roman Empire there seem to have been a significant number of persons of a fairly exalted rank who possessed books of magical spells and who practised magic, presumably on their own behalf. Nor again do they belong to the very lowest strata of society, the slaves who worked in the mines and as agricultural labourers and herdsmen. From the point of view of contemporary observers they occupied the more debased regions of society: they were to be found in taverns and brothels, in the vicinity of the circus, at the crossroads or at the shrines of certain deities such as Isis; they belonged to a netherworld with whom contact was made, at least in the Roman Empire, through servants and clients.

This study will attempt to assemble the evidence for the existence of sorcerers and sorceresses and will at the same time try to address the question of their identity and social origins. There are a number of other questions that need to be asked. Were sorcerers more common at some times and places than their female counterparts or was the reverse true? Was there any differentiation between the sexes in the forms of magic practised? Were women consulted about some matters and men about others? Or did it also depend on the place in society and financial resources of a person as well as his or her sex whether he or she turned to a sorcerer or to a witch? Where were magicians to be found or encountered? How did people make contact with them? The nature of the evidence precludes definitive solutions to these questions.

4

There are nonetheless some pointers and it is possible to offer provisional answers.

The starting point of the study will be the beginning of the fifth century BC and it will end in AD 650. The starting point will be justified at greater length in the following chapter, where it will be argued that the concept of magic only came into existence in the Greek-speaking world in the fifth century BC. If magic was not a category of thought with which people operated until that date, it follows that there were really no magicians in the sixth and seventh centuries, although there were certainly persons who performed acts that would later be classified as sorcery. The Arab conquest of Palestine, Syria and then Egypt is a convenient point at which to bring the inquiry to its conclusion. The geographical scope of the study will at the beginning be confined to Greece and the Greek cities on the coast of Asia Minor and will then be extended over the larger Hellenistic World. From there it will pass to Rome and Italy and then to the Roman Empire.

I am conscious of not having been able to isolate particularly marked regional and chronological variations in the forms in which magic-workers came, or, at any rate, not as many of them as might be expected. That the cadre of persons from whom magicians were drawn should have remained largely unchanged over a period of almost a thousand years and that the indigenous traditions of an area should not have affected the behaviour of magicians in that region and the way in which they presented themselves defies belief. Yet these variations are on the whole difficult to document. In some areas and at some times, for instance, men may have played a larger rôle than women. It is very difficult to detect such differences. There is not much to be done about this, except to acknowledge that our sources have their shortcomings and that the pattern which emerges from them is almost certainly too homogeneous.

## Sources

The student of witchcraft in Early Modern Europe has the records of judicial proceedings on which to base his reconstruction; he has the references contemporaries make in their writings to those famed in their own day as wizards; in some cases he has the treatises written by these wizards. The anthropologist has his native informants and his own observations to work from. These sources of information are not without their drawbacks, but historians of antiquity can only envy the good fortune of historians of Early Modern Europe and anthropologists in having such rich resources at their command. The historian trying to recreate the world in which in Classical Antiquity sorcerers and witches operated does not possess court proceedings to work from. The closest he can come to such records are the vivid pictures of trials for sorcery in Rome in the first century AD with which the historian

Tacitus regales us, but a worked-up literary account of a trial and its background is a far cry from the transcript of an interrogation.

The historian of antiquity has for the most part to rely on imaginative literary accounts of the activities of witches and sorcerers. These begin in the fifth century. The Homeric epics, the *Iliad* and the *Odyssey* and Greek elegiac and lyric poetry of the seventh and sixth centuries BC must be excluded from consideration, since magic is not a category of thought that informs the thinking of the authors of these works. The pickings from the Athenian tragic poets of the fifth century BC, Aeschylus, Sophocles and Euripides, are thin, though not negligible. The fragments of Athenian Old Comedy and the plays of the one poet of that form of whom whole plays survive, Aristophanes, are disappointing in what they yield. Greek New Comedy is more helpful. There is even more to be gleaned from its Roman imitators, Plautus and Terence. When we move away from Athens to Hellenistic Alexandria, we encounter for the first time portrayals of magic-working and of sorceresses in action. These themes were not invented by the poets who lived and worked in Alexandria. There is nonetheless in the poets of this era a greater interest in portraying social reality. The accounts of low life in the Alexandrian poet of the first half of the third century BC, Theocritus, are a rich repository of information and one poem in particular sheds a good deal of light on the milieu in which sorcery was performed. His contemporary, Apollonius Rhodius in his *Argonautica*, portrays Medea, the princess from Colchis at the east end of the Black Sea who helps Jason gain the Golden Fleece, as a votary of the goddess Hecate and as an expert sorceress. It hardly needs to be said that there were no such women as Medea. The forms of sorcery that she is portrayed practising are nonetheless an indication of what sorceresses did.

Witches or wise women, though not sorcerers, play a considerable part in the Roman elegiac poets of the late first century BC, Tibullus, Propertius and Ovid. Their younger contemporary, Horace, describes the doings of witches with great verve in his *Epodes* and *Satires*. Vergil has less to offer on that subject, but does throw light on Roman attitudes to magic-working. It is particularly disappointing that the Epicurean poet of the Late Republic, Lucretius, though eager to free the minds of men from the fears that superstition engenders, has nothing to say about magic or its practitioners. Silver Latin epic, especially Lucan's poem on the Civil War, the *Pharsalia*, tells us more about the techniques of magic-working than it does about its actual practitioners. More helpful from that point of view are the epigrams of Martial, written in the early second century AD. There is much of interest in the two surviving Roman novels, the *Satyricon* of Petronius and Apuleius' *Metamorphoses*, which belong respectively to the time of Nero and to the second half of the second century AD.

The Greek novel, with the exception of a late example of the genre from the third or fourth century AD, Heliodorus' *Aethiopica*, does not have much to contribute. There are nonetheless rich seams to be mined in the *Aethiopica*.

The satirical writer of the late second century AD from Samosata in Syria, Lucian, although openly hostile to magic-working because of his Epicurean sympathies, deals frequently and at length with wise women and sorcerers and is an invaluable source of information. Philostratus' *Life of Apollonius of Tyana*, written around AD 220, deals with the wanderings and adventures of a holy man of the late first century AD from Cappadocia. It throws a good deal of light on the sort of figure who in the eyes of some men was a holy man and who to others was a sorcerer and magician.

Non-imaginative literature also has a contribution to make. History and more especially philosophy shed some light on the figure of the sorcerer. The great historians of the fifth century BC, Herodotus and Thucydides, make virtually no mention of magic. The subject was presumably below their dignity and in any case had little bearing on the events they described. Of Greek historians, most is to be gleaned from Diodorus Siculus, a universal historian of the late first century BC. There are passing references in the historians of the Roman Empire to the sorcerers and sorceresses with whom members of the senatorial class were accused of having had dealings, but the focus of the historian's attention is not on these lowly persons but on the fate of the grandees who consulted them. Plato has something to say about sorcerers in several of his dialogues, but particularly in the *Republic* and the *Laws*. Reference is made to them in the fifth- or early fourth-century Hippocratic tract, *On the Sacred Disease*. Plutarch, writing in the early second century AD, mentions them from time to time in his *Lives* and in the treatise *On Superstition*. We have only two forensic speeches dealing with accusations of witchcraft: one of them, Apuleius' *Apologia*, is generally thought to have been delivered, although not perhaps in exactly the form it now exists, while the other, the speech that Philostratus says Apollonius of Tyana would have given in his own defence, had not the Emperor Domitian acquitted him, is not believed by most scholars to be genuine. The subject of magic-working as such is almost wholly, though not entirely, absent from the corpus of Attic oratory of the fourth century BC. Demosthenes does, however, shed an oblique light on magic-working in Athens in the vivid description he provides of the part that he says his opponent Aeschines had played as an acolyte in initiation ceremonies into a private mystery-cult. The one substantial corpus of speeches in Latin, that of Cicero, has almost nothing to offer, although there is valuable information contained in the treatises of the same author on divination and on the nature of the divine. Pliny the Elder's encyclopaedic work on natural phenomena, the *Natural Histories*, which must have been written by AD 79, since its author perished as a result of the eruption of Vesuvius in that year, is an invaluable repository of information about the men, principally from the Hellenistic Period, who composed books consisting of collections of magical lore. With its help something of the world of the learned magician can be reconstructed. It also contains a brief history of magic, which tells us where magic was believed to have originated and how it had spread from its birthplace in Persia.

The epigraphic record does not on the whole have much to contribute to our understanding of the world of the witch and sorcerer. That was only to be expected. Inscriptions are by and large public records or public announcements. As such, they are unlikely to mention magic-workers. However much one might hope to find an inscription that dealt with measures to be taken against magic-working or that recorded police or judicial actions against magicians, it seems that with one exception the hope is not to be fulfilled, despite tantalizing reports of just such an inscription from the Hellenistic Period.[10] The lead tablets that record both the questions directed at the oracle of Zeus at Dodona and the answers given throw some light on the practitioners of magic-working in north-western Greece in the fourth century BC. The one branch of epigraphy that does make a considerable contribution to our understanding of ancient magic-working are the sheets of lead on which spells or curses were written. They enable us to reconstruct something of the groups within which magic particularly flourished and that produced many of its practitioners.

Much of the evidence from the Late Roman world bearing on the identity of witches and sorcerers is of a rather different order from anything that we possess from Classical Antiquity and presents its own peculiar problems of interpretation. The accounts that Ammianus Marcellinus gives of trials for witchcraft in the fourth century AD resemble those in Tacitus but in fact provide a richer mine of information. The sermons in which Church Fathers inveigh against Christians turning for help to those expert in magic are a particularly valuable resource. More is to be learned from them than from any other source about who it was people called upon when they needed someone skilled in magic, on what occasions they did so and also something of the rituals performed. They also tell us something about the social groups particularly devoted to magic-working. The lives of saints are another source that can be exploited with advantage. Finally, there are the proceedings of Church Councils, whether in Greek or Latin, or in Syriac translations of the Greek original. They are as close as we come to the transcripts of the judicial interrogations and trials that survive in the archives of Western Europe from the Late Middle Ages and the Early Modern Period.

On the face of it this is not a very impressive array of sources. It is certainly not such as to encourage the hope that the task of recovering the ancient reality will be an easy one. But quantity is not our only problem. There is also the matter of quality. What we should like to know but cannot determine is what sources of information were available to the authors upon whom we have to rely when they wrote about witches, sorcerers and the world in which they lived. In other words, did they really know what they were talking about? We assume that most authors were not themselves practising sorcerers, although there are those who believe that Lucan's account of magic-working betrays a rather too intimate knowledge of that subject. It does not, however, follow that because an author does not himself engage in witchcraft, he does not know those who did practise it and does not have a very good idea what they did. Literary influences will have certainly played a part in shaping ancient accounts of sorcery, but personal experience should not be discounted. Despite the pretensions of magicians to have access to arcane and secret knowledge, there was in fact nothing very arcane or secret about what they did. A good deal of magical lore circulated more or less surreptitiously in the form of magical handbooks and men and women will have known either from their own experience or at second-hand what went on in a magical ceremony. To the proposition that almost all accounts of ancient magic are written from the outside there is in all likelihood at least one exception, Apuleius' *Apologia*. Although Apuleius in the *Apologia* defends himself against a charge of sorcery he is, in the version of the speech that he has chosen to publish, sympathetic to the view that magic (*magia*) and philosophy, the latter a subject in which he openly professes to be engaged, are inextricably bound up.[11] The *Apologia*, then, arguably gives us entry into a world in which the borderline between philosophy and magic is blurred and one which is inhabited by highly-educated men who risked being charged by their enemies with practising *magia* or *veneficium*.

It would be fatuous to doubt that there were in most communities of any size in the Greek and Roman worlds people who practised magic. Their identities will have been widely known and what they did will have been no secret. There is no mystery in a Greek village or in Athens, for that matter, about whom it is to whom a mother should turn, if she feels her child has been bewitched. There are, of course, differences between Classical and Late Antiquity and the present. One does not now necessarily have to know where the woman expert in taking the Evil Eye off lives. All that is needed is that her telephone number should be known, since it is now possible to cure the effects of the Evil Eye over the phone. To be rather more precise, the phone line between the afflicted party and the woman performing the ritual that nullifies the influence of the Evil Eye has to remain open.

Let us consider the case of Theocritus, who is one of our most important sources of information for magic-working and magic-workers in the Early Hellenistic Period. He conjures up a vivid picture of a *demi-monde* in which a disappointed courtesan turns to sorcery to bring back her lover. It is reasonable to ask how accurate a portrait he gives or can give of a world in which we perhaps wrongly assume he had no part and of which he knew nothing. The strict segregation of rich and poor that exists in most cities of the modern western world has made scholars take it for granted that the same held good for the cities of the ancient world. It is an assumption that would have surprised some of our not too distant ancestors. Rome, Pompeii and Herculaneum provide us with an idea of how people lived in some ancient cities: the houses of the rich very often, especially if they were on a main thoroughfare, had commercial establishments incorporated in them; amongst these shops there would have been taverns and inns, centres in both the Greek and Roman worlds of prostitution.[12]

It does not follow, however, that because Theocritus had perforce a fairly intimate knowledge of low life, the picture he draws of the practice of witch-craft is an accurate one and is not based on or affected by stereotypes. Two points need to be made here: Theocritus would not have had to go out of his way to observe prostitutes and their world; and the stereotypes that shaped his vision of the lives of the prostitutes and flute-girls he describes may themselves reflect a general reality. Even more acute doubts are aroused by the picture of low life drawn by the Roman elegists and by Lucian in his *Dialogues of the Courtesans*. The influence of New Comedy on both of these literary forms does nothing to allay the suspicion in the reader that it is not reality pure and unadulterated which is being depicted.

In trying to recreate ancient realities, we have in general to come to terms with the degree to which in the texts that we read stereotypes or, as it is fashionable to call them now, representations, come between us and reality. The portrayal of magic-working on the part of women is at many removes from reality, if we are to believe those who have in the recent past written about representations of that subject in the ancient world. An attempt, for example, has been made to demonstrate that the literary portrayal of women engaged in erotic magic reverses what really happened. Its author contends that the female magic-workers portrayed in literature are entirely the products of the fevered male imagination, which through a process of denial transferred to women actions that were in reality performed by men; the truth is to be found not in literature but in the recipes in the magical formularies recorded on papyrus; they take it for granted that it will be men who will make use of the spells they contain.[13] The figure of the hideous old crone as witch is also explained away. It is argued that such frightening hags as Empousa, Lamia and Mormo reflect the hatred and fear inspired in men by old women as a category; behind the hatred and fear lies the feeling on the part of men that old women are persons who have fulfilled their natural functions in life and who have now no proper rôle to play.[14] To this basic explanation further refinements have been added: the fear and hatred aroused by old women was reinforced by the memory men had of the frightening women who had been the most important figures in their upbringing; and the ominous magical powers with which old women were credited came from the part that they played in the 'mysterious, disturbing and polluting events surrounding life and death'.[15]

There is very little, if anything, in such explanations that is not questionable. They tell us more about the preoccupations of their authors than they do about the past. The categorical assertions that men feared and hated old women and that they did so because, in their view, old women had no proper part to play in life, can hardly be sustained. Nor are the psychological propositions advanced as self-evident truths invulnerable to attack. The Freudian notion of denial and transference is particularly suspect. The propositions that the notion of denial and transference is used to explain are in any case questionable. It is by no means true that only women are portrayed practising erotic magic; nor do the formularies assume that only men will use their spells. There is a further problem with explanations in which the figure of the witch as hideous old crone is invoked in the underlying assumption that there was in the Greek mind a figure exactly comparable to the frightening figure of the witch, *hexe* or *strega*, as she is imagined in the modern western world: that is, a malign old hag who performs extraordinary supernatural feats. It is not that such creatures do not exist in the Greek and Roman imagination, but to the extent that they do, they belong to the category of the demonic and semi-divine and not to the human. The woman who performs sorcery, the *pharmakis*, *pharmakeutria* in Greek-speaking lands and the *saga* or *venefica* in the Latin West, is for the most part by no means as sinister and terrifying a figure as our witch, nor does she inhabit some wild and deserted space, but is to be found living amongst other more or less ordinary persons in the poorer quarters of ancient towns and cities.

To return to the more general question of getting behind the stereotype in ancient literature to the reality it conceals or distorts, we can either renounce the attempt as hopeless and confine ourselves to the not very demanding task of recording ancient representations or tackle the problem. It is a very much more difficult and dangerous undertaking to make sense of the ancient evidence than it is to opt out of the fight and to allow ourselves to succumb to the nihilism of an ill-understood and internally incoherent philosophical position, which on the one hand would deny that a text can ever draw a picture of reality not in thrall to forces beyond the control of its author, but which at the same time reserves for its proponents a privileged and independent standpoint from which to comment on the dependence and frailty of others. What has immunized the critic against the false consciousness that afflicts everyone else is a mystery.

There is nonetheless a very real difficulty about reconstructing the world of the ancient witch or sorcerer when what we have to work from is largely the literature of the imagination. That there is certain consistency to the portrayal of the sorceress could mean that she was in fact generally a poor old woman, perhaps a former prostitute and now a procuress, and was very often tipsy. It could also mean that the sorceress in literature conforms to a stereotype. If that is true, it has to be asked what gave rise to the stereotype, since it can hardly have been concocted out of thin air. The obvious, though not the only, answer is that the literary figure of the sorceress has its roots in a type of women with which men and women were thoroughly familiar.

There is a source of information about magic-working that is not obviously vulnerable to the criticism to which a purely literary text is exposed. It tends to corroborate the picture of the rôle played in particular by women in sorcery that can be constructed from imaginative pagan literature. The homilies of John Chrysostom, Clement of Alexandria's *Paedagogus*, and to a lesser extent the writings of Basil the Great and of Athanasius suggest that the sorceress existed in Antioch and Constantinople in the late fourth century and in Alexandria in the late second and fourth centuries in a milieu remarkably similar to the one that we can recreate from the novel, the love-elegy, Horace's epodes, Herodas and New Comedy. This body of writing gives us a picture of the low life quite as vivid as anything to be found in Petronius and Apuleius.

It is, in sum, an exceedingly difficult task to track down the magicians of Classical Antiquity and of the Late Roman world. They are relatively seldom the primary focus of attention in our literary or historical sources. At best they receive passing mention. Nor again do they make anything but the most fleeting appearances in the epigraphical and papyrological record. Traces of their existence are indeed hard to find. It is customary for scholars, after making depreciatory remarks about the sources with which they have to work, to announce that there is still a ray of hope and that the darkness can be illuminated. The ray of light as often as not comes from cross-cultural comparisons. It is not one that will illuminate this study. I have read about magic-working in other cultures, sometimes with interest, but often with dismay at the conceptual confusion inherent in the account of the ethnographer. Any faint hope that I may have had that such studies might help me fill in the many gaps in the picture I have tried to draw has been abandoned.

There is every reason to think that conditions in most of the societies studied are or were sufficiently different to render any sort of cross-cultural comparison largely meaningless. There is also the very real danger in using such studies that we may be putting our trust in an analysis of witchcraft which has itself been influenced by the preconceptions entertained by modern Western man about the nature of magic. That means in effect that a notion or category which has its roots in Greece and Rome is being used in the investigation of a society in which it has no place. It is not then a very sensible procedure to reconstruct the lives of magic-workers in Roman Egypt on the basis of pictures of non-Western societies drawn by anthropologists unable to see the society they are studying except in the categories they have inherited from Greco-Roman Antiquity. There is no particular reason to believe that these categories have universal application and are an accurate representation of phenomena to be found in every culture.

## Terms for witches and sorcerers

Something needs to be said at this point about the fairly wide array of terms employed in Greek and Latin to denote witches and sorcerers. In Greek, they may be called, if male, *epodoi* or *epaoidoi* (sing. *epodos*), *goetes* (sing. *goes*), *magoi* (sing. *magos*) and *pharmakeis* (sing. *pharmakeus*), and, when female, *pharmakides* (sing. *pharmakis*) or *pharmakeutriai* (sing. *pharmakeutria*) and less commonly *goetides* (sing. *goetis*). Sometimes also the masculine forms *goetes* and *magoi* are used for female practitioners. The craft practised by *goetes* is known as *goeteia*, while the transitive verb used to refer to the effect of that activity is *goeteuein* or in an intensive form, *ekgoeteuein*. The craft practised by *magoi* is *mageia* or *mageutike* (*techne*) and the verb used to refer to their actions *mageuein*. As for *pharmakeis* the craft they follow is *pharmakeia*; the transitive verb used to refer to the effects of their activities is *pharmakeuein*. In Latin, sorcerers are *magi* (sing. *magus*) or *venefici* (sing. *veneficus*) when male, and *cantatrices* (sing. *cantatrix*), *sagae* (sing. *saga*) or *veneficae* (sing. *venefica*) when female. Although these terms have very different origins, they come to be used interchangeably to refer to the same people.

It is natural and tempting to suppose that there was originally a distinction in meaning between *goes* and *magos*, and *goes* and *magos* as against *pharmakeus*, and that these were names for different kinds of magical specialists. It has indeed been argued that *goetes* were originally shamans, who in an ecstatic state conveyed the spirits of the dead on their perilous journey to the other side. That hypothesis rests on the etymological link between the masculine noun *goes* and the verb *goan*, 'to utter a cry of lamentation over the dead'.[16] That the substantive *goes* does derive from the verb *goan* can hardly be doubted.[17] If *goes* originally designated a shaman who conveyed the souls of the dead to the great beyond, it has to be said that very little trace of the original meaning is to be found in the way in which the word is used in the literature of Classical Greece, although some of those called *goetes* undoubtedly did induce in themselves the trances characteristic of shamans. While it may readily be conceded that Greek magicians did on occasion go into shaman-like trances, it does not follow that the practices of Northern Asian shamans had made their way into the Greek world by means of the contacts that Greeks in the Black Sea had had with Scythian shamans. There is little secure evidence for the existence of shamans in Northern Asia in antiquity and no evidence for the transfer of shamanistic practices from Asia to Greece.[18]

There are indeed simpler explanations of the derivation of *goes* from *goan*. The most straightforward of these is that magicians came to be called *goetes* because of the cries and incantations they characteristically uttered.[19] Since the verb *goan* and its cognates are used specifically as cries of lamentation, it might just be that originally *goes* was a term applied to one who summoned up the dead with an incantation in which there was a strong element of lamentation.[20] Support for that suggestion has been found in the Byzantine lexicon dating to the end of the tenth century AD called the Suda, where the practice of being a *goes*, *goeteia* is defined as the summoning up of corpses.[21] The trouble with that explanation is there is no evidence that *goetes* originally specialized in summoning up the dead. As for the entry in the Suda, it can be used neither as testimony to the original function of the *goes* nor to actual Greek usage. It has to be looked at in its context, which is an attempt at making a distinction amongst *mageia*, *goeteia* and *pharmakeia* by showing that they refer to different kinds of magic-working. The distinction is artificial and runs contrary to Greek usage and in the case of *goeteia* rests on the etymological link with the word used of lamentations for the dead. The testimony of the Suda has, accordingly, no independent authority. It has also been suggested that *goetes* have the name they do since the ill they inflicted on others caused those unfortunates to lament.[22] This etymology is unnecessarily convoluted and rests on a view of Greco-Roman magic as essentially harmful. There is no reason to suppose that *goes* was originally applied only to those who practised what we would call black magic. It should not, furthermore, be assumed that our distinction between white and black magic was one that would have meant much to ancient man.

In the case of the word *magos* it might be expected, because it is a loan-word from Persian, where it is employed to refer to a fire-priest, that it would be used in a sense reflecting its origins.[23] That expectation is borne out to some extent: the word continues to be used of the exponents of Zoroastrianism; at some point in the fifth century BC it comes to be a term for a magician; and from the Hellenistic Period on it is applied to persons from the East and not only Persians who were believed to have been authoritative sources of magical knowledge. It has been suggested that some time after the middle of the sixth century BC the Greeks settled on the seaboard of Asia Minor became familiar with members of the Median priestly caste of Magi driven westwards by the defeat that their people had suffered at the hands of the Persian leader, Cyrus.[24] This is an interesting and attractive hypothesis, but there is unfortunately no secure evidence to sustain it. It is nonetheless the case that a hypothesis along these lines is needed to explain the adoption by the Greeks of the Persian term *magos* to mean not a fire-priest but a magician, often with the implication that the credentials of the person referred to were not entirely trustworthy and that his good faith was in doubt. That the term was originally spread by displaced persons who made a living from performing rituals supposed to be efficacious in curing ills and solving problems and who laid claim to Eastern wisdom to bolster their authority is not unlikely and is in accord with certain other indications.

To call a man an *epodos*, which means literally 'one who sings over' or 'one who directs song at something', does not mean that the man in question engaged in a specialized form of magic-working in which incantations were more than usually important. It is a fair guess, nonetheless, that the *epodos* was not originally a magician, but a man who specialized primarily in singing over persons afflicted with various physical ills to cure them of the ill or at any rate to alleviate their suffering. Despite their name, *pharmakeis* and *pharmakides* did not confine their activities to the use of drugs or poisons (*pharmaka*), although they too will have had their origins in persons expert in *pharmaka* and in the allied calling of the cutting of roots (*rhizotomia*).

To sum up, although there are indications that *goetes*, *epodoi*, *magoi* and *pharmakeis* originally pursued quite distinct callings, there is no indication

14

when the terms are first encountered in the fifth century that they refer to specialized forms of magic. The terms seem, so far as their denotation goes, to be interchangeable. Although in practice there were inevitably those who specialized in particular aspects of magic-working, their specialization is on the whole not reflected in the words used to refer to them. That generalization needs some qualification. Those who specialized in creating illusions tend to be called *goetes*. It may well be that there is some difference in the emotional charge associated with these words and that to call someone a *goes* is more insulting than to call him a *magos* and that *goes* carries a stronger suggestion of fraudulent behaviour. The assertion of the lexicographer of the second century AD, Phrynichus, that *goes* is more Attic than *magos*, is worth noting at this point.[25] The observation is to some extent borne out by the frequency with which *goes* is used in contrast to *magos*, but it tells us nothing about the meaning of the terms, and it may be that all that lies behind the comment is an awareness on the part of Phrynichus or his source that *magos* is a loan-word from the Persian and not properly Greek. It nonetheless looks as if Phrynichus assumed that *goes* and *magos* were synonyms.

In Latin, it is equally impossible, for the most part, to assign separate spheres of activity to *magi* and *venefici*. Poisoners and sorcerers are, however, both encompassed under the terms *veneficae* and *venefici*, as indeed they are in Greek with *pharmakeis* and *pharmakides*. We know too little about the activities of *cantatrices* to assert with any confidence that they did very much more than intone incantations and perform a few simple rituals in conjunction with their incantations. The evidence such as it is suggests that *cantatrix* denotes a woman practising a much narrower and more modest range of activities than an *epodos* in Greek practised. The women called *sagae* are, however, credited with doing everything from nullifying the effects of a bad dream to summoning up ghosts. There seems to have been a general assumption that to be a *saga* a woman had to be old.

Magic-working was very often practised in conjunction with some related calling. Persons who presented themselves as expert in one or the other of the sub-specialities of the craft of the seer, for whom the most general term in Greek is a *mantis*, frequently turned their hand to magic-working. Similarly, the creators of illusions or conjurors, who in Greek are called *planoi* and *thaumatopoioi*, will very often have been indistinguishable from *goetes*. There were no very strict lines of demarcation here.

Not all of those on whom the appellations *goes*, *magos*, *pharmakis*, *saga* or *venefica* were bestowed will have been given these names because they offered their expertise in sorcery to others. All of these words, with the apparent exception of *saga*, were employed as terms of abuse. Many women, for instance, who had formed a relationship with a man, whether licit or illicit, will have been denounced as *pharmakides* or *veneficae* by distressed relatives or disappointed rivals unwilling to acknowledge that the charms of the woman had won over the man. Men might also be denounced as sorcerers for the same reason or because they had enjoyed success greater than seemed natural. The use of the terms to denounce people will not be the main focus of our attention, because it tells us very little about who witches and sorcerers were.

Finally, a word on the English terms employed in this book to refer to magic-workers. In anthropological writing of the recent past a distinction of the following form is made between witches and sorcerers: witches are persons possessed of an inherent but disordered power; sorcerers are persons who engage in magical manipulations to achieve their ends. The distinction goes back to Evans-Pritchard (1937). Whatever the merits of the distinction may be for describing the way in which the tribe Evans-Pritchard was studying, the Azande, viewed the world in which they lived, it is certainly not in accord with normal English usage and cannot safely be applied universally. The distinction has no application in the Greek and Roman worlds and does not reflect Greek or Roman ways of looking at magic-workers. The terms magician, magic-worker, sorcerer and wizard will be used indifferently to refer to the persons whom the ancients called *goetes*, *magoi* or *venefici*. For the sake of brevity and convenience the women who are consulted or summoned because of their reputed skill in magic-working will generally be referred to as witches or sorceresses. It would in some ways be better to use the older and less loaded English term 'wise woman' to refer to many of them. 'Wise woman' suggests simply a woman who knows how to cure certain conditions, whether physical or psychic, and whom persons consult about the source of the ills afflicting them. Since the term is no longer in current use and has a distinctly antiquarian ring to it, I have had to make do with 'witch' and 'sorceress'. By these terms I mean only a woman who is believed to be skilled in magic-working. Sorceress and witch will, accordingly, have to encompass not only women, such as Lucan's Erichtho, who perform the spectacular and horrific feat of revivifying corpses and the women who transform themselves into birds or animals to prey on children or the dead, but also the poor old woman called in to take off the Evil Eye or to cure a child of sickness. It is above all the last with whom we are concerned.

## Terms for the activities pursued by sorcerers

The most general term in Greek for the procedures pursued by magicians is *manganeia* or *manganeuma*. The term does not seem to be related to the words *magos* and *mageia*, but there is reason to suspect that most Greeks will have believed that *manganeumata* took their name from their being performed by *magoi*.[26] The spells that sorcerers deploy against others are in Greek called *pharmaka* (sing. *pharmakon*) and in Latin *veneficia* (sing. *veneficium*). In both languages the word is used of poisons, magical substances, spells in which substances and words are used, and perhaps magical formulae. The word *philtron* in Greek and its calque in Latin *amatorium* have roughly the same range of meanings, although the terms are restricted to the procedures used in erotic magic.[27] A *philtron* or *amatorium* may then be the substance put into food or drink to induce sexual passion in the person who consumes or imbibes it; it may be a substance used as an ointment; it may be a substance accompanied by a spoken spell designed to elicit the same result; and it may be a spoken spell intended to provoke sexual desire.

The term used for the special form of words uttered by the sorcerer to effect his purposes is in Greek an *epaoide*, very often contracted into *epode*, and in Latin an *incantamentum* or a *carmen*. The simplex of the forms *epode* and *incantamentum* is also found in poetry: in Greek *aoide* and in Latin *cantus*. Since the terms suggest a form of singing, it is to be imagined that the *epodai* were originally always sung and it is indeed the case that the earliest instances of the genre are in hexametric verse.

There is a further form of spell that must have been very much part of the stock-in-trade of many magicians. It is the spell very often now called a binding-spell. Spells of this form were very often written on thin beaten-out sheets of lead, which were then generally rolled up and in Greek times pierced by a nail, before they were deposited in a recent grave or in the sanctuary of a deity whose sphere of activity was the Underworld. In later times they were placed in wells or in the vicinity of the place in which their intended victims either lived or conducted their activities. Such spells directed at charioteers have been found, for example, in hippodromes. The older name for what is the common surviving form of spells of this class is a curse-tablet. The Greek for these spells is *katadeseis* or *katadesmoi*, terms that literally mean 'a means of binding down'. They take their name from the use to which the lead tablets were originally put, which was to impose constraints on the activities of an opponent. Curse-tablets were employed, for instance, to inhibit an opponent speaking in court. The earliest surviving lead tablets have been found in Selinus on the south-west coast of Sicily.[28] They are to be dated to the early fifth century and come either from a cemetery or from the sanctuary of Demeter Malophoros.

The original function of *katadeseis* and *katadesmoi* may have been to impose constraints on an opponent, but by the fourth century BC, if not earlier, spells intended to inflict harm on enemies rather than just impose temporary constraints on them are denominated *katadeseis* or *katadesmoi*.[29] By the middle of the fourth century BC lead tablets were used not only to constrain and harm enemies, but in erotic magic to secure the affections of another.[30]

In Latin, the verbs *defigere* and *devovere* are employed to denominate the process of employing a curse-tablet against an opponent. *Defigere* refers to the fixing or binding down of the victim symbolized in the piercing of a rolled-up sheet of lead by a nail; it is presumably an attempt at rendering in Latin the Greek verb that gives rise to the nominal forms *katadeseis* and *katadesmoi*, namely, *katadein*. *Devovere*, on the other hand, is used of prayer consigning victims to the gods of the Underworld.

# 1

# THE FORMATION AND NATURE
# OF THE GREEK CONCEPT
# OF MAGIC

To devote the first chapter of a book on magicians in the Greek and Roman worlds to a discussion of the concept of magic with which the Greeks operated and which the Romans inherited from them requires explanation and justification. There will be those who feel that such preliminaries can be dispensed with, since they are largely irrelevant to the real business in hand. These are feelings with which I can sympathize, since my own reactions on coming across yet another attempt at defining the notion of magic is dismay combined with a sense of foreboding.

Anxious examinations of the nature of magic and of its relationship to on the one hand religion and on the other to science abound in the literature of anthropology.[1] Discussions of the nature of magic have very often been motivated by the desire to provide a definition of the notion that will hold good for all cultures and that will at the same time explain what it is that all procedures thought of as magical have in common. Such enterprises are doomed to failure on two scores: firstly, they do not give sufficient recognition to the fact that the notion of magic is the product of a particular set of historical circumstances in Ancient Greece and that the concept of magic in Judaeo-Christian cultures is the direct offspring of that notion; secondly, all such attempts at capturing the peculiar nature of magic make the mistaken assumption that all concepts have at their heart a core or essence.

Let us begin with the assumption that magic is a universal notion and not one that is culturally specific.[2] In a general work on social anthropology written towards the end of his career, the distinguished anthropologist Sir Edmund Leach, confronted with the problem of applying the concepts of magic, religion and ritual to societies that seemed to him to lack these notions, was moved to write of magic:

> As for magic, which readers of Fraser's *The Golden Bough* might suppose to lie at the very centre of the anthropologist's interests, after a lifetime's career as a professional anthropologist, I have almost reached the conclusion that the word has no meaning whatsoever.[3]

It was specifically the realization that the notion of magic is not a universal one and may, accordingly, have little or no place in the description of the conduct of societies lacking any such concept that prompted Leach to write in these terms.

The realization that the concept of magic as opposed to religion has no application in many non-Western societies has led some scholars to suggest that the notions should not be employed in the study of societies in whose thinking they play no part. Critics of this persuasion would argue that applying the notions of religion and magic to societies that lack these categories is tantamount to projecting our own parochial prejudices and attitudes onto these societies.[4] What such critics are in essence proposing is that societies should be described in the categories that they themselves employ; alien notions should not be used to explain their thinking. That is a point of view with which many students of Greece and Rome will be sympathetic, since for a good many years now classicists have consciously attempted to understand the Greeks and the Romans in their own terms. In the study of Greek popular morality, for instance, there is now widespread agreement that it is necessary to understand Greek thinking from within and not to impose our own categories on it. What aroused admiration in a fifth-century Greek and what moved him to moral indignation would not provoke the same feelings in most modern Western men. The rather different moral outlook of the Greek is not to be captured if we do not attempt to look at the world in the way he did. What seemed important to him does not seem important to us, but it is nonetheless possible by paying careful attention to what he says to recreate some of his world.

There will be those who object that it is impossible for someone from an alien culture to look at a culture other than his own in quite the way that a person born within the culture does, since he will be unable to free himself from the presuppositions that he brings with him from his own culture.[5] There is no doubt a good deal of truth in the objection, but it does not follow that it is by definition impossible, as has been suggested, for a stranger to understand an alien society from within. All that follows is that it is a difficult enterprise. There is no overwhelming reason, accordingly, to abandon the attempt to see the world through the eyes of the members of the society studied, even though our own preconceptions and prejudices may from time to time affect our judgment and understanding. That is to say, the emic approach to the study of culture should not be abandoned in favour of the etic.[6] That said, it has to be granted that there are some situations in which it would be crippling to confine our descriptions of an alien culture to the categories that the culture examined has at its disposal. In discussing medical matters, it is necessary to translate, so far as that is possible, the understanding of the society studied into modern terms. Where there is no understanding, we have little choice but to use the distinctions and classifications modern Western medicine employs. That means that a student of birth control in the Roman Empire, while acknowledging that contraception was not distinguished from abortion, must use the notion of contraception in his study of practices and substances that in fact had a contraceptive effect.[7] There are also some higher level concepts peculiar to modern Western society and of which the society studied knows nothing that nonetheless help explain features of that society. The Marxist notion of a false consciousness, whether in its original form or in its various recent transmogrifications, may be one of these. Magic and religion are not, however, scientific terms that help us better understand natural phenomena of whose meaning the alien culture studied has only a limited grasp, nor are they higher level concepts, consciously devised to illuminate the workings of society. They are rather categories constitutive of certain societies and not of others. Applying them to societies to which they mean nothing can only cause confusion.

The student of Greek and Roman magic is in a rather peculiar situation: he is not an anthropologist conducting researches into a culture in which magic as opposed to religion is a meaningless opposition; he studies societies in which the opposition existed, but which at an earlier stage in their existence did not make any such distinction. He is, furthermore, studying the societies that gave birth to the concept of magic with which modern Western man operates. He needs, however, to be sensitive to the differences that exist between what the ancients saw as magic and what he himself might be inclined to call magic. If he does not make that effort, he will fall into the trap of labelling as magic what in the eyes of those using them were perfectly legitimate and unobjectionable procedures.

Credit for recognizing that the concept of magic to which we are heir is the product of a very special set of circumstances and emerged at a particular time and place is due to a historian of Greek and Roman religion, Fritz Graf.[8] In Graf's view, two factors gave rise to the hiving off of magic from religion, of which it had for Graf been an integral part: on the one side, self-conscious philosophical reflection on the nature of the divine had led to a purified conception of the gods completely at odds with the assumptions about the nature of the divine made by those who practised *mageia*; on the other side, natural science, especially in the form of medicine, had begun to look at nature as a closed system free from divine intervention within which changes were to be attributed to physical causes only. The combination of these two factors produced a radically altered conception of the relationship between the world of the gods and the world of men that marginalized the rôle traditionally played by certain religious specialists; their activities were now classified as *mageia*. The *mageia* of the religious specialists was not co-extensive with what magic is now understood to be, but embraced a much wider spectrum: private religious practices that were not part of civic cults, Bacchic mystery-cults, purificatory rites, black magic, rites connected with controlling the weather and conjuring up the dead.[9] The conception of *mageia*, to which opposition on the part of doctors and of philosophers such as Plato, concerned to create gods purified of all moral blemish gave rise, did not at first affect the thinking of the mass of their contemporaries. It was basically the product of a debate between two groups of people who stood on the margins of society, the doctors and the philosophers on one side and the religious specialists on the other. Proof that this new conception of *mageia* as an enterprise, opposed on the one hand to religion and on the other to science, had made no impression on the civic authorities is to be seen in their failure to pass laws against it as such, although they were prepared to take action to deal with it to the extent that it threatened the physical well-being of the members of the community. The punishments that Plato in the *Laws* suggests should be exacted from those practising *mageia* reflect his own particular concerns about *mageia*, not those of the state. As Graf sees it, Plato campaigns against *mageia*; his contemporaries use it freely and unabashedly.[10]

If Graf is correct, the concept of *mageia* was at first very far from being co-extensive with the notion of magic with which we operate; it was not much more than a way of distinguishing between acceptable and unacceptable forms of religious behaviour to which only a few philosophers subscribed; at the same time it was a view of what was effective and what was not in medicine shared by some doctors (*iatroi*), although presumably by only a relatively small number of those who pursued that calling. The common ground between the two groups was that both condemned essentially the same religious experts, though from very different perspectives: the philosophers, because the religious experts treated the gods as corruptible by bribes; the doctors, mainly because the healing techniques employed by the religious experts assumed the intervention of the divine in natural processes. How these two rather different ways of condemning the motley crews of religious experts who stood apart from the official cults of the cities came together to make up the notion of *mageia* Graf does not explain. Nor is any explanation given of how and when this view of *mageia*, shared at first by only a few exalted spirits, came to be more widely adopted. Nor yet again are we told how and at what point the notion of *mageia* took on a much sparer aspect and was stripped of the private cults and Bacchic mysteries that it had previously embraced. When the latter process was completed, *mageia* would have become more or less co-extensive with the concept of magic with which the modern Western world operates.

First, a word about the wider implications of Graf's realization that magic as a discrete category of thought had its origins in the Greek world of the fifth and fourth centuries BC. It goes far beyond the study of Greek and Roman religion and affects not only our understanding of other ancient religions, but also the study of religion in general. It may be that notions analogous to the Greek concept of magic came into being in other cultures where tensions similar to those existing in Greece obtained. There is some reason to think that an idea akin to the Greco-Roman concept of magic was present in

Ancient Israel. At any rate, in Deuteronomy 18.9–14 various forms of divination, spell-casting and consultation of the dead are declared to be the practices of the nations that will not enter the land of Israel and pronounced abominable.[11] The practices abominated are, accordingly, alien to the religion of Israel and for that reason occupy a position akin to that of magic in relation to religion. That is not quite enough to say that the practices abominated were thought of as magical. It would, on the other hand, be very difficult to demonstrate that the notion of magic had any part to play in the conceptual system of the Ancient Egyptians, at least until they were influenced by Greek ways of thinking.[12] It is true that in Coptic texts the term *hik* is identified and associated with loan-words from Greek such as the noun *mageia* and the participle *mageuon* and that *hik* is related to the divine personification of pharaonic times, *Heka*.[13] But these identifications and relationships do not warrant the conclusion that *Heka* was the personification of what we would call magic. It can hardly be that, since *Heka* was quite openly worshipped and the force of which he is the personification is said in a text of the Tenth Dynasty to have been given by God for the protection of mankind. *Heka* is not a hidden and illicit force, but a force that is recognized as a boon to mankind.[14]

It is of the utmost importance for the present enterprise to come to terms with the Greco-Roman conception of magic. Without a description of the complex of ideas and practices that constituted magic in the eyes of the ancients the risk is always present that persons whom no ancient man or woman would ever have imagined to be magicians will be categorized as magicians. The need for definition is also necessary because many of the techniques and practices that were later held to constitute sorcery were in existence in the Greek-speaking world long before there is any sign of the emergence of magic as a distinct category of thought. Odysseus, for instance, in the *Odyssey* summons up the spirits of the dead from the Underworld.[15] By the fourth century BC, if not earlier, those who professed to be able to conjure up the ghosts of the dead to consult them or to send them to haunt others are treated as magicians, but there is no suggestion in the *Odyssey* that Odysseus is acting as a sorcerer or that there is anything untoward about his conduct. Again in the *Odyssey*, the poet mentions a drug which Helen mixed with wine and which had the effect of making men forget their woes for the moment. He says that she obtained it from Polydamna, the wife of Thon, whose land Egypt provided drugs in profusion, some beneficial, some baneful.[16] Later writers believed that the poet had in mind the fame of Egypt as a nursery of magicians, but what he goes on to say belies such an interpretation: 'Each man there is a doctor of surpassing skill, since they are the descendants of Paion (the god of healing).'[17] In other words, the skill that the Egyptians display in using the drugs in which their land is so rich is proof for the poet of their medical ability and not of their facility in sorcery. There are other incidents in the *Odyssey* that appear to have all the hallmarks of sorcery: Circe throws baneful drugs (*pharmaka*) into a concoction of cheese, barley, honey and Pramnian wine which she gives to Odysseus' men to drink so that they may completely forget their homeland; she then strikes them with a rod to herd them into a pig-pen, where they lose their human form and take on that of a pig, although their minds remain unimpaired and they weep; Hermes gives Odysseus a root that he calls a *pharmakon*, hard for mortal men to pull from the ground, that will protect him from Circe, which it in fact does, keeping him from being entranced (*akeletos*) by her.[18] In the *Iliad*, there is Agamede, who is the eldest daughter of Augeias and the wife of Moulios, the first man killed by Nestor in battle. Of her it is said that she knew all the drugs the earth nourished.[19]

The root that Hermes pulls up to protect Odysseus against Circe looks to our eyes to be an apotropaic device designed to ward off the effects of sorcery. Circe's conduct is certainly presented as frightening and sinister. Hers is a particularly puzzling and complex case; it has to be conceded that it is not at all clear how she fitted into the world-picture of the poet of the *Odyssey*. It is hard to believe that people did not have a category of thought in which they placed underhand assaults on others in which potions were employed.[20] However difficult it may be for us to think of Circe as anything but a sorceress, it should be acknowledged that there is nothing in the Greek text to suggest that its author possessed the concept of magic and that he thought of Circe as a sorceress. The poet gives no indication, for instance, that Circe's conduct is to be seen as impious or sacrilegious. There is no hint, in short, that her actions are invested with the same significance that the actions of magicians are invested with at a later date. Yet in Athens in the early fourth century BC Circe is not surprisingly assumed to be a sorceress.[21] By the Hellenistic Period, Agamede also had become a sorceress and not only that but a sorceress of the same order as Circe and Medea.[22] There is even less reason to believe that Agamede was in the eyes of the poet a sorceress. What she was to his way of thinking was almost certainly an expert in the cutting of roots, a *rhizotomos*. Hermes will also have displayed the same expertise.

References to what later ages would certainly have seen as magic-working are also to be found in other forms of poetry. A poem of the first half of the sixth century BC celebrating the goddess Demeter portrays the goddess in the guise of a poor old woman promising to bring up and nourish the son of Metaneira, who was the wife of Celeus, the king of Eleusis, and to protect the child from ills.[23] The ills from which Demeter undertakes to protect the infant Demophon and to provide antidotes against are sickness, which here is conceived as a hostile visitation, and the cutting of roots performed with malicious intent. Demeter promises that through no stupidity on her part will her charge be harmed, that she knows how to cut a root capable of counteracting anything cut with hostile intent and, furthermore, that she has a device to check the illness. The structure of the verses in which Demeter makes her promise are in their incantatory effect reminiscent of later magical spells and charms designed to ward off or cure ills.[24] The hymn gives us a glimpse into a world that we can only partly understand in which nurses protect the infants in their care from hostile forces, whether supernatural or human, and in which in all likelihood incantations in verse existed designed to ward off such ills from children. What lies beyond our understanding and what cannot be extrapolated from the hymn is the conceptual framework within which the activities that the nurse seeks to counteract and her own actions fitted.

The difficulties to which importing our own preconceptions about what constitutes magic into the interpretation of ancient practices gives rise occur in a particularly acute form with the songs that we call incantations. In the admirable article published in 1924 on incantation in Pauly-Wissowa's *Realencyclopädie der classischen Altertumswissenschaft*, the author, a distinguished historian of Greek religion of a markedly rationalist character, says that incantation was an essential element in magic as far back as we can go in Greek history.[25] In making that assertion the writer had in mind the passage in the *Odyssey* in which incantations stop a flow of blood.[26] Now one of the techniques used in ancient medicine to cure conditions not in need of sterner measures was singing over the affected part.[27] The technique seems to have been used mostly to relieve pain and to stop bleeding, but there are indications that it may have had a wider application: a passage in Plato's *Euthydemus*, for instance, speaks of incantation being used to charm or soothe vipers, spiders, scorpions, wild beasts and illnesses.[28] The author of the article makes no allowance for the fact that incantation was in some circumstances treated as an accepted and acceptable medical practice and he takes no account of the very real possibility that in the Greek-speaking world of the eighth, seventh and sixth centuries there was no category of magic. Greek medicine from at least the seventh century BC used procedures that are to our eyes indistinguishable from the techniques employed by sorcerers. Yet there is no evidence, even in the fifth and fourth centuries, of anyone accusing the doctors who employed the procedures of having resorted to sorcery and of having abandoned medicine, despite the fact that the idea of magic was by that time well entrenched in the Greek consciousness.

The word in Greek for a song that heals or relieves is the word that is used for incantation in general, *epode* or *epaoide*. In Latin, the verbs *incantare* and *praecantare*, which have roughly the same basic meaning, are used. Besides incantations there was the technique of wrapping substances, whether animal, mineral or vegetable, or a combination of these, about a limb or the neck of the patient. This wrapping was called in Greek a *periamma* or a *periapton* and in Latin an *amuletum*. Incantation and the application of an amulet to a patient were probably very often performed in conjunction. Plato has Socrates speak of a certain leaf that was useless as a remedy (*pharmakon*) unless an incantation (*epaoide*) was intoned over it, but which was an effective cure for headache if the incantation was performed.[29]

24

Although it is not altogether clear, it does rather look as if Plato has in mind a leaf that is to be attached as an amulet or *periapton*. The poet Pindar, in a poem composed in the 470s BC, provides a list of the techniques employed by the mythical father of ancient medicine, Asclepius, to cure patients of their ills: (1) gentle incantations (*epaoidai*); (2) soothing potions; (3) the wrapping (*periaptein*) of antidotes (*pharmaka*) about limbs; (4) cutting or surgery.[30] A century later, amongst the techniques employed to heal the sick that Socrates in Plato's *Republic* lists, are incantations and amulets.[31] The use of incantations by doctors continued into the second century AD, if not later, and was sanctioned by the greatest physician of the time, Galen.[32]

To return to the fifth century BC, it may fairly be inferred that Pindar thought incantations and amulets were healing devices sanctioned by the father of medicine. In the middle of the fifth century in the *Oresteia* of Aeschylus we find an implicit distinction made between incantations used to reverse or cure other ills and incantations that were employed to raise the dead: the latter were forbidden and their use punished; other forms of medical incantation, it is implied, were allowed.[33] It is less clear what Plato's own position was, but he does speak of amulets and incantations as though in the eyes of his contemporaries they were on a par with surgery, drugs and cauterization. There is, accordingly, every reason to suppose that medical incantation was a recognized and respectable procedure not infected by the taint of sorcery.

The conclusion to which the foregoing discussion is intended to lead is that it cannot safely be assumed that actions we would classify as magical seemed so to an Athenian of the fifth or fourth centuries BC. Curing physical disorders by uttering incantations over them is in our eyes a quintessentially magical technique. It is so for two reasons: the procedure looks to us to be unscientific and so magical, since we cannot imagine how it could be effective; and we are predisposed to suppose that an incantation must of its nature be magical. The latter assumption makes no allowance for the possibility that for a Greek *epode* did not have the same denotation, not to speak of connotations, as incantation does for us. Our intuitions, in sum, of what counts as magic are not necessarily the same as those of an Athenian of the late fifth century BC. If we are not going to flounder helplessly, we have to come to terms with what the defining characteristics of magic were for a Greek of the late fifth century BC. It is true that what is seen as magic in Classical Greece, as even now, depends in some measure on the eye of the beholder, but it does not follow that calling an action magical is a purely subjective matter. The person who puts that label on the action will generally have done so because it possessed some of the characteristics that marked out what was magical from what was not. That does not mean that the notion of magic was tightly defined and that one can point to what its essence was in late fifth-century Greece. There was almost certainly a degree of fluidity to the notion, in the sense that different criteria would have been brought into play at different times in applying it.

The idea of defining characteristics needs clarification. My concern is with the criteria that Greeks used as a matter of intuition in classifying an action as magical, not with what a Greek would have said, if asked, magic was. It is not a self-conscious definition of magic that is being sought. For most Greeks and Romans it looks as though the defining characteristic in this latter sense was that the magician, in contrast to a priest or worshipper following the practices of proper religious observance, did not humble himself before the gods, but treated them as creatures who could be bent to his will, as beings to whom he was prepared to apply force and coercion. The idea that the magician coerces the divine and lacks proper respect for it is first found in the Hippocratic treatise *On the Sacred Disease* and can be traced down to the end of Classical Antiquity and beyond.[34] The idea that magic coerces the divine and is on that account impious has its roots in the feeling that the procedures of magicians must differ in some radical way from those pursued by normal worshippers of the divine. The magicians themselves no doubt contributed to the suspicion by pretending to be able to extract more from the gods than other men could and by maintaining that they could alter the course of nature. How soon they came to realize that they could use their reputation for coercing the divine to their advantage and began to play up to it is obscure, but there are strong indications that they did so. Study of the way in which the gods were addressed in fourth-century Athenian curse-tablets and in the magical formularies of the fourth century AD do not, however, show coercion being applied to the gods, but, if anything, an approach that is prayerful and supplicatory.[35]

Ancient definitions of magic do not, accordingly, really help us understand the concept of magic with which the Greeks and then the Romans operated. What they tell us is what the Greeks and then the Romans thought was different and wrong about magic. That is in itself helpful to know, but the accepted definition of a concept should not be confused with the way in which the concept is in fact applied. It is mainly the application in which we are interested, since it is its intuitive application that shows what was seen as magical and what was not.

The account that will now be given of the formation of the concept of magic in the fifth century is based on the assumption that the complex concept that is magic was not the product of conscious shaping and defining, but was a spontaneous and ever evolving creation. In this I differ from Graf who credits doctors and philosophers with consciously shaping the concept. It can hardly be denied that some concepts are the conscious inventions of men, but they tend to be highly theoretical constructs that need to be accommodated within a larger existing theoretical framework. Magic is not on the face of it such a creature. It is not so tightly defined a notion. An account of its evolution in which there is less emphasis on consciously-taken decisions and more on an organic growth fostered by strains and tensions within the religious life of Greece would seem to be in order. Magic is better viewed as the creation of a very special set of circumstances in which different forms of religious practice came into conflict. It would almost certainly be too simple-minded a solution to the problem to treat the growth of the notion of magic as the product of a conflict between new and old, although that is how the matter may have seemed to those who wished to exclude and condemn the body of practices they grouped under the heading of *mageia, pharmakeia* or *goeteia*.

Long before there is any evidence of philosophers or doctors trying to give definition to the notion of magic, the disparate practices, lacking any common thread to tie them together, that were later held to constitute magic were already being treated as of a piece, were already exposed to the same moral condemnation to which they were later subjected, were already viewed as being at odds with accepted religious practice and were already thought to be able to upset the normal course of nature. That would seem to be sufficient evidence to posit the emergence in the fifth century of a concept with a close resemblance to our concept of magic. There is nothing exclusive about the category of thought just characterized: tragic and comic playwrights appeal to it in such a way as to suggest that it was widely understood and accepted. That suggests that what the author of the Hippocratic tract *On the Sacred Disease* and Plato have to say about magic does not play a decisive rôle in shaping the concept; they merely articulate and, in the case of the medical writer, draw out the implications of ideas that are already there.

## The crystallization of the concept of magic: some straws in the wind

It is in the latter part of the fifth century BC that the first sure signs of a consciousness of magic as an activity apart are to be detected. At this point men are to be found placing a variety of quite disparate procedures under the single heading of *mageia, goeteia* or *pharmakeia* and expressing abhorrence for a form of conduct that is at the same time mysterious, secretive, audaciously wicked, irreligious, that seeks to upset the due course of nature and that does not accord the gods their proper dignity, but treats them as creatures to be manipulated at will. Before that time there is no secure indication of the formation in the minds of men of such a category of thought, although there are some tantalizing but insubstantial signs that earlier in the century the concept had in fact taken shape or was in the process of taking shape. Since the developed concept of magic is a complex and open-ended one, it is not only difficult to point to a date by which it had assumed its final form, but misguided to do so. At best what can be done is to isolate the first appearance in literature of some of the elements that go to make it up.

We should not delude ourselves into imagining that we are privy to all of the stages in the evolution of the notion of magic. It is a fair guess that it was a long and complex process of development in which quite disparate elements were absorbed and digested. That there is no one word for a magician, but that it is possible to refer to him as a *goes*, an *epodos*, a *magos* and a *pharmakeus*, points to the absorbing and homogenizing of quite separate forms of expertise. All of this has taken place by the latter part of the fifth century when most of the terms in question are first encountered. The process will not have been a short one. Yet we have really have no inkling of how it happened.

The earliest witness to the confluence of forces that eventually came together to produce magic is the East Greek philosopher from Ephesus of the late sixth century BC, Heraclitus. He is reported by a Christian writer of the early third century AD, Clement of Alexandria, to have prophesied that a fiery punishment after death awaited those who wander by night ( *nyktipoloi*), *magoi, bacchoi, lenai* and initiates in the mysteries ( *mystai*), on the ground that such persons practised unholy initiations into the mysteries.[36] That he should have made some such statement fits well with his recorded concern with the way in which mystery-cult was celebrated in his day.[37] Were we certain that we had Heraclitus' own words or an accurate paraphrase of them, what is said would shed light on the process by which sorcery came to be associated with the persons called *magoi*. The authenticity of the fragment is, not surprisingly, hotly disputed.[38] The first question to be asked in connection with it is whether it makes sense to have a man of the time of Heraclitus speak in these terms or whether its language is wildly anachronistic. *Bacchoi* and *lenai* are both terms for followers of Dionysus. There does not seem any very good reason to suppose that *bacchoi* and *lenai* were unknown to Heraclitus and that he could not have mentioned them in the same breath as initiation into the mysteries. As for *magoi*, although there is not a scrap of evidence for their appearance either in Western Asia Minor or in the wider Greek world in the latter part of the sixth century BC, it is a fair guess that men claiming to be Iranian fire-priests turned up in the Greek cities of Asia Minor in the aftermath of Persia's expansion into Ionia and Aeolia at the beginning of the second half of the sixth century BC. Ephesus, when Heraclitus was writing, had been under Persian suzerainty for some forty years. There is then a fair degree of probability that Heraclitus will have met or known of wandering mendicants who pretended to be *magoi*.[39]

The vocabulary employed is certainly not that of Clement of Alexandria, who is not otherwise known to have composed pastiches. It follows that Clement is unlikely to have concocted the whole fragment. The possibility remains that the word *magoi* has at some stage been interpolated into the fragment and that the rest of the passage is genuine. There seems to be no terribly compelling reason for anyone to do this. It is, in sum, entirely feasible that the words quoted by Clement represent what Heraclitus wrote. If so, we have an extraordinarily interesting glimpse into what was going on at the end of the sixth century BC in the religious life of at least one corner of the Greek world.

The picture that Heraclitus sketches suggests at first glance a world in which holy men who characterized themselves as acolytes of Dionysus or as Iranian *magoi* offered initiation into mysteries that were suspect in the eyes of Heraclitus and no doubt of others. We may surmise that the impiety Heraclitus saw in these ceremonies of initiation lay in part in their being performed privately and apart from the cults that the city sanctioned. He may also have suspected that there was something fishy about them. What that was we cannot say. Caution is called for, however, in identifying the *magoi* of whom Heraclitus speaks with persons representing themselves as Iranian fire-priests. Heraclitus could have meant by *magoi* a number of different things. He might have intended to refer to men who passed themselves off as Iranian fire-priests; he might have used the word as a term of abuse to mean wandering religious charlatans without any suggestion that they were Iranian fire-priests; or he might have used the term primarily to refer to men passing themselves off as Iranian fire-priests but with connotations of charlatanism. What may be cautiously asserted is that by the end of the sixth century in the world of the East Greeks, persons who could be referred to as *magoi* offered initiation into private mystery-cults. There is nothing in the fragment to support the idea that *magoi* had any connection with what we would call magic.[40] It is nonetheless extremely significant that persons called *magoi* should at this stage be found alongside figures from the cult of Dionysus offering initiation into the mysteries, since the associations that magic had with mystery-cult played, as we shall see, an important part in the form that magic was to take. That there was thought to be something impious about the mystery-rites practised by the *magoi*, *bacchoi* and *lenai* of whom Heraclitus complains is a precursor of the later suspicion that magicians adopted or mimicked the ceremonies of mystery-cult for impious purposes.

Heraclitus, accordingly, in all likelihood illuminates an early stage in the formation of the concept of magic in which *magoi* are associated with impious mystery-rites. There is no warrant for inferring that the real burden of Heraclitus' attack on *magoi*, *bacchoi* and *lenai* was that they were engaging in sorcery under the guise of conducting initiations. In fact, there is no sure indication of an association between practices that came later to be thought of magical and *magoi* until well into the second half of the fifth century BC. That is not to say that the association could not been made earlier, only that the evidence for it is missing. There is, however, an episode in Aeschylus' *Persians* which raises the suspicion that necromancy is presented there as a form of *goeteia* peculiar to the Persians. It is, however, unclear exactly what the force of the word *goeteia* will have been at this point. *Persians* was produced in Athens in March 472 BC, some seven years after the Persian navy was routed at the Battle of Salamis and some six years after the defeat of the Persian army at Plataea. Aeschylus portrays the response of the mother of the Persian king,

Xerxes, and of the Council of Elders left behind in the capital Sousa to the news of the calamities that had befallen the Persian forces, in a fashion which is by no means unsympathetic. The Greek stereotype of the Oriental, however, gives shape to much of the way in which the Persians are portrayed acting and speaking in the play, even though it is wildly at odds with Persian reality. There are, accordingly, grounds for thinking that the decision of the queen-mother, once she has learnt of the disasters that have overtaken the forces of the Persians, to summon the ghost of her husband Darius, the previous king, from his grave by means of placatory libations that she herself will pour and a song of invocation to be sung by the Council of Elders, is imagined to represent a characteristically Persian action.[41]

There can be nothing approaching a conclusive demonstration that Aeschylus thinks of the necromancy of the Persian Elders, aided and abetted by the Persian queen-mother, as *goeteia*, let alone as sorcery. Yet there is in the speech with which the ghost of Darius addresses the Council of Elders when he first rises up above his tomb something that suggests *goeteia* has been performed: Darius speaks of the Elders standing near his tomb uttering a lament (*threnein*) and calling on him in piteous fashion, raising their voice in spirit-drawing cries of woe (*psychagogoi gooi*).[42]

*Psychagogia* is a term used for drawing up the spirits of the dead from the Underworld. As for *gooi*, the term Darius twice employs to refer to the cries with which he is summoned from the grave, it is a word generally used of a funeral lament and belongs to the same root as the word for a sorcerer, *goes*.[43] In the same breath that he speaks of the *psychagogoi gooi* with which the Elders summon him he calls the song that they sing standing by his tomb a *threnos*. A *threnos* is also a funerary lament. There is unquestionably an element of lament in the song that the Elders sing calling on the gods of the Underworld to let Darius go and appealing to him to come to their aid, but it is certainly no straightforward funerary lament and to describe it first as *threnos* and then as *goos* is to single out one element in the song to the exclusion of others.[44] A play on the etymological link between *goos* and *goes* or *goeteia* implying that what a *goes* does is utter *gooi* summoning the dead from their rest below would explain the emphasis that is placed on the song as a lament or *goos*.[45]

It cannot be confidently asserted that Aeschylus, in the scene in which the Persian Elders summon up the ghost of Darius, exploits the association of necromancy with Persian *magoi* and the etymological link between *goos*, a funerary lament, and *goes*, the possibility nonetheless exists that this is what is he is doing. If so, it means that by the 470s there was in Athens, if not a developed, at any rate a developing consciousness of *goeteia* as a discrete entity and, in addition, a tendency to imagine that Persians were particularly adept at its practice.

There is a further indication that Aeschylus associated necromancy and *goeteia*: Phrynichus, a lexicographer of the late second century AD, says that men in times past had used *psychagogia* to mean bringing up the spirits of the dead by means of certain forms of sorcery (*goeteia*) and that Aeschylus' play *Psychagogoi* was on that theme.[46] Phrynichus, accordingly, implies that in Aeschylus' *Psychagogoi* sorcery was employed to summon up the spirits of the dead. His testimony has to be treated with some caution, since he was hardly in a position to say whether the techniques employed by necromancers to raise the dead counted as magic in Aeschylus' day, unless there were very clear indications in the play that the process of summoning up the dead was presented as sorcery. There are some tell-tale signs, nonetheless, that in *Psychagogoi* necromancy is a disreputable activity.[47] In Aristophanes' comedy of 414 BC, *Birds*, there appears to be a reminiscence not only of the *Odyssey* but also of *Psychagogoi* in an ode sung by the chorus of birds in which they speak of Socrates and Peisander practising *psychagogia* by the Lake of the Shadow Feet.[48] The ode is one of two odes in which the birds describe the disreputable activities in which from their vantage-point overhead they have seen Athenians engaging.[49] The inspiration for *Psychagogoi* is the passage in Homer's *Odyssey* in which Odysseus summons up the spirit of the dead seer Teiresias from the Underworld, but in the play the entrance to the Underworld is beside a lake where grass-grown graves are to be found and not as in the *Odyssey* at the confluence of rivers;[50] furthermore, *Psychagogoi* does not take Odysseus' calling up the departed seer seriously, but seeks to extract humour from it. That much is to be inferred from a fragment of the play in which Teiresias, it seems, prophesies that a heron flying overhead will ease itself and strike Odysseus with its excrement, causing his skin to rot and his hair to fall out.[51] Tragedy does not tolerate anything so vulgar or farcical. A satyr-play is a much more natural home for improprieties of this order.

There is an indication in the epic poem known as the *Phoronis* that the term *goes*, already at the beginning of the fifth century BC if not a little earlier, had associations with the activities with which sorcerers were later associated. In a fragment of the poem the figures known as the Idaean Dactyls are credited with having invented metal-working in the glens of Phrygian Mount Ida and are called *goetes*.[52] The *Phoronis* was a poem about a Prometheus-like person, Phoroneus, who is supposed both to have been the first of men and to have been the first man to make a number of important discoveries. The date of the poem is probably later rather than earlier, but was certainly drawn upon by Acusilaus of Argos, a mythographer writing in the first half of the fifth century. The context does not make clear what the author of the poem had in mind in calling the Dactyls *goetes* and it will not do to argue from the later associations of smiths and sorcery that sorcery was precisely what was at issue for him. The historian Ephorus, who belongs to the early fourth century BC and who takes the same view of the origins of the Idaean Dactyls as the *Phoronis*, says that they were *goetes* who practised incantations (*epodai*) and mystery-rites.[53] The tradition followed by Ephorus that the Idaean Dactyls were *goetes* will go back to the *Phoronis*, but we cannot be absolutely confident that the activities attributed to them as *goetes* by Ephorus were also to be found in the *Phoronis* and were not the invention of Ephorus or some intermediary source.

Securer evidence of the association of *goeteia* with one of the activities later associated with sorcery is to be found in the Athenian genealogist and historian of the middle of the fifth century BC, Pherecydes, who is reported to have said that the left Dactyls – the word means 'a finger' – were *goetes* and the right Dactyls were *analyontes*, which is to say they undid the effects of bindings, *katadeseis*.[54] It is very likely, accordingly, that *goetes* were in Pherecydes' view associated with some of the activities later attributed to sorcerers and were maleficent and sinister figures. We may further infer that the spells that bound men down were thought to be the province of *goetes*.

The Sicilian philosopher and holy man Empedocles, a somewhat younger contemporary of Aeschylus, provides evidence that by the middle of the fifth century men lumped together, as though they were of a piece, some of the disparate activities that were at a later date to be classified as sorcery. It very much looks as though he thought that the activities had something in common. That is another way of saying that he was operating with an overarching concept that encompassed the various feats sorcerers claimed to be able to perform. It is true that Empedocles does not subsume the list of marvellous powers which he professes to possess under the heading of magic or sorcery, but that is really neither here nor there, since a concept is a device with which or a category under which we organize our thoughts, not an abstract noun. The powers that Empedocles boasts of having and which he declares that he will bring to fruition for the addressee of his poem alone are antidotes (*pharmaka*) for evils, a defence against old age, the ability to stop the winds blowing and to make them blow again, the ability to cause drought in place of rain and tree-nurturing rain in place of drought and finally, a means of bringing from Hades a man who is dead.[55] The verses are quoted by Diogenes Laertius, who in the third century AD wrote lives of philosophers. He cites them on the authority of Satyrus, a writer of biographies of the Hellenistic Age.[56] Satyrus had said that Empedocles was a doctor and an orator and that Gorgias of Leontini, the expert in rhetoric, had been his pupil and that, furthermore, Gorgias had been present when Empedocles had engaged in sorcery (*goeteuein*). Perhaps to corroborate this assertion, Satyrus had said that Empedocles had himself professed to be able to perform sorcery and as proof that he did so had cited the verses which have just been paraphrased.[57] It would be prudent to suspend judgment on the question of Gorgias' having been a pupil of Empedocles, since Hellenistic and later writers had a penchant for making one Presocratic the pupil of another, even though they can have known hardly anything about the personal lives of these men.[58]

There is no common element that ties together the quite disparate powers Empedocles maintains he possesses other than that they represent an upsetting of the course of nature and that in later times they would have fallen under the heading of magic. That suggests that they were already thought of as a piece by Empedocles' time. Yet it certainly does not follow that Empedocles' consciousness of magic as a category apart was fully developed; he does after all quite openly announce that he has special knowledge. On the other hand, it has to be acknowledged that he promises to realize these special powers only for the recipient of the poem, which is precisely the kind of promise that we find being made in very much later magical texts. What we may tentatively conclude is that Empedocles in the boast that he makes about his powers does show an incipient awareness of the existence of a special category of thought.

## The developed concept of magic in the later fifth century BC

So much then for the fragmentary early history of the crystallization of the concept of magic. By the end of the fifth century BC, the existence in the Greek world of a developed consciousness of magic as a discrete activity is to be inferred. If we put together what is said and implied about magic-working on the one hand, and about *magoi*, *goetes* and *pharmakeis* or *pharmakides* on the other, the conclusion to be drawn is that people were by the end of the century operating with a concept tallying in large measure, but not entirely, with the notion of magic which we employ. The principal testimony to the existence of the concept is provided by the plays of Sophocles, Euripides and Aristophanes and the Hippocratic treatise just referred to, *On the Sacred Disease*.

It is best to begin with the activities associated with the persons known as *magoi*, *goetes*, *pharmakeis*, *epodoi* and their female counterparts, *pharmakides* and *epodoi*. Thessalian *pharmakides* are specifically credited with an expertise in bringing the moon down from the sky.[59] *Magoi* hold out the promise of prolonging life.[60] They also practise incantations and purifications.[61] The incantations they intone in their purificatory rituals are characterized by barbaric and unintelligible sounds.[62] *Goetes* and *epodoi* offer initiation into ecstatic mystery-rites (*teletai*).[63] *Magoi* are able through the techniques they employ to bring about the disappearance of persons.[64] They are also able, through engaging in a mystery-rite (*telete*), to pull the moon out of the sky, cause the sun to disappear and effect alterations in the weather.[65] Further light on the activities pursued by *magoi* in the Greek-speaking world is shed by the rituals that Herodotus credits the *magoi* of Persia with performing. They were for Herodotus the religious experts and priests of the Persian people. It would not be quite true to say, however, that in the eyes of the historian they were no more than Iranian fire-priests: he employs terms that are never used of the actions of a Greek priest to characterize some of their doings. One explanation for Herodotus' portraying them in such a way is that his picture of them has been coloured by the activities in which the *magoi* known in the Greek-speaking world were believed to engage. For instance, he describes the song intoned by a *magos* when a sacrifice takes place in such a way as to suggest that it was first and foremost an incantation (*epaoide*):

> When the man who has performed the sacrifice has laid out the meat, a *magos*, who takes up his stance beside him, chants (*epaeidei*) a theogony – that is what they say the incantation (*epaoide*) is.[66]

Then there is the sacrifice of white horses that the *magoi* accompanying Xerxes' advancing army performed in Thrace at the River Strymon. It and some other rites they carried out there are described as affecting the river with a spell (*pharmakeusantes*).[67] That was not all they did at the River Strymon: they also buried alive nine boys and maidens of the local people at a crossing-place called *Ennea Hodoi* or Nine Roads.[68] Later in the journey, when the expedition had reached Thessaly, a severe easterly gale struck the fleet and did great damage. To get the storm to cease, the *magoi* performed placatory sacrifices, perhaps using human victims, and sang incantations (*kataeidontes*) to the wind.[69] If we can argue back from Herodotus' portrait of the *magoi* of the Persians to the *magoi* he knew in the Greek world, by the historian's time *magoi* had come to be associated with incantation, the casting of spells and human sacrifice.

The range of activities in which the persons denoted as *magoi, goetes, pharmakeis* and *pharmakides* and *epodoi* engage corresponds roughly with what we would expect of a sorcerer. It is in general fair to say that *magoi, goetes*, and *pharmakeis* have as their province the reversal of the normal order of nature. There is little to show that *magoi, goetes* and *pharmakeis* have specialized spheres of activity; they are all credited with performing the same types of feat. The conclusion to be drawn is that the terms are virtually interchangeable. Their interchangeability suggests a further inference is in order: *goeteia, mageia* and *pharmakeia* no longer have an independent existence, but have coalesced to form one overriding category encompassing what must at some stage have been rather different activities. The overarching category so formed is surely to be identified with a concept that denotes much the same set of activities as does our concept of magic. A shared denotation, however, does not mean concepts are identical, since the intellectual and moral framework within which they exist may be quite different.

Confirmation that *goeteia, mageia* and *pharmakeia* are essentially interchangeable, in spite of a residual feeling or memory that *goeteia* and *mageia* are two different crafts, is to be found in a speech composed by Gorgias, *Encomium of Helen*.[70] To explain how incantation, *epode*, can through *goeteia* alter the disposition of the mind, Gorgias says that two crafts (*technai*) have been discovered, *mageia* and *goeteia*, both of which produce delusion and cause the mind to make mistakes.[71] Whether it is anything more than a difference in name that leads Gorgias to speak of *mageia* and *goeteia* as separate crafts it is impossible to say. However that may be, what is clear is that Gorgias cannot in fact distinguish between the pair, which is to say that they are not really separate concepts. In a discussion of the power that words possess Gorgias brings up the capacity of incantation to effect an alteration in the disposition of the mind and in effect compares the ability words have to cause pleasure and remove pain to an incantation. From that theme he turns a little later to make a comparison between the power words exert over the disposition of the mind to the power that drugs (*pharmaka*) have over the condition of the body: just as drugs can cause disease and life to cease, so can words induce pain and pleasure, produce fear and confidence and through the evil force of persuasion cast a drug (*pharmakeuein*) and a thorough-going spell over (*ekgoeteuein*) the mind.[72] To bring out Gorgias' play on the word *pharmakon*, the verb *pharmakeuein* has been translated by 'cast a drug over', but in reality in contexts such as this the verbs *pharmakeuein* and *goeteuein* or the more intensive form *ekgoeteuein* are indistinguishable. If *mageia* is not to be distinguished from *goeteia* and *goeteia* is not to be distinguished from *pharmakeia*, it follows that all three terms are virtual synonyms.

Further evidence that by the second half of the fifth century Greeks were operating with a category of thought that covered activities of a quite disparate nature, some of which had nothing very much in common with each other, is to be sought in the existence of a goddess who presides over not only the use of very different kinds of *pharmaka*, but over the assaults of ghostly forces. This is the goddess Hecate. There is no sign until the latter part of the fifth century of Hecate cast in the part of a malign and threatening goddess. For reasons that are far from clear she has assumed the rôle of tutelary goddess of magicians well before the end of the century.[73] It will be that Hecate whom Medea invokes in 431 BC in Euripides' play of that name as she sets to work against those who have wronged her. Medea swears by her mistress that no one who has caused her anguish will get away with it, apostrophizing the goddess as the one whom she worships above all others and has chosen as her helper, Hecate, who dwells in the inmost recesses of her house.[74] The deed to which Medea proceeds that leads her to invoke Hecate is the application of a deadly salve (*katachriston* or *epichriston*) to a garment to be given to a woman who has usurped her place. In the play, Medea is credited with expertise in two very different kinds of *pharmaka*: those that kill;[75] and those that enable a childless man to sire children.[76] Hecate is also invoked in another play of Euripides, *Ion*, by the chorus of maidservants as an elderly manservant sets out on behalf of his and their mistress, Creousa, to deposit a *pharmakon* in the wine of a youth who seems to Creousa to present a threat to her. In this case, Hecate is apostrophized as she who presides over assaults by day and by night and is asked to speed on its way the filling of the mixing-bowl with a *pharmakon*.[77] Hecate is then the goddess who presides over the use of very different kinds of *pharmaka*, but also of hauntings by day and night. The very wide domain over which Hecate presides and the special rôle she plays for

Medea point very strongly to the existence of a category that encompasses quite diverse practices under its aegis.

So far, all that has been established about *goeteia*, *mageia* and *pharmakeia* is that they are used to denote much the same set of activities as magic now covers. Their further significance, moral and religious, remains to be explored. The persons who engage in the activities denoted by *mageia* and its synonyms and the activities themselves are not regarded as morally neutral. To call a man a *magos*, *goes* or *epodos* is to speak abusively. It is to suggest that he is dishonest and engages in questionable activities. Oedipus, in Sophocles' *Oedipus Rex*, for instance, calls the seer Teiresias a scheming *magos* and a devious begging-priest who has only an eye for his own material advantage but is blind in his craft.[78] In Euripides' *Bacchae*, Pentheus speaks of Dionysus as a *goes epodos* from Lydia who consorts with women by day and by night, offering them the prospect of initiation into ecstatic mysteries.[79] It does not follow from *magos'* or *goes'* being a term of abuse that the activities which defined a man as a *magos* or *goes* were in themselves suspect, only that some of the activities pursued by such men were thought questionable. From *Oedipus Rex* it is to be inferred that *magoi* are associated with deviousness and greed, while quite what negative associations *goes epodos* carries in *Bacchae* is unclear.

It is theoretically possible, though not very likely, that the magical activities in which *magoi* and *goetes* engaged were considered perfectly reputable and that it was only the greed and deviousness of some of those who passed themselves off as *magoi* and *goetes* which gave the whole group a bad name. There is, however, some evidence that tends to tell against such an inference. It is to be found in Sophocles' *Trachiniae*. In that play, Hercules' wife, Deianeira, in desperation at seeing a younger woman usurping the affections of her husband and supplanting her in his bed, anoints a garment to be given to Hercules with a substance that will bring him back, as she thinks, to her. She had acquired the love-potion from the centaur Nessus, who had told her that it would act as a charm (*keleterion*) on the mind of her husband, so that no woman would engage his affections more than she.[80] The gift that the centaur offers Deianeira on the face of it looks to belong to the category of spells used by men or women to bind the affections of the persons they love to keep them from straying in other directions. In the magical papyri there are recipes for just such spells and we have lead tablets with spells written on them designed to bind someone's sexual affections. No examples of such tablets, however, quite as old as Sophocles' play have been found.[81]

An older woman's use of a spell to retain the affections of her husband, when her position is threatened by a younger woman in the full bloom of youth, would not seem to be the most heinous form of offence, nor one that would inspire moral indignation of the most violent kind. Nonetheless, perhaps to highlight the dilemma in which Deianeira finds herself, Sophocles has Deianeira speak of what she does in terms that reflect extreme repugnance. She declares that she wishes to know nothing of wicked acts in which leave is taken of the moral senses (*kakai tolmai*) nor to learn them, and that she hates (*stygein*) those who engage in them; in spite of these feelings, she has gone ahead and devised a way of defeating the girl with a love-philtre (*philtron* and *thelkterion*) aimed at Hercules, but she will desist, she says, if her action seems unrestrained and wanton (*mataion*) in the eyes of the chorus, who in this play represent the young women of the community.[82] The young women of Trachis, who are presented as shielded by their youth from the pains of life but at the same time all too ready to offer gratuitous moral advice, do not dissuade Deianeira but give her qualified encouragement.

The words which Deianeira uses to voice her loathing for the use of a love-spell and the women who have recourse to it are terms expressive of the deepest sense of outrage and of the strongest abhorrence. In Greek, as in English, a speaker expresses moral disapproval that comes from the core of his being by saying that he hates (*misein* or *stygein*) someone or something or that a person or action is hateful (*echthros*) to him. The verb used by Deianeira, *stygein*, conveys a sense of physical abhorrence or repugnance. The earliest instance of such an expression of moral detestation in Greek literature is Achilles' telling Odysseus in the *Iliad* that the man who says one thing but keeps another concealed in his heart is as hateful to him as the gates of Hades.[83] Such expressions are not uncommon in Sophocles.[84] To take just one example, Achilles' son Neoptolemus, a true heir to his father, declares that whatever it pains him to hear, he hates (*stygein*) to do.[85]

What Deianeira says she hates are acts that spring from a total lack of moral restraint on the part of the agent. Acts of that character are in Greek called *tolmai* and *tolmemata* and the agent who performs them is said to *tolman*. The noun *tolme* and the denominative verb *tolman* that derives from it are used basically of boldness or endurance, but, when employed as terms of moral disapprobation, are used to refer to the kind of boldness that suffers from no moral restraint and that would stop at nothing. There are parallels, to look no further than Sophocles, for this form of expression.[86]

The one other instance in tragedy of a woman yielding to the temptation to cast an erotic spell is Phaedra in Euripides' *Hippolytus*. She has succumbed to an overmastering passion for her stepson Hippolytus that Aphrodite has sent upon her. Nonetheless, out of a deep sense of shame and guilt she does her best to resist and keep quiet about her condition. Eventually her old nurse succeeds in extracting from her what is wrong, and, after an initial reaction of shock and outrage, offers to help her with incantations (*epodai*) and words that beguile (*thelkterioi*).[87] Phaedra's response to the whole tenor of the speech of the nurse, which has essentially been to propose curing Phaedra's passion by using incantations to draw Hippolytus to her, is disgust: the words that the nurse speaks are shaming and base (*aischistoi*).[88] The nurse admits that the proposal is base and shaming (*aischra*), but for all that better than preening oneself on taking a high moral stand (*kala*) and dying for it.[89] Phaedra continues to insist on the baseness of the nurse's proposal and begs her not to go on.[90] The nurse at first accedes to the request and grants that if that is Phaedra's view, she ought not to do wrong (*hamartanein*). She then recovers herself and suggests that there is another possibility: she has at hand love-philtres (*philtra*) that will put an end to Phaedra's sickness, but not at the cost of base and shameful actions (*aischra*) and without doing harm to the mind, provided that Phaedra is not herself a wicked woman (*kake*).[91]

The nurse's claim that her love-philtres will do no damage to the mind is a reference to the belief, widespread in antiquity and perhaps not unfounded, that love-philtres might adversely affect the minds of those to whom they were given.[92] In the interchange between Phaedra and the nurse it is at first difficult to separate Phaedra's response to the suggestion that she should have an illicit affair from her reaction to the nurse's proposal that magic should be employed to further that end. As the exchange develops, it becomes clearer that Phaedra is certainly shocked by the idea of using love-philtres and incantations to win Hippolytus. It is precisely the moral disgust that such a course of action arouses in her that the nurse eventually realizes she must overcome. She does so by inventing a love-philtre that can be used without doing anything shameful, provided the user is not wicked in the first place. Phaedra accepts this and yields to the blandishments of the nurse, giving the woman something belonging to Hippolytus to help her cast an effective spell.[93] The conclusions to be drawn from all of this are that for a woman such as Phaedra the use of love-philtres is morally repugnant (*aischra*), that those who use them err morally and that their users are wicked women (*kakai*).

Before we jump to the conclusion that the feelings about love-spells to which Deianeira and Phaedra give expression constitute proof that the doings of *magoi* and *goetes* were universally condemned in late fifth-century Athens, a number of points need to be made about what can legitimately and safely be inferred from what the two women say. First of all, the abhorrence Deianeira and Phaedra express about casting spells to bring an errant lover to heel or to win a new lover is not necessarily shared by everyone. Yet in the case of Deianeira and Phaedra it would be strange if Sophocles and Euripides had chosen to portray women holding views peculiar to themselves and not shared by the audience watching. The way in which Deianeira in particular expresses her feelings suggests that she speaks from a well-understood and widely-shared standpoint. Secondly, a certain degree of caution is called for in extrapolating from what may be granted were widely-held misgivings about the morality of casting erotic spells to a general abhorrence of everything *magoi*, *goetes* and *pharmakeis* did. It is, nonetheless, a fair inference that erotic spells were not the only form of charm thought suspect.

Those who perform magic are, accordingly, prepared to fly in the face of the moral scruples that restrain other people. They also do not feel the same religious constraints as do others, since they are believed not to respect the gods in quite the same way as other persons do. The author of the tract *On the*

*Sacred Disease* maintains that in his view those who promise to pull the moon down from the sky and to control the weather, despite their protestations about being god-fearing men who respect the divine, do not in fact accord the gods the honour that is their due, do not believe in them and do not think that the gods have any power.[94] Such persons are, in short, impious.

Finally, secrecy as a defining characteristic of magic. It is easy to take it for granted that magic is necessarily performed in secret, until we step back a little to consider why this should be so. Part of the reason is obviously that many magical acts are intended to harm others; if their perpetrator became known, there would be a distinct risk of revenge being taken or punishment being exacted. That does not entirely explain why secrecy seems to be an inherent characteristic of magic. When, for example, Deianeira anoints the robe she is going to send to Hercules to win his love back, she does so in secret within the confines of the house.[95] Since from a practical point of view there is no call for Deianeira's doing what she does in a covert fashion, it looks as though the secrecy of her actions is an integral part of the procedure she carries out. Then there is the deception Iphigenia in the *Iphigenia Taurica* works on the attendants sent by the Taurian king to take her brother Orestes away: she forbids them to advance further forward, since she is going to perform a purificatory rite that will involve carrying out a sacrifice whose flame it is forbidden to see (*aporreton*); she is then heard to utter magical incantations, as though she were washing blood away.[96] The attendants are, accordingly, deceived because of their willingness to believe that magical actions have to be carried out in secret. The adjective that the messenger applies to the fire that will be part of the sacrifice is *aporretos*, a word that means 'forbidden', and that is specifically used of those features of the mysteries that initiates are forbidden to reveal.[97]

The similarities between magic and mystery-cult in respect of exclusiveness and secrecy are worth dwelling on a little further. Magic – here what is being talked about is the modern Western conception of magic – is by its nature something exclusive and mysterious. It is a form of hidden knowledge that can only be attained with some difficulty and through instruction by an adept; it promises the initiate all manner of advantages over other men and women. Mystery-cult also promises its initiates advantages in this life and in the next life. It too is exclusive, since initiation is in theory only open to the pure. What the initiate sees and learns he is forbidden to reveal. The ceremony itself is cloaked in secrecy and takes place invariably at night. Since mystery-cult played an important rôle in the genesis of magic, it is hardly surprising that magic should mimic many of its features and that it should have some of the same appeal which mystery-cult possessed.

The secrecy in which magic is performed is not an incidental feature of magic but of its essence. Without secrecy magic loses its *raison d'être*. Its attraction disappears and it becomes just another cult-activity. There is another factor that fosters the secrecy of magic: it is the peculiar symbiosis in which it stands with religious orthodoxy and the authority that underwrites it. Magic becomes meaningless if it does not exist in opposition to an authority that forbids it or at least frowns upon it. There has to be a form of religious orthodoxy against which it can set itself off. Its secrecy is in part imposed on it from outside by those who disapprove of it, but it also imposes secrecy on itself, so that the sense of opposition, exclusiveness and illicitness may be fostered. If it is something that can be freely practised and becomes an activity in which everyone can expect to attain expertise, it loses its allure. The magician performs his ritual in secrecy, partly because he has to keep up the pretence that he has access to a special and exclusive body of knowledge and partly to feed the feeling that he stands apart and in opposition to regular and sanctioned forms of religion and conduct. Once magic loses the aura of being something illicit that can unlock powerful hidden forces, it no longer attracts those who hope to be able to bypass the natural order of things by employing the sort of subterfuge it seems to offer.

Augustine has an excellent analysis of the psychology of ancient magic in which he points out how the mystery in which magic is clad makes it the more attractive to its would-be disciples, since the acolytes think they are being given access to a secret and illegally-acquired body of knowledge. He speaks of those who are learned in magic adding the spice of the occult to the potions that they have to offer those who are imbued with a preternatural curiosity; their aim is to make the inquisitive imagine that they are learning something important just because it is secret, and to make them drink in with greater pleasure nonsense as knowledge in the conviction that they are acquiring something stolen.[98] The psychological relationship that obtains between a magician and his client is *mutatis mutandis* almost exactly the same as that which Augustine suggests holds between the adept in magic and those who want to participate in his wisdom. The ancient magician is rather like the man who seeks to give the impression that the goods he hawks in the street or in a subway-car are stolen, smuggled or in some way illicitly acquired, even though they may well not be, since the gullible customer fondly imagines in his greed that he is getting something for less than it is really worth because it is illicit. In the same way the magician's client persuades himself that he will gain advantages he would not otherwise obtain by being party to a transaction that is illicit and secret.

The concept of magic, present in the Greek world of the fifth century BC and particularly in Athens, that emerges when we bring the disparate pieces of information about it together, tallies in large measure but not entirely with the concept of magic with which the Western world is familiar. It promises to effect the disappearance of persons, to upset the natural order and to instil passionate love in the breast of another. It is an activity that men and women feel is disreputable and shameful. Those who engage in it are believed to be bound by no moral inhibitions and to be prepared to go to any lengths in their criminality. The fact that a verb characteristically used of audacious acts of criminality, *tolman*, is employed to describe the state of mind of those who engage in magic suggests that such persons are ready to fly in the face of the moral and religious forces which impose a check on the behaviour of others. The absence of religious scruple in such persons is also evident in the lack of respect for the divine that they manifest in forcing through actions contrary to nature. The practitioners of magic nonetheless put on a pretence of sanctity and claim to have special access through the mysterious and hidden rites they practise to the divine.

There remains the question of how the notion of *mageia* came into being and what forces gave shape to it. This is necessarily a highly speculative endeavour, since so many pieces in the jigsaw puzzle are missing. It looks at first sight as if the obvious place to begin the quest is with the term *magos* and with the presumed though unattested emergence, in the Greek world, of either genuine Iranian fire-priests or persons passing themselves off as such. Since those who are foreign or at any rate live on the margins of a society are frequently suspected of being expert in magic, it would make sense of a sort, if magic was from its very beginnings felt to be an alien set of practices imported from afar. It is also true that until it is replaced by Egypt, Persia, understood in a very broad sense to include Babylon and Assyria, is thought to be the home of magic. It is an open question, however, in whose imagination it is that the *magoi* of Persia are the ultimate experts in magic: are we to suppose that they occupied such a rôle in the popular imagination or was it a learned conceit contrived by those who knew where the word *magos* had come from? By the time – and this is at a very early date – we encounter in a Greek setting persons who are referred to as *magoi* there is no trace left of Zoroastrianism. What we find instead are men who offer initiation into the quite unPersian institution of the mystery-cult.[99] That is puzzling. The puzzle is compounded by the knowledge that offering initiation into the mysteries is hardly the exclusive possession of *magoi*: Pentheus in Euripides' *Bacchae* says he has been told that there is a stranger in his land, who is a *goes epodos*, who pretends to do just that, so that he may consort with young women by day and night.[100] The trail, accordingly, does not take us back to Persia, but only to persons offering initiation into mystery-cults that did not apparently enjoy the official auspices of the city. Yet it is not to be doubted that persons either calling themselves *magoi* or who were thought to be *magoi* must have appeared in the Greek world. Their connections with anything Persian may have been slight to the point of vanishing. What they certainly fastened on and exploited were the possibilities presented by offering initiation into the mysteries. In other words, they exploited what was, however they may have presented it, an essentially Greek institution.

The theory that the *magoi* were bearers of Eastern wisdom should not be abandoned quite yet. Magical techniques did come, if not from Persia, at least from Western Asia, to Greece. Raising the ghosts of the dead to consult them appears to have been a practice that has its roots amongst the Assyrians and to have spread during the seventh century from Assyria to Anatolia, the Levant and Egypt.[101] It will have reached Greece in the second half of the seventh century and not too long after its arrival will have been seized on by the poet of the *Odyssey* and exploited by him to some effect. The technique may have been re-introduced or re-invented in the early fifth century with one major modification: the ghost is now summoned by an incantation. Mesopotamia is also in all likelihood the source of the peculiar practice of arousing the ghost of a dead person to send it to haunt an enemy or opponent, either to terrify him or to drive him mad.[102] This is the technique known in Greece as *epagoge*, a noun deriving from a verb, *epagein*, that means 'to bring or send towards or against'. It is also a Mesopotamian trick that the Thessalian *pharmakis* whom Strepsiades in Aristophanes' *Clouds* contemplated employing to pull the moon from the sky has learned, for reference is made in a Neo-Assyrian letter of the seventh century BC addressed to King Esarhaddon to women bringing the moon down from the sky, apparently with malign intent.[103] Ventriloquism, which in the Ancient Near East and in the Greek and Roman worlds was used for prophetic utterances, is also likely to have been a technique the Greeks acquired from Western Asia. It is a ventriloquist, the Witch of Endor, whom, in 1 Kings, Saul gets to summon up the ghost of Samuel.[104] Kings belongs to the post-exilic Persian period – that is, the second half of the sixth century BC – and reflects the concerns and realities of that time.[105] The earliest reference to a ventriloquist in Greece comes from the 420s. He was called Eurycles and operated in Athens. He contrived to make people believe that the prophetic utterances they heard emerged from the bellies of others.[106] The list could probably be extended, but it is enough to show that some of the feats the magicians of the fifth century professed to be able to perform had come from Mesopotamia. That raises the possibility that persons claiming to be *magoi* brought them with them.

If there is any substance to the hypothesis that the *magoi* who appeared in the Greek world from the late sixth century on did bring magical techniques that had their origin in Mesopotamia with them, and that, furthermore, these persons made much of their eastern origins, then we would expect to find indications that magic was in the eyes of the Greeks an eastern craft. One of the signs that in later times speakers of Greek and of Latin were firmly persuaded that the centres of magical expertise lay in the lands of the East is in the use in incantations of words imagined to come from these parts. There is already, in the passage in Euripides' *Iphigenia Taurica* that has been used to establish the secrecy inherent in magic, proof that barbarian words, which will generally have been understood to be words spoken by Easterners or Asiatics, were thought to be characteristic of magical incantation: the messenger not only says that Iphigenia, to conceal from him and his companions what she was up to, had ordered them to stay their distance, but also that she had, to give herself time, ululated and intoned barbarian songs in a performance of magic (*mageuousa*), as if to wash away blood that had been spilled.[107] The sound of barbarian incantations, in other words, convinces the attendants of the Taurian king that a magical rite from which they must keep away is being enacted. Evidence of a more straightforward kind for the assumption that Asiatics will by their nature be skilled in magic is to be found in the accusation that a Spartan woman, Hermione, who has aborted a child and whose husband has turned against her, directs at the woman whom she believes to be responsible for her misfortune, Andromache, the widow of Hector. The accusation is that Andromache, as a woman from the mainland of Asia, will be skilled in such matters.[108]

We may never be able to explain how it came about that persons calling themselves *magoi* presented themselves as experts in magic and at the same time offered initiations into the mysteries. What can hardly be gainsaid is that magic, because of its early associations with mystery-cult, took on some of the colouring of the mysteries and that some of its ceremonial became inextricably confused with mystery-rites. That partly explains, as has just been noted, its preoccupation with secrecy, although there are unquestionably other factors at work, and its professed exclusiveness. The hostility that the purveyors of initiations into privately-organized mystery-cults encountered and the feeling that there was something impious about the form their initiations took almost certainly led to the isolation and marginalization of such initiatory rites and to their being condemned as impious. The criticism that Heraclitus levels at *bacchoi, lenai, magoi* and *mystai* is precisely that they perform initiations in an unholy fashion into rites that do have a proper form.[109] It is not that Heraclitus disapproves of rites of initiation conducted in a proper form, by which he may mean rites that are performed publicly as part of civic cult; his disapproval is directed at those carried out in private and so irregularly. To the extent that magic-working was bound up with mystery-rites that were privately conducted, the opprobrium which such ceremonies attracted may have rubbed off on it and have led to the feeling that it was impious and wicked. That is not to say that the attempts magicians made to harm and manipulate others against their will did not contribute to their bad reputation.

The close ties that bind magic and mystery-cult together do explain something of the form that magic takes as a distinct institution. It is still a puzzle how the various forms of magic-working came together to form a whole and secondly how the purveyors of initiation into the mysteries came to double as magicians. Despite the intimate connection between magic and privately-conducted mystery-cults we should not imagine that these activities formed an indistinguishable unity in the Greek mind and were referred to as *mageia*. There is no evidence for their coalescing conceptually, although the same people may have turned their hands to both activities.

## The fourth century BC: Plato's conception of magic

No one in the fifth century, so far as is known, attempted to analyse the concept of magic and say what it was. The same holds good for the following century: no philosopher tries to define its essence. From one point of view that is just as well, since the definition would almost certainly not have done justice to a complex and open-ended notion. It would nonetheless have been interesting to see how philosophers grappled with so elusive a concept and what particular aspect of it they fastened on to the exclusion of the several other facets of the notion. Although Plato does not discuss magic as an abstract idea, he is at one point in the *Laws* forced to distinguish between two different kinds of *pharmakeia*, one in which one body acts directly on another and one in which that does not happen. This is as close as he comes to defining magic. The topic comes up when the Athenian Stranger, who is the principal interlocutor in the work, proposes penalties for those who hurt, but do not kill, other persons through *pharmaka*. The Athenian Stranger distinguishes between two forms of *pharmakeia*: one acting in accordance with nature on physical bodies by means of other physical bodies; the other, through *manganeiai, epodai* and the actions called *katadeseis*, persuading those who try to do such harm that they have just such a capacity and those at whom the harm is directed that those engaging in *goeteia* against them are able to do them the greatest harm. He adds by way of comment that it is not easy to understand what the nature of all of these actions is, nor again is it easy for those who do understand to persuade others what the truth is; nor is it appropriate for those who have no clear conception of what is happening to attempt to persuade men who have seen likenesses in wax at doors, crossroads and ancestral tombs to treat such objects with contempt.[110] Our understanding of what Plato is driving at is hampered by uncertainties about the meaning of the Greek text, but what is quite clear is that he is attempting to make a distinction between the form of *pharmakeia* that roughly speaking we would call poisoning and something that does not depend on the direct action of one body on another but on what people believe, and that consists in various forms of *goeteia* such as incantations and techniques for constraining others. When the Athenian Stranger actually comes to lay down the penalties for the non-physical kind of *pharmakeia*, he speaks not only of *katadeseis* and *epodai*, but of the summoning of ghosts to haunt others (*epagogai*) and other such *pharmakeiai*.[111] Although Plato does not try to define the non-physical type of *pharmakeia*, there can be no question that it is in his eyes a distinct entity encompassing the various forms of *pharmakeia* or *goeteia* of which he provides a catalogue.

In general, Plato uses the term *goeteia* in preference to *pharmakeia*, but in the passage under discussion finds it more convenient to speak of *pharmakeia*. The terms are for the most part virtually interchangeable, otherwise Plato would not be able to write that those who are the objects of *pharmakeia* in its various forms are convinced that they may suffer harm at the hands of those able to perform *goeteia* (*goeteuein*), but it possible that the extension of *goeteia* is broader.[112] It encompasses in Plato, besides binding-spells and hauntings, the creation of illusion by making objects appear to be present that are not really there;[113] the illusions that consist in the *goes* himself taking several different forms;[114] drawing and alluring persons, presumably whether they like it or not;[115] casting spells over fierce wild animals and reducing them to submission;[116] knowing what *pharmaka* to put into food to effect alterations in states of mind;[117] reducing men by incantations (*epodai*) and *pharmaka* to an inarticulate numbness;[118] and finally calling up the dead from the Underworld.[119] As for *mageia* or *mageutike*, it is impossible on the basis of the two references to it in Plato to say whether its extension coincided for Plato with that of *goeteia* or *pharmakeia*, but since attraction-spells fall within the province of both *goeteia* and *mageia*, there is some reason to think that it did.[120]

Despite the dismissive tone he takes to the threat presented by magic, Plato still wishes to punish with death those seers (*manteis*) and interpreters of wonders (*teratoskopoi*) who direct sorcery at others and who employ the craft of the seer in practising magic.[121] It may be the social disruption that fear of magic causes which prompts him to impose just as severe a penalty on the experts in magic as on those expert in using physical substances to harm others. Magic-working does nonetheless arouse his moral indignation: he speaks in the same passage of those who resort to harmful magic as persons who display *tolme*, that is, as persons whose moral effrontery and audacity know no bounds.[122] It is the term that he reserves in the *Laws* for those who feel no compunction about committing the most heinous of criminal offences.[123]

In sum, there is no evidence in any of Plato's writings that he gave serious theoretical thought to defining the notion of magic. Nor it might be added is there any evidence that anything he may incidentally have said on the subject greatly affected the views of his contemporaries or of later generations. On the one occasion on which he might have been expected to attempt a definition he fails to do so and contents himself with giving a list of instances of what he has in mind. The complexity of the concept of magic makes his failure to define it understandable. It is certainly never at the forefront of his interests, but is always a peripheral issue. There is nothing, however, to suggest that the concept of magic with which he operates differs one iota from that which men used in the second half of the previous century. It is difficult to say whether Plato thought that magic was an empty sham, although prepared to concede that magicians believed in the efficacy of what they were doing, or whether he supposed there was something to it. He had perhaps not given the topic sufficient thought to come to a fixed opinion on it or his views may have changed over time. What he was in no doubt about was the audacious wickedness and impiety of those who practised magic.

## Conclusion

To sum up, by the latter part of the fifth century BC magic was a distinctive category in the minds of men, characterized by an ability, real or pretended, to upset the course of nature, by its being akin to conventional forms of religious behaviour, while at the same time being at odds with it, by its impiety, by the secrecy of the rites it performed and finally by its immorality. It follows that there is no question of anachronism in speaking of magicians and sorcerers in Greece from the latter part of the fifth century onwards. While it is entirely appropriate to speak of magicians and sorcerers in the fifth century BC, at the same time care has to be taken not to imagine that the range of activities in which the persons variously referred to as *magoi, goetes* and *pharmakeis* engaged coincided with what magicians in Early Modern Europe were imagined to do. Nor again should we make the mistake of supposing that procedures that seem to us to smack of magic fell within the province of the magic-worker of the fifth and fourth centuries BC and were not thought to be perfectly innocent actions.

# 2

# SORCERERS IN THE FIFTH AND FOURTH CENTURIES BC

## Introduction

Evidence bearing on the identity of sorcerers and witches in Classical Antiquity varies in quantity and quality from place to place and from time to time. It is never particularly plentiful, but we are relatively well endowed with information about sorcerers in Athens in the fifth and fourth centuries BC for the very simple reason that more literature survives from Classical Athens than from anywhere else in the Greek world of the period. There is just enough information from other parts of the Greek world to suggest that Athens was not peculiar and that magic-workers were to be found elsewhere.

There is only one substantial text that can legitimately be used to throw light on magic-working and on the identity of its practitioners in the wider Greek world, the Hippocratic tract *On the Sacred Disease*. Who was its author is not known. That it was written in Ionic, the dialect used in a band that stretches across the Aegean from east of Athens to the coast of Asia Minor, and not in Attic tells us nothing about its place of origin, since medical works were by convention composed in Ionic. Whoever composed it and wherever it was composed, it is almost certainly not addressed to an audience made up solely of Athenians, but looks to the wider Greek world. That means it does not confine itself to parochial Athenian concerns, but deals with situations that other Greeks would recognize. That in its turn suggests that the practitioners the tract attacks as magicians were to be found in cities other than Athens. Then there are the lead tablets containing questions put to the oracle of Zeus at Dodona in North-western Greece. The questions put to the oracle and the answers, which were sometimes inscribed on the same tablet on which the question was submitted, confirm that magic-working was in the fourth century BC a preoccupation in parts of Greece far from the Aegean seaboard. It is not possible to be absolutely certain where the questioners came from, but since the dialect in which the questions were put is Northwest Greek and since the questioners themselves seemed to have inscribed their questions, it is a reasonable presumption that the majority of them will have come from North-western Greece itself.[1]

Then there is the indirect evidence for the presence of magic-workers in places other than Athens. It consists in curse-tablets and in protective spells inscribed on sheets of lead. Until very recently Sicily and Attica were the only two areas in which substantial numbers of curse-tablets from the fifth and fourth centuries BC had been found. An increasing number of curse-tablets are beginning to emerge from Macedonia proper and in one case from a colony on its periphery.[2] The formulae used in these early Macedonian curse-tablets bear a resemblance to the formulae in use in Attic curse-tablets of the same period, even though they are written in the Northwest Greek dialect in use in Macedonia. A family likeness to Attic curse-tablets is also to be detected in the considerable body of curse-tablets from Sicily from the fifth and fourth centuries.[3] It is clear from the features that the tablets have in common and from their being used for very much the same purposes in all three areas that a body of shared magical lore was in circulation throughout the Greek world.

The formulae used in curse-tablets were not the only form of magical lore in circulation in the Greek world in this early period. Versions of a hexametric incantation written on lead tablets promising the happiness enjoyed by initiates and ending with a guarantee of protection from various forms of magical assault have been found in places as far afield as Phalasarna in Crete, Epizephyrian Locris in Magna Grecia and Selinus in Sicily.[4] All of the tablets belong to the fourth century BC. The persons responsible for the diffusion of this body of knowledge are difficult to identify, but it is plausible to surmise that they were persons with special knowledge, some of whom moved from place to place.

There are a number of reasons for thinking that curse-tablets are largely the work of specialists. We may begin with the testimony of Pherecydes, who implies that *goetes* were responsible for the spells said to bind people down (*katadeseis*).[5] Since curse-tablets are a sub-category of this class of spell, their creation presumably fell within the province of the *goes*. The simplicity of some curse-tablets, consisting basically as they do in a list of names, perhaps with a verb in the first person singular in which the person on whose behalf the curse-tablet is laid announces, though without giving his own name, that he registers with the powers below the person or persons named does not in itself suggest that a specialist has been at work. Other considerations make it likely that such tablets were composed and written by professionals. There is first of all the very real possibility that a rather more elaborate ceremonial attended the creation of the curse-tablet and its dedication than has left any trace. Not everyone will have known what the appropriate ritual was. A further reason for thinking that a professional hand is at work is that the ability to read and write will have been confined to a relatively small number of persons in most communities in the fifth and fourth centuries BC. Finally, even though the formulae used in most curse-tablets from the fifth and fourth centuries are not particularly elaborate and mastering them would be no great burden, it is to be imagined that people will have placed greater faith in the efficacy of the actions of persons whom they had been persuaded were expert in the deeper mysteries of magic than they will have placed in their own unaided efforts. It is fair to conclude, accordingly, that when we find curse-tablets deposited in graves or in the sanctuaries of chthonic deities, persons who would have been thought of as specialist magicians had been at work in the communities in which the curse-tablets were found.

Most of the specialists who produced curse-tablets will have remained in their own community and will not have moved out of it. The existence of a common body of magical lore, on the other hand, does very strongly suggest that some specialists were on the move and brought their learning with them. Athens, in short, was not the only place in which magic-workers were to be found. It enjoyed no monopoly on magic. The counterparts of the various forms of magical specialist to be found in Athens were almost certainly present in other Greek city-states.

Who the magic-workers were in Sicily and Macedonia who were responsible for producing the curse-tablets found in these regions we are not in a position to say. At the same time, we have to acknowledge that we really do not know who in Athens it was who wrote the curse-tablets found there. The high literary texts that we possess from the fifth and fourth centuries BC have nothing to say about the magic-workers to whom the humbler residents of Athens, the tavern-keepers and prostitutes, approached to have a curse-tablet produced for them. The magicians about whom we hear seem to have been the kind of persons who inveigled themselves into the lives of the rich and powerful and who cut quite a broad swathe. They were for those reasons a source of interest and concern. It was almost certainly beneath the dignity of Plato and the tragic poets to mention the magicians to whom the humbler sort of person turned for help. We can, accordingly, only infer their presence in a community from the existence of curse-tablets. That means that any picture we may draw of magic-working in the Greek world in the Classical Period will necessarily be a distorted one: because of the overwhelming predominance of literary texts produced in Athens, the picture will largely be one of Athens; but even that picture will be an inadequate one, since it does not portray the humbler kind of magic-worker.

## The legal position of the magician in Athens

Before turning to the question of who it was in Classical Athens to whom men and women went for help when they wanted magic performed for them and to the question of the place of the magician in society, it will be helpful to look at some of the constraints under which magicians operated, so that a sense can be gained of the world within which magic-workers lived. Information about this topic is particularly hard to come by and none of it is straightforward, but there is just enough to give us a very general idea of the legal perils that a sorcerer might encounter.

In Rome, there was a law laid down towards the end of the Republic under which sorcery certainly came to be prosecuted, the *Lex Cornelia de sicariis et veneficiis*. That sorcery was also one of the crimes the law was intended to suppress seems likely, but is not demonstrable. The same situation did not obtain in Athens: there is no trace of legislation aimed at sorcery as such. The absence of legislation does not mean that the Athenians did not have legal remedies available, should they have wished to take action against a magician or someone whom they felt had used sorcery to harm them. It is a matter of some dispute what legal measures were taken in Athens against magic-workers. There are those such as Graf who deny that any cognizance was taken under Athenian law of sorcery as such, although action might be taken against a magician when the consequences of his deeds violated the law of the city, and who argue that the legislation Plato proposes in the *Laws* to promulgate against sorcery as a form of *asebeia* or impiety does not reflect Athenian practice, but Plato's own idiosyncratic position on magic.[6] Others are more cautious, preferring to reserve judgment on whether magic-working would have been prosecuted under the law of impiety.[7] Finally, there are those who believe that magic-working was prosecuted under the law of impiety.[8]

### Cases involving sorcery falling under the graphe asebeias.

There is from fourth-century Athens one fairly well-attested prosecution and execution of a woman who is called a sorceress (*pharmakis*). It is necessarily the prime exhibit for those who believe that sorcery was prosecuted under the heading of impiety, but it may not bear the weight that is put on it. To put a precise date on the trial is impossible, other than that it took place at some time in the middle of the fourth century. The evidence for the case comes from three sources: from Philochorus, an Athenian who was active both as a historian and a politician in the latter part of the fourth and in the early years of the third century BC; from a speech transmitted in the manuscripts containing the collected speeches of Demosthenes; and from Plutarch's *Life of Demosthenes*. Harpocration, who composed a lexicon designed to help in the reading of the Attic orators, records under the lemma 'Theoris' that a woman bearing the name was mentioned by Demosthenes in the speech *Against Aristogeiton* and that she was a seer (*mantis*) who was condemned for impiety (*asebeia*) and executed for the offence according to the account given by Philochorus in the sixth book of his history;[9] the speech in the Demosthenic corpus declares that the Athenians put the foul Lemnian sorceress (*pharmakis*) Theoris and all of her offspring to death for the *pharmaka* and the incantations (*epodai*) that the twin brother of Aristogeiton had himself used as his own, after receiving them from his mother, Theoris' maidservant, who had in fact informed against her mistress;[10] finally, Plutarch gives an account of the trial different from that in the *Against Aristogeiton* and in the fragment of Philochorus, but that can be reconciled with what they say: Demosthenes, who prosecuted the case, accused Theoris of having engaged in many criminal deeds (*radiourgesa*) and of teaching slaves how to deceive and succeeded in having her executed, which was the penalty he had asked for.[11]

The technical heading under which Theoris was prosecuted will have been impiety. This is the kind of detail that Philochorus, a man who was interested in cult and wrote on the topic, is likely to have got correct. The same inference is to be drawn from the fact that the woman was tried and condemned, after being denounced by a slave. Slaves were encouraged to denounce their masters only in cases where the vital interests of the state were threatened; in other cases their evidence had to be taken under torture.[12] *Asebeia*, since it might draw down the wrath of the gods on the state as a whole, will be one of the offences for which denunciation (*menysis*) on the part of slaves was encouraged.[13] Despite her birth on Lemnos, an Athenian possession, the woman was presumably an Athenian citizen and subject to Athenian laws affecting impiety. If we can trust *Against Aristogeiton* on this detail, it was not only the woman who was executed but her offspring also. The execution of the children can hardly have been contained in the sentence passed on her; if they were indeed executed, they must have been indicted and convicted separately for their involvement in the misdeeds of their mother. One does not, however, have to take at face value everything that is said in a speech delivered in an Athenian law court and then worked up for publication; speakers did not feel honour-bound to tell the exact truth, let alone to give a pedantically correct description of the niceties of the charge. The Greek of the speech nonetheless suggests that the woman and her offspring were executed for sorcery, pure and simple. It is, however, also possible to put a broader interpretation on the Greek, in which case what is meant is that the woman was executed on account of her magic-working, but not necessarily under the heading of magic-working. The speech and Philochorus can thus be reconciled.[14] After we have considered the next two cases, we shall return to Theoris' offence.

One of Aesop's fables tells the story of a female magician (*magos*) who boasted in the older recension of the fables of expertise in incantations (*epodai*) and in the laying to rest (*katathesis*) of divine wrath and in a more recent version of averting divine wrath, and who made a considerable living from performing these services; she was indicted for making innovations in matters concerned with the divine (*kainotomein*) or in the more recent recension of impiety (*asebeia*), brought to trial and condemned to death; as she was being led away from the law court, someone said to her: 'How was it that you were not able to persuade men, although you profess to be able to avert the anger of gods?'[15] A fable of Aesop is not the obvious place to turn for enlightenment on a point of Athenian law. It is, however, the case that the first known collection of Aesopic fables was made towards the end of the fourth century BC by the Athenian statesman and philosopher, Demetrius of Phalerum.[16] It was long ago recognized that the Athenian colouring of some of the fables in the older recension of the fables, the Augustana, reflected their origin in the collection made by Demetrius.[17]

The version of the fable in the older recension contains an otherwise unattested expression for laying the wrath of the gods to rest, *katathesis*, and a term that we find in Attic in connection with impious actions, *kainotomein*; the other recension essentially paraphrases and explains.[18] The vocabulary, the use of what is evidently the Athenian procedure against impiety and finally the feat the female magician professed to be able to perform point very firmly to the fable's having its origins in Demetrius' collection and to its having been composed in the fourth century BC in Athens.[19] The taunt directed at the female magician as she leaves the court after having been convicted, that although she boasted of being able to avert the wrath of the gods, she had proved unable to persuade men, taken in conjunction with the feats that the woman herself had advertised, incantations and laying the wrath of the gods to rest, make it fairly certain that she belonged to the number of those who professed to be able to persuade the gods, presumably by incantations, to lay aside their wrath and thus save men from the punishment that their crimes would otherwise have brought upon them.[20] The offence committed by the woman was not then sorcery, but attempting to placate the wrath of the gods by means that were felt to be at odds with Athenian tradition, presumably because they involved sorcery. It looks then as if the innovatory character of the procedure was what made it vulnerable to a charge of *asebeia*.[21] The fable does not then constitute evidence that sorcery itself could be prosecuted under the law of *asebeia*, but only that those who employed incantations in trying to placate the gods were liable to be charged with impiety.

The only other instance of what may be a prosecution and conviction under the law of impiety for an offence that involved sorcery belongs to the 350s or 340s. It is the case of a woman called Ninos, who is described in our principal source, Demosthenes, as a priestess (*hiereia*). Demosthenes alludes to her execution in speaking of the low birth of his political opponent Aeschines, whom he says was the offspring of Atrometos, an elementary teacher, and Glaucothea who brought together *thiasoi*; he then adds that another priestess was executed for doing what Glaucothea did.[22] The groups of worshippers known as *thiasoi* that Glaucothea had brought together she had convened, as Demosthenes tells the story, in carrying out initiations into the mysteries of the god Sabazios. An ancient commentator on the passage gives the relative clause in which Demosthenes comments that another priestess was executed for what Glaucothea did to an antecedent, *pharmaka*, and then says that the woman was called Ninos and that she was accused by a certain Menecles of having made love-philtres for young men; another explanation of the passage, which appears to belong to an alternative tradition of interpretation, says that Ninos was executed because the ceremonies she performed were felt to have made a mockery of the real mysteries, but on the gods issuing an oracle, the Athenians allowed the mother of Aeschines to conduct initiations into the mysteries of Sabazios.[23] There is one final piece of testimony that needs to be taken into consideration: Josephus, a Jewish historian from Palestine of the latter part of the first century AD, says that a priestess was executed by the Athenians, accused of having conducted initiations into the mysteries of foreign gods.[24] The execution of the woman who can only be Ninos is the final item in a catalogue of instances of persons accused of impiety in Athens that Josephus gives to illustrate his contention that the Jews were not the only people jealous of their own religious traditions. Josephus' list begins with Socrates, who is followed by Anaxagoras, Diagoras and Protagoras and finally Ninos.[25]

The trial of Ninos was evidently a notorious one, since in a speech included in the Demosthenic corpus Menecles is identified as the one who secured the conviction of Ninos.[26] It is significant that the speaker says of Menecles that he was a member of a gang of men who made a practice of bringing accusations against others. That suggests that not everybody thought Ninos deserved to be convicted and executed. Her son at a later date brought a suit against Menecles and had a speech written for him.[27] The family, accordingly, must have had some standing in Athenian society. The context in which Demosthenes makes mention of the execution of Ninos strongly suggests that she was put to death for activities connected with the private ceremonies of initiation that Aeschines' mother – at least on Demosthenes' account of her activities – was also wont to conduct. The charge in that event was almost certainly *asebeia*.

Josephus and the ancient commentator who said that the woman was accused of making a mockery of the mysteries can be taken, if one can place any trust in them, to confirm the nature of the charge.[28] The question that needs to be asked is whether Ninos was accused of having employed sorcery in conducting initiations. The issue is whether any weight can be placed on the ancient commentator who assumes that Ninos was charged with magic-working and who asserts that Menecles accused her of having manufactured love-philtres for young men. Ultimately, the information, if accurate, can only have come from a speech or from an Atthidographer. The difficulty is that it is quite common to find ancient commentators, confronted by an allusion they cannot explain, inventing an explanation based on the text they have in front of them and presenting it as a fact. That is not what has happened here: the story told by the commentator does not emerge from anything in the text of Demosthenes; it puts an unexpected interpretation on what Demosthenes has said and credits Menecles with having made accusations that fit such an interpretation. Menecles may, accordingly, have argued that a woman sullied by her connections with magic-working profaned the mysteries by conducting initiations into them. Whether the commentator is to be trusted or not, it remains the case that Ninos' offence lay in something to do with the way in which she conducted initiations into mysteries.

The cases of Theoris, the female magician, and Ninos do not enable us to assert confidently that magic-working on its own was ever prosecuted under the Athenian law of *asebeia*. We cannot, on the other hand, entirely exclude the possibility that the charge of *asebeia* was used to prosecute magic-working. Although magic by itself may not have been subject to prosecution under the law of *asebeia*, there is reason to believe that those who used magical procedures in performing religious rituals might find themselves accused of *asebeia*. It is an open question whether someone who was known to be a magician was vulnerable to the charge of *asebeia*, if he took an active part in carrying out a religious ceremony, even though magic played no part in what he did in the ceremony. It was certainly true at a later date that known magicians were excluded from the precincts of temples and from the rites enacted in them.[29] The feeling seems to have been that the effectiveness of the ceremonies conducted in them was compromised by having an impure person participate in them.

There is, in sum, no very good ground for thinking that the threat of a *graphe asebeias* constantly hung over the head of those magic-workers in Athens who kept to magic and did not presume to play the part of priests in private religious ceremonies. Not only is it uncertain whether the procedure for *asebeia* was used against magic-working in general, there is reason to doubt whether the trials of Theoris and Ninos were representative proceedings. If we read between the lines, it sounds as if Theoris and Ninos were quite well-known personages with connections in the larger Athenian world; they were not obscure and humble women known only to the little people who lived around them. Their conviction and execution had certainly not passed unmarked and seems to have sent shock waves through Athens that had lasted for quite some time. There may, accordingly, have been more to the trials than meets the eye; they may have had political ramifications. Caution is then called for in extrapolating from what may have been two quite extraordinary events to the legal dangers facing other magic-workers in Athens. Those who were out of the public eye may not have been exposed to the dangers which confronted their more prominent contemporaries. It is also possible that very different legal procedures were used against those forms of magic-working designed to harm or manipulate another.

### Legal remedies for persons harmed by sorcery

There must have been cases in which people thought that they or theirs had suffered actual physical harm at the hands of a sorcerer. Some idea of what might have happened in this eventuality can be gained from a case cited by the author of the *Magna Moralia*, a work attributed to Aristotle and certainly written by someone belonging to his school, to illustrate the notion of an unintended consequence: a woman gave a man a love-philtre to drink that then caused his death; the woman was acquitted by the Court of the Areopagus, the tribunal within whose purview fell cases of intentional poisoning, on the ground that she had not given the man the philtre with a view to killing him, but out of love.[30] It is worth pointing out here that such a death was a very real possibility, since at least in Late Antiquity hemlock seems to have been one of the principal ingredients in love-philtres. The acquittal by the Areopagus of the woman, on the ground that she had not intentionally caused the death of the man by poisoning, raises two interesting questions. Would the Areopagus have been the appropriate court before which to bring someone thought to have caused a death by sorcery? And would that person have been charged under the heading of causing death by administering *pharmaka*? The Areopagus was the court which tried cases of deliberate homicide, cases involving the administering of *pharmaka*, which is normally understood to mean poisoning in our sense, and cases of arson.[31] The ambiguity inherent in the meaning of the term *pharmakon* and the use of physical substances in combination with verbal spells and rituals as *pharmaka* raise the possibility of prosecutions before the Areopagus of persons accused of bringing about the death of another by sorcery on the ground that they had administered *pharmaka*. Even if legal recourse by that means was unavailable, it would still in theory have been possible to bring someone suspected of having encompassed a death by sorcery before the Areopagus charged with deliberate homicide.

There is also the question of what legal remedies were open to a man who felt that he or someone for whom he was legally responsible had suffered harm, short of death, at the hands of a sorcerer. There are two pieces of evidence, both from the fifth century, that have a bearing on the question: one of them is a story told by Herodotus about a woman from Cyrene called Ladice who was given in marriage to the Egyptian pharaoh, Amasis;[32] the other is the issue around which the plot of Euripides' *Andromache* turns. The story in Herodotus is that Amasis, whenever he lay with Ladice, was unable to perform sexually, although he had no difficulty having intercourse with other women; he had, accordingly, accused the woman of having cast a spell on him (*katapharmassein*) and announced that there could be no escape for her from being put to death in the most terrible fashion; Ladice had then made a silent vow to Aphrodite, promising to send a statue of the goddess back to Cyrene, if she were to be saved from the peril surrounding her. The result of the prayer was immediate: Amasis had intercourse with her on the spot. Whatever would have happened at the court of the pharaoh, had such a situation really arisen, is almost certainly neither here nor there. The story reflects what Herodotus or his source, if he had one, thought would happen to a woman accused of sorcery by an absolute monarch. That he imagined a

55

terrible punishment would befall her is an indication that persons in the world he himself knew would have been punished, if convicted of performing sorcery against others. It is unlikely that there was complete uniformity throughout the Greek world in the measures taken against sorcerers, but it is equally unlikely that there were enormous variations. What happened in Corinth was probably more or less what happened in Athens.

What happens in *Andromache* goes some way towards corroborating that supposition. In that play, the protagonist, Andromache, is accused by another woman of having by sorcery – specifically by employing a *philtron* – alienated the affections of her husband and of having caused her to abort.[33] The accuser is Hermione, the daughter of Menelaus, who has married Achilles' son, Neoptolemus. Andromache, the woman who stands accused, is Hector's widow and now Neoptolemus' concubine. Because of the accusation and because Neoptolemus is not present to defend her, Andromache takes refuge at an altar. The safety it affords turns out to be illusory, since Menelaus, who has come from Sparta to support his daughter, gets hold of the son whom Andromache had sent into hiding and offers Andromache the choice of abandoning her suppliant-station to die at his hands or having her son die. She chooses the former course, but not before arguing that she would willingly have suffered such punishment as should befall her at Neoptolemus' hands for having cast a spell over Hermione and for having made her abort; the harm (*blabe*) that Neoptolemus had suffered by her having deprived him of offspring was after all greater than any harm suffered by Menelaus.[34] Andromache's point is apparently that it is appropriate for Neoptolemus as the party who has suffered the greater harm to take action against her for her sorcery. Since the play is set in the Heroic Age, there are no courts before which to have the case tried. The monarch deals with the matter himself. Yet there is in the legalism of Andromache's argument a hint of what might have happened in Athens, if a married woman had been rendered childless by sorcery: her husband would have been the appropriate party, since he had suffered the most harm, to proceed against the person suspected of sorcery. The woman herself could not have initiated proceedings. To the extent that Andromache's language affords any clue to the legal procedure that would have been followed, we might infer that the proper course of action for the husband to take was for him to bring what in Athenian law was called a *dike blabes*, that is, a private suit for damage.[35] Most such suits were brought because of damage to real property, but it is just possible that the notion of damage might have been extended to encompass damage done by sorcery. Speculation on the precise legal procedure followed is just that. Andromache's words do nonetheless suggest that sorcery was not necessarily always considered an offence which affected the well-being of the whole community, but a wrong done an individual. In Athenian law that meant only the party wronged could prosecute.

The case of Ladice and Andromache suggests that severe penalties were exacted from persons thought to have used sorcery to harm another. It remains completely obscure what the injured party or a man acting on behalf of an injured woman would have needed to do to secure that end. What the two cases tell us, if they tell us anything, is what would have happened to a woman who used sorcery against her husband or against a rival. Presumably a man convicted of attempting to harm someone through sorcery would have suffered the same fate.

There is one further indication that in Athens sorcerers believed to have harmed other persons were punished. In Plato's *Meno*, Meno jokingly suggests that Socrates had been well advised to stay put in Athens, since were he as a stranger (*xenos*) in some city other than Athens to bewitch (*goeteuein*), cast a spell over (*pharmattein*) and perform an incantation (*katepaeidein*) over people, so that they became numb with perplexity, he would be subject to summary arrest (*apagoge*) as a sorcerer (*goes*).[36] Meno's joke turns on the belief that sorcery could make a person quite helpless and, in particular, render him totally inarticulate in a court of law. *Apagoge* was the name in Athens for the summary arrest of one citizen by another.[37] The citizen arrested was either a homicide discovered in a place in which he was not allowed, someone deprived of civic rites who persisted in using them or a malefactor (*kakourgos*) caught in the act. Most of the malefactors subject to such arrest would have been thieves of one sort or another.[38] They were brought before the magistrates called The Eleven, who executed on the spot those who confessed to what they had been caught doing, while those who denied the matter were kept in prison to await trial. Three different constructions can be put on what Meno says: (1) sorcerers in cities other than Athens were subject to summary arrest, while in Athens they were quite free to ply their trade, since no laws had been passed against them there;[39] (2) were a foreigner to be caught performing sorcery in a city other than his own city, he would be subject to summary arrest; (3) it was just as well that Socrates had remained in Athens where he was well known, since were he to have gone to a city where he was a stranger, his conduct would have immediately secured his arrest as a sorcerer. The last interpretation is the most likely, although the other two cannot be ruled decisively out of court. What gives the last explanation the edge over the others is that they do not fully take account of the emphasis that is placed on the danger Socrates would face in another city where his ways were not known. It does not then follow from Meno's joke that there were no laws against sorcery in Athens, but that they existed in other cities and that sorcerers elsewhere were subject to the form of summary arrest to which malefactors caught *in flagrante delicto* in Athens were liable. The conclusion to be drawn from Meno's gentle banter is not that there were laws in Athens specifically directed at sorcery, but that someone who had the effect on others that Socrates had was likely to have action taken against him as a sorcerer. What the legal source of the action was must remain obscure. It is true that Meno speaks of Socrates being subject to summary arrest as a *goes*, but there are dangers in taking a joke too literally. It would, in consequence, be prudent to suspend judgment on whether sorcerers in Athens were liable to the same form of summary arrest to which other categories of malefactor were subject.

To sum up, there is just enough evidence to warrant the conclusion that Athenian citizens could and did take legal action against persons possessing Athenian citizenship whom they suspected of having used sorcery against them or theirs. Laws against sorcery as such do not seem to have existed, but other forms of action were no doubt available. Since all lawsuits were undertaken by private citizens, there could be no concerted efforts on the part of the authorities in Athens to rid the city of citizen magic-workers. It may well be that sorcerers who confined their operations to the lower reaches of society went unprosecuted, because their victims did not feel that they could successfully use the legal remedies available to them. They will have taken their revenge in other ways.

### The control of magic-workers who were not Athenians

It is easy in discussions of the administration of criminal justice in Athens to lose sight of the fact that we know virtually nothing about the way in which non-Athenians with no legal standing in Athens were treated. There is every reason to think that they did not possess the same legal rights and privileges enjoyed by Athenians and persons permanently resident in Athens as aliens, the so-called *metoikoi*. We may well wonder what would have happened to a wandering holy man accused or suspected of sorcery in Athens. Pentheus' treatment of Dionysus in Euripides' *Bacchae* may afford a clue to the way in which in Athens at the end of the fifth century BC wandering holy men suspected of magic-working were treated: Pentheus, as the ruler of Thebes, has Dionysus, who is in his eyes nothing but a sorcerer (*goes*) and enchanter (*epodos*) from Lydia, arrested and imprisoned near the stables.[40] It goes without saying that Euripides is perfectly capable of imagining a king behaving in a high-handed and arbitrary fashion and that Pentheus' arrest of Dionysus does not necessarily reflect what the Athenian authorities in the late fifth century would have done if confronted by a mendicant holy man from the East offering initiations into new and unheard of mysteries. There is nonetheless the possibility that Pentheus' summary arrest of Dionysus is a fair indication of one of the dangers faced by wandering holy men in Athens and in other cities in the late fifth century.

There were other dangers that magicians who had no legal standing in Athens had to face. One of Demosthenes' speeches alludes to one of them, that of being unceremoniously driven out of Athens. The relevant passage is one in which the orator, who is addressing the Athenian Assembly, is trying to give his hearers a feeling for what life was like at the court of Philip of Macedon and of the kind of men with whom that monarch surrounded himself:

he speaks of Philip's rejoicing that the company of men such as the Athenians are united in seeking to drive out of their city, men even more licentious than *thaumatopoioi*, men such as the public slave Callias, the actors who perform in farcical mimes and composers of vulgar songs.[41] The passage would seem to suggest that *thaumatopoioi* were a standard by which licentiousness was judged and the sort of person whom the Athenians sought to drive out of Athens. Since *thaumatopoioi* or wonder-workers often doubled as *goetes*, it is to be inferred that sorcerers were also encouraged to move on. How the Athenians discouraged the presence of such persons is not clear, but it does sound as if they took more active measures to move the unwelcome element on than just turning their backs on them and shunning them.

Police measures of an informal nature, perhaps instituted by the magistrates in charge of certain aspects of public order, the *astynomoi*, may have been one of the ways in which the problem was dealt with. It is true that none of our sources for the activities of *astynomoi* in the fourth century tell us that regulating performers in public and private places in Athens and the Peiraeus was one of their concerns, much less that they had the authority to march offending foreigners out of Attica, but there are indications that they may well have done just that. Besides the *astynomoi* there were also the officials in charge of the market known as the *agoranomoi*. Their main concern was with ensuring that what was sold was pure and unadulterated, but they had other wider responsibilities. Aristotle in the *Politics* has a general and fairly abstract discussion of the rôle played by *astynomoi* and *agoranomoi* in the larger Greek cities. He credits both sets of officials with responsibility for maintaining a seemly and orderly state of affairs (*eukosmia*) in their respective spheres of activity.[42] His readers will have known what he meant by that, but what the term encompassed is not at all self-evident. Plato, for his part, in his treatment in the *Laws* of *agoranomoi* and *astynomoi* says that *agoranomoi* should be responsible for good order (*kosmos*) in the marketplace. Since he believes that *astynomoi* are their counterparts in the larger sphere, it is fair to conclude that they too were charged with maintaining good order.[43] Plato's *agoranomoi* are to have the authority to impose a fine of up to one hundred drachmas on those native to the city guilty of contraventions of good order in the marketplace, but if the fine to be imposed is larger, the *astynomoi* are to sit on the tribunal with them. Slaves and foreigners are to be punished with blows and imprisonment; *astynomoi* are in their province to have the same powers of punishment.[44] It is by no means certain that the much greater latitude accorded *agoranomoi* and *astynomoi* in the punishment of foreigners and slaves reflects Athenian practice, but it is likely enough that it does. It is entirely conceivable that *goetes*, *thaumatopoioi* and other forms of mountebank who were not Athenian citizens were, when they seemed to threaten public order, beaten and driven out of Athens by the responsible authorities.

59

## Magic-working in the Laws of Plato and Athenian law

In the *Laws*, Plato mentions magic-working in two different contexts: he refers to it on a number of occasions in his discussion of impiety or *asebeia*; and he treats it in its own right as a non-physical form of *pharmakeia*. Magic comes up for mention in the discussion of *asebeia*, either because the impious persons who particularly engage Plato's wrath use magical techniques to effect their purpose, which is to deflect the moral indignation of the gods from those who have done wrong, or because they perform magic on the side.[45] It is never quite clear which of the two Plato has in mind. He does not, however, propose that magic should be punished as a form of *asebeia*, although he may well have believed that magic-working entailed *asebeia*. That said, it is necessary to insist that magic-working is only an incidental feature of the *asebeia* that is his concern. It is undoubtedly the case that the impious persons whom Plato wishes to confine in a place where they can have no contact with the rest of the free population do engage in magic-working, but that is not their main offence in Plato's eyes: it lies in promising that they can bend the gods to their will. That they also practise magic and that they use magic in getting the gods to do their will aggravates their offence, but it is not the real gravamen of Plato's charge against them. The penalties that he proposes to impose on the impious should not then be conflated with the measures he suggests should be taken against magicians pure and simple. The punishments reserved for the two groups are quite different: the impious are to be imprisoned in an isolated spot for the rest of their days, to be seen by no one of free birth, and when they die, their bones are to be cast outside the boundaries of the state;[46] the persons found guilty of practising binding-spells, summoning ghosts to haunt opponents or employing certain incantations are, if they are amateurs, to be punished appropriately, but if professional practitioners, are to be put to death.[47] In laying down the penalties for magic-working in its own right, Plato has nothing to say about impiety; the harm, *blapsis* or *blabe*, such actions do is his concern.[48] In Athenian law, the appropriate form of legal recourse for *blabe* was a *dike blabes* or a suit seeking punishment for harm done. Plato then provides some slight support for the thesis that a *dike blabes* would have been the normal form of legal redress for someone who felt that he or his had been harmed by sorcery performed by an Athenian.

# Holy men as magicians

The magician pure and simple in Classical Athens is an elusive figure. The magic-workers of whom we hear anything are almost always something else besides magicians; most of them are specialists in some form of religious activity. The closest that we seem to come to the magic-worker whose magic is not an extension of his religious expertise is the miracle-worker-cum-sorcerer, the *thaumatopoios* who is also a *goes*. Even so, it is likely that many miracle-working illusionists laid claim to a special understanding of the divine and sought to give the impression that their intimacy with the supernatural bestowed unusual powers on them. Since magic in the Greek world grew out of the rituals of religion and retained many features that derive from its origins, it is not altogether surprising that persons who laid claim only to an expertise in magic should be difficult to uncover. Very often the magician is a soothsayer (*mantis* or *chresmologos*) or an interpreter of prodigies (*teratoskopos*); he may also offer ritual purifications (*katharmoi*); he may provide initiations into mystery-rites; and finally, he may be a mendicant holy man (*agyrtes*). Sometimes the same man turns his hand to all of these callings. A concern with the divine is the common thread that ties together all of the rôles played by such men. That there is no strict differentiation in rôle between seers and magicians and between other forms of holy men and magicians is hardly an Athenian peculiarity, but is a phenomenon that is to be observed until the end of pagan antiquity and continues to be a problem in an increasingly Christianized Roman Empire.

The impression to be gained from our sources is that magicians were more likely than not to be seers or *manteis* and that some of the seers who performed magic could also be described as *agyrtai*, a term used to refer to mendicants. The earliest instance of a man being characterized as a *mantis* and *agyrtes* as well as a *magos* is in Sophocles' *Oedipus Rex* of about 430 BC. There Oedipus, searching to find the killer of his predecessor as ruler of Thebes, Laius, is dumbfounded to be told by the *mantis* Teiresias, whose advice and help he has sought, that he himself is Laius' killer. He assumes that Teiresias must have been put up to doing this by his brother-in-law Creon to deprive him of his throne by subterfuge and that Creon had suborned Teiresias, whom he characterizes as a *magos*, cunning in his scheming, a devious and underhand *agyrtes*, who can only see where there is profit to be made, but who is blind in his own craft (*techne*). These reflections on the prophet's craft lead Oedipus to address Teiresias directly and to ask him when had he ever shown himself to be a clear-sighted *mantis*.[49] The implication of the passage is that there was a class of persons who presented themselves as *manteis* but who were also *magoi* and *agyrtai* and that the last category of person was prepared to turn its hand to all sorts of underhand schemes, provided it made a profit from it. There is nothing in the context that makes it certain that a *magos* is for Sophocles a magician, but it is hard to see what other rôle the unscrupulous *mantis* who doubles as a *magos* can have.[50]

It sounds then as if the *magos*-cum-*agyrtes* who represented himself as a *mantis* would have been a familiar figure for Sophocles' audience. That to some extent is confirmed by the author of the treatise *On the Sacred Disease*, who hypothesizes that the first persons to treat epilepsy as a divinely-sent condition must have been men of the kind who are now *magoi*, purifiers (*kathartai*), *agyrtai* and charlatans (*alazones*), but who present themselves as being especially punctilious in their worship of the gods and at the same as the possessors of a superior understanding.[51] There is little doubt in this case that the persons referred to under this composite description are called *magoi* because they practise magic; the author asserts that these same people profess to be able by their *mageia* and sacrifices to pull the moon down from the sky, make the sun disappear and create storm or calm.[52] Although the author of the treatise does not call the persons he attacks *manteis*, what he describes is undoubtedly a form of *mantis*: they interpret the sounds made by epileptics while having a convulsion and the form the convulsion takes as signs of possession by particular deities.[53] The author is also at one with Oedipus in believing that the principal motivating factor in the lives of such persons and the factor that leads them into all manner of deviousness is their need to make a living.[54]

The figure of the *agyrtes*-cum-*mantis* is next encountered in Plato's *Republic* in a speech in which Adeimantus challenges Socrates to present a case for living a morally upright life, if it is possible by assuaging the anger of the gods to be cleansed of the consequences of any wrongdoing. According to Adeimantus, there are persons who claim to be able to perform this service: they are the *agyrtai* and *manteis* who come to the doors of the rich and seek to persuade them that they have acquired the capacity from the gods through sacrifices and incantations (*epodai*) to heal in a pleasurable and festive form not only any crimes the party approached may have committed but also any crimes his ancestors may have committed; the *agyrtai* and *manteis* also let it be known that if anyone wishes to harm an enemy, he will be able to do so at no great expense, whether by conjuring up a ghost (*epagoge*) or by employing a binding-spell (*katadesis*), as they will persuade the gods to serve them.[55] That is not all that Adeimantus has to say about the *agyrtai* and *manteis* who come to the doors of the rich; he also maintains that they cite lines from Homer to support the view that the gods can be bought off by prayer and sacrifice and that they provide what he calls a hubbub of books by Musaeus and Orpheus that lay down the rules for the sacrifices they perform and, furthermore, that they seek to persuade not only individuals but whole cities that releases and purifications (*katharmoi*) can be procured for men while they are still living by means of sacrifices conducted in a pleasant and joyous manner and that they are good also for death, in which event the ceremony is called *teletai*; what it does is free men from the ills in the afterlife that would otherwise affect them.[56]

Plato in the *Laws* makes mention of persons whose conduct bears a marked resemblance to the *agyrtai* and *manteis* of the *Republic*, although he does not refer to them under such a description, but only as *asebeis* or impious persons. He refers to them in explaining what the purpose is of a law forbidding the performance in private of religious rites. Part of the *raison d'être* for the law is to prevent anyone from engaging in sacrifice and prayer in private, but it is also intended to keep the *asebeis* from establishing shrines and altars in private houses and making, as they at any rate imagine it, the gods propitious in secret.[57] The persons who commission the *asebeis* to perform these services are described as being their betters.[58] In this context that is likely to mean that they are the social superiors of the *asebeis*. It is virtually certain that Plato has the same group of *asebeis* in mind at this point in the *Laws* as those whom he has a little earlier characterized as having a bestial nature (*theriodeis*); they are persons who in their contempt for their fellow-men perform *psychagogia* on many of the living and who attempt out of greed to destroy root and branch individuals, whole households and cities, asserting that they can perform *psychagogia* on the dead and undertaking to win over the gods by acts of sorcery (*goeteia*) involving prayer, sacrifice and incantation.[59] Their actions have the same catastrophic consequences for those who hire them as those that attend on engaging *asebeis* to perform private religious ceremonies designed to propitiate the gods: those who hire the *asebeis* draw down the wrath of the gods on their own heads and cause the whole city to pay for the actions of those they have hired.[60] Since the actions of the *asebeis* of the *Laws* are virtually identical with those that the *agyrtai* and *manteis* of the *Republic* promise to perform for the rich men to whose doors they come, namely, to cure the effect of wrongs committed through a power acquired from the gods by sacrifices and incantations, and since the persons who commission the *asebeis* seem to be persons of the same social standing as the rich men whose doors are besieged by *agyrtai* and *manteis*, there are grounds for thinking that the *asebeis* of the *Laws* and the *agyrtai* and *manteis* of the *Republic* are either the same people under different descriptions or persons who have a good deal in common.

Plato refers on two other occasions in as many words to *manteis* who practise magic. In the *Laws*, shortly before he discusses the *asebeis* of a beastly nature, he digresses from his argument to dilate on the kind of person who emerges from the number of the *asebeis* who do not believe in the existence of the gods, but who conceal their disbelief from others. At the head of the list of the talented but devious and treacherous individuals who do not believe in the gods but conceal their atheism from others Plato places many *manteis*, actively engaged in all manner of magic-working (*manganeiai*); he adds that sometimes persons of this type become tyrants, demagogues and generals and then that there are those who devote themselves to private initiations, and sophists of a guileful character.[61] It is above all then seers who practise magic who most conspicuously emerge from the ranks of the naturally gifted but devious and treacherous persons who dissemble their atheism. The suspicion must be, even though it can be no more than a suspicion, that many of the *asebeis* of beastly nature would fall into this category.

The one other reference to *manteis* who engage in magic is also in the *Laws*, in this case in the discussion of the penalties to be exacted from those who practise *pharmakeia*, whether it be the *pharmakeia* in which one body acts on another or the *pharmakeia* that consists in *manganeiai, epodai* and *katadeseis*. In both cases there is to be a distinction in the penalties imposed on those who practise *pharmakeia*, between those who are professionals and those who are not: the court is to assess the penalty to be paid by a non-professional who does not understand what he is doing, whereas if a doctor or a seer (*mantis*) or interpreter of prodigies (*teratoskopos*) is convicted of engaging in their respective forms of *pharmakeia*, there is a mandatory penalty of death.[62] The principle governing the imposition of a more severe penalty on persons skilled in the craft of the seer (*mantike*) would seem to be that, just as doctors know about drugs, so binding-spells, the summoning of ghosts to haunt people and other such harmful forms of *pharmakeia* are in some sense the special province of the seer.

We should beware of supposing that the relationship between doctor and non-professional and seer and non-seer is strictly analogous and that in both cases the difference turns on the doctor's and seer's knowing what they are doing and their non-professional counterparts' not knowing what they are doing. The Athenian Stranger in this passage of the *Laws* is in fact sceptical of the efficacy of the craft of the magician, although he does not go so far as to say that there is nothing to it.[63] The analogy between the doctor who employs poison and the seer who engages in magic with hostile intent is rather between a man for whom a knowledge of drugs is part of his craft and those for whom magic-working is almost an integral part of their professional activity. In short, while other persons may on occasion resort to magic-working, there is a presumption that seers and interpreters of prodigies were more likely to be versed in magic-working than anyone else. There seems to be no very good reason to think that Plato is unfairly blackening the name of *manteis*. There is after all the conviction and execution for *asebeia* of a *mantis* who was notorious as a sorceress, the Lemnian sorceress, Theoris, whom the historian Philochorus described as a *mantis* condemned for *asebeia*.[64]

Who then were the *manteis* who practised magic and in what kind of religious environment did they operate? The question is a difficult one to answer, not least because there is reason to believe that considerable differences existed amongst the *manteis* who practised magic: different kinds of *mantis* will have served very different clienteles and will have offered somewhat different services. Some *manteis* combined the performance of purificatory ceremonies that involved initiation into the mysteries with the practice of magic; others performed purifications, but not of the kind carried out for those being induced into the mysteries, and also practised magic; and yet others may have been *manteis* and have engaged in magic without acting as purifiers of any sort. Even amongst the class of persons who combine the practice of magic with purifications and initiations there may be major differences. The persons falling under this description to whom Plato refers in the *Republic* and the *Laws* may well constitute a rather special class of religious entrepreneur, who should not be confused with those persons who in their own houses inducted initiates into the mysteries or with those who went around more humble dwellings performing purificatory rituals.[65] Nor can there be any certainty that the purifications they offered in the seclusion of the houses of their patrons took the same form as the purificatory ceremonies performed in a more humble setting. All we can note is that their purifications, while unquestionably having something of the character of an Orphic-Bacchic ritual of purification, differ from Orphic-Bacchic ceremonial in inserting incantation (*epode*) into the ritual.[66]

Our quest into the identity of the holy man who performs magic will begin with a figure with whom he is on several occasions associated, the *agyrtes*. When Plato speaks about *agyrtai* and *manteis* making their way around the doors of the rich he almost certainly does not have separate categories of person in mind, but a single category. He is thinking of *manteis* who were at the same time *agyrtai*. The term *agyrtes* means basically 'someone who collects a living by begging'.[67] It is very often translated as 'beggar-priest'. The translation is misleading to the extent that it suggests all such persons owed allegiance to a particular divinity. Some certainly did, but others presented themselves as seers (*manteis*) and others yet again were probably oracle-mongers.[68] Men will have given to *agyrtai* for a variety of reasons: sometimes it will have been in return for services rendered; on other occasions, they will have imagined that in supporting a beggar-priest they were winning the favour of his god.

The figure of the *agyrtes* is to be encountered first in Aeschylus' *Agamemnon*: the Trojan princess, Cassandra, who has been given the gift of prophetic vision by Apollo, asks the Chorus of Argive elders, when she sees revealed before her what turns out to be the feast of Thyestes, whether she has hit on the truth or whether she is a false *mantis* of the sort who knocks on doors and babbles nonsense;[69] when at a later stage in the series of visions that roll before her eyes she sees a two-footed lioness who will kill her lying in bed with a wolf in the absence of the lion, she throws off the insignia of the seer's (*mantis*) craft that she wears and complains of having to endure being called a wandering *agyrtes*, a wretched beggar half-dead from starvation.[70] There are a number of lessons to be drawn from the episode: one is that by 458 BC, when the play was performed, *agyrtai* were so well-established a feature of Athenian life that Aeschylus is not conscious of the anachronism involved in introducing them into a drama set in the Heroic Age; secondly, some *agyrtai* presented themselves as *manteis* and specifically as the kind of *mantis* whose prophetic gift consisted in ecstatic visions; thirdly, some of them made their way from door to door; and finally, those who pursued the calling were often destitute and were greatly despised.

The *agyrtai* about whom we hear most are the acolytes of the Mother Goddess, Cybele.[71] They were known as *metragyrtai* or *menagyrtai*. Such persons were probably already a presence in the Greek world early in the fifth century; the ecstatic ravings of *metragyrtai* may be what Aeschylus has in mind when he makes Cassandra complain that she is treated as an *agyrtes*; and Pindar knows of the drums (*tympana*) and the castanets that were a feature of the worship of Cybele.[72] Confirmation that *metragyrtai* were a familiar feature of the religious landscape is not to be found until later in the century: the comic poet Cratinus, who was a somewhat older contemporary of Aristophanes, alluding to the eunuch-acolytes of the Mother Goddess, the *Galloi*, calls the famous seer Lampon a Cybele-collectress (*agersikybelis*);[73] and there is a play by Sophocles called *Tympanistai*, the chorus of which, to judge from its title, must have been made up of the drummers who played a part in the cult of Cybele. Lampon was not the only religious expert to be subject to such insults:[74] in the 380s or shortly thereafter the Athenian military man Iphicrates called a member of the family who provided the torch-bearer in the Eleusinian Mysteries a *metragyrtes*.[75] *Metragyrtai* will generally have moved around in bands with different persons in the band performing different rôles. That is implicit in the story told by the Peripatetic philosopher Clearchus, who was active in the latter part of fourth century and in the early third century, about the ultimate fate of Dionysius the Younger, who had once upon a time been tyrant of Syracuse: he brought his life to a miserable close in Corinth as a *metragyrtes* and drum-bearer.[76] The story is without question *ben trovato*, but it does tell us something about the place of such priests in the social hierarchy: there was no lower and more demeaning calling than being a begging-priest of the Mother Goddess; it represented the ultimate form of degradation. The moral standing of *metragyrtai* was also low: they served as a touchstone for turpitude.[77]

The persons called *agyrtai* will have been a heterogeneous group and will have come from very different backgrounds. It would be natural to assume that *metragyrtai* had their roots in the north-western part of Anatolia, in Phrygia, and that they had emerged from there to spread the cult of the Mother Goddess. The cult may, however, have had a long sojourn in Ionia and have become thoroughly hellenized before it made its way west.[78] It was certainly not the case in the fourth century BC that all of the votaries of the Mother Goddess were Asiatics. Had they been, Clearchus could not have told a story about Dionysius the Younger ending his days as a *metragyrtes*.

That *agyrtai* were vagabonds, persons of no fixed abode who made their way from city to city begging for a living, may be a largely correct assumption, but it is not one that can easily be proved. Plutarch, in his life of the early Spartan lawgiver, Lycurgus, does say that Lycurgus allowed no sophist nor mendicant soothsayer (*mantis agyrtikos*) nor keeper of courtesans to set foot in Laconia.[79] The implication of the anecdote is that *manteis agyrtikoi* wandered from place to place. Plutarch's source is probably Hellenistic. The passage has certainly nothing to tell us about conditions in Sparta in the seventh century BC, but will be testimony to the wanderings of *agyrtai* in the period from which it comes.[80] Not all *agyrtai* will necessarily have spent their lives wandering from place to place; some of them may well have been rooted in a city and confined themselves to making their way around it begging. The mother of Epicurus is a case in point. There is some reason to think that she would have been called an *agyrtria* if she had really, as an opponent of Epicureanism maintained, made the rounds of humble dwellings in Athens accompanied by her son, who read out purifications (*katharmoi*) for her.[81] While there may well have been persons who could be called *agyrtai* who were permanently, if not necessarily legally, resident in a community, the suspicion must be that many *agyrtai* did wander from city to city. It is likely, therefore, that *agyrtai* will for the most part have lacked legal standing in the communities in which they sought their livelihood. They would have been able to move around fairly freely; the boundaries of ancient states were porous. Such persons were no doubt subject to summary expulsion as well as summary punishment.

We are still a long way from being able to pin down who *agyrtai* actually were. It is virtually certain that anyone who owned enough land to live off or who had a craft to make a living from would not have gone out on the road as an *agyrtes*. *Agyrtai* by their nature are basically persons who are destitute, although some of them may eventually become sufficiently successful to settle down and establish themselves in a community. The real question is where can persons with a knowledge of ritual practice of whom a fair number must have been literate have come from. The anecdote told by Clearchus about Dionysius II of Syracuse suggests that some of them may have been men who were down on their luck. Although destitute and essentially beggars, *agyrtai* were not necessarily utterly obscure and nameless individuals. Some of them seem to have made a name for themselves, if the way in which Plutarch identifies the butt of a pithy saying uttered by a Spartan is anything to go by: he is Philippos the *Orpheotelestes*, a man who was utterly destitute, but who nonetheless told people that those who had been initiated under his supervision became prosperous and happy, once they had died. This had led to the Spartan saying to him: ' Why don't you die as soon as possible, you silly fellow, so that you may in one fell swoop put an end to your misfortune and stop lamenting your poverty?'[82] Since the story is likely to be Hellenistic in origin, it does not necessarily tell us very much about those wandering mendicants who in the Classical Period made a living from inducting persons into the mysteries.

It is possible to get a little closer to who the wandering mendicant religious experts were by looking at a kind of religious expert who has a good deal in common with the *agyrtes*, but about whom we are rather better informed. He may very well have been called an *agyrtes*. He is the *chresmologos*. In the second half of the fifth century, the *chresmologos* is in our sources the most conspicuous of the religious entrepreneurs who professed to be able to mediate between the human and the divine. His authority rested on his having access to collections of oracular utterances that were said to have been delivered by the Sibyl or by Bakis or Musaeus.[83] He is variously described as a *chresmologos* or a *mantis*. The stock-in-trade of the successful soothsayer of the entrepreneurial type was characteristically his possession of a book or books of oracles, that is to say, of a papyrus-roll or -rolls. We learn from a speech written by Isocrates of the career of such a *mantis*. The story told by Isocrates is worth recounting, since it does give us some idea of the background of one religious entrepreneur and of how he made his way in the world. It is very unlikely that other religious specialists followed precisely the same path, but some of them must have had similarly humble beginnings and have used some of the same devices in seeking their fortune. Isocrates' speech was written for a man who claimed to be the heir of a certain Thrasycles. Thrasycles was the son of a *mantis* called Thrasyllus from the island of Siphnos in the Cyclades. Thrasyllus, who had inherited no property from his ancestors, had laid the foundations of his fortune by becoming friends with an established *mantis* from somewhere other than Siphnos with whom he had formed a close attachment. The older man, who was called Polemainetos, had on his deathbed left Thrasyllus the books of his mantic craft and part of his property. Equipped with this stock-in-trade, Thrasyllus wandered from city to city, taking up residence for a time in a place. Wherever he settled, he would consort with the local women, although he did not acknowledge the children he fathered as his legitimate issue. When he had accumulated a very large amount of property, he felt the call of his native island of Siphnos and went back there. On his return to Siphnos, by now the wealthiest man on the island, he made an ambitious marriage, taking as his wife the sister of the father of the plaintiff, a woman whose family enjoyed a certain social standing on Siphnos. When she died, he married a cousin of the father of the plaintiff. The second wife also died and at this point Thrasyllus married into a family from Seriphos, another small island in the vicinity. The family was much grander than was to be expected from so small an island.[84]

The books of oracles that Thrasyllus inherited were the key to his success. With their help he had come from nowhere to accumulate enough wealth to be able to return to the island of his birth and marry into one of its leading families. That the possession of a book of oracles invested its possessor with power and authority we can see in a general way from Aristophanes' *Knights*. Amongst the devices that the new Paphlagonian slave uses to keep his master, the Athenian people, in his pocket are the oracles he recites to the master, who has a passion for Sibylline oracles.[85] The other slaves are discomfited at their loss of authority and can only retrieve it by stealing the Paphlagonian's book of oracles from him.[86] Aristophanes' *Peace* and *Birds* also both show us how important possession of a book of oracles was to a soothsayer. In *Peace*, a *chresmologos* called Hierocles, who is known from an inscription to have been a real person, turns up just when a character called Trygaeus is about to perform a sacrifice to consecrate the peace he has engineered.[87] Hierocles starts to interfere by quoting oracles that contradict what Trygaeus has done, and when Trygaeus quotes Homer in support of his actions, Hierocles declares the Sibyl does not agree.[88] Hierocles continues to make a nuisance of himself and complains when Trygaeus does not invite him to share in eating the entrails from the sacrificial victims. He is told by Trygaeus to eat the Sibyl.[89] In *Birds*, a soothsayer (*chresmologos*) appears and forces himself into the picture as the sacrifices are being made by a disaffected Athenian called Pisthetairos to inaugurate the foundation of Cloud-Cuckoo Land. When Pisthetairos questions whether the oracle pronounced by the *chresmologos* could really have contained the provisions for gifts to the seer, the man repeatedly bids Pisthetairos take the papyrus-roll and see for himself. Pisthetairos does not do so, but retaliates by citing an oracle which he maintains he had himself transcribed at Apollo's bidding. It says that when a quack appears unbidden wanting to eat the entrails that are cooked when sacrifice is made, then that man should be beaten. The *chresmologos* does not believe this and Pisthetairos bids him take the papyrus-roll and see for himself.[90] It is clear enough from the exchange that the authority of such soothsayers rests on their having a book of oracles in their possession to which they can appeal. It is less clear whether seers would actually have invited those from whom they wished to extract a fee to take their book and read it for themselves, to persuade them of the authenticity of what they had said, although it is entirely conceivable that this was one of their tricks.

From Thucydides we can get a sense of how soothsayers who traded on their possession of collections of oracles might intervene in public life and gain publicity for themselves. There are three occasions that the historian mentions in which *chresmologoi* seized the psychological opportunity afforded by momentous events in the offing to insert themselves into the public eye: just before the outbreak of war between Athens and Sparta in 431 BC, when the whole Greek world was in a high state of excitement, oracles were recited by *chresmologoi* both in the cities that were going to participate in the war and in those that would have no part in it;[91] later in the same year, when the Spartan king, Pleistoanax, and his army had come within sixty stades of the city of Athens and there was debate in Athens over what should be done, *chresmologoi* were again at work reciting oracles, which people interpreted as their inclinations took them;[92] finally, in 415 BC *chresmologoi* and *manteis* again inserted themselves into events, encouraging the Athenians to think that they would conquer Sicily; on this occasion, news of the calamitous failure of the expedition led the Athenians to be angry with those who had invoked an understanding of the divine to mislead them.[93]

Some of the men who possessed collections of oracles were respectable and respected Athenian citizens, securely rooted in the life of the city. The well-known seers, Lampon and Diopeithes, seem to have belonged to this category. Most soothsayers were probably not respected. They seem to have been thought of as sharp operators and not as respectable members of society. Thucydides, for instance, clearly did not approve of the opportunism of *chresmologoi*. In Aristophanes, they are presented as opportunists whose good faith is in doubt. The favoured term of abuse for them in *Peace* and *Birds* is *alazon*, a word that in this context means a man who lays claim to an expertise that he does not possess.[94] 'Quack' or 'charlatan' is the appropriate English equivalent.[95] Herodotus tells a story about an Athenian *chresmologos* and organizer of the oracles of Musaeus called Onomacritus, who was expelled from Athens by Hipparchus, a son of the tyrant Peisistratus, after he was caught by the lyric poet, Lasus of Hermione, in the act of inserting a prophecy that foretold the disappearance into the sea of the islets in the vicinity of Lemnos into the oracles of Musaeus. According to Herodotus, a reconciliation between Onomacritus and the sons of Peisistratus was effected, and they took the man with them when they travelled overland to Sousa to try to persuade the Persian king, Xerxes, to invade Greece and restore them. The Peisistratids spoke glowingly of Onomacritus, who then quoted selectively from his collection of oracles, leaving out all oracles that predicted failure on the part of the Persians and only citing those that announced Persian successes, interpreting them to mean that the Hellespont should be bridged and an expedition mounted.[96] Whatever the reality behind the story may be, it is an indication of the suspicion that surrounded such soothsayers and their *modus operandi*.

To return to the Siphnian *mantis* Thrasyllus. Isocrates tells us that he had been left no property at all by his forebears, which is to say he was very poor but of free birth. It is probably fair to say that his ancestry was obscure. Somehow or other he had learned to read, since otherwise he would not have been able to use the books of oracles that his friend Polemainetos had left him. One suspects that the relationship between Polemainetos and Thrasyllus was not quite what Isocrates represents it as being, which is one of guest-friendship, since it is far from clear what hospitality Thrasyllus, a propertyless man, could have afforded Polemainetos. Thrasyllus was perhaps the apprentice and helper of the older soothsayer and it may have been from Polemainetos that Thrasyllus learned to read and from Polemainetos that he acquired his craft. To what extent Thrasyllus' career as a soothsayer represents a common pattern we cannot say, but we may surmise that the origins of many religious entrepreneurs were wrapped in mystery and that they served some sort of apprenticeship as the helper of an older man from whom they learned the rudiments of reading and the tricks of their trade. Why anyone who had any property of his own and some standing in his own community would have taken up the life of a soothsayer is a puzzle. Where we do find a man with roots in the community acting as a *chresmologos* it may be that this was an inherited calling and one that he pursued only intermittently when called upon by the state or a prince. With the exception of men of that sort, soothsayers will generally have belonged to the class of the dispossessed and rootless.

One feature of Thrasyllus' life as a soothsayer, his wandering from city to city, living in each place for a time, does have parallels: Hierocles, the soothsayer at whose expense Aristophanes has some fun in *Peace*, is not an Athenian but comes from Oreos on the island of Euboea.[97] Despite the fact that the prophet Diopeithes was a man of some standing in Athens, he was in 410 BC to be found adducing and interpreting an oracle for the Spartan king Leotychides; that is to say, in the middle of hostilities between Athens and Sparta Diopeithes was apparently present in Sparta advising a Spartan king.[98] Whether the story about the Athenian seer Onomacritus' going to Sousa in the company of the Peisistratids is true or not, it does bear witness to the opportunism of such men and to their willingness to travel to exploit the gullible.

Further confirmation that in the fifth century there were seers on the move throughout Greece comes from the pages of Herodotus' *Histories*. Of the nine *manteis* mentioned in Herodotus only one seems to have practised his craft in his native city and even that is not clear.[99] A disproportionate number of them come from Elis.[100] Two of that number belong to the clan or guild of the Iamidae, a group who boasted that they were descended from Iamus, a son of Apollo.[101] In Herodotus, seers are characteristically to be found with armies, pronouncing on the sacrifices taken before military expeditions or before battles, but armies and battles are the stuff of which Herodotus' narrative is made. It is likely that these men also played a part in the peacetime activities of the cities to which they made their way. The seers mentioned by Herodotus were the famous ones who made their mark on public life. They are probably the tip of an iceberg. Run-of-the-mill seers will, like their more famous counterparts, have provided themselves with a pedigree or with credentials of some sort. They could, if they were especially ambitious, lay claim to being members of one of the two main guilds of seer, the Iamidae, whose centre was Elis, or the Melampodidae. That itinerant seers sometimes appropriated to themselves a lineage that was not theirs is to be inferred from what Herodotus says about Deiphonus, the seer who performed the sacrifices for the Greek force at Mycale before the battle there in 480 BC. He came from Apollonia, a joint foundation of Corinth and Corcyra, and was said to be the son of a citizen of that city, Euenius, who had been given the gift of prophecy by the gods and had become renowned for his abilities in that quarter, after having been deprived of his eyesight by the authorities in Apollonia as punishment for failing to guard a flock of sheep sacred to the Sun.[102] What Herodotus reports about Deiphonus is that he had heard it said that Deiphonus had appropriated the name of Euenius and had, in consequence, found work all over Greece, even though he was not the son of Euenius.[103] The truth or falsity of the story cannot be recovered, but it does bear witness to the existence of itinerant seers who made their way around the Greek world trading on their name, whether it was rightly theirs or not.

Isocrates' account of the career of Thrasyllus gives us some idea of the background from which the wandering *manteis* who offered their services as magicians will have come. Like Thrasyllus, they must almost inevitably have been propertyless persons, driven by their lack of means to seek a living by their wits. We know where Thrasyllus came from, but we are not in a position to venture any opinion on where in the Greek world or in the areas surrounding it the mendicant wandering holy men came from. Some of them may in fact have come from the hinterland of the Greek cities on the coast of Asia Minor; others will have represented themselves as Phrygians, versed in the cult of the Great Mother; others again will have been runaway slaves; and yet others persons down on their luck. Whatever their origins, they will have been persons who lacked legal standing in the communities to which they came on their travels.

Thrasyllus was taken up by an older man from whom he not only learned his craft, but who left him the tools of his trade, a collection of oracles. The same situation must have obtained for many of the wandering holy men: they too will have begun their careers as the helpers of an older man or in some cases possibly of a woman and obtained the rudiments of their craft from that person as well as eventually acquiring the texts that gave their master some of his authority. The texts that mendicant holy men who turned their hands to magic needed will very much have depended on the rôles they played. Those who undertook to perform purificatory ceremonies that were part of an initiation-rite will have required the texts to whose authority Plato says the *agyrtai* and *manteis* who came to the doors of rich men appealed.[104] These will have been poems ascribed to Musaeus and Orpheus and perhaps to other legendary figures, composed mostly in the sixth century. Such persons will also have been in possession of incantations appropriate to the various forms of magic they boasted of being able to perform. Plato speaks of their carrying out binding-spells and of their summoning up ghosts to haunt enemies. A binding-spell did not necessarily take the form of a lead curse-tablet, but incantation is likely to have played some part in its performance. The same will be true of the summoning up of ghosts. The earliest known collection of magical spells belongs to the first century BC, but spells will have circulated in writing at a much earlier date. Precisely what form they will have taken is a mystery, but there is some evidence from the middle of the fourth century of incantations being passed on, presumably in a written form. Aristogeiton's brother is said to have received from his mother, who was the maidservant of the Lemnian sorceress put to death by the Athenian people, the *pharmaka* and the *epodai* that had belonged to the woman and with these he had set up in business as a magician in his own right.[105] The underlying assumption of the slander is that the stock-in-trade of a sorceress including her incantations exists in a physical form that can be passed on.

The fact that reading was a necessary accomplishment for many wandering mendicant holy men calls for comment. It is a matter of some dispute how widespread in the period in question literacy of any sort was in Athens and in the wider Greek world. There are those who would still maintain that most Athenian men could read, although they would concede that the ability was not for the most part exercised very extensively.[106] The main argument against that position is that most Athenians would not have had the wherewithal to pay for the education of their sons, nor would they have been able to release their sons from the work that they needed to have done to let them go to school.[107] In view of these considerations, it is likely that a very restricted class of persons would have been taught to read and write. They will have been very much the same group who would later be enrolled as hoplites, that is to say, men who had the means to purchase the equipment of heavy infantryman. Since there is no very good evidence for widespread literacy in ancient Athens and because the idea of universal male literacy flies in the face of economic realities, it should follow that having access to books containing arcane and mysterious texts and owning these same books would have had a cachet that it would not have had in a society in which literacy was more widely distributed. Limited literacy tends to endow those who can read and who possess books with power, authority and charisma. The difficulty then is how to explain an ability to read and probably to write also on the part of persons who come from the margins of society. These mendicant seers and purveyors of mysteries will not have come by their ability to read and probably also to write by attending an elementary school accompanied by a slave-paedagogus; they will have acquired these attainments from the men or women whose helpers or apprentices they were.

We may now turn to look a little more closely at the persons who combined the practice of magic with the promise of being able to cure men of the effects of their and their ancestors' wrongdoing by initiating them into the mysteries. It is to be inferred from Euripides' *Bacchae*, a play that belongs to the last decade of the fifth century, that wandering holy men offering initiations into the mysteries and at the same time practising magic were at the end of the fifth century a feature of the Greek religious landscape. That is what Pentheus' decrying the god Dionysus as a foreigner from Lydia and a *goes epodos* who conducts ceremonies of initiation would suggest.[108] The portrait that Ephorus paints of the Idaean Dactyls and their pupil Orpheus tends to support that supposition. They are on Ephorus' account sorcerers (*goetes*) who practised incantations (*epodai*), initiations (*teletai*) and mystery-rites (*mysteria*); they had crossed to Europe from their place of origin on Mount Ida in Phrygia with Mygdon, the eponymous ancestor of the Thracian people called the Mygdones;[109] during the period in which they dwelt in Samothrace they had terrified the inhabitants of the island; a further feature of their sojourn on Samothrace was that Orpheus, a man who had extraordinary poetical and musical abilities, became their pupil and was thereafter the first man to introduce mystery-rites (*teletai* and *mysteria*) to the Greeks.[110]

Not all of those who conducted private initiations into the mysteries wandered from city to city. There is no question of Aeschines' or his mother's having moved from place to place. Yet he was said by his opponent Demosthenes to have assisted his mother when a boy in initiating men into the mysteries of the Phrygian god Sabazios.[111] The ceremonies appear to have been conducted in the dwelling-place of the family, although this is not absolutely certain. Demosthenes' attack on Aeschines inspired a Stoic opponent of Epicurus to attribute the same sort of upbringing to Epicurus: Epicurus had accompanied his mother when she went around humble houses (*oikidia*) to read out purifications (*katharmoi*) for her; alongside his father he had taught elementary letters for a miserable fee; and one of his brothers had been a pimp who consorted with Leontion the hetaera.[112] It looks as if the man who invented the calumny wanted to have Epicurus spring from even humbler stock than Aeschines; hence ceremonies of purification performed in other people's houses and humble houses at that. The reality, however, must be that purificatory-cum-initiatory rites that mimicked Orphic-Bacchic ceremonial were performed for fairly humble people by women who came to their houses and that these women occupied an even more degraded place on the social ladder than those who conducted initiations in their own houses.

Those who conducted ceremonies of initiation in their own premises must on the whole have been people from the margins of society, such as slaves and ex-prostitutes. That much is to be inferred from the story that Demosthenes makes up about Aeschines' origins. He says that his opponent's father had been the slave of a man teaching elementary reading and writing near the temple of Theseus in Athens; not only was he a slave, but he had suffered from the further indignity of being a slave of the lowest sort, one who was shackled; he went under the slave-name of Tromes, to which his son had added two syllables to create the entirely respectable name of Atrometos; Aeschines' mother, who had brought him up, had been a prostitute whose place of work was a hut near the shrine of a certain hero; there she had plied her trade, even in the middle of the day, until eventually a slave called Phormion had removed her from that calling; not only had the son created a new and grander name for his father, he had done the same for his mother: she was now Glaucothea, a much more dignified name than her nickname as a whore, Empousa, which she was given because she was prepared to do anything and put up with having anything done to her.[113]

## The miracle-worker as magician

There is another category of person who sometimes doubled as a magician in Athens and no doubt elsewhere in the fifth and fourth centuries of which account needs to be taken. These are the persons known as *thaumatopoioi* or less frequently as *thaumatourgoi*. A *thauma* is a wondrous event that can very often only be explained by invoking a supernatural agent. *Thauma* is, in consequence, the word that is used in the New Testament for a miracle. A *thaumatopoios* is literally 'a wonder-worker'. *Thaumatopoiia*, however, covers not only conjuring-tricks, but also juggling, acrobatics and marionette shows.[114] A closely related form of entertainment was provided by the persons known as *planoi*. The noun *planos* is derived from a verb that means in the active 'to cause to wander, to lead astray', and in its intransitive form 'to wander'. It is interestingly never altogether clear in the way in which the word is used in practice whether it is the active or the intransitive form that is the root. The original root was probably the active form, but because of the associations of the root with wandering from place to place, the word not only has the sense of impostor but also of vagabond. Plato repeatedly speaks of *goetes* assuming forms other than their own and associates them with *thaumatopoiia*.[115] Although Plato links *goeteia* and *thaumatopoiia*, there is no reason to suppose that all *thaumatopoioi* were considered *goetes*, nor that all *goetes* practised *thaumatopoiia*. There was nonetheless an overlap. The fragmentary information that we have about the illusion-creating *goes* or *thaumatopoios* who wanders from city to city seeking his living necessarily limits what can confidently be said about him, but there is the distinct possibility that magicians of this kind form a specialized sub-class of magic-workers and are not to be identified with the wandering holy men who use the pretence of privileged access to the divine to win clients for themselves.

There are indications that already in the fifth century *magoi* and *goetes* claimed to be able to effect miracles, which is to say, they performed conjuring tricks. A Phrygian slave in Euripides' *Orestes*, trying to account for the disappearance of his mistress Helen, has three explanations to offer: spells (*pharmaka*) were involved; the craft of *magoi* was responsible; she was spirited away by the gods.[116] It may be that *magoi* promised to make persons vanish without actually doing so in front of spectators, but it does rather sound as if the slave is referring to what we would call a conjuring-trick. In Euripides' *Bacchae*, Dionysus is in the eyes of the king of Thebes, Pentheus, a *goes epodos*, but for the seer Teiresias he is a god.[117] When the attendant who has been sent to arrest the ecstatic followers of Dionysus, the maenads and Dionysus himself, comes back with Dionysus in bonds but without the maenads, he also brings with him a report of the miracles (*thaumata*) that have attended the arrival of Dionysus in Thebes. They consist principally in the effortless escape of the maenads from the public prison in which they had been held fettered; the fetters had been loosed from their feet without their doing anything, the bolts on the doors had come undone, and the doors had opened without any human hand touching them. Pentheus is unimpressed and orders that Dionysus be released from his bonds, since he is confident that his prisoner will not be able to escape.[118] The miracles are in fact proof of Dionysus' divinity, but for Pentheus they are presumably the tricks of a *goes* and as such not to be taken seriously. Then there is the story that is for Herodotus justification for concluding that the Neuroi, a people whose territory borders that of the Scyths, are likely to be *goetes*. It is a story, according to Herodotus, told by the Scyths and by the Greeks living amongst them: every year for a few days each of the Neuroi changes into a wolf before returning to

75

his former self.[119] If that were all that there were to the tale, we might fairly infer that the Neuroi were shamans and that *goetes* had a shamanistic side to them. Herodotus, however, says that those who tell the story have not persuaded him of its truth, although their failure to do so has not prevented the tellers of the tale affirming its accuracy and swearing to its truth. It is not then because the Neuroi are shamans that Herodotus supposes they are *goetes*, but because they are not what they purport to be. Herodotus' reason for calling the Neuroi *goetes* turns out, accordingly, to be that the Neuroi have deceived the Scyths and the Greeks into thinking that they become wolves. In other words, a *goes* is for Herodotus a person who is able to create in the mind of others an illusion of what is not.

To sum up, it is virtually impossible to point to men who were magicians and magicians only. They are almost always found to follow some other calling, but one that is closely related to their magic-working. It would nonetheless be dangerous to assume that magic-working was only practised by those who were wandering holy men, seers and wonder-workers. Allowance should be made for the possibility that there were men who were magicians pure and simple. Who they would have been we cannot even begin to guess. There is no evidence from Athens that some men specialized in some forms of magic-working and other men in others. Nor again is there any positive evidence of men practising one kind of magic-working and women another. The careless assumption that love-philtres are the province of the female magician and that the clientele these women served was female needs to be guarded against: Ninos is said to have provided young men (*neoi*) with love-philtres;[120] Deianeira, on the other hand, gets the magical ointment that will keep Hercules from any other woman from a male, Nessus; and Hercules, when told by his son that his wife, convinced she was applying a love-philtre, had anointed his robe, asks what sorcerer (*pharmakeus*) of the people of Trachis had helped her.[121] There is nonetheless a consideration that makes it possible that there was some differentiation in rôle amongst magicians. It is that the different branches of magic had very different origins. That could have meant, for example, that the persons who practised one of the forms of magic that had its roots in *rhizotomia* would not also have conjured up the ghosts of the dead.

It is very difficult to capture the texture of life in Classical Athens, since our sources give us so sanitized a picture of conditions there. There are large areas of human existence that they ignore or that were in some sense invisible to them. Stray scraps of information may betray something of the reality. We are told, for instance, that one of the tasks of the *astynomoi*, or rather of their slave-attendants, was to pick up the corpses of those who had expired in the streets.[122] These are presumably the bodies of persons who lived on the streets and who had no relatives to take care of their burial. Who they were beyond that must be a matter for speculation, but that the *astynomoi* had such a task points to the presence in Athens of homeless persons, probably very often from elsewhere, who had gravitated to the city to find a livelihood. Such details remind us that the medley of sights, smells and noises that would have assailed us, had we walked through the *agora*, would no doubt have been overwhelming. The variety of persons present and the goods and services they had to offer is not readily grasped. It is too easy to be lulled into imagining that the population of Athens was made up of citizens, resident aliens and slaves and to forget that there will have been many people in the city who fell into none of these categories or who fell between them. While it is difficult enough for us to imagine what the life of the well-to-do in Athens will have been like, it is even more difficult for us to make sense of what it will have been like to be destitute, to lack the right to legal residence and to have to live by one's wits. The precariousness and misery of such a life are not easily recaptured. This will have been the situation of many of the persons who practised magic-working. They were in all likelihood subject to beatings at the hands of the slaves of the *agoranomoi* and the *astynomoi*, to summary arrest and imprisonment, and to expulsion from Attica, if their activities were believed to have been a threat to public order.

## Magic-workers in places other than Athens

If a proportion of the persons who practised magic in Athens were itinerant holy men or wonder-workers, it follows that they will have engaged in the same activities elsewhere. The trouble is that we are desperately badly informed about their doings anywhere other than in Athens. There is nonetheless something to be said about magic-working in the larger Greek world of the fifth and fourth centuries BC and those who engaged in it. Amongst the sheets of lead recording questions put to the oracle of Zeus at Dodona that survive are a number that ask questions about sorcery. One of the concerns of those approaching the oracle is to find out whether sorcery had been performed against themselves or against someone connected with them. The questions put to the oracle complement the binding-spells inscribed on lead that have survived from the period. They testify to a tendency to blame sorcery when something was amiss and show that sorcery was a very real fear and not just a figment of the literary imagination. We can only guess at the reasons the questioner had for asking the oracle whether a ship-owner or perhaps a ship-captain was being harmed by spells (*pharmaka*).[123] It is a fairly safe bet that the financial interests of the questioner were at risk, but was he afraid lest the spells might create adverse weather and prevent the successful completion of the voyage or was it something quite different that was the focus of his fears? The questioner gives no hint in what remains of the lead sheet of who might be casting spells against the ship-owner. Other tablets are more illuminating. One questioner asks at the end of the fourth century whether someone, whose sex is unclear, has put a spell (*katapharmassein*) on a woman whose name is Aristoboula on behalf of a man called Timos.[124]

It is to be imagined that the questioner is a man and that the question he asks is about a woman in whom he has some sexual interest but who is unresponsive. There is nothing very surprising in this. What is much more interesting is the assumption made by the questioner that Timos has employed someone, apparently known to the questioner but unnamed, to put a spell on Aristoboula. That points to the presence of known magic-workers, whether male or female, in the community. Some corroboration for that inference is to be found in a question that asks whether an unnamed party has brought a spell (*pharmakon*) acquired from Lyson to bear on his own family, on the wife and, finally, on the questioner.[125] What the questioner is asking is far from clear, but it may be that he has got his personal possessive pronouns mixed up and is asking whether his own family, his wife and himself have been the object of sorcery. Whatever the solution to that problem may be, what is not in doubt is the assumption made by the questioner that if a spell has been cast, it has been acquired from a third party, who is known and named.

A question put, to judge from the script in which it is written, at the beginning of the fourth century bears further witness not only to the existence of known magic-workers in the community but also to specialization within that calling. The questioner asks the presiding deities of the oracle Zeus Naos and his consort, Dione, whether or not they are using Dorios, the *psychagogos*.[126] It may be that the inquiry to the oracle is couched in the third person and that the inquirers are asking whether they themselves are to employ Dorios, the *psychagogos*. It is on the whole slightly more likely that the questioner is asking whether unnamed third parties are using a *psychagogos* against him. Certainty is not obtainable here. But it is at least clear that the questioner or questioners know of a man to whom people turn when they need someone expert in raising spirits.

# 3

# SORCERESSES IN THE ATHENS OF THE FIFTH AND FOURTH CENTURIES BC

We are on the face of it infinitely better informed about male magicians in Athens in the fifth and fourth centuries BC than we are about their female counterparts. It is possible that our sources reflect a reality and there were indeed more men at work as magicians than there were women. There are, however, complications. The common ancient assumption was that women were more likely to be expert in magic than men.[1] It sounds as though it was already a commonplace by 428 BC when Euripides' *Hippolytus* was performed: the Nurse, speaking in the presence of the women of Troizene, who form the chorus of the play, and with the charms and incantations that can cure the lovelorn of their sickness in mind, says to her mistress Phaedra that men would be slow to find their way to such cures without the inventiveness of women.[2] The Nurse uses the first person plural in speaking of the inventiveness of women. The context suggests that she embraces in her remarks not only women in general, but more immediately herself and the women of Troizene. Of course it can be and in fact has been argued by those with a certain *parti pris* that utterances of this type express a stereotyped view of women as scheming and devious and are not in consequence to be relied upon. That the Nurse is giving expression to a stereotyped view can certainly be conceded. The question that needs to be asked is whether the stereotype reflects a reality or only male prejudice and fear. There is ultimately no way of settling the matter, since those who like to think that the figure of the sorceress is largely a figment of the male imagination are not going to be persuaded by any of the counter-examples that might be brought against their position. It is nonetheless not easy to see why, if the notion that women are all potential sorceresses is a construct of the male mind, male magicians enjoy a much greater prominence in the writings of male authors in the fifth and fourth centuries BC than do their female equivalents.

When we dig a little below the surface, we discover that holy men have their female counterparts and that these holy women engage in very much the same set of suspect practices as do some holy men. Not only that, we also find evidence of women who are far from being holy women or wandering mendicants practising magic. In fact it is here that we get much closer to finding persons whose magic-working is not just an offshoot of religious activity but has an independent existence. In other words, we get closer to someone who conforms to our preconceptions of what a magician should be.

The world of the wandering holy man is, as we have seen, the matrix out of which many male magicians emerge. The same probably holds good for some sorceresses, although the evidence linking religion to magic-working in the case of women is more tenuous. The existence of mendicant holy women in this period is certainly not to be gainsaid. There were at least two forms in which these women might come: they might either be mendicant seers or priestesses who begged on behalf of a deity. Cassandra in Aeschylus' *Agamemnon* exemplifies the former type: she feels that as an inspired seer (*mantis*) reduced to slavery she suffers the indignities endured by mendicant holy women (*agyrtriai*) who wander hither and thither.[3] The other kind of mendicant holy woman is exemplified in the begging-priestess (*hiereiai*) into whom Hera transforms herself in Aeschylus' play, *Xantriai*. In that play, Hera begs on behalf of the nymphs of the River Inachus in Argos.[4] It is clear both from the *Agamemnon* and from the indignation implicit in Socrates' adducing in the *Republic* the example of Hera transformed into a begging-priestess as an instance of what poets should not be permitted to do that to be a mendicant holy woman was an extremely degrading form of existence.

It cannot be shown that wandering mendicant holy women of the types represented by Cassandra and Hera respectively practised magic, nor even that they conducted initiations into the mysteries, unless we are to count the mother of Epicurus as an example of the type. What can be demonstrated is that women who are described in our sources as priestesses (*hiereiai*), but who are certainly not priestesses of one of the official cults of the city, did conduct ceremonies of initiation and that one of them, Ninos, was condemned to death for activities connected with these rites of initiation.[5]

Any inclination we might have to imagine that the grander kind of magician in Athens was likely to be male and to belong to the ranks of wandering, mendicant holy men and that the simpler forms of magic were performed by local women who did not have the aura of authority that possession of arcane texts conferred on the mendicant holy men should be resisted. The example of Theoris, whose magical drugs and incantations the brother of Aristogeiton is supposed to have acquired from his mother, who was the maidservant of Theoris, is salutary in this regard.[6] From the way in which Theoris is spoken of it is apparent that the speaker in the case against Aristogeiton thought that the jury would recognize her name. She was clearly a figure of some renown or notoriety. She must also have been important enough in her own right or perhaps more likely because of her connections to have been thought worthy of prosecution. Theoris was no local witch. Nor was she some poor destitute old woman. She did after all own a maidservant, who seems to have been her accessory, until she informed against her mistress. Theoris was also said to have possessed both magical drugs and incantations.[7] The latter, since the maidservant was able to pass them on to her son, look as though they will have existed in the form of a book. That is significant, since it means sorceresses of this level were credited with possessing books of spells and with being able to read. In the speech in the Demosthenic corpus in which she is mentioned she is referred to as the sorceress (*pharmakis*).[8] Yet the Atthidographer Philochorus calls the woman a *mantis*.[9] There is, as we have seen, no inconsistency in the woman's being referred to both as a *pharmakis* and a *mantis*. Male seers engaged in magic; they will have had their female counterparts. What we end up with when we put all of these pieces together is a woman who comes from Lemnos, an Athenian possession, and is apparently an Athenian citizen, living, so far as can be judged, independently and on her own with her maidservant, apparently making a living as a seer and extending her activities as a diviner into magic-working. She is also a woman who possesses the ability to read. She does not exist in obscurity, but probably has contacts who occupy prominent places in Athenian public life.

The only other women in Athenian life who have both independence and fame of whom anything is known are the great courtesans.[10] Theoris looks as though she belongs to the same *demi-monde*. Her origins may be not unlike those of some of the courtesans. Something of this culture can be pieced together from remarks about famous courtesans preserved in various sources and from the account of the career of a hetaera, prominent in Athens and in other parts of the Greek world, given in a speech delivered in court by a plaintiff called Theomnestus. Theomnestus' motive in telling his highly-coloured story of the career of the courtesan was to take revenge on the man who treated the hetaera as his legitimate wife. Whatever reservations may be entertained about accepting what Theomnestus says about the woman, who is called Neaera, we can be fairly confident that his picture of life in the *demi-monde* had for his hearers a degree of verisimilitude and corresponded to something they knew. Neaera was purchased as a child by a woman whose name was Nicarete. Nicarete was at that time resident in Athens. She was herself the freedwoman of a man from Elis in the western part of the Peloponnese. She lived with a man who was a cook by trade. Nicarete had a knack of picking girls who would later become beauties. Neaera was only one of a stable of seven girls purchased by Nicarete. She ran the girls as prostitutes in Athens and then had Neaera working in Corinth, where she sold her to some of her clients, who had formed a partnership to purchase the freedom of the girl. Neaera moved back to Athens to consort with one of the men, but his mistreatment of her caused her to decamp to Megara, taking with her household effects that belonged to the man, the gold ornaments and clothes he had given her and two maidservants. She spent two years in Megara working but had difficulty keeping up the expensive establishment she ran, because the Megarians were too stingy to pay her enough. Finally, she was brought to

Athens from Megara by Stephanus, the man who was later to pass her off as his wife. In describing the extent of Neaera's wanderings, Theomnestus says that she had plied her calling throughout the Peloponnese, in Thessaly and Magnesia, on the island of Chios and in a large part of Ionia.[11]

The historian Theopompus provides another example of a courtesan on the move and of the world from which she came in the person of Pythonice, the kept woman of Alexander the Great's paymaster, Harpalus. It was a scandal to Theopompus' way of thinking that Harpalus should have honoured the woman with a funerary monument in Babylon, where she had died, and also with one in Athens, which had been her principal base. She was a slave of the flute-player Bacchis, who in her turn had been the slave of a Thracian woman called Sinope, who had worked as a prostitute in Aegina before leaving it for Athens.[12] The same historian recounts that what happened after the death of Pythonice was that Harpalus summoned another courtesan from Athens, Glycera, whom he wished people to do obeisance to as his queen.[13] He does not reveal what her antecedents were.

Isaeus, a speech-writer of the second half of the fourth century, all of whose surviving speeches deal with disputed inheritances, presents a variation on Neaera's rise from a girl hired out to entertain men to great courtesan, except that the woman in question begins at an even lower point on the hierarchy of prostitutes and does not reach the heights scaled by Neaera. This time the woman is called Alce and had been the property of the freedwoman of a well-to-do man called Euctemon. The freedwoman had run a lodging-house (*synoikia*) in the Peiraeus where she had kept prostitutes. These would have been youngish girls, who were presented half-naked for the customers to choose from. They each had cells (*oikemata*) to themselves, where they did their work. They were not quite the lowest form of prostitute since there were those who had to work outside. Both the Peiraeus and the area near the Dipylon-Gate in what was the potters' quarter in Athens, the Ceramicus, were centres of prostitution. Alce worked in her cell for a good number of years, before she became too old to earn a living in that way. She might then have been in her twenties. While she worked in the lodging-house, she had cohabited with a freedman called Dion and maintained that the children to which she had given birth were his. Dion went along with this and brought them up as though they were his own. That arrangement came to an end when Dion had to leave Athens for Sicyon to avoid the consequences of a crime that he had committed. At this point, Euctemon put Alce in charge of the running of a lodging-house, presumably also a brothel, near the gate in the Ceramicus where wine was sold. He then began to spend time with her, even dining in her company. This caused his wife and children some considerable distress. Their annoyance did no good and Euctemon ended up living with Alce. Worse was to follow: Euctemon tried to get the quasi-kinship organization or phratry of which he was a member to accept the elder of Alce's two boys as his legitimate son. The attempt failed.[14]

It is to this sort of female *demi-monde* that Theoris will have belonged. The women in it move relatively freely from place to place. They tend to be slaves by origin but either have their freedom purchased for them or establish a *de facto* freedom for themselves. They set up their own establishments with the help of well-to-do male patrons and admirers, have maidservants, and when their days as prostitutes or courtesans are over, the more intelligent and enterprising become madams and live off the earnings of younger women, while the others have to revert to living as common prostitutes. Xenophon portrays a visit that Socrates makes to the establishment of such a woman. She is called Theodote and lives in some style. A painter is painting her likeness when Socrates and his companions arrive, but withdraws. The house is well furnished, Theodote is well turned out, as is her mother, who lives with her, and there are numerous attractive and well-clad maidservants in attendance. When Socrates asks the woman what supports the establishment, she replies that she depends on the benefactions of male friends (*philoi*). It emerges, however, that this is by no means an assured source of income nor one in which Theodote can feel any great confidence.[15] We may imagine that the mother, if we are really supposed to believe that she is Theodote's mother, is herself a former courtesan and runs the undertaking. The whole enterprise rests on rather shaky foundations and will collapse, once Theodote loses her charms. At that point she will either have to find a successor to live off, who may or may not be her daughter, or become a common prostitute.

The literary evidence showing that in Athens in the fifth and fourth centuries BC the worlds of the female magic-worker and prostitute or procuress and madam intersected is thin, but even here there are indications that their worlds did indeed come together. Let us take the case of the ex-prostitute called Alce whom Euctemon in his old age put in charge of a brothel in the Ceramicus and for whom he ended up abandoning his wife and family. When Euctemon tries to register one of her sons in his phratry, probably to secure recognition that the boy was his legitimate son and so able to inherit from him, Isaeus is able to suggest that anyone whose state of mind was such as to attempt such a deed had been moved to act against his better judgment, either by *pharmaka*, a sickness or some other factor.[16] It looks then as if Isaeus' thinking is governed by the assumption that a man who is in the hands of a prostitute or ex-prostitute and who acts against his own best interests to promote hers may have been persuaded to act in this way by her magic-working. That is to say, there is the presumption that women who are prostitutes or courtesans will be expert in magic.

There is also Theodote, the courtesan on whom Socrates pays a visit. When she invites Socrates to spend more time with her, he excuses himself by saying that he has great deal of business to which he must attend and he also has female friends (*philai*), who have learned from him how to use love-potions (*philtra*) and incantations (*epodai*); they prevent him from leaving them. On hearing Socrates say this, Theodote asks whether that means Socrates also knows about such matters. Socrates' response is to ask Theodote why does she imagine Apollodorus and Antisthenes never leave his side and why does she imagine that Cebes and Simias have come all the way from Thebes. The answer is that this could not have happened without the aid of many love-potions, incantations and magical wheels (*iynges*). Theodote now asks Socrates to lend her his magical wheel, so that she may begin by drawing him to her.[17] What is happening here is that Xenophon is exploiting the irony inherent in a conversation in which Socrates tells a courtesan that the men who seek out his company do so because they are drawn inexorably to him by the devices used in erotic magic, and that he in his turn is in thrall to the magical devices that his female friends have learned from him. Theodote is surprised or feigns surprise at Socrates' being expert like herself in erotic magic. What is interesting from our point of view is the assumption governing the conversation, which is that erotic magic is an integral part of the equipment of a courtesan and that it is needed to make sure that lovers are drawn to her and remain faithful to her.

Our next exhibit is a song from Aristophanes' *Plutus* in which the Corinthian courtesan Lais is presented as a Circe who mixes *pharmaka* and brings magic to bear on (*manganeuousa*) the comrades of Philonides, an Athenian whom Aristophanes pillories.[18] It is a matter of some interest that by 388 BC, the year in which *Plutus* was performed, Circe has come to be seen as a sorceress. It is for our purposes still more interesting that Lais is imagined as a Circe-like figure entrapping men by her magic. It may be inferred from the identification of a courtesan with a figure emblematic of sorcery that courtesans were credited with practising magic to ensnare men. We should be careful to remember that it is an inference and that the identification of Lais with Circe does not necessarily mean courtesans were generally believed to engage in sorcery. There is always the possibility that Lais was notorious as a sorceress and that her notoriety had nothing to do with a general prejudice against women of her kind as magic-workers. It is, on the other hand, much more likely that Aristophanes has no particular knowledge of Lais and that he endows her with one of the attributes courtesans were widely supposed to possess.

Finally, there is the ex-prostitute, nicknamed Empousa because of her sexual versatility, who goes on to conduct purificatory and initiatory ceremonies into private mysteries. She may at one level be the product of Demosthenes' imagination, but at a deeper level she represents a type that Demosthenes did not invent; she is not just a convenient stereotype on which Demosthenes drew to vilify Aeschines. There is no other direct evidence for the existence of women of her type. Yet it is hard to see from where the priestesses who conducted private initiation-ceremonies in Athens emerged, if not from the *demi-monde*. That such women also engaged in magic-working is likely, but not demonstrable.

Whatever inadequacies the literary evidence may have as a source of information about the links between magic-working and prostitution in Athens, the material record leaves us in no doubt that prostitutes in Athens in the fourth century BC lived in a milieu in which sorcery was, if not endemic, certainly present to a degree that it was not in other sectors of society. If we exclude the curse-tablets whose aim it was to prevent a case coming to court or to render tongue-tied and mute opponents-at-law, a disproportionate number of the spells that seek to impede the success of an enterprise are directed at women who are, to judge from their names, either prostitutes or courtesans or at the persons who live alongside them and with whom they associate, which is to say, pimps, procuresses, brothel-keepers and the keepers of taverns. It is not that persons following other callings are not attacked, but not to the degree that the men and women running brothels and taverns or working in them or out of them are the target of such assaults. As often as not several of these categories of persons are mentioned in the same spell, which is a fair indication of how intertwined their lives were; in the eyes of the person casting the spell, they certainly belonged together. What all of this suggests is that magic-working was especially at home in this section of society. It is not proof positive that prostitutes or courtesans themselves engaged in magic, but it does create the very strong presumption that they will have had a good deal to do with it.

The spells that we have from Athens are on the whole intended to disable or put out of commission the persons who are their targets. Getting behind the spells to the identity of the persons casting them and their motives for doing so is a perilous undertaking, but it can be asserted with some confidence that when a curse-tablet is directed at a group of pimps, tavern-keepers and prostitutes, the person who commissioned it belonged to the same world as that of his would-be victims. Reconstructing that world on the basis of curse-tablets aimed at its denizens is difficult, since only a very small part of the jigsaw puzzle survives. What does remain does, however, provide a perspective on the lives of these people that is not to be obtained from any other source.

There are, for instance, five spells in which the same persons or some of the same persons are named that in effect constitute an archive of documents emerging from the lives of a group of prostitutes, brothel-keepers, tavern-keepers, pimps and assorted other persons. Four of the spells belong together, both because they were found in the same place and because in three of them the same parties are named, although in association with different persons in each instance.[19] The fifth spell has in its rich and varied cast of characters only one person in common with the persons mentioned in the other spells, Agathon the tavern-keeper, but that is enough to show us that all five spells are the products of the same sub-section of Athenian society.[20] In two tablets the names of two men, Ophilion and Olympus, are closely associated: one binds down Ophilion and the tavern Olympus, then Melanthius and all his doings and the tavern Agathon, next is Syricus and all his doings followed by Pistias and Manes;[21] in the other the names Ophilion, Ophilime and Olympus are given before the caster of the spell binds down the work-shop (*ergasterion*) of Ophilion, which is followed by a list of names, Hecataeus, Manes, Phime and Eirene, which is in its turn succeeded by a binding-down of the work of Eirene.[22] A third tablet binds down all of these persons and some others, including Pistias from our first spell.[23] Their names are characteristic of either slaves or prostitutes. Ophilion and Olympus are the main targets of the spells and the persons who run the establishments in which the other persons named are either employed or use as their base. Olympus runs a tavern, a *kapeleion*, but Ophilion controls an *ergasterion*, which is a word that covers both workshop and brothel. It will be the latter here. Why the owners of the two establishments are so closely linked is not altogether clear. Perhaps they were run in conjunction with each other. Eirene, whose work is singled out for special attention, is surely a prostitute who works in the brothel of Ophilion and may have been a big draw.

The tavern Agathon, as it is styled after the name of the man running it, is the target of one spell alongside the tavern Olympus and that of Syriskos. Syriskos does not appear again, but Agathon does in a very wide-ranging curse-tablet.[24] He is bound down along with five other taverns run by men and one run by a woman, that of Mania beside the fountain. Mania from her name is either a slave or a freedwoman. Agathon is quite specifically identi-fied as the household-slave of Sosimenes, who is himself bound down along-side another household-slave of his, a linen-seller called Karpos and a woman called Glykanthia, also known as Malthake.[25] Sosimenes is himself identified as being brother to one of the tavern-keepers previously mentioned. It is vir-tually certain that Glykanthia, with the by-name Malthake, is a courtesan. We know of a courtesan of the name Malthake from a comedy of the fourth cen-tury.[26] Glykanthia has some connection with Sosimenes: he either owned her or kept her. The first tavern-keeper bound down by the spell is a man called Kallias, described as the neighbouring tavern-keeper. Bound down along with him is his woman, Thratta. Her name is an indication of her or her mother's origins as a Thracian slave. So we are again in an interlocking world of tavern-keepers, prostitutes and courtesans. Some of the tavern-keepers are slaves or freedmen or freedwomen.

Very much the same sort of world is to be discerned in another very large curse-tablet found outside the ancient city. Although it begins by taking aim at a miller, the rest of the spell is devoted to an assault on prostitutes, their brothels, female tavern-keepers, who seem to run brothels, a procuress (*mastrope*) with what was surely the nickname of Areskousa, the one who pleases, a woman described as a seller of sexual favours, *charitopolis* (whether her own or those of others is unclear from the context), sundry men who appear to run brothels, and the concubine (*pallake*) of one of them, Lakaina.[27] One of the brothels is referred to as the *ergasterion* Lyde. It was clearly known by the name of the woman who ran it. The spell goes on from there to bind down a man and then a lodging-house or *synoikia* and all those having rooms in it or all the rooms in it (*synoika*). The *synoikia* was evidently one of these establishments in which the prostitutes had their separate rooms or cubicles. The prostitutes or madams have slave-names such as Lyde or have the kind of name only a prostitute would be given such as Posis or Drink. The spell was unfortunately difficult to read, but there is still enough left to give us a hazy picture of what seems to have been a self-enclosed society.

It is difficult to penetrate the complexities of the world of prostitutes, tavern-keepers and brothel-mongers and the assorted ancillaries associated with them to form any idea of how it operated. It is important to remember that male prostitution was also part of this world and that could mean the selling of the bodies of boys. One curse-tablet on one of its sides binds down two men.[28] One of them is called Androcles. His evil tongue, evil spirit and evil soul and his *ergasterion* and his boys are all bound together. But in the first line on the other side of the tablet in writing that has proved hard to interpret we find in the accusative case the following list: the matters of Aphrodite (*aphrodiasia*) at a certain indecipherable location, what is presumably the name of a person, the *ergasterion* and the *pallakai*.[29] The last word, which is normally taken to refer to concubines, may in fact have a wider application. The accusative case is an indication that we have to supply the word *katado*, 'I bind down'. But what is bound down is a brothel in which women are supplied. So what we have on the same tablet are assaults on brothels containing respectively boys and women.

If magic-working was so much part of the world in which prostitutes and courtesans lived, it might reasonably be expected that there would be some sign in the material record of courtesans, if not common prostitutes, practising magic on their own behalf when their interests were threatened. The anonymity in which persons casting curse-tablets designed to harm others cloak their identity makes it in most cases ultimately impossible to say whether it is a man or a woman who has commissioned the tablet. There is really only one Athenian curse-tablet from the fourth century of which it can plausibly be maintained that it shows a courtesan engaging in magic against a rival. It was directed at a certain Theodora and was intended to break up any relationship the woman may have had with two named men, Callias and Charias, but above all the latter, and all other men.[30] It is virtually certain that Theodora was a courtesan and that what we have is an attempt on the part of a rival to end Theodora's relationship with Charias and win him away from her, but at the same time to destroy Theodora's career as a whole.

Magic-working amongst women was unquestionably not confined to women who sold their bodies for sex and to holy women, whether resident in Athens or itinerant mendicants. The implications of what the Nurse in Euripides' *Hippolytus* has to say about the facility women display in contrast to men in the matter of erotic magic has already been remarked upon. They are that women in general are adepts in this kind of magic and more immediately that the Nurse herself and the women who are present are not without resources here. Phaedra, on the other hand, is presented as an innocent in these matters and, like Deianeira in Sophocles' *Women of Trachis*, unhappy at having to have recourse to magic. The women present are citizens of Troizene, a small city on the eastern coast of the Peloponnese lying across the Saronic Gulf from Athens. To the extent that they are given a distinct and coherent identity and character, they are relatively humble women, although still apparently citizens of Troizene, who gossip about the doings of their social superiors, as they do their washing on the rocks of a river.[31] That such women existed in Troizene is likely, but Euripides' experience of them will have been in Athens. He will have transposed what he knew about them from Athens to Troizene. They represent a class of woman about whose way of life we are singularly ill-informed. The women about whom we do know something, because they are mentioned in speeches to be delivered in the law-courts, are either courtesans of some standing or the wives of men of some substance.

Euripides' treatment of the contrast between the ignorance and discomfort that Phaedra confronted by magic displays and the knowingness of the Nurse, a knowingness in which the Nurse leads us to believe the local women participate, has to be handled with a delicate touch. It nonetheless does look as though Euripides supposes that a knowledge of erotic magic is restricted to female servants such as the Nurse and women of humble, if free, birth and that for well-born women such as Phaedra magic is very much an unknown territory. It goes without saying it would be a mistake to imagine that all elderly female servants and all low-born women were expert in love-magic. A more nuanced and better balanced assessment of what may fairly be extracted from *Hippolytus* would be that in Euripides' view a knowledge of erotic magic was to be found principally amongst women of the humbler sort and amongst elderly servant women and that these were the persons to whom well-born women would go for assistance, if they wanted to have sorcery performed. The Nurse presents herself as having a certain expertise in erotic magic and tells Phaedra that she has love-philtres within the house; all she needs from Phaedra is some token from the object of Phaedra's longing, Hippolytus, if she is to accomplish her end.[32] That the Nurse represents a recognized type, an old woman who acts as a procuress for her mistress and uses magic to bring to fruition the illicit longings of the woman she serves, is likely, but not demonstrable on the basis of any evidence available from Athens in the fifth century BC. The type is amply attested in later times and was probably to be found in New Comedy.

A speech of the Athenian orator Antiphon, composed towards the end of the fifth century BC, suggests that a knowledge of erotic magic was not by any manner of means entirely confined to freeborn women of humble birth and to servant-women. The speech in question purports to be a forensic oration delivered before a court by a young man prosecuting his stepmother for having poisoned his father. It is a rhetorical exercise built on an imaginary case. It is for all that an invaluable social document, since it is not based on a particular reality that may be quite unusual but on a distillation of a more general reality as its author sees it. The gist of it is that the speaker charges his stepmother with having got the concubine of a friend of his father to administer to the father what the concubine imagined to be a love-potion but which was in fact a poison from whose effects the father was to die eighteen days later. The stepmother had contrived to bring about that end by befriending the concubine of Philoneos, the friend of the father, who, when in Athens, lived in the upper part of their house. She had subsequently learnt that Philoneos was about to set the concubine up in business as a prostitute. That information gave her the opportunity to summon the woman to tell her what was going to befall her and to put before her a way in which she could retrieve her position: she possessed the ability to secure the affections of Philoneos for the concubine and of her husband for herself.[33] The concubine had then administered what she supposed to be a love-philtre to Philoneos and to the father of the plaintiff. Philoneos had expired on the spot, because the woman in her anxiety to win back his love had given him an extra large dose; the father, who had been given a smaller amount, lingered on for the best part of three weeks before finally succumbing.[34] The occasion at which the supposed love-philtre was administered was a dinner party in the Peiraeus following a sacrifice performed in connection with a voyage that the father was to make to Naxos.

The story is illuminating in a number of regards: it dispels any illusions that we might have about its being only humble women who were interested in erotic magic; it throws some additional light on one of the segments of society in which erotic magic flourished and on the reasons for its flourishing; and it shows a concubine accepting what she thinks is a love-philtre from a woman of some social standing.

## Drunkenness in sorceresses as a clue to their identity

Drunkenness is one of the characteristics of the sorceresses encountered in Old, Middle and New Comedy. This will reflect in part the ancient conviction that old women were drunken, but the drunkenness of these old women also affords a clue to their social status.[35] The old woman is very much a stereotyped figure in Old, Middle and New Comedy. Her main attribute is an unquenchable thirst for strong wine, which she drinks in large measures; she may in addition be lecherous.[36] It has been suggested that the figure of the bibulous or drunken old woman reflects the greater freedom allowed old women in contrast to the strict controls imposed on young unmarried women or married women of child-bearing age.[37] There may be something to this explanation, but it is decidedly Athenocentric in its focus and does not explain the persistence of the figure in other ancient societies in which controls on women were not as strict as they are imagined to have been in Athens. More importantly, it takes no account of the social station of the drunken old woman. Her position in life is invariably, so far as it can be determined, a humble one. Well-born old women are not portrayed in this fashion. The freedom of old women to drink to excess both in public and private may then be not so much a function of the liberties that her age allowed her as of her place in society. Prostitutes and courtesans, whom it is safe to suppose were generally young, if not very young, women are after all drinkers and are regularly depicted drinking on Attic vases.[38] In Old Comedy, the old women who are portrayed as drinkers lead humble lives: in Aristophanes, they drink in dram-shops, have the owners of these establishments as their neighbours and complain about being given short measure there;[39] in Pherecrates' *Korianno*, a hetaera with a daughter is an eager drinker.[40] From the *Antilais* of Epicrates, a comic playwright from the first half of the fourth century, we learn that the character who is the inspiration for the comedy, the Corinthian courtesan Lais, has in her declining years become lazy and a drinker, living only for her drink and food.[41] It hardly matters whether Lais was really a hard drinker or not and whether she was now in fact prepared to go to bed with anyone for a small fee. What is significant is that the playwright is playing up to his audience's expectations: they expect aging courtesans to be heavy drinkers.

The strongest evidence for drunkenness as a characteristic of sorceresses is a fragment of Pherecrates in which a woman is called lewdly wanton, a drunkard and a sorceress (*pharmakis*).[42] The mythical witch-figure Lamia, who gives her name to Crates' *Lamia*, may well have been drunken. Diodorus Siculus, at any rate, speaks of the drunkenness of the Libyan Lamia, as though it were an accepted fact.[43] From Middle Comedy there is a fragment of Ephippos' *Circe* in which a character who may well be Circe, and who will by this time have come to be thought of as a witch, expresses the preference characteristic of old women for strong wine.[44] A fragment of Menander's *Thettalai*, a play which on the testimony of Pliny the Elder dealt, not surprisingly given its title, with women attempting to pull down the moon, has someone who is accused of having opened a wine container and is denounced as reeking of wine.[45] The person reeking of wine is in all likelihood one of the sorceresses.[46] This is not very much to be going on but still enough to suggest that the figure of the drunken old sorceress was a standard one in comedy.

What all of this adds up to is that sorceresses were imagined to come from the lower orders of society and to share the prevailing vice of old women of humble origin. As to who the drunken old women sorceresses of Comedy were beyond being humble old women there are only the most meagre of clues. One of them is perhaps to be found in the fragment of Pherecrates that speaks of a woman as lewdly wanton, drunken and a sorceress. This might be a reference to a prostitute who is somewhat over the hill but who still tries to sell her wares, although she now needs sorcery to get any customers. In the absence of any context other interpretations of the fragment are equally legitimate.

## Sorceresses as purifiers and healers

It turns out to be rather easier to get a handle on the identity of female magic-workers than that of their male counterparts; they belong to a part of Athenian society of which we have some understanding, whereas the world of the male magician is less accessible. Coming to terms with what female magic-workers did is a more difficult task. That some of them practised erotic magic is certain, but what they did beyond that is less clear. It is not in doubt that women performed purifications and that some of the purificatory ceremonies were intended to cure the persons purified of the effects of the wrath of the gods, that others were designed to heal the party purified of physical ailments, others again of mental ills and yet others of the consequences of having seen an untoward dream or sight. It is also known that women were brought in to heal the sick by applying amulets to them, over which they probably intoned an incantation. All of these activities are well attested. The problem is knowing how to classify them: were those who performed the rituals thought to be practising magic or was it the way in which the rituals were performed that determined the view people took of them or was it partly the way in which the ritual was performed and partly who it was who was performing that made the difference?

The ceremonies of initiation carried out by women such as Ninos and Glaucothea had a purificatory aspect to them. Just because purification was an important element in initiation it does not follow that every private ceremony of initiation was thought to be tainted with magic and those performing it a magician. It is nonetheless the case that Ninos was executed for something that was thought to be impious about the way in which she had conducted such a ritual. The Aesopic fable in which a woman, described as a female magician, is executed for *asebeia* because she promised to lay to rest the wrath of the gods, apparently by using incantations, is relevant here.[47] The lesson to be drawn from the case of Ninos taken together with that of the female magician is that initiations and purifications could be construed as magic, if performed in a certain way, and that those who performed rituals of that pattern were believed to be magicians. The indications, such as they are, suggest that introducing incantations into these ceremonies was one of the factors that caused trouble. It will suffice to point to the mention of incantation in the Aesopic fable and to the three references in Plato to incantation, in one instance characterized as *goeteia*, in the purificatory rituals enacted by *agyrtai* and *manteis* and by impious persons of a beast-like character.[48]

There is, accordingly, a case for thinking that there were women who conducted purificatory-cum-initiatory rites who were considered to be magic-
workers.

What of the women who cured people of psychic or real ills or of the dangers consequent on having seen an untoward vision? Were they thought of as
magicians? Theophrastus in his sketch of the man who is unduly afraid of the
divine says that such a man will, if he sees a shrine at a crossroads wreathed in
garlic, go away from it, have his head doused in water and summon priestesses (*hiereiai*) to purify him thoroughly (*perikathairein*) with either a squill or
a puppy.[49] Who are these so-called priestesses and how are the purifications
they performed viewed? The priestesses in question are not the priestesses of
one of the official cults of the city, who in any case could hardly be summoned in this way, but women of a humbler sort who made a living from
their calling as holy women. Such women were by the Hellenistic Period
thought to belong to the world of the sorcerer. They are to be read about in
Plutarch's tract *On Superstition*, a work that probably derives from a Hellenistic work on the same topic, where we learn that mendicant holy men (*agyrtai*)
and sorcerers (*goetes*) tell someone troubled by a dream that he has to
employ an old woman expert in purifications or a *perimaktria*, literally a
woman who kneads a substance all around something, to cleanse him of the
effects of the dream.[50] The same view was probably taken in the fourth century of women who performed such purifications. Women who purify those
who have had disturbing dreams or visions are not said to perform magic,
but the author of the Hippocratic treatise *On the Sacred Disease* certainly takes
the *katharmoi*, intended to cure epilepsy, performed by the persons he refers
to as *magoi, kathartai* and *agyrtai* as acts of *mageia*.[51] The *katharmoi* in question
consist in the application of substances such as blood and in incantations.[52]
Did we not possess the speech *Against Aristogeiton*, in which Aristogeiton's
brother is said to have taken over the magical paraphernalia of the mistress
of his mother and set up as a magician himself and to have promised to cure
those afflicted with epileptic seizures, even though he himself had been
seized by wickedness, it would be theoretically possible to discount what the
Hippocratic author has to say and to treat it as unrepresentative.[53]

There is a further facet of Theophrastus' portrait of what the man who is
unduly afraid of the divine does when confronted by an alarming sight that
calls for comment: he summons priestesses, not just a single priestess. This is
the earliest instance of a phenomenon that is attested throughout much of
antiquity. Literary portrayals of female magic-workers very often have them
working together in pairs or in larger groups. It has been suggested that the
image of sorceresses operating in tandem which we find in poems and novels
is a figment of the deluded male imagination.[54] This attempt at explaining
away what is to be found in ancient texts has more to do with current sexual
politics than with any serious attempt at getting to grips with an ancient reality. The vision of reality reflected in poetry and novels is no doubt highly

coloured, but there will be a kernel of truth embedded in it. What really needs to be asked is why women should have performed magical rituals in concert with each other. There are almost certainly a number of factors at work here. One of them will be that more than one person was needed to perform the ritual. Another will have been the desire to orchestrate a more impressive show for the benefit of the client. What was essentially a maidservant helping her mistress would in the eyes of the customer eager to delude himself have become another sorceress. A procuress with her girls would in the proper circumstances constitute another group of sorceresses.

Closely related to the priestesses summoned to the house to cure someone of the effects of dreams and visions will be the old women who were brought to a house to cure the illnesses of its inhabitants by applying amulets to them. A story that Theophrastus tells in his *Ethics* in connection with the problem of whether misfortune and bodily suffering lead to alterations in character points to the part that women played in the fourth century, if not in the fifth, in these mundane forms of magic: when Pericles was ill with the plague, he showed a friend who had come to visit him the amulet (*periapton*) that the women had hung around his neck as an indication of the straits to which he was reduced in being prepared to submit to such nonsense.[55] That the story is in all likelihood apocryphal does not greatly matter.[56] It does suggest that by the late fourth century amulets were already the special province of women.[57] There is one clue to the identity of the women who carried out this task: they are referred to with the definite article as 'the women'. Since no other specification of identity is given, it may be inferred that it was the women of the household who had attached the amulet to Pericles' neck. In later times, we find serving-women or women known to the serving-women of the household who performed this service.

## Women performing harmful magic on behalf of others

There can be no question that women did commission magicians to write curse-tablets for them out of a desire to harm and disable their opponents. They might even be imagined engaging more directly in magic: Medea in Euripides' play of that name anoints, with a salve that will kill, a robe to be given to the woman who has supplanted her in Jason's affections. When she produces the *pharmaka* that she will use to accomplish the task, she does not say that she had acquired them from someone else.[58] The assumption that the audience is meant to make is that the *pharmaka* are of Medea's own devising. She has after all already told the women who make up the chorus that she will rely on the craft in which she and they are skilled (she uses the first person plural as does the Nurse in *Hippolytus*), namely, *pharmaka*, to dispatch her enemies and then swears by her mistress, Hecate, whom she reveres above all other gods and has chosen to be her helper, dwelling as she does in the innermost part of her house, that no one who has caused her distress will escape scot-free.[59] Whether Medea is by this date the quintessential sorceress is not altogether certain. It is nonetheless plausible to suppose that the rôle in which she is cast in *Medea* reflects what sorceresses in the real world did or were believed to do.

Medea may have been portrayed practising harmful sorcery in other tragedies. In Sophocles' *Rhizotomoi* or *Root-cutters* someone certainly described her cutting roots with a bronze sickle, naked, turning her eyes away as she did so and uttering loud cries, and then draining the foaming juice from the roots into bronze boxes that were to be kept hidden.[60] Our source of information is a Late Roman author, Macrobius, who to illustrate his contention that Sophocles portrayed Medea cutting maleficent plants and turning her head away, lest she be killed by their smell, cites the seven lines of the play that have just been paraphrased.[61] It is not altogether certain that Macrobius does not go rather beyond what Sophocles had written to interpret Medea's actions in the light of his own understanding of the ritual. In Euripides' *Ion*, Creousa, who rules Athens as a descendant of Erichthonius, attempts to kill Ion with a *pharmakon* secreted in his wine by an old servant of hers. Her maidservants, who constitute the chorus, call on Hecate as mistress of hauntings by night and by day to speed the filling of the deadly wine-bowl in which the *pharmakon* is to be placed as the servant sets out to perform his task.[62] The larger significance of Creousa's actions is complicated by two factors: it is the old servant who initially encourages her to kill, whether with a sword, by guile, or by *pharmaka*;[63] the *pharmakon* that she herself produces, when she settles on that course of action, is not the normal *pharmakon* of sorcery, but turns out to have been one of two drops of the blood of the Gorgon, one beneficial, the other deadly, given to her ancestor Erichthonius by Athena and handed down within the family ever since.[64] In light of these complications it would be unwise to draw any general conclusions from the case of Creousa about women and malign magic. The only moral to be drawn from the episode with reasonable confidence is that servants were imagined to encourage well-born women to such drastic actions as the use of baneful drugs.

In sum, it cannot be proved that women actually engaged in malign magic, but it seems likely enough that they did so. Plato's use of the masculine gender in describing the magic-working of *agyrtai* and *manteis* proves that he believed men practised black magic, but does not mean that he was not speaking generally and not also thinking of women. Medea's speech gives some encouragement to the idea that women were particularly expert in the department of black magic that involves the use of harmful drugs. They were certainly believed to have that capacity. The reality may not have been so different, if *rhizotomia* had traditionally been in their hands.

## Conclusion

There is a good deal of evidence for women practising sorcery on their own behalf in Athens in the fifth and fourth centuries BC, but rather less for women who put their expertise in sorcery at the disposal of others. Such women unquestionably existed; identifying them is largely a matter of guess-work. We would probably not be too far off the mark, if we surmised that they were drawn from the ranks of those women in whose own lives magic-working played a considerable part and who had as such a reputation as experts in magic. The one discrete group of women who fall into this category of whom something is known are prostitutes and courtesans. Some at least then of the women to whom people turned to have magic performed for them will have been prostitutes or former prostitutes. There is also a persistent tradition that begins with the Nurse in Euripides' *Hippolytus* that well-born women got help in magic-working from their maidservants, since magic was something that lay outside their experience.

# 4

# SORCERERS IN THE GREEK WORLD OF THE HELLENISTIC PERIOD (300–1BC)

## Introduction

The conquests of Alexander the Great extended the horizons of the Greek world and established Greek cities in the interior of Anatolia, in the Near and Middle East and in Egypt. It is customary to assert that the extension of the Greek world into Egypt, Syria and points still further east, the subjugation of the Greek city-states by Macedonia, the loss of autonomy entailed by their subjugation and the elimination of democratic institutions that followed induced in men a sense of dislocation, made them feel that they had lost familiar bearings and caused them to search for a new identity. The feeling of rootlessness effected by these changes is supposed to have led men to a quest for personal fulfilment that centred on the emotional well-being of the individual and not in his realizing his potential by participating in public life. We are told that philosophical systems promising personal fulfilment and happiness now came to the fore. We are also informed that the less educated took other routes to allay the anxieties with which the age filled them: they gave themselves up to the irrational, by enrolling in mystery-cults and turning to the practices of astrology and magic.[1] A further factor is sometimes added to explain the supposed flight to the irrational and the occult from the rationalism of the Classical Age. It is that the non-rational cast of mind of the Egyptians and the Semitic-speaking peoples of Syria had led to an erosion of the Greek commitment to rationalism.

There is much that is questionable about such a picture of the religious and intellectual life of the Hellenistic Age. Two assumptions call for particular attention: one is that a two-tier model of religious and intellectual life adequately describes reality;[2] and the other is that the discontinuities of the period outweigh the continuities. It will emerge from the present chapter that making philosophy the province of the educated élite and restricting an interest in magic and mystery-cult to the uneducated underclass is too simple a dichotomy and does great damage to the truth. Mystery-cults had, long before Alexander, been a conspicuous feature of the religious life of many Greek cities. All of the evidence that we possess suggests that, if anything, it was especially the well born and well educated who turned to the mystery-cults for sustenance. There is no reason to think that the situation alters greatly in the Hellenistic Age and that the poor in their deluded ignorance now flock to mystery-religion in the hope of the blessings in this life and the happiness in what was to come thereafter that their better-educated superiors know is not to be found in that quarter.

The discontinuities in life that the Hellenistic Period brought with it were probably far outweighed by the continuities. The Greek city-states continued to function very much as before, although their autonomy in foreign affairs was necessarily diminished, an annoyance perhaps for the very ambitious, but for most people not a pressing concern. The energies of ambitious men were now channeled in other directions. It is true that democracy seems to have disappeared, but whether its disappearance had much effect one way or the other on the tone of intellectual and religious life is by no means clear. Long before the Athenian defeat at Chaeroneia in 337 BC by Philip of Macedon the dramatic forms for which Athens was famous had run their course. Even if democracy had prevailed in Athens and the few other cities in the Greek world in which it had a hold, there would have been developments in Greek culture and new forms would have come into being. A very good case can be made for thinking that Alexander's conquests had a beneficial effect on the Greek world by releasing new energies, by creating several centres of cultural activity and by broadening horizons.

The evidence of actual magic-working from the Hellenistic Age in the form of lead tablets, amulets whether of stone, metal or papyrus, spells written on papyrus and the formularies in which such spells were collected is very thin indeed. There are many more lead tablets from fourth-century Athens. Not too much weight should be placed on how few signs of magic the material record shows, since chance plays a very large rôle in the survival of such objects and styles of performing magic may well have changed. To illustrate that point, it is worth considering the discrepancy that exists between the evidence in the literature of the Hellenistic Age for what would seem to be a widespread preoccupation with the belief popularly known as the Evil Eye and the almost complete absence from the period of apotropaic devices designed to ward off the effects of the Evil Eye. In a case such as the Evil Eye, it is fair to conclude that people protected themselves against it in ways that have left no physical trace, either because they relied on gestures and words or because the amulets they wore to guard themselves against its effects were made of perishable substances. That it is very much a matter of chance what has survived is also suggested by the large number of places spread over a very wide area from which single curse-tablets have emerged. It is exceedingly unlikely that these were the only curse-tablets deposited in these places. What is much more significant than the absolute numbers is how widespread the custom was and how it passed from the Greek colonists of the West to the peoples with whom they came into contact. The existence of curse-tablets written in Etruscan and Oscan is a far better indicator of the prevalence of this form of magic-working than the discovery of a large number of tablets in any one place. As for the literary record in the Hellenistic Age, it cannot be said to betray any great preoccupation with magic, although references to magic-working in it are certainly more abundant than they are in the Classical Period. There is, in sum, little to indicate any upsurge in magic-working in the centuries after Alexander's death.

Although there are few signs that magic in the Hellenistic Period had any more of a hold over the minds of men and women than it had in the fifth or fourth centuries BC, changes did occur: there was probably an influx of new magical practices, new kinds of magic-worker made their appearance and educated and literate men began to make collections of magical lore and perhaps to experiment with it. One of the reasons for the changes that took place was the opening up of the Greek world to new influences. Techniques used in the Near East and to a lesser extent in Egypt for effecting wondrous changes on the natural world became known to the Greeks and to persons who had learned Greek and who had absorbed something of the Greek world-view. The new techniques were then added by them to the body of Greek magical knowledge.

Our sources of information about magic-workers in the Hellenistic Period are of a different order from those for Athens in the Classical Period. The most striking difference from our perspective for the understanding of ancient magic is that we now have poets who write about ordinary and humble people engaging in sorcery. The difference in this regard between the literature of Classical Athens and that of the Hellenistic Period should not, however, be exaggerated. That there is a degree of realism in Euripides' *Hippolytus* in the portrayal of the relationship between the Nurse and Phaedra and the help in the form of sorcery that the Nurse affords her mistress is likely. We should also bear in mind that had the mimes of the Syracusan writer of the late fifth century BC, Sophron, survived, we would have had a very different view of Classical Greek Literature, since there would have been at least one sketch of magic-working in the *demi-monde*, if not two. It is also likely that magic-working was portrayed in New Comedy: Menander had a play, the *Thettalae*, in which witches played a part and more intriguingly he wrote a *Menagyrtes*, which must have had something to do with one of the begging-priests of the Mother Goddess. The depictions of low life to be found in Theocritus in the first half of the third century BC and in his contemporary, the writer of literary mimes, Herodas, do not, accordingly, emerge from a complete vacuum but have definite antecedents.

The two historians who survive from the fifth century BC, Herodotus and Thucydides, and the one who survives from the fourth century, Xenophon, have, for whatever reason, with a few minor exceptions in the case of Herodotus, nothing to say about sorcery. Hellenistic historians, geographical and ethnographical writers and the authors of the genre called paradoxography, that is, the description and cataloguing of natural wonders, are more interested in the topic. They do not on the whole describe magic-working or magicians in the Greek world. The sorcerers who attract their attention belong to foreign and distant lands and places or to the remote Greek past. What is said in this connection is nonetheless invaluable, not for what it tells us about other lands and peoples and about the distant past, but for what it reveals about the Greek present. The patterns and categories that the historian uses to make sense of alien practices shed a certain amount of light on the way in which sorcerers operated in the Greek world and about who they were.

## Magic-working amongst prostitutes and courtesans in Cos in the early third century BC

There is in Theocritus' Second Idyll a vivid portrait of a young woman trying to win back by magic a lover who has deserted her for someone else. She does so by performing a binding-spell (*katadesis*) designed to draw the errant lover burning with desire back to her. It is a binding-spell in which no lead tablet is deposited in a grave: it takes the form of incantations accompanied by a complex ritual in which a variety of substances are burned on a fire. In the first part of the poem the young woman issues instructions to her maidservant about the preparation of the materials needed for the spell she is engaged in casting, all the while chanting an incantation that acts as a refrain throughout the earlier part of the poem. In the second part of the poem, when the maidservant has gone off on an errand, there is a monologue in which the young woman rehearses for herself the history of her love affair.

Theocritus' poem may owe something to the mimes of Sophron. An ancient commentator on the poem maintains that the figure of the maidservant Thestylis has been tastelessly transposed from the mimes of Sophron.[3] It is probably the same commentator who says that the spells are taken from the mimes of Sophron.[4] Theocritus is unlikely to owe an enormous debt to Sophron. Ancient commentators characteristically exaggerate the debt that authors owe to their predecessors when they come across indications of borrowing. Whatever the nature of Theocritus' debt is to Sophron, it can hardly be gainsaid that the poem is firmly set in the Hellenistic World and not in Classical Greece.

The story told in the poem is of a young woman called Simaetha, who had encountered a young man, Delphis, on her way to a procession in honour of Artemis and had been attracted to him. She had then suffered the usual pangs of love, which had driven her to resort to the houses of old women skilled in incantations. The help given by the old women seems to have been of no avail and Simaetha had ended up taking a more direct course of action: she had sent her maid, Thestylis, to Delphis to tell him she wanted to see him. He had responded to the summons by coming to her house, they had made love and he had continued to visit her for some time, but had stopped doing so. It is now twelve days since he paid his last call. Not only that, there are rumours that he has fallen in love with another. It is at this point that Simaetha has had recourse to magic. She ends her soliloquy by threatening to use the harmful magical substances that she had learned from an Assyrian stranger and that she now keeps in a box.

Such is Simaetha's predicament. Theocritus introduces us to a world in which single women send their maidservants to act as their go-betweens in arranging assignations with young men, in which there are old women expert in incantations to be visited by women anxious to capture the affections of a man, and finally, a world in which women can learn noxious spells from an Assyrian visitor. We need to know what sort of world this is in which Simaetha lives and who she and the people with whom she consorts are. The events take place in a town which, though not definitely identifiable, does have certain distinguishing characteristics. Such indications as there are point to the town of Cos on the island of Cos.[5] Theocritus had connections with Cos: the setting of his Seventh Idyll is that island and it is evident from the poem that Theocritus must have spent some time on the island. The town which is the setting for the Second Idyll is large enough to have what is evidently a proprietary palaestra or gymnasium, known by the name of its owner or the man who ran it, Timagetus.[6] This is where Delphis is generally to be found.[7] Delphis himself is not a native of the city, but comes from Myndos, a city on the south-west coast of Anatolia that faces the island of Cos.[8] The city of Myndos, which in the fifth century BC had paid tribute to the Athenian-dominated Delian League, was refounded by Mausolus of Halicarnassus some time before the middle of the fourth century BC and for most of the third century BC was under the suzerainty of the Macedonian rulers of Egypt, the Ptolemies.[9] It would have been natural to find a Myndian just across the strait in Cos, which, while Theocritus was active, was closely tied to the Ptolemies, although autonomous.[10] Myndians, it is true, seem to have travelled widely. One of them is found in the third century BC as an official of the Ptolemaic administration on the island of Thera.[11] That Delphis has not wandered further afield and is in Cos is strongly indicated by the compliment he pays Simaetha on his first appearance: her message to him had only anticipated his coming by the same narrow margin that he had beaten Philinus in a race.[12] There was a well-known Coan runner of the second quarter of the third century BC of that name. His native land was sufficiently proud of his achievements to have commemorated them with a statue at Olympia.[13] It will be that Philinus who is meant. A further reason for thinking Cos is the setting is the grove of Artemis to which Simaetha is on her way when she encounters Delphis. The mythographer Antonius Liberalis records a Coan myth that seems to reflect a cult of Artemis in a grove and, furthermore, a cult in which Artemis is worshipped as Hecate, an identification which is made throughout our poem.[14]

The principal town on the island of Cos is, accordingly, by far the most likely candidate as the setting for Theocritus' Second Idyll. Cos in the second quarter of the third century BC enjoyed a higher degree of prosperity than it did at any other time in antiquity. Ptolemy Philadelphus, who had been born on the island, quite clearly had a fond regard for it. The political alignment of the island was with Ptolemaic Egypt, but it seems to have been left free to direct its internal affairs. Its School of Medicine was its greatest embellishment: Coan doctors and Coan-trained doctors were dominant in Alexandria. In the field of literature, the best-known Coan figure is the poet Philetas. His presence on Cos probably drew Theocritus to the island and we may surmise that the writer of literary mimes, Herodas, whose Second Mime is unquestionably set in Cos, will also have visited the island, brought to it by its literary connections, as Meleager of Gadara seems to have been at a later date. There is evidence of the presence of foreigners of a less exalted sort than Theocritus and Herodas. Many of them came from Caria and more especially from the Myndian peninsula and its principal city, Halicarnassus.[15] Syro-Palestine provided a considerable contingent: there were men from the Phoenician cities of the coast and Nabataean and Gerrhaean Arabs from the interior.[16] The opportunities that the thriving commercial activity of the island afforded will have been what attracted most of the men and women who came to it from the East.

Others came because it was a cultural centre. One of them was an expert on astrology from Babylon, where he was a priest of the god Bel. The evidence for Berosus' presence in Cos is a statement by Vitruvius in his work on architecture to the effect that Berosus, the first of the Chaldaeans, settled on the island of Cos in the city of Cos and opened a school there.[17] Vitruvius says this in discussing the contribution of the Chaldaeans to astrology. Berosus was not only a priest of Bel in Babylon, but wrote a history of the Babylonians that he dedicated to the Seleucid monarch, Antiochus I, who ruled an empire whose centre was Syria from 281/0 to 262/1 BC.[18] In the past doubt has been expressed about the veracity of the story of Berosus' visit to Cos.[19] The idea that Berosus would have abandoned his living as a priest of Bel in Babylon to open a school in Cos has also caused disquiet.[20] New evidence has turned up that tends to confirm Vitruvius' reliability. Vitruvius mentions as the immediate successor of Berosus a man called Antipater. An inscription of the mid-second century BC from Larissa in Thessaly honours a native of Syrian Hierapolis, a Chaldaean astrologer called Antipater, who is said to have been for some considerable time a citizen of Thessalian Homolium.[21] The Antipater recorded in the inscription is virtually certain to be the man mentioned by Vitruvius. He was evidently a man who had made a considerable impression in second-century Thessaly. It does not necessarily follow that because Vitruvius' reliability is vindicated in the case of Antipater, the information he gives us about Berosus is also accurate. The presumption must nonetheless be that a Babylonian priest of Bel, who was both a historian and an astrologer, established himself in Cos in the second quarter of the third century BC.

So much then for the rich cultural and commercial life of Cos. Its underside is represented by women such as Simaetha preying on the well-to-do young men who were drawn to the island. Her lover, Delphis, spends his time in a proprietary palaestra. We may imagine that he represents a type common enough in Cos, a member of the *jeunesse dorée* of a city on the Myndian peninsula, attracted by the glamour of a larger cultural centre and the fame of its gymnasia and athletes. Philinus with his five Olympic, four Pythian, four Nemean and eleven Isthmian victories may have made Cos something of an athletic mecca for youths from the surrounding area. Delphis will belong to the category of young men who have passed through the two years of athletic and military training required of youths of their class and who now made the gymnasium or palaestra the centre of their lives. They were an obvious target for the resident *filles de joie* and the old women who kept them or acted as their go-betweens.

Herodas in his First Mime, which may well be set in Cos, has a portrait of the type of girl with whom these young bloods formed associations.[22] The girl in Herodas' mime is called Metriche. She has a Thracian maid, who answers the door to an old woman, Gyllis by name, who identifies herself as the mother of Philaenis. Metriche wants to know why she has not seen Gyllis for five months, to which Gyllis' answer is that she lives a long way off, the back-alleys have been loin-deep in mud and old age has diminished her strength.[23] Gyllis has come to persuade Metriche to abandon hope of the return of her current lover and to take in his place or in addition to him another lover, on whose behalf she is acting. To further her cause, since Metriche's lover has gone off to Egypt and nothing has been heard from him for ten months, she draws a picture of the attractions of Egypt for a such a young man: it has wealth, palaestras, power, settled weather, fame, sights to be seen, philosophers, gold, clubs of young men, a sanctuary of the Brother and Sister Gods, a good king, the Museum, wine, all the goods one could want and as many women as the stars in heaven.[24] Metriche's young man quite clearly comes from the same milieu as Simaetha's erstwhile lover: he belongs to the world of the palaestra, to the associations of young men (*neaniskoi*), the centre of whose activities was the gymnasium. Wine and women occupy the rest of his time. The young man on whose behalf Gyllis has come has a similar background, although his credentials as an athlete are very grand: he has five victories as a boxer in the crown games of which to boast: one as a boy in the Pythians, two in the intermediate category at the Isthmians and two in the Olympics as a man; he is also rich and chaste.[25] Metriche is not pleased by Gyllis' suggestions and turns her down, but to allay the disappointment of the old woman bids her maid clean out a black cup and pour into it three large measures of unmixed wine and a drop of water. Gyllis gratefully drinks the wine and hints that she would like more, prays that no ill may come to

Metriche and that Myrtale and Sime may remain in the bloom of youth, so long as she is alive.[26]

What Herodas lays before our eyes is a world of impoverished but by no means destitute women, who live by themselves with one slave. Their dwellings are, it would seem, in the back-alleys, which in the winter, when it rains, are a sea of mud. The cup or more likely bowl from which Metriche is to drink is specified as the black one and has to be wiped out for Gyllis' use, indications that Metriche has a limited number of drinking vessels and not very grand ones at that. The vessel in question has the black glaze common to the eastern Mediterranean in the third century BC. The old woman Gyllis is, to judge from her daughter's name, Philaenis, the mother of a prostitute, and depends for her livelihood on two other prostitutes, as well as such money as she can get by procuring. She is old and bibulous. Metriche evidently also prostitutes herself, but has a certain independence and lives alone. She is not a common prostitute, but one of those women who form an association with well-to-do young men. They then provide her with enough money to keep her. The associations that such women form with young men are not completely commercial transactions, since they may fall in love with them and forget that relationships of this nature are necessarily transitory and can lead to nothing more.

Simaetha is part of the same world. It has been suggested that she is an impoverished member of the bourgeoisie and no hetaera.[27] This is unlikely. It is true she complains of having sacrificed her virginity to Delphis and of his not having made her his wife.[28] The complaint should probably not be taken at face value. It is the sort of complaint that prostitutes were typically supposed to make and no doubt did.[29] Furthermore, neither Simaetha's name, the acquaintances she keeps nor her conduct suggest respectability. Her name, Simaetha. is that of a prostitute. She goes to see a procession in honour of Artemis with the Thracian nurse who had lived next door to her, and she is on friendly terms with the mother of a flute-girl.[30] She is in and out of the houses of old women expert in incantations and she sends her maid to the palaestra to summon Delphis to an assignation.[31] Finally, it is she who leads Delphis to her bed.[32]

Theocritus' Second Idyll brings three different kinds of magic-worker before us: a courtesan who lives by herself with her maidservant, old women expert in incantations and an Assyrian stranger. There is no indication that any of them are part of the citizen-community. They belong to a *demi-monde* made up of foreigners from the east, prostitutes, flute-girls, courtesans and procuresses. It is a world largely of women and of women who live on the margins of society. It is, accordingly, a courtesan and her magic-working with which we have to deal in the person of Simaetha. It will be no accident that Theocritus portrays Simaetha as expert in magic and as able to summon *Selene* (the Moon) and Hecate to help her. Indeed at the end of the poem Theocritus has Simaetha, once she has finished with her magic-working, dismiss *Selene* and bid her go on her way, as though she no longer needed to delay her further.[33] The especial affinity for this deity that Simaetha displays rather suggests that as a magician she views Artemis-cum-*Selene*-cum-Hecate as her tutelary deity. Simaetha is assisted in her magic-working by her maid-servant, who also acts as her go-between in arranging assignations. This too is probably intended to be a realistic touch. One further feature of the portrait calls for comment: Simaetha displays no inhibitions about what she is doing; she shows none of the hesitation of a Deianeira or Phaedra, forced by pres-sure of circumstances to turn to magic. What all of this adds up to is that Theocritus takes it for read that women of Simaetha's type will be expert not only in erotic magic, but in more harmful forms of sorcery also, that they will turn to it quite naturally and that the servant-women who attend them will assist in their magic-working. There is no very good reason to think that Theocritus is deluded here and that he is projecting his own male fantasies onto Simaetha. It can readily be conceded that there is a degree of literary artifice in the evocation of Simaetha's magic-working. Theocritus is not nec-essarily concerned to give an accurate picture of what actually went on in such a session, if indeed he knew. It does not follow that he fantasizes about courtesans resorting to magic when they want to attract a man or to win back his affections, if those affections have strayed elsewhere. The sheer force of economic necessity makes it likely that, if anyone was going to resort to erotic magic, it would be a courtesan or prostitute who saw her source of livelihood disappearing.

The poet tells us nothing about the identity of the old women who per-form incantations to whom Simaetha has recourse when she wants initially to win the affections of Delphis. They are evidently old women who live on their own, which rather suggests that they do not have family connections, but for some reason or other pursue an independent existence. It is a fair guess that they are former prostitutes who have acquired an expertise in magic from the older women who had looked after them or with whom they were intimate.

## Magic-working in Cnidus in the first century BC

Theocritus gives us a picture of magic-working on the part of a courtesan viewed from outside and above that is also no doubt somewhat embellished. His portrayal may be complemented by the testimony to magic-working amongst persons belonging to the world of which Simaetha is part, provided by the lead tablets deposited in the first century BC in the sanctuary of Demeter and other gods of the Underworld in Cnidus. We do not exactly hear the direct voice of prostitutes and courtesans, since the tablets have been written by a professional in a formulaic form. The tablets do nonethe-less tell us what the preoccupations of these people were and give us some impression of the degree to which magic-working and accusations of magic-working were part of their lives. Those who have deposited the tablets are humble people concerned over the loss or theft of a tunic; there are women whose men have been stolen away from them;[34] and there is a man who has been beaten and whipped.[35] We have no reason to suppose that those who take action against the persons who accuse them of having practised or been involved in magic-working are in any way different from the other petitioners. The tablets offer a picture of magic-working and of accusations of magic-working within a community that cannot be matched from elsewhere. It gives us some idea of the apparently ungrounded suspicions that could circulate and of the counter-measures that could be taken against them.

One woman consecrates to Demeter and the other gods of the Underworld another woman called Antigone, evidently for having suggested that a man called Asclepiades had been subjected to an underhand attack of some kind. The traduced woman spells out the charges of which she wishes to clear herself: they are that she had given Asclepiades a *pharmakon*, that she had conceived in her mind of doing him any ill or had summoned a woman for a fee of three half-mnas to come to the sanctuary to remove him from the living.[36] This sounds like an instance of a man becoming sick and of his sickness having given rise to accusations, which were that a woman with whom he had enjoyed a relationship other than marriage had used hidden means to harm him. The women involved sound as though they are courtesans and rivals. What is most interesting about the tablet is the notion that a woman could be summoned to the sanctuary for a fee of three half-mnas to perform a magical ceremony designed to kill someone. There is no sign here that the more serious forms of magic-working were in the hands of men. As for the amount of money that the woman has to be paid, three half-mnas would seem to be an enormously large sum of money to have to pay anyone for any service, but since the spell goes on to speak about giving bronze coins to pay for the woman, the amount cannot really be so great.[37] The sum involved would appear to be a known fee for such services. The sanctuary to which the woman is summoned is in all likelihood the sanctuary of Demeter and the other gods of the Underworld in which the lead tablets were found. We can only speculate on what kind of ceremony the woman was supposed to perform, but it almost certainly involved a binding-spell, no doubt accompanied by suitable rituals. It also looks as if the ceremony was performed in the presence of the party who commissioned the spell.

The slanders that Antigone had put about may well have been false, since the woman who deposits the spell seems to be confident that she will be seen to be innocent in the eyes of Demeter and the other gods, but the woman hired for three half-mnas to perform a ritual whose purpose was to secure the death of someone will be a real enough figure. The world in which these events take place would seem to be the *demi-monde* in which courtesans live, a society in which women live independently and have the means to hire other women to perform magic for them. It is finally a world in which there are female magic-workers who can be called on to carry out sorcery of a very serious nature.

Then there is a woman accused of making *pharmaka* for her man, confronted by a much graver danger than gossip, that of being tried.[38] She does not name the person responsible, nor the man who had brought the charge against her. It is hard to know what to make of this failure to name names. Finally, there is a man who defends himself against the person or persons who had said that he had been involved in the use of magic and apparently wishes to clear his name of the accusation that he had employed a woman to do his dirty work, though the Greek is not entirely clear and it is just possible that the woman had been acting against him and his. There appear to be three different procedures that the woman may have carried out either for the man or for one of his family: she may have made a *pharmakon* for him to be drunk (*poton*), to be applied as a salve or ointment (*katachriston*) or that involved conjuring up a spirit against someone (*epakton*).[39] What the last-named procedure was is not wholly clear, but if the adjective has been correctly read, it would appear to have been an *epagoge*, which is to say, the summoning up of a spirit to haunt someone. Whatever force is assigned to the disputed word, we do at least have a woman who is imagined to be skilled in three different kinds of sorcery.

Even if all of the charges of sorcery that the tablets seek to combat were false, there is still a good deal to be learned from them about magic-working in Cnidus. Men, at least on the evidence of the three tablets, are not the active partners in it. Women, who can be hired for a certain price, are the only experts of whom we hear. It is a world in which there is a good deal of suspicion of sorcery and in which there is much loose talk about who has been engaging in it, which somehow or other gets back to the ears of the persons accused. That loose talk results in counteractions which are themselves in a way sorcery.

## The larger Hellenistic world

If we turn from Theocritus' picture of magic-working in the *demi-monde* of Cos and from the execration-spells from Cnidus and the glimpse that they afford us from a different perspective of that same world to the wider Hellenistic world, we find further instances of the types of magician to whom Theocritus and the Cnidian tablets introduce us. One scrap of information is to be found in the earliest of all of the Greek magical formularies. It contains three different spells to cure sickness composed in accomplished hexameters. Two of the spells are attributed to women. A woman of Gadara called Syra is credited with a spell to cure a burning-condition. Not much can be made of her identity, since Syra is an ethnic given as a proper name to slaves of Syrian origin. The name, if it is a proper name at all, is very much a generic name appropriate for someone from Gadara. A spell to cure headache is

106

attributed to the Thessalian woman Philinna. In light of the reputation of Thessalian women as witches the attribution of a spell to a woman of that country is very much what we would expect. The best-known Philinna of Thessalian origin is a woman from Larissa. She bore to Philip II of Macedon a son, Philip Arridaeus, who ruled Macedonia after Alexander's death. She was notorious in later times as a harlot and as, what was to all intents and purposes the same thing, a dancer.[40] Whether there was any truth to the charges is immaterial. What is important is that to give the spell a proper pedigree it should be attributed to a Thessalian woman with a reputation as a whore.

The presumption that prostitutes or, at any rate, Thessalian prostitutes will practise magic also lies behind an anonymous Hellenistic epigram in the *Palatine Anthology* which purports to be on the dedication to Aphrodite by a sorceress (*pharmakis*) called Niko from Larissa in Thessaly of a magic wheel (*iynx*) made rather strangely of amethyst decorated with gold and with a thread of wool dyed purple bound around it. Niko had used the wheel to draw men across the sea and to bring girls from their beds.[41] She had, in other words, used it on behalf of both men and women. The poem belongs to a group of epigrams on the dedications made by courtesans to Aphrodite or Priapus put together by Meleager in the first century BC. Apart from the fact that the dedication is to Aphrodite, an indication that it is the dedication of a prostitute or courtesan, the name of the woman, Niko, is a further sign of her calling. It was the name of famous Samian hetaera and is employed in three epigrams by the early Hellenistic epigrammatist, Asclepiades, as the name either of a courtesan or of the mother of a courtesan.[42] Niko is then a courtesan or former courtesan who has made a second career out of her expertise in erotic magic.

The idea that prostitutes and procuresses are expert in magic-working may also be reflected in the account that the historian Polybius gives of the conduct of Oenanthe, the hetaera of Ptolemy IV Philopator, in the aftermath of his death in 204 BC: in fear for her life she had taken refuge in the temple of Demeter and Kore at Alexandria, which she was able to enter because it happened to be open for an annual sacrifice; at first she tried to prevail on the goddesses by dropping to her knees and engaging in magic (*manganeuousa*) and then sat herself at the altar and kept quiet.[43] Magicians when they want to conjure the gods or spirits of the Underworld with incantations do just what Oenanthe does: they fall to their knees to utter their repeated incantations.[44] Prayer to the gods above is normally performed standing with the arms raised upwards and held somewhat apart.[45] It is generally only the deities of the Underworld who are addressed on bended knee.[46] Demeter and Kore are not unambiguously chthonic deities, but it is to that aspect of them that Oenanthe turns in her hour of need.

## Old women as purifiers and healers

The old women who sing incantations to whom Simaetha goes when she wants to attract Delphis are well attested in the Hellenistic world. It is not to be imagined that they spent all of their time helping courtesans and prostitutes in their intrigues. Much of their activity will have been of a more humdrum nature and will have consisted in curing sicknesses, whether in humans or in animals, through the application of amulets and the uttering of incantations, forestalling or curing the effects of the Evil Eye, purifying those who had experienced a frightening dream or who felt that there was something else amiss about themselves. Especially when curing the sick, they will have gone to the houses of those who summoned them. One striking feature of their activities is that they very often operate in conjunction with other women.

From Menander's play *Phasma*, 'The Vision', a fairly vivid idea can be gained of what would have happened if someone had had a disturbing dream. A young man called Pheidias sees a beautiful girl, but is persuaded that it was merely a dream. He is upset by what has happened and is advised by a slave that the remedy he needs is that women should stand around him in a circle purifying him and burning sulphur about him and that he should have himself sprinkled with water from three springs into which have been cast salt and lentils.[47] There can be no doubt that more than one woman is imagined to take part in the ceremony. The same phenomenon has already been encountered in the story about the amulets that Pericles, when desperately ill, had put around his neck.[48]

The presence of more than one woman during ceremonies of purification encourages the suspicion that on some occasions a hierarchy of rôles may have been observed with one woman taking a dominant part and the others acting as her acolytes. One woman may have uttered incantations, while her helper or helpers performed the symbolic acts that went hand-in-hand with the verbal part of the ceremony. This is in effect what is portrayed in Theocritus' Second Idyll: Simaetha pronounces the spell that she hopes will bring her lover back to her and performs some of the symbolic acts that accompany the spell, while her maid, Thestylis, has charge of the paraphernalia necessary for the ritual and brings them into use as they are needed, but also performs some of the magical actions necessary for the success of the spell. Thestylis has first of all to have the laurel-leaves and the love-philtres at hand and is required to garland a basin with a thread of red wool.[49] She has next to scatter barley-groats on the fire and to say as she does so: 'I scatter the bones of Delphis.'[50] Finally, the girl is sent off to the threshold of the lover, there to knead some herbs and to whisper as she does so: 'I knead the bones of Delphis.'[51]

Amulets seem to have been the special province of old women. Plutarch says that Bion of Borysthenes, a wandering sage of the end of the fourth century BC, maintained that old women carried amulets with them and that they affixed these amulets to whatever they came in contact with, as though it were a peg.[52] Diodorus Siculus in his discussion of the identity and origins of the Idaean Dactyls gives a glimpse into what women did when they were preparing and putting on an amulet. He cites authorities, whom he does not name, who propounded the theory that there was an Idaean Dactyl called Hercules, who was a wizard (*goes*) and practised mystery-rites; as proof Diodorus' authorities adduce the custom still well attested in Diodorus' day of women using Hercules in incantations and in making amulets (*periammata*).[53] What exactly Diodorus means by this is by no means perspicuous. The general lineaments of what the women were doing can nonetheless be discerned, since quite a lot is known about Hercules as a talisman against evil. Formulaic inscription are to be found near the doors of houses that declare: 'Hercules dwells within, let not evil enter.'[54] His club, carved in relief on the walls of houses, is found on the island of Delos.[55] It will have conveyed the same message. If Hercules was felt to ward off evil, his name may well have been intoned by old women as they applied an amulet. Incantations were after all regularly intoned as amulets were affixed.[56] The incantation reinforced the power of the amulet to protect and at the same time endowed it with magical potency.

There are passing references in Theocritus to old women performing apotropaic actions to ward off the threat of the Evil Eye. The one-eyed giant Polyphemus declares, after he has admired his reflection in the sea, that he has spat thrice into his breast, as he had been taught by an old woman called Cottytaris, so that he might not be bewitched by the Evil Eye of Envy.[57] In another poem by the same poet a singer ends his song with the wish that there may be peace between himself and another singer and that an old woman may be present to ward off ill by spitting on them.[58] What has moved the singer to utter the prayer for an old woman is the danger created by his public expression of a wish for peace between himself and his fellow-singer. In the ancient world friendship and concord between two persons was thought to invite the assaults of envious and malign forces and to mention it was considered especially dangerous. This is the danger that the singer wishes to avert by having an old woman perform the apotropaic action of spitting. From an ancient commentator on the passage we learn that when old women performed the apotropaic act of spitting over the object they wished to protect, they very often did so after uttering an incantation.[59]

## Holy men and women from the East

The Assyrian stranger from whom Simaetha learns of the especially deadly drugs that she keeps in a chest as a weapon of last resort is an interesting figure. At the most superficial level he represents the type of man who was drawn in the Early Hellenistic Period from the East to Cos. He is a precursor on a rather less grand level of the Babylonian priest and historian Berosus who arrived in Cos in the second half of the third century. The Assyrian stranger represents not only the sharp-witted foreigner attracted to the rich pickings that Cos afforded, but a man who exploits the reputation enjoyed by the lands of the East as the centres of older and more profound cultures. Simaetha's weapons of last resort, the drugs that will kill her one-time lover, come from the Assyrian, not because he is, as has been suggested, a man and as such superior in talent to the local women whom Simaetha had approached earlier, but because he is from the East, from Assyria.[60] There must in reality have been partly hellenized men like the Assyrian stranger who made their way west from Mesopotamia and from points even further east to take advantage of the reputation that their homelands possessed for wisdom and religious understanding.

The Assyrian is of particular interest because he is the earliest example of an Easterner other than a Persian credited by a Greek with a knowledge of magic. It is of some importance to learn where exactly he comes from to determine who could in the eyes of the Greeks plausibly pass himself off as an expert in magic at this date. The issue is complicated by a marked tendency on the part of Greeks, beginning with Herodotus, to use the terms Syrian and Assyrian interchangeably.[61] They are followed in this by the Romans. The area from which those designated as Assyrians or Syrians normally come is Syro-Palestine rather than Assyria.[62] The poet and anthologizer of the first century BC, Meleager, in one of the funerary epigrams that he wrote for himself says that his fatherland was Gadara amongst the Assyrians; he then refers to himself as a Syrian.[63] But Assyrian can on occasion also mean someone from Babylon or from Assyria more generally and be used interchangeably with Chaldaean. Somehow or other the fame of the Persians in magic rubbed off on the Babylonians and the Chaldaeans and the distinction between these peoples became blurred. An ancient commentator on Theocritus, evidently to explain why it is from an Assyrian that Simaetha gets her most malign spells, says of the Assyrians that they were a Persian people and skilled in magic who lived between the Tigris and Euphrates.[64] Because the Assyrian is imagined to be an especially potent magician, it will be Assyria proper or Babylonia that is his home.

Theocritus introduces the Assyrian with no word of explanation about who he is. That he is mentioned without further ado suggests that he was a known type in the Hellenistic world or even a known person. There are few clues to the identity of such magicians. It is possible that some of them emerged from the ranks of the priests expert in conducting healing and exorcistic rituals who continued to be a presence in Babylonia under the Seleucids. Incontrovertible evidence exists to be examined shortly that Babylonian ritual recipes became in this period part of the pharmacopoeia of Greek magic. Whether any of them were brought into the Greek world by ritual experts who had assumed the guise of magician is uncertain but possible. Of the presence of one group of ritual experts with roots in Babylonia, although they spawned many imitators, there can be no doubt: they are the persons expert in astrology, who are variously referred to as Chaldaeans, *astrologoi* or *mathematikoi*. At a later date, some of them certainly had a reputation as magicians. Since astrology in Babylon was employed in healing and exorcistic rituals, it would not be surprising that those expert in such techniques were viewed as magicians by Greeks predisposed to believe that Persia and Babylonia were the home of magic. It very much depended on the outlook of the observer whether he saw the Chaldaeans as magicians or as heirs to a body of wisdom older and more profound than anything to which the Greeks had access. Diodorus Siculus, who depends in this instance on the Stoic philosopher of the late second and early first century, Posidonius, gives an extraordinarily admiring account of the way in which the Chaldaeans preserve their ancient learning unchanged, handing it on from father to son.[65] Diodorus declares that the Chaldaeans devote their lives to *philosophia*, that their main fame lies in their astrology, but that they lay claim to wide expertise in the art of the seer (*mantike*), making pronouncements about the future, and that by use of purifications (*katharmoi*), sacrifices, and incantations (*epodai*) they attempt to ward off ill and bring benefits to fruition.[66] Someone less favourably disposed on philosophical grounds to astrology and the other predictive arts than Posidonius and so less prepared to put a favourable construction on the activities of the Chaldaeans of Babylonia might have seen them as mere sorcerers and purifiers.

How widely people calling themselves Chaldaeans travelled can be seen from a warning given in a work on agriculture written around the middle of second century BC by a prominent figure in Roman political life, Cato the Elder. What Cato warns against is allowing the slave-overseer (*vilicus*) of a farm to consult various forms of fortune-teller, amongst them a Chaldaean.[67] What this in effect means is that by the middle of the second century BC and as far west as Italy men known as Chaldaeans were taken for granted and were consulted by quite humble persons. In 139 BC, Cn. Cornelius Scipio Hispanus, the *praetor peregrinus*, issued an edict expelling Chaldaeans from Rome and ordering them to leave Italy within ten days to keep them, in the words of our source, from purveying their foreign knowledge.[68] Of these Chaldaeans the most famous and the first of whom we know to have come west was Berosus from Babylon itself. A generation or so later we find another Chaldaean of some note, Soudines, at the court of Attalus I of Pergamum.[69] The identities of two of the three eminent Chaldaeans whom Vitruvius names are known and also that they took up residence in Greece. The same will be true of the third member of the triumvirate, Achinapolus, whose fame rested on his calculating horoscopes from the date of conception rather than birth.[70] All of these men are called Chaldaeans, but they did not necessarily come from Babylonia. Antipater, who, although he is called a Chaldaean in the decree from Larissa, is described in the same document as a Hieropolitan of Seleucia. He comes, accordingly, from the Syrian city of Bambyce or Hierapolis that lies 75 km north-east of Aleppo and 24 km from the Euphrates.[71]

There were besides Chaldaeans other kinds of Eastern holy men and women, the strangeness of whose religious practices both gave them a certain purchase over the minds of some of the Greeks and Romans with whom they came in contact and made them suspect in the eyes of others. They were men and women who exploited their exotic origins to win authority for themselves. All of the Syrian holy men whom we encounter in the Hellenistic Period possess the gift of prophecy. It is on this gift that their authority rests. The dividing line between inspired seer and magician is a fine one and is overstepped, if the holy man is suspected of using wonder-working to enhance his authority. The magician-cum-wonder-worker is not a new phenomenon. There are already hints of his existence in the Classical Period. We shall meet him increasingly frequently in the centuries that follow. In addition to having the gift of prophetic utterance, the two Syrian holy women and one Syrian holy man at whom we shall look have something else in common: they are all taken up by a patron and become more or less part of his household. This too is a pattern that we shall meet again and again.

There is first of all the peculiar phenomenon of the Syrian prophetesses to be found in the train of generals on campaign. Aristoboulus of Cassandreia in Macedonia, a contemporary of Alexander the Great, reported that one of the camp-followers of that monarch was a Syrian woman subject to divine possession. She was at first a source of merriment to Alexander, but when it became clear that everything she said during her seizures had turned out to be true, the king became more interested in her. She was, in consequence, granted access to him by day and by night and often stood over him when he was asleep. Her greatest claim to fame was that she was credited with having saved Alexander from being assassinated.[72] The Roman general Marius had in 102 BC another Syrian prophetess called Martha in his retinue during his campaign against the Celtic tribes of the Cimbri and the Teutones.[73] Finally, Spartacus, the leader of the slave revolt in Italy in the late 70s, was accompanied by a Thracian slave-woman with mantic gifts.[74] Such women were a characteristic feature of the much larger train of camp-followers that accompanied Hellenistic armies. Plutarch says that the army of the reforming king of Sparta, Cleomenes, was quite unlike that of any other royal or Hellenic army, in that no mimes, wonder-workers (*thaumatopoioi*), female dancers or players on the lyre followed in its train, but that it was free of all elements of licentiousness, vulgarity and of the atmosphere of the fair.[75] Whether Cleomenes' army in the second half of the third century BC was, as Plutarch would have us believe, such a model of rectitude and decorum is another matter, but it is hardly to be doubted that Hellenistic armies resembled travelling fairs.

The two female Syrian soothsayers belong to the class of wandering holy persons. Our sources vouchsafe no more information about their background beyond the fact that they were Syrian. There can be no question that they were native Syrians and not Greeks resident in Syria. The name of Marius' prophetess, Martha, makes that clear. The native language of the women will have been Aramaic or some other Semitic tongue. Beyond that not much can be said about them. The same is not true of the man who was at the centre of the slave revolt in Sicily in the 130s BC. Our information about him comes ultimately from Posidonius.[76] Posidonius' place of birth was the Greek settlement in Syria of Apameia. His account of the slave revolt lies behind the narratives of Diodorus Siculus and Livy, the latter of whom we possess only in the summaries of two late historians, Orosius and Florus. Posidonius, who first came to Rome some forty years after the suppression of the revolt, will have been reasonably well informed about its origins and progress. His picture of its leader and his actions, although not necessarily trustworthy in its details, will portray a type of man familiar to Posidonius. It is inconceivable that what the leader of the revolt, Eunus, said and did was recorded at the time and that the records were preserved.[77] The account that we have of Eunus' career will be in some measure an imaginative recreation on Posidonius' part based on patterns of behaviour with which he was familiar. It is no less valuable for our purposes than a portrait based on autopsy.

The man at the centre of the revolt was a Syrian slave called Eunus, who belonged to a citizen of Enna in Sicily named Antigenes. Eunus, who is characterized by Diodorus Siculus as a *goes*, came from Apameia in Syria, Posidonius' own city. He gained authority and credence at first by pretending to foretell the future in obedience to commands given him in dreams by the gods. He went on from there to assert that he saw the gods when awake and heard them telling him about the future. People increasingly came to believe him, because a number of his impromptu predictions came true. His most impressive feat was to prophesy in an inspired state, while breathing fire from his mouth. The reality was that he had a walnut in his mouth, pierced in two spots and containing sulphur and some fire.[78] Before the revolt took place, he had said that the Syrian Goddess had appeared in an epiphany to him and told him that he would be king. He went around telling everybody this including his master, Antigenes. Antigenes was taken in by his miracle-working and brought the man to dinner parties, where what we could call his conjuring-tricks, but what his audience would have thought of as wonders or miracles, provided amusement. That was the state of affairs when the slaves of an especially rich citizen of Enna, whose treatment of them was outrageously harsh, came to Eunus to ask him whether the gods would permit the revolt that they were plotting. Eunus' reply, backed up by a miracle, was that the gods would indeed grant them permission. He urged them, furthermore, to press on with their enterprise. They gathered a body of four hundred slaves and fell upon Enna with Eunus at their head breathing flames. Once Enna was in their hands, they held an assembly at which they crowned Eunus as their king with the name of Antiochus; they made the woman with whom he cohabited, who herself came from Apameia, his consort. They chose Eunus as their king for no other reason, according to Diodorus, than his ability to perform miracles.[79] That they did in fact make Eunus their king under the name Antiochus is confirmed by a coin from Sicily, minted probably in Enna, that has on its reverse the legend: King Antiochus.

The career of Eunus has a good deal in common with those of the two Syrian prophetesses. In all three cases they succeed in convincing those around them that they do indeed possess visionary powers. Their charismatic power lies in part in their ability to exploit the conviction of Greeks and Romans that as Syrians they were endowed with special powers and had access to especially potent and mysterious deities. Eunus invokes the Syrian Goddess to good effect. His conduct diverges from that of the others only insofar as he was prepared to perform even more outrageous tricks to gain credence. He is the first identifiable instance of the magician-cum-miracle-worker whom we have encountered. The milieu in which a successful miracle-worker performed his miracles was, as in Eunus' case, not so much the street-corners but symposia or dinner parties. Pliny the Elder and other sources tell of recipes for conjuring-tricks to be performed by the magician on such occasions. Eunus is said to have won the confidence of his master and have been taken up by him as something of a prize turn. That was no doubt something that did occur. What happened to such men in the long run is an imponderable. Some of them may have been manumitted, become freedmen and set themselves up in business on their own.

The career of Decaenus, a holy man from the Danube-frontier who had helped Burebistas become the leader of the Getae, follows, if Strabo is to be believed, a similar path to that of Eunus. Strabo says that Decaeneus was a *goes*, who in the course of his wanderings had travelled to Egypt and had there learned certain premonitory signs that enabled him to interpret the will of the gods; shortly afterwards he had become a god in the eyes of the Getae and such were his powers of persuasion that he succeeded in persuading the Getae to cut down their vines and live without wine.[80] The events described by Strabo would, if they had really happened, have taken place in the 60s BC. It is to be doubted whether they took the form that Strabo says they did. He will have imposed on the story of Decaeneus a pattern familiar to his readers: a prophet who used the tricks of a *goes* to secure acceptance for his prophetic utterances and who had begun his career by claiming to have acquired the wisdom of Egypt and to be able through it to foretell the future and who had then gone on from there to have himself proclaimed a god. That such men were also able to effect major alteration in the way people lived seems also to have been part of the pattern. Men of this type will be encountered at a somewhat later date in Syro-Palestine.

## Mendicant sorcerers

The Syrian women found in the entourages of Alexander and Marius are likely to be essentially mendicant-priestesses of some Syrian deity. The persistence into the Hellenistic Period of mendicant-priests who practised magic is not attested in the Greek or Roman worlds themselves. Their existence can nonetheless be inferred. The terms and categories used by Hellenistic authors to describe the religious life of alien peoples or to make sense of the legendary past enable us to reconstruct the forms of religious life with which they were familiar. The *Indica*, a history of India in four books, that come from the pen of the Ionian man of letters, Megasthenes, are based in some degree on what he had learned as the ambassador of Seleucus I to India, but the categories in which he describes life in India betray the impress on his thinking of his own late fourth-century world. There is unfortunately no adequate modern study of this writer. Amongst the people he describes is a tribe he calls the Garamanes. He divides them into three sub-groups. Those who enjoy the highest repute are called *Hylobioi* or Forest Dwellers, a name that reflects their mode of life in the forest where they remain, eating leaves and wild fruit and abstaining from sex and wine; they communicate with the kings through messengers and supervise their religious rituals. Second in esteem are a group of mendicant healers called the *iatrikoi*, who live simply; they through their skill in *pharmaka* (*pharmakeutike*) are able to make people have a large number of children and also to make them have male or female children; most of their doctoring, however, is done through diet, not through drugs (*pharmaka*); their skill in *pharmaka* lies especially in salves (*epichrista*) and plasters; besides these *pharmaka* most of their other *pharmaka* are maleficent; they display great powers of endurance and can remain in the same position for a day. Then there are the soothsayers (*mantikoi*), utterers of incantations (*epodoi*) and those skilled in matters pertaining to the deceased; they go from village to village and city to city begging; the more tasteful and refined of the group do not refrain from the rites that are widely said to be performed in connection with the Underworld; they, however, only perform those that are pious and holy.[81] It is not worthwhile speculating on what Indian caste, if any, Megasthenes has in mind. What is apparent is that he has described two groups of people in categories familiar to himself. They become begging-priests, making their way from community to community, in one case acting as doctors and at the same time offering various maleficent forms of sorcery and in the other professing to be able to foretell the future, performing incantations and practising necromancy. It will be no accident that Megasthenes casts these vagabond holy men as doctors and sorcerers and as seers and magic-workers. The combination of rôles in both cases will have seemed natural and familiar to him. The gradation in esteem in which the three categories of holy men are held is also revealing: at the top of the pyramid come those who live apart in the forest and communicate through messengers; then there are the mendicant doctors-cum-sorcerers-cum-wonder-workers; and finally, at the bottom of the heap, there are the vagabond seers, utterers of incantations and necromancers. The division in function between mendicant vagabonds, persons expert in medicine and in physically-based *pharmaka*, whether magical or medical, and persons expert in divining, incantation and necromancy perhaps reflects the specializations followed by the wandering mendicants whom Megasthenes himself knew.

The author who quotes the account that Megasthenes gives of the Garamanes is the geographer Strabo, who wrote at the end of the first century BC. At a slightly later stage in his discussion of India Strabo mentions a people called the Pramnai, the opponents of the Brahmins. They, like the Garamanes, are made up of three groups: the Mountain Pramnae; the Naked Pramnae; and the City or Neighbouring Pramnae. The Mountain Pramnae wear deer-skins and carry pouches filled with roots and *pharmaka*; they claim to be experts in medicine, which they practise in conjunction with sorcery (*goeteia*), incantations (*epodai*) and the application of amulets (*periapta*). The Naked Pramnai live naked, spending their lives in the open air, and engage in feats of endurance.[82] Strabo does not say what his source of information is here, but uses a third-person plural verb whose subject the context suggests is writers on Indian life. The Pramnae sound very like the Garamanes with the parts assigned the three groups who make up the Garamanes distributed differently. Megasthenes is then Strabo's source for the Pramnai or, if not his source, the inspiration for someone else's ethnography of that people. The Mountain Pramnai are, accordingly, another group of wandering mendicant healers offering a combination of medicine and sorcery whose activities will owe as much to the vagabond healers of the Hellenistic Greek world as they do to any Indian reality. We have then some reason to picture for ourselves wandering mendicant healers-cum-sorcerers carrying the knapsacks (*pera*) characteristic of Greek beggars, filled with the *pharmaka* they needed for their activities and making their way from community to community.

## Magic and mystery-cult

The idea that magic-working is intimately connected to the practice of mystery-rites also persists into the Hellenistic Period, but there is no direct testimony to the existence of magicians whose magic-working went hand-in-hand with initiations into the mysteries. It is, however, a connection to which Hellenistic writers appeal to make sense of the lives of certain figures from the mythical past. That suggests that persons who made a living from initiations into the mysteries and sorcery were still a presence in the Hellenistic Period. The unnamed Hellenistic authorities on whom Diodorus Siculus draws in his account of the Idaean Dactyls said that the custom observed by women even in their day of invoking Hercules in incantations and in the preparation of amulets was evidence that the Hercules invoked must have been a sorcerer and one who practised secret rites.[83] The argument is based on the interesting assumption that those whose authority is invoked in spells and incantations will be magicians and secondly that there is an intrinsic relationship between the mystery-rites practised by *agyrtai* and magic-working. The latter assumption also underlies the euhemeristic account that Strabo, who relies here on some earlier Hellenistic source, gives of the career of Orpheus: he was at first a sorcerer (*goes*) who made a living as a mendicant (*agyrtes*) from music, the seer's craft (*mantike*) and mystery-rites, before he became more ambitious and went on to attempt greater things.[84] It is to be suspected that behind this conception of Orpheus lurks the presence of *Orpheotelestai*, the wandering mendicant holy men-cum-sorcerers who, relying on their possession of books written by Orpheus, offered initiation into the mysteries. A similar rationalizing pattern of explanation is to be found in another passage in Strabo in which the geographer tries to relate to a reality that makes sense to him the legends told by men of old about such figures as the Idaean Dactyls. The rationalization he offers for the stories told about the journeys through the mountains the Idaean Dactyls undertook and for their ecstatic possession by the divine (*enthousiasmos*) is that their mountain-walking signifies their concern with mining and hunting and in general with acquiring the necessities of life, while a mendicant way of life (*agyrtikon*) and sorcery (*goeteia*) are closely related to divine possession, the performance of religious ritual and the craft of the seer (*mantike*).[85] That surely means that in the world Strabo knew there were wandering holy men with pretensions to being experts on the proper worship of the gods who engaged in ecstatic prophecy and practised sorcery.

## The emergence of the learned magician

The Hellenistic Period did not exactly give rise to new and revolutionary types of magic-worker. The magic-workers whom we have encountered all have precursors in the Classical Period. There is one distinctly new creation of the Hellenistic Age and that is the educated man who takes an interest in magic and perhaps collects and organizes magical lore. The term 'learned magician' is something of a misnomer, since such men were not necessarily practising magicians, although they may have on occasion experimented a little, but men who collected magical lore. Bolus of Mendes, an Egyptian, but educated in Greek, which suggests that he belonged to the priestly caste, is the best known instance of the type.[86] He is likely to have been active in the first half of the second century BC.[87] He may well have had predecessors. It was certainly the case that he drew on the work of men who had brought together information about the properties of natural substances. It is, however, a good deal harder to show that anyone before Bolus self-consciously set out to collect magical lore on its own.

There are two figures who may have mapped out some of the road that

Bolus was to follow. They are Hermippus of Smyrna and a doctor called Cleemporus. In the case of Hermippus we cannot be certain what exactly the character of his work was and, in that of Cleemporus, when it was he wrote. About the date of Hermippus of Smyrna there is not much room for doubt. He belonged to the same generation as the great Alexandrian scholar and poet Callimachus, who was active in the first half of the third century BC. Hermippus made use of the system for the organization and classification of literary works that Callimachus had invented. He wrote biographies of eminent men that were, for example, mined in the second century AD by Diogenes Laertius in his *Lives of the Philosophers*. To judge from what survives of Hermippus in Diogenes, he was a man who had a distinct taste for the scandalous anecdote. He must have lived a long life, since he seems still to have been alive at the end of the third century BC. Pliny the Elder in his chapters on the history and dissemination of magic informs us that Hermippus wrote in painstaking fashion about the whole art of magic and did an explanatory commentary on two million lines of Zoroaster, the individual volumes of which he equipped with indices.[88] The treatise on the art of magic of which Pliny speaks is presumably the work to which Diogenes Laertius gives the title *On the Magoi* and in whose first book he says the *magoi* are credited with believing in a good divine element and an evil divine element, known respectively as Zeus or Oromandes and Hades or Areimanius.[89]

The account that Pliny gives of Hermippus' classificatory and exegetical activity has provoked a great deal of debate centring on the vast number of ancient book-rolls that would have been needed to accommodate the two million lines attributed to Zoroaster. Some scholars have been quite happy to believe that the Library in Alexandria really had six hundred books of what they imagine was Persian religious lore; other scholars have been inclined to doubt whether the Library could have had room for so many book-rolls. The scepticism of the latter group of scholars does not go far enough: more radical questions need to be raised. It is proper to ask how Hermippus could have read works written in Old Persian. No one would deny that Greeks were interested in foreign customs and religious practices. The problem is that they did not, except under duress, learn foreign languages. They had, accordingly, to satisfy their curiosity about the strange and barbarous by reading about it in Greek. There were bilingual foreigners who were willing to meet the need and who wrote books specifically designed to supply Greeks with the information they sought in the form that they wanted.[90] In addition, there was a thriving pseudepigraphical industry that on occasion catered to the Greek taste for alien knowledge. It is overwhelmingly likely that it was basically a pseudepigraphical work on which Hermippus wrote his commentary. There is also the very real possibility that the two million lines attributed to Zoroaster are a fiction concocted by

Hermippus himself to give authority to material that he had either assembled or invented.

Whether Hermippus attributed magical recipes to the *magoi* in his book on them must be a moot point. Pliny certainly says that Hermippus discoursed on the whole art of magic, but it is to be doubted whether Pliny had himself seen the book. His information will have come from some intermediate source, perhaps the Alexandrian grammarian Apion, who was active under Tiberius, Caligula and Claudius and who wrote a work entitled *On the Magoi.*[91] Although Pliny may not have been terribly well informed about the contents of Hermippus' writings, it is difficult to believe that Hermippus can have found enough material to fill up a whole book on the *magoi* without including magical lore in it. Whatever sort of book it was on which Hermippus wrote his exegetical commentary and whatever it was that was contained in his treatise *On the Magoi*, the writings of Hermippus do testify to an interest on the part of Alexandrian intellectuals and scholars with the wisdom of the Persian *magoi*.

It is virtually certain that Hermippus was Bolus' predecessor. It is rather less clear whether the work on the magical properties of plants whose author was probably Cleemporus was older than Bolus and an influence on him. It purported to be a treatise composed by Pythagoras on the basis of what that sage had learned from the *magoi* of the East, whom he was supposed to have visited.[92] Pliny, who chose to believe that Pythagoras was the author, admits there were persons who took the opposite view and attributed the work to Cleemporus.[93] Cato the Elder knew the book, which means that it belongs to the first half of the second century BC or earlier.[94] That Cato in far-away Italy should have read the work is some indication of the widespread interest that such pseudepigraphical writing must have aroused.

There are indications that Cleemporus' work on magical plants was the model that Bolus followed in his much more wide-ranging study of the magical properties of not only plants, but birds, fish, mammals and stones. Bolus' work was apparently called the *Cheiromecta*, a title that suggests the book dealt with what was kneaded, moulded or worked by hand. There was perhaps in the title a reference to the substances that were ground or cut up by *rhizotomoi*. Bolus, as Columella informs us, pretended that Democritus was the author of the compilation.[95] Pliny, for his part, maintains that there was general agreement about Democritus' authorship, although he does later concede the existence of sceptics.[96] That the work on magical plants is ascribed to Pythagoras and the *Cheiromecta* to Democritus, Pythagoras' follower, may mean that Cleemporus had pre-empted Pythagoras' name and that he was the earlier writer.

The *Natural Histories* of Pliny the Elder are our principal source of information about what was contained in the *Cheiromecta*. The only material that Pliny specifically assigns to that source is a selection of entries from the section of the work on magical plants.[97] On other occasions Pliny adduces the authority of either Democritus himself or the *Magi*. These are not separate sources, but alternative ways of referring to the same source, since in the *Cheiromecta* the fictitious figure of Democritus will have appealed to the authority of the *magoi*. Whether all of the magical lore attributed to Democritus and the *Magi* in the *Natural Histories* comes from the *Cheiromecta* is uncertain. It is possible that Pliny had recourse to pseudepigraphical works attributed to Democritus written by an author or authors other than Bolus in which the authority of the *magoi* was invoked. Even if that were the case, the chances are that most of the magical lore for which Pliny gives Democritus and the *Magi* as his source still comes from Bolus.

One of the fictions of the *Cheiromecta* was that Democritus had sought out magical lore not only from the *magoi* of Persia and Babylon, but also from *magoi* in Arabia, Ethiopia and Egypt. That should mean that the work contained material purporting to come from all of these areas. There is a good deal of evidence that in fact it did. Pliny, for instance, in the selection of magical plants that he makes from the *Cheiromecta* cites two plants from Ethiopia, one of which is called Aethiopis or Merois and the other, Ophiusa, from Elephantine.[98] Merois, we are told, is good for dropsy, while Ophiusa, when drunk, causes visions of snakes to appear before the eyes; so terrifying are these apparitions that they lead to the suicide of the person experiencing them. We may imagine that Bolus adduced an Egyptian or Ethiopian *magos* as the source from which Democritus acquired this knowledge.

It would be extremely useful to know how in reality Bolus set about making his compilation and in what form it came. If we could get some idea of the raw material from which he worked, we would be so much better placed to ascertain what exactly his contribution was. It would be most surprising if Bolus did indeed have the authority of the Persian *magoi* for any of the lore that he published under Democritus' name. We should beware, however, of assuming that Bolus did not sweep up genuine Near Eastern material in his net. A closer study of Pliny the Elder, the herbal of Dioscorides and whoever else drew on Bolus' Democritus than has been undertaken might reveal more of Bolus' borrowings. As it is, only one instance of his borrowing has been uncovered. There is a Babylonian cuneiform tablet that presents a series of recipes all of which are concerned with women whose affections have been alienated by another man. One of the recipes is inscribed under the heading 'To Make a Woman Talk'. It prescribes taking amongst other things the tongue of what may be a bat, wrapping it in wool and placing it at the head of the bed of a sleeping woman to extract from her answers to the question about whom she was having sexual relations with.[99] In two papyri from Roman Egypt containing magical formulae we find virtually the same recipe: one of them from a papyrus of the fourth century AD prescribes placing the heart of a hoopoe on the private parts of a sleeping woman and then questioning her;[100] the other from a rather older papyrus suggests putting the tongue of a hen under the lips of a sleeping woman or on her breast to get her to reveal the name of the man she loves.[101]

There is not much room for doubt that the procedures found in the papyri, which also crop up in lapidaries from Late Antiquity in the same form or in a slightly varied form, are the same technique as that found in the cuneiform-tablet. There is, however, an enormous gap between the eighth century BC and the second or third century AD, the date of the older papyrus. There is also the question of how a recipe in cuneiform came to be translated into Greek. Pliny the Elder records two instances of the procedure, one of which he ascribes to Democritus and the other to the *Magi*. The procedure attributed to Democritus recommends that the tongue of a frog with nothing else adhering to it is to be removed from the creature while alive; the frog is then to be released in water; and the severed tongue is to be placed above the beating heart of a sleeping woman, so that she may give true answers to the questions put to her.[102] Versions of the same procedure are to be found in two late Greek manuscripts now in Athens and in a Greek manuscript of the fifteenth century now in Paris.[103] Pliny, immediately after he has described the procedure, recounts another recipe for which a frog is needed, also for dealing with an errant woman: if a frog is transfixed by a reed from its private parts to its mouth and the reed is then placed in the menses of a woman, the woman will find the man with whom she has been having adulterous relations no longer to her taste. The latter recipe Pliny ascribes to the authority of the *Magi*. The second formula for extracting a confession is virtually the same as the recipe in which a frog is employed except that it prescribes placing the heart of an owl above the left breast of a sleeping woman to make her utter all of her secrets when questioned.[104]

The probabilities are that both the recipe ascribed to Democritus and that ascribed to the *Magi* go back to Bolus of Mendes. There is also reason to suspect that the two recipes employing frogs, one of which is attributed to Democritus and the other to the *Magi*, were to be found together in Bolus' Democritus, and that Bolus himself found them side by side in a source of much the same form as the Babylonian cuneiform-text. In it procedures for dealing with wives whose affections had wandered will have been assembled. Bolus of Mendes may have collected material emanating from Mesopotamia that was originally inscribed on cuneiform-tablets, but it is highly unlikely that he was responsible for unearthing and translating the recipes he recorded. There must, in other words, have been a further intermediary or intermediaries. He will have been a subject of the Seleucid rulers of Syria who knew cuneiform itself or had access to Babylonian texts that had been translated into Aramaic.[105]

Bolus of Mendes invented or made a substantial contribution to a new literary genre, magical recipes collected together and organized alphabetically and according to the nature of the substances employed in them. Such works are emphatically not the handbooks of working magicians and were not intended to have that rôle. Quite what function they were expected to perform is less than clear. Many of the recipes in them prescribed ingredients that must have been either difficult or impossible to obtain. Pliny the Elder says of one of a series of recipes which made use of the parts of the *bubo* or eagle owl that it is a wonder just to have seen the bird, let alone to have found its egg.[106] The point is a good one, if the recipes in the collection were intended to be taken seriously, but misses the point, if their purpose is primarily literary. It looks then as if those who assembled the collections were not much concerned with the practicalities of employing a given recipe. If the recipes were not practicable, two questions then arise: what can their origin be; and why have they been included in a collection? Answers to such questions are very much a matter of guesswork, but there is the distinct possibility that recipes of a particularly exotic nature were intended to impress and that even the handbooks of working magicians may have contained a certain number of such formulae.

Although collections of magico-medical recipes may have been primarily literary artefacts, it does not follow that their recipes were not taken over by magicians, and if not put into effect, were at least incorporated into their handbooks. We have instances of the spell for extracting a confession from an adulterous wife while she slept in two magical formularies written on papyrus. Whether these were the handbooks of actual practitioners or more likely were collections of spells put together by men whose sense of power was enhanced by having such books in their possession and who liked to think that if they wanted to, they had the means at hand to perform the feats that the recipes they now had in their possession promised is unclear. But even if the two formularies do not represent the handbooks of working magicians, we should still allow for the possibility that spells from literary texts found their way into the handbooks of magicians.

## Democritus' *Paignia*

A large part of the stock-in-trade of many ancient practitioners of magic will have been what we would call conjuring-tricks, but what a Greek would have called *thaumata*, wonders or miracles. The leader of the Sicilian slave revolt, Eunus, is a case in point: the walnut with burning charcoal in it that he held in his mouth and breathed through to produce flames is a characteristic trick for an ancient magician. The extension of the term *thauma* is a good deal wider than our conjuring-trick and takes in any phenomenon that runs counter to what we expect of nature. There is some evidence that Bolus, again under Democritus' name, made a collection of recipes for tricks, amongst which conjuring-tricks probably played an important part. In all likelihood he gave his collection the title of *Paignia*, which means in Greek 'Tricks'. There is in a magical papyrus of the fourth century AD a collection of tricks of assorted kinds written out under the rubric *Tricks of Democritus*.[107]

It cannot be demonstrated that any of the tricks go back to Bolus and one of them in the form we have it can be shown, because of a reference in it to gladiators, to be later than Bolus. The title of the collection does nonetheless testify to a tradition of tricks associated with Democritus.

Indirect evidence for Democritus' having made a collection of tricks is to be found in the work of one of Bolus' spiritual descendants, Anaxilaus of Larissa, who was expelled in 28 BC from Rome and Italy by Augustus as a *magus* and Pythagorean. We know that Anaxilaus looked back to Bolus or at any rate to Bolus' recreation of Democritus as a Pythagorean holy man, since a late alchemical papyrus records the ascription by Anaxilaus to Democritus of a recipe for transmuting copper into silver.[108] Anaxilaus will have followed in Bolus' footsteps in putting together a collection of tricks. Those which are recorded are principally conjuring-tricks.[109] Quite in what spirit Bolus made his collection of tricks eludes our understanding, but his calling them *Tricks* rather than bestowing some more pretentious title on them suggests that he saw them as a sub-class of magic, distinguished from the magic that had more serious ends in view.

## Bolus' successors

Of Bolus' successors we know virtually nothing. That there were such persons is certain, but we only know the name of one of them. He is Zachalias of Babylon, who wrote a work on magical gem-stones, which he dedicated to King Mithridates. He too invoked the authority of the *magoi* for what he had to say.[110] According to Pliny, Zachalias believed that stones had a controlling effect on man's lot. The sample of the work that Pliny gives us is about the gem hematite, which Zachalias maintained not only was beneficial for the liver and the eyes, but was helpful for those petitioning a king, useful in lawsuits and a boon on the field of battle. Since Pliny does not identify the Mithridates in question further, the presumption must be that it is the most famous of the many men who bore the name, Mithridates VI Eupator, ruler of Pontus from roughly 111 BC until his assassination many years later in 65 BC.[111] More than a little caution is called for in accepting as true Pliny's statement that Zachalias the Babylonian dedicated his work on magical gems to King Mithridates. What is cause for concern is the existence at a later date of pseudepigraphical magical works that contain fictitious dedications to famous rulers. The dedications are designed to give the impression that the treatises have received a royal *imprimatur.*

# 5

# MAGIC AS A
# DISTINCTIVE CATEGORY IN
# ROMAN THOUGHT

## Introduction

One of the difficulties of describing and interpreting almost any aspect of Roman culture is that of preserving a proper balance between overemphasizing what is peculiarly Roman and overstating the degree to which Roman culture had been hellenized.[1] It is altogether too easy in this matter to take too extreme a stance: to adopt either the position that Roman institutions and literature are the products of native Roman genius or that Rome is little more than an extension of the Greek world. To make due allowance for what is distinctively Roman is a difficult business, since Greek influences were at work in Rome from its earliest beginnings and the resulting amalgam is hard to separate. So it is with magic.

There is evidence, archaeological and epigraphical, that the earliest Romans were in contact with Greeks. To what degree Early Roman culture was influenced by Greek culture is difficult to assess, but, if the Etruscans are anything to go by, Greece must have made a strong impression on the shape that culture took. That the Greek colonies of Southern Italy exerted an influence on Rome is likely but not easily documented. It is to be imagined that peddlers, performers and entertainers of different sorts and holy men and women in various guises made their way north to Rome and Etruria, but their influence will have waned as Samnites and other peoples took over many of the Greek colonies in Italy. More substantial merchants from Greece itself certainly sailed to Rome to do business. Greek-speaking slaves will also have played a rôle in shaping Roman modes of thought and speech by introducing their masters to new institutions, practices and ways of looking at the world. These were present in Rome in increasing numbers from the beginning of the third century BC. There is dispute over what percentage of the total population of Rome were slaves and within the number of slaves how many were Greek-speakers.[2] It is really impossible to give a satisfactory answer to either question, but what can be said with some confidence is that slaves from the Greek East played a significant rôle in the household and in the upbringing and education of young upper-class Romans. Rome from the third century BC on had a sizeable Greek community made up of slaves, freedmen and foreigners from Greece itself and the Greek-speaking East. Such communities may, because they are self-contained and isolated, have little influence on those around them. That does not seem to have been true of the Greek colony in Rome.

From the early second century BC onwards an important part of the formal education given young Romans of the ruling class was the study of Greek literature followed by a training in Greek rhetoric. By the middle of the century a substantial number of the senatorial class will have known Greek and some of them will have absorbed a great deal of the higher Greek culture. It may be that many young Romans, since they were brought up by Greek-speaking slaves, knew Greek almost as a first language.

If we go outside the world of the rich and the privileged, evidence for a knowledge of Greek is harder to come by, but there is nonetheless some. Bilingual word-plays in the comedies of Plautus show that at least at the beginning of the second century BC a knowledge of Greek, albeit of a fairly elementary level, must have been widespread in Rome.[3] But it does not amount to a much greater knowledge of Greek than that of the Englishman who knows how to say *merci beaucoup* in French. Much work still remains to be done on how widely Greek was known in Rome in the last centuries of the Republic and on how profound a knowledge of the language different strata of society possessed. We would, however, probably not be too far off the mark in supposing that a considerable body of men from the senatorial and equestrian classes possessed a sound knowledge of the Greek language and of Greek literature and that some knowledge of the language was diffused amongst other strata of society.

The effect that a training in the language and literature of Greece will have had on those upper-class Romans who were exposed to it should not be underestimated. It will certainly have brought them into contact with the concept of magic and they will have had to come to terms with it to make sense of some of what they read. Those of them with a taste for the spectacular and wondrous will even have read Hellenistic treatises on the magical powers of plants, stones and animals. Cato the Elder, as we have already noted in another context, had read the pseudo-Pythagorean treatise on magical plants and seems to have drawn on it liberally in his discussion of cabbage. It cannot on that score be confidently concluded that the category of magic had any meaning for him and that he had made it part of his thinking, but he must at least have been aware that there were persons called *magoi* to be found in the East who had in their possession secret information about substances capable of effecting miraculous transformations. It could be argued that if Cato had realized what was entailed in the notion of magic, he would have been more cautious about the sources on which he drew. That is a weak argument. It is quite possible for a reader to pick and choose entertaining oddities from a magical text without feeling that he shows himself to be a devotee of the magical arts.

What, however, matters more is not whether the members of senatorial class possessed a passive knowledge of certain Greek concepts, but to what extent had the ways in which Romans thought about the world been moulded by Greek ideas. It may well be that Cato the Elder knew in a certain sense what a *magos* was in Greek and what *goeteia* was, but these were not necessarily ideas that governed his own thinking about the world. It is not then a question of how much Greek was known in Rome, although that will have been a factor in the absorption of Greek ways of categorizing the world, but of which Greek ideas had become part of the fabric of Roman thought.

The precise mechanisms by which ideas are passed on are elusive and hard to recapture. It is, nonetheless, a fair guess that the increasing contacts of a more mundane type which Rome had with the Greek-speaking world from the late third century BC on will have furthered the process. Men and women from Greece and the Greek East who were peddlers, soothsayers, jugglers, conjurors and even magicians will have been familiar figures. Greek-speaking slaves will from the beginning of the second century on have been a growing presence in Roman Italy. On the purely religious front there is in the passage in which Cato warns landowners against allowing their stewards to consult those who divine from entrails, those who interpret the flight of birds, inspired prophets and Chaldaeans, proof that travelling seers and soothsayers were in evidence before the middle of the second century BC.[4] Cato does not say that he is worried, lest the head of the steward should be filled with mistaken notions. His stated concern is that the steward should waste money consulting vagrants and then begin to steal from his master. It may nonetheless be observed that if Cato had been more favourably disposed to these wandering prophets, he might not have felt so strongly about this side of the activities of the steward. Some of the itinerant seers will have been Greek-speaking. The Chaldaeans, in particular, are likely at this date to have come from Greece or the Greek-speaking East.

Besides itinerant fortune-tellers in various guises, new forms of religious life of Greek origin began to appear in Rome in this period. Their presence must necessarily have introduced new ways of thinking and new forms of behaviour. The most notorious of the religious innovations was the cult of Dionysus, which had existed in the Greek cities of Southern Italy from at least the fifth century BC. The reaction of the Roman Senate in the 180s to the popularity of the cult resembles the response that we find in Athens in the fifth and fourth centuries BC to those offering initiation into mystery-rites and especially to Plato's concerns about religious activity conducted in private. There is no scholarly consensus on what the reasons were for the extreme reaction of the Senate to the popularity of the cult and for its requiring, at least in Southern Italy, those wanting to hold a Bacchanal to get permission from the authorities and for its confining the numbers attending to no more than five. It would be unwise to insist that the Senate saw it only as a conspiracy and that there was no religious dimension to their response.[5] However that may be, what cannot be in doubt is that the notion of initiation into the mysteries must by the middle of the second century BC have been familiar to many Romans. It will have been an idea that had negative associations for many people and the ill-understood rituals connected with initiation into the mysteries will have aroused deep suspicions and fears.

Imaginative reconstructions of scenes from ancient life are dangerous, but it is probably not too risky to try putting ourselves into the shoes of a Roman crowd staring at a conjuror or wonder-worker from the Greek East and trying to make sense of what they saw. There may have been Greek-speakers present, familiar with such performances and only too eager to enlighten the ignorant Romans about how it was done. They may have told their neighbours that the wonder-worker was an adept in the Persian art of magic or they may have told them that the wonder-worker was a charlatan skilled in creating illusions. Some explanation will have been given that will have enabled the Romans to make sense, as they imagined it, of what they saw and will have led them eventually to an understanding of what magic was. Although it can only be an informed guess, my feeling is that it was in this way people came to understand what magic was and not by some more intellectual and abstract process.

## The effect of the transfer

Whatever the mechanisms involved may have been, there can be no doubt that there was a one-way traffic in ideas and the institutions that went with them from Greece to Rome. Romans came increasingly to look at the world with Greek eyes and to react to it accordingly. The notion of magic is just one of many ideas of greater or lesser complexity that found a home in Rome.[6] It would be very surprising indeed, if it had not at a fairly early stage been naturalized in Rome.

What did the naturalization of magic mean in Rome? It is generally now taken for granted that ideas and the institutions that go with them undergo major transformations in the passage from one culture to another. The transformation may take a number of forms: the institution may be fitted into an existing framework of ideas and made sense of within it; practices already present may be grafted onto the new stock and adapted to fit it, coming to be thought of as an integral part of it. Change, in short, is what is to be expected and what we have to be alert to. That expectation might lead us to predict that native Roman and Italic institutions will have come to have been thought of as magical and that magic itself will have taken on a new significance and will have been set within a new conceptual framework. It would not be occasion for surprise that the Roman conception of magic should have differed from its Greek parent. That is what might have been expected;

the reality is somewhat different. It turns out to be exceedingly difficult to distinguish between a Greek and Roman conception of magic; and it is not at all easy to demonstrate that native Roman ritual practices have taken on a new meaning and have come to be incorporated in the body of practices that the Romans thought constituted magic.

### Greek magical practices in Italy and Rome in the Middle and Late Roman Republic and their bearing on the transfer of the concept of magic

Greek magical practices were adopted by the indigenous peoples of the Italian peninsula from as early as the third century BC. The testimony of the material record to magic-working either in Early Rome or in the Late Roman Republic is, as matters now stand, virtually non-existent. There are, for instance, no curse-tablets written in Latin and inscribed on lead sheets and then rolled up and pierced by a nail to be placed in a tomb or a well from Italy, let alone from Rome or Latium. The earliest such spell belongs to the reign of Augustus.[7] There is reason to suppose, however, that it is only a matter of time before such a lead tablet turns up in Rome. There is first of all evidence that other Italian peoples adopted the Greek practice of casting a spell on others by writing the charm out on a lead tablet and consigning it to the powers below. Three lead tablets with what are certainly lists of names on them were found in an underground tomb-chamber in the Etruscan town of Volterra.[8] That they are curse-tablets is not in doubt. Another spell was found in a necropolis on the northern coast of Etruria.[9] The tombs amongst which it was found are dated to the end of the third century BC. Its precise interpretation like the three tablets from Volterra must remain in doubt, until Etruscan is deciphered. From Campania south of Rome there are two curse-tablets written in the Italic language Oscan.[10] Whatever else may be in doubt about their interpretation, what is unmistakable is that they have been inspired ultimately by Greek models. Finally, there are three curse-tablet, again in Oscan and written on lead tablets, from still further south, from the territory of the Bruttii, from sites in the modern province of Catanzaro: two of them, directed at the same persons, come from a tomb in the community of Cirò and belong to the fourth or third centuries BC;[11] the third was found in a tomb in the community of Tiriolo.[12] All three spells conform to the same pattern: a name in the nominative followed by one in the accusative, presumably respectively that of the person directing the spell and that of his victim. There are no parallels in Greek for such a pattern, although many early binding spells consist of no more than a list of names. It is interesting to note that from another tomb in Tiriolo a further lead curse-tablet of the late fourth century BC has emerged, but this time written in Greek and with Greek names on it.[13] At the time at which it was written the area had already fallen under the control of the Bruttii.[14]

What the curse-tablets in Etruscan and Oscan show is that Greek magical practices had been taken up by the peoples living to the north and the south of Rome. Whether there were specialized practitioners who wrote out the spells for the clients who came to them, as seems to have been the practice in Athens in the fourth century BC, is on the basis of the slight volume of evidence we possess impossible to say. Nor again are we in a position to say how an Etruscan or an Oscan-speaking Samnite understood what he was doing in casting a curse-tablet. The existence of the spells nonetheless serves to remind us that Greek magical practices had been adopted at a fairly early date by many of the peoples of Italy.

There may be no curse-tablets written in Latin found in a Republican context, but a lead tablet with a curse inscribed on it in Latin from Carmona (Seville) in the province of Baetica makes it virtually certain that spells taking this form were being written in Latin in Italy. The tablet asks that the gods of the Underworld should cause the head, heart, mind, health, life and limbs of a woman called Luxia to be affected by illness. The tablet from Carmona is on grounds of palaeography and orthography to be assigned to the second half of the first century BC.[15] If in the second half of the second century BC in one of the most heavily Romanized parts of Spain curses were being written in Latin on lead by a person clearly well acquainted with the formulae used in such curses in Greek, then it is very likely that the ultimate source of the practice was Italy, if not Rome itself.

It may be impossible to point to direct evidence in the archaeological record of magic-working in Rome before the Augustan Period, but there is unequivocal testimony in our literary sources of the existence in Rome, at least in the Late Republic, if not earlier, of objects which in the Greek world had magical associations. The Romans adopted the Greek practice of wearing amulets to ward off threats to their well-being and may even have pursued the practice with a greater enthusiasm than anything known in the Greek-speaking world. The most general term in Latin for an amulet is a *remedium*. The term was already in use in the Late Republic.[16] The amulets worn by the sick and those who feared sickness went under that name as did those worn by those fearful of the baneful effects of envy. We know from a variety of sources that boys of high birth wore an amulet called a *bulla* around their necks in which was enclosed a phallus.[17] The purpose of the phallus was to ward off the dangers to which the envy that they provoked might give rise. That the device was already in used by the second half of the third century BC is to be inferred from its mention by the early poet Naevius in a comedy called *Stigmatias*.[18] A little later Plautus has a joke about cutting off the private parts of an adulterer to provide what he calls a rattle (*crepundia*) to be worn around the neck of a boy.[19]

There is an intriguing passage in a poem on hunting belonging to the reign of Augustus that pours scorn on the customs of a simpler age and on those who suggested tying the hair of badgers, coral, necklaces made of shells and plants over which incantations have been uttered to the collars of hunting dogs to protect them from the harm that an evil eye might inflict.[20] Since works on hunting, *Cynegetica*, were written by Greek authors in prose and verse, there is a temptation to suppose that the poet, Grattius, is referring to such a work. There are two reasons to doubt whether it is only Greek hunting practices that he has in mind. For one thing his reference to the arts of old and the discoveries of a simple age does not sound as if Grattius was thinking primarily of hunting manuals.[21] Secondly, the attaching of badger-hair to the collars of hunting dogs is almost certainly an Italian custom, since badgers do not seem to have been known in Greece. It can, on the other hand, hardly have been a custom of immemorial antiquity, since hunting in the Greek fashion was introduced into Italy no earlier than the middle of the second century BC.[22] If hunting dogs wore protective devices on their collars, horses too, animals still more valuable and susceptible to injury and disease than dogs, will have had amulets attached to them.

As for the amulets the sick or those who felt threatened by disease wore on their person, Valerius Maximus, writing in the time of Tiberius, says that three temples were built to *Febris* or Fever and that to these temples were brought the *remedia* that had been attached to the persons of the sick.[23] Presumably the amulets were brought as thanks-offerings either by persons who had recovered from a fever or who had avoided an attack of the fever. The fever that the temples of *Febris* were built to combat was most likely malaria. Amulets designed to protect against malaria are well attested from the Late Roman Period in the Greek East and Egypt. To judge from Valerius, they must have been widespread still earlier. Yet he writes as if the practice of bringing amulets to the temples of *Febris* was no longer observed, which should mean the wearing of fever-amulets was one of some antiquity in his time.

There is, in sum, little room for doubt that amulets were widely used in Rome by the Late Republic. That should mean there were people who manufactured them, sold them and applied them. These people have disappeared almost without trace from the literary record, but not entirely. If the Greek precedent was anything to go by incantations will have been employed in the creation of the amulet and in its application. Fever-amulets may have had what were in effect incantations inscribed on them. Grattius bears witness to the use of incantation in the preparation of amulets: the plants that were applied to the collars of dogs were, in his words, helped by mighty incantations.[24] In other words, an empowering-incantation was intoned over the amulet. It is to be surmised that these incantations were the special and jealously guarded property of persons who posed as expert in their use. The existence of the amulets leads us back into a hidden world of experts in the rituals of the manufacture and application of amulets, not to speak of those who sold them.

There are extensive indications in the literature of the second century BC and that of the first half of the first century that the Romans had taken over a great deal of magical lore from the Greeks. What they made of it is another matter. Plautus is an especially rich source of information. He brought to a Roman audience the comedies that had been composed and performed in Athens in the late fourth century and in the third century BC. Yet he was no slavish and mechanical translator of the Greek, but displayed a good deal of invention in his writing. In his comedies, *veneficus*, *venefica*, and the intensive forms, *terveneficus* and *trivenefica*, are used with some frequency.[25] In Latin, these terms cover both sorcerer and poisoner. It is not so much that the terms in one context mean 'sorcerer' and in another 'poisoner', as that sorcery and poisoning tend not to be distinguished. In Plautus, the context in which the term is used shows in most cases that what we would call sorcery is at issue rather than poisoning. For the playwright, it is generally a term of abuse and is mostly found in passages that are likely to have been composed *a novo* by the playwright himself. Plautus is not, accordingly, merely taking something from his Greek original that has very little meaning for his Roman audience. He plays on a notion that is thoroughly familiar to the Romans. Now the way in which this group of words is employed is a good indication of how familiar most Romans must have been with various forms of magic-working. They were after all expected to pick up from contexts in which no actual magic is involved why a speaker rounds on someone as a *venefica* or *veneficus*.

There is some additional evidence from later in the second century for a familiarity on the part of the Romans with erotic magic and the milieu in which it flourished. Apuleius in the speech in which he defends himself against the charge of magic cites six verses in iambic dimeters that must be part of a description of witches gathering the ingredients for love-spells (*philtra*).[26] Apuleius says of the verses that they will be recognized by those who have read Laevius.[27] The verses were, in other words, composed either by Laevius, a poet who was active around 100 BC and who was the earliest of the group of poets called the Neoterics, or by a member of that school. In the six lines quoted everything referred to belongs to the paraphernalia of Greek erotic magic and of the terms used three are Greek. The fragment looks to be evidence that Romans of the late second century BC had a more than passing acquaintance with the details of Greek erotic magic. The inference could in this case be a dangerous one, since the Neoterics looked to the learned poetry of Hellenistic Alexandria for their inspiration and do not necessarily reflect what was common knowledge in Rome.

A further and better, though indirect, indication that the practice of erotic magic was known in Rome in the second century BC is to be found in a fragment of the satirist Lucilius. The fragment speaks of the effect of age on the appearance as a topic proverbially brought up by the woman who combines the rôles of wise woman or sorceress (*saga*) and go-between (*conciliatrix*).[28] There is also a fragment of the comic poet Turpilius, who will have been a slightly older contemporary of Lucilius, in which a character declares that he does not manage his affairs by hiring a wise woman (*saga*) as is commonly done.[29] To judge from the comment of the grammarian who cites the fragment, the speaker is talking of the practice of hiring wise women to act as go-betweens in love-affairs.[30] Now if it was the case that in Rome in the second century BC procuresses doubled as sorceresses, the presumption must be that their sorcery was an extension of their activities as procuresses and that they practised erotic magic. It must be conceded that the procuress warning her charge to seize her opportunities while she can has antecedents in Greek literature.[31] In Latin they are known as *lenae*. There is therefore a certain literary flavour to the fragment of Lucilius. Yet it seems unlikely that both Lucilius and Turpilius operate only at the level of literature and that the institution to which they refer of women combining the parts of procuress and sorceress was unknown in Rome in their day.

Finally, the comic playwright Lucius Afranius of the second half of the second century BC has a character in his play *Vopiscus* declare that if men could be trapped by devices of enticement (*delenimenta*), every old woman (*anus*) would have a lover, but in fact youth, a tender body and good character are the drugs (*venena*) that beautiful women possess; old age finds no enticements.[32] It is easy to discount the lines, since they echo what Menander had said about love-philtres.[33] Afranius did not, however, as Plautus and Terence did, write comedies whose setting and characters were Greek (*comoedia palliata*), but comedies set in a Roman or Italian setting (*comoedia togata*). If a character in such a comedy can speak about love-philtres, that is a very good indication that love-philtres were known and used in Rome in the second half of the second century BC. Furthermore, the lines create the presumption that love-philtres were the special province of old women.

The testimony of Lucilius, Turpilius, Afranius and the unknown poet who composed the verses on love-philtres shows that Greek love-magic had made its way to Rome and had its specialist practitioners. Part of the reason for the spread of erotic magic to Rome will have been that in that city in the second century BC the same environment existed which in the Greek world fostered erotic magic. In Rome too, high-class prostitutes formed associations with well-to-do young men and competed for them. They were aided and abetted by older women, themselves often former prostitutes, who acted as the protectors of the girls and as their agents. There is every reason to think that some of the women will have been slaves from the Greek-speaking world and that they will have brought with them a knowledge of magic.

There is some further information to be gleaned from Plautus that adds considerably to our knowledge of magic-working in Rome in the second century BC and reminds us how much in this period Rome will have had in common with Hellenistic Greek cities. In the *Miles gloriosus*, Periplectomenus explains his unwillingness to marry by giving a catalogue of the demands that a wife will put on him for money. The passage has a profoundly Roman flavour to it and can, therefore, be used as evidence of what life was like in Rome.[34] Amongst the requests Periplectomenus imagines a wife making is her asking for money on the 19th of the month to pay the woman who utters incantations, the woman who interprets dreams, the inspired prophetess and the woman who divines from entrails. He goes on to picture her complaining that it will be a crime if she sends off the woman who observes the sky without giving her anything.[35] This extraordinary vignette of female superstition gives an idea of the varied cast of holy women who made their way to the doors of rich women to prey on them. At the head of the line is the woman who utters incantations, the *praecantatrix*.

There are only two instances of the use of the word in Latin besides that in Plautus: one of them is in a fragment of the *Logistorici* of Varro; the other is in a commentator on Horace of the late second century AD, Porphyrion. Varro speaks of it being women in the main who employ *praecantatrices* and of their not showing something to the doctor.[36] This suggests that *praecantatrices* were women who professed to be able by their incantations to cure people of their ills and that women as against men resorted to them in preference to doctors. Confirmation that the inference is sound is to be found in two lines of Lucilius in which someone, speaking in the first person, uses in succession the verbs *praecantare*, *exigere*, 'to drive out', and *excantare*, 'to remove by song', to refer to what he or perhaps more likely she is doing.[37] The context makes it virtually certain that *praecantare* is being used here of incantations that cure ills.[38] Porphyrion uses the term *praecantatrix* to define the word *saga*: *sagae* are *praecantatrices* who employ incantations to summon ills to harm people or who employ incantations to drive such ills out.[39] Although it is impossible to be quite certain whether Porphyrion means that *praecantatrices* employ incantations to do harm and to dispel harm or whether that part of the definition applies only to the term to be defined, *sagae*, it is on the whole likely that Porphyrion is dilating on what a *praecantatrix* is in the relative clause. It goes without saying that over two or more centuries shifts can occur in the meaning of terms. What should not be in doubt is that women who performed healing incantations of some sort were a feature of Roman life in the early second century BC and that they were only one amongst a larger cast of female religious experts.

It is to be concluded that since by the second century BC Rome was in some degree part of the larger Hellenistic world, one aspect of its membership in that wider world was that Greek forms of magic-working along with the social institutions fostering them had become naturalized there. That this was so does not warrant our drawing the inference that in the eyes of the Romans *veneficae* and *praecantatrices* engaged in a suspect activity mimicking proper religious observance but which was in fact a perversion of it. The most we can say is that in Plautus *veneficus*, *venefica*, *terveneficus* and *trivenefica* are used as terms of opprobrium. There are at least two reasons, compatible with each other but sufficient in themselves, why the words should carry so negative an emotional charge: the activities of *veneficae* fall into the disapproved category of magic; the harmful spells that *veneficae* sometimes cast make them a suspect group. It is, in sum, impossible to say for certain on the basis of references to magic-working and magic-workers in the second century BC whether the Greek notion of magic had taken root in Rome by that date.

There is, however, one piece of evidence from the latter half of the second century BC to suggest that the Romans not only had taken over many of the magical practices of the Greeks, but possessed a discrete category of thought into which they placed them. It is an aetiological myth told by a contemporary of Lucilius, a historian called Gnaeus Gellius, designed to explain why the Marsi, a people of the Central Apennines whose territory lay around the Fucine Lake, were endowed with certain special powers.[40] The story Gellius tells is that Aëtes had three daughters, Angitia, Medea and Circe; Circe had settled on the Circeian Hills and by her malevolent incantations created various illusory visions; Angitia had taken up residence in the vicinity of the Fucine Lake and because of her powers of healing was worshipped there as a deity; Medea had been buried by Jason at Buthrotium and her son had ruled the Marsi.[41] The Circeian Hills lie to the south of Rome and form a promontory projecting out into the Tyrrhenian Sea from the territory of the Volsci. When the promontory was first identified with Circe's island is unclear, but Circe was worshipped there at the end of the Republic and this is where she is to be found when Vergil has Aeneas sail past her.[42] Angitia was a goddess worshipped by the Marsi and other central Italian peoples.[43] The exact nature of her cult is obscure, but the Romans imagined, perhaps rightly, that it was connected with preventing and curing snake-bites. The Marsic priest in the *Aeneid* who joins the Latin alliance against Aeneas and whose death is lamented by the grove of Angitia certainly possesses these abilities: he knows how by incantation (*cantus*) and touch to make poisonous snakes sleep, how to calm their wrath and to alleviate their bite.[44]

Vergil is by no means the first Latin author to credit the Marsi with the power to charm snakes. The tradition goes back to Lucilius and beyond. Lucilius compares a person whose stomach is about to burst to a snake that the incantations of a Marsic man has caused explode.[45] It is apparent from what Lucilius says that the ability of the Marsi to make snakes explode was already by his day proverbial. In addition to having a reputation as snake-charmers, the Marsi were certainly famed at a later date for other forms of magic-working.[46] It is these two aspects of their reputation that Gellius seeks to explain by having Angitia settle in Marsic territory and by making the son of Medea their ruler. Circe and Medea are by the Hellenistic Period the quintessential sorceresses. If a sister of Medea and Circe settles amongst the Marsi and a son of Medea is their ruler, it is proper to infer that in Gellius' eyes the special powers which the people possess are those of magicians. In other words, magic-workers are for Gellius a category of persons marked off in some way from their fellows. It is significant that it is the Marsi, a hill-people of the Abruzzi whom the Romans supposed to be utterly different from themselves, who are credited by Gellius with having magical powers. Magicians in the ancient world are very often the other, the foreign, those on the margins who are not part of the community. The Romans by the late second century BC were, to judge from Gellius' attempt at explaining the special powers with which the Marsi were believed to be endowed, inclined to think of magic-working as a capacity that belonged to the foreign and alien.[47] Beyond their otherness we are unfortunately not in a position to say what the distinguishing marks of the magician and magic were in the eyes of Gellius and his contemporaries.

The evidence marshalled up to this point cannot be said to be conclusive testimony to the domestication in Rome by the end of the second century BC of the concept of magic, but it constitutes a fairly compelling case. Anyone who wishes to explain it away will have to go to some considerable lengths to do so and will have to engage in some fairly fancy footwork. Now it is true that the term *magus* with its plural *magi* is not found in Latin until the 50s BC. Its absence and that of the term *magia*, which is the form for the abstract term that in Latin renders the Greek *mageia*, do not warrant the inference that the Romans had no conception of magic as a discrete category of thought and that they did not distinguish the rituals used in casting spells and necromancy from those sanctioned for proper religious observance. We should not make the mistake when we come to deal with the notion of magic amongst the Romans of supposing that, before an idea can exist and be expressed, an abstract term has to exist with which to name it. We have seen that the concept of magic in Athens in the fifth and fourth centuries BC was made up of a complex of ideas and attitudes. These ideas and attitudes can be expressed in a variety of ways. If the Romans characterized sorcery in the same way as the Greeks, distinguished it from proper religious observance and expressed abhorrence of it, then they are operating with the same concept of magic as the Greeks, whether or not they label what they are talking about under the heading *magia*. A consciousness that *magus* and *magia* are Greek terms may in any case have kept Roman authors from using them.

The earliest instances of the use of the term *magus* in Latin are in the poet Catullus and in Cicero. Cicero uses *magus* to refer to Iranian fire-priests and diviners rather than to magicians.[48] The distinction in Greek in this period between a *magos* in the sense of an Iranian fire-priest and a *magos* who is an expert on magic is not clear-cut, since the former is often imagined to be identical to the latter. Cicero must inevitably have encountered the term used in such an ambiguous sense. Some of what he says about *magi* may well be influenced by that experience. He speaks of its being permissible to add the portentous fantasies of the *magi*, the madness of the Egyptians and the beliefs of the masses to the erroneous statements Greek poets make about the divine.[49] Now Pliny the Elder speaks in exactly the same terms about the portentous or fantastic statements made by *magi* on magic.[50] The adjective that both Cicero and Pliny use to characterize the promises made by the *magi*, *portentosus*, in this context in Pliny means 'fantastic', 'surpassing belief'. It is for Pliny a manifestation of the empty pretensions of the *magi*.[51] He speaks of the fantastic promises made by the *magi* for the magical lore that they purvey in the same breath as he speaks of their lies and fictions.[52] Pliny assumes that *magi*, who are for him Persian priests or priests of the Persian persuasion, are a major source of magical lore. It may, accordingly, be the tradition that credited the *magi* of Persia with being a source of wondrous magical lore that Cicero has in mind when he speaks of their portentous fantasies. There are grounds, accordingly, for concluding that Cicero knows of the *magi* as the source of a great deal of magical lore. *Magus* for Cicero is not then necessarily a neutral ethnographic term, but may also carry connotations of expertise in magic.

Catullus, writing perhaps ten years earlier than Cicero, employs the word *magus* in one of a series of insulting epigrams that he directs at a certain Gellius.[53] The way in which Catullus uses the word does at the very least betray a great deal of prejudice against the religious practices of the Persian *magi*, which is hard to explain, unless Persian religious observance was thought suspect.[54] In the epigram, Catullus plays on the widespread though false belief that Persians and more especially *magi* had sexual unions with their wives and daughters:[55] he suggests that the product of the union between Gellius and his mother should be a *magus*, who should learn the Persian art of divination from entrails; the product of this incestuous union will then be a suitable person, if the impious religious observances of the Persians are true, to please their gods with the song that they find acceptable, while he melts in flame the fatty covering of the intestines. Why Catullus should characterize Persian religious practices as impious is hard, though not impossible, to explain, unless there is already in the Roman mind a connection between magic-working and *magi*. Secondly, there has to be something pointed about the veneration in pleasing song that the *magus*, still to be born, will pay the gods of the Persians. The word here for song, *carmen*, is in Latin ambiguous and may mean 'song' or in a religious context 'hymn', but it may also have the meaning 'incantation' or 'spell'. There is then the distinct possibility that what is implied is that the gods of the Persians will be worshipped in the kind of song appropriate to deities of their nature, namely, incantation.

However suggestive the epigram of Catullus and Cicero's references to the *magi* may be for Roman attitudes towards magic, we have to look beyond the word *magus* and the adjective derived from it, *magicus*, if we are going to trace the evolution of a consciousness on the part of the Romans that magic-working belongs to a different and inferior sphere to proper religious observance. As we have seen, there are clues to be found elsewhere that point to the existence by the end of the second century BC of a developed awareness of magic-working as both a discrete and a suspect activity. What is lacking, however, is clear-cut evidence of a consciousness of magic as an illicit and wicked activity that hides itself in the shadows. Here what is lacking in the second century BC is to be found in the succeeding century. We should beware of concluding that in the meantime an evolution in moral consciousness had taken place. It needs to be borne in mind that, where evidence is fragmentary, evolutionary hypotheses are all too easy to frame. We are very much dependent on the nature of our sources and it is not until the closing years of the century that the literary forms that deign to mention and describe magic-working come into existence.

Roman literature in the last century of the Republic does not add greatly to what we know about techniques of magic-working and those who practised it. Cicero's *Brutus* does contribute to our knowledge in one significant respect: we learn from it that the Romans were familiar with the binding-spells Greeks used against their opponents in lawsuits and could invoke the notion to explain their failures in court. In that work, Cicero recalls an incident from a trial in the 70s in which he had summed up the case for a woman called Titinia; the opposing counsel, a Gnaeus Sicinius, had, when suddenly all that he had to say went from his head, blamed his loss of memory on the spells and incantations of the same Titinia.[56]

It can be argued that the verses cited by Apuleius in which various forms of love-philtre are mentioned are nothing more than a learned imitation of Greek poetry and are not rooted in any Roman reality. That is possible, though not very likely. What cannot be gainsaid is the import for the existence of love-magic in Rome of the story told by Cornelius Nepos about the effect that a love-philtre given to L. Licinius Lucullus by a freedman who wanted to secure his love had on the unfortunate victim, a general who had distinguished himself in warfare in Asia Minor and who had on his return home retired from public life to devote himself to a notoriously sybaritic existence: far from achieving its intended aim the drug had had a catastrophic effect on Lucullus' powers of reason and had reduced him to a state of help-lessness.[57] Lucullus died shortly thereafter in 57 BC.[58] The tale shows that at least by the Late Republic love-philtres and their effects were well known in Rome and could be invoked, no doubt wrongly, to explain a man's losing his wits. Cornelius Nepos, the source of the story, was a rather younger contemporary of Lucullus, but not a young man at the time of the events he described. The story that he reports will, in the immediate aftermath of Lucullus' losing his senses, have gone the rounds in Rome and have been remembered by Nepos when he came to write the life of Lucullus for his book *On Famous Men.*[59]

Cicero makes one further contribution to our catalogue of the Greek magical practices known to the Romans, but also, more importantly, to our understanding of Roman attitudes to these practices. In a speech delivered in 50 BC and designed to undermine the credibility of the testimony of Publius Vatinius, he asks Vatinius how, after engaging in wicked and unheard of rites, after being in the habit of summoning up the spirits of the

Underworld, after honouring the gods below with the entrails of boys, he is so insane and morally degenerate as to treat the auspices undertaken by the augurs on behalf of the Roman state with contempt.[60] It is very difficult to say whether Cicero is speaking of one or two different magical rituals here and it may be that he is not speaking with any precision and is merely trying to conjure up a vision of Vatinius' unrestrained criminality. Boys were believed to be killed for a variety of magical purposes: their famished livers might be used in love-magic;[61] the future might be found in their entrails;[62] and it is very likely that they were sacrificed by necromancers.

Whatever the other magical practices may be that Cicero has in mind, necromancy is certainly one of them. It is quite clear Cicero expects his audience to agree with him that the practices pursued by Vatinius are a form of religious observance (*sacra*), but of a new and hateful kind. They are, in other words, a perversion of true religious practice. The degree of Vatinius' moral degeneracy is to be seen in his being prepared to upset the proper religious customs of the Roman State, after having engaged in such heinous practices. The contrast between the magical rites that Vatinius has performed and proper religious observance could not be more strongly put. It is of no particular significance that Cicero does not use the term magic to characterize the rituals practised by Vatinius. What is significant are the terms with which the practice of magic is excoriated and the conceptual framework implicit in the use of these terms. Cicero's attitude to magic is essentially that of Plato.

It is not until we reach Vergil's *Aeneid* that reservations about magic are expressed in as many words. There we find Dido, who when she asks her sister for help in performing magical rites, which she suggests will either give Aeneas back to her or free her from her love for the man, calls the gods to witness that only reluctantly does she have recourse to the arts of magic (*magicae artes*).[63] Dido says that she was shown the spells by a priestess of the Massylian race from the western extremities of the world; the expertise of the priestess in magic encompassed freeing people from infatuations and inducing infatuations in them, stopping rivers, reversing the path of the stars, summoning the dead, making the earth groan and causing trees to descend from mountains.[64] The implication of the lines is that it is only in desperation that Dido has been driven to the use of magic and that she seeks the pardon of the gods for resorting to a course of action of which they will disapprove. For our present purposes it does not greatly matter whether we are supposed to imagine that Dido has consulted the Numidian priestess or that she has invented her to fool her sister Anna. What is significant is that a priestess living in distant parts is imagined to possess a knowledge of the magical arts. It is the stranger, as we have just remarked, who is characteristically believed to be expert in magic, because magic is thought to be an arcane and exotic secret. The Numidian priestess who comes from the furtherest extremities of the earth conforms to this pattern. Secondly, it is no accident that it is a priestess who imparts her arcane knowledge to Dido. What lies behind that transaction is the idea that magic is a special form of religious behaviour. It will, accordingly, be priestesses of strange foreign cults who are credited with having a knowledge of magic.

We can piece together from a poem by Horace that will have been composed some time before the *Aeneid* an even fuller picture of the concept of magic in Rome in Vergil's time. Horace's *Epode* 5 is a dramatic poem that depicts witches burying a boy alive with his head protruding from the ground so that, once he has starved to death, they may use his famished liver as a love-philtre. In the poem, both the boy and the chief witch, whose name is Canidia, speak. It is principally from what they say that we can reconstruct what Horace thought of magic. The poem begins with the bewildered and frightened boy begging the witches by whatever may move them, if perchance they have any children, to tell him why they look at him so.[65] He concludes his plea by appealing to the name of Juppiter, who, he adds, will disapprove of what they do.[66] The witches continue their activities unmoved, it is to be inferred, by the prayers of the boy. We are no doubt meant to imagine that they are so lacking in moral conscience and in the normal human sensibilities to remain unaffected by any appeal to their better feelings. Horace, in fact, says of one of the witches, Veia, that she was unaffected by any sense of conscience, while she dug the trench in which the boy was to be laid.[67] The women are also lacking in respect for the divine. That is apparent in the unconcern with which they greet the invocation of Juppiter. Juppiter's disapproval of their activities will in the context mean that he looks with disfavour on their magic-working. It does not just mean that he will disapprove of the witches' taking of an innocent life.

In the course of the preparations the sorceresses undertake Canidia prays to Night and Diana as faithful witnesses to what she does to be present and to direct their wrath and divine power against the house of an enemy.[68] Diana, in particular, is prayed to as she who rules over the silence in which the hidden sacred rites are performed.[69] The rituals the sorceress performs are from her point of view mystic rites confined to those adept in an esoteric form of wisdom, performed in secret, in silence and in the darkness of the night. Similarly in the *Argonautica* of Apollonius Rhodius, the magical rituals that the sorceress Medea performs are for her the mystery-rites of Hecate.[70] The expression that Canidia employs in speaking of these mysteries, *sacra arcana*, is in fact used by Ovid in the *Heroides* to translate the Greek term *orgia* employed by Medea in the prayer in the *Argonautica* in which she invokes the mysteries of Hecate.[71]

Canidia in her invocation of Night and Diana explains why she seeks their aid. Once she has finished, the narrator says the boy no longer attempted to mollify the impious women with soft words but pronounced a terrible curse on them.[72] The women in the eyes of the narrator are impious, not just because they are prepared to sacrifice an innocent life, but because they engage in magic. The boy begins his curse by asserting that spells do not have the power to alter man's lot.[73] The ineffectiveness of magic is one of the standard charges made against it. It is already found in the Hippocratic tract *On the Sacred Disease.*[74] This is never a charge brought against what was believed to be regular religious observance, even though the requests made of deities are very often indistinguishable from those made in magical rituals. What lies behind the charge is the feeling that magic presumes to be able to subvert the order of nature in a way that regular religion does not. There is a case for thinking, as we have remarked, that those who take the position that natural substances and incantations cannot alter the course of nature and that the miraculous claims for them are untrue have formed a conception of magic that sees it as a specious form of knowledge.

The picture of sorcery that emerges from the Fifth Epode of Horace is the following: it is an activity that bears a close resemblance to the mystery-cults of regular religion, but which is in fact a travesty of or perversion of proper religious practice; it is not only at odds with regular religious practice but seeks to overturn the natural order of things; those who engage in sorcery are not only devoid of any sense of moral scruple, they are also impious and lacking in due respect for the divine. This is essentially Plato's conception of magic with the addition of the idea that magic is an essentially misguided attempt to defeat the ordinary course of nature.

Essentially the same view of magical practices is to be found in the second book of Ovid's *Ars amatoria.* The topic of the book is how young men are to retain the affections of girls. At the very beginning of the discussion the possibility of using herbs, incantations and love-philtres to secure that end is dismissed out of hand.[75] Two reasons are given for rejecting such a course of action: (1) herbs and incantations do not work; (2) love-philtres harm the girls on whom they are used by damaging their minds and driving them mad. The writer concludes his treatment of the subject with a command: keep away from all actions contrary to the moral and religious order (*nefas*). The implication of the exhortation is that herbs, incantations and love-philtres represent a transgression of the moral and religious order. In other words, actions constitutive of what would later certainly be understood to be magic are wrong.

Once someone is found asserting that practices associated with magic do not have the power to alter the course of nature, we have as good an indication as we are going to get that the person in question has grasped the notion of magic. The speaker has understood the pretensions of magic to subvert the natural order and has decided that it has no such power. He has seen that magic presents itself as a way of bypassing or cheating the constraints that nature imposes. If he also calls it impious that is even more persuasive evidence of his having a firm grasp of the notion. Grattius expresses the same doubts as does the boy in Horace. Grattius' doubts are specifically directed to the effectiveness of protective magic and to its reinforcement by incantation. He introduces the topic of protecting dogs from the Evil Eye by attaching apotropaic devices to their collars by asking what is to be said of the arts of an earlier age and of the inventions of a simple age, a rhetorical question which he answers by saying that they offer solace to false fears but that they do not win credence in the long run.[76] He rounds off the discussion with another rhetorical question, prompted by the thought of the vegetable substances whose effectiveness has been reinforced by incantation that are to be tied to the collars of the gods: does a protective peace won in this fashion from the gods master the harmful spells cast by malicious eyes?[77] The message conveyed is that such incantations cannot secure protection from the gods. Grattius does not explain why, but the implication is that there is something importunate and too pressing about the request. It is unlikely for that reason to win the favour of the gods.

To sum up, the Romans by the middle of the first century BC and in all likelihood earlier had come to disapprove of the rituals practised by persons claiming to have the power to upset the normal course of nature and had come to think of these practices as aberrations from proper religious observance. This development almost certainly came about because of the hellenization of Roman culture and was not something that came into being spontaneously and independently of the influence of Greek culture. Some Romans by the time of Horace and Vergil not only considered impious the secret rites performed by persons who boasted of being able to subvert the natural order, but had formed the view that the self-serving assertions made by such persons were untrue. Others again no doubt viewed the activities of those engaging in secret rituals whose aim was that of altering the course of nature as immoral and abhorrent to the gods, but were prepared to believe that the rituals were effective. Both groups can reasonably be said to have been operating with the concept of magic.

# 6

# CONSTRAINTS ON MAGICIANS
# IN THE LATE ROMAN
# REPUBLIC AND
# UNDER THE EMPIRE

Magicians in the Roman world did not enjoy complete freedom of action. There were three forms of constraint that the community imposed on them: there was the danger of being prosecuted for magic-working under the law; then there were the police actions that the authorities might take at any given time to eliminate magic-workers from their midst, either executing them or expelling them; finally, there were spontaneous actions on the part of the populace to drive out a known or suspected magician who was felt to be a threat to the well-being of the community. It is the two latter forms of action that are likely to have posed a greater threat to magic-workers than the danger of prosecution under the law. The dangers that magic-workers faced from prosecution under the law are not, however, to be discounted. It was unquestionably an instrument that could be used against them. The account that follows will encompass restrictions on being a magician not only in Rome itself, but also in the provinces of the Roman Empire and will cover the period from the Late Roman Republic to the time of Constantine.

For sheer lack of evidence it is impossible to describe the legal constraints on magic-working in the Hellenistic world. That they existed is likely, but what they were we cannot pretend to say. The situation in Rome is very different or rather gives every appearance of being so. Pliny the Elder, as proof of the early spread of magic to the peoples of Italy, cites the legislation against magic in the *Twelve Tables*.[1] The *Twelve Tables* were said to be the product of a special legislative commission of ten men (*decemviri legibus scribundis*) set up in 451 BC to codify Rome's laws.[2] This version of events is not without its difficulties, but it is at least likely that the *Tables* go back to the Early Republic.[3] The story in Livy that an embassy was sent from Rome to Athens to copy down the Laws of Solon and to acquaint themselves with the institutions, customs and laws of other Greek states is apocryphal.[4] It is nonetheless the case that there are distinctively Greek elements in the *Twelve Tables*. We cannot unfortunately be fully confident that all of the laws attributed to the *Twelve Tables* were in fact part of that codification. There may have been a tendency to assign any law that seemed to have an archaic flavour to it to the *Twelve*

*Tables,* nor can we be certain that the *Twelve Tables* were not periodically recodified and updated.

The clauses in the *Twelve Tables* that Pliny takes to be proof of the spread of magic to Rome were a measure that laid down penalties for using incantations to charm the crops belonging to another off his land into one's own possession and a regulation forbidding the utterance of harmful incantations.[5] It is understandable that Pliny should have seen these particular clauses in the *Twelve Tables* as evidence of the spread of magic. Vergil and the Rome elegists, who were two or three generations Pliny's seniors, do after all treat the charming of crops out of the possession of their owner as one of the characteristic attainments of an accomplished sorcerer or sorceress.[6] There are a number of questions that need to be asked about the clauses: did those who formulated the laws think of the practices they were condemning as magical; if they believed them to be magical, did they condemn them for that reason or because they believed them to be harmful; and finally, are the practices in question entirely Roman in origin?

What we know of the one legal process that would appear to have fallen under the clause in the law that dealt with the charming of crops out of the possession of one person into that of another is at first glance not very illuminating. The suit, which is to be dated perhaps to 191 BC, was directed at something rather less fantastic than crops being made to march, like the trees that followed the music of Orpheus, from one field into another.[7] The story of the lawsuit is told by Pliny the Elder, who draws on the *Annales* of Lucius Calpurnius Piso Frugi, a man renowned for his probity and frugality.[8] Piso's political career culminated in his censorship in 120 BC. The *Annales* brought events down to their author's own time. The story in question is about a freedman, whose name, C. Furius Chresimus, suggests he was a Greek-speaker. Chresimus incurred the envy and hostility of his neighbours because he had succeeded in growing much larger crops on his small patch of land than those with much greater acreages. This led to the neighbours accusing him of having employed spells to entice the fruits of others into his plot.[9] He was formally accused. When the curule aedile, who would have acted as the prosecutor in what rather interestingly would have not have been a trial on a capital charge, named the day for the trial before the assembly of the Roman people known as the *comitia tributa,* Chresimus, fearing that he would be condemned, brought into the forum, where the trial was to take place, all of his farm equipment, which was well made, all of the members of his household, who were well fed and well clad, and his sturdy oxen. Pointing to them, he declared these were his spells; he could neither display, nor bring into the forum, however, the night watches he had kept, the midnight oil that he had burned and the sweat that he had expended. The result was that all of the tribes voted for his acquittal.[10]

The accusation was a response to the puzzling phenomenon of one piece of land producing larger yields than the fields and trees around it. It may also reflect the tensions induced in a community by the presence of a successful outsider.[11] It is unfortunate that the nature of the evidence on which the prosecution rested its case is no part of the story. Had we possessed the arguments of the other side, or those attributed to them, we might then have been able to form some impression of what those who charmed crops out of fields were imagined to do. As it is, all that we have is the speech in his defence that Chresimus is supposed to have given. Grave doubt about its authenticity is in order. The story makes a point that Piso would have wanted to make all too neatly, namely, that what is important for agricultural success is hard work, not the amount of money that is expended.[12] What the tale does reveal is that Piso or whoever worked up the story assumed that spells designed to draw crops out of fields would be performed at dead of night. That is the meaning at one level of the night watches and the burnings of midnight oil that Chresimus could not bring into the forum. The assumption of the storyteller that spells designed to draw crops out of fields would be performed at dead of night does not of itself mean that such spells belonged in the mind of the story-teller to the sphere of magic, but it is *prima facie* evidence that it did. It follows that we have some reason to suppose that by the second half of the second century bewitching crops had come to be treated as a form of magic-working and that the legislation of the *Twelve Tables* was used against it.

The bewitching of crops and fruit may have come by the second century to have been thought of as magic, but it cannot be assumed that at an earlier date it was invested with the same significance. So far as is known, the idea that spells may draw off fertility is a peculiarly Roman or Italian notion. It does not seem to be at home in the Greek world. The closest that we come to the belief are those spells designed to draw the object of the sexual desire of a man or a woman to the man or woman. Nor is there any very close parallel in the Greek language for the verb used in the law, *excantare*, meaning in this instance 'to charm out of or away by song'.[13] There is a Greek verb meaning 'to draw out of by singing', *exaedein* or *exepaeidein*, but it is only used of drawing spirits and illnesses out of a person by a process akin to exorcism. That is not to say that Greek incantatory practices may not have been adapted at a fairly early date to fit Roman needs. The law against drawing off the crops of other people seems, accordingly, to reflect a native Roman or Italic preoccupation. Needless to say, it is quite possible to have the idea of summoning crops out of a field by song and to have no notion that there is a larger conceptual category under which such activity might be subsumed. If the law indeed pre-dates the codification of the mid-fifth century BC, it is very unlikely that the Romans at that point had any concept of magic. It follows that the purpose of the law cannot have been to punish magic-working *per se*, but that it must have had some other aim. Its aim is in any event likely to have been economic. It will belong to those provisions in the *Twelve Tables*, of which there are several, designed to safeguard agricultural property from various forms of harm.

The other clause in the *Twelve Tables* that was for Pliny proof of the spread of magic from Persia to Rome has to be distinguished from a clause laying down the penalty of death for anyone composing or uttering a song that affected the good reputation of another. The clause forbidding evil incantations does not forbid incantations *per se*, but only incantations taking the form of song intended to harm (*malum carmen*). Whoever framed the law was clearly aware of a wider category of incantation within which there were incantations uttered to harm another. The harm effected will not have been harm to the reputation but harm to the physical or psychological well-being of the person at whom the incantation was directed. Since Pliny says the clause was to be found elsewhere in the *Twelve Tables* from the clause on songs that cause crops to disappear, magic was clearly not the overarching category under which the clauses were grouped. What is to be gleaned from the *Twelve Tables* is that incantation in general was familiar to the Romans at a fairly early date and that incantations directed at harming another were a matter of concern. That is certainly not adequate ground for inferring that the clause in the *Twelve Tables* was framed to deal with what was seen as a form of magic-working.

Whatever the original intent of the laws against spiriting crops away and evil incantations may have been, both clauses could have been used to suppress certain forms of magic-working. It is hard to believe that the law against evil incantations was not used against those who were felt to have worked magic, but actual instances of its application cannot be cited. Nor again are we in a position to say whether it was used only against those who actually uttered the incantation or also against those who procured others to perform incantations on their behalf. The likelihood is that both categories of person were prosecuted under the law.

The prevailing opinion is that the law passed in 81 BC by Sulla as dictator against cut-throats and against *veneficia* (*Lex Cornelia de sicariis et veneficiis*) was not originally used to prosecute cases of magic-working as such, although persons who had administered love-philtres (*amatoria*) that resulted in a death might be prosecuted under it.[14] That the law could potentially be directed not only at poisoners, but at the casting of spells is suggested by the use in it of the highly ambiguous term *veneficium*. It was an ambiguity of which the Romans were conscious. Two passages in Quintilian's *Institutions of Oratory* pay testimony to the ambiguity and to the possibility that the ambiguity could give rise to discussion over the precise scope of the law. Quintilian, in dealing with the part that the definition of a term plays in legal proceedings, gives *veneficium* as an example of a term over whose meaning there might be debate. What would be in dispute in its case is whether it encompassed the incantations of magicians, even though it was acknowledged that an incantation and a deadly potion were quite different things.[15] Another instance of a problem of the same order that Quintilian cites is whether a love-spell (*amatorium*) and a *venenum* should go under the same name – presumably *venenum* – even though they both have their own names.[16] Since Quintilian does not say what the resolution was to these problems, they may be hypothetical questions that never in fact arose in a court and were never settled by a resolution of the Senate.

It is impossible to ascertain what the intent of the *Lex Cornelia* was when first it was promulgated, since there are no known cases from the Late Roman Republic of magic-working being brought to trial. There is not much room for doubt that in the Early Empire some aspects of magic-working were subject to legal action. Pliny the Elder says of the small fish called the *echeneis*, which means literally 'a ship-holder', that it is infamous for its use in erotic spells (*amatoria veneficia*) and for causing delays in court cases, but that balanced against these crimes (*crimina*) is the good reputation that it has won for preventing miscarriages.[17] Unless Pliny is using *crimen* very loosely and intends by it something like 'a morally outrageous action', he has to be taken to mean that criminal charges might arise out of the use of the *echeneis* in love-potions and in spells intended to delay a trial.

Of actual trials in which magic-working was prosecuted only two are known. The likelihood is that these were tried under the *Lex Cornelia*. The earlier of the trials belongs to the reign of Tiberius and occurred in the year AD 23/24: a woman called Numantina was prosecuted for having made her former husband insane by using incantations and spells (*carminibus et veneficiis*).[18] Numantina was acquitted of the charge. For our knowledge of the events that gave rise to the trial we are dependent on the historian Tacitus. What had led to the prosecution was the strange behaviour of the former husband, a man of some prominence, who was at the time a praetor. His name was Plautius Silvanus. He had thrown the wife he had married after Numantina either downstairs or out of a bedroom window to her death and when brought before the Emperor by the aggrieved father-in-law had answered in such a way as to suggest his mind was deranged, giving the impression of someone who was heavy with sleep and for that reason unaware of what he was doing. Under questioning he had said that his wife had taken her own life. Tiberius had immediately made his way to the house of the accused man, where evidence of a struggle and of the woman's having been pushed to her death were visible. That led to the Emperor's referring the matter to the Senate and to arrangements being made for a trial. Before the trial could take place, Silvanus killed himself by having his veins opened, after having made a vain attempt at dispatching himself with a dagger sent him by his grandmother, who had done so, it was believed, on the prompting of the Emperor.[19]

It very much looks as if Numantina was prosecuted under the heading in the *Lex Cornelia* that dealt with *veneficia*. In her case, *veneficia* was certainly not given a narrow construction and taken to mean 'poisoning', but was understood to encompass an act of magic of which incantations (*carmina*) were a part. It is particularly to be noted that the law was used to take cognizance of a crime other than homicide, namely, causing insanity by means of *veneficia* and *carmina*. Those who brought the prosecution must have done so under the conviction that the actions Silvanus had committed in his deranged state were exactly those that the magic of a jealous and spurned woman might induce.

The other case is the trial in AD 158/59 at Sabratha in Africa proconsularis of the Platonist philosopher Apuleius of Madaura. The trial took place before the proconsul governing the province. Apuleius was charged with having through magic seduced a rich widow into marrying him. There should be little doubt that this was the offence with which Apuleius was charged and that he was tried under the *Lex Cornelia*. He himself understood the charge to be one of magic: he interpreted the account of his interests and conduct presented by his accusers as one designed to support such a charge.[20] After he had disposed of what the prosecution had adduced as evidence of his being a magician, Apuleius turned to the basic charge that confronted him. What in his own words he did was to come to the root of the accusation, to the charge of magic or *maleficium*.[21] He then asks his accusers to explain what possible financial advantage there was for him, even if he was the greatest of magicians, in seducing a woman into matrimony by incantations and spells.[22] Apuleius was, in sum, charged with having used spells and incantations to compel a woman to marry him under a law that forbade the use of such devices. The *Lex Cornelia de sicariis et veneficiis* was surely the operative law.

The two fairly secure instances of the prosecution of magic-working tried under the *Lex Cornelia*, one a case in which a man is rendered insane and the other a case in which a woman marries someone whom she would not have married if fully in command of her senses, do not enable us to say exactly what the scope of the law was understood to be.[23] What is certain is that the clause in the *Lex Cornelia* dealing with *veneficia* was subject to interpretation over the course of the years and its scope widened. Modestinus, a jurist of the first part of the third century AD, refers to a *senatus consultum* which asserted that persons making evil sacrifices or having them in their possession were subject to punishment under the *Lex Cornelia*.[24] There is no point in speculating on the date of the *senatus consultum*. Its intent is also not as clear as it might be, since it could refer either to sacrifices intended to effect evil or to sacrifices that were in themselves evil, such as the killing of children for divinatory purposes. There is some reason to suppose that sacrifices performed for evil purposes are what are meant.[25] In the legal opinions ascribed to the jurist of the early third century AD, Paulus, which are known as the *Sententiae Pauli*, but which in fact in the main belong to the end of that century, the *Lex Cornelia* is said to impose a penalty on those who perform or initiate the performance of impious sacrifices or sacrifices carried out at night whose aim it was to bewitch or put a binding-spell on someone.[26] The same work also describes the penalties prescribed for those giving a potion designed to effect an abortion or intended to induce love and for those who possess magical books.[27] It draws a distinction between the penalty imposed on those who are a party to magic-working and that imposed on the magician himself: the former is to be thrown to the beasts or crucified; the magician is to be burned alive.[28] When first such punishments were imposed is a question not readily to be answered.

That a fairly broad construction was placed on the meaning of *veneficia* by the second half of the second century BC is to be inferred not only from the case of Apuleius, tried on a capital charge for having used magic to win the hand of his wife, but also from an imaginary legal situation sketched in a text-book on rhetoric dating to that time from the pen of an expert on the theory of that subject, Hermogenes of Tarsus. It is the case of a magician (*magos*) who had approached a father asking for the hand of his daughter and had been rejected; the girl had then conceived a passion for a ghostly image (*eidolon*), which had led to the prosecution of the magician for sorcery (*pharmaka*).[29] It sounds as if the imaginary magician is being prosecuted for *veneficia*. His offence seems to consist in getting the girl to fall in love with an image that he had sent.

That magicians, meaning those expert in magic and making a living from it, were actually burned alive by the middle of the second century AD is certainly the case.[30] That much is clear from a rhetorical exercise from the pen of a contemporary of Apuleius, the sophist and rhetor, Hadrian of Tyre.[31] Whether the women in the hypothetical case that Hadrian constructs were subject to the provision in the law mentioned in the *Sententiae Pauli* is quite another matter. Hadrian does say that the law refers to sorcerers as such and not just to crimes arising out of *veneficia*. The issue dealt with by Hadrian in the exercise is whether the law affecting sorcery takes cognizance only of those who have engaged in sorcery towards an evil end or those who possess the art of the sorcerer, even if it has not yet been exercised. In arguing that the law is in fact directed at those in possession of the sorcerer's art, Hadrian imagines the case of a woman who successfully undertakes to set alight the pyre of a woman convicted of sorcery that obstinately refuses to burn. Hadrian argues that the woman should herself by burned alive, on the ground that, since the law speaks not of one who has committed sorcery but of a sorceress (*pharmakis*), it applies its punishment to the art of sorcery and expresses its detestation of the power the art gives. Hadrian's interpretation of the law looks like a clever piece of casuistry, but what can hardly be in doubt is that he is referring to a clause in a law that explicitly mentioned the burning of sorcerers. Hadrian's credentials in matters of sorcery were not insignificant: he himself had the reputation of being a *goes*, a reputation that Philostratus in his *Lives of the Sophists* surmises came from Hadrian's having dealt in a spectacular way in his rhetorical exercises with the conduct of magicians (*magoi*).[32] Hadrian was, in other words, something of an expert on magicians and their ways.

Modern scholars have posited a law or a *senatus consultum* passed in the Late Republic against magic as such.[33] The grounds for positing such legislation are slight. The known cases of magic-working that were prosecuted look as though they could have fallen under the *Lex Cornelia*. What also tells against the existence of such legislation is the existence of forms of magic-working that were never prosecuted. Necromancy may have been one of these;[34] the old women who performed incantations over the sick and who attached amulets to them were almost certainly left alone. There are indications, nonetheless, from the late second and from the early third centuries AD that magic was generally understood to be illegal and that those who practised it were thought to do so at their peril. That is the understanding of Apuleius, who argues that it makes no sense to maintain that he had performed a magical ceremony in the presence of fifteen of his slaves by putting a slave-boy into a dreamlike trance to use him as a medium for divination, if magic was forbidden: his accuser must either acknowledge that what was done was not illicit, in which event Apuleius would have had no reason to fear that others knew, or that it was illicit, which would mean so many persons ought not have been privy to the deed.[35] Mention of the illegality of magic leads to Apuleius' enlarging on the subject and on how long magic had been treated as illegal: he points out that magic is a matter of concern to the law and had been so since the *Twelve Tables* in the distant past.[36]

Philostratus in his *Life of Apollonius of Tyana* writes with the same understanding. He makes Apollonius argue that his accuser takes the absurd position of charging him with practising sorcery (*goeteia*) without being able to show what Apollonius would have gained from doing so. Apollonius goes on to argue in essence that sorcery, since it is illegal and brings in its train lawsuits, is dangerous and that no one would engage in it unless there were some financial advantage attached.[37] Philostratus himself in a digression on sorcery, which is mainly concerned to demonstrate that those who give credence to it and use it practise a systematic form of self-deception, concludes his discussion by asking rhetorically why he should continue to attack something that is contrary both to nature (*physis*) and to law (*nomos*).[38] There is one further passage in the *Life of Apollonius of Tyana* that tends to show that magicians were subject to prosecution: in it Philostratus in support of the contention that magicians are the most wretched of men adduces as evidence their confessing, when accused before a court, that they are skilled in subjecting ghosts to examination, and performing barbarous sacrifices, incantations and anointings to change the course of what is fated.[39]

It is one thing to be able to show that the *Lex Cornelia de sicariis et veneficiis* came to be more widely interpreted and that those who practised sorcery in its various aspects were at least in theory liable to be prosecuted, but that does not mean very much from a historical point of view, unless some impression can be gained of how often the law or laws were pressed into service and how great a degree of anxiety men and women felt, lest they should fall foul of the law. If the effect of the legal provisions against sorcery is to be properly understood, it is also necessary to know who it was who was prosecuted under them: was the law primarily aimed at persons who had recourse to magic to further some end of their own or was it mainly directed at the practising magicians such persons employed? A complete dossier of the lawsuits that took place in Rome between 80 BC and the time of Constantine, let alone those that were conducted outside the city, certainly does not exist. Since statistics cannot be compiled, we have to deal in impressions. But even that is difficult, since texts in which men betray their anxieties are hard to come by. Some indirect light is, however, shed by ancient astrological texts on the fears that haunted men. The dangers that these texts predict for men born under a certain conjunction of the stars may be taken to reflect the threats men felt hung over them. When the danger predicted is condemnation for a particular crime, it is reasonable to conclude that such crimes were actively prosecuted. A particularly rich mine of information about such suits is provided by the *Mathesis* of Iulius Firmicus Maternus, a lawyer active in Rome between AD 334 and 357. It is on the whole unlikely that Firmicus Maternus himself made up the horoscopes he recorded. He is much more likely to have taken them over from the work of a predecessor, though they may well still be relevant to the conditions of his own day. The predecessor or predecessors on whom Firmicus Maternus draws for his predictions about condemnations in lawsuits do nonetheless belong to the Roman Empire and not to Hellenistic Egypt.

On at least seven separate occasions Firmicus cites nativities that will give rise either to a condemnation for sorcery or a related offence or to the danger of being charged with such an offence. If Mars and Mercury are present equally in the horoscope of one born during the daytime, then persons with such nativities will be unfortunate and short-lived, either because of a woman or because of the enticements of love or because of secret writings (*absconsae scripturae*) or it will cause their condemnation for sorcery (*de maleficiis*) or for forgery.[40] On the other hand, if the Sun, Saturn and Mercury occupy a certain conjunction, then there is the danger of being accused of having been in possession of secret writings (*absconditae litterae*) or of having forged public documents or of having counterfeited currency.[41] Mars, Saturn and the Moon in a certain combination give rise to persons who will perish by the sword, after having been publicly accused of sorcery (*maleficia*) or of engaging in unlawful religious rites (*inlicita sacra*) or of having adulterated the coinage.[42] Mars and Mercury combined in another setting will produce those charged with forgery or persons associated with sorcerers and magicians (*malefici et venenarii*) in a criminal form of life.[43] Mercury and Saturn or Mars found in conjunction with the Moon in a certain position create forgers, sorcerers (*malefici*), and those who adulterate the coinage, persons destined to be severely punished by a judge for their crimes.[44] Finally, there is a text that tells of men who are down on their fortunes turning to the illicit arts and being condemned and punished for so doing. Again it is Mercury and Mars in conjunction that produce such persons; it is their fate first to stand surety for others and then as a result to suffer financial collapse and to be reduced in legal status to *humiliores*, at which point they either actively engage in certain of the illicit arts or become the helpers of others or are privy to what is going on, which in its turn leads to their arrest, condemnation and execution.[45]

Firmicus draws on a source or sources who inhabit a world in which sorcerers, the possessors of secret writings and those who practise illicit rites, which may be presumed to be some form of magical ceremony, are executed alongside forgers and counterfeiters for their crimes. Other references in the *Mathesis* suggest a society populated by persons who are expert in secret or illicit writings, who may be born under the same conjunction of signs as *magi*, philosophers and astrologers.[46] It looks then as if the authors of astrological texts constructed their horoscopes to take account of a world in which many men were the possessors of magical texts and spent their time poring over them.[47] That is interesting, but it is even more interesting for our immediate purposes to learn that such texts were illegal. The author or authors of the horoscopes contained in the *Mathesis* do envisage a world in which magic-working and magic-workers are actively prosecuted. The horoscopes unfortunately do not distinguish between those whom circumstances force into having recourse to magic, those who without exactly being professional magicians have a more than passing interest in magic and those who make all or part of their living from magic. The impression with which the horoscopes leave us is that it is the two last-mentioned categories of person who are meant.

A summary of what we know about the law affecting sorcery in Rome should first of all acknowledge the gaps in our knowledge. To begin with, we cannot, in spite of what Apuleius may say, assert with any confidence that the clauses in the *Twelve Tables*, which were in later times understood to prohibit magic, were in fact ever consciously used to prosecute magic as such. Nor are we in a position to say whether the *Lex Cornelia de sicariis et veneficiis* was conceived as a tool for dealing with magic-working. It is not until we reach the reign of Tiberius that we have any evidence of legal action being taken against sorcery. That the *Lex Cornelia* was the law under which cases involving sorcery were tried is extremely likely, but not strictly provable. It nonetheless does look as though the scope and intent of the law were extended and defined over time, so that eventually it could be used to prosecute most serious forms of magic-working. The testimony of the *Mathesis* of Firmicus Maternus does suggest that magic-working and, more significantly, magic-workers were actively persecuted. Due allowance must be made for the possibility of peaks and troughs in this activity.

The account that has just been given of what in Rome and the Roman world until the reign of Constantine the legal consequences were of practising magic or of engaging a magician is in general agreement with accepted scholarly opinion.[48] It is only fair to point out that an attack of an extremely radical nature has recently been made on the scholarly consensus. Its contention is that it was only in the reign of Diocletian at the beginning of the fourth century AD that the Roman authorities tried to exert any control over magic-workers, soothsayers and diviners; up to that point, magic, soothsaying and divining had not been thought sufficiently important to merit legislative action.[49] The principal reason given for this major rewriting of the history of Roman legislation against magic is the absence before the beginning of the fourth century AD of any discussion of the subject on the part of the experts on Roman Law. This indeed would be very strange, if legislation against magic-working had been in existence at an earlier date. The explanation offered for the change in policy is that the Emperor and his advisers extended the degree of control they felt it necessary to exert over men to their beliefs as well as their actions. As the earliest indication of that change in outlook a rescript of Diocletian is cited that lays down the severest penalties not only for those who advocate Manichaeanism, but also for those who adhere to the tenets of the sect. The ground given for the legislation is that such actions represent a contravention of what the gods have thought fit in their concern for humanity to establish as good and true.[50]

That the Roman state came more and more from the time of Diocletian to resemble a modern police state in which not only were men's actions controlled, but also their thoughts and beliefs is to make too much of certain measures and to ignore the considerable degree of latitude the Late Roman state allowed its subjects. Nor is it quite true to say that no Roman jurisconsult had anything to say about the law of magic before the beginning of the fourth century AD: Modestinus in all likelihood did so and the author of the opinion recorded in the *Sententiae Pauli* certainly did, unless we choose to believe that he belongs to the fourth century or later. What cannot be argued away are the cases of Numantina and Apuleius. They were tried for engaging in magic. Finally, if there was no legislation against magic, we have to contend with the belief of Apuleius, the sophist Hadrian and Philostratus that the law forbade magic. It is not very likely that they were deluded in this matter.

## Police actions against magicians in Rome and Italy

Those who brought actions for magic-working under the *Lex Cornelia* either did so on their own behalf, because they believed that witchcraft had been employed against them, or on behalf of persons who felt that they had been subjected to sorcery. These were emphatically not prosecutions initiated by the state. If the *Lex Cornelia* was the only mechanism for checking magic, most magic-working would have gone unchecked, since those who used the instrument of the law against magic-working must either have been persons of some standing or have acted on behalf of persons of standing. Prostitutes who were slaves, freedwomen or foreigners will not have used the *Lex Cornelia* to exact punishment for the wrong done them from a rival who was believed to have employed sorcery against them. Nor again was the *Lex Cornelia* a very suitable instrument for dealing with a practising magician who was notorious but against whom no one had laid a complaint.

There were other more effective ways of handling the latter category of person. The Roman authorities from time to time took police action against magicians and astrologers and either expelled them from Rome and Italy *en masse* or did so individually. These actions are part of a larger pattern of suppressing sacrificial rites felt to be foreign and non-Roman and performed for profit. Just when these actions began and to what extent our sole source for these measures, Livy, projects contemporary practice back into the past is hard to say. In his narrative of the events in the year 186 BC at the height of the uproar over privately organized Dionysiac groups in Rome one of the consuls, Spurius Postumius, in a speech at a public meeting, declared that in the time of their fathers and grandfathers instructions had been given to the magistrates to forbid sacrifices of a foreign nature being performed, to ban sacrificial priests and prophets (*sacrificuli vatesque*) from the forum, circus and the city, to seek out and burn prophetic books and to put an end to sacrificial practices not sanctioned by Roman custom.[51] One of the events that Livy has in mind is the crackdown that took place in 215 BC during the Second Punic War when crowds of women were to be seen sacrificing and praying in public in the forum and the Capitolium in a non-Roman manner. The explanation that Livy gives for the phenomenon was that sacrificial priests-cum-prophets (*sacrificuli vatesque*) had established a hold over men's minds and were reaping easy profits from the dissemination of mistaken foreign practices. He relates that there was criticism in the Senate of the officials responsible for public order, the aediles and the *triumviri capitales*, for not having put a stop to what was going on; in fact when they had tried to move the parties responsible from the forum and break up their cultic equipment, they had come within an ace of being attacked themselves. In consequence, a praetor was given instructions to free the minds of the people from their attachment to these practices and a resolution of the Senate was passed that required those who had in their possession prophetic books or prayers in writing or instructions on the art of sacrifice to hand them in by the Kalends of April and that there be no further sacrifice in public using a new or foreign rite.[52]

Whatever may in fact have happened in 215 BC, it clearly made sense to Livy that books of prophetic utterances should have been sought out and burned and that the priests-cum-prophets that he refers disparagingly to as *sacrificuli vatesque* should have been driven out of their haunts in the forum and around the circus and from Rome generally.[53] These will have been private religious entrepreneurs who made a living from performing sacrifices for those who sought them out in the forum and the circus. A Greek would have called them *agyrtai*. The banishing of magicians and astrologers is a manifestation of the same concern with non-Roman practices and with religious operators preying on the gullible for a profit.

On one of the occasions the Roman authorities took action against astrologers and magicians, they drove citizen magicians and astrologers into exile, but put the foreigners to death. The occasion in question was early in the reign of Tiberius, either in AD 16 or in the following year, in the aftermath of the conspiracy of Scribonius Libo Drusus. Tacitus says simply that the Senate passed decrees about expelling astrologers and magicians from Italy and then goes on to report the execution of two of these persons, who from their names sound as if they were Roman citizens.[54] Dio Cassius, on the other hand, gives a more detailed account of what would appear to be the same set of events in which he speaks of Tiberius executing everyone who was an astrologer or magician (*goes*) or who engaged in any other form of divination, if they were not Roman citizens, and of his exiling as many of the citizens who had persisted in pursuing these arts after the promulgation of the former decree (*dogma*) forbidding their practice in Rome.[55] The only earlier decree recorded by Dio Cassius that looks as if it might be the measure referred to is an edict belonging to the last years of the reign of Augustus. We are told that in AD 11 Augustus forbade seers (*manteis*) to deliver prophetic utterances to anyone who was not accompanied by other persons and that he absolutely forbade prophesies concerning death, even if they were presented to a group of people. The historian remarks on the lack of concern that Augustus personally felt about such matters, which showed itself in his publishing his own natal horoscope.[56] That suggests that Augustus was responding to pressures from below and that he did not issue the edict on his own initiative. It is to be surmised that the pressure came from the authorities in Rome, since the edict appears to have applied to Rome and Italy rather than the whole Empire. If Dio is giving a faithful record of the measures taken in AD 11 and then again in AD 16 and 17, it looks as if what Augustus and then the Senate wanted to clamp down on were first of all consultations about the future undertaken in secrecy and then prophesying about death. Magicians were obviously one of the categories of person at whom Augustus' measure was aimed, precisely because a large part of their business was bound up in divination. It would be unwise to assume, however, that only those magicians found to have engaged in divination in private were in AD 16 or 17 executed or driven out of Rome and that other magicians did not suffer. All known practising magicians may have suffered, because of the presumption that divination was one of their principal activities. The events of the year AD 16 did after all lead to a surprisingly large number of deaths. The *Chronicle of the Year* AD 354 records, because it had not happened before, the execution in the reign of Tiberius of forty-five sorcerers and eighty-five sorceresses.[57] It is presumably the events of AD 16 or 17 that the chronicler has in mind. As many again will have been driven into exile.

The earliest known instance of the expulsion of magicians as such from Rome took place in 33 BC at the hands of an exceedingly active aedile, Octavian's right-hand man, Marcus Agrippa. He is said to have expelled on that occasion not only magicians but also astrologers.[58] It will be in virtue of the police powers vested in him and his general concern with maintaining public order in Rome that Agrippa as aedile acted against magicians and astrologers.[59] It is natural to assume that Agrippa's motive in getting rid as aedile of the magicians and astrologers had to do with the preservation of public order in Rome and with keeping it free of the hucksters and charlatans who preyed on its population, but if the events at the end of the reign of Augustus and the beginning of that of Tiberius are anything to go by, Agrippa may have had a more specific reason for expelling these two very closely related categories of person.

One hundred years before in 139 BC Chaldaeans were expelled from Rome and Italy by the *praetor peregrinus*, Cn. Cornelius Hispalis, because, in the words of one of our sources, they were deriving gain from a false art by imposing on feeble minds.[60] The same praetor is credited with making Jews, who were accused of attempting to corrupt Roman tradition with the cult of Juppiter Sabazius, return to their homeland.[61] Certainty is not to be attained about Hispalis' motives in expelling the Chaldaeans, but it has to be acknowledged that there is a certain consistency to the explanations our sources give for the measures that in the second century BC the Roman authorities took against foreign cults, which are the preservation of Roman religious practice and a desire to prevent religious operators from making a profit from the simple and gullible.[62] It is entirely possible then that the praetor took the action out of a desire to defend what he saw as traditional Roman religious practice from the inroads that foreign cults were making and out of a concern to keep *agyrtai* from profiting from the ignorance of the masses.[63]

A decree of the Senate that might just come from the same period has been associated with the same concern. The decree sought to protect and encourage the practice of Etruscan haruspicy or divination from the examination of entrails. It made provision for boys who came from the leading families – it is unclear whether Roman or Etruscan – to be sent to Etruscan communities to study the art, lest, because of the small numbers active in it, the art should lose its religious authority and be taken over by persons whose motive in practising it was purely gain.[64] That at any rate is Cicero's reading of the matter. The motive of the Senate must in part have been to preserve what it had come to assume was an integral part of Roman religious observance, but the threat in this case came not from foreign cults but from freelance *haruspices* and their female counterparts, *haruspicae,* who sought to make a living from the art of divining from entrails. That such *haruspicae* were already a presence in Rome in the first half of the second century BC and something of a nuisance has already been noted.[65] It is then conceivable that the motive of Cn. Hispalis in banning astrologers from Rome and Italy was to protect traditional Roman religious observance. At the same time, it is also very likely that his edict was motivated by a genuine dislike of priests making a living from selling their expertise, which is to say, acting as *agyrtai*.

It should not be assumed that the persons swept out of Rome in 139 BC put too strict a construction on what it was to be a Chaldaean, confining their activities to giving horoscopes, and that some of them did not venture into other forms of divination and even into magic. There is a story that probably comes from the memoirs of the Roman dictator Sulla about an encounter that Sulla had with a man described as a Chaldaean, who, after looking intently at Sulla's face, observing his mental and physical movements and setting what he had seen against the teachings of his craft, declared his astonishment that Sulla tolerated not being the first of all men. The Chaldaean was part of the entourage of an envoy from the Parthian king who in 92 BC had had a meeting with Sulla on the banks of the Euphrates.[66] In Velleius Paterculus' version of the episode, it is *magi* amongst the envoys who prophesy on the basis of Sulla's physical characteristics that he will have a great future.[67] The moral to be drawn from the story is that persons who might be variously described as Chaldaeans or *magi* engaged in forms of divining that had nothing to do with casting horoscopes.

Five years after Agrippa drove astrologers and magicians out of Rome, Augustus is credited with having expelled a single magician from Rome and Italy, Anaxilaus of Larissa.[68] It is true that this was no ordinary magician and that we only know about his banishment because he was well known and the event was thought worth recording. The banishment of Anaxilaus of Larissa nonetheless raises the possibility that other less renowned magic-workers were routinely driven out of Rome and Italy on their own and not as part of a mass expulsion. It would be prudent to keep an open mind about the factors that led to the periodic expulsion of astrologers and magicians from Rome and not to attempt to assign any one cause to them. What look to us to have been very similar events may have arisen out of very different circumstances. Magicians in Rome may not have spent their lives in constant fear of being driven out of Italy or of being executed, but the risk was there. We know about the more spectacular episodes in which large numbers of them were expelled or executed, but we know nothing about the more routine dangers that magic-workers faced. We should particularly like to know whether the aediles took action against a man or woman if he or she became particularly notorious and began to pose a threat to public order. After AD 68 we hear of no more expulsions of astrologers and magicians from Rome. It is difficult to know what to make of this: whether it reflects a failure on the part of our sources or a real change in policy. It is interesting, nonetheless, to note that the Senate is concerned only with public order in Rome and Italy. Its concerns do not extend to the larger Empire. The effect of the measure on the greater Roman world is none of its business.

## Actions against magicians in the provinces

It presumably fell to Roman provincial governors to move against magic-workers or persons they saw as magic-workers who were causing trouble in their jurisdiction. That at least in one case this happened is known from an edict of AD 198/99 emanating from the prefect of Egypt. It takes the form of a letter addressed to local governors commanding them under penalty of death to root out those professing to know the future.[69] It is specifically directed at two forms of divination, the latter of which was peculiar to Egypt: (1) oracular response given in the form of written answers; (2) processional divination. The former kind of divination consisted in submitting questions on ostraka or papyri, one of which might contain a positive response and the other a negative. The god was then supposed to indicate what his answer was. The process is sometimes called a ticket-oracle. Processional divination had a long history in Egypt. Images of the gods were taken out of their temples on a tour of the vicinity. In the course of that procession people addressed questions to the statue, which then responded, perhaps by moving in an appropriate way. The interpretation of that response probably then fell to the priests accompanying the statue on its outing.[70]

The prefect sees those who attempt to look into the future in these ways as men who engage in a risk-fraught form of curiosity (*periergia*) and as men who profess to know what lies beyond human ken.[71] He suggests that they use magical devices (*manganeiai*) to bolster their claims to knowledge.[72] In describing the pursuit of knowledge from ticket-oracles and processional oracles as curiosity or *periergia*, the prefect, Q. Aemilius Saturninus, uses a loaded term. *Periergia* and its Latin equivalent *curiositas* are in such contexts not neutral terms used to denote a disinterested spirit of inquiry. They refer rather to the pursuit of the occult and of that which properly lies hidden from human view. Saturninus, accordingly, saw ticket- and processional oracles as centres of magic-working in which the tricks of magicians were used to impose on the gullible. He is not interested in prosecuting those who consult them. His ire is reserved for those who profess to be able to see into the future. It does not, however, sound, from the instructions that Saturninus gives about rooting out those professing to be able to see into the future, as if he was moving against official public cults. His target seems to be individual entrepreneurs.

It has been suggested that the decision to move against the ticket- and processional oracles was not that of Saturninus himself, but reflects imperial policy and is to be connected with the visit that in AD 199 Septimius Severus made as Emperor to Egypt.[73] That there was some connection between the edict and the imperial visit cannot be ruled out, but since the practices

Saturninus tries to stamp out are quite specific ones, it very much looks as if he is attempting to attend to a particular set of local problems. From the preamble to the letter it also sounds as if Saturninus had been moved to act out of a feeling that abuses were being perpetrated on the populace. We would probably do Saturninus an injustice if we were to interpret his actions as a failure to understand or respect Egyptian traditions. It is more likely that what he was attempting to do was to stamp out the abuse of a tradition.

How the municipalities of the Latin-speaking provinces of the Roman Empire dealt with magicians who set up shop in their midst is not known. Cases of magic-working falling under the *Lex Cornelia de sicariis et veneficiis* would, to judge from what happened to Apuleius, have been tried under that law, but what the municipal authorities would have done, had they been confronted by the presence in their towns of a person making a living from magic-working, is quite another matter. It is to be imagined that one course of action open to the aediles of the town would have been to use the police powers vested in their office to expel the offending person. Informed guesswork is in order for the Latin West. The same holds true for the Greek East.

## Informal actions against magicians

It would probably be a mistake to imagine that the only recourse a community had when it wanted to drive a magician out of town was to wait for the local council to act. More informal measures may have been taken. The expression of public sentiment may have led to the magician finding it convenient to leave town. The astrological texts from Late Antiquity are full of predictions of public pointings out (*deigmatismoi*) of unpopular persons, of shoutings and outcry (*periboesia*) directed at the same persons and of communities rising up (*epanastaseis*).[74] One text seems to envisage a progression from enmity to public outcry to a trial for *pharmakia*.[75]

An ancient reader would automatically translate such terms in his mind into a concrete reality. It is a good deal less easy for us to do so, but by no means impossible. One of the ways in which public opinion could be aroused against interlopers who threatened the well-being of the community or the established religious order we know from the story told in the Acts of the Apostles about what the silversmiths of Ephesus did when they felt their trade in silver likenesses of the temple of Artemis at Ephesus was threatened by the missionary activities of Paul and his companions in Ephesus and Asia. One silversmith had succeeded in so stirring up the crowd that they rushed to the theatre of the city dragging two of Paul's fellow-workers with them. There confusion reigned, although there was orchestrated chanting lasting for two hours. The sole cry of the mob during this period was: 'Great is Artemis of the Ephesians'. The matter was brought to an end by the Secretary of the City Council, who warned the crowd that they were in danger of being charged with riotous behaviour and that there were proper legal channels for dealing with their complaints.[76] The outcry at Ephesus was in fact quelled by a representative of the city-government and led to nothing, but it is quite conceivable that on other occasions the authorities found it easier to go along with the mob and drive the offending party or parties out of town.

Apuleius in the *Metamorphoses* certainly envisages public outrage prompted by the wickedness of a sorceress (*saga*) leading to a meeting at which it is decided to stone the woman to death. The meeting at which the decision is taken is definitely not a properly constituted trial, but an informal assembly instigated by one man. The sentence is not carried out, since the spells of the witch completely imprison the inhabitants of the town in their houses. The witch only agrees to release them, if they will swear off what they have planned and promise to help her, should anyone else think of taking action against her. As for the instigator of the meeting at which the decision had been taken, he and his house are transported lock, stock and barrel to a city perched on a mountain-top that has no water.[77] The events described are set in Thessaly, somewhere in the vicinity of Larissa, where the sorceress runs an inn. The element of fantasy in the story and its setting in Thessaly does not mean that in its basic outline it does not reflect a reality. Legal remedies against witchcraft must have seemed slow, cumbersome, expensive and uncertain. That will have encouraged people to take the law into their own hands and to band together with their neighbours to rid themselves of persons they suspected of practising magic in their community.

Finally, Philostratus tells of persons he calls Egyptians and Chaldaeans making their way to the western shore of the Hellespont, after the area had been rocked by a series of earthquakes. They then tried to hold up the inhabitants of the cities there for what was in effect an exorbitant ransom: they said they would only perform a placatory sacrifice if they were paid ten talents. Apollonius, since he found this intolerable, appeared on the scene and drove the Egyptians and Chaldaeans away, on the ground that they were profiting from the misery of others. He then successfully placated the offended deity at no great expense.[78] There is no mystery over the identity of the Chaldaeans. They will have been astrologers. The Egyptians present more of a problem. They are best understood to be persons trading on the renown that Egyptian priests had as experts in the divine and in the occult. What is more difficult to understand is how Apollonius is to be imagined to have driven out the Chaldaeans and Egyptians. It rather sounds as if we are to think of him orchestrating public opinion against them and in that way bringing about their departure.

## Sanctions against magicians entering religious sanctuaries

Punishments inflicted by the state and expulsion from a city, whether by legal or extra-legal means, were not the only disadvantage in being a magician or having a reputation as a magician. A known or reputed magician, at least in the Greek-speaking parts of the Roman Empire, would have encountered other difficulties. He or she might have suffered the embarrassment of being barred from entering a religious sanctuary and from participating in religious rites. Philostratus reports that when Apollonius of Tyana came to Eleusis seeking initiation into the mysteries there, the hierophant refused to initiate him, on the ground that he would never initiate a sorcerer (goes), and declined to give him access to the precinct at Eleusis, since in matters pertaining to the divine Apollonius was not pure (katharos).[79] Much the same thing happened at a later date when he came to consult the oracle of Trophonius at Lebadaea in Boeotia: the priests refused to allow him to question Trophonius; they told other people that their reason for refusing him entry was that they would never allow a goes to question Trophonius, but what they said to Apollonius himself was that the religious calendar forbade consultation at that time.[80] Finally, when at the end of his life he approached the temple of Dictynna in Crete and the dogs which were supposed to guard the temple, far from barking at him, fawned on him, the men in charge of the temple arrested him and put him in bonds as a goes and thief, charging him with having thrown the dogs a titbit to placate them.[81]

The incidents may very well be fictitious, since they all reflect well on Apollonius and on his superior piety and wisdom, but the theme of the goes who is refused admission to a sanctuary because he is impure is unlikely to be Philostratus' invention; it will be grounded in reality. There is independent evidence that the episodes Philostratus describes could well have happened. It takes the form of an inscription forbidding entry to a shrine to those tainted by the practice of magic. The inscription comes from Philadelphia in Lydia and belongs to the first century BC.[82] It purports to record the instructions given in a dream by Zeus to the man, an individual called Dionysus, who set up the shrine.[83] Those who entered the shrine, whether they were free men or free women or slaves, were to swear an oath testifying to their never having employed guile against another, nor an evil pharmakon, nor that they knew or had used evil incantations (epodai), nor love-philtres, nor abortifacients, and they were also to swear that they had never forcibly carried off anyone or killed them, nor had they been party or privy to such doings.[84] Those who are aware that there are persons attempting to enter the shrine who have contravened any of the regulations are to make that information public.[85] Men who have corrupted a woman other than their wife are not to be admitted to the shrine, nor are women who have known a man other than their husband.[86] The overriding concern of the regulations is to ensure both that those who take part in the mysteries in the shrine should be of good character and that they should be ritually-pure. Although parallels for the regulations against magic-working are not attested in the epigraphic record, they are unlikely to be the product of one whimsical individual; they will reflect the concerns of a larger group than Dionysus himself. The priests who refuse to let Apollonius enter their temples or participate in the rites they supervise may be the invention of Philostratus, but priests will in reality have refused entry to the sanctuaries they ran to known sorcerers, either relying on the authority of regulations such as those from Philadelphia or moved by the fear that they themselves would be held responsible by the god for allowing a polluting force into the sanctuary. What in effect the existence of such regulations or of the feeling that gave rise to them meant is that known magicians were at a disadvantage in trying to taking part in religious activities, since they were liable to be denounced.

Recovering the thinking that lies behind the debarring of sorcerers from sanctuaries is not an easy task. The decree from Philadelphia does not explain what the reason for the regulations is and why magicians are classified with other forms of impure person such as women who have known a man other than their husband and men who have seduced and ruined either boys or women other than their wives.[87] The hierophant at Eleusis does say that Apollonius as a *goes* is not pure (*katharos*) in matters relating to the divine.[88] Very much the same view of the impropriety involved in allowing a *goes* access to the sanctuary of a god as that underlying the inscription is likely to be at the back of the punishment that Plato in the *Laws* imposes on the man who commits a major impiety in performing sacrifices to the gods, whether public or private: he is to be executed for having performed a sacrifice when not pure (*katharos*).[89] Plato does not spell out in what the impiety consists, but the overall context would suggest some form of magical ceremony. The reason for the state's taking such drastic action against persons who perform sacrifices when they are in an impure condition must be the risk it faces of incurring the wrath of the gods in allowing tainted sacrifices to take place.[90] It remains unclear why exactly magic is thought to make a man impure. It may very well be that different people would have given different answers, if asked that question.

In sum, there is more than enough evidence to suggest that magicians in the Roman Empire, both in Rome and Italy and the provinces did not lead an untroubled existence, but faced threats from various quarters: they might be prosecuted for engaging in magic-working against someone; they might be driven out of town by the authorities or even executed; and the population might rise up against them to banish them; sometimes the actions of the populace might encourage the public authorities to move against them. Astrological texts provide a very good indication that these were very real threats.

# 7

# SORCERERS AND SORCERESSES IN ROME IN THE MIDDLE AND LATE REPUBLIC AND UNDER THE EARLY EMPIRE

## The Middle and Late Republic

### The background to magic-working: the religious fringe

Far more is known about the private religious entrepreneurs present in Rome in the Middle and Late Republic than is known about this aspect of religious life in any other Hellenistic city. It is clear that at any given time in the period Rome contained a substantial number of persons of indeterminate origin who offered religious services of various kinds. Many of them were men or women expert in divination. The varied cast of religious experts with whom Periplectomenus' wife in Plautus' *Miles gloriosus* consorts and whom she feels obliged to pay on the 19th of the month have already been mentioned.[1] There are not only the woman who performs incantations (*praecantrix*), the woman who interprets dreams (*coniectrix*), the inspired prophetess (*hariola*), the woman who inspects entrails (*haruspica*) and finally, the woman who observes the sky. It is conspicuous that they are female. They have their male counterparts: in a tragedy by Ennius, a contemporary of Plautus, a character complains about ecstatic prophets (*superstitiosi prophetae*) and shameless inspired seers (*harioli*) who are either idle or insane or driven by need; they are men who do not know their own way, yet propose to show the way to others and who promise wealth to those from whom they seek a drachma as their fee.[2] It is amongst persons of this type that many of Rome's magic-workers will have been found.

The type of seer most frequently mentioned in the plays of Plautus is the inspired seer, *hariolus* or *superstitiosus*.[3] If the frequency with which he is mentioned is anything to go by, his presence must have been particularly felt in Rome. The *hariolus* is certainly one of the characters whom Cato feels may get the steward of a farm into trouble.[4] His prophetic utterances were listened to in 87 BC when Rome was in the grip of civil strife.[5] Forty or so years later Cicero declares rather forcefully that he accords no respect to those who engage in ecstatic prophecy for the sake of gain.[6] Others very clearly did listen to them.

Chaldaeans were already a force in Rome and its vicinity by the middle of

162

the second century BC. That much is to be inferred from Cato's warning against them.[7] By 139 BC their presence in Rome was obviously felt to be enough of a threat to justify their expulsion *en masse*.[8] They probably drifted back fairly soon afterwards, although little is heard of them for some time. They were definitely back in Rome by the middle of the following century, since they are said to have predicted not once but several times that Pompey, Crassus and Caesar would die at home in their beds, full of years and glory.[9] These were presumably a higher class of Chaldaean than the astrologers for whom Cicero expresses his contempt.[10] They and other types of fortune-teller were to be found hanging around the circus and forum.[11]

Local or freelance diviners from entrails or *vicani haruspices*, to use the contemptuous term for them that Cicero employs to distinguish them from the official *haruspices* of the Roman state, are part of the Roman colouring in Plautus.[12] The playwright knows of both male and female *haruspices*.[13] Some *haruspices*, both male and female, seem to have gone from door to door;[14] others again were to be found where people congregated. In a scene in Plautus' *Curculio*, *haruspices* are said to be found in the Velabrum, an area between the Capitoline and the Palatine where there was a market, in the company of bakers, butchers and those who change form or provide the means for others to change form.[15] Who the last category of persons is is obscure. They may be either cheats or mountebanks of some kind.

The interpreter of dreams (*coniector* or in the feminine *coniectrix*) is also a familiar figure in Plautus.[16] By the Late Republic there is a special category of dream-interpreters connected with the Egyptian deity Isis known as *Isiaci coniectores*.[17] Cicero predictably has no time for them nor for the figure known as the Marsian augur.[18] He was a freelance interpreter of the flight and the cries of birds. Finally, there was what seems to have been the humblest form of seer of all, the *sortilegus*, or drawer of lots.[19] Other kinds of seer undoubtedly existed, but there is no record of their existence in this period.

A somewhat different type of religious operator was the sacrificial priest-cum-prophet (*sacrificulus vates*), who is said in Livy to have been associated with foreign cults and to have been periodically driven out of the forum and circus by the Roman authorities.[20] Whatever may have happened in the Early Republic, persons presenting themselves as the priests of foreign cults were probably to be encountered in the forum and around the circus in the Late Republic. The persons contemptuously referred to as *sacrificuli* performed a variety of religious functions. Some of them like their counterparts in Athens offered privately conducted ceremonies of initiation into the mysteries. The person who Livy says was responsible for the spread of Dionysiac mystery-cult into Rome was such a *sacrificulus vates*, a Greek of obscure origins who came first to Etruria and who acted as the officiant in secret ceremonies of initiation conducted at night; he was not one of those religious operators who, while they filled men's minds with error, could be said to seek quite openly a livelihood from the cult they propagated.[21] Whatever the truth may be about the existence of the Greek, he represents a known type. It is a type that in Livy's view is to be distinguished from another known type, the mendicant priest who openly makes a living from his cult. They too will have been referred to as *sacrificuli*. Other *sacrificuli* conducted religious ceremonies in private. The *sacrificulus* called Licinius who informed Pompey that certain slaves and freedmen of Milo had been organized to assassinate him is to be assigned to that category. Licinius had emerged from the common people and his speciality was purifying families.[22]

A Greek-speaker asked to find a general term that covered all of the forms of seer and priest described in the preceding paragraphs would have called them *agyrtai* or perhaps would have used the hendiadys *agyrtai kai manteis* to characterize them. Plutarch, at any rate, uses the latter form of expression to refer to the varied cast of Chaldaeans, *haruspices* and interpreters of Sibylline oracles (*sibyllistai*) with whom the consul of 87 BC, Gnaeus Octavius, kept company and who persuaded him to stay in Rome when the forces of Marius were threatening it.[23]

### Sorceresses

The testimony of Plautus very strongly suggests that prostitutes and the women who ran them were in the early second century BC believed to practise magic against men and to be expert at it. There are two scenes that presuppose a familiarity on the part of the audience with erotic magic and its practice by prostitutes. In both scenes a man enraged by the conduct of a woman denounces her as a *venefica*. In *Mostellaria*, Philolaches overhears an old woman called Scapha encouraging his beloved Philematium, a prostitute whom he has just freed from slavery, not to place all of her eggs in one basket but to have more than one lover while she can. This upsets Philolaches, making him wish to be turned into a snake so that he may throttle the *venefica*.[24] The slave who gives his name to *Epidicus* describes for Periphanes, the father of a young lover called Stratippocles, soldiers returning from a successful military expedition and the concourse of prostitutes who have gathered to greet their lovers and entrap them. The main focus of his account is the woman with whom Stratippocles is infatuated and the ambush she is laying for him. The picture that Epidicus draws leads Periphanes to ask whether Epidicus has seen the *venefica*.[25] What lies at the back of Philolaches' calling the old maidservant Scapha a *venefica* and Periphanes' use of the same term to refer to the mistress of his son is the idea that Scapha as a procuress and the mistress as a prostitute are likely to be expert in entrapping men by the use of erotic magic. It is true that the masculine *veneficus* may be used as an empty term of abuse with no real suggestion that the person so called is a sorcerer or poisoner, but the context in which Philolaches and Periphanes employ the word *venefica* makes it probable that they have in mind the erotic magic which prostitutes and procuresses were believed to practise.

Turpilius and Lucilius show that the figure of the procuress or go-between who doubles as a *saga* was a recognized one.[26] They write of her as though the two activities were inseparable. That rather implies that erotic magic was her main concern. Perhaps it was, but it was probably by no means all that she did. Porphyrion gives reason to think that she is to be identified with the *praecantrix*.[27] If that is so, much of her time will have been occupied with relatively mundane forms of magic-working such as performing purificatory ceremonies for those who had experienced an ominous dream or uttering an incantation over a sick child. Periplectomenus in the *Miles gloriosus* of Plautus complains, as we have noticed, that should he marry, his wife will seek money from him on the 19th of each month to pay off the *praecantrix* as well as various other forms of female seer.[28] *Praecantrices* must, accordingly, have been a feature of Roman life from the early second century BC. The fragment of the *Logistoricus* of Varro that speaks of *praecantrices* is one of the few scraps of evidence that such women were a continuing presence from the early second century BC down into the Late Roman Republic. The fragment comes from a work of Varro whose subject-matter is the upbringing of children. It says that most women employ female singers of incantations (*praecantrices*) in preference to showing their sick children to doctors.[29] The fragment, accordingly, testifies to the almost universal tendency, if Varro is to be believed, on the part of the women bringing up children to summon these females to the house when a child was sick rather than showing it to a doctor. It is to be inferred from what Varro and Plautus say that these women were mainly consulted and employed by other women rather than by men. The testimony of Plautus and Varro on this matter unquestionably reflects the male conviction that women are superstitious and easy prey for unscrupulous religious experts. While due allowance must be made for male prejudice here, it is still likely that it was mostly women who consulted *praecantrices*. Finally, it is worth noting that Varro speaks not just of single women being brought in but of more than one. In Rome too, magic, it seems, was performed by women acting in groups.

There is some further information to be extracted from the sources about *sagae*, but about *sagae* whose lives have a very different conformation from the procuress-cum-*saga* who is an independent operator. They are the *sagae* who are part of the entourage of a great man. The activities and origins of one of these women are well documented. She is the Syrian holy woman Martha. Plutarch's *Marius* gives the fullest account of the career of this extraordinary figure. The philosopher Posidonius is known to be one of the authorities on whom Plutarch relies in recounting Marius' life. The chances are very high that it is Posidonius whom Plutarch is following at this point.[30] It is exactly the kind of story that Posidonius would have told. Its ingredients are very much the same as those in the tale spun by Posidonius about Eunus, the Syrian from Apamea who led the slave revolt in Sicily in the 130s: a holy man or woman from Syria who uses his or her special powers to win their way to a position of authority. Posidonius evidently knew and was interested in the way in which these people operated.[31] Posidonius was unquestionably in a position to give a more or less accurate account of Martha's rise in the world, but that may not have been how he conceived of his responsibilities as a historian. The value of his account as with that of Eunus may lie not so much in its strict historical accuracy as in its portrayal of a type known to the author.[32]

At the very end of the second century BC, the Roman general Marius took Martha with him on his campaigns against the Germanic tribes of the Cimbri and the Teutones.[33] He employed her predictions of victory to boost the morale of his troops. Her case is of particular interest because it illustrates, more clearly than does that of the possessed prophetess who accompanied Alexander, how such people wormed their way into the confidence of the famous and powerful and became part of their households. Martha's first move had been to try to gain entry to the Roman Senate to foretell the future for that body. Repulsed, she had taken herself to the women, presumably the wives of prominent men, and had in their presence given proof of her abilities. She had made a particular point of sitting by Marius' wife at gladiatorial games and predicting what the outcome of particular contests would be. Her success in this endeavour had persuaded Marius' wife to recommend the woman to her husband. Marius had taken her up. He gave her a litter to be carried around on, and whenever she bade him sacrifice, he did so. When she needed to participate in a sacrifice, she abandoned the litter and appeared wearing a crimson gown pinned at the shoulder and carrying a spear to which were tied fillets and wreathes. Plutarch says there was doubt in the minds of men whether Marius was acting in good faith or whether he was cynically playing along with the woman to put on a theatrical display.[34] The story, as Plutarch tells it, about the way in which Martha inveigled herself into Marius' good graces again, takes it for granted that women are particularly vulnerable to the approaches of holy men and women.

Martha is variously described in our sources as a prophetess (*mantis* – Plutarch), the devotee of a divinity (*sacricola* – Valerius Maximus) and as a wise woman or sorceress (*saga* – Frontinus). The different terms under which Martha is referred to do not signify any disagreement over who she was, but reflect the difficulty of finding any one expression to describe a wandering Syrian holy woman, apparently the acolyte of some deity and an inspired prophetess, who adapts to the circumstances of her new environment to exploit it with a certain theatricality for her own benefit and that of her patron. There is a further lesson to be drawn from this seeming terminological confusion: it is that there was in the minds of the Romans no sharp line of demarcation between the inspired prophetess and the sorceress or for that matter between quite uninspired prophets and sorcerers. If we look at what Frontinus, writing under the Flavians in the second half of the first century

AD, has to say about the woman, that becomes apparent: 'Marius had a *saga* from Syria, from whom he pretended to have foreknowledge of the outcome of military engagements.'[35] What to our eyes looks like a failure to mark a distinction may mean that persons calling themselves prophets would at the drop of a hat turn their hand to magic and that their ability to foresee the future was thought to be part of their magical powers.

There is one other inspired prophetess who attached herself to the commander of an army known from the Late Republic. She is the Thracian woman and compatriot of Spartacus, who lived with him and shared his adventures. The woman, whose name is never given, is said by Plutarch to have been a prophetess of the kind who becomes possessed through the mystery-rites of Dionysus. Her one recorded prophetic utterance, which was that there had been a sign that a great and fearful power would come to an unfortunate end, was certainly designed to encourage Spartacus and his followers to pursue their rebellion.[36] It is likely to be Posidonius who is the source of this story also.[37] If the details of the story are to be trusted, the woman will have been sufficiently hellenized to know how to exploit her Thracian origins to present herself as an inspired prophetess of Dionysus.

Marius is said to have been responsible for taking Martha with him on the campaign. That is as may be. What was certainly the case was that military campaigns attracted seers and religious experts along with other camp-followers such as pimps and prostitutes. Roman armies were in this respect no different from Hellenistic armies. In 134 BC, Scipio Aemilianus, confronted with indiscipline and poor morale in the force besieging Numantia in Spain, expelled from the camp all the merchants, prostitutes, seers (*manteis*) and *haruspices* (*thytai*) and forbade anyone to perform a sacrifice in future for divinatory purposes.[38]

One other report of a *saga* who is part of the household of a great man is to be found in the commentator on Horace, Porphyrion. In explaining who a sorceress called Sagana is, he remarks that he remembered reading in Helenius Acron that Sagana was a *saga* of Horace's time belonging to Pompeius, the senator whom the Triumvirs proscribed.[39] The Helenius Acron mentioned was also a commentator on Horace, but of an earlier vintage than Porphyrion. He seems to have lived under the Antonines. A good deal of the information that comes down to us about the identity of persons mentioned in Horace ultimately goes back to Acron.[40] Who the Pompeius was who was a senator and proscribed by the Triumvirs is a puzzle. He can hardly be the son of Pompeius Magnus, Sextus Pompeius, despite the tradition that Sextus dabbled in witchcraft.[41] Sextus was never a member of the Roman Senate. Porphyrion, in any case, refers to him as Sextus Pompeius and not merely as Pompeius. Whoever Pompeius is, he is a man of some standing who is said to possess his own *saga*. She appropriately takes her name from her calling. Precisely what is meant by saying that Sagana was the *saga* of Pompeius is not at all obvious: does it mean that Pompeius owned and used the woman as a *saga* or is something quite different to be understood? The very simple way in which the relationship is expressed and the case of Marius suggest that Pompeius kept the woman as his household *saga*. It is very difficult to know how much credence to place in the report and to what extent Acron's identifications are to be trusted. It is nonetheless hard to believe that Acron himself invented the whole story, which suggests that it goes back to a time closer to Horace's own day. That does not make it true, but it does make it more likely that it represents a reality of the late first century BC. It is certainly the case that at a somewhat later date there were in Rome rich men who had male magicians amongst their entourage. The cases of Martha and Sagana also rather strongly suggest that there were *sagae* in Rome in the Late Republic who were known personalities.

Early in the second century AD, Juvenal complains that Rome has been turned into a Greek city and that the Syrian Orontes – the river that flowed through the great Seleucid capital Antioch – ran into the Tiber.[42] The Syrian holy woman whom Marius takes up reminds us that the tide from the Orontes was already flowing into the Tiber in the late second century BC. The Greek East was not the only source of inspired prophetesses. To judge from the story of Spartacus' companion, others will have come from partly hellenized areas such as Thrace that were a major source of slaves. Religious life in Rome in the Late Republic will have had a rich diversity to it, which, because of the paucity of our sources for the period, it is all too easy to lose sight of.

### Learned magicians

Male magicians will have existed in Rome in the Late Republic. No trace of their presence survives, except in the form of the learned magician. His existence is quite well attested. Cicero tells us nothing about magic-working amongst the lower orders in Rome, but he does introduce us to three members of the senatorial class who took an interest in the occult. One of them we have met already, P. Vatinius, the second is a member of the patrician family of the Claudii, Appius Claudius Pulcher, consul in 54 BC, while the third is the polymath P. Nigidius Figulus. Cicero in his work on divination, speaking of various forms of fortune-telling whose intellectual legitimacy he does not acknowledge, mentions the consultation of the souls of the dead (*psychomantia*) and adds that Claudius was wont to practise it.[43] The summoning up of the souls of the dead was not a native Roman procedure; Cicero has to use a Greek word, *psychomantia*, to refer to it. By the time Claudius took up the practice the summoning of the souls of the dead had in the Greek world strong associations with magic-working. It is to be presumed that it brought these associations with it to Rome. Not so many years after Cicero wrote on divination, there is very good evidence that consulting the souls of the dead is considered a form of magic-working: one of the feats with which the elegiac poets credit *sagae* is calling up the dead.[44] Cicero mentions *psychomantia* alongside those who offer predictions by drawing lots (*sortilegi*) and those who practise inspired prophecy for gain (*harioli*), although he does imply that people place more credence in *psychomantia* than in these socially disreputable forms of divination. That Claudius should in this way have sought insights into what was otherwise hidden from mortal view is not altogether surprising. He was, after all, a man who was ridiculed by his fellow augurs in the College of Augurs for his credulity and superstitiousness: they called him the man from Sora and the Pisidian.[45] In calling him a Pisidian they alluded to the reputed devotion of the Pisidians, a people living in a remote region of southern Anatolia, to using the flight and cries of birds to predict the future.[46] The significance of their calling him a man from Sora is less clear, but it would seem to lie either in the reputation for magic-working that surrounded the Marsi to whose territory the town of Sora lay close or perhaps in their superstitious credulity. Cicero, at any rate, in the *On Divination* alludes to the credulity with which the Marsi greeted bird-signs, which suggests that they were a byword for their simple-minded faith.[47] A certain openness on Claudius' part to what from the Roman point of view must still have constituted exotic religious experiences is suggested by his erecting a propylaeum at Eleusis and by his consulting the Delphic oracle at a time at which it barely functioned.[48] The propylaeum at Eleusis almost certainly points to initiation into the mysteries. Claudius wrote a book on augury, probably with a strongly antiquarian flavour to it. The interest that the man took in necromancy is of a piece with these other activities. He is the first example from Rome or for that matter from anywhere else, although it is to be presumed that Claudius had predecessors in the Hellenistic East, of a well-to-do man who dabbled in magic and the occult arts whom we have encountered. Such persons were very different from the sorcerers and witches who made a living from magic-working or who used it to supplement their income. Nor again is he to be placed in the same category as the compilers of magical lore about plants, animals, fishes and stones. Claudius belongs to a class of persons not only inclined by temperament to believe that there is a hidden scheme of things waiting to be uncovered that will give them a key to the manipulation of nature, but also prepared to put their beliefs into practice.

So far as we know, Claudius did not try to fit his religious convictions into any overarching philosophical system and there is no hint of any interest in Pythagoreanism in our sources. There are, however, two prominent figures in the Late Republic in whom an interest in the occult seems to have gone hand-in-hand with Pythagoreanism. One of these has already been encountered. He is the Caesarian, Vatinius, who reached the consulship in 48 BC under the aegis of his patron. The other is P. Nigidius Figulus, praetor in 58 BC, a man strongly opposed to Caesar. Nigidius died in 45 BC in exile from Caesar's Rome. Caesar, to judge from Cicero, was irreconcilably set against

Nigidius' return.[49] Despite their political differences, Vatinius and Nigidius were united in their interest in Pythagoreanism. An ancient commentator on Cicero even implies that Vatinius was one of those who were drawn to Nigidius because of his Pythagoreanism.[50]

We hear of Vatinius' Pythagoreanism from Cicero, who mentions it in the speech that in 56 BC he delivered against Vatinius: he says that he wishes to ask Vatinius, who is in the habit of calling himself a Pythagorean and of using Pythagoras' name to cloak his monstrous and barbarous ways, how he could be so depraved or mad as to ignore auspices taken by members of the College of Augurs, after having engaged in rites of an unparalleled wickedness, after having summoned up the spirits of the dead and after having sacrificed boys to the *Di Manes* of the Underworld.[51] The implication of this is that the wicked and sacrilegious rites, the summoning up of the dead and the sacrifice of boys were all done under the guise of Pythagoreanism. The ancient commentary on the speech says that Cicero in the speech he delivered two years later in defence of Vatinius made a very full job of clearing Vatinius of these charges, defended him on that score and even praised him for his Pythagoreanism.[52] That means that in the *Pro Vatinio* Cicero must have dealt with Vatinius' Pythagoreanism, explained and defended it and showed that whatever it was Vatinius did *qua* Pythagorean was laudable. Later in the speech against Vatinius Cicero turns the black toga that Vatinius affected as a Pythagorean against him and suggests that Vatinius' wearing it at a banquet on a public religious holiday and on entering the temple of Castor has some sinister political meaning to it.[53] We learn from the commentator on the *In Vatinium* that in the *Pro Vatinio* Cicero had maintained that the black toga was a symbol of Vatinius' devotion to a harmless brand of Pythagoreanism.[54] The adage that there is no smoke without fire must be used with some caution in assessing what speakers in the Late Roman Republic have to say about their political opponents. It certainly looks as if an allegiance to Pythagoreanism might be seized on by those who were not well disposed towards a man as *prima facie* evidence of an interest in the occult. Vatinius' known Pythagoreanism, accordingly, laid him open to the charge that he engaged in necromancy. It was a short step from there to suggesting that Vatinius' necromancy took the especially heinous form of consulting the spirits of young boys who had been ritually sacrificed.[55] It is impossible to say whether Vatinius' Pythagoreanism did encompass necromancy, but in view of his associations with Nigidius Figulus it is likely enough that his Pythagoreanism was not free of the taint of magic.

Nigidius Figulus was after Varro probably the most learned figure of the Late Republic. His learning like that of Varro had a strongly antiquarian and nationalistic bent to it. In his writings he covered very much the same areas as Varro. There was a lengthy work, the *Commentarii grammatici*, on the Latin language and one on gesture in oratory (*De gestu*), accounts of human physiology (*De hominum natura*) and of animals (*De animalibus*) and a book on meteorology (*De vento*). Nigidius had a particular interest in ways of predict-ing the future: there was a work on augury (*De augurio privato*); one that prob-ably dealt with the Etruscan discipline of divining from entrails (*De extis*); and finally, an astrological work (*De sphaera*). His concern with the divine shows itself in a long and encyclopaedic work on the gods (*De deis*).

Cicero, who was on friendly terms with Nigidius but who seems to have had reservations about the direction taken by Nigidius' inquiries into nature, says in the preface to his translation of the *Timaeus* that Nigidius was responsible for reviving Pythagoreanism, after it had become extinct.[56] It was a pretty, though not perhaps wholly accurate, compliment to pay to Nigidius' memory in the preface to the most Pythagorean of all Plato's works, but in the way in which Cicero introduces Nigidius to us there is a hint of some-thing amiss. He begins generously enough saying that Nigidius was equipped in all of the liberal arts, but it is what he says next that causes disquiet: Nigidius was a keen and diligent searcher after that which nature keeps veiled.[57] That is a somewhat ambiguous way of describing the man. There is just a suggestion in the characterization of someone who searched after what was forbidden. Cicero gives expression in the *On Divination* to his own view of how the mysteries kept veiled by nature should be handled. There, in speak-ing of physical prodigies and happenings that presage the future, he declares that he refuses to look into what lies behind them, on the ground that the cause stays hidden, veiled by the obscuring force of nature, since the divine does not wish men to know the cause of prodigies and significant happen-ings, but only to use them.[58] Cicero's description of Nigidius' activities comes, accordingly, very close to saying, although in the politest possible way, that Nigidius delved into the occult.

Jerome in his notice on Nigidius' death in 45 BC is more straightforward: he calls him a Pythagorean and magician.[59] The ancient commentator on the *In Vatinium* was aware of the same tradition: he says that spiteful detractors derided those who flocked to Nigidius' side as a disreputable gang, although the men so characterized liked to think of themselves as the sectaries of Pythagoras.[60] The ancient sources hint at Nigidius' magic-working, but do not say what it amounted to. There is one exception: Apuleius in the speech in which he defended himself on a charge of magic brings up as an example of the employment of boys for magical divination the boys who were able, after Nigidius had uttered an incantation over them, to find five hundred denarii that had gone missing; they pointed out where some of the coins had been buried and to where the remainder had found their way.[61] How much weight should be placed on the anecdote is hard to say. The story certainly testifies to Nigidius' reputation as not just a man learned in the lore of sor-cery, but as one who had some practical expertise in it.

The precise nature and extent of Nigidius' magical activities can never be known, but it is possible to recover something of what he had to say on the subject. Jerome's description of Nigidius as a *magus* and Pythagorean need mean no more than that Nigidius collected magical lore. It need not mean that Nigidius actively practised magic. Pliny the Elder cites Nigidius on a number of occasions alongside the collective authority to which he refers as the *Magi*.[62] According to Pliny, Nigidius ascribed great power to the cricket and the *Magi* greater still, since it walks backwards, bores into the ground and screeches during the night.[63] After having discussed the apotropaic and curative powers with which the *Magi* credit ticks plucked from the ears of dogs, Pliny adds that Nigidius left amongst his writings the story that dogs will avoid for a whole day the sight of a man who has extracted a tick from a pig.[64] Pliny now goes on to relate what the *Magi* have to say about sprinkling the blood of a mole on a demented person and what they teach about the calming effect that a concoction made from the tongue, eyes, gall and innards of a snake has on those driven mad by nocturnal deities and Fauns. Finally, in the course of some chapters devoted to the teaching of the *Magi* on amulets to be made from snakes and on cures for snake-bite, Pliny tells us that Nigidius took the position that a snake by a necessity of nature returns to the victim it has struck.[65]

It is probably not just a question of the *Magi*'s and Nigidius' having had similar views on the magical properties of ticks and crickets, but of Nigidius' having read the *Magi* and of his having cited them in his own writings, adding to what they had said and sometimes qualifying it. There is in the commentary of the late fourth century AD by the grammarian Servius on the *Eclogues* of Vergil a passage that goes some way towards corroborating the hypothesis that Nigidius had read the *Magi*: Servius quotes a passage from Nigidius' *De Deis* in which Nigidius cites the *Magi* as an authority for the thesis that there would some day be a reign of Apollo in which there was a danger of a general conflagration taking place.[66]

Whom Nigidius understood the *Magi* to be is not an easy or straightforward question to answer. To judge from Pliny the Elder, Pythagoras and Democritus might be spoken of as *Magi*. Pliny speaks of them in this way apparently because they are imagined to transmit the magical lore of the Persian *Magi*. In other words, Pythagoras and Democritus become identified with the people whose mouthpiece they were believed to be. It is a fair guess that the source of much of the magical material assembled by Nigidius was Bolus of Mendes. Nigidius, in sum, belongs to the tradition of Pythagoreans who take a learned interest in magic. He will have been one of the conduits by which the body of magical lore collected by Bolus was translated into Latin and became naturalized in Italy.

Under the year 28 BC Jerome reports the expulsion from Rome and Italy by Augustus of the Pythagorean and *magus*, Anaxilaus of Larissa.[67] How long Anaxilaus had been in Rome before he was expelled is not known. Thessaly and its largest city Larissa were traditionally the breeding ground of magicians. Whether it is pure chance that Anaxilaus was from that city and developed an interest in magic we have no means of ascertaining, but there is always the possibility that he adopted Larissa as his birthplace to give himself an appropriate *nom de guerre*. What is positively known about the man is that he put together a collection of spells of an amusing character such as would entertain those present at a drinking-party. They were like the *Tricks* of Democritus called by the Greek name of *Paignia*. Irenaeus, Bishop of Lugdunum (Lyon) in the latter half of the second century AD, accuses the Gnostic heresiarch Marcus of using conjuring-tricks from the *Paignia* of Anaxilaus to impress his followers.[68] One of the tricks Marcus is said by Irenaeus to have performed was that of making the cups of wine over which he was saying Grace appear red or purple, as though the Grace (*Charis*) of Christ had entered the cups in response to his appeal. The other trick that Irenaeus accuses Marcus of practising was that of filling a larger cup to overflowing from a smaller vessel. Another still later Christian source written in Latin speaks of tricks of Anaxilaus that make fire appear to dance above water.[69] Pliny the Elder attributes to Anaxilaus four tricks for deceiving the senses.[70] Three of them are certainly meant to be party-tricks performed at symposia. One of them was to put the ink of a cuttlefish on a lamp-wick to make those present look as though they were Ethiopians.[71] Another was to burn the discharge from a mare in heat in a lamp, so as to cause the heads of horses to appear to those present.[72] Finally, there was the trick that made those attending a symposium look as though they were dead: some sulphur was added to a cup of wine below which was a piece of burning coal; the cup was then carried around the company; when the sulphur flared, a deadly pallor was cast on those present.[73] Pliny in fact describes the last device as another of the tricks of Anaxilaus.[74] That means that by Pliny's time Anaxilaus' collection of what were essentially conjuring-tricks was circulating under the title of *Paignia*. It is virtually certain that Anaxilaus will have given that title to his work. There is one further recipe that Pliny ascribes to Anaxilaus: to keep the breasts of a woman from sagging they should from maidenhood onwards be rubbed with hemlock.[75] It is just conceivable that the recipe for keeping the breasts of a woman firm was included in the *Paignia*, since it was thought of as more of a trick than a serious medical prescription.

Anaxilaus was clearly not the kind of magician to be found at the crossroads or marking time at a shrine of Isis in the hope that someone would approach him there to consult him. He will have presented himself as a Pythagorean and will have displayed the outward trappings of membership in the sect, the black cloak and linen garments and shoes. It is frustrating that we know nothing of the philosophy of those Pythagoreans like Anaxilaus with a leaning towards the occult. All that can be said of Anaxilaus is that he represents a version of Pythagoreanism that goes back at least to Bolus of Mendes and almost certainly further. Anaxilaus' expulsion not only from Rome but also from Italy in 28 BC in the year in which the new Augustan dispensation came into place suggests that his activities went rather beyond putting together a collection of conjuring-tricks designed to amuse the guests at a symposium, but what he had been doing is a mystery. The puzzle is in no way lessened by the fact that since he wrote in Greek, only a limited number of persons can have had access to his work.

Men such as Nigidius Figulus and Anaxilaus will have been responsible for the dissemination in Rome and in the larger Latin-speaking West of a good deal of the magical lore that had previously only been available in Greek. Their principal audience will have been those members of the educated classes with a taste for the marvellous. The story that Irenaeus tells about the heresiarch, Marcus, using conjuring-tricks drawn from the *Paignia* of Anaxilaus to fool his followers cannot be accepted as evidence that Anaxilaus' tricks eventually found their way into the hands of real magic-workers to be exploited to good effect by them. The most common accusation made against members of heretical Christian groups is that they resort to magic to impress people into casting their lot with them. No great weight can for that reason be placed on such accusations. It is still possible that some learned magical lore, especially tricks drawn from Anaxilaus' *Paignia*, did become part of the repertoire of magicians in Rome and the West, but since no magical handbooks have survived from the Latin West and are unlikely ever to be found, the supposition can be no more than speculation.

There is a figure with whom the learned magician merges imperceptibly who needs to be considered before we turn away from the magic-workers of the Late Republic. He is the man from the upper reaches of society who either always has a magician at hand or who consults magicians with some frequency. Intimations of his existence are to be found in the stories told about Marius and Pompeius. It also looks as if Sextus Pompeius, the son of Pompey the Great, was, if not an example of the type, at any rate accused of being just such a person. The *tour de force* that Lucan performs in portraying the necromancy of the Thessalian witch Erichtho has drawn a lot of attention, but the part that Sextus Pompeius plays in the proceedings has not been subjected to quite the same degree of scrutiny. It is after all Sextus who initiates the necromantic ritual: he goes to Erichtho to learn what the outcome of the battle that looms at Pharsalus between the forces supporting his father and those of Julius Caesar will be and what fate lies in store for himself. The explanation that the poet provides for Sextus' seeking of information from such a source is that Sextus had never been content with legitimate means of divination, but had known the secrets loathed by the gods above of cruel magicians (*magi*), baleful altars on which funereal rites had been performed and the deliverances of the shades and of the god of the Underworld.[76] Put in more prosaic terms this means that Sextus had engaged in magic and in particular the form of necromancy that required the sacrifice of young boys. He is being tarred with precisely the same brush with which Cicero had tarred Vatinius. The freshly-killed corpse who is summoned back to life to offer information on what will happen at Pharsalus refuses to tell

Sextus what awaits him, but predicts that when Sextus is in Sicily, the ghost of his father will tell him what lies before him.[77] That suggests that Lucan had conceived of a *De Bello Civili* in which Sextus, while in Sicily, was to engage in a second act of necromancy and summon the ghost of his father from the dead. The idea that Sextus was a necromancer is unlikely to be Lucan's invention, but will belong to the tradition surrounding Sextus. It will have had its origins in the very negative way in which Sextus was portrayed by writers favourable to those who were opposed to him. Whether there was any substance to the charges made against Sextus does not greatly matter. What counts is that it made sense to Sextus' contemporaries that he should be depicted in such a light; they could readily believe that a man from the ruling classes would spend his time with magicians and be addicted to the practice of magic.

## Sorceresses in Rome and Italy in the Early Empire

### *Preliminaries*

With the expulsion of Anaxilaus from Rome in 28 BC the learned magician with philosophical pretensions disappears from view for a time, only to re-emerge later in the reign of Tiberius. Something is then known about learned magic under the Early Empire, but our sources have very little to say about ordinary working male magicians in this period. There can be no doubt that such men existed, but for a variety of reasons they do not surface in the literature of the age. The person who engages the attention of the literary world is the sorceress. In consequence, a good deal can be learned about who she was and what she did. It is then because of the nature of our sources that we hear so much more about the sorceress than we do about the male magician in the first century of the Roman Empire. It is nonetheless likely that there were more female practitioners of magic than male. Quintilian speaks of a presumption that men will thieve and women will engage in sorcery.[78] Pliny the Elder puts the same point in a slightly different form in speaking of popular beliefs about magic: the great mass of people are as firmly convinced that plants and drugs have the capacity to effect changes in the sun and the moon as they are that this is the one area of expertise in which women are predominant.[79] That the prejudice had a basis in fact may be seen in the proportion of sorcerers to sorceresses arrested and punished in the city of Rome under Tiberius: forty-five sorcerers to eighty-five sorceresses.[80]

The figure of the sorceress plays a prominent rôle in Horace, in his *Epodes* and *Satires*, in the three Roman love-elegists, Tibullus, Propertius and Ovid, in Petronius' picaresque novel, the *Satyricon*, and in the epigrams of Martial. The elegiac poets present themselves as resigned to having to live with the *sagae* who are part of the world that their girlfriends inhabit without being fully convinced there is anything to the magic the women claim to be able to perform. Propertius calls on those who pretend to be able to pull the moon down from the sky and who perform sacrifices at magic hearths to change the mind of his mistress and make her pale at the sight of him. If they can do that, he says, he will believe their pretensions to be able to alter the direction of the stars and rivers by means of Thessalian spells.[81] The implication of this is that he does not believe that sorceresses are capable of doing what they say they can. Ovid rather half-heartedly contemplates the possibility that magic of some sort may be responsible for his impotence and that a *saga* may have carried out a binding-spell against him.[82] The same poet rejects out of hand any suggestion that the loss of hair his girlfriend has suffered may have been caused by plants over which incantations had been sung or by the Thessalian water in which a perfidious old woman had washed the girl's hair.[83] In the *Ars amatoria*, Ovid says that those who have recourse to magic to win the love of a girl delude themselves; the only way to a girl's heart is to be lovable.[84] Finally, Tibullus tells his girl that a *saga* has composed incantations for him that will keep the partner of the girl from recognizing her infidelity, even if the evidence of it is immediately in front of his eyes.[85] Yet the question that the poet now asks himself betrays a lack of confidence in what the *saga* has told him: he asks whether he is to give any credence to any of what he has been told.[86]

The sorceresses of poetry are consistently portrayed as old, drunken and as often as not as procuresses. The question of the relationship of this picture to reality needs to be addressed. The possibility that the Roman sorceress is nothing more than a creation of the literary imagination is a source of concern. It is not only the sorceress who must be suspect but the whole world to which she belongs. In Roman love-elegy it is a *demi-monde* made up of prostitutes (*meretrices*) and procuresses (*lenae*) and of well-to-do young men who have nothing better to do with themselves than to have affairs with prostitutes. The prostitutes may be in love with the young men, in which case their mothers or their protectors and procuresses will warn them against putting all of their eggs in one basket and in placing any trust in the fickleness of a lover. The young men for their part may be in a state of despair, because the prostitutes with whom they have become infatuated have deserted them for a richer lover. This world of love bears a marked resemblance to the situations portrayed in Theocritus' Second Idyll and in Herodas' First Mime. It is also in large agreement with the world of love in Greek New Comedy and in its Roman adaptations by Plautus and Terence, although it lacks both the angry old fathers anxious to keep their sons from being trapped by prostitutes and wicked and cruel panders. Because the characters of this world are stock literary figures, it is easy to jump to the conclusion that it corresponds to nothing in Roman reality and that it is all an amusing literary exercise. If that is true, Roman elegy cannot be used as a source of information about the life of love in Rome, let alone about the sorceresses who frequent that world. At best we can use it to fill out our picture of sorcery in the Hellenistic Greek world.

A powerful case has been made against the legitimacy of that inference, resting on the recognition that Rome was by the Late Republic in many ways indistinguishable in its institutions and mores from a Hellenistic Greek city.[87] The life of luxury as lived in Rome was not very different from that to be found in Athens or Alexandria. The picture that the Roman elegists paint of the life of love is indeed shaped by literature but it is not a fantasy of the literary imagination. What is missing is a good deal of the sordidness and violence. The drunken fights outside brothels are allowed no place. The mercenary nature of the relationship of the young man with the prostitute is never in the forefront of the picture and is only alluded to when the prostitute leaves him for a richer lover. We hear nothing of the premises in which the sexual encounters take place, where they were and who owned them. The unappealing figure of the brothel-keeper is suppressed. The vulgar abuse that irritated prostitutes rained on the heads of those whom they scorned has no place in this idealized and stylized world.

In Roman elegy, accordingly, we have to do a certain amount of reading between the lines to get to the reality that lies behind the stylized picture of the life of love. Horace, on the other hand, in his *Epodes* and *Satires* portrays the life of love and luxury in more realistic colours and adds touches of local detail. Ovid in his account in verse of the Roman calendar, the *Fasti*, in his work on the art of love, the *Ars amatoria*, and in his renunciation of that work, the *Remedium amoris*, gives us vignettes of Roman life that throw light on the less glamorous aspects of prostitution and procuring. Petronius describes in sordid detail the escapades of some young men in the cities of Southern Italy.

Besides these authors, there is another source of information about prostitution and sorcery in Rome: the minor and major declamations ascribed to Quintilian. The so-called minor declamations appear to be the lecture notes of a teacher of rhetoric.[88] There were originally three hundred and eighty-eight of these. Only the last one hundred and forty-four have survived. They consist in examples of orations illustrating what could be said in an imaginary lawsuit or what could be said in a public assembly about an issue and of notes made by the teacher on how the case or issue was to be presented. If this body of material does not come from the pen of Quintilian himself, it was certainly written by somebody who had read long and deeply in Quintilian.[89] It is to be dated, if not to the late first century AD, to some time in the second century AD. The so-called major declamations are mostly on forensic themes and are just declamations. They are definitely not by Quintilian. There are no very good pointers to the date at which they were composed. They were in existence by the late fourth century AD and seem already to have been circulating under Quintilian's name at that date.

It is the declamations to be delivered in lawsuits in which someone is accused of having given a love-potion or a potion designed to engender hatred that principally concern us. It cannot be assumed without further ado that such declamations reflect a reality. For one thing the lawsuits in them are very often the product of the ingenuity of the teacher of rhetoric. One of them has a pimp suing a lover for the loss he has incurred because one of his girls had fallen in love with the lover after the lover had given her a love-phil-tre.[90] Another presents an impoverished lover suing a prostitute who has given him a potion designed to make him hate her, so that she may get him off her hands.[91] Secondly, the speakers appeal to stock images to make their case. The stereotypes on which they draw may well have been formed in part by Roman love-elegy or by Plautus and Terence, but since it was teenage boys who were expected to compose the declamations, they must also have had to draw, if not on their own experience, at least on common lore about prosti-tutes, their lovers and their ways. That this collection of beliefs was com-pletely divorced from reality defies belief.

### The prostitute as witch

It would hardly be wise to believe everything that the Romans have to say about prostitutes. It is nonetheless interesting that the litigant in one of the declamations ascribed to Quintilian tells the judges, if they wish to learn whether the woman being tried had indeed administered a harmful potion, that they should take a look at the circumstances of her life. The condition of life that he hopes will prove the woman to be guilty is that she is a prostitute. The speaker puts the matter more forcefully: 'The whole life of a prostitute is *veneficium.*'[92] He proceeds to elaborate on the aphorism: prostitutes, since they cannot rely on pandering, lies and the attention they lavish on their bodies to succeed in taking men's minds by assault, have both by day and by night to devote their energies to *veneficium* to ensure that men's lusts are channeled in the right direction and to keep their desires from departing elsewhere. The judges are at this point asked whether they imagine the woman does not know how to master the eyes and how to destroy minds burning with desire when she certainly knows how to break up the passionate kisses and embraces of lovers.[93] A little later in the speech the litigant returns to the same theme: the prostitute has devised a *venenum* that separates hus-bands from the affections of their wives and young men from the clutches of other prostitutes.[94] The argument, in brief, is that since the woman is a prosti-tute, she can be expected to know what potions will attract a man, which ones will keep his affections from wandering and finally, what potions can drive husband and wife apart and separate a young man from another prostitute. What may fairly be concluded is that there was a presumption that if a woman was a prostitute, she was probably expert in the whole gamut of erotic magic. That does not mean that every prostitute without exception was suspected of practising magic, but only that magic-working was believed to be endemic amongst prostitutes.

In Horace's portrayal of the witch Canidia there is a good deal to be learned about the prostitute as sorceress. There are three poems in which

Canidia is the central figure, *Epodes* 5 and 17 and *Satire* 1.8; passing reference is made to her in three other poems of Horace.[95] *Epode* 5 describes Canidia's burying alive in the floor of her dwelling a young boy of good family by covering him up to his neck, so that she might use his famished liver to win back a lover who has deserted her and on whom less powerful spells have had no effect. In *Epode* 17, the last poem of the book of *Epodes*, Horace recants the ill that he has spoken of Canidia and begs her to desist from her sorcery against him. The speaker in *Satire* 1.8 is a wooden statue of Priapus set on the Esquiline Hill, where the bodies of the poor were buried. He describes Canidia and her fellow-witch Sagana performing a necromantic sacrifice to summon up the spirits of the dead to seek answers from them and their carrying out a binding-spell with the help of wax dolls. It has to be conceded that Horace cannot refrain from imparting a certain literary colouring to the speeches made by Canidia both in *Epode* 5 and 17 that seems implausible, even in an especially talented courtesan: in *Epode* 5, Canidia complains that the magical substances used by Medea to impregnate the cloak that burned Creon's daughter up have not worked for her;[96] in the other poem, she compares the likelihood of her releasing the poet from the spell with which she tortures him to that of Juppiter's setting Tantalus, Prometheus or Sisyphus free.[97] It does not follow that because the influence of the rhetorical schools is to be discerned in the speeches made by Canidia that the basic theme of *Epode* 5 should be discounted, which is a deserted prostitute trying through magic to regain the affections of her lover, or that of *Epode* 17, which is the vindictiveness of a prostitute who has been mocked. It is very hard for a Roman poet to surmount his initial training in rhetoric. Sometimes that training stands him in good stead, but on other occasions it lets him down.

Who is Canidia as Horace presents her? She is first and foremost a prostitute, but more specifically a prostitute of the kind who has formed a relationship of some permanence with one or more men that provides her with the wherewithal to live. She refers to herself at one point as a *paelex*, a word that derives from the Greek *pallakē*.[98] A *pallakē* is essentially a kept woman as against a common prostitute. The magic to which Canidia has recourse in *Epodes* 5 and 17 is magic performed in her own interest, in the one case to bring a lover back, and in the other to gain revenge. To the particularly horrendous act of magic that she performs to bring her errant lover back to her, starving a boy to death to use his famished liver in a love-philtre, she is driven by the actions of a more skilled *venefica* who has anointed the bedchamber of her lover to make him forget her.[99] Whether the other *venefica* is a rival or someone employed by a rival Canidia does not say. In *Epode* 5, she is already as a prostitute on her way downhill. That inference is to be drawn from the prayer she addresses to Night and Diana: may they turn their wrath against the house of her enemy and may the bitches of Subura, when all wild beasts lie asleep, bark at the old adulterer, so that everybody may laugh at him.[100] What this means is that Canidia's elderly lover has deserted her for the common prostitutes who frequent the low-lying area between the Viminal and Esquiline Hills. *Epode* 17 makes Canidia's age and lack of charms and what that means for her career more explicit: her youth has deserted her, sallow skin clothes her bones and her hair is white; her customers are hucksters and sailors.[101] Age has reduced her, in other words, from something approaching a courtesan to the lowest form of prostitution.

Porphyrion, in commenting on the identity of Canidia, says that under the name of Canidia is to be understood a Neapolitan unguent-maker called Gratidia whom Horace was always attacking as a witch (*venefica*); he did not attack her under her own name, since it was illegal to write scurrilous poetry; he therefore followed the practice of other poets in concocting a name similar to the real name; the name Vergil gives Cytheris, Lycoris, in the *Eclogues* is an instance of the custom.[102] The commentator, accordingly, assumes that behind Canidia there is a real person and that Horace employs the practice, also used by the Roman elegiac poets, of giving the women of whom they wrote a pseudonym of the same metrical pattern as the real name. It is likely that his information goes back to Helenius Acron. Part of the identification is probably suspect; it looks as though it rests on a misunderstanding of something Canidia herself says in the poem, which is that her former elderly lover is anointed with an unguent that even she could not surpass.[103] Since salves and unguents were very much part of the business of a magician, Canidia might well only be referring to her facility in the preparation of magical ointments. As for her Neapolitan origins, Acron may have inferred that she was from Naples, because Naples is said to have known something of the activities of another of Canidia's helpers.[104] It is difficult to believe, however, that Acron can have invented the name Gratidia. Acron may then somehow or other have had access to a tradition that Canidia was really a known person called Gratidia. That does not take us very far. We have, accordingly, to fall back on such scraps of information that can be wrung out of Horace himself. Of Canidia's identity and origins Horace has nothing other to say than to deny in his recantation that she is worn out and reduced to the sordid condition of her father.[105] This is unfortunately not a very precise way of describing the background of the woman, but suggests that a man whose station in life is that of the hucksters and the sailors who now use her services had begotten her. We would know more about her lot in life had we been told who her mother was, but perhaps it is implied that the mother was some old drab like herself. Although the origins that Horace imputes to Canidia are of the most sordid kind, this does not keep him from crediting her with the ability to read: when he begs Canidia to desist from her magic, he invokes in his prayer Proserpina, Diana and the books of incantations that have the power to call the stars down from the sky.[106] There are complications in using the scraps of information provided by Horace in conjunction with what is to be learned from Porphyrion about Canidia to draw a composite portrait. The principal difficulty is that if Canidia is indeed a real person for whom Horace did not care, then he is as likely as not attempting to blacken her name, which means that what we have in front of us is to all intents and purposes an invective with all of the problems that an invective presents for those who seek the truth. If it is an invective, it will nonetheless represent a reality of a kind: Gratidia cast in the rôle of prostitute and sorceress.

Canidia has in *Epode* 5 three helpers, Sagana, Veia and Folia. There is a fair chance that Sagana is a known *saga*. Her rôle in the proceedings is to sprinkle the house with water from a river of the Underworld to purify it; she is dressed as witches are supposed to dress for such ceremonies: her gown has no belt holding it in at the waist, her hair flows unchecked and she is barefooted.[107] Veia's task is to dig the trench into which the boy is to be placed; she is a woman whose criminality knows no bounds.[108] Her name suggests that she is from Etruria, but Folia is the only one of the trio about whom the poet provides any personal details: she comes from Ariminum and was believed by the inhabitants of Naples and the surrounding towns to have had a man-like passion for other women. She is expert at pulling the stars and the moon down from the skies using Thessalian incantations.[109] Folia comes from modern-day Rimini, which was in Horace's time an important porttown near Venice. She had found her way to the area of the Bay of Naples, where she had been a prostitute of some specialized sort. She is obviously now supposed to be in Rome.

Although Horace only portrays Canidia practising magic on her own behalf, we are almost certainly not meant to suppose that that was the extent of her sorcery. Her possessing magical books and Horace's reported jibe in *Epode* 17 at her being the High Priest of Esquiline Sorcery suggest otherwise.[110] She also speaks of the *venefica* whose incantations and salves have kept her lover from her as a more knowledgeable *venefica*, which suggests that she also thinks of herself as a sorceress.[111] Furthermore, as a *venefica* Canidia practised both sorcery and poisoning: in *Epode* 3, a poem on the ill effects that eating garlic has had on the poet, Horace suggests that the offending meal may have been a poisoned feast prepared by Canidia.[112] Canida, accordingly, represents the aging prostitute who has turned or is turning herself into a sorceress and who has acquired or inherited books of spells as one of the tools of her trade. The world she inhabits is one in which she has to defend herself against the magic-working of rivals. She operates very often in conjunction with other women of her kind. Her possessing books of spells suggests that she can read.

### The procuress as witch

One of the minor declamations ascribed to Quintilian deals with the case of a pimp or brothel-keeper (*leno*) who is suing a young man for a loss he has incurred: his maid-servant (*ancilla*) had been given a love-philtre by the young man and has, in consequence, fallen in love with him.[113] Very little survives of the declamation, but there is a fascinating collection of notes on topics that the students given the theme to speak on might develop. One of them offers help on what a speaker taking the part of the young man might say, if the accuser were to ask him why he gave the girl the love-potion. It is suggested that he say that unhappy men very often attempt what is not particularly reasonable; in his case what happened was that an old woman (*anus*) had come up to him when he was in a dejected state and had shown him the love-potion; he, before he administered the potion, had drunk it himself to make sure that it did no harm.[114] If we can place any weight on the advice that Ovid gives young men in the *Ars amatoria*, administering love-philtres to the persons the poet calls girls (*puellae*), but who were in fact prostitutes, was just one of the things that young Roman males got up to when they felt that their hold on a girl was diminishing. Ovid tells young men not to turn to magic in the hope that an incantation will enable them to retain the affections of a girl: it will be of no avail, since it just does not work.[115] Next he warns against the use of potions: love-philtres given to girls will be of no benefit; they cause harm to the mind and result in madness.[116] We do not, however, have to believe that young men who had a hangdog look about them were regularly approached by old women offering them love-potions. They must nonetheless have got the love-philtres from someone and must have known where they were available. What does call for comment is the easy assumption that there were old women with love-potions to offer. The teacher feels no need to explain who she is. It is apparent that he can take her existence for granted. Her identity presents us with something more of a puzzle. Who can the old woman be who has love-philtres in her possession?

In trying to track her down we shall transfer our attentions from the aging prostitute and sorceress Canidia to the procuress who is a sorceress. What that in effect means is that the focus of our attention is now on the rôle that Canidia will eventually fill. The *lena* is a figure who has a large part to play in Roman love-elegy. The elegists do not explain who the *lenae* of the girls they love are and where they come from. We have to turn to Plautus for that information. It is for a number of reasons unlikely that the *lena* of Plautus is a figure transferred lock, stock and barrel from Greek New Comedy and that she had no counterpart in the Roman world. There is also no very good reason to suppose that matters had changed much in this area between the time of Plautus and Augustan Rome. In Plautus' plays, the *lena* takes a variety of forms; in *Curculio*, she is an old woman who is the gate-keeper for the pander (*leno*) who keeps the maiden Planasium in his house;[117] in *Asinaria*, she is the mother of the *meretrix*;[118] the *lenae* in *Cistellaria* are respectively the mother and supposed mother of the *meretrices*;[119] she is the maid-servant of the *meretrices* in *Mostellaria*, *Persa* and *Truculentulus*.

From *Cistellaria* we get an insight into the social and economic standing of these women and how they came to be what they were: the *lenae* in *Cistellaria* became *meretrices* because they were freedwomen; their daughters were the products of their encounters with men; the motive behind the prostitution of one of these daughters is that her mother should be able to eat.[120] In *Asinaria*, the *lena* cannot afford to allow her daughter to have a love affair and have no other clients, since that would spell starvation for the family.[121] In *Mostellaria*, Scapha, the maid-servant and *lena*, warns her mistress against placing too much faith in one lover; her own bitter experience in being deserted by a lover when she grew too old should be a warning to her mistress.[122]

The curses that disappointed lovers call down on the heads of *lenae* who thwart them, or look as if they will, also provide an indication of the sort of world from which these women are believed to have emerged and was thought always to be around the corner. It was a life of rags, hunger, coldness and poverty. In *Mostellaria*, Philolaches curses Scapha with a death caused by thirst, hunger and cold, significantly in that order.[123] In *Asinaria*, Argyrippus, whom the *lena* Cleareta has kept from Philaenium, because he has spent all of his money, prays that Cleareta and Philaenium may be reduced to the extremes of poverty in which they had formerly existed: destitute, having only rags to wear and filthy bread to eat.[124] The *lena* is then an impoverished old woman whose sole resource is the income she derives from the *meretrix* or *meretrices* she looks after or a woman who has been reduced to being the maid-servant and *lena* of a prostitute. She herself will often have been a prostitute and the prostitute she lives off may well be her daughter.

The *lena* who is a sorceress or *saga* appears in a number of poems by Tibullus, Propertius and Ovid that are built around the theme of the dislike felt by the poet for the *lena* who has advised his girl to seek a richer lover. The *lena* argues that there is nothing to be gained from having a poet as lover. For the purposes of the present inquiry the most striking feature of the poems is the presumption that the *lena* engages in magic-working. Ovid gives the most elaborate and conventional account of the attainments in sorcery of the *lena* responsible for his discomfiture, the accomplishments of Propertius' *lena* are scarcely less remarkable, while Tibullus alludes only obliquely to the sorcery of his *lena* in the curse that he pronounces on her.[125] The sorcery of these women goes well beyond the practice of erotic magic and extends into necromancy, effecting changes in the weather and, in the case of Tibullus' *lena*, poisoning.[126] Dipsas, in addition, employs astrological arguments in attempting to persuade Ovid's girl to abandon him for a rich lover.[127] It is true that she did not need to possess any very profound knowledge of astrology to say that when Mars was in the ascendant, conditions were unfavourable for the match, but since Venus had replaced him, matters were more auspicious.[128] That a *saga* is credited with having any knowledge of astrology at all and that she should deploy it in making her case is interesting and is an indication that astrology will very often have been bound up with the practice of magic. The presumption that procuring goes hand-in-hand with sorcery is also to be found in an elegant epigram by Martial on a woman called Philaenis, who had died at a great age: the poet, affecting to mourn her passing and her chattering tongue's falling silent, asks who now will know how to draw the moon down from the sky with a Thessalian wheel and what procuress will know how to sell beds. The punch line of the epigram is to be found in the wish in the last couplet that the earth may lie light on Philaenis, so that dogs may be able to root up her bones.[129] She is, in other words, to be rewarded in kind for the wrongs that she as a *saga* did in digging up the bones of the dead to use them in her magic-working. That poets can take it for granted that procuresses will practise sorcery does not give us warrant to conclude that all procuresses could turn their hand to magic-working, but it does make it likely that a certain number of the poor old women who made a living from procuring supplemented their earnings by sorcery.

Besides being sorceresses what the *lenae* of the three elegies have in common is that they are old and bibulous or drunken. Dipsas, the subject of Ovid's poem, is specifically said to be an old woman and Propertius' Acanthis has bones that are visible through her skin, a wrinkled neck and decayed teeth.[130] Dipsas is never sober when she sees the dawn, her eyes are lacrimose with wine and part of the curse that Ovid pronounces on her is that she may always be thirsty. Tibullus curses his unnamed *lena* with the wish that the cups she drinks may be laced with much bitter poison. Finally, the fate that Propertius wishes on Acanthis is that her shade may feel thirst and that her grave-marker may be an old amphora with its neck broken off.[131] The broken amphora as grave-marker for a drunken old woman has literary antecedents: there are two Hellenistic epigrams by Leonidas and Antipater of Sidon respectively on the cup that surmounted the grave of a bibulous old woman, aptly named Maronis, whose only regret in the grave was that the cup was empty.[132] The broken amphora may be a literary motif, but the emphasis on the alcoholism of these old women is so marked in all three poems that it is hard to believe it is just old age that makes them as they are and that the trait is not more specifically connected with their calling in life.

The thirsty procuress is a familiar figure in the plays of Plautus and before him of Menander. Plautus may take over the figure of the bibulous procuress from Greek New Comedy, but it is highly unlikely that he would have done so, and would have made so much of her, if she had not been a type already familiar in Rome in his day. It is interesting that the *lena* is never presented as drunk but only as a heavy drinker who in her cups becomes excessively loquacious and who at the same time has an insatiable capacity for yet more wine. Leaena in *Curculio* has an astounding appetite for unmixed wine, is brought to the door by the smell of wine poured there, and functions as a sort of measure, since she can hold an amphora or *quadentral*.[133] Less spectacularly thirsty is the *lena*, Cleaerata, in *Asinaria*: if she breaks the contract Diobolus has drawn up to keep her daughter from having contact with anyone else, her punishment is that she is to be deprived of wine for twenty days.[134] In *Cistellaria*, when Selenium, the supposed daughter of the *lena* Melaenis, entertains the other *lena*, Syra, and her daughter, Gymnasium, Syra rather ungraciously complains that the servant has been niggardly in pouring the wine and has, furthermore, polluted it with water.[135] Syra herself says that it is the vice of a large proportion of the women who ply her trade that once they are loaded, they say more than they ought.[136] The god who is to speak the prologue of the play then complains that she has scarcely left anything for him to say, as she is an unduly loquacious and bibulous old woman.[137] Melaenis for her part needs to be bribed with a barrel of wine to get her to say anything.[138] The boastful soldier who gives his name to the play called *Miles gloriosus* wins over the mother, who is a *lena*, of the prostitute he is pursuing with, amongst other gifts, that of wine.[139]

It is possible to treat the drunken old woman as no more than a stock literary figure and leave the matter at that without inquiring further into why old women are thought to be drunken and whether it is all old women or only some who are portrayed as drunken. There can be no question that old women were a byword for drunkenness and loquacity.[140] The *Greek Anthology*, for example, has a series of epitaphs for drunken old women. The names given these old women reflect their fondness for wine.[141] In the magical papyrus that contains the *Paignia* of Democritus, amongst the tricks there is even a recipe to keep an old woman from being too voluble and drinking too much.[142] The little pen-portrait of the magic-working old woman with her girls at the festival of the Feralia left us by Ovid will serve as an introduction to a brief excursus on the culture of alcohol amongst female magic-workers.[143] After the old woman has finished her magical ritual, she and her companions finish off the wine that has been used to pour a libation to the goddess Muta. The garrulous old woman is naturally the person present who drinks most of the wine and who departs in an inebriated state. She conforms to the stereotype of the old woman as drunkard. But it is not only she who drinks; the girls who are with her also drink. Ovid does not give any indication of age. It is likely, nonetheless, that these are youngish girls whose ages will range from twelve or younger to eighteen at the most.

The reader who is in thrall to the casual modern assumption that in Mediterranean societies wine is from an early age an accepted part of daily life for both boys and girls will see nothing amiss in young girls helping finish off a container of what presumably was unmixed wine. A Roman reader would have had a very different understanding of the scene: he would not have been surprised by it and would have expected no more and no less of the girls in question; their conduct conformed exactly to the preconceptions he possessed about girls of their type. What he would have seen in the scene was not just an old woman with some girls having a drink, but an old procuress or *lena* and her girls. His understanding of the scene was governed by the feeling that respectable women would not or should not drink wine, whereas prostitutes and their keepers were exactly the kind of women who might be expected to drink. The prejudice against women drinking wine can be traced back to the early second century BC. The earliest of Roman historians, Fabius Pictor, tells a story of a Roman matron who was forced by her relatives to starve herself to death because she was found to have broken the seals of the boxes in which the keys to the wine-cellar were kept.[144] The Elder Cato in a speech that was in all likelihood delivered in the 190s maintained that a husband would punish his wife if she was found to have drunk wine.[145] Fifty years later, the Greek historian Polybius in an excursus on the constitution and manners of the Romans reports that Roman women were forbidden to drink wine.[146] A century later still, Cicero in a treatise on what a good state should be says categorically that there is no woman who has any truck with undiluted wine.[147]

Many more statements of the same order about women and wine could be brought forward, but the testimony of Fabius Pictor, Cato the Elder, Polybius and Cicero demonstrates clearly enough that there was in the last two centuries of the Roman Republic a feeling against drinking on the part of women. The prejudice did not die out with the Republic but continues on into the Empire, though perhaps not in so marked a form. Valerius Maximus, writing about 30 AD, at one point speaks as if women in his day were no longer forbidden to drink wine, but elsewhere, in commenting on Egnatius Mecenius' clubbing his wife to death for having drunk wine, remarks that an excessive appetite for wine on the part of a woman closes the door on all virtues and opens it to every sin.[148] The sentiments that Valerius voices about the deleterious effect of wine on the moral character of women put in more general terms what had long been said in Rome about the adulterous proclivities of women who drank.[149]

In contrast to the prejudice against women who drink, implied in the stories about women being punished for drinking and the categorical statements made by Cicero and others that women did not drink wine, Ovid in his *Ars amatoria* is found declaring that drinking is much more becoming for girls than eating and that had Paris seen Helen eating greedily, he would have taken against her and announced that he had made a mistake in abducting her.[150] The reason that the poet gives for making such a pronouncement is that Bacchus does well with Cupid, by which he means that wine is conducive to love. He does, however, qualify his commendation of wine somewhat by warning against drinking to the point of becoming uncoordinated. He gives two reasons: a woman lying sodden with wine on a couch is a base sight, and a woman in such a condition is a fit object for all sorts of couplings.[151]

What Ovid has to say might at first sight seem surprising, if we supposed Cicero and Polybius were really saying that drinking was unknown in Rome amongst women of all classes and conditions. They are, of course, saying no such thing, but only that respectable women do not or should not drink. Had the Romans who condemn drinking in women had in mind women of every class and condition, they would not have justified their condemnation by appealing to the power that wine has to incite the female sex to adultery.

What concerns them are the morals of respectable Roman women. They are not interested in the conduct of women who do not contract regular marriages and who are not freeborn Roman citizens. The morals of that category of women are of no concern to them. Ovid is in the event not turning Roman morality on its head in saying that drinking, since it is conducive to love-making, is more becoming in a girl than eating, but only that wine is a useful lubricant in the kind of social intercourse engaged in by the high-class prostitutes for whose assistance in attracting lovers he pretends to write this part of the *Ars amatoria*.

It is to be inferred from Ovid's recommendation that drinking was an accepted element in the lives of high-class prostitutes; it was what made them merry, sociable and free with their favours. Somewhat further down the economic scale were the prostitutes to be found in drinking and eating establishments. It is reasonable to imagine that wine was at least as much a part of their lives as it was that of the better-looking and more socially adept courtesans to be found in the company of well-to-do young man at louche dinner parties. All of these prostitutes were very young. They will have begun their careers in their early teens and so will have spent much of their lives in a society in which drinking played a large part. It will have been the constant exposure to a culture of drinking that helped produce the procuress who is dependent on alcohol. There will have been other factors at play besides exposure to wine from an early age in creating the procuress who is always on the look out for wine. Not the least of these will have been the misery and precariousness of the situation of these women. Cheap wine must have served as a cushion against the grim realities of life and helped women who lived constantly on the verge of destitution to forget the true horror of their situation; it will also have been an anodyne against the very high level of physical discomfort that in the ancient world older people had to endure.

The prostitutes and women for whom the poets of Roman elegy proclaim their love are far from being common prostitutes but women whose status comes closer to that of a kept woman. The procuresses, accordingly, who work on behalf of these women are by no means at the bottom of the social pile. Yet it requires no great imaginative effort to see that they must have lived on the verge of destitution. If they were unsuccessful in their trade, they were finished. When Ovid prays that the gods may bestow no house, a destitute old age, long winters and a permanent thirst on Dipsas, what he prays for must have been a reality that many of these women faced.[152] Destitution, cold, hunger and homelessness were always lurking around the corner. The grim details of the way in which the *lena* might end her days are spelled out by Propertius with some relish when he describes the death of Acanthis: she coughed up bloody phlegm, which she spat through her rotten teeth, before breathing her last on her paternal rush-matting in a curved lean-to (*pergula*) whose fire was cold.[153]

The possession of books of spells and the ability to copy out binding-spells were important weapons in the armoury of the magician. The assumption that the ability to read and write contributed in no small measure to the authority of most magicians is probably not far off the mark. That raises the question of how many prostitutes and procuresses possessed the degree of literacy necessary to copy out a spell or use a book of magical recipes. Ovid in his work on the art of love, the *Ars amatoria*, suggests that the high-class courtesans to whom he offers advice on how best to seduce a man and then hold on to him should number amongst their cultural accomplishments a knowledge of Callimachus, Philetas, Mimnermus and Sappho and in Latin of Propertius, Gallus, Tibullus, Varro Atax and Vergil.[154] Part of Ovid's reason for naming these authors is the aspiration he proceeds to voice that he himself may some day be counted amongst their number.[155] It does not greatly matter whether Ovid for his own purposes gravely overestimates the reading abilities of courtesans. The idea that a courtesan should have some acquaintance with poetry is still *prima facie* evidence for a degree of literacy amongst these women. How courtesans acquired that attainment we cannot confidently say, but it is not unlikely that the men or women who ran them as well as training them in dancing and singing also had them taught reading and writing as a necessary accomplishment. If that were the case, there is no great mystery how they could have come to possess books of magical recipes and have been able to copy out binding-spells. At a rather humbler level prostitutes may have picked up from the *lena* in whose charge they were the rudiments of writing and learned to copy out spells.

We should now turn to the question of what kind of magic it was that these women practised and who it was who consulted them. There are in Greek and Latin poetry more or less conventional catalogues of the feats that particular sorceresses can perform such as raising the dead, changing into the form of a bird or animal, splitting the ground, bringing the moon down from the sky, effecting changes in the weather and causing rivers to reverse their course. The Roman elegiac poets are no exception and have no scruples about attributing these powers to *sagae*, but these are not forms of magic-working that play any real part in love-elegy.

A good deal of the magic practised by procuresses probably consisted of binding-spells, many of which they will have directed against each other. It is this form of magic in which Ovid portrays what looks to be a *lena* and her girls engaging at the festival of the Feralia.[156] The vignette that Ovid paints is a suggestive one, since it offers us an insight into the conditions that fostered magic-working amongst *lenae* and prostitutes and shows how a knowledge of magic might be passed on by the *lena* to the girls under her charge. It is just one of many such scenes from real life with which the poet enlivens his account of the Roman calendar in the *Fasti*. Ovid presents his little picture of the procuress and her girls engaging in magic-working, apparently outside the door of a rival, as an example of the activities that took place on the last day of the *Feralia*. On that day the spirits of the dead were placated with offerings. What the *lena* does is to perform rituals in honour of the spirit of a nymph called Muta or Tacita, the mute or silent one, who had been consigned to the Underworld. The *lena* is a woman who has many years to her name. She sits in the middle of her girls and performs sacred rites in honour of the goddess Tacita, although she herself is anything but silent.[157] The rite that she carries out takes the following form: using three fingers to perform the action, she places three grains of frankincense in the hidden passage that a mouse has made below a door step; she next ties ribbons, over which incantations have been uttered, around a piece of lead, turns seven black beans around in her mouth and burns in a fire the head of a sardine whose mouth has been sown up, bound together with pitch and pierced by a bronze needle; a libation of wine is poured and what is left of the wine is drunk by the old woman and her companions, although she drinks more of it than they; as she departs, now drunk, she declares: 'We have bound enemy tongues and hostile mouths'.[158] The purpose of the ritual is transparent, although it is hard to provide parallels for every detail in it:[159] the spell performed is designed to silence hostile tongues, presumably either those of the rivals of the procuress or that of a disgruntled client. Reading behind the lines what emerges is how highly competitive must have been the world in which procuresses and prostitutes lived, and how that competitiveness must have given rise to hostilities and tensions that fostered various forms of magic-working.

The magical operations which the elegiac poets credit *sagae* with performing are various forms of erotic magic and healing or purificatory magic. In the former category there is first of all making a woman fall in love with a man, causing impotence by a binding-spell, causing a girl to lose her hair, making the partner of a girl blind to her infidelity and finally, freeing a man or woman from the love they feel for another by a form of purificatory ceremony.[160] These are, with the exception of the spell that causes loss of hair, all well-attested magical operations. Such spells will have been the basic stock-in-trade of the procuress-cum-sorceress. The procuress-cum-sorceress is likely also to have been one of the persons from whom love-philtres were procured. That they might display a degree of inventiveness and compose incantations designed to fit a particular situation and to be especially effective is suggested by the *saga* who composes an incantation for Tibullus that Delia is supposed to intone when she wants to deceive the man with whom she is living.[161] It is hard to see how such an incantation could have been passed on and preserved, unless the *saga* wrote it out and handed it over to her client. Tibullus, in other words, assumes that some *sagae* can write and do not mechanically reproduce old incantations, but are capable of concocting incantations themselves.

When it is a question of performing purificatory magic, *sagae* come to the house to which they are summoned. One of the themes of Roman love-elegy is the lover summoning a *saga* when his girl falls ill or has disturbing dreams.

Here the lover does not call the *saga* to the house of his mistress because he feels that she will do any good but because he believes that the girl will feel the better for it and will think the more kindly of him for spending money on her behalf. This is very much a concession to female superstition. In the *Ars amatoria*, Ovid advises the lover to be both happy and willing to hear his girl-friend recount her dreams and suggests that he make sure an old woman is summoned to purify the bed and the area around it with sulphur and eggs carried in a shaking hand.[162] It is services of this order of which Tibullus reminds Delia when he wants to win her back from the embraces of another: when she was ill he himself had gone round the bed purifying it with sulphur, after an old woman had sung a magical incantation; he himself had taken steps to make sure that the bad dreams Delia had dreamt had done her no harm; he had thrice uttered apotropaic prayers over a barley-cake and it was he with a ribbon around his head and his tunic loosened who had made nine vows to Hecate at dead of night.[163] Tibullus, in short, was so devoted to Delia that he had carried out himself most of the magical rituals a *saga* would in normal circumstances have been called on to perform. That, the poet says, will be taken to be a sign of concern.[164] The mundane business of curing the sick and relieving anxieties induced by disturbing dreams probably made up a large part of the practice of the *saga*.

Martial also exploits the motif of the expenses that a lover incurs in bring-ing in a *saga* to perform purificatory rituals for his girlfriend, if she has had a frightening dream. He has two poems on the subject. In both, a significant feature of the expense the lover incurs in trying to accommodate his girl-friend is the amount of wine the *saga* drinks.[165] In fact, the implication of one of the epigrams is that the *saga* is paid off principally in wine. In one of Lucian's *Dialogues of the Courtesans*, the old Syrian witch who brings about a reconciliation between Bacchis, a courtesan, and her lover costs very little, only a drachma and some bread, but she did have to have a *krater* of wine to herself to drink, while she performed the ritual.[166] The old woman who is paid off mainly in wine for the sorcery she performs is undoubtedly a conven-tional figure and there can be little question that the cost of expiating the dreams of a girlfriend is a stock theme. That can easily be granted. It remains likely, nonetheless, that it was women principally who called in sorceresses for purificatory purposes and that prostitutes had especially close associa-tions with *sagae*. The *saga* will not only have been called in by prostitutes when their health was threatened or when they had a disturbing dream; respectable women will also have summoned her, whether on their own behalf or out of concern for a child. Finally, there is no very good reason to doubt that one of the expenses incurred in employing such an old woman was the wine she was given to drink and probably also to take away with her.

Men too will have consulted *sagae* not only for the sake of their girlfriends, but on their own behalf. They will certainly have got love-philtres from them and they will no doubt have paid them to perform spells for them. They may also have approached these women if they felt they had been bewitched. In Petronius' *Satyricon*, the hero of the novel, Encolpius, is introduced to an old woman to cure him of his impotence. She performs various magical rituals, but ultimately fails in her attempt and sends him on to another old woman, who performs a rather more elaborate ritual with the help of some other old women.[167] The second old woman is said to tend a shrine of Priapus. All of this takes place in Croton in Southern Italy. Petronius extracts a good deal of comedy from his description of the procedures to which Encolpius has to submit, but that does not mean the notion of men consulting *sagae* in the hope of being cured of impotence was a fantasy and that there was not something of a hierarchy amongst these women.

## Sorceresses and wise women in Rome and Italy in the late first and early second centuries AD

The *sagae* or wise women whom we have encountered hitherto were to be found in Rome and in a large town of Greek origins in Southern Italy. It would be wrong to assume that wise women were a purely urban phenomenon and that they did not exist in smaller communities in the countryside. Their existence in that setting is attested in a work on agriculture written in the third quarter of the first century AD, Columella's *De re rustica*. Columella, following the example of Cato, whose authority he cites, has towards the beginning of the work a discussion of the duties of the farm manager or steward (*vilicus*). Columella advises that the farm manager should make no sacrifices, except on the instructions of his master, and that he should not allow access to diviners from entrails (*haruspices*) and *sagae*.[168] This corresponds to Cato's warning against allowing the farm manager to consult soothsayers, whether they be diviners from entrails or birds or inspired prophets or Chaldaeans, lest it lead to his cheating.[169] Columella, for his part, does not want the farm manager to let in diviners and *sagae*, on the ground that both types of persons, because of the empty superstition they promote, encourage untutored persons to spend heavily and then to engage in wicked and shameful conduct. There are two significant additions that Columella makes to the advice given by Cato: he does not want the farm manager to conduct sacrifices not sanctioned by his master; and he does not wish him to allow entry to *sagae*. The coupling of forbidding unauthorized sacrifices with the banning of *haruspices* and *sagae* from the premises is an indication that in Columella's mind the measures were linked. He forbids these unauthorized sacrifices, perhaps partly out of concern at the costs the farm manager may incur, but also perhaps because he fears that the man may be encouraged to perform magical and illicit sacrifices by the *haruspices* and *sagae*. The addition of the *sagae* to the list of the persons whom Cato would ban must reflect the widespread presence of wise women in Columella's time. The *saga* and the *haruspex* are an especial menace in the view of the writer to a household of slaves in the country, because their rude and untutored minds are more than usually prone to superstition and so susceptible to being mulcted of their own money and that of their master as well as being encouraged to engage in criminal activities. Columella does not say where the diviners and the *sagae* who present a threat to the well-being of the slaves on a farm come from. It is impossible to say whether they had their base in the nearest village or town or made their way through the countryside preying on the gullible. The *Metamorphoses* of Apuleius, although admittedly a century later than Columella and set in the towns and countryside of Thessaly, suggests that fortune-tellers conformed to the latter pattern.

The one other reference to a *saga*-like figure in this period, besides that in Columella, is to be found in Juvenal's Sixth Satire in his catalogue of the shortcomings of wealthy Roman women. Amongst the dubious religious practitioners from the East such women patronize, there is the old Jewish woman who for a small fee interprets dreams in a manner calculated to please.[170] Juvenal describes her as an exegete of the laws of Jerusalem, a mighty priestess of the tree and faithful intermediary between heaven and earth.[171] Much ink has been spilled over the interpretation of these words. What we can usefully extract from them is that the authority of the woman rested on her being taken to be a holy woman of some sort. The stray mentions that we have in Latin literature of holy women of this type such as the Syrian seer Martha should keep us from imagining that all *sagae* were ex-prostitutes. There is the very real possibility that *sagae* emerged from quite other milieux and that there were some *sagae* whose authority rested on their having access to the arcane mysteries of Eastern cults.

## Magicians in the first and second centuries AD

Although their identity is elusive, there were in Rome and Italy in the Late Republic and the Early Empire professional magicians. The sources for the period testify to repeated attempts at expelling them, almost always in conjunction with astrologers (*mathematici*): in 33 BC, Agrippa drove astrologers and magicians from Rome;[172] then there is the expulsion and execution of astrologers and magicians in AD 16 or the following year;[173] again in AD 68 at the end of Nero's reign an attempt was made to expel magicians and astrologers. Sometimes our sources speak only of the expulsion of astrologers, although persons whom we might regard as magicians may have been expelled on these occasions also. The record of the repeated attempts at cleansing Rome of magicians should leave no room for doubt that male sorcerers were present in Rome and in Italy. It is not, however, to be assumed that on these occasions only men were driven out of Rome and Italy and that the humbler female magician was left alone. The *Chronicle of the Year* AD 354 shows that to be a dangerous inference: it records, because it had not happened before, the execution in the reign of Tiberius of forty-five sorcerers and eighty-five sorceresses.[174] It is presumably the events of AD 16 or 17 that the chronicler has in mind. It is likely then that our other sources for the expulsions of sorcerers are using the generic masculine when they speak of magicians (*goetes* Gk.; *magi* Lat.) and that both sexes are encompassed under the term. Even though more women than men may have been expelled from Rome in these periodic purges, it still remains the case that there were men who were driven out of Rome for practising magic.

The problem is not then to demonstrate that in Rome and Italy there were men who made a living from magic-working but to put a face to them and to invest them with an identity. We can get a handle of a sort on their identity from the persons in whose company they were periodically driven out of Rome, the astrologers. The historical sources for the period speak of the cleansing of Rome of astrologers and magicians, a way of speaking that suggests there were two distinct categories of person expelled, astrologers and magicians. That distinction may not be intended. A fragment of the jurist Ulpian gives what purports to be a decree of the Senate of the year AD 17. It must have been passed in the aftermath of the affair of Scribonius Libo Drusus in AD 16 and may be one of the *senatus consulta* to which the historian Tacitus refers. The decree speaks of an interdiction from fire and water and of the confiscation of their goods, of astrologers, Chaldaeans, inspired prophets and others who engage in similar endeavours and of the interdiction and punishment of anyone from a foreign nation who undertakes such practices.[175] There is no word here of magicians as such. Dio Cassius under the year AD 16 describes measures taken by Tiberius against astrologers, magicians and anyone who engaged in any form of divination. The measures described by Dio coincide in good part with the provisions of the *senatus consultum* as given by Ulpian: foreigners were put to death and citizens still practising the craft after the previous decree were banished, if they were indicted.[176] Either Dio Cassius and Tacitus are referring to completely separate measures taken against magicians from those of the *senatus consultum* of AD 17 or these are the same measures. If the latter is true, then the way in which the historians couch the matter reflects the assumption that those who engage in divination and those who practise magic are not really separate categories of person. It should be no occasion for surprise that for many Romans there was no sharp distinction between magic-working and divination in general. The distinction, in particular, between magic and astrology was blurred.[177]

It is not to be assumed that all of the sorcerers and astrologers who lived in Rome in this period were independent operators. Some of them were the clients of rich patrons and formed part of the households of their patrons. There are intimations of their existence in the form of the Syrian woman called Martha who was part of the entourage of Marius and of the *saga* named Sagana who belonged to the Pompeius proscribed by the Triumvirs. Although Martha may have accompanied Marius on his campaigns, in Rome a magician would not have been resident in the house of his patron, but would have lived apart as a client, coming each morning to the house of the great man for the levee. The speaker in Juvenal's Third Satire complains about the Greeks who have abandoned their birthplace, whether it be Sicyon in the Peloponnese or Amydon in Macedonia, or the islands of Andros and Samos, or Tralles or Alabanda in Caria, to make their way up the Esquiline and Viminal Hills into the houses of the great to be the vital components of these houses and their future masters.[178] These men, the speaker says, can be whatever their patron wants: teacher of literature or rhetoric, surveyor, painter, masseur-cum-coach, augur, tightrope-walker, doctor or magician.[179] A half-century or so after Juvenal, Lucian, in an essay on the fate of educated Greeks who sought their living in the houses of rich Romans (*On Those Hired for Pay*), warned the young man to whom the essay is addressed that once he was old he would be cast off like a worn-out horse and that nobody would wish to employ him, since people would take it for granted that he had been dismissed because he was an adulterer or a magician or some such thing; men were prejudiced against Greeks and naturally assumed that they had easy morals and turned readily to criminality. The causes of the prejudice were entirely understandable: a large number of the Greeks who entered private households, because they had no other useful form of knowledge to offer, professed to be adept in prophecy and sorcery, specifically in the spells that made people attractive to those for whom they felt sexual desire and in summoning up spirits against enemies; they told their patrons that they were educated in these matters, while at the same time wrapping themselves in worn cloaks and sporting long beards.[180] Lucian, in other words, says that some of the educated Greeks who found their way into the households of rich Romans professed themselves expert in prophecy and magic-working and at the same time wore the badges of office of the philosopher.

It is very difficult to assess to what extent the essay *On Those Hired for Pay* is a literary set piece and to what extent it reflects a Roman reality. The matter is complicated by the similarities that it bears to a number of Juvenal's satires, not least the Third. The points in common between it and the Third Satire seem adventitious and there is a good deal of difference between the picture in Juvenal of the hungry Greek turning his hand to everything including magic and the philosopher who practises magic and prophecy.[181] We must also bear in mind in assessing the worth of Lucian's essay as evidence for a social reality the generally hostile stance that Lucian adopts in his satires when he speaks of philosophers: the philosopher is the hypocrite *par excellence*.[182] It may readily be granted that Lucian draws on previous literary exercises on the subject of the fawning educated Greek trying to earn a living in the employ of rich Romans and that in accusing philosophers of practising magic he is attacking his favourite target. Yet the very distinct possibility still remains that some of the Greek philosophers who were the clients of rich

Romans did engage in magic-working on behalf of their patrons and in the closely related activity of divination.[183]

The educated Greeks who practised magic on behalf of their Roman patrons of whom Juvenal and Lucian speak were men who had gone through what counted as a higher education and had been trained in rhetoric and in some cases in philosophy. They were men whose families had been able to pay for a prolonged period of education, but who were not themselves independently wealthy. They did not, in short, belong to the curial class in the Greek cities of the East, but were men who had to make a living from their wits. There is an example of such a man in the person of the Alexandrian philosopher and astrologer Thrasyllus, who was taken up by Tiberius during his enforced sojourn on Rhodes and became part of his household. As a result of Tiberius' patronage, Thrasyllus, while still with Tiberius on Rhodes, became a Roman citizen.[184] None of his astrological or philosophical writings has survived, although we can form a general picture of their character from fragments and summaries. Thrasyllus' philosophical interests and activities throw more light on his intellectual bent and sympathies than what is known of his astrological writing. He was a Platonist, but a Platonist whose Platonism was heavily influenced by Pythagoreanism.[185] He was responsible with Dercyllides for dividing up Plato's works into the four groups in which they are still published.[186] Diogenes Laertius also credits him with having performed the same task for Democritus.[187] There is, however, reason to think that the arrangement of Democritus' writing antedates Thrasyllus' activity. He did, however, compose a *Prolegomena to the Reading of the Works of Democritus.*[188] His conception of Democritus as a philosopher is apparent in the way in which he characterized Democritus' intellectual lineage: he was a devotee of Pythagoras, mentioned that philosopher admiringly in the work called *Pythagoras* and took all of his ideas from Pythagoras, so much so that he might have been thought to be a pupil of Pythagoras, were such a supposition not at odds with chronology.[189] Thrasyllus' Democritus is not the robust critic of superstition, but the Pythagorean holy man who published all manner of strange and wonderful lore. That Thrasyllus cherished such a picture of Democritus tells us more about Thrasyllus than it does about Democritus. It may be inferred from it that in Thrasyllus philosophy, mysticism and occultism overlapped. To characterize Thrasyllus as no charlatan nor adventurer but as a serious inquirer and philosopher is a little misleading, if we take Thrasyllus to be a philosopher in the modern sense.[190] His intellectual commitments were no doubt sincere enough. It is the direction they took that is interesting. Furthermore, Thrasyllus does represent a Greek who becomes a member of the entourage of a rich and powerful Roman while engaging in an activity which many men thought suspect and which had close ties with sorcery. This is how the relationship is seen two centuries later by the historian Dio Cassius. In discussing inconsistencies in Tiberius' character, Dio reports that Tiberius through daily intercourse with Thrasyllus reached a high degree of proficiency in the craft of the seer, so much so that when he had a dream in which he was bidden give a certain man some money, he realized that a demon had been conjured up through sorcery (*goeteia*) to impart this information to him; he therefore put the man responsible to death. Dio goes on immediately after this to describe the measures Tiberius took in AD 16 against all other astrologers, sorcerers (*goetes*) and diviners of any guise.[191] The inconsistency, accordingly, lay in Tiberius' action in letting Thrasyllus, from whom he had learned to detect sorcery, stay on, while executing all foreign astrologers and sorcerers and expelling all of the other astrologers and sorcerers in Rome who did not abandon their profession. As for the other historians who mention Thrasyllus, both Tacitus and Suetonius assume in speaking of Tiberius' relationship with Thrasyllus that taking an interest in astrology was a guilty secret which a man such as Tiberius might go out of his way to conceal.[192]

There is evidence from the late second century AD of a somewhat different kind of magician being admitted to the salons of the rich and powerful in Rome. A Christian document of that time presents a magician performing party-tricks at séances in private establishments and putting on displays in public. The work in question is an account, originally written in Greek, composed towards the end of the second century or in the early decades of the third century AD, describing the career of the Apostle Peter in Rome. It is known as the *Acts of Peter*.[193] Only the last portion of the work survives in Greek, although the whole work exists in a Latin translation of a later date. The familiarity of the author of the work with places in Rome and its environs suggests rather strongly that it was written either in Rome itself or by someone who had lived in Rome.[194] The surviving portion in Greek describes the jealousy that Peter's curing the sick on the Sabbath in the name of Jesus Christ aroused in the Palestinian magician, Simon Magus, who vowed in front of a crowd that he would confute Peter within a few days, by showing that the god in whom Peter placed his trust was not a true god but a make-believe one. Those of Peter's disciples who were secure in their faith used to ridicule the illusions Simon created. It was his practice to use dining-rooms (*triklina*) as a venue for conjuring up spirits (*pneumata*) which were not real but had only a seeming existence. He was also caught using magic (*magia*) to make cripples appear whole for a short time, of making the blind seem to see and finally, on one occasion of having given the impression of having brought back a large number of corpses to life.

During all of these performances the unfortunate Simon had Peter at his elbow exposing his trickery and discomfiting him. The mockery which he had to endure from a now hostile and sceptical crowd finally led him to announce that on the following day he would leave behind the present impious and godless crowd to fly to the god of whom he was the Power, feeble though he now was; despite the crowd's having turned away from him, he was still the Standing One; he would go back to his father and say to him that

196

they wished to lay low in sickness the Standing One, his son, but that he had made no compact with them and had returned to his father. On the following day, an even greater crowd gathered at the *Via Sacra* to see Simon fly. Peter came to the spot where the performance was to take place to expose Simon. Now Simon on first arriving in Rome had put on a display of flying and had filled the spectators with amazement. This episode is mentioned earlier in the work and by Simon's own account he had flown around the gate of the city in the same clothes in which he had entered it.[195] Because Peter was not present in Rome at that point to expose him, Simon had been able to lead Rome astray and fill her eyes with such fantastic visions that some members of the crowd were quite overcome by what they had seen. When the time came for Simon to make his flight, Peter prayed to the Lord Jesus Christ that Simon might fall without killing himself and break his leg in three places. The prayer was answered and Simon fell to the ground duly breaking his leg in three places. The crowd, after stoning the wretched Simon, went home. Simon, for his part, was carried on a litter-bed through the night to Aricia, from which town he made his way to Tarquinia to join a certain Castor, who had been exiled from Rome for his magic-working.[196]

It is greatly to be doubted whether the description given by the *Acts of Peter* of Simon Magus' activities in Rome bears much relationship to reality. By the time the *Acts of Peter* was written the doings of Simon Magus in Rome had long been part of Christian myth. The apologist Justin Martyr speaks of Simon's presence in Rome in his *First Apology*. That work must have been written before AD 161. What Justin says about Simon is that he came from the village of Gitta in Samaria and was present in Rome during the reign of Claudius, where he had put on displays of great magical power with the help of demons which had been made active. Justin adds that these performances led to Simon's being thought a god by the Romans and to the erection of a statue in his honour between the two bridges over the Tiber; on the statue was inscribed in Latin: *Simoni Deo Sancto.*[197] Although the tales told in the *Acts of Peter* of Simon Magus' magic-working in Rome belong to a well-established tradition, they do bear witness to the existence of men who came to Rome from distant parts with pretensions to being more than mere magicians and who through their private and public performances of thaumaturgy tried to persuade their audience that they were more than human. The Simon Magus of the *Acts of Peter* is a holy man of this type. He puts on his more spectacular displays of wizardry in public in front of large crowds. The public displays consist in healing the lame, curing blindness and revivifying corpses and in some form of levitation. Simon Magus' activities are not just confined to the public forum. He manages to get himself into the houses of the well-to-do where he performs parlour-tricks more suitable for such a setting. It is in the confined and intimate space of the Roman dining-room (*triclinium*) that Simon conjures up spirits for the amusement of the company. The description of the performance leaves it unclear whether the author of the *Acts of*

*Peter* has in mind a séance in which spirits are questioned or the creation of optical illusions.

The magic-working of Simon Magus consists essentially in putting on a show. Sometimes the performance is in public and sometimes again in private. Holy men who put on such performances were probably a relatively common phenomenon, although much better attested in the Greek East than in Rome itself. The evidence is just not there to say whether magicians of Simon's sort expected their performances to lead to private commissions to perform magic on behalf of someone. The magicians, on the other hand, of whom Juvenal and Lucian tell perform in private and engage in more culpable forms of magic. What gives them their entrée to the salons of the rich is their education: the eastern holy men of the type of Simon Magus depend on the charisma given them by the aura of holiness that surrounded them.

There must also have been magicians who were rather less grand and whose magic-working did not consist either in spectacular public display or in performances at drinking parties, but in forms of sorcery that were necessarily kept more secret. They emerge only intermittently into the light of history from the obscurity in which their existence is cloaked. That happens when a great man is publicly accused of conspiring against the emperor and the magicians he has consulted are brought into the public gaze. Tacitus in his *Annals* records two such cases: one in AD 16 early in the reign of Tiberius; the other in AD 66 towards the end of Nero's rule.

It was the earlier case that had repercussions for astrologers and magicians practising in Rome and resulted in their execution or their expulsion from Italy by the Roman Senate. The protagonist in the affair was a young man of good family, Libo Drusus by name, who was accused of having designs on the throne. Tacitus gives a full account of the affair, since in his view it represented the first of a series of trials that ate away at the heart of the state.[198] Although Tacitus promises to present a painstaking history of Libo's case, it must be borne in mind that he was in no position to know what really had happened. His aim is as much with creating a highly-charged dramatic episode that will culminate in two spectacular public executions in one of which an ancient ritual was revived.[199] The picture that the historian paints of Libo is of a young man, lacking in prudence, egged on to indiscretions by someone who pretended to be a friend but who really wished to entrap him. The indiscretions in which the friend, a senator called Firmius Catus, encouraged Libo to engage were consulting Chaldaeans, having magical rites performed and approaching the interpreters of dreams.[200] When Firmius had acquired witnesses to these goings-on and was able to lay his hands on slaves who knew about them, he brought the matter to Tiberius' attention through an intermediary. Tiberius refused to meet the accuser but bided his time until his hand was forced by a well-known accuser called Fulcinus Trio, who had Libo arrested and brought before the consuls. Fulcinus then demanded that the Senate should conduct an investigation. The accuser had taken this course of action, after being approached by a certain Iunius with the information that he (Iunius) had been encouraged by Libo to summon up the spirits of the dead by means of incantations.[201] At his trial before the Senate papers were produced which showed amongst other follies attempted by Libo that he had asked parties whom Tacitus does not name whether he would acquire resources great enough to allow him to cover the Via Appia from Rome to Brundisium with coins. More damaging was the document that the prosecutor maintained was in Libo's own hand in which were the names of the Emperor and his family and those of the senators, with terrible notations or at least notations of an occult nature against them.[202] The upshot of this was that Libo, after unsuccessfully petitioning Tiberius, took his own life.[203] His goods were then divided up amongst his accusers, days of thanksgiving were voted by the Senate and decrees were passed about expelling astrologers and magicians from Italy. Two of their number were singled out for more drastic punishment: a Lucius Pituanius was thrown off the Tarpeian Rock; and the consuls ordered the execution outside the Esquiline Gate, in the manner of the olden days and after the sounding of trumpets, of a Publius Marcius.[204]

The only expert in the occult with whom Libo had dealings actually named by Tacitus is the necromancer Iunius. Knowing that the name of the man was Iunius does not take us very far, but the dismissive manner in which Tacitus speaks of him as a certain Iunius (*Iunius quidam*) shows that he was a disreputable person of humble origins. Tacitus employs the same device on a number of other occasions of referring to a man by his *cognomen* only and qualifying it with the word 'certain' to mark the man's ignoble and insignificant place in society.[205] Tacitus, accordingly, uses the expression when he wishes to record his distaste for a man, his origins and his way of life.[206] All of this is implied in his referring to Iunius in the terms he does. Iunius, in short, was a man from the lower reaches of society. Whether he was a Roman citizen or not is unclear. It is equally obscure whether he was a freedman or not.

Tacitus does not say that the two men executed in the wake of the affair of Libo Drusus were implicated in it, but it is hard to explain why they were singled out from their fellow-astrologers and magicians for condign punishment, had they not been involved in the matter. They sound from their names, Lucius Pituanius and Publius Marcius, to be Roman citizens or at least freedmen. Yet Dio Cassius writing of events in AD 16 says that Tiberius banished Roman citizens who practised astrology, magic and any form of divination, but put to death non-Romans who did the same.[207] The way in which Pituanius and Marcius were executed, on the other hand, tends to suggest that they were Roman citizens. In the riots following Caesar's death in 44 BC, the consul, Dolabella, crucified slaves, but had freeborn men thrown from the Tarpeian Rock.[208] The same pattern obtains in the Principate: those who are thrown from the Tarpeian Rock are Roman citizens and sometimes persons of some standing.[209] Execution in the manner of old was under the Principate a punishment reserved for those Roman citizens who were thought to have committed particularly heinous crimes.[210] This was the sentence that the Senate passed on Nero. The condemned man was stripped naked, his head was placed in a forked stick and he was whipped to death.[211] There is no evidence that anyone besides Marcius actually suffered such a fate, although two prominent men, one in the reign of Tiberius and the other in that of Nero, were threatened with that form of execution. In the event neither was put to death in this way, largely because a punishment that was thought too barbarous for the times would not have redounded to the credit of the emperor. It looks, accordingly, as if Pituanius and Marcius were Roman citizens and that Marcius' crime was more serious than that of Pituanius. Hence his execution as a public spectacle, signalled by the sounding of trumpets and in a form designed to make those who might think of doing whatever it was he had done have second thoughts. The conclusion to be drawn from the execution of Pituanius and Marcius is that the experts in the occult with whom Libo Drusus had dealings ranged from men whose origins were obscure and humble to Roman citizens who were by no means the lowest of the low.

Tacitus is also our main informant about the case of Soranus in AD 66.[212] A professional accuser, by name Ostorius Sabinus, had charged a former proconsul of the province of Asia called Soranus with having overreached himself in the administration of the province, with having stirred up sedition in its cities and finally with his daughter Servilia's having lavished money on magicians.[213] The last event had taken place when Soranus was already facing trial. The girl was not yet twenty years old and recently married. She had, says the historian, confined her consultation to three topics: the safety of her family; whether Nero could be placated or not; and whether the trial of her father in front of the Senate was a threat to his life. Under cross-examination by Ostorius before the Senate she was asked whether she had sold some of the ornaments given her as part of her dowry and whether she had taken the collar from her neck to sell it to raise money to pay for the performance of magical rites.[214] The girl had wept at this but kept silent and had then thrown herself on the ground before embracing an altar, from which vantage-point she had declared that she had invoked no impious gods, uttered no binding-spells and had called for nothing else in her prayers than that her father, Nero, and the members of the Senate should be kept safe and well; she had given the precious stones, clothing and marks of her status, just as she would have done had her life and blood been asked for; she had not known the names of the magicians before she met them nor what they did.[215] Tacitus says nothing about the identity of the magicians whom Servilia consults during the trial of her father. He probably had no idea who they were. It is tempting to make something of Servilia's having had to sell her gems and jewellery to pay for their services, but there is the possibility that something of this may be embroidery on Tacitus' part to heighten the pathos of an innocent girl's foolishly having consulted sorcerers out of concern for the fate of her father. It does nonetheless look as if consulting professional magicians could be expensive. Such magicians must have cost much more than the poor old women brought in to cure an upsetting dream who could be paid off in wine. Servilia professes neither to have known the names of the magicians whom she consulted before she was brought into contact with them nor to have known what they did. The implication of what Servilia says is that the names of magicians were known as a matter of course to other persons who acted as go-betweens. It is worth remarking finally that Servilia consults not just one magician but magicians. Tacitus apparently assumes that more than one magician would take part in a magical rite. It is reasonable to suppose that he knew what he was talking about.

What emerges from the accounts of the trials of Libo Drusus and Soranus given by Tacitus is that besides the educated Greeks who might turn their hand to magic and the holy men who performed miracles for public consumption and did conjuring-tricks at private parties there were magicians of obscure origin who engaged in more private forms of magic on behalf of others. They were found by the grandees who used them through intermediaries, presumably servants or clients. Such persons belonged, in other words, to a world to which the well-born had no immediate access and of which they knew nothing. Magicians of this order were generally not Roman citizens, but people of obscure origins and of low social standing. Yet the spectacular public executions in the aftermath of the affair of Libo Drusus are a warning against the too easy assumption that all magic-working in Rome was performed by the humble and the obscure. Persons of more exalted social standing who were Roman citizens might also engage in it.

# 8

# WITCHES AND MAGICIANS IN THE PROVINCES OF THE ROMAN EMPIRE UNTIL THE TIME OF CONSTANTINE

## The learned magician

Educated men who collected magical lore or whose philosophical interests extended into the occult are a phenomenon that we have already encountered in the Rome of the Late Republic and Early Empire. Perhaps because the evidence is more plentiful, one gets the impression that persons of this type were increasingly visible. Philosophers whose basic philosophical tenets derived from Plato, but who believed that Plato was the intellectual heir of Pythagoras and who therefore saw themselves as Pythagoreans seem from the second century BC to have had a peculiar fascination with the occult. The type continues to exist: at least three can be named, two of them certainly real persons and the third possibly also. Besides Pythagorean philosophers, there are doctors of a Pythagorean tendency who made the not very difficult transition from medicine to magic. From the late second century AD, it becomes harder to distinguish between philosophy in some of its manifestations and magic. To effect union with the divine and to heighten their perceptual powers Platonist philosophers adopt techniques and rituals that have in fact been borrowed from the repertoire of the magician. The ritualistic and mechanical procedures used by these philosophers for gaining intimacy with the divine are most generally known as theurgy, a term whose meaning was contested by those who thought of themselves as theurgists. In the eyes of many of their contemporaries theurgists were no different from magicians. Serious philosophers who engaged in theurgy certainly neither thought of themselves as magicians nor presented themselves as such. They viewed themselves as adepts in a higher branch of wisdom that went beyond philosophy to attain knowledge of the divine. There were probably others, however, whose motives were not quite so pure who exploited the cachet that theurgy had because of its connections with Platonism. Elements of theurgy come to be incorporated in magical performances. The effect must have been to invest the magician with a new authority. Cross-fertilization, in short, takes place between the more rarefied realms of philosophy and magic.

There are further additions to the galaxy of characters who used their education to advance a reputation that hovered between that of wise man and sorcerer. Wandering holy men-cum-wonder-workers presented themselves as Pythagorean sages. People reacted in very different ways to such characters: for some they were saintly figures whose lives and deeds were to be enshrined in hagiographies; for others they were charlatans, rascals and sorcerers whose wickedness needed to be exposed. Then there is the figure of the young man who had gone to Alexandria to further his education, but who had fallen by the wayside and succumbed to the allure of the occult. What that meant was that they went to study under Egyptian priests, who initiated them into the arcane secrets of Egyptian magic. Since the temples of Egypt had by the end of the first century BC largely replaced in the public imagination Persia and Babylon as the true home of magic, it was almost inevitable that magicians should have been credited with having studied their subject under an Egyptian expert. Unfortunately the only instances of educated men who had studied magic in Egypt are to be found in the pages of literary fictions. They are not attested in the historical record. The question that needs to be addressed is to what extent, if at all, the stories reflect a reality. Did some of the young men who went to Alexandria to enjoy the advantages that it offered as a seat of higher learning in fact end up consorting with Egyptian priests and being initiated into what they were told was Egyptian magic? Or are all such tales pure fictions based on nothing other than the popular stereotype of Egypt?

One way of approaching the issue is to look at the degree to which terminology, ideas and images drawn from Egyptian religion have been absorbed on the one hand into Greek magical texts and on the other into the iconography of magical amulets. If they have been, then it is fairly good evidence in the case of the magical literature that men familiar with Egyptian sacred texts have played a part in the formation of the magical lore that in antiquity circulated in various forms, both in Greek and Latin. Those familiar with the sacred texts are primarily the literate élite of Egyptian society, the personnel of the temples. The one class of magical texts that betray Egyptian influence are the Greek magical papyri. Most of them belong to a period later than that with which we are concerned and many of them seem to have been in the possession of a single individual who lived in Thebes in Upper Egypt and to have been copied out by the same hand, though not necessarily that of their owner.[1] The fact that many of the papyri are to be dated to the fourth century AD does not mean that the influence of Egyptian priestly lore on them occurred only at that late date. The temples had long been in decline and Christianity did not help their cause any. Egyptian influences are likely to have been absorbed at an earlier date. The same type of case could almost certainly be made from the magical amulets, could a date be affixed to them. Since the context in which they were found is not recorded and there are no known internal means of dating them, they are not a great deal of help. But it would be very surprising if the iconographical transfer had not taken place long before the Christianization of the Roman Empire. It cannot be said that either the magical papyri or the magical amulets provide unimpeachable evidence for magic being practised within Egyptian temples, but they do encourage the suspicion that the figure of the priest who is a magician is not entirely a figment of the literary or the popular imagination.

In the second half of the second century AD, the philosopher with an interest in the occult was almost certainly a familiar type. He does not emerge suddenly from nowhere. In the Late Roman Republic those who subscribed to Pythagoreanism were suspected, probably with good reason, of having more than a passing interest in the occult. The association of Pythagoreanism with magic and the occult goes back, as we have seen, to a much earlier date in the Hellenistic Period. The most prominent representative of the tradition, at least in the eyes of Late Antiquity and the Middle Ages, is Apuleius of Madaura. It certainly does not follow that, because there was a tradition to the effect that Apuleius was a magician, he in fact was. Tracing the evolution of the tradition would be an interesting enough exercise in intellectual history, but it would still leave open the question of whether Apuleius can fairly be called a magician. Very different opinions have been expressed in modern times on whether Apuleius was a magician or not.[2] There are those who find it difficult to imagine that a man of Apuleius' standing and education could possibly have been a practising magician. Then there are others again who think that Apuleius displays all too great a familiarity with the details of magic-working not to have actively participated in sorcery himself. The most that probably can be said is that Apuleius' intellectual tastes and affinities are not too different from those of the Pythagoreans who did go on to dabble in magic.

In the latter part of the second century AD it is not only in North Africa that we find philosophers interested in Pythagoreanism and sympathetic to the occult. They were also to be found in the Greek-speaking East. Lucian has a dialogue called the *Philopseudeis* that records tall stories about the supernatural and magic told in a gathering that consists at the beginning of four philosophers, a doctor and a man of sceptical disposition and that is joined later by a Pythagorean called Arignotus. Amongst the initial group there is a Peripatetic, a Platonist and a Stoic. The philosophers and the doctor tell such outrageous stories that the sceptic, Tychiades, is relieved when the Pythagorean Arignotus appears on the scene, since he imagines that Arignotus will put a stop to the tales of the miraculous that are being told. It should be noted that the tales told by the philosophers and the doctor are about the magical powers possessed by others and not by themselves. Arignotus affects long hair, wears a grave and dignified expression, is famed for his wisdom and is generally known as Arignotus the Holy.[3] It is an appearance that mimics that of Pythagoras as it was imagined in the late second century AD.[4] It is to be surmised that Lucian's portrait of Arignotus is based on a well-known type, if not an actual person.[5]

The Pythagorean, far from giving Tychiades the support he had looked for, is worse than a disappointment. He asks what the subject of conversation has been and is told that the assembled company have been trying to persuade Tychiades of the existence of ghosts. Arignotus inquires next whether Tychiades would also deny that the spirits of those who have died violent deaths wander around on earth. On being told that he would, Arignotus launches into a story designed to confute Tychiades' disbelief. It is about driving a demon out of a house in Corinth that the demon had made uninhabitable. Arignotus had accomplished the feat after discovering where in the house the body of one who had met a violent death had been buried. This he had done after spending the night in the house armed with his considerable library of Egyptian books. He needed to have them at hand to consult about the appropriate procedures for dealing with the problem. When the demon appeared and tried to scare him by taking on a number of different shapes, Arignotus had responded by uttering in the form of an incantation the most fearsome formula in Egyptian that he knew. That had led to the demon's disappearing into the corner of a dark room. It was there the next day that Arignotus had told those who came to look for him to dig. They had expected to find him dead. Predictably the excavators found a skeleton at the spot at which they were invited to dig.[6]

Tychiades remains unpersuaded by the tale and this encourages the host to tell a story of a voyage up the Nile that as a young man he had undertaken in the company of an Egyptian sacred scribe from Memphis, who was said to have spent twenty-three years in an underground chamber studying magic under the guidance of Isis. These details are sufficient to enable Arignotus immediately to recognize the man and name him. The man turns out to be his teacher, Pancrates by name, a holy man whose head was always shaven. According to Arignotus, Pancrates was a man of acute intelligence, but with a shaky command of Greek; he was long and slender, snub-nosed with protruding lips and skinny legs.[7] Whether or not Arignotus himself was a known historical figure does not matter greatly. He almost certainly represents a recognizable type: the Pythagorean holy man who affects a certain appearance and demeanour and who pretends to be acquainted with Egyptian sacred texts, which he claims to have studied in Egypt under the aegis of one of the priests of that country. It is difficult to know what to make of the pretensions of such men to have studied magic in Egypt under the instruction of a priest. Scepticism would seem to be in order so far as the notion of serious study goes, but it would be wiser to reserve judgment and allow for the possibility that men such as Arignotus did come to Egypt in search of its hidden wisdom and consort with hellenized Egyptians such as Pancrates, who was a very real person.

The philosopher whose interests coincide with those of the magician becomes even more of a presence from the end of the second century AD onwards. The Neoplatonist philosopher Iamblichus, who came from Apamea in Syria, is generally credited with having in the latter part of the third century AD made fashionable in philosophical circles the use of theurgy to attain union with the divine. The true story is probably more complex and will have its beginnings much earlier than the end of the third century. Iamblichus found inspiration for the rituals he employed to effect communion with the divine in the text known as the *Chaldaean Oracles*. They were composed in hexameters and were presumably known as the *Chaldaean Oracles* because they purported to have been given as an oracular response. Iamblichus wrote a commentary on the work. He was not the first Neoplatonist to take an interest in the *Oracles*: his somewhat older contemporary Porphyry had already devoted some attention to them and in fact he too had written a commentary on them. If we may judge from what Porphyry and Iamblichus respectively have to say about theurgy, they must have taken a very different view of the *Chaldaean Oracles* as a guide to attaining union with the divine: Iamblichus voices no reservations about the practice of theurgy as he understands it, whereas Porphyry, as Augustine was happy to note, was torn by doubt.[8]

The *Chaldaean Oracles* were in antiquity associated with a father and son, known respectively as Julian the Chaldaean and Julian the Theurgist. Julian the Theurgist's image as a worker of magic in the popular imagination is reflected in the story told about his activities when he accompanied Marcus Aurelius in his campaign of AD 174 against the Marcomanni, which was that he had performed various magical feats that helped the Romans. Of these the best known was his getting rain to fall on a parched Roman army.[9] It is significant that an Egyptian called Arnouphis, who is variously described as a philosopher or magician, is also credited with having performed the same feat on the same or a related campaign.[10] The *Oracles* were in fact probably composed in the reign of Marcus Aurelius. The philosophical matrix that gives rise to them is Platonism and it was not unsurprisingly Platonists who embraced them. What ultimately lies behind the aspiration to union with the divine that the theurgist tries to engineer by mechanical means is a passage in Plato's *Phaedrus* that evokes the ascent in the company of the gods of the disembodied soul to view the eternal forms.[11] It is very much to be doubted whether the *Chaldaean Oracles* were the only source of all of the theurgical rituals that magicians and holy men performed to enable them to come into contact with the divine. They were in all likelihood a particular manifestation of a much larger movement.

To the eye of most modern scholars magic and theurgy seem indistinguishable. It is not only the modern scholar who is shocked that philosophy should have come to such a pass. Augustine could see no difference between theurgy and magic.[12] Both judgments can be discounted: the modern, because its perspective on magic is not that of an ancient; the Christian, because the Fathers of the Church are all too ready to condemn any pagan practice as magic. It is quite another matter to have Porphyry in a book devoted to the ascent of the soul to the divine (*De regressu animae*) warn those who engage in theurgy to be careful because what they do comes perilously close to being magic.[13] The warning that Porphyry delivers to those who would venture into theurgy is that care needs to be taken in its use, since it is deceptive, dangerous and forbidden by the laws. If we did not know that Porphyry had theurgy in mind, we might be forgiven for thinking that he was speaking about magic. The demonic forces that magic brought into play were thought to deceive the senses and make the onlooker imagine he saw what was not in fact there. They were also believed to be dangerous to whoever conjured them up, hence the constant warnings given the would-be magician in the magical papyri to don a protective amulet before he summoned up spirits. As for Porphyry's warning against engaging in a practice prohibited by the laws, that must mean that the authorities would have proceeded against a theurgist as they would have done against a magician.

That the unsympathetic should have thought theurgy and the text on which a good deal of theurgical practice was based, the *Chaldaean Oracles*, smacked of magic is not surprising. In the theological system expounded in the *Chaldaean Oracles* the goddess whom magicians conjure up from the Underworld to help them, Hecate, plays an important part.[14] Furthermore, the rôle that Plato assigns demons as intermediaries between gods and men the *Chaldaean Oracles* gives to the entities it calls *iynges*. What exactly these *iynges* are imagined to be or to look like is obscure. The associations, however, of *iynges* with magic are not in doubt. They are the wheels magicians spin to cast a spell over their victims. It will not have been an accident that the author or authors of the *Chaldaean Oracles* gave names suggestive of magic to elements in their cosmological system. The interpreters of the system responded accordingly: theurgists took the mention of *iynges* in the *Chaldaean Oracles* as a licence to use magical wheels to assert their will over nature.[15]

Some of the stories that were put into circulation about the remarkable powers possessed by some of the great names in Neoplatonism will have done nothing to quell the suspicions aroused by theurgy. It was Neoplatonists who put the stories about, no doubt eager to persuade themselves and the larger world of the almost divine nature of the stars of their movement. Some of those who heard the stories will have been impressed by them: others again will have taken the stories as proof of dealings with demons and base spirits. We are told, for instance, that Iamblichus' servants saw him, when he engaged in his private devotions, levitating some distance above the ground with a golden penumbra surrounding his body. When his pupils accosted him and asked whether the report was true, he denied that it was, but in such a way as to leave the truth of the matter open.[16] He was also credited with possessing visionary powers that enabled him to see what was happening elsewhere.[17] He was said in general to have been reluctant to display his superhuman powers, but to have yielded on one occasion in Gadara in Syria to the blandishments of his pupils, who were always pressing him to perform some wondrous feat in their presence. It was when he and his pupils had come to Gadara to enjoy the warm springs there. What he did was to summon out of two fountain-houses the attendant-spirits of two of the warm springs there. They were called Eros and Anteros and took the form of good-looking young boys. After they had embraced each other, Iamblichus sent them back to their respective domains.[18]

Theurgy is not the only movement of the second century AD in which magic and philosophy come together; there is also Gnosticism. It too encourages a belief in revelatory transcendental experiences. Given the nature of that doctrine, it is hardly surprising that magic should make common cause with it. Its essence is the belief that there is a wisdom whose acquisition by a select few through revelation has a transforming and redeeming power.[19] The esoteric nature of Gnostic wisdom with its promise of personal transformation makes it attractive to the same sort of personality that is drawn to magic. Despite the kinship between magic and Gnosticism it should by no means be assumed that many Gnostics were magicians. Here we have to contend with the hostile picture painted in the *Acts of the Apostles* and in the Apologists, Justin Martyr and Irenaeus, of two early leaders of Gnostic communities in Samaria and Antioch respectively, Simon Magus and his pupil Menander.[20] Both are accused of being the agents of demonic forces and of practising magic. These are standard accusations against heretics and cannot be accepted unquestioningly. We have already had occasion to take note of the conjuring-tricks drawn from the *Paignia* of Anaxilaus of Larissa that Irenaeus complains the Gnostic heresiarch Marcus used to impress his followers.[21]

The influence of Gnosticism nonetheless does make itself felt in the magical papyri. There is, furthermore, from the middle of the third century AD the interesting testimony of Plotinus about Gnostic practices. Plotinus contends that the Gnostics known to him used incantations to make the higher powers obey them and do their bidding and more specifically that the incantations in question were songs, cries, breathings-upon, hisses and other noises that in the writings of the Gnostics were said to have a magical effect.[22] There is some reason to suppose that Plotinus has a Gnostic theurgic ritual in mind. Hissing and whistling are a well-attested part of the repertoire of strange noises and sounds that magicians make. The breathings-upon of which Plotinus speaks are perhaps the popping noises called *poppysmoi* in the magical papyri and elsewhere. They are regularly used in conjunction with the sound of hissing.[23] These noises are specifically employed in theurgic rituals. In the great Paris magical papyrus, for example, popping and hissing noises are prescribed in a theurgic ritual whose purpose it is to present a revelation of the divine.[24] There is also an excerpt from a work on music by a Pythagorean mathematician of the very early second century AD called Nicomachus of Gerasa which relates that theurgists use hissing and popping noises as well as the seven vowels when they perform an act of worship.[25] The seven vowels were of particular significance in magical rituals. One of the factors that lies behind their use is the Pythagorean doctrine that there was a sympathetic tie between the seven vowels and the seven planets.

The philosopher whose curiosity led him to investigate and manipulate the occult is a familiar enough figure, but the doctor who crossed over the not very clearly defined line between medicine and magic is less well documented, but probably also a recognized type. Lucian provides us with on the one hand a credulous doctor who happily believes in supernatural happenings and on the other a doctor who engages in sorcery. The credulous doctor is to be found in the *Philopseudeis*, where he is ignored by the others and takes little part in the discussion. He nonetheless rather confounds the expectations that the sceptic Tychiades has entertained about him: once by backing up a story about a statue that during the night wanders around the house with a tale of his own about a bronze statue of Hippocrates that ran around his house after dark upsetting things; and on a second occasion by declaring that there was nothing amazing about the visit to and return from Hades of their host, since he had himself treated a man who had on the twentieth day arisen from the dead after having been buried for all that time.[26] The other doctor is the man who had kept the pre-pubescent boy who was later to found a famous oracular shrine at Abonuteichos on the Paphlagonian coast of the Black Sea. Publicly he was a doctor, but privately he was a sorcerer (*goes*) who advertised incantations and spells that guaranteed success in love and in acquiring inheritances; in addition, he promised to conjure up ghosts to haunt enemies and maintained he was able to find buried treasure. He was, Lucian adds, as though that explained everything, a citizen of Tyana in Cappadocia who was one of those who were associates of Apollonius of that city and who had a thorough knowledge of the performances put on by Apollonius.[27] The doctor is almost certainly a real person and will have belonged to the circle of Pythagoreans who looked to Apollonius of Tyana as their leader. The Pythagorean sympathies of the doctor are to be inferred not only from those of Apollonius, but also from those of his protégé, Alexander of Abonuteichos. The accusation that the doctor was a full-blown sorcerer has to be taken with more than a grain of salt. Lucian employs many of the techniques used in ancient invective in creating his portrait of Alexander of Abonuteichos, whom he loathed, and of the milieu from which he had emerged. That is to say that we should not feel particularly surprised if Lucian is found to have engaged in exaggeration or to have told outright lies. What remains is the figure of the Pythagoreanizing doctor who practises magic. Is it credible to believe that there were such men? Lucian evidently expected his readers to recognize the type.

Lucian's portrait of the philosopher who takes an interest in the occult is one of unvarnished hostility. He paints them as charlatans and opportunists. It is a one-sided and one-dimensional picture that does less than justice to the type. Philostratus in his biography of the Pythagorean holy man,

Apollonius of Tyana, gives a much more sympathetic portrait of men of the kind pilloried by Lucian. The biography adds a dimension to our understanding of the itinerant holy man-cum-philosopher missing from Lucian's more hostile account. It has at the same time to be acknowledged that Philostratus will err on the side of generosity and put the best construction possible on the activities of Apollonius and his kind. Part indeed of Philostratus' brief, as he saw it, in writing the biography was to set the record straight by demonstrating that Apollonius was no *goes*. He says at the beginning of the work that some men thought Apollonius was a *magos*, since he had consorted with the *magoi* of Babylon, the Indian Brahmins and the Naked Ones of Egypt, and that these same men had slanderously put it about that the wisdom Apollonius possessed was of the kind which employed force in its application.[28] Apollonius, in other words, stood accused of being a magician and of compelling nature and the gods to act against their will. Since Philostratus wrote his *Life of Apollonius* one hundred and twenty years or so after the death of its subject, there will be a good deal in the biography that is anachronistic and that reflects conditions in Philostratus' own time.

Apollonius, according to Philostratus, was born in Tyana in Cappadocia of a family that was descended from the founders of the city. It was a family whose wealth was great. Apollonius received his initial education in letters and literature in Tyana and despite his provincial upbringing spoke impeccable Attic Greek. From Tyana he was sent at the age of fourteen to Tarsus to study rhetoric. He was fond enough of his teacher, but the immorality of Tarsus led him to ask his father that he should be allowed to move to Aegae in Cilicia, whose peaceful character, serious young men and shrine of Asclepius made it a suitable haven for one whose ambition was philosophy. In Aegae he sampled the teaching of the Platonists, Stoics, Peripatetics and Epicureans, but was drawn to Pythagoreanism, even though his teacher was more of an Epicurean than a Pythagorean. At the age of seventeen he adopted the Pythagorean way of life: he forswore meat for a diet of fruit and vegetables, put aside wine for water, went unshod, wore linen rather than woollen garments, let his hair grow long and began to live in the precinct of Asclepius.[29] From Aegae he returned at the age of twenty to Tyana to bury his father and to divide the brilliant inheritance his father had left him with a somewhat older and very dissolute brother. After he had succeeded in reforming the character of his brother, he gave the rest of his wealth away to relatives and kept a very small portion for himself.[30] The next stage in his career was a period of silence that lasted for five years. It was spent travelling around Pamphylia and Cilicia. The mere presence of Apollonius in a city served to quiet the factional strife in which the supporters of chariot-teams and pantomimes were wont to engage. The period of silence ended in Antioch and it was at that point that he decided to journey to India by way of Babylon to learn about the philosophy of the Brahmins.[31]

There is much in Philostratus' hagiography of Apollonius that is pure fiction, but the account that he gives of the early life and background of the sage is probably reasonably accurate. It is very much to be doubted whether Apollonius' journeys were quite as extensive as those with which Philostratus credits him. It is nonetheless likely that in Philostratus' day figures comparable in some ways to Apollonius made their way from place to place. Apollonius is, accordingly, a young man of good family who has had the benefit not only of an education in literature and rhetoric, but also of one in philosophy. All of this he renounces for the ascetic and self-denying life of a Pythagorean. It was a regimen designed to purify the mind of the taint of the material creation, so that it could enter more fully into communion with the divine. In Apollonius' case it means the development of heightened powers of perception that enable him to see what lies hidden from others. Whether there were Pythagorean sages of good family who detached themselves from the communities in which they had standing and gave up everything to wander from place to place is difficult to say. It is to be suspected that most such wandering holy men and sages did not come from so exalted a background. They were nonetheless men who possessed certain educational attainments, which means that they cannot have come out of nowhere. Philostratus takes it very much for granted that such a man will be constantly on the move, travelling from city to city, even going as far west as Spain. It is not altogether clear to us why such holy men have always to be on the move, but journeys do seem to have been a feature of their existence. Their moving from place to place will almost certainly have had an economic motive. Philostratus chooses to portray his hero as financially self-sufficient. The reality may have been rather different.

It is what wandering holy men such as Apollonius do on their travels that laid them open to the charge of being sorcerers: not only does Apollonius perform exorcisms, when needed, as he travels from community to community, he also settles disputes in the cities to which he comes and generally gives the inhabitants of the cities the benefit of his wisdom. His ability to perform exorcisms rests in large measure on his divinatory powers. When a plague, for instance, descends on Ephesus, its citizens at first ignore Apollonius' advice, and it is only when it has taken a firm hold that he is able to persuade all age-groups to assemble in the theatre, where there was a shrine dedicated to Hercules Averter of Ills. At the shrine was to be seen an apparition that had the appearance of an old beggar. Apollonius encouraged the citizens of Ephesus to stone it, despite their unwillingness to treat a stranger and a suppliant in that fashion. Some of the Ephesians did, however, begin to stone the beggar, who now opened his eyes to reveal eyes blazing with fire. The Ephesians, realizing that they were in the presence of a demon, began to stone it vigorously. A pile of stones accumulated around the apparition which, when it was dismantled, revealed not a beggar, but a dog whose appearance was that of a Molossian hound, but whose size was that of a lion.[32] What the critics of the Pythagorean sages fastened upon was the exorcisms they performed and their wonder-working; the wise counsels they offered individuals and communities, the latter perhaps imparted in a speech delivered in a public setting such as a theatre, are ignored.

There is a further aspect to the godly or divine aura in which men such as Apollonius of Tyana were enveloped. It is their mysticism. Apollonius enters into union or communion with the divine. The real Apollonius is most unlikely to have pursued such mystical unions. They are a feature of the Platonism of Philostratus' day and not that of the second half of the first century AD. How important an element union with the divine was for magicians of a certain elevated sort is apparent from the four different prescriptions that the great magical papyrus of the early fourth century AD, now in the *Bibliothèque Nationale* in Paris, contains for effecting such a union.[33] They are to be found amongst a host of recipes for the more mundane forms of magic. From their presence in the Paris magical papyrus and in other papyri containing collections of magical recipes we can get an insight into the aspirations of a certain sort of magician: he is interested not only in collecting spells that will effect changes principally in the behaviour of other people or that will enable him to see what is hidden from normal view, but he also hopes to effect a union with the divine, sometimes so that he can question the god, but on other occasions for nothing more than the revelatory experience that such a union brought with it.

From the Pythagorean sage we may turn to the figure of the highly-educated Egyptian who poses as an expert on magic and appeals to his Egyptian heritage to support that claim. Pancrates, the teacher of Arignotus, is a striking instance of the type. He was in fact an identifiable historical figure. He is the Pachrates, a *prophetes* from Helioupolis, mentioned in the great Paris magical papyrus. According to that text, Pachrates had displayed the power of a certain spell for the edification of the Emperor Hadrian: it brought a man to the spot in one hour, laid him low in bed in two hours and dispatched him to his final reward in seven hours, and, in addition, it sent a dream to the Emperor himself. The papyrus goes on to record Hadrian's amazement at Pachrates' powers, which was such that he gave the man a double salary.[34] More still is known about Pachrates: an Egyptian Greek, Athenaeus of Naucratis, the author of the *Deipnosophistae*, a miscellany of material on a great array of topics, in discussing wreathes mentions a Pancrates, whom he describes, probably with a hint of disdain, as a poet who was one of the natives, by which he will mean a native-Egyptian rather than a Egyptian Greek like himself. This Pancrates, he says, had recited a poem for Hadrian's benefit in which a miracle was described with a great deal of fanfare. The performance had taken place when the Emperor was present in Alexandria. The subject of the poem was a lotus with a rosy hue, which Pancrates suggested should properly be called Antinoeios after Hadrian's favourite, Antinous, since it sprang from the blood of the great lion that Hadrian and Antinous had killed while hunting in the desert west of Alexandria. Hadrian was delighted by the conceit and rewarded Pancrates with the privilege of meals in the Museum of Alexandria.[35] As it happens, papyrus fragments of a hexametric poem on the same subject have been found.[36] They will come from the poem that Pancrates composed either in AD 130, just before the death of Antinous by drowning in the Nile or just after that event.[37] It is curious that Athenaeus refers witheringly to the miraculous element in the poem. The explanation may be that he is alluding to Pancrates' reputation as a magician. A poem on a miracle is at any rate a suitable topic for a poet who is also a learned magician. The magician-cum-priest and the poet are almost certainly one and the same person. It would be nice if we could flesh out the picture further and get an impression of what manner of man Pancrates was and what exactly he did to gain a reputation as a magician. We may suspect that it rested on his writings and that he exploited the authority that his priestly calling gave him to pronounce on matters magical.

Pancrates had his predecessors of whom the most famous is the extraordinary figure of Apion. Apion is best known as a *grammatikos* and as the spokesman of the delegation from Alexandria to the Emperor Gaius on the occasion of intercommunal strife in Alexandria between the Jews and the Greco-Egyptian population.[38] As his name suggests, he was probably of Egyptian descent. He came from the oasis of El Kargeh, a circumstance of which the Jewish writer Josephus makes much, but became a citizen of Alexandria. By so doing, he acknowledged in Josephus' view the baseness of his Egyptian heritage and tried to forswear it.[39] Josephus is not being fair to Apion, who, to judge from the five-book work he wrote on matters Egyptian, was not at all inclined to disavow his Egyptian ancestry.[40] Apion is one in a long line of Egyptian authors, starting with Manethon in the early third century BC, who assume the rôle of interpreters of their native land to the Greeks. Apion clearly made an impression on those he met. He was nicknamed *Pleistonikes*, a name that derives from the formal nomenclature of athletics and meant that he had won many victories, and, less flatteringly, *Mochthos*, a somewhat ambiguous term that suggested he was capable of great endurance or that it required great endurance to hear him. The Emperor Tiberius rather wittily called him the Cymbal of the World, because he was very much inclined to blow his own trumpet.[41] He succeeded the *grammatikos* Theon in Alexandria, but he also taught in Rome and performed in Greece. Apion was clearly something of an international star. The remains of his Homeric glossary do not exactly convey the flavour of the man, but they do represent his most lasting achievement.

Aulus Gellius, writing of Apion a century later, says of the Egyptian's *Aigyptiaka* that he recorded in them all that was wondrous in Egypt.[42] There was, in other words, a strong element of paradoxography in his writing. Apion did, however, provide his own personal twist to the paradoxography: he would boast that the story he was about to tell he had witnessed with his own eyes and that it was not just hearsay or what he had read. He had in fact introduced the story of Androcles and the lion in just these terms.[43] Apion's interest in the miraculous was not just a literary pose but was very real. He was one of those Greeks and Romans who made their way up the Nile to Thebes to visit the colossi of Memnon, one of which was supposed at dawn to emit a sound. Some of the tourists then recorded their impressions of the experience in the form of graffiti scratched on the flank of the colossus. Apion was not only one of these but perhaps initiated the practice.[44] His experiences characteristically outdid those of most of his fellow-tourists: he heard Memnon sigh three times.[45]

In Bolus of Mendes a fascination with the miraculous went hand-in-hand with an interest in magic. Apion was no different: he too was a devotee of the occult. Pliny the Elder, who as a young man had seen Apion, presumably in Rome, found the misinformation he purveyed quite appalling. It was quite as bad as anything in the writings of the *magi* of old. To illustrate his point, he cites what Apion had written about the plant called *Cynocephalia* or Dog's Head, which Apion had said was called in Egyptian *Osiritis* or the Osiris Plant: it was divine and afforded protection against all maleficent spells, but if uprooted in one piece, it brought about the immediate death of the person who had dug it up.[46] Apion had evidently tried to impart an Egyptian colour to the lore on magical plants he furnished, which in this case looks to be of a spurious character. Pliny also regales us with one other instance of what Apion had said about plants with magical properties, although in this case he does not actually mention Apion by name, but chooses to refer to him as one renowned a little before his own time as a *grammaticus*. According to Pliny, that person had said that being touched by the plant called *Anacampserotes* or Love's Return caused either the return of passions or their dismissal and replacement by hate.[47]

It is impossible to say in what form Apion had published the lore on plants. Since the information contained in his *Aigyptiaka* is by no means confined to Egyptological subjects, there could have been herbal learning in the book. If Apion's proven interest in magic amounted only to a few cases in which he described certain plants and their magical powers in a work not specifically devoted to a magical theme, then it would be silly to assign him to the category of learned magician, however loosely the category may be defined. There are two other pieces of information that affect our assessment of the man. The more striking of these is the story that Pliny proceeds to tell about Apion, after complaining that there is no need to go back to the *magi* of old to find people prepared to tell whopping lies: Apion had put it about that he had summoned up the shades to ask Homer what his homeland had been and who were his parents, but that he did not dare divulge the answer he had been given to the questions.[48] Implicit in the story is a claim on Apion's part to magical expertise and specifically to an expertise in necromancy, which seems to have been the form of magic-working most favoured by the educated. Apion with the coyness characteristic of magicians had evidently said that the most dreadful punishments would befall him if he disclosed the results of his inquiries. The second and equally intriguing piece of information about Apion's concern with magic is that he had written a book called *On the Magus* or *On the Magi* or even *On Homer as Magus*.[49] There is unfortunately confusion in the manuscript-tradition over the precise title, but we can be fairly confident that it was a book about *magi*, since a well-known magician called Pases was mentioned in it. Something of the flavour of the book can be gleaned from a story about Pases that must have been told in it. Much of the information in the article on Pases in the Suda is likely to derive from Apion's treatment of him. He is mentioned there to explain the origin of a proverbial expression, 'The Demi-Obel of Pases'. The explanation for the expression will come from Apion. It runs as follows: Pases had a demi-obel that he could bring back into his possession after having paid it over for a purchase; he was able to do so because, although an effeminate, he surpassed all other men in his magical powers: his incantations could make expensive dinners with the necessary staff to serve them appear out of the blue and yet other incantations could make them vanish again. There are parallels for both of these feats in stories told about other magic-workers. One of the magical feats that Eucrates in Lucian's *Philopseudeis* said he saw Pancrates perform was to utter an incantation over some such object as a bar on a door and turn it into a servant to perform his bidding. Pancrates was loath to give Eucrates the appropriate magical formula, which led Eucrates to spy on him and to his overhearing Pancrates uttering a trisyllabic word. Eucrates, when Pancrates was gone, uttered the incantation and bade the upright of a door pour water for him. The upright was transformed and set about its assigned task and continued to perform it, until the whole room was flooded with water, since Eucrates did not know what to say to reverse the process. Pancrates reappeared, grasped what had happened and turned the servant back to wood, before vanishing into thin air.[50] Simon Magus is also credited with having been able to make household equipment serve him.[51] Later in the chapter we shall encounter itinerant Egyptian sorcerers who stand in the marketplace and conjure up visions of sumptuous meals. It would appear then to have been stories of this type with which Apion regaled his readers.

There are many things that one would like to know about Apion, not least whether he assigned a special rôle to Egypt in his writings on magic. There is not very much to go on here, but his assertion that the Egyptian name for *Cynocephalia* was *Osiris* rather suggests that he wished to give an Egyptian dimension to magic. If he did so, it is reasonable to suppose that he exploited his Egyptian ancestry and pretended to have privileged access to the magical mysteries of Egypt. It would also be interesting to see how Apion presented his stories about magicians, since with the exception of the magical papyri stories about magicians are never written from a perspective favourable to them.

Some idea of Apion's later renown as an expert on magic is to be gained from the *Homilies* falsely ascribed to Clement of Rome, but in fact written long after Clement's day. In one of them Clement encounters an Appion Pleistonikes in Tyre, who is an Alexandrian *grammaticus* and follower of the heresiarch Simon Magus.[52] Despite the misspelling of the name, there can be no doubt that this is Apion. Clement also meets the man in Rome during Appion's sojourn there. On this occasion he comes to visit Clement on his sickbed. Clement is aware of Appion's hatred of the Jews, that he had written many books against them and that Simon Magus' affection for Appion and association with him had nothing to do with any desire on Simon's part to learn from the man, but came from his sharing with Appion a profound antipathy to the Jews. By pretending that the sickness he suffers from is love Clement gets Appion to offer to perform erotic magic for him, an art which Appion says he had himself acquired from an Egyptian, expert in magic, encountered when he himself was sexually obsessed with a woman. Clement rejects the offer of help on the ground that it involves compulsion. Appion then offers to write an encomium of adultery that will persuade the woman to agree to come to Clement. Clement agrees and the encomium is written. It draws heavily on Greek myth to make its point and represents in Clement's eyes what Hellenic culture really stands for.[53] In what form Apion's fame as an expert on magic lived on into the third century AD is far from clear, but what is certain is that his writings on magic made a sufficient impact on the Christian imagination to make him a close associate of the arch-magician, Simon Magus.

The persistent tradition that highly-educated young men came to Egypt to be inducted into the mysteries of magic by the Egyptian clerisy needs to be examined further. Lucian's Arignotus, for instance, claims that Pancrates was his teacher.[54] We are not told, however, how a Pythagorean philosopher had come to have an Egyptian priest as his teacher. There is, however, a piece of pseudepigraphy from the High Roman Empire that describes the circumstances in which a student of literature who had come to Alexandria to work under the great men who taught there ended up becoming a student of magic. The young man was called Thessalus. He was supposed to have been the author of the work of astral-herbal lore that bears his name. An astral-herbal is a herbal which specifies under what conjunction of heavenly signs certain plants should be plucked if they are to be effective.[55] In the dedicatory epistle that precedes the work Thessalus explains how he came to acquire the information contained in the herbal.[56]

Thessalus' story was that in Asia Minor he had trained as a *grammatikos*, a teacher of letters, and had been successful in that endeavour. He had then decided to take himself with a substantial sum of money to Alexandria to consort there with the persons most expert in *belles lettres*. This he had done and had won golden opinions for his industry and intelligence. He had also made a habit of attending the lectures of those who discoursed on medicine, since that subject had a special fascination for him. When the time came for him to return home, he had already made a good deal of progress in the study of medicine. He had made a search of the libraries and found in the course of the search a book by the Pharaoh Nechepso that contained 24 cures for all parts of the body. The cures were effected by stones and plants employed in conjunction with the signs of the zodiac. Thessalus was impressed by the wonders the book promised to produce, but when he attempted to effect the cures, they all ended in failure. What made the failure the more galling was that he had impetuously written to his parents boasting of the effectiveness of the book, before he had actually tried out the recipes in it. He had also made a fool of himself in the presence of his rivals in Alexandria. He could not now return home, nor could he remain in Alexandria, where his fellow-doctors mocked him. To cut a long story short, he eventually came to Thebes and persuaded one of the older and more sober priests there, and not one of those who made exaggerated boasts about their knowledge of magic, to have the god Asclepius appear to him and impart his wisdom to him. The priest uttered some secret words and left the room, so that the god could appear to Thessalus.[57]

Although the preface to Thessalus' herbal unquestionably belongs to the genre of pseudepigraphy, it is nonetheless interesting for the light that it sheds on what we may infer was a recognized pattern in the career of a certain type of young man in the Greek East. It introduces us to a young man of respectable family who has pursued a literary education in one or more of the great cities of Asia Minor and has then gone on from there to further his education in Alexandria. In Alexandria, he decides to specialize in medicine and hopes in consequence to be able to return to his native city as something of a conquering hero. To attain that end, he needs to bring back from Egypt something special that will mark him off from other men.

It looks then as if there were in Asia Minor and in other parts of the Greek-speaking world also well-educated men who had come back from Egypt, where they had gone to advance their education, and who put it about that they had brought back with them special secret books containing information of the greatest value which they had acquired in very special circumstances from or with the help of an Egyptian priest who was an adept in the higher forms of magic. There may indeed have been a trade in Egypt in various forms of magical text, some of which will have been sold to persons from elsewhere in the Greek-speaking world who had come to Alexandria because of its fame as a centre of higher learning. The Egyptian books that Arignotus takes with him to the haunted house in Corinth to help him in exorcizing the unquiet spirit there are a case in point.[58] They are presumably Egyptian only in the sense that they have an Egyptian flavour to them. They will be like many of the recipes found in the magical papyri and will have prescribed incantations containing strings of Egyptian or Egyptian-sounding words.

Not all of the educated young men who dabbled in the occult acquired their knowledge of that subject in Egypt. It would be very surprising if they had done so. Nor again will they always have taken their magic so seriously. For many of them it must have been little more than a more or less danger- ous ploy, a venture into forbidden territory in which some fun was to be had. It was an area for experiment and high jinks. We get a hint that this was so from the continued existence of the *Paignia* of Democritus, which were still being copied out in Egypt in the fourth century AD, no doubt altered and added to. The tricks that such collections of *Paignia* contained could be used to impress the gullible with the superhuman powers of the magician or they could be performed as a prank, as a way of making a fool of the company at a symposium. The motives of those experimenting with such tricks will have varied and there may well have been cases where motives were mixed. All of this would be fairly empty speculation and word-spinning, were there not a passage in Philostratus in which that author, speaking in his own voice, dis- cusses a tendency on the part of those who have recourse to magic to blame its ineffectiveness on their own failure to carry out the ritual properly. In bringing his digression on magic to a close, Philostratus says that the tech- niques by which sorcerers (*goetes*) create miraculous signs from the gods and other wonders have been exposed by those who mock the pretensions of the craft of the magician; he will content himself with announcing his opposi- tion to young men consorting with sorcerers and by so doing becoming accustomed to playing such tricks (*paizein*).[59]

Philostratus is here talking about young men playing tricks (*paignia*) amongst which will be those that take the form of natural prodigies or won- ders (*terata*). He will have in mind such natural phenomena as thunder and earthquakes. That is to be inferred from something that is said earlier in the *Life of Apollonius of Tyana* by Thespesion, the leader of the Egyptian Gymnosophists, who complains that the Indian Brahmins are thaumaturges who rely on the magician's art and compares them to their disadvantage with Apollo: Apollo, when asked a question at Delphi, says what he knows without engaging in wonder-working (*terasteuomenos*), although it would be no great feat for him to cause Parnassus to shake, to have Castalia make her springs flow with wine instead of water and to keep the Cephisus from being a river.[60] Creating thunder and giving the impression of an earthquake are two of the tricks that magicians are known to have performed. The techniques employed are described by Hippolytus, a bishop of the first half of the third century AD, in his work on heresies. In that work there is an exposé of the procedures used by magicians and it is there that we learn of two ways of making thunder-like noises and of how to give the impression of an earth- quake so that everything seems to be moving.[61] One way of making thunder- ous noises is to push stones of different sizes over a precipice, so that they fall onto thin sheets of beaten bronze; the other is to tie a light cord around the kind of thin board used by fullers for pressing clothes and then to pull the cord away causing the board to vibrate. Since there is a lacuna in the manuscript at the point at which we are to learn how to create an earthquake, we shall never find out how the trick was performed other than it involved the droppings of an ichneumon, a magnet and burning coals.

Hippolytus gets this information from a text called *The Art of Thrasymedes*. Who Thrasymedes is supposed to have been or when the work was written is not known. Part of it, though not necessarily all of it, nonetheless clearly belongs to the tradition of making collections of *paignia* that goes back to Bolus of Mendes. How the author of the work referred to his tricks is uncertain, but Hippolytus uses the verb *paizein*, 'to play tricks', to denote the procedures used to create noises resembling thunder and calls the helper of the magician 'his fellow-trickster', *sympaiktes*.[62] If Hippolytus, a bishop in Rome, had access to a text of *The Art of Thrasymedes*, high-spirited young men will also have been able to get hold of such works. Some of them will certainly have done so, but that is not how Philostratus says they learned about performing *paignia*. His worry is that they acquired that knowledge by keeping company with magicians. This is mildly surprising, since it suggests that upper-class young men could find magic-workers with whom to associate and that Philostratus took this to be well known. Did the young men encounter the magicians when they went out whoring or were there other contexts in which the meetings took place? However bitterly we may regret it, we do not have the information to fill in the background to these encounters and to bring alive the occasions in which young bloods and their social inferiors came together to practise mischief. It is, however, worth noting that Philostratus does not treat the matter as a joke and appears to think that such associations had serious implications. It is possible that he is just being priggish, but there is also the possibility that he is worried, lest the young men should move on from a form of magic that amounts to no more than playing tricks to more serious magic-working.

## Magicians in the households of the rich or powerful

Lucian introduces us in his essay on the educated Greeks who offer themselves for hire to rich Romans to the educated Greek who enters the household of a rich Roman patron and passes himself off as an expert in magic-working and divination, because he finds that magic-working and soothsaying give him an importance he would not otherwise have enjoyed.[63] He nonetheless continues to affect the style of a philosopher: he sports a long beard and wears the philosopher's cloak. Magicians who were part of the household of rich and powerful men and women were to be found not only in Rome, but also in the eastern provinces of the Empire. Our knowledge of the social origins and education of these figures is extremely sketchy, but we may surmise that since the rich and powerful found them acceptable company, they must have had some social and educational attainments to recommend them.

Alexander of Abonuteichos was at least on Lucian's account of his doings a man of this sort. Abonuteichos was a small port on the Black Sea coast of Paphlagonia, where Alexander, who was a native of these parts, established an enormously successful and popular oracle of the healing god Asclepius. There can be no question of the existence of the oracle; coins testify to its presence. Lucian's account of Alexander's career and conduct is another matter. How much reliance can be placed on it is an open question. There is unquestionably a good deal of personal animus in Lucian's portrait, but more significantly Alexander represented in Lucian's eyes a particularly abominable example of a type of person whom Lucian loathed or affected to loathe, the religious charlatan. The worth of the account lies in the type that it delineates rather than in the portrait of the actual man.

On his return to Paphlagonia and Abonuteichos Alexander put it about that on his mother's side he was descended from Perseus and on his father's from Podalirius, a son of Asclepius, who had fought at Troy. That should mean that he belonged to some old and distinguished family. Lucian mocks the Paphlagonians, a people proverbial for their stupidity, for believing this, when they knew full well that both of the parents of the man were obscure and humble persons.[64] Now it is the case that ancient invectives almost invariably attribute humble, if not disgraceful, origins to the object of abuse. Not too much reliance should, accordingly, be placed on what Lucian says about Alexander's parentage. It was almost certainly not as humble as Lucian maintains it was, since Alexander clearly had received a literary education in an age in which education was by and large confined to those who could pay for it. Rather more weight can be placed on the picture that Lucian draws of the physical and intellectual endowments of the man and of the impression he made on people: he was a large and good-looking man with a white skin, and, Lucian concedes, a godlike demeanour; he had a beard but not an especially shaggy one; his hair was partly his own and partly a wig, but it was a very good wig that was hard to detect; his eyes had a certain brilliance and a divine quality to them; his speech was both very sweet and extraordinarily clear. These were his physical attributes. His intellectual capabilities were in no way inferior: he had an extremely sharp mind and was endowed with an extraordinarily good memory and with the ability to take in rapidly whatever he was taught. Yet he put these gifts to the worst possible uses. Lucian rounds off his thumbnail sketch of Alexander by saying that Alexander had in a letter to his father-in-law, a Roman of consular rank called Rutilianus, claimed a likeness between himself and Pythagoras. In Lucian's view, the comparison did an injustice to Pythagoras, who, however great a monster his worst detractors made him, was no match for Alexander in rascality and criminality. People nonetheless, on first meeting Alexander, came away with an impression of great probity, simplicity and sincerity.[65]

Lucian's next topic is Alexander's youth and how he had spent it. On Lucian's account, Alexander had as a lad exploited his good looks to earn money from prostitution. Amongst his lovers was the doctor-cum-magician from the circle of those who not only kept company with Apollonius of Tyana but who emulated him. The man took Alexander on as his apprentice and helper. At this point Lucian breaks off his narrative to address the man to whom the biography is dedicated, Celsus, to say that Celsus will now see out of what sort of school Alexander had emerged.[66] The key then in Lucian's eyes to an understanding of Alexander was the doctor who formed a link between Alexander and Apollonius of Tyana. Lucian's view of Apollonius of Tyana is quite evidently not that of Philostratus: Lucian's Apollonius is not the Pythagorean holy man, but the Pythagorean impostor and sorcerer whose existence Philostratus is at some pains to deny.[67]

Another standard feature of ancient invective was to accuse a man of having prostituted himself in his youth. Celsus, the opponent of Christianity, not the Celsus to whom Lucian dedicates his exposé of Alexander, maintained that Jesus was a man of illegitimate birth who had gone to Egypt and prostituted himself there and while in that country had acquired the magical powers that enabled him to pass himself off as a god.[68] No particular credence can be given to the charges that Lucian and Celsus make about the early years of Alexander and Jesus, but the form that the slanders take do suggest that the background of many of the holy men-cum-magicians of the type represented by Alexander will have been somewhat obscure and will have lent itself to slander. The more interesting part of the attack on Alexander is the charge that he had been the apprentice of a sorcerer, who had concealed his true vocation under the guise of being a doctor and who had, furthermore, belonged to the school of Apollonius of Tyana. There are two points worth remarking on here: one is that magicians do seem very often to have undergone an apprenticeship with an older man, while the other is the link with Apollonius of Tyana. Alexander, accordingly, in Lucian's eyes belonged to the same tradition of miracle-working holy men and charlatans as Apollonius of Tyana. The doctor from the circle of Apollonius was presumably the source of Alexander's Pythagoreanism. He will also have been responsible for Alexander's interest in Asclepius. Apollonius too was a devotee of Asclepius and, if Philostratus is to be trusted on the point, lived in the precinct of the temple of Asclepius throughout his sojourn in Aegae. Alexander's Pythagoreanism may have taken a more subtle and edifying form than the golden thigh which Lucian says the subject of his exposé was wont to lay bare to persuade those who saw it that the soul of Pythagoras had been reborn in him.[69] A less hostile witness than Lucian might have seen Alexander in a more favourable light as a Pythagorean holy man and devotee of Asclepius who followed a tradition established by Apollonius of Tyana.

By the time the doctor died, Alexander had begun to grow facial hair. The death of the doctor and the change in his own appearance meant that Alexander had no ready means of supporting himself. Throughout much of antiquity, once puberty set in, boys tended to lose their sexual appeal in the eyes of the men who had hitherto been drawn to them. Alexander had, accordingly, to find a new way of earning his livelihood. He had teamed up with a man from Byzantium called Cocconas who wrote lyrics to be performed in competition by choruses at festivals. They had then travelled around cheating the public of their goods by displays of magic and sorcery. One of their victims was a rich Macedonian woman from Pella, whose looks had faded but who still wanted to be the object of the sexual attentions of men. She had paid for their food. They for their part had followed her from Bithynia to Macedonia. When they were in Macedonia, they had purchased a large tame snake, which Alexander was later to use in the oracle he established in Abonuteichos.[70] The implication of Lucian's account is that the woman took Alexander and Cocconas into her entourage so that they might cast spells that would attract men to her.

It should be apparent that Lucian's account of the career of Alexander of Abonuteichos cannot be taken at face value. It requires a certain amount of inspired guesswork to get below the surface to the real Alexander. What can be salvaged from it is the picture of a certain kind of career. Men in the Greek East such as Alexander had to make their own way in the world because they had neither land nor property to support them. They had nonetheless received an education of a sort and may well have had a certain facility with words. Some of them were even well-enough trained and sufficiently talented to belong to the class of persons who wrote choral lyrics to be performed in the games. Lucian conspicuously does not criticize Alexander's education. In fact the terms in which he speaks of Alexander's powers of memory and of the ease with which he could absorb new ideas are reminiscent of the language employed by Philostratus to describe the powerful memory that Apollonius of Tyana displayed when he received his primary education from a *grammatikos* in his native city.[71] It looks as if Alexander had had a more than adequate education in language and literature at the feet of a *grammatikos* and that he may have had some training in philosophy. The stories that he made up about his heroic ancestry and the verses he presumably composed testify not only to a familiarity with Greek literature, but to a facility in composing hexameters. Lucian says it was Alexander's looks that recommended him to the doctor from Tyana with whom he served his apprenticeship. Where the apprenticeship took place Lucian fails for whatever reason to say. The doctor passed his Pythagoreanism and interest in Asclepius on to his apprentice. To judge from the case of Apollonius, the two interests went hand-in-hand. Pythagoreanism will have meant not only an ascetic form of life, but a belief in transcendental experiences and an interest in experimenting with the occult. Alexander's doctor evidently died when his apprentice was still too young to establish himself on his own and it was at this stage that Alexander teamed up with Cocconas to travel the circuit with him. They were then lucky enough to be taken up by an older woman and to be made part of her household.

Lucian does not pretend that Alexander was not a physically attractive and able person. He possessed, in particular, two qualities that must have been invaluable in a man of his sort: the brilliance of his gaze suggested to men that there was an element of the divine in him; and those who met him took away an impression of moral rectitude, goodness and sincerity. That impression would have been reinforced by his beard and hair, which seem to have been allowed to grow long in the Pythagorean fashion. He was, in short, admirably equipped to play a holy man of the type that Apollonius of Tyana had invented, the holy man who is both a follower of Pythagoras and a devotee of Asclepius. Some of these wandering sages will not have been averse to practising wonder-working to impress those whom they encountered with their divine powers. The particularly fortunate ones such as Alexander will have been taken up by rich patrons.

In the Acts of the Apostles and in the Jewish historian Josephus a rather different kind of magician is encountered, Jews who were part of the household or entourage of high Roman officials serving in the East. The Acts of the Apostles say that Paul at the beginning of his mission to the Gentiles, when he had made his way from Salamis – which was where he had landed on Cyprus – to Paphus, found in the company of the governor, the proconsul, Sergius Paullus, a Jewish magician and false prophet called Bar-Jesus. Sergius summoned Paul and Barnabas so that he might hear the word of God from them. The magician did not like this and tried to keep the proconsul from believing God's word. Paul, now filled with the Holy Spirit, looked the man in the eye and announced that he would be struck blind for attempting to lead Sergius away from the path of the Lord. The magician was promptly deprived of his eyesight and Paullus was converted.[72] These events would have taken place between AD 46 and 48. The Sergius Paullus in question, a man of Italian descent with land in Galatia, came from Pisidian Antioch, which was to be Paul's next destination, and was in AD 70 the first senator from the East to hold the suffect consulship. Paul probably made Pisidian Antioch his next stopping point, precisely because of Sergius Paullus' influence there.[73] It is of some significance that the author of Acts can take it for granted that his readers will not have been puzzled by the presence of a Jewish magician and seer in the entourage of a high Roman official. That suggests that Jewish magicians and magicians who were part of the court of Roman administrators were in their eyes familiar figures.

The existence of Jewish magicians as a known presence and, furthermore, of Cypriot magicians is to be inferred from the paragraph in Pliny the Elder's history of magic in which Pliny speaks of another branch of the magical art, many thousands of years more recent than that of Zoroaster, that descends from Moses, Iannes, Lotapes and the Jews, and yet another, still more recent, in Cyprus.[74] Notwithstanding its interesting confusions, the notice in Pliny represents an extremely important testimony to the fame in the first century

AD of Jewish and Cypriot magic-workers. Whether the Cypriot magicians were Jewish or not is unclear from Pliny, but some of them must have been.

Bar-Jesus will have belonged to the Jewish community in Cyprus. Amongst the close associates of Felix, the Roman procurator of Judaea, at roughly the same time as Paul visited Sergius, was another Jewish magician from Cyprus. This is the man called Atomus, whom Josephus says Felix counted amongst his friends. Felix employed Atomus as his go-between when he tried to persuade a certain Drusilla to leave her husband for him.[75] For a high Roman functionary to have had a Jewish magician amongst his friends almost certainly means that Atomus was part of Felix' entourage. Atomus is likely to have been a hellenized Jew with sufficient education to make him fitting company for a Roman procurator.

## Itinerant magicians in general

An in-house magician, let alone a philosopher-cum-magician, was a luxury reserved for a very limited group of people. Nor will any but a very select few have had anything directly to do with the Neopythagorean holy men who dabbled in the occult, although the curious may have had heard them dispense their wisdom when they came to town to perform. Most people will have had to look elsewhere for help in magic-working. Where they looked is the question. The obvious answer would seem to be that they consulted their local magician. Since magicians were periodically expelled from Rome, it looks as though there were magicians who were more or less permanently domiciled in the capital. It is hard to believe that the same did not hold true for Carthage or Antioch or Alexandria or even Athens. The difficulty is that there is little or no record of their existence. This is almost certainly a reflection of the kinds of sources that exist for the period, since magicians who are permanently resident in a city are well-enough attested in the Late Roman Empire.

The magician about whom our sources for the period do tell us is the itinerant sorcerer. He has already been encountered in the person of Alexander of Abonuteichos, who, after the death of the doctor to whom he was apprenticed and before he was taken up by the rich woman from Macedonia, was a wandering sorcerer. That was in the period in which he had teamed up with Cocconas from Byzantium and had travelled around Bithynia with him putting on displays of magic and performing sorcery to fleece the masses or, as the pair themselves would have put it, using what Lucian says was the patois handed down from magician to magician, 'the fat and the thick'.[76]

The questions that need to be asked about these itinerant magicians are first of all who they were, then what they did do and finally, where they were to be found. To begin with the terminology used in speaking of itinerant magicians: in Greek they continue to be classified as *agyrtai* or begging holy men, although sometimes they are also called *ageirontes*, a participle from the same root as *agyrtes* that means 'those taking up a collection', and sometimes yet again as *planetai*, 'wanderers or vagabonds', or *planoi*, the deeply ambiguous term that means primarily 'one who creates delusions in the minds of other men', then 'sorcerer', but that may also have connotations of vagabond or wandering beggar;[77] the term *laoplanos*, 'one who deludes the masses', is also found;[78] in Latin there is no term that is the exact equivalent of *agyrtes*, but in practice a *circulator* was what in Greek would have been called an *agyrtes*. In Late Latin glossaries, *agyrtes* is given as an equivalent of *circulator*. A *circulator* gets his name from his gathering a circle (*circulus*) of onlookers about himself and this is precisely what most *circulatores* will have done. The term is likely to be an attempt at rendering in Latin references in Greek to persons who perform or beg *en tois kyklois*, that is, surrounded by a ring of spectators. An example of that type of expression is to be found in Maximus of Tyre's criticisms of the kind of person who believes that the gods are prepared to prophesy to anyone, no matter who he is and no matter what his purpose is: they suppose the gods to differ not a whit from those collecting money in the centre of a circle of onlookers (*en tois kyklois ageirontes*) who are happy to produce prophetic utterances for every Tom, Dick and Harry for two obols.[79] In Greek astrological texts, the word *ochlagogos* occurs, which means 'one who gathers a crowd about himself'.[80] In a glossary, *circulator* is given as its equivalent. It will be no accident that in astrological texts the *ochlagogos* belongs to the category of those who abuse their fellow-men and of those who conduct their business in a deceitful manner.[81] The astral configuration that produces *ochlagogoi* also gives birth to *magoi, planoi*, persons who perform sacrifices for the purpose of divination (*thytai*), doctors, astrologers, bankers, counterfeiters and forgers.[82] *Ochlagogoi* are also mentioned in two Christian texts that set out the categories of person to be excluded from admission to the catechumenate unless they renounce the callings they currently pursue. In the earlier text, the so-called *Traditio apostolorum*, which belongs to the first half of the third century AD, they are mentioned alongside performers of incantations, astrologers, diviners, interpreters of dreams and makers of amulets.[83] In the later text, the *Constitutiones apostolorum*, the *ochlagogos* is found in the immediate company of the magician (*magos*), the utterer of incantations (*epaoidos*), the astrologer, the diviner (*mantis*), the snake-charmer (*therepodos*),[84] the *agyrtes*, the maker of amulets and the purifier.[85] These are not all discrete categories of person, but in some cases different ways of referring to the same person.

Not all *agyrtai, ageirontes* and *circulatores* were magicians. In fact the majority of them will have had different, though related, accomplishments. The itinerant magicians and holy men of the High Roman Empire belong to a much larger world of travelling performers, astrologers and salesmen, not to speak of beggars, who were to be found at street-corners, in marketplaces, and around the theatres, amphitheatres, hippodromes and temples of the more substantial towns. All of these persons fall into the category of *ageirontes*, although beggars were probably not thought of as *circulatores*. *Circulatores* were after all persons about whom a circle of persons gathered in the expectation of seeing a performance of some kind. The sophists who moved freely around the cities of the Eastern Roman Empire putting on virtuoso displays wherever they went would not have been classified as *circulatores* or *ageirontes*, even though in some sense they earned their living from such public performances. No doubt unkind critics sometimes labelled them as *ageirontes*, but *circulator* and *ageiron* were on the whole terms of disparagement reserved for those reduced to having to beg for their living.

To get some idea of the world of which the itinerant magician and holy man were part, it will be useful to look at who it was who was a *circulator* or an *ageiron* and at what exactly he did. We should look first at the *circulator*. In Apuleius' *Metamorphoses*, the narrator Lucius, who is dilating on the theme of there being more on heaven and earth than meets the eye, speaks of his having almost choked the previous evening on a large morsel of cheesecake, and then, continuing on the same theme, speaks of his having seen in Athens in front of the Stoa Poikile with his own two eyes a man swallow a sharp-pointed cavalry sword, and with the encouragement of some small pieces of change thrusts a hunting spear down his throat as far as his bowels. Not only does Lucius say he had seen that, he also maintains that he had witnessed an effeminate boy performing sinuous manoeuvres, while perching on that part of the spear that had not been swallowed.[86] The man who swallows the cavalry sword and then the spear Lucius calls a *circulator*. Who he is we are not told. But we do learn that he performs in the Athenian Agora, that he has a boy who is part of his act and that he draws his initial audience by putting on a free show for them, which leads, once he has been paid a small sum, to his doing something more spectacular. Now what elicits the story is the disbelief that one of Lucius' travelling companions has expressed about the power of magic to alter the natural order.[87] The *circulator* from the Athenian Agora is, accordingly, in Lucius' eyes something of a magician.

The snake-handling *circulatores* mentioned both by the medical writer of the first century AD, Celsus, and in the *Digest* of Justinian were no doubt also sometimes classified as *goetes* because what they did seemed to contravene the natural order.[88] The *Digest* speaks of the penalties to which such *circulatores* were liable if the snakes they carried around and exhibited instilled such fear as to cause harm. Celsus is more revealing: he explains how *circulatores* were able to place the heads of poisonous snakes in their mouths without experiencing any harm: they drugged their charges and, unless the handler was bitten, the saliva of the snake did no harm. The large tame snake from the vicinity of Pella that Alexander and his comrade-in-arms Cocconas acquired and employed to promote their oracle is an extreme example of a snake used by a magician to persuade the gullible of his special relationship to a god.[89] Indirect evidence for *circulatores* who get the animals in their charge to perform amazing tricks is to be found in the reaction of

Encolpius, the narrator in the *Satyricon*, to the introduction of some pigs to the banqueting chamber of Trimalchio, a vulgar parvenu: he is convinced that acrobats have entered and that the pigs are going to perform miraculous tricks as is wont to happen in the middle of circles of persons.[90]

There were no doubt many other kinds of person besides magicians, jugglers and acrobats who would have been called *circulatores*, but the two other kinds of *circulator* who are referred to in as many words as *circulatores* of whom our texts tell us were respectively the man who declaimed in the forum of a town and the man who recited poetry or perhaps put on plays in a similar venue. The style of declamation of these marketplace orators was violent and overdone and they were a byword for unchecked volubility.[91] The *circulatores* who did poetic recitals had kindred faults: a slave who has learned to imitate *circulatores* reciting poetry causes the over-refined sensibilities of the narrator of the *Satyricon* great distress by the way in which he raises and lowers his voice when he performs for the company at Trimalchio's symposium. The rebarbative style of recitation favoured by *circulatores* also emerges from the proud boast made by the owner of the slave: he has no peer in his imitations of *circulatores* and muleteers.[92]

It is Tertullian who is our principal source of information about the magicians who were *circulatores*. He does not say who they were, but he does tell us quite a lot about what they did. What emerges from the four passages in which he brings up *circulatores* and their doings is that the magic they performed was of the spectacular variety that lent itself to public display: apparitions of Castor were conjured up; water was carried in sieves; beards were turned red by a touch of the hand; the spirits of the dead were called up; men were made to have dreams; prophetic utterances were elicited from boys, goats and tables.[93] *Circulatores* who performed magic in public were in some ways the ancient counterparts to the modern conjuror or magician. There was another aspect to the displays they put on in public that resembles the performances of a modern medium rather than a conjuror: they practised forms of divination using boys, goats and tables. How tables and goats were employed for the purpose of divination is something at which we have to guess, but there is a good deal of information about the use of boys as mediums. Most commonly they were made to gaze into a bowl of water, a mirror or a lamp in which they saw deities or demons whom they questioned.

The information to be gleaned about *ageirontes* and what they did, from our Greek sources and especially from Philostratus' celebration of Apollonius of Tyana and from the criticisms of Christianity to be found in the fragments of Celsus' *True Account* contained in Origen's *Against Celsus*, complements and supplements what is to be learned about *circulatores* from authors writing in Latin. The strolling players, for instance, whose existence may be inferred from Petronius are to be found as large as life in Philostratus. Apollonius and his companions encounter just such a person in Rome: after arriving in the city they were settling down to dinner in their inn near the city gates when a drunken figure burst in on them. He was a man who made his way around Rome singing passages from tragedy that were set to music. The passages were ones that the Emperor Nero himself had sung. The man had purchased the privilege of singing these passages and he was allowed to arrest anyone who did not listen respectfully to the songs or who did not pay him a fee.[94] The reality behind the episode is likely to be the existence of travelling singers who sought audiences not only at street-corners but also in inns and drinking establishments. There was also the tragic actor who collected a living (*ageiron*) by going around the culturally-deprived cities of the western provinces. He did this at a time when the cities of Spain were being compelled to celebrate Nero's victories in the Crown Games of Greece, although the actor himself had not been thought worthy to compete against the Emperor at these festivals. In the more civilized communities his performances gained him some renown, if for no other reason than that the inhabitants of these cities had never heard a tragedy, but also because he pretended to give an accurate rendition of the lyrics that Nero sang. On the other hand, the inhabitants of Hispalis were so overcome by his appearance on a high stage that when he raised his voice in a shout, most of them fled as though they had heard the cry of a demon.[95] Lions and other large wild beasts being led around on a tether by persons who used them to collect money from passers-by were no doubt one of the sights to be seen in the cities of the Roman Empire. Philostratus tells a story about a lion on a leash which Apollonius met in Egypt. It and its owner travelled over a wide area begging for money. Its particular trick was to nuzzle not only its owner but whomever it approached.[96]

Philostratus places sorcerers or *goetes* firmly in the category of those who earn a living as wandering mendicants (*ageirontes*). In a speech that Apollonius is supposed to have composed to deliver in front of Domitian, which he did not in the event give, but with which Philostratus nonetheless regales us, Apollonius divides up the crafts by the different levels of knowledge displayed in them: at the top of the hierarchy are those in which real knowledge is involved such as poetry, music and astronomy; then there are those in which a kind of sub-knowledge subsists such as painting and sculpture; and finally there are the practitioners of crafts that lay claim to a pseudo-knowledge; they are the persons who make their living as mendicants. Into this last category Apollonius places *goetes*.[97] *Goetes*, in other words, belong to a larger category of wandering mendicants who lay claim to a kind of pseudo-knowledge. Who the persons who make up the rest of the category are Apollonius does not exactly say, but since he excepts as much of the prophetic craft as is true from the category of pseudo-knowledge, we may infer that he also has in mind false prophets of various kinds as well as other forms of charlatan.

The figure of the wandering magician also springs readily to Celsus' lips when he speaks of Christians or Jews. Moses, according to Celsus, traces the lineage of the Jews back to men who were vagabonds and sorcerers;[98] Christians he likens to those who are vagabonds, sorcerers and summoners of apparitions.[99] Elsewhere, to remind his readers that Jesus was just one of many such men, he points out that men like Jesus went around begging in the cities and the military camps of Phoenicia and Palestine and would, as though divinely inspired, proclaim themselves God or the Son of God or the Holy Spirit.[100] Celsus' repeated mention of vagabond-magicians makes it likely that wandering holy men who practised magic-working were a familiar feature of the world in which he lived.

## Wandering Egyptian and Jewish magicians

In Apuleius' *Metamorphoses*, a guest at the dinner party recounts how in Larissa in Thessaly the father of a young man who has been murdered had brought forward an Egyptian prophet (*propheta*) called by the foreign-sounding, though in fact not Egyptian, name of Zatchlas, to raise his son from the dead, so that the revivified corpse might reveal what had happened to him.[101] Zatchlas then raises the man from the dead and gets him to explain how he had met his fate. All of this takes place in the forum of Larissa. The bereaved father calls Zatchlas both a prophet and a priest (*sacerdos*). The Egyptian turns out to be a young man dressed as an Egyptian priest: his garments are made of linen; he wears sandals made of palm-fibre; and his head is completely shaven. He undertakes to revivify the corpse and make it speak, for a considerable fee.[102]

Itinerant Egyptian magicians and persons passing themselves off as such will have exploited the widely-held view that as Egyptians they were expert in magic, which in its turn rested on the belief that Egyptian religion was essentially magic and that those who had access to its secrets were particularly powerful magicians. In Heliodorus' *Aethiopica*, Calasiris, who is a priest of Isis, tries to correct that image of Egyptian sacred wisdom, explaining that he had once been able to exploit it to his own advantage when the hero of the story, Theagenes, had sought him out, supposing that as an Egyptian *prophetes* he would be able to help him through magic to win the love of the heroine of the novel. Calasiris says that he had gone along with Theagenes' deluded view of his nature and had played up to the expectations entertained by the youth about what an Egyptian priest-cum-magician should be able to do.[103] In recounting the incident, Calasiris tells his hearer that there are in fact two different kinds of Egyptian wisdom: one is a vulgar and earthly kind that is concerned with ghosts, the bodies of corpses, plants and incantations and, in general, with illicit and licentious activities, whereas the other is that which priests practise from their youth; it looks heavenwards, consorts with the gods and shares in their supernatural power and is concerned to promote good.[104] Although he attempts to correct the widespread misapprehension about the nature of Egyptian priestly wisdom, Calasiris does not deny that there is a form of Egyptian wisdom whose subject matter is sorcery. It is to be surmised from Calasiris' protestations about the heavenly form of wisdom practised by Egyptian priests that there were persons calling themselves priests of Isis who made a living from the earthly form of wisdom he describes. Zatchlas will be an example of the type. The Egyptian magician, Pancrates, familiar to us from Lucian's *Philopseudeis* is certainly a priest; he is supposed to be of the number of the sacred scribes in Memphis and to have spent twenty-three years underground in the holy of holies learning at Isis' hands how to be a magician.

A telling indication of the existence of persons presenting themselves as Egyptian magicians or as authorities on magic because they are Egyptian is to be seen in the Egyptian whom Pausanias, a travel-writer of the second half of the second century AD, cites as the source of the story that, at the spot on the racecourse at Olympia where horses tended to take fright, Pelops had buried an unspecified object which he had received from Amphion the Theban and that the buried object had scared the horses of Oenomaus and all subsequent horses. Pausanias adds that the same Egyptian had put down Orpheus' success in getting wild beasts to come to him and Amphion's ability to draw stones with which to build the walls of Thebes to their skill in magic-working.[105] This is just one of several explanations to be rejected that Pausanias gives on the authority of persons who are not named for the strange phenomenon of horses taking fright at a certain point on the racecourse at Olympia. The practice of citing the explanations of suitable authorities only to reject them is a device best known from Herodotus. In Herodotus' case the authorities are very often of his own invention. The Egyptian is almost certainly Pausanias' creation.[106] He is an Egyptian, since the explanation that would spring to the mind of such a person for horses panicking in a hippodrome was that someone had buried on the racetrack a curse-tablet received from a magician.

What all of this adds up to is that Egyptian magicians were a known feature of some areas of the Roman world. Many of them will have played the part of priests, and priests of Isis, in particular, will have dressed appropriately in linen, shaved their heads and made much of their holiness, the mysterious nature of Egyptian religion and the powerful forces it knew how to unlock. Not all of the itinerant magicians who presented themselves as Egyptian priests were frauds. A case can be made for the existence in Egypt of persons associated in a more or less official capacity with its temples who exploited the fame that attached to them as magicians and either practised magic themselves or pretended to be able to teach it. That some of them travelled to foreign parts and turned the fame that they enjoyed as magicians to their own advantage would not be surprising.

Some idea of the activities in which itinerant priests of Isis might engage is to be gained from the story that Porphyry tells about an extraordinary event at which his master Plotinus was present. An Egyptian priest, who had come to Rome, made contact through a friend with Plotinus. He did so because he wished to impress Plotinus with a display of his wisdom. It was to consist in his summoning up the personal demon of Plotinus. The philosopher assented readily enough to the proposal. The evocation of the demon took place in the temple of Isis, since the Egyptian declared it was the only pure place in Rome. When the demon was in fact called up, it was a god who appeared, which led the Egyptian to exclaim that Plotinus was blessed in having a god as his personal demon and not one of the inferior race of demons. Unfortunately, there was no time to see any more of the god or to ask him questions, since the friend who had acted as the go-between was present at the session, and had, either out of envy or out of fear, wrung the necks of the chickens he had with him for the sake of protection.[107] The story is told after another anecdote illustrating Plotinus' supernatural powers. Its aim was clearly to demonstrate Plotinus' close relationship with the divine. It lacks the authenticating details of the names of either the friend or the Egyptian priest and cannot, on that account, be accepted as an actual instance of magic-working. The story is nonetheless *prima facie* evidence that persons calling themselves Egyptian priests did participate in magic-working.

The Acts of the Apostles tells of wandering Jewish exorcists who, hearing of Paul's success in Ephesus in curing the sick and driving out evil spirits, were moved to try to exorcize evil spirits in the name of Jesus, saying: 'I exorcize you in the name of Jesus, whom Paul proclaims'. Amongst those attempting to perform this feat were seven sons of a certain chief priest (*archiereus*) Sceva. The evil spirit, however, refused to acknowledge their invocation of Jesus and Paul and said to them: 'I recognize Jesus and know Paul, but who are you?' Worse still, the man possessed by the evil spirit attacked and wounded the would-be exorcists and drove them from his house. When this became known, we are told, fear fell upon the inhabitants of Ephesus, both Greeks and Jews. Many of those who had been persuaded of Paul's power confessed their doings, while a significant number of those who had pursued curious practices (*perierga*) collected their books and burnt them in the presence of all.[108]

There can be no doubt that the wandering Jewish exorcists are for the author of Acts magicians. Pagans, such as Marcus Aurelius and Lucian, took very much the same view of the practice.[109] No stigma attaches to exorcism in the eyes of our Christian sources when it is practised by Jesus or by his apostles, but if a pagan or Jew performs the same act, then its associations with magic-working come to the fore again. Amongst the charges that Irenaeus directs at the followers of Simon Magus, the so-called Simonians, is that they engage in magic. He gives a fairly extensive catalogue of the kinds of magic that they perform. The list begins with exorcisms and incantations and moves on to amatory spells and spells that draw a person and ends with the use of familiar spirits and the sending of dreams and whatever other curious and excessive practices (*periergia*) they pursue.[110] In view then of the associations of exorcism with magic it is not surprising that in the story told in Acts one of the effects of the discomfiture of the Jewish exorcists when they try to use the name of Jesus in an exorcism is that a significant number of those who had engaged in what the author of *Acts* calls excessive or curious practices (*perierga*) are moved by fear to bring their books to a central spot and burn them in the presence of all.[111] Now excessive or curious practices in this context mean interfering in what ought to be left undisturbed, which is to say, practising magic. The books that are burned are, therefore, magical books and their owners consign them to the flames, because they are convinced of the inefficacy of magic in relation to the Word of the Lord. This incidentally is our first indication that a significant number of people, Jews and Hellenes, who are not themselves magicians might own books of magic.

From the perspective of at least some Jews exorcism was a perfectly legitimate practice with ancient and respectable antecedents. Josephus traced its history back to Solomon and the incantations he composed and the techniques he devised under the guidance of God for combating demons.[112] It was a technique that was still very much in use in his own day, according to Josephus, who goes on to describe an exorcism he had witnessed. The exorcism had taken place in the presence of Vespasian, his sons, officers and army and had been performed by a certain Eleazar, a countryman of Josephus. Eleazar had placed a ring containing a root below a seal of the kind prescribed by Solomon before the nostrils of one who was possessed and had then drawn the demon out through the nostrils of the man as he smelled the root; when the man fell to the ground, Eleazar conjured the demon not to return, using Solomon's name and the incantations that Solomon had composed; as proof that the demon had departed Eleazar ordered it to overturn a vessel containing water as it left the man.[113]

Josephus saw the exorcism performed by Eleazar as proof of God's love of Solomon, manifested so that all persons under the sun might know it.[114] Very few pagans or Christians will have viewed Jewish exorcists in this light. Solomon and his seal were soon appropriated by Gentile magic-workers. The very words 'Seal of Solomon' came when inscribed on metal or clay to have a talismanic force against the powers of evil. Jewish exorcists continue to be a presence well into the second half of the second century AD. For Lucian, Jewish exorcists are just magicians, although there is the trace of a hint in one passage that they are the exorcists *par excellence*. Ion, the representative of Platonism in the *Philopseudeis*, says that he expects all of those present know the Syrian from Palestine who can charm spirits out of the possessed and are aware that for a substantial consideration he will stand over people who have fallen to the ground and whose eyes whirl and whose mouths foam and ask the spirit in them whence he has come and, furthermore, that when the spirit answers, whether in Greek or some other language, he compels it to leave by uttering threatening oaths.[115] Again in Lucian's *Podagra*, the personification of gout in rehearsing the number of useless cures to which men have recourse in trying to get rid of her mentions the Jew who gets hold of a fool of a patient and tries to charm the disease out of him.[116]

Celsus, the Platonist critic of Christianity, introduces us to a further type of wandering holy man-cum-magician: the inspired prophet with a message of salvation. He maintains that Jesus was just one of many such persons to be found in Phoenicia and Palestine; they were men of obscure origins, some of whom were to be encountered in temples or outside temples, others again went to and fro as mendicants visiting cities and army-camps where, in a state of great agitation, as though divinely-inspired, they would make a prophetic utterance to the effect that they were God or the Son of God or the Divine Breath. According to Celsus, the wandering holy men supplemented these grandiose pronouncements with utterances of an obscure and demented nature, which no reasonable man would be able to decipher, but whose obscurity made it possible for every fool and sorcerer (*goes*) to appropriate them in whatever way they wanted and for whatever purpose they desired.[117] Celsus says rather specifically that inspired prophets of the type he describes were a phenomenon peculiar to Phoenicia and Palestine.

## The settings in which wandering magicians performed

There were a number of settings in which itinerant holy men, performers of a humbler kind, wandering preachers and popular philosophers operated, but there are three that are mentioned above all others, temple precincts, marketplaces and crossroads. Dio Chrysostom, for instance, speaks of the large number of men who passed for Cynics in Alexandria to be found at crossroads, in narrow alleys and at the gates of temples, where they collected money (*ageirein*) and put one over on a mob made up of boys or possibly young slaves (*paidaria*), sailors and other persons of that order, by stringing together jests and gossip and giving responses characteristic of the market-place (*agora*).[118] It is true that in Apuleius' *Metamorphoses* the votaries of the Syrian Goddess, who rig themselves out in their gaudy costumes at the start of each day, begin their ecstatic dance while wending their way through a few hovels, although they reserve their best efforts for the country-house of a rich landowner, where they begin to whip and mutilate themselves and engage in inspired prophecy.[119] Few other itinerant holy men will have made their way through the countryside in a noisy and colourful procession that drew whoever was around to it. Even the priests of the Syrian goddess will mostly have performed in marketplaces and at crossroads. It is after all the case that their leader is said to be one of the scum of the common people from the cross-roads that carried the Syrian Goddess from marketplace to marketplace and town to town, forcing her to beg.[120]

It is also the case that these same priests when they come to one village succeed in persuading the inhabitants of one village to let them make the sanctuary of the Mother Goddess their headquarters.[121] This is not altogether surprising, since temples in general, and especially the temples of Oriental deities, tended to be places where a variety of dubious characters congregated. In Rome, temples were notoriously one of the spots where men went to pick up prostitutes.[122] The temple of Isis was especially infamous in this regard.[123] In the Greek East, the same situation prevailed. Temples were one of the locations where mendicant priests of all varieties were to be found. Celsus says that in Phoenicia and in Palestine men proclaiming themselves God or the Son of God or the Holy Spirit were to be found both in temples and outside them.[124] As in the Hellenistic and Classical Periods, these men, and perhaps women, mixed religion with magic-working. The temples of the gods were, accordingly, one of the spots to which men and women who were in need of a magician made their way.

A speaker in a dialogue by Plutarch in which the decline of oracles uttered in verse is discussed explains the passing of such oracles by the disrepute that the hucksterish, mendicant (*agyrtikon*), altar-besieging and vagabond element to be found at shrines of the Great Mother and Serapis had brought oracles delivered in verse; some of them made up their own verse-oracles, others chose them by lot from tablets; slaves and women were entranced by the metre of the oracles and by their poetic diction. The speaker concludes that poetry by prostituting itself to cheats, sorcerers (*goetes*) and false prophets has lost its reputation for being truthful and has been banished from the Delphic tripod.[125] Plutarch does not explain who the people were who produced oracles in verse and who hung around the shrines of the Mother of the Gods and Serapis beyond saying that they belonged to the hucksterish and mendicant element who wandered from place to place and besieged altars (*bomolochon*). He almost certainly has in mind begging-priests in their various manifestations. Philo Judaeus, writing in Alexandria two generations at least before Plutarch, speaks of a *magike* coined in a false form that is pursued by begging-priests of the Mother Goddess (*Menagyrtai*), by those who frequent altars (*bomolochoi*) and the basest of women and slaves.[126] The false *magike* of which Philo speaks is simply sorcery, which he distinguishes from its true form, as it is practised in Persia. The latter in his view is an enhanced form of vision that enables its practitioners to see more clearly into the workings of nature.[127] Although Philo seems to speak of the begging-priests of the Mother Goddess and those who frequent altars as though they were quite separate categories of person, he almost certainly should not be taken to do so. His meaning is rather that magic is practised by begging-priests and others who hang around altars. What we have here is a form of hendiadys, the rhetorical device by which a complex idea is expressed by two coordinated nouns. Philo goes on to say that these sorcerers profess to be able to perform purification and to reconcile those who are at odds with each other and make those who are in love come to hate each other through philtres and incantations.

It is difficult to tell whether Philo also means that the base slaves and women who promised to effect purifications, bring about reconciliations and engender enmities were to be found in temple precincts hanging about the altars there, but there is a passage in another author from Alexandria that suggests this is exactly Philo's meaning. He is the Christian author of the early third century AD, Clement, who adapts and amplifies Philo's somewhat laconic account to meet his own needs. In the course of a denunciation of the conduct of rich women he speaks of their spending their time with men who regale them with erotic tales that lead to their physical and mental corruption. The next or another stage in their descent into wickedness follows: they are carried on litters to various shrines, there to perform sacrifices and to seek oracular advice; they are accompanied on their daily rounds by mendicant priests, begging-priests of the Great Mother and by the kind of old woman who hangs around altars and contributes to the destruction of the home; they put up with old women's whisperings over their cups and they learn from sorcerers love-philtres and incantations whose purpose is the destruction of marriages; they already have possession of some men, they pray for others and the seers promise them possession of yet others.[128]

Clement's description of the life of the idle rich matches in its vividness and in its detail anything in the pages of Petronius or Juvenal. The picture that he paints of rich women consorting with magicians and sorceresses is nonetheless ultimately inspired by Philo Judaeus. Although Clement has drawn on Philo here, it does not follow that Clement's picture is nothing more than the amplification of a literary motif and does not represent a reality. There is no reason to suppose that conditions had changed so radically between Philo's and Clement's day that temple precincts were no longer the haunt of begging-priests and other ne'er-do-wells. Nor does it seem likely that the rich women filling in their time each day with trips in litters to the sanctuaries of various deities accompanied by begging-priests and old women who were part procuress and part sorceress does not correspond to some aspect of life in Alexandria. It is true that a Church Father in full cry denouncing sexual irregularity may get somewhat carried away and may embellish and exaggerate the truth in some measure, but that does not mean there were not irregularities there to be denounced.[129]

Clement's account helps to bring to life and make sense of the more allusive references that we have in Philo and Plutarch to the women and mendicant holy men who were to be found frequenting altars in temple precincts. It is easier now to form a picture of who it was, at least in Alexandria, who went to the altars of the Mother Goddess or Serapis to sacrifice and seek oracular advice and why it was that they were vulnerable to the approaches of the mendicant holy men who lay in wait for their prey around the altars. Not only women looking for love or sexual adventure will have made their way to these shrines, but the sick, the distressed and the ambitious or greedy will also have visited them and will in their own way have been as vulnerable to the advances of the motley cast awaiting them in the temple precinct.

Celsus' attacks on Christianity present a vivid picture of wandering magicians operating in marketplaces in comparing the miracle-working of Jesus and Christian evangelism in general to what vagabond-magicians did in the agora. The miracles that Jesus performed he is prepared to concede did in fact happen, so that he can then point out the striking similarity of the healing of the sick, the raising of the dead and the matter of the loaves and the fishes to what sorcerers (*goetes*) and the pupils of the Egyptians did in the middle of agoras: they sold for a few obols their sacred doctrines, they drove demons out of people, called up heroes from the dead, produced tables laden with expensive foods that were not really there, brought alive what was without life and created other illusions.[130] Elsewhere, in attacking Christians for only attracting an uneducated riff-raff to their cause, he compares Christian proselytizers to the mendicants (*ageirontes*) who put on contemptible displays in the agora and who are careful to avoid coming into contact with groups of intelligent men, but who are happy, when they catch sight of some adolescents or a crowd of house-bred slaves or other half-wits, to shove their way through the crowd to show off in front of them.[131]

## The activities of wandering magicians

The comparison that Celsus draws between the miracles Jesus performed and the performances that sorcerers and the pupils of the Egyptians put on in the agora will serve as a transition to the subject of what wandering sorcerers did in public places. A cursory reading of the texts suggests that there may have been something of a distinction to be drawn between those who frequented shrines, particularly those of such Eastern deities as the Mother Goddess and Sarapis, and those who found their way to the places in towns and cities where people congregated. Those who frequented shrines were essentially on the lookout for clients to whom they could purvey their wares, while those who sought out places where people gathered did so because they wanted spectators for their performances. There were almost certainly exceptions such as the Cynic preachers mentioned by Dio Chrysostom who were to be encountered at the gates of temples in Alexandria.[132]

The men who sought out the places where people in a community gathered were in a somewhat different position from those who made a shrine their base of operations. They had to do something to draw attention to themselves and to get a crowd to form around them. That meant performing deeds that would pique the curiosity of the idle throng. The most straightforward way of accomplishing that goal was to deceive the senses of the onlookers into making them think that they were witnessing a miracle. There are indications from Plato that conjuring-tricks were a large part of the stock-in-trade of many of the men characterized as *goetes*. Apollonius in the speech in which he classifies *goeteia* as a false art practised by wandering mendicants declares that the skill of the *goetes* such as it is rests on the silliness of those who are deceived into believing in the existence of the non-existent and into distrusting the existence of that which really is.[133] It looks as if Apollonius has the conjuring-tricks or thaumaturgy of *goetes* chiefly in mind here. That displays of thaumaturgy in which a spell is cast over the eyes and ears of the audience are an integral part of *goeteia* emerges from the exchange that Apollonius has with Thespesion, the leader of the Egyptian Gymnosophists, who attacks Apollonius for admiring the Indian Brahmins, who followed the practice at noon and at midnight each day of performing purificatory rituals, which led to their being propelled by the ground some feet into the air to hang suspended there, all the while singing a hymn in honour of the Sun;[134] Philostratus says that the Brahmins' motive in levitating is not to put on a performance of wonder-working (*thaumatopoiia*), which would be inconceivable in their case, since they eschew personal ambition; what they do when they leave the earth represents a fitting form of worship of the Sun.[135] For Thespesion, however, their levitating is wonder-working and a technique for exerting a compelling force on nature, which is another way of saying magic. He concludes his denunciation of Apollonius for admiring them by declaring that if he rejoices in the actions of these wandering beggars (*ageirontes*), he flatters his eyes and ears, but shows a lack of sense.[136] Apollonius, for his part, when he comes to reply to Thespesion, paraphrases the accusation that the latter has made against the Brahmins: the Brahmins do nothing sound and healthy, but cause stunned amazement and cast a spell over the eyes and the ears.[137] Celsus' account of sorcerers and pupils of the Egyptians producing tables laden with expensive food and of their bringing to life what was without life gives some idea of some the tricks that *goetes* performed in the agora to draw a crowd.[138] Exorcisms performed publicly were also part of the repertoire of the wandering-magician, and, to judge from the New Testament, from other Christian sources and from pagan authors such as Philostratus occurred with some frequency.

Prophecy of various forms will have made up an important part of the stock-in-trade of the itinerant holy man. Such men had a public all too ready to believe that there were ways of divining the future, even though it might be forced to acknowledge that there were false prophets. Amongst the more spectacular forms of divination a holy man might employ was the summoning up of the spirits of the dead. Celsus speaks of magicians practising in the agora a particularly recherché form of necromancy, that of calling up heroes from the dead. A hero in this context is the spirit of a man or woman whose life had ended unhappily or violently.[139] It is a spirit that resents its death and is imagined eating its heart away and whistling savagely.[140] Its anger makes it a potent force in magic. That such spirits should have been summoned up in the agora is astonishing and it is hard to imagine to what end they were called up on such a public occasion, but not hard to imagine the effect on the audience. An even more spectacular form of necromancy that was apparently practised in public was the revivifying of a corpse to question it. Celsus speaks darkly of sorcerers and the pupils of the Egyptians bringing alive in the middle of the agora what was without life, but it is the story told in Apuleius' *Metamorphoses* about the corpse brought to life in the agora of Larissa by the Egyptian priest Zatchlas to reveal the identity of its killer that spells out what holy men may have done to achieve an especially striking effect.

A sorcerer with a crowd gathered around him publicly announcing that he knew how to consign men to death and then bring them back to life again must have been a not unfamiliar sight. Polemon, a sophist who lived in the time of Hadrian, accuses a rival sophist, Favorinus, of doing just that. His feud with Favorinus had begun during a tour of Greece in the course of which Favorinus had performed in Athens and in Corinth. Polemon portrays Favorinus, however, not as a touring sophist, but as a sorcerer who got crowds of men and women to gather around him by promising to lay low in death the living and to bring the dead back to life and who at the same time was successful in convincing men that he knew how to make women pursue men with the same ardour that men pursued women. To attain that end he employed what Polemon calls a hidden voice. Polemon also charges Favorinus with collecting deadly poisons to sell secretly.[141] In the real world what the crowd then witnessed was the magician putting an assistant into a trance, probably by whispering into his ear and then bringing him back to life by again murmuring into his ear. One of the tricks performed in Rome by Simon Magus in the apocryphal *Acts of Peter* is to speak into the ear of a slave belonging to the *praefectus urbi* causing the man to fall dead.[142] Tertullian, for his part, leaves us with the impression that one of the feats that magicians who gathered a crowd around them were in the habit of performing was calling a man away from the living.[143] Predictably enough one of the magical formularies gives an incantation that will arouse a corpse.[144]

In practice, the corpse will very often have been brought back to life so that it might be consulted about the future or about what had befallen it.[145] The crowd, once it had seen a man apparently die, only to be revived by the magician, will have been readier to believe that the man might be able to help them. At this stage they might have heard a voice emanating from somewhere other than the mouth of the magician telling of the powerful spells of which the magician knew and of their capacity to draw women maddened with desire to men. The voice would have purported to have been that of a dead man or a demon. The technique of ventriloquism, which in Greek is *engastrimythia* or *engastrimanteia*, goes back to the fifth century BC.[146] It is associated in the first place with a voice that seems to emerge from the belly of the ventriloquist, hence its name in Greek. *Engastrimythia* was used above all for prophetic utterance. What gave authority to the utterance in the mind of those who heard it was their conviction that they were hearing a dead person, a god or a demon speaking.[147] Although ventriloquism may originally have been a voice that appeared to come from the belly, it sounds as if magicians had by the second century AD adapted the technique to make those around them believe that a corpse or an apparent corpse was speaking.

Artemidorus, the author of a work on the interpretation of dreams written in the second half of the second century AD, tells us a little more about the diviners, most of whom must have been *agyrtai* and some of whom will have combined that calling with being a sorcerer, to be found in the agora and wherever great crowds of people congregated. To one category of these persons he was well disposed, those who interpreted dreams. He asserts in the preface to his work that he had for many years consorted with the diviners (*manteis*) of the agora, in spite of the way in which the haughty and disdainful chose to speak of them, calling them beggars (*proictai*), sorcerers (*goetes*) and besiegers of altars (*bomolochoi*). He had met them in the cities of Greece, Asia Minor and Italy and at the festivals in these areas as well as in the largest and most populous of the islands and had been prepared to listen to the ancient dreams they recounted and to their outcome.[148] Diviners of dreams (*oneiromanteis*) were, in other words, to be found in the agoras of cities throughout a great deal of the Roman Empire. They belonged to what for Artemidorus was a discrete category of persons, the diviners of the agora. When there was a festival they deserted the agoras of the cities to make their way to it. They will also have moved from city to city. Since Artemidorus was interested in what diviners from dreams had to say and naturally thought that oneiromancy was a legitimate technique, he was inclined to give this class of diviner the benefit of the doubt and not label them as *agyrtai*, *goetes* and *bomolochoi* in the way that supercilious people did. Artemidorus himself, on the other hand, takes exactly the same attitude to diviners who are either not *oneiromanteis* or who do not pursue one of the forms of divining sanctioned by the Roman State. He gives a list of some length of the diviners whose predictions are unreliable and false: they are Pythagoristae, those who divine from the physiognomy, diviners from knuckle-bones (*astragalomanteis*), cheese-diviners (*tyromanteis*), diviners who employ sieves (*koskinomanteis*), scrutinizers of form (*morphoscopoi*), palmists (*cheiroscopoi*), bowl-diviners (*lekanomanteis*) and finally, necromancers. Diviners who follow these techniques, he declares, fleece those whom they encounter by subjecting them to *goeteia* and by deceiving them.[149] Such persons are *goetes* in Artemidorus' eyes because they trick those who consult them into thinking that they possess real knowledge. Artemidorus does not say where the diviners of whom he disapproves are to be found, but some of them will certainly have been encountered in the agora and wherever large crowds of people gathered.

Conjuring tricks, divinations, exorcisms and necromancy, all performed in front of an audience, are what might be expected from itinerant holy men, but Celsus also speaks of these same *goetes* selling their sacred doctrines in the middle of the agora for a few pence.[150] This must mean that itinerant holy men actually purveyed the sacred teachings of their sect in the marketplace and that this was one of the routes by which these doctrines were disseminated to a wider public. It is unclear whether Celsus means that people were sold what were in effect pamphlets or that those who paid were taught some of the key tenets of the sect. However that may be, the passage does remind us that it was not only Christians who proselytized, but that the votaries of other sects did the same thing.

If Polemon is to be believed the wandering magicians who put on shows of thaumaturgy in the marketplace or at the crossroads also advertised their expertise in other more private and personal forms of magic. This is no doubt what happened. The public display will have served to persuade spectators of the skill of the magician and encouraged them to approach him for help with their own problems. There is after all nothing in our sources to suggest that there was a specialized category of *goetes* who confined their activities to public performances. The *goes* who performed conjuring tricks was one and the same person as the *goes* who was hired to direct spells at others. Apollonius in the speech in which he defends himself against a charge of being a *goes* speaks as if *goetes* did not just put on public performances, but in their eagerness to make money practised real magic in private.

Our discussion of the activities of itinerant magic-workers may be brought to a conclusion by examining the latter part of the career of Alexander of Abonuteichos. Alexander achieved a measure of success of which few of his fellows can even have dreamed: he was able to set up an oracular shrine that brought him renown, wealth and social position. Lucian's account of the devices Alexander used to create the impression that the god Asclepius had taken up residence in the shrine in Abonuteichos and then how he deceived those who came to put questions to the god is necessarily suspect, so far as it concerns Alexander, but it does give us some idea of the tricks in which magicians-cum-prophets engaged to hoodwink the gullible.

Lucian's story is that there was some disagreement between Alexander and his partner Cocconas over where they should establish their oracle: Cocconas was in favour of Calchedon because of its central location; Alexander preferred his homeland, Abonuteichos, because of the superstitious nature of the people there. In the end Alexander prevailed, although they did decide to use Calchedon to promote the fraud to the extent of burying in the precinct of Apollo's sanctuary there bronze tablets that told of Asclepius' coming to Pontus in the company of his father, Apollo, to take possession of Abonuteichos. The discovery of the tablets was contrived and the prediction written on them was then widely disseminated. The result was that the inhabitants of Abonuteichos voted to build a temple for Asclepius and began forthwith to dig its foundations. Cocconas was left behind in Calchedon, where he died, while Alexander made an impressive formal entry into Abonuteichos dressed to look like the hero Perses, whose descendant he pretended to be. Oracular verses that predicted his arrival in Abonuteichos were concocted;

they gave him a suitable heroic pedigree that not only included Perses, but Podaleirius, a doctor mentioned in the *Iliad.*

Once in Abonuteichos, Alexander feigned periodic episodes of divine possession, made the more convincing by his frothing at the mouth. The latter effect was achieved by chewing on the root of a certain plant. Even before he got to Abonuteichos, Alexander had had the head of a snake with human features made up in linen. Its mouth could be opened by pulling on horse-hairs, which also were used to control its forked tongue. The stage was set for the epiphany of the god. Alexander achieved that end by planting at dead of night in some mud in the foundations of the temple the egg of a goose that had been sucked out and had had a young snake placed within in it. He had then rushed into the marketplace of Abonuteichos clad in a gilded loincloth, carrying a sickle as though he were Perses and tossing his hair after the fashion of the mendicant priests of the Mother Goddess. Mounting a high podium, he pronounced the city blessed indeed because of the god whom it was about to receive into its midst. He uttered strange and unintelligible sounds partly in Hebrew and partly in Phoenician to impress his audience, but was careful to intermingle the perfectly intelligible words 'Apollo' and 'Asclepius' amongst them. That done, he went at a run to the temple to the place in which he had buried the egg and standing in the water he sang hymns to Apollo and Asclepius in a loud voice, calling on the god to come to the city and bring it good fortune. At that point he dipped a large cup into the water and mud and brought up the egg, which to outward appearances looked whole, since the aperture in it had been covered over with wax and white lead. Taking the egg in his hand, Alexander announced that he now had Asclepius in his possession and, with the onlookers watching him intently, he broke the egg open to release the snake, which then entwined itself around his fingers. The spectators greeted the god and pronounced their city blessed.

After this successful *coup de théâtre* Alexander retired to his house to lie low for a few days to allow the story to spread throughout Paphlagonia. People gathered in Abonuteichos and were received by Alexander who reclined on a couch in a small room, attired as if he were a god. The tame snake he had acquired in Pella was wrapped about his body with its tail showing. Its head he kept under his oxter. The linen snake's head emerged from his clothing at one side of his beard as though it were part of the snake. The crowds poured in and were properly impressed. Alexander was now ready to announce that the god would on a set day answer for a fee of a drachma and two obols questions put to him; those who wished to seek his help were required to write their questions on a papyrus-roll, which they were to seal with clay or wax or whatever substance they wanted. Alexander took the rolls into the temple, which had by this time been completed, broke open the seals and read the questions. To conceal what he had done he employed three techniques of some considerable ingenuity to replace the seals. The answers he gave were suitably ambiguous. The oracle was successful and Alexander gathered a considerable staff around him. Fairly frequently he would appear with the snake wrapped round him and would then declare that the god would make his utterances without the aid of an interpreter. That was done by having a helper who was outside the room answer the questions by speaking into tubing made from the windpipes of several cranes that led into the linen snake's head.[151]

It is difficult to say how much, if any, of Lucian's account we should accept so far as it concerns Alexander. If Alexander, as seems likely, did in fact receive sealed requests for advice from the god, then he will have used the techniques or techniques very like them for unsealing and replicating the seals that Lucian describes, and if he did have a talking snake, then he will have got up to tricks of the kind portrayed by Lucian. Some of the same techniques as well as others for replicating the seals on documents that have been opened are described by Hippolytus, drawing on *The Art of Thrasymedes*.[152] Hippolytus also explains how pipes made from the windpipes of cranes and other long-necked creatures are used to make skulls seem to speak or to supply answers to a boy-medium.[153] There is, accordingly, the possibility that the exposé Lucian pretends to give of Alexander's tricks derives from a handbook on the techniques for deception employed by magicians and is not rooted in the real world. Alternatively it may come from an exposé of such tricks. Philostratus tells us there were such exposés written by those who found the pretensions of magicians ridiculous and we know that the Epicurean Celsus, who is the dedicatee of Lucian's *Alexander*, wrote just such a work.[154] Lucian may have known what kind of oracle Alexander ran without knowing what the techniques he employed were. If that is what happened, it is very likely that the techniques set out in the exposé come from a handbook. The question that then arises is what the relationship of the handbook is to what actually went on in the real world: was it based on observation or was it a literary exercise? The answer is that it was probably a bit of both. The techniques described seem real enough and it is hard to believe that anyone would have gone to the trouble of thinking them up as a purely intellectual exercise.

As for the wider import of the tale, it reflects a more general reality that there were men of obscure origins like Alexander who succeeded in setting themselves up as religious authorities. In Alexander's case it is as the priest and prophet of an oracular shrine. That was not the only form that such an undertaking could take, but the techniques used to achieve the end will have had a certain similarity. The wandering mendicants in Phoenicia and Palestine were like Celsus and Alexander in working themselves up into a state and then proclaiming themselves in temples and outside temples, in cities and in army camps God or the Son of God or the Divine Breath; like Alexander, they descended into unintelligible speech.[155] Since they did so in Phoenicia and Palestine, the message that they proclaimed was adapted to fit the particular circumstances of the religious culture there. That the same thing happened in other parts of the Greek East seems likely, although appropriate adjustments for local conditions will have been made to the message proclaimed. That a number of them used tricks employed by magicians to convince the public of their divinely-inspired state seems likely.

## Other kinds of magician

It is hard to believe that all magic-workers were wandering mendicants and that there were not magicians who lived quietly in one place and pursued their calling there. Such men surely existed, but do not engage the attention of our sources. Glimpses of their presence are caught in the fourth and later centuries. A distinct hint of the existence of such persons is nonetheless to be found in a cache of curse-tablets, inscribed on lead sheets and then deposited in a well in the agora of Athens, a procedure intended to transfer the chilling effect of the water to the men and women cursed.[156] Their date is difficult to determine on palaeographic grounds, but archaeological considerations suggest that they belong to the third century AD. A later date is excluded. Twelve of them are written by the same hand. Six of them are directed at athletes, three of them are designed to upset sexual relationships, two are too fragmentary to discern their purpose and one summons up a ghost. The writer has a number of stock formulae that he uses in these spells, both in season and out of season. The misfortunes, for instance, that he wishes on wrestlers in their matches he also asks to be visited on prostitutes.[157] It is true that love-making in some literary texts is imagined as the grappling that takes place in a wrestling match, but this is unlikely to be the explanation for the formula. It looks as if the writer had mechanically transferred something that might appropriately be wished on a wrestler to a prostitute. Although no instances of the same combination of formulae that the Athenian writer uses have been found in formularies, his extremely repetitive style suggests that he was following an exemplar. His writing out curses for different persons point to his being a professional. The formulae that he falls back on may afford a clue to his identity.

It is fair then to infer that the writer was a known magician and, furthermore, one who lived close to the Athenian Agora. His help was sought by persons who were either themselves athletes or who had some interest in causing an athlete to lose; prostitutes or persons who had an economic or sexual interest in the affairs of prostitutes also came to him for help. It is possible that the magician was a woman, but not very likely. It would be very unwise to state categorically that men would never have come to a woman to seek help in ensuring that an athletic contest had the outcome they wanted, but the little that is known about such magic-working suggests it was in the hands of men. To the extent that it is possible to infer from the station of the persons cursed what the background was of the party who commissioned the curse we may cautiously conclude that there was no uniformity to his clientele and that it cut across social lines. One of the athletes who is cursed is an ephebe who is on the point of competing in a wrestling competition in which there are several rounds.[158] He belongs to the select group of young Athenian males who spent two years together training in the gymnasium and competing in contests against each other. The object of another curse is a man called Alcidamus who is going to run in the Panathenaic Games.[159] He and the ephebe will come from a very different social milieu from the two other wrestlers who attract curses.[160] The latter are men who have not emerged from the gymnasium, but are slaves or ex-slaves whose livelihood depends on their wrestling. It is they who can perhaps provide a clue to the identity of the magician.

It will be no accident that so many of the decipherable curse-tablets recovered from the well are directed at athletes and prostitutes. They are precisely the groups of persons whom we know to have been most deeply involved in magic-working. Philostratus in discussing the tendency of the simpler kind of man to credit sorcery with performing wonders brings up as an example of the type athletes (*athletai*) and those who engage in competitions (*agonistai*): he says of them that out of a desire to win they have recourse to the art of the magician; if they lose, they do not find fault with the magical arts, but blame themselves for not having performed an adequate sacrifice or for not having burned the right incense. He goes on to remark on the existence of the same trait in merchants and those consumed by sexual passion for boys: the merchant credits the *goes* with any success he may have enjoyed and puts down to his own stinginess in failing to sacrifice enough anything untoward that happens; those who are in thrall to sexual passion do exactly the same thing.[161] Then towards the end of the third century the North African Christian Arnobius asks in the form of a rhetorical question who does not know that amongst the deeds magicians (*magi*) perform is that of causing horses which are part of a chariot-team to become enfeebled, speeding them up and slowing them down.[162] The competitors whom Philostratus has primarily in mind are very unlikely to be gentlemen-athletes competing in the crown games or in local athletic festivals. They will be charioteers, members of professional troupes of wrestlers and other such competitive performers. The target of three of the curse-tablets is a certain Eutychianus, who was a wrestler, while another curse-tablet has as its victim a wrestler called Petres the Macedonian.[163] Eutychianus is referred to in one spell as the Eutychianus whom Eutycha bore and whom Aethales set free and in another as the pupil of Aethales.[164] Petres known as the Macedonian is further identified as the pupil of Dionysius.[165] Additional clues to their identity are to be found in the curses directed against them. Eutychianus is to be matched with one Secundus.[166] Matches are, in other words, arranged against particular opponents. There was not a series of rounds from which a winner emerged, which was the pattern at the athletic festivals in which freeborn athletes competed. Secondly, it is not only Eutychianus and Petres who are cursed; persons referred to as 'those with them' are also part of the curse.[167] What all of this adds up to is that Eutychianus and Petres belonged to a troupe of wrestlers that was run by a master. It is from the astrological handbook of Firmicus Maternus that we learn of masters of troupes of athletes and that there were such things as troupes of athletes. In that work Firmicus gives the nativities of persons whom he refers to as the leaders of *palaestritae* or those placed over them and of persons whom he calls the masters of athletes or those placed over them.[168] The nativities of the latter category are the same as those of the persons Firmicus calls the master of the *palaestra*. These are probably not distinct callings, but different ways of referring to the master of a troupe of athletes.

The magician whose curse-tablets turned up in the well in the Athenian Agora was a man of whose clientele athletes, whether upper-class or humble, were a considerable component. The formulae that he used were those with which someone who specialized in placing binding-spells on wrestlers would have equipped himself. The magician in question was apparently part of the probably small and close-knit world in which wrestlers from wrestling troupes moved. In a milieu in which magic-working was so much a part of life it is hard to believe that professional competitors always turned to persons outside of their own ranks for help and that some magicians did not emerge from within the system. It is entirely possible then that the magician whose curse-tablets were deposited in the well in the Athenian Agora had at one time been a member of a troupe of wrestlers. It is to be surmised that there were in the great cities of the Roman Empire other magicians whose backgrounds were similar to his. They become visible in the fourth century, but they were probably a presence at a much earlier date.

## Sorceresses

### General standing of women as magic-workers

There are strong indications that women generally occupied a lowly position in the hierarchy of magicians in the Roman Empire. Plutarch, in the essay in which he treats of excessive fear of the divine, says that those who suffer from it when they have frightening visions in sleep do not laugh off the vision on waking up or rejoice at its only having been a dream, as others would, but get into a state of upset and take themselves to mendicant holy men ( *agyrtai* ) and sorcerers ( *goetes* ), on whom they spend money; these persons then advise them to find some old woman to cleanse them of the demonic visitation that they have experienced, to wash themselves in the sea and spend the day sitting on the ground.[169] It is first of all to be remarked that Plutarch is in all likelihood not speaking about two separate categories of person, *agyrtai* and *goetes*, but that there is a hendiadys and that the persons really intended are mendicant holy men who turn their hand to sorcery. The rôle of the mendicant holy man is to identify the cause of the dream as a demonic visitation and then to give instructions on the purificatory rituals to be followed. The old women carry out the rituals. The implication of the passage is that the old women who perform the ritual of purification are mere technicians, while the *agyrtai* are the true experts.

Corroboration that the magic performed by old women was pretty routine stuff and that it was men from whom the real *tours de force* were to be expected is to be found in Lucian's *Philopseudeis* in a passage in which a speaker asks the sceptic Tychiades whether he does not even believe in the sending away of periodic fevers, the charming of snakes, the cure of swellings of the groin and all of the other things that even old women can perform.[170] It has already been noted that in the Hellenistic Greek world and in Rome certain areas of magic were the peculiar preserve of women, and old women especially. These are not the more spectacular forms of magic-working, but the run-of-the-mill cures and snake-charmings that the speaker in Lucian's *Philopseudeis* feels even old women can perform. The same pattern seems then to have obtained in the Greek-speaking provinces of the Roman Empire.

There is no mention in the *Philopseudeis* of the purifications necessary after a troubling dream, but this was surely one of the areas of magic-working that was the special preserve of women. To judge from Plutarch's *On Superstition*, there were old women whose speciality it was to perform such purifications.[171] Philo might be taken to suggest that the begging-priests of the Mother Goddess who hung around altars as well as the base women and slaves to be found there all offered purifications, help with love affairs and help in turning love affairs into bitter enmities.[172] It is, however, probably mainly women he has in mind performing purifications. There is a very good reason for such purifications being the exclusive preserve of women: it is very often performed in the bedchamber where the disturbing dream has taken place. The presence of a strange man is hardly going to be tolerated in the midst of the household, whereas an old woman presents no threat.

It is also old women who are brought in to cure those who have been bewitched by the Evil Eye of Envy, *baskania*. In Heliodorus' *Aethiopica*, the Egyptian priest Calasiris goes through the motions of curing the heroine Charicleia of the Evil Eye, although he knows perfectly well that her lassitude is caused by her pining away with love. He first calls for a tripod, laurel, fire and frankincense to be brought in and gives instructions that no one should interrupt him until he summons them; he then begins the ritual by burning the incense; next, while whispering prayers, he waves the laurel-branch over the girl from head to foot; finally, as he comes slowly and late to the end of the procedure, he yawns sleepily in the manner of an old woman.[173] Calasiris yawns in this way because what he is doing is simulating what would normally be done by an old woman called in to remove the Evil Eye; his old-womanish yawn is an attempt at verisimilitude, since old women yawned in the course of the ritual. From Heliodorus himself it is to be learned that those affected by the Evil Eye were wont to yawn: the hero of the novel, Theagenes, is seen to yawn and this is taken to be a symptom of *baskania*.[174] Presumably then a transference takes place and the lassitude-inducing effects of the Evil Eye are imagined to pass to the old woman. There are no ancient parallels for this happening, but spells from present-day and early nineteenth-century Crete have been collected that specify yawning on the part of the old woman whose job it is to take off the Evil Eye.[175]

Not only will many female magic-workers have enjoyed a low standing in the hierarchy of their calling, there is also reason to think that they suffered from certain other disadvantages, not the least of these being that they were exploited by men or by other women. Since our sources have very little to say about the circumstances of female magic-workers beyond mentioning their being summoned to a house or being encountered in the precincts of a temple, it is easy to assume that they were independent operators. This may not in fact have always been the case. Luke in Acts tells a story about a visit that Paul and Silas made to the Roman colony of Philippi in Macedonia at the centre of which is a slave-girl owned and exploited by her owners. The story is that Paul and Silas encountered a girl who earned a considerable income for her masters by uttering prophesies using the technique of a ventriloquist. In Luke's words, she possessed the spirit of a Python. For a number of days she followed Paul and Silas around screeching out: 'These men are the slaves of The Most High God and announce the path of salvation to you'. This was eventually too much for Paul and he turned round and bade the spirit depart from the girl in the name of Jesus Christ, which the spirit promptly did. The masters of the girl, seeing their source of income vanish, dragged Paul and Silas to the marketplace into the presence of the authorities to complain that they were Jews who were disturbing the peace of the city by promoting forms of conduct that the complainants as Romans could not practise.[176] The girl sounds as if she is the female equivalent of the boy-mediums used by magicians for divination. She is obviously a slave. How she came to be owned by a number of masters is unclear, but perhaps what Luke means is that there was a family operation running her. It is likely that Luke is describing a not uncommon phenomenon and that many female magic-workers with special gifts worked for a master or mistress and provided them with an income from the fees that they collected.

### Prostitution and sorcery

The character of our sources for the Greek East under the Roman Empire is such that very little is said about prostitutes, ex-prostitutes and procuresses engaging in sorcery. That they did so is hardly to be doubted. The two curse-tablets directed at a prostitute and her clients from the well in the Athenian Agora do, however, afford a glimpse into the world of prostitution and the magic-working to which it gave rise. One tablet consigns to the demon of the spring two men, Leosthenes and Pius, to prevent them from paying visits to Juliana, the daughter of Marcia, in her brothel (*ergasterion*).[177] The other spell consigns Juliana herself to the same chilling influence to keep her from pursuing a relationship with a man called Polynices.[178] The spells are unquestionably aimed at separating Juliana from certain of her regular customers. Although sexual jealousy cannot be ruled out as a factor, the motive for the spells is as likely as not to be economic.

There is one potentially valuable source of information about prostitution and magic in the Greek East in the form of Lucian's *Dialogues of the Courtesans*. In them courtesans in conversations amongst themselves or with their mothers refer to the subject of sorcery and speak about it in what at first sight looks to be an interesting and illuminating way. The success, for instance, of one courtesan is put down to her mother's being a sorceress (*pharmakis*) and to the potion the mother had given a young man, which had made him quite besotted with the daughter. There is a wife who attributes the infatuation of her husband with a courtesan to drugs he has been given, when in fact his problem is that he is being driven mad by jealousy.[179] Then there is a prostitute who recommends a Syrian sorceress, expert in love-magic, to another prostitute whose lover has deserted her; the sorceress will not cost much to employ, but will need a mixing-bowl of wine to sustain herself while she is performing her magic.[180] The value of the information is unfortunately seriously compromised. The problem is that Lucian sets the *Dialogues* not in some indeterminate city in the East, but in Athens in the late fourth or third centuries BC. He has chosen that period and an Athenian setting for the conversations because the principal inspiration for the situations and the conversations of the *Dialogues* is transparently Greek New Comedy.[181] The vignettes that Lucian draws are not then necessarily an accurate reflection of the world of the Athenian courtesan in his own day. They need, in consequence, to be approached with the greatest of caution. What Lucian takes above all from New Comedy are the basic situations in which the courtesans find themselves and the topics that they bring up in their conversations. Many of the details he probably supplies from his own world. It is possible to argue that it does not greatly matter that Greek New Comedy lies behind the dialogues, since the situations in which the courtesans find themselves are timeless in the sense that young men in Athens in the late second century AD still probably got entangled with courtesans anxious to keep them to themselves, so long as they had money to spend on them. That may be so, but it still remains the case that Lucian is not drawing entirely on his own direct and unmediated experience in creating his little sketches.

Lucian's *Dialogues of the Courtesans* have nothing to say about male brothel-keepers or *pornoboskoi*. That brutal reality is left to the side as it is in Roman Elegy. Astrological texts, however, have no qualms about presenting a true picture of the underside of life. One of the astrological poems that goes under the name of Manetho gives a list of particularly abominable persons born under a certain configuration of Saturn; amongst them are the sorcerers who nourish prostitutes (*hetairotrophoi goetes*), which is no more than a poetic way of saying *pornoboskoi goetes*. The text goes on to dilate on the wickedness of these masters of licentious prostitution who seek profit from a base source.[182] That *pornoboskoi* characteristically engaged in sorcery is hardly surprising, but it is helpful to have a text that explicitly says that they did.

Another of the versified astrological texts ascribed to the pen of Manetho is a useful reminder that not all of the sorcery performed in the world of the prostitute was carried out by prostitutes or their keepers. The young men with whom the prostitutes became involved might also turn to sorcery out of jealousy. That will happen, the poem says, when Venus lies between Mars and Saturn, since men with such a horoscope have relations with prostitutes, fall in love with them and become jealous of them; the result is that they kill the women through the love-philtres they administer to them.[183] What is envisaged is young men becoming involved with prostitutes and out of sexual jealousy giving the girls love-philtres that kill them.

### Mendicant holy women

The last category of female magic-worker to be examined is the mendicant holy woman. That such women were more of a presence than our sources reveal seems likely. For one thing it is possible that some references to *agyrtai* are generic and encompass both men and women. The one reference that there is to a female mendicant, an *agyrtria*, is in Philostratus' *Life of Apollonius of Tyana*. A certain amount of information is nonetheless to be extracted from it. It is to be found in a comparison that Damis, the companion of Apollonius, makes of his meagre prophetic gifts with those of an old mendicant woman (*agyrtria*) who prophesies about little sheep and such like things.[184] The comparison affords a glimpse of a world that is almost wholly lost to us in which humble people consult elderly mendicant holy women about their flocks, but it also inadvertently tells us of a hierarchy amongst seers and magicians in which old women with some sort of pretension to holiness who go from community to community begging stand on the very bottom rung of the ladder. Exactly what service the old mendicant woman offers those who consult her about their sheep is not at all clear from the passage, but there is another passage in the same work of Philostratus that almost certainly has some bearing on what these women did.[185] In it the wisdom of the Egyptian Gymnosophists in relation to that of the Indian Brahmins is compared to the powers of divination displayed by old women with sieves attached to them who approach shepherds and sometimes even cowherds promising to cure their animals of illness by divination. Apollonius, who is the speaker in the passage, goes on to remark that these old women like to be called wise women (*sophai*). How divination with a sieve (*koskinomanteia*) worked is not known.[186] It is dismissed by Artemidorus as one of the forms of divination used by sorcerers (*goetes*) and cheats to swindle those they chance upon out of their goods.[187] It was, at any rate, a fairly lowly form of divination and one that old mendicant women were likely to have used.

# 9

# CONSTRAINTS ON MAGICIANS UNDER A CHRISTIAN EMPIRE

## Civil legislation

While the conversion of Constantine to Christianity and the subsequent triumph of that faith over its pagan competitors, whether monotheistic or polytheistic, may in some ways have made life more difficult for magicians, it certainly did not lead to their disappearance. Magic-working now came under attack on two fronts: it was prosecuted both by the civil authorities and by the Church, sometimes acting in concert. On the secular front, the imperial authorities periodically tried to tighten up legislation against magic-working, but this was hardly part of a concerted policy to clamp down on magicians and seers.

It is exceedingly difficult to assess what the rôle of Christianity was either in giving definition to what was to be considered illicit in magic-working or in tightening up the penalties for those who practised magic or soothsaying or consulted magicians or soothsayers. Part of the problem is that we do not know what latitude was in earlier times allowed magicians and soothsayers and those who consulted them. It is not altogether certain, for instance, whether the *Lex Cornelia* was used to punish persons who employed love-philtres, either to seduce someone or make him hateful to another. It is well-enough known that it was dangerous to consult soothsayers on certain subjects and above all on the subject of the imperial succession. But the danger arose not from any law governing the consultation of soothsayers, but from the law defining *lèse-majesté*. To the best of our knowledge there was no law against soothsaying or consulting soothsayers. That Christianity had some part to play in Christian legislation against magic and soothsaying can hardly be gainsaid, but it is not altogether clear that much of the legislation could not equally well have emanated from a pagan emperor who felt that his life was in danger. The particularly severe measures of the years AD 357 and 358 and their unusually harsh language, for instance, are best explained as a response to the dangers that the Emperor Constantius II believed threatened his regime at that time.[1]

The earliest recorded Christian legislation dealing with magic or soothsaying belongs to the year AD 319 and to the reign of Constantine the Great. On the face of it, the legislation is startling. It is possible, nonetheless, to interpret it as a delicate balancing act on the part of the Emperor between allaying Christian concerns about soothsaying and pagan forms of worship and not upsetting pagan sensitivities too much. Constantine forbids diviners from entrails (*haruspices*), priests and those accustomed, in the words of the decree, to minister to that rite from crossing the thresholds of private houses, even on the pretext of friendship, but permits those whom he describes as desiring to pay service to their superstition to perform such rites in public.[2] The penalty imposed on a diviner for contravening the decree is the drastic one of death by burning, while the man who summons the diviner is to be mulcted of his goods and sent into exile on an island.[3] On the face of it this is the legislation of a Christian prince concerned with pagan superstition. The rhetoric of the decrees with its talk of those desiring to serve their superstitious beliefs sounds Christian and undoubtedly is so, but the actual content of the decrees reflects a long-standing pagan preoccupation with religious rites performed in the secrecy of private houses, away from the scrutiny of the public gaze.[4] Despite its talk of serving superstition, the language of the law does not really allow us to say whether the boundaries of what was considered to be magic had shifted under the influence of Christianity or whether they remained in place.

A few years later Constantine felt it necessary to define what forms of magic should be punished and what should go unpunished: those who with the help of the magical arts either attempted to harm the well-being of other men or to seduce chaste minds into succumbing to lust were to be punished under the most severe laws; no criminal prosecutions were to arise out of the use of devices employed to protect human bodies or when devices were employed in the countryside to protect the grape-harvest from rain or hail.[5] It looks as if there had been attempts to extend the scope of the *Lex Cornelia* to forms of magic-working not hitherto prosecuted under it and that Constantine had resisted any such extension to the scope of the law. It should follow then that the *Lex Cornelia* had as a matter of course been invoked not only against those who employed magic to harm others, but also against those who tried to manipulate the sexual feelings of others through love-philtres. What is rather less clear is whether Constantine was moved to promulgate the edict out of a desire to check attempts on the part of zealous Christians to extend existing criminal sanctions against magicians to those who made use of amulets and incantations. There is little room for doubt, however, that for Constantine the forms of activity that he excludes from criminal prosecution are also magic, but differ from the preceding category in that they are aimed at preserving human beings and their crops from harm.

One authority does assert on a number of occasions that sometimes even those engaging in the more harmless forms of magic were subject to judicial prosecution and execution. The authority in question is the historian Ammianus Marcellinus, who was born in Antioch around AD 330 and died towards the end of the century in Rome, where he had settled after a career in the imperial administration. Ammianus himself had obviously enjoyed a superior education. He had read and been influenced by the Neoplatonist philosophers, Plotinus and Porphyry.[6] There is in his writing a discernible bias against Christianity: he is predisposed to see the best in pagan adminis-trators and to put the worst construction possible on the actions of their Christian counterparts. It may be that he was a Christian apostate.[7] Ammianus' debt to Tacitus is now a matter of some dispute.[8] Both historians certainly aim at the theatrical. There is a difference: Tacitus develops a plot, while Ammianus concentrates his attention on creating a series of arresting but disconnected tableaux.[9] It is nonetheless the case that both writers try to conjure up the terror of certain episodes in the history of the Roman state and to give their readers a pleasurable *frisson* of horror. That means that the writer has few scruples about regaling his readers with horrific stories, if they suit the rhetorical purpose of his work, even though he was in no position to vouch for their truth. We generally have to rely on informed impressions in pronouncing a work rhetorical, but in the case of Ammianus there is rather more to go upon.[10] It is known from a letter of Libanius written in 392 to a Marcellinus in Rome that the said Marcellinus had divided up his writings into a large number of sections and had given declamatory readings from them in Rome. These had been received with acclaim and more were called for.[11] There is a fair chance that the Marcellinus in question is the historian Ammianus.

Extreme caution, accordingly, needs to be exercised in taking as evidence of what actually happened Ammianus' highly coloured account of the prose-cutions that occurred under Constantius II between AD 357 and 359 and again under Valens in AD 371. Especially suspect are the references that Ammianus makes to the prosecution of trivial forms of magic-working. He either speaks in the most general terms about them or where he does give instances of people being condemned to death for some harmless act, the persons condemned are not named. In his account of the reign of Constantius II, he twice speaks of the danger people faced of being executed for minor superstitious acts. Once, to illustrate the climate of terror that overtook the headquarters of the Emperor in Milan in AD 356, he says that if anyone consulted an expert about the cry of a shrew or about a weasel run-ning across his path or about any such significant event or employed an old woman to utter an incantation over him to relieve some ill – a practice that Ammianus asserts medical authorities endorsed – he was informed against, accused and condemned to death.[12]

Three years later in the reign of the same emperor, in AD 359, Constantius sent a high legal official of the regime, a man called Paulus, nicknamed the Chain, to the East to investigate instances of *lèse-majesté*. According to

Ammianus, the Emperor's concern was aroused by questions that had been asked an oracle of the Egyptian dwarf-god Bes at Abydus in the Thebaid. The questions had been written down on papyrus or parchment and some of them had been left around the shrine after the responses had been given.[13] Paulus made Scythopolis in Palestine the headquarters of his investigation, since it was midway between Alexandria and Antioch. Ammianus' account of the investigation does not suggest impartiality. He begins his narrative by giving the names and identities of four men who were brought before the court of inquiry; two of them were sent into exile and two were acquitted; he then goes on to speak of the inquisition spreading its tentacles further; of torture and death and of the confiscation of goods; of the fertility of Paulus' mind in inventing charges.[14] It is at this point that Ammianus speaks of people being denounced and condemned to death for wearing amulets on their necks to protect themselves against the quartan fever and other ills and of malevolent accusations of necromancy inspired by nothing more than someone's having gone past a tomb in the evening.[15]

Ammianus is certainly tendentious in suggesting that the use of incantations or amulets was sanctioned by the authorities on medicine.[16] Some doctors and veterinarians unquestionably did believe in the efficacy of amulets and incantations, but most of the profession probably thought that such devices had nothing to do with proper medical practice. More troubling is his failure to name names and his use of the same formulaic device to introduce the sentences in which he gives a catalogue of the superstitious acts that had met with condign punishment during the two different prosecutions.[17] It is hard to avoid the suspicion that Ammianus in trying to evoke the atmosphere of a reign of terror in which even the most trivial forms of magic were prosecuted has gone rather beyond what he knows to have happened.[18]

Some of the same doubts are aroused by Ammianus' account of the prosecutions in the reign of Valens in AD 371 that a certain Festus Tridentinus, as the consularis of the province of Asia, initiated. According to Ammianus, he had undertaken the prosecutions in imitation of the prosecutions in Rome that had brought Maximinus, the prefect in charge of the corn supply for the capital, to positions of great authority.[19] Ammianus paints a picture of an instantaneous change in Tridentinus' behaviour brought about by the realization that the enormity of Maximinus' behaviour had actually helped him attain the prefectship of the city: his mask changed like that of an actor and his eyes now blazed, intent and staring, with fire; he declared that the day of his own prefectship would now be at hand, if he too had dipped his hands in the blood of the innocent. In recounting what Festus had done, Ammianus says he is choosing a few select examples of widely-known cases to make his point.[20] His first example is a philosopher of some merit called Coeranius whom the tortures to which he was subjected had killed; he had written to his wife using a proverbial expression for looking into a matter more deeply. His three following examples are instances of the execution of unnamed persons for having engaged either in a harmless form of magic-working or for having cast a horoscope: there was the simple old woman who cured periodic fevers with soothing incantations who was executed as a criminal, despite in the past, with Tridentinus' full knowledge, having been summoned to his house and having cured his daughter; there was the member of the town council of some city in whose papers was found astrological data about the birth of someone called Valens, whom the accused maintained was his deceased brother and not the Emperor; and lastly there was the young man who was seen both alternately touching the marble of a bath-house and then his chest and reciting the seven vowels of the alphabet under the impression that this was a capital remedy for his stomach problems.[21]

Ammianus' depiction of the sudden change in character that overtook Tridentinus is, while a splendid piece of dramatic narrative, psychologically implausible and owes more to Ammianus' powers of invention than it does to any reality. The widely-known instances of Tridentinus' harshness that Ammianus says he selects to illustrate his case will at best be the product of an oral tradition that has simplified matters to the point of caricature and at worst the product of Ammianus' creative genius. It is quite clear from the way in which Ammianus speaks that the record on which he relies is not a documentary one but anecdotes whose authority rests on their being well known.[22]

The lesson to be drawn from this examination of the techniques Ammianus employs in describing the prosecutions for *lèse-majesté* that periodically convulsed parts of the Roman world is that it is far from clear whether people were ever really executed for wearing an amulet or consulting an expert over the significance of the cry of a shrew or whether old women who performed incantations over the sick were ever put to death. What is clear is that the prosecution of such minor derelictions would have been considered quite extraordinary. There is no reason, accordingly, to suppose that these were offences to which the civil authorities paid much heed. That conclusion is borne out by the testimony of the Church Fathers, who, while greatly exercised over the use that the members of their flock made of amulets and much troubled by their summoning Jewish magicians or old women expert in incantations to their homes to cure them or their children of sickness, at no point suggest that such activities bring any other danger in their wake than the loss of eternal salvation.

If we look carefully at the legislation of Constantius, Valens and Valentinianus affecting divination and magic of the years of some of the great prosecutions, AD 357, 358 and 371, there is no hint that their edicts are directed at the more harmless forms of magic-working. They are directed at those persons who sought to learn what the future held and at those whose goal it was to do harm to others. There can be no question that in these years consulting seers in their various forms and magicians about the future was now completely banned, but the legislation is very much the product of particular circumstances and not of a concerted effort on the part of the authorities to eliminate pagan forms of divination. In a decree of January AD 357, Constantius forbids the Roman people to consult any form of fortune-teller on pain of execution by sword and specifically orders 'Chaldaeans, *magi* and the other persons who are commonly called *malefici*, (sorcerers), on account of the enormity of the crimes that they commit' not to practise any form of divination.[23] A decree of the same ruler of July of the following year removing the immunity from torture of those members of his entourage whose rank had traditionally exempted them from that form of interroga-tion, when it speaks of *magi* and those accustomed to try their hand at magic, specifies that they should be the kind of magicians who in the vulgar accep-tance are called *malefici*.[24] Constantius' legislation is, accordingly, clearly directed at those who practise the more harmful forms of magic. A decree of the year AD 357 emanating from Milan speaks of those who through the use of the magic arts disturb the elements, who have no hesitation about threat-ening the lives of innocent persons and who dare to boast of their being able to kill their enemies by summoning up the spirits of the dead, and declares that since their conduct is foreign to nature, they should be killed.[25] Again it is forms of magic that threaten the well-being of men that are at issue.

There is an edict of Valentinian of the year AD 364 aimed at magic-working that looks to be the product of specifically Christian concerns. It bans the car-rying out at night of baneful prayers, magical operations and funereal sacri-fices on pain of death.[26] On one interpretation it looks to be an attempt at banning incantations intended to harm others and necromancy, if per-formed at night. In practice, it could be construed to mean that mystic rites performed at night were no longer permitted. That at any rate is the inter-pretation put on the law by the pagan historian Zosimus. He cites in support of that reading of the law what the proconsularis of Greece, Praetextatus, is supposed to have said, namely, that life would be insupportable for Hellenes if they could no longer carry out their mystery-rites. According to Zosimus, Praetextatus did not enforce the law and allowed the mystery-cults to carry on as before.[27] Whatever its original intent may have been, the law will have had a chilling effect on the small number of persons who still participated in the mystery-cults, since the intent of their rituals could easily be misconstrued.

Our survey of the legislation of the first Christian emperors directed at magic and divining may be rounded off with an edict of Valentinian from May of AD 371 addressed to the Roman Senate. The Emperor acknowledges that haruspicy has of its nature no necessary connection with the harmful forms of magic-working and he calls to witness the laws promulgated at the beginning of his reign allowing men to worship in the way that they have been used; he finds no fault with haruspicy itself; he only bans haruspicy employed for harmful ends.[28] The decree in effect concedes that haruspicy employed for public purposes and in public is permissible. What the authorities are frightened of are private forms of divination performed with an ulterior motive in mind.

The upshot of all of the foregoing discussion is that the civil authorities in the Late Roman Christian world had little interest in repressing forms of magic that did not present a serious threat to the well-being of men or to the stability of the regime. The old woman who was summoned to a house to cure a child of sickness through the use of incantations and amulets was not guilty of any offence in the eyes of the law, nor again were the persons who summoned her. It may be that in extreme circumstances such actions were persecuted because they were thought to have been performed with some sinister ulterior motive in view. It is also more than likely that prosecutors will have dragged up instances of old women being summoned to a house to perform incantations when they wanted to build up a case against those whom they accused of having had dealings with magicians.

## Church rules and Canon Law

By the beginning of the fourth century AD most educated Christians will have taken it for read that magic was the province of the Devil and that he used magic to entrap Christians and enlist them in his cause. The concern of the Church with magic is, accordingly, of a rather different order from that of the Roman civil authorities. Their concern is with the maintenance of public order and with protecting the subjects of the regime from harm. Forms of magic that do not immediately threaten these ends are of little or no interest to the ruling power. Since engaging in magic-working and making use of a magician represented in the eyes of the Church enlistment in the legions of Satan and the loss of all hope of eternal salvation, the Church exercised itself over magic-working of every sort. The very different nature of its concern can be seen in Canon Law and in the sermons and homilies that were delivered on the subject of magic. It is precisely the areas of magic ignored by secular law as harmless and of no importance that engage the concern of the Church, for the very good reason that the greatest temptation faced by a Christian was not with the spectacularly wicked forms of magic but with the pressures that sickness placed on him to summon an old woman skilled in incantations and amulets. This was the vulnerable point at which the Devil might gain entry.

Canon Law deals with the conduct of members of the Church, whether they be the laity or the priesthood. The Church had not only to take cognizance of what its members did, but also of who it was who was to be admitted to membership. Here too magic was a concern. There are two documents, one belonging perhaps to the third century, and the other belonging to the 380s that provide a list of the categories of person to be excluded from the catechumenate, unless the person is prepared to renounce his or her calling. Prominent amongst the callings excluded are magic-workers in various forms. What is almost certainly the earlier of the two texts, the so-called *Traditio apostolorum*, declares that magicians are not even to be examined for admission to the catechumenate, while performers of incantations, astrologers, diviners, interpreters of dreams, those who gather crowds around them and the makers of protective amulets are either to desist from these callings or be rejected. In Book 8 of the later document, the *Constitutiones apostolorum*, the exclusions of the *Traditio* have been elaborated and amended: one who engages in unmentionable practices, one who is a sodomite, a fool (*blax*), a magician (*magos*), an utterer of incantations (*epaoidos*), an astrologer, a diviner (*mantis*), a snake-charmer (*therepodos*), a gatherer of crowds about himself (*ochlagogos*), a maker of amulets, a purifier (*perikathairon*), an interpreter of birds, an expert on signs, an interpreter of palpitations, one who is on the look out for distortions of the face or feet and for weasels, chance utterances, or words overheard of meaningful significance is to be subject to long scrutiny, since his vice is hard to eradicate, but if he desists is to be accepted into the catechumenate.[29]

Speculation on why the regulations have in some respects been tightened and in others relaxed, to the extent of giving serious consideration to someone who has been a magician, would in the absence of any information on what the factors were that led to the changes not be a fruitful exercise. It is more important to acknowledge that the position of the Church on the admission of magicians to the catechumenate does not constitute a break with what had gone before. There is no new beginning here. As we have seen, attempts were made to keep known magicians from worshipping in pagan sanctuaries, as their presence was felt to be particularly offensive to the deity.[30] Magicians were, not surprisingly, barred from initiation into the Eleusinian Mysteries.[31]

The Canons of the Church belonging to this period that deal with magic and divination are basically concerned with defining the penalties to be imposed by the Church on those Christians guilty of engaging in the practices in question. The purpose of the penalty is to cleanse the sinner of his sins and to lead him back after a period of penance and contrition into the body of the faithful. The penalties that the Church imposes on those who engage in magic-working or who employ some other party to practise magic on their behalf do not correspond in their degree of severity to those of secular criminal law. On the other hand, delinquencies that secular law ignores are treated with the same degree of severity as homicide. The severity of the penalties is a reflection of the seriousness with which the Church took all dealings in magic.

The Canon Law of the Church on the subject of magic, so far as it affects the laity, rests principally on the rulings of two important Church Fathers of the latter part of the fourth century, Basil, the Bishop of Caesarea in Cappadocia, and his brother, Gregory of Nyssa. The penalty prescribed by Basil for women who, while not intending to do harm, kill someone with a love-philtre and who employ incantations and binding-spells in conjunction with it is that they should be treated in the same way as those guilty of intentional homicide. The reasoning behind the decision is that magic and a forbidden practice are involved in the offence. Basil goes on to add that women who supply abortifacients and those who take them should be placed in the same category as persons guilty of voluntary manslaughter.[32] It is to be inferred that a similar pattern of reasoning lies behind the rulings issued by Basil concerning those who have confessed to sorcery (*goeteia*) and those who have given themselves over to diviners: they should be treated in the same way as those who have admitted to homicide.[33] In a further ruling, we learn what the penalty is to be for those who have consulted diviners or who have brought into their houses persons who will work spells or will perform purifications: they are to fall under the six-year Canon, which is to say that they are to lament for one year, follow instruction for another year, be in an inferior position for three years and consort with the faithful in the final year.[34] Gregory of Nyssa's contribution to the treatment of those who have recourse to sorcerers, diviners and those holding out the promise of effecting through the invocation of demons protection and purification is to propose that they be asked with great care whether they still abide by the Christian faith and whether it was under duress that they had turned to wrongful courses of action or whether they did so contemptuous of Christian witness; if it turns out that a degree of compulsion beyond the capacity of their mean spirits to handle was responsible, they are to be treated with the same indulgence shown those who have succumbed to the pressures of torture.[35] It is apparent from the Canons cited that the Church took cognizance of forms of magic-working that fell outside the scope of the secular criminal law: it was concerned with persons who had summoned to their houses those expert in expiations and in purifying the house from evil and in performing rituals meant to have an apotropaic and protective effect.

In addition to the Canons of Basil and Gregory of Nyssa that were absorbed into the corpus of Canon Law, there are Canons emanating from Alexandria that belong to the second half of the fourth century or to the early fifth century at the latest. They are preserved in Arabic and less fully in Coptic in the form of a detailed and reasoned set of prescriptions for the behaviour of the clergy and the laity. In the Arabic manuscripts, the prescriptions are ascribed to Athanasius, Patriarch of Alexandria, who reigned from AD 326 to AD 373, although his tenure of office was interrupted by periods of exile. The Canons were originally written in Greek by someone who was a high official of the Church in Alexandria. Their contents are consonant with their having been written by Athanasius, and, if not by him, by someone living not too long after his death.[36] By the seventh century at least they had been translated into Coptic and in the eleventh century from a text in the Bohairic dialect of Coptic into Arabic.

The Canons are important not only because of the offences with which they are concerned, but for the light they shed on conditions in Alexandria. Basil and Gregory have, for whatever reason, nothing to say about the treatment of magicians or diviners themselves. The Alexandrian Canons do deal with the issue. The impression to be gained from them is that magicians and diviners of various kinds were very much part of the fabric of life in Alexandria at this time. Perhaps such persons were more of a problem in Alexandria than in Cappadocia.[37] There is at any rate in the Alexandrian Canons a certain acceptance of the existence of magicians and diviners: presbyters are not to give communion to wizards, conjurers or soothsayers; if such persons should enter the church, they are to be placed amongst the catechumens; the doorkeepers are also to take care not to let such persons enter the church and to make sure that they should be set apart.[38] This set of Canons has nothing to say about the consultation of magicians and diviners on the part of the laity. Their concern is with magicians. If the son of a cleric is found to be studying books of magic, he and his father are to be kept apart from the Church, until such time as the father hands his son over to the civil authorities, so that everyone may know that the father has had no part in the sin of the son.[39] It should be said here that the son would almost inevitably have been executed. The next clause deals with the penance to be imposed on such magicians as are prepared to burn their magical books: they are to fast cheerfully for three years, and if they undertake a greater penance, they are to be given communion.[40] The following clause deals with the penance to be imposed on persons who are fortune-tellers, conjurors and enchanters: they are to fast for a year.

Since the penalty for fortune-tellers, enchanters and conjurors is so much less severe than it is for magicians, it is reasonable to suppose that there is a difference between a magician and a conjuror or enchanter. It is likely that in the Greek original the term for a magician was a *magos. Epodos* may have been used for an enchanter. Conjuror is more difficult. The crucial difference between the magician and the conjuror and enchanter appears to be that the magician has books. The others will be uneducated persons who perform cures and exorcisms. The magician is presumably felt to be more deeply involved in the work of the Devil by his possession of magical books and perhaps because he engages in the more harmful forms of magic. In the matter of clerical discipline the Canons from Alexandria prescribe a period of bitter penance lasting three years for any cleric who approaches an augur, a magician, a wizard or a sorcerer. Three witnesses of the misdeed are needed.[41]

Most of the Canons affecting the behaviour of the clergy rather than the laity have their origins in the pronouncements of Councils of the Church. The primary concern of ecclesiastical councils was with matters of dogma and with questions of discipline within the Church. Canons emanating from such bodies tend, accordingly, to govern the behaviour of the clergy rather than that of the laity. The penalties prescribed by such councils are on the whole slightly more severe than those which Basil lays down for a member of the laity found doing the same thing. The earliest Canon emanating from a synod that deals with magic-working comes from a synod at Laodicea in Phrygia. The date of the Synod is unfortunately unknown and to complicate matters further the Canons attributed to the Synod of Laodicea do not all come from the same synod in that place. For our purposes it does not greatly matter whether the Canon forbidding clergy to engage in magic comes from the time of Theodosius I at the end of the fourth century or from the first half of the fifth century. What it says is that a priest or a cleric ought not to be a *magos* or one who performs incantations or an astrologer or one who makes phylacteries. It pronounces phylacteries to be a prison for the soul and prescribes the expulsion of those who wear them from the Church.[42] The Canon was taken over by the Latin Church, but without the clause commanding that those wearing phylacteries be cast out of the Church. It is to be found in a compendium of Canons made sometime before AD 550 by Ferrandus, a deacon of the Church in Carthage.[43] It is surprising that those guilty of wearing a protective amulet should suffer so extreme a penalty, but perhaps what is meant is that persons who are irremediably committed to such conduct are to be excommunicated.

Finally, there is a Canon that comes out of the so-called Council in Trullo of AD 692. The council was held in a domed building in Constantinople in the palace of the Emperor, hence its name. Although it falls at the end of the period studied, it is worth citing because it reasserts the rulings of the Fathers of the Church and specifies various forms of magical divination and magic-working that almost certainly existed within the period which is our concern but which are not otherwise attested:

> Those surrendering themselves to diviners and the so-called *hekatonarchai* or to other such persons, so that they may learn from them what they wish to be revealed, let them fall under the Six-Year Canon as defined by the Fathers in the past; those dragging bears around or animals of that kind for the amusement and harm of simpler persons should be subject to the same penalty, as should those who utter fortunes, fates, horoscopes and all the multitude of such nonsense and as should the so-called chasers of clouds, sorcerers (*goeteutai*), makers of amulets and diviners; those who persist in such pursuits and do not set them aside and flee from these forms of Hellenic perdition we say ought to be thrown out of the Church, just as the Holy Canons prescribe.[44]

The Canon is of particular interest because it does not distinguish between those who avail themselves of magicians and those who actively practise magic. All are subject to the same penalty of a penance lasting six years and to excommunication, if they persist in such practices.

## The application of Canon Law and Civil Law

There is no great difficulty in demonstrating the hostility of the institutional Church to magic-working. Nor is there much room for dispute that the suppression of magical practices was a major preoccupation of the higher clergy. What is less easy to document are the formal steps taken by the Church to suppress magic and to enforce the Canons that dealt with the subject. About ecclesiastical courts devoted to the investigation of magic on the part of laymen next to nothing is known. It is not even known whether such a mechanism to root out magic existed. The Church, nonetheless, did play an active part in extirpating magic. Since magic-working represented an acknowledgment of Satan's powers, the Church was naturally enough thought to have a special authority and interest in cases of sorcery. That was no doubt one of the reasons that investigations into magic sometimes devolved on it. Yet because there are only one or two cases to go by, it is hard to determine the extent to which the rôle of the Church in investigating and dealing with magic was formalized. There is nonetheless a rescript of 1st February AD 409 issued in Ravenna by the Emperor Honorius requiring that unless astrologers were prepared to have their books burned in the presence of bishops and give their allegiance to the Christian faith, they were to be expelled not only from Rome but from all the cities of the Empire.[45] In some cases proceedings against magicians seem to have been initiated by the Church and then to have received the backing of the civil authorities. In these circumstances the civil authorities do not seem to have been interested in pursuing the matter further and applying the criminal law in its full severity to the accused magicians. Finally, what little we do know about the intervention of the Church in public life to stamp out magic does not suggest it took action against the more trivial forms of magic that fell outside the scope of the criminal law.

There is also the question of what happened when a member of the clergy was accused of magic. Did his being a cleric mean that he was subject only to the jurisdiction of the Church or could he be brought before the civil authority? The evidence, such as it is, suggests that either course of action was possible, but that for the most part the civil authorities preferred to leave such matters to the Church. The Church for its part clearly preferred to try its own. The Canon from Alexandria requiring clerics to hand sons found studying books on magic over to the civil authorities on pain of being excluded from communion is strictly speaking in conformity with this general rule.

The concrete cases on which these contentions rest are an investigation into magic-working in Beirut in the late 480s, an accusation of sorcery against a Syrian bishop heard by a synod that met in Ephesus in AD 449, the trial in Trier in AD 386 and subsequent condemnation and execution of the Spanish bishop, Priscillian of Avila, and finally, in the 620s the trial before the governor of Cyprus of a presbyter from a village near the capital Constantia and his condemnation to being burned at the stake.[46] The first two cases tell us a great deal not only about the procedures used against persons accused of sorcery, but also about some rather surprising manifestations of the learned magician. They are worth recounting in some detail, since they come as close as anything from antiquity does to providing a first-hand account of the magician and his world. The story of the trial in Constantia also merits being told, not for anything it tells us about the magician, but because it gives us something of the flavour of a trial before the civil authorities of a magician who was a churchman. Priscillian's trial before the Emperor Maximus and execution were very unusual events, from which general lessons are not to be drawn.

The case from Beirut offers a particularly striking example of the Church in the form of the local bishop, backed up by the muscle of the imperial administration, taking measures to suppress the practice of magic. Beirut at this time was the centre to which students from the Greek East who aspired to be lawyers came to study Roman Law. The story of the Church's investigation of magic-working amongst some of the students of Roman Law then present in Beirut is told by Zacariah of Mytilene in his *Life of Severus*. Zacariah came from Gaza, which in his time was famed for its school of rhetoric. He had got to know Severus, the subject of the *Life* and the later monophysite Patriarch of Antioch, when they were in Alexandria together. Severus had gone on from Alexandria to Beirut to study law a year before Zacariah himself came to that city to pursue the same course of study. The *Life of Severus*, which Zacariah had written in Greek, exists only in a Syriac translation. It is to some extent possible to recreate the Greek original, a task which is made the easier by the translator's having done no more than transliterate Greek and Latin administrative titles and technical terms.

The story that Zacariah recounts has its beginnings in the infatuation of a young man with a woman. The young man in question was a student of law in Beirut called John Foulon. He had come to Beirut from Thebes in Egypt. The woman with whom he had become infatuated had turned out to be chaste and had resisted John's advances. He had, accordingly, had recourse to the recipes contained in books of magic to get the better of her, but that had made her hate him the more.[47] It was not only he but several of his fellow-students who had resorted to magic in their desire to seduce the woman. Matters had come to a head when John and some of his companions had at dead of night on some pretext or other taken an Ethiopian slave belonging to John to the circus in Beirut, where they planned to sacrifice him, so that demons might be summoned up that would help bring the woman to them. The proceedings were interrupted by the arrival of some strangers. The would-be sacrificers fled and the Ethiopian escaped. He went to a compatriot of his master, a good Christian, and told him what he had narrowly escaped. John's compatriot out of compassion for the slave and out of concern for John informed Zacariah and his friends of what had taken place. The reason for his following such a course of action was that Zacariah belonged to a group who took delight in toiling on behalf of Christ and who called themselves in consequence the *Philoponoi*. The *Philoponoi* now asked whether the slave had said anything about John's having books on magic in his possession and were told he was indeed the owner of such writings.

Zacariah and his group went to John's place of residence and told him that they had come to him out of concern for his well-being, since he was rumoured to own magical texts; it was their wish to quell the rumour if it was found to be untrue. John, who had hidden the books in a box concealed below the seat on which he had placed himself for the interview, invited them to search the premises. They made a search and could find nothing, until the Ethiopian slave signalled to them where the hiding-place was. Once his secret was revealed, John burst into tears and begged them not to hand him over to the judicial authorities. They replied that they had not come there for any such purpose, but to save his soul and advised him to burn the books with his own hand. Arrangements were made to have a fire brought. The books to be burned contained strange images of demons and barbaric names. Some of them were attributed to Zoroaster, others to Manetho and others yet again to Ostanes. It was at this point that John was moved to tell them what had happened to him and to give them the names of the other young men who had for the same reason as himself become addicted to magic. They too, he said, had magical books. When the fire appeared, he threw the books into it with his own hand and confessed his gratitude to God for having saved him from a life of servitude to demons; he was a Christian and the son of Christian parents but had taken up the worship of idols to win over maleficent demons. The group then shared a meal with him and went off to the Church of the Apostle Jude and asked the priests there to pray for John.[48]

What had been a private affair now became a public matter. The story of John's burning his books on magic had got around and had led to a man called Martyrius approaching one of the *Philoponoi*, Polycarpus, a native of Beirut, who was a soldier in the cohort of the prefect. What Martyrius, who was a scribe and a lector in a church in Beirut, had to say to Polycarpus was that George of Thessalonike, a law student and associate of John Foulon, had approached him with a book of magic that he wanted copied. The *Philoponoi* at this juncture laid the names of George, Asclepiodotes of Heliopolis, Chrysaorius of Tralles, who were all studying law in Beirut, and Leontius, a teacher of law, before John, the Bishop of Beirut. The Bishop gave them the support of his clergy and told them to examine the books of the accused. There were also officers of the civil authority in attendance. The search was not wholly successful: the magical books of George and Asclepiodotes were discovered and were brought into the centre of the town; the books of the others could not be found because their owners had fled and hidden the books. One of those who had fled, Chrysaorius, stirred up a crowd of persons called the *Companions*, whom Zacariah says were of low moral character. In response, one of the *Philoponoi*, Constantinus, who was an advocate in Beirut, brought in the peasants from his estates to seize the leaders of the *Companions*. They laid hold of Leontius, the teacher of law, who was only saved from bodily harm by Zacariah.

When the time came to burn the books, Zacariah and his party had at their side, in accordance with the orders of the Bishop, a judicial official of the imperial administration known as the *defensor civitatis*, other civil officials, whose exact positions cannot be recovered from the Syriac text, and members of the clergy. The books and their diabolic symbols were duly burned. According to Zacariah, the books contained instructions on how to cause upset in cities by arousing the people and arming fathers against their sons and grandsons, on how to break up legitimate marriages and cohabitations, on how to win over to illicit love against her will a woman who wished to live in chastity, on how to commit adultery and murder, on how to conceal a theft and on how to make judges render a favourable verdict.[49]

The sequel to the affair was that Leontius, who at the first sign of trouble had fled from Beirut, decided to be baptized in some city other than Beirut in the Church of the Martyr Leontius. That gesture enabled him to re-enter Beirut, where he sought public pardon. As for Chrysaorius, he shortly afterwards got himself mixed up in some further sinister business involving magic-working and a search for hidden treasure. A group of vagabond-magicians had appeared in Beirut with a story that they said they had from the mouths of the Magi and the Persians about Dareius' having hidden gold in certain places. Chrysaorius accepted the story unquestioningly and asked how the hidden treasure could be recovered. The vagabonds told him that necromancy was needed and that that they had in their number one skilled in that art, but that he needed a hidden spot in which to exercise his craft. At this point, Chrysaorius got the help of the watchman (*paramonaorios*) of a chapel called the Second Martyrium on the understanding that the watchman would get a share in the treasure. The man said there was in the chapel beside some tombs an isolated spot where at dead of night the deed could be performed. The vagabonds, for their part, declared that they needed silver objects both to invoke by the sea the demons who were the guardians of the treasures and for the necromancy. Chrysaorius provided them with some silver objects with which they fled, after making a pretence of invoking the demons who were the guardians of the treasures. As for the watchman, he gave the man who was to perform the necromancy a silver censer from the chapel treasury to aid him in invoking the souls of the dead who were supposed to say where the treasure was to be found. As the necromancer was carrying out his ritual, an earthquake sent by God occurred. The vagabond-magician and Chrysaorius took to their heels, while the poor people, whose only home was the chapel, cried out and shortly afterwards made known in Beirut what had happened.

The events seem to have occurred just before the festival of John the Baptist, since at the festival there was a public outcry against the watchman and Chrysaorius. The Bishop had the watchman arrested and sent to a monastery, while Chrysaorius fled from the town, but was able to use his wealth to buy his way back to Beirut. He remained unrepentant, convinced that it was his magic, the demons in his service and his wealth that had enabled him to overcome the forces opposed to him. Proof that Chrysaorius was mistaken Zacariah found in the loss of the ship that Chrysaorius had hired to take back to Tralles not only his books of magic, his law-books and his silver, but also his children and their mother, his concubine, despite his not having allowed the ship to set sail until he had consulted a magical book and had had calculations made based on the movements of the stars.[50]

The episode is instructive in several respects, not least because it explains in part how it was that responsibility for the investigation devolved on the Bishop of Beirut and not the local civil authorities. The explanation would seem to be that the matter fell to the Bishop to deal with because the persons who had first become involved in the business were concerned Christians whose primary goal was to save men from the consequences of their sins. The implication of Zacariah's account is that only when the affair began to get out of hand did the *Philoponoi* go public with the matter and bring it to the attention of the Bishop. When the Bishop decided to take action, he seems to have had the power to commandeer officers of the state to help his agents, in this case the *Philoponoi*, in prosecuting their quest. The one identifiable official was the *defensor civitatis*, whose jurisdiction in this period was confined to hearing civil cases not involving sums of great value.

At this point, it is proper to step back and ask what gave the Bishop the authority to take command of officials who answered to the Roman State. His personal charisma and the respect that men felt for religious authority may have been factors. It has also been suggested that a law, dating probably to the same decade as the incident in Beirut, was what empowered bishops to give such orders.[51] The law commands the officials of the Roman State to search out with the help of the local bishops the teachers of Hellenism.[52] There is nothing in this imperial rescript, however, that bestows on bishops the authority to give orders to public servants responsible to the Roman State, and it stretches the imagination somewhat to have to suppose that even in the mind of the most fervent Christian teachers of Hellenism and magicians were one and the same.

To return to the investigation in Beirut, it had two outcomes: such magical books as were found were burned publicly with both ecclesiastical and civil authorities in attendance; those who publicly repented of their wrongdoing were allowed to return to Beirut and resume their life there. There seems to be no question of the persons concerned being tried, even though the possession of magical books was unquestionably a capital offence at this period. There can be no doubt that John Foulon would have suffered a terrible punishment had he been convicted of necromancy, an offence in his case compounded by his being prepared to sacrifice a human being to further his aims. The outcome of the investigation suggests that the primary concern of the ecclesiastical authorities was with the salvation of souls. So far as we know, this was in any case the extent of their jurisdiction at the time.

These are the inferences to be drawn from Zacariah's account of the episode. We have to remember that Zacariah is our only source for the affair and, furthermore, that he was an interested party. It would, accordingly, be naïve to imagine that Zacariah has not shaped his tale to put the best possible construction on his own actions, those of his comrades and those of the local bishop. It is also likely that story has been told in such a way as to make the reader believe that the sole concern of the parties involved was with the salvation of souls. There may well have been occasions in which the Church was more zealous in its pursuit of magic than the civil authority and was eager to see the agents of the imperial administration exact harsh penalties.

The second case gives us some idea of how the Church dealt with magic-working within its own ranks. It comes from the proceedings of the second session of the Ecumenical Synod of Ephesus of the year AD 449, the so-called *Latrocinium Ephesinum* or *Robber Synod*. Theodosius II was responsible for convening the Synod. It gets its name from its exploitation by the Monophysite followers of Cyril of Alexandria. They had seized control of it and turned it into a tribunal before which the Dyophysite or Nestorian bishops of Syria and Phoenicia were arraigned and condemned. No account of the proceedings of the second session of the Synod has survived in Greek, but there is a translation into Syriac of some of the Greek record, preserved in a single manuscript that is now in the British Museum.

The principal business recorded in the fragment of the proceedings in Syriac was the deposing of Ibas, the Nestorian Bishop of Edessa, who was head of the See of Osrhoene, and the removal of certain other Nestorian bishops.[53] Ibas was an important figure at this time; his presence had attracted a number of Christians from the realm of the Sassanians to study in Edessa.[54] It was in the second session of the Synod that Sophronius, Bishop of Constantia or Tella, a bishopric that fell under the authority of Edessa, was accused of magic-working.[55] Sophronius was a son of Ibas' brother and was not surprisingly also accused of being a Nestorian. The suspicion that there is nothing to the charge of sorcery is in the circumstances a natural one and is heightened by the knowledge that Ibas too was accused of being a magician. The story begins with the arrival at the city limits of Edessa of Flavius Chaereas, the Count of the Province of Osrhoene. There he was greeted by the assembled higher clergy, monks and men and women of the city. They acclaimed the Emperor, orthodoxy in the Church and Chaereas before beginning a chant in which they demanded the dismissal of Ibas and his relatives. On the following day, April 4th, another group, this time consisting only of the clergy of Edessa, had come to the council-chamber of Flavius Chaereas to greet him and had then struck up a second chant intended to lead to the ouster of Ibas. Amongst their cries they had called out:

> No one accept Ibas the Bishop! No one accept Nestorius! No one accept Simon Magus' adherent.[56]

Towards the end of the demonstration the assembled group had chanted:

> The one Ibas, the one Simon! Mighty was Musarius the magician, mighty now is Ibas!

The point of the pseudo-acclamations is on the one hand to acclaim Ibas as a matchless magician who is the equal of Simon Magus, and on the other to compare Ibas in his magical power with another obviously notorious but otherwise unknown magician. There was then a third session of orchestrated chanting, which was said to have lasted for three or four days and in which all the clergy and laity joined. During it Ibas and Simon Magus were again linked and sarcastically acclaimed as they had been in the session at the council chamber on April 4th. After some more cries, the crowd had gone on to dilate further on the theme of Ibas as magician and specifically as magician-cum-charioteer:

> Another bishop for the metropolis! We do not accept this one! No one accepts the magician! No one accepts the charioteer! No one accepts the charioteer-bishop! He has worn as clothing in the Church of the Holy Barlaha consecrated linens! Abraham has organized races in the circus for him![57]

They come back to Abraham in the course of a set of chants in which they demand that those who are of the party of Ibas be driven into exile:

> Archdeacon Basil into exile! Abraham the guest-master (*xenodochos*) into exile![58]

We know about these orchestrated denunciations because they were entered as evidence into the proceedings of the Synod. A year earlier at a synod in Beirut the disaffected clergy of Edessa had presented a summary list of wrongs, amounting to some seventeen items, committed by Ibas and his nephew Daniel. The fourth count against Ibas was that he had tried to advance to a bishopric men involved in magic-working. Specifically, the charge said that when the deacon Abraham, who had entered into a partner-ship in magic with a man named John, who had himself been caught red-handed in an act of sorcery, was called to appear before Ibas and his clergy to give account of himself and when Abraham had confessed to being guilty, Ibas, instead of having the deacon excommunicated and driven into exile, as Abraham himself had fully expected, had attempted to appoint him bishop of the city of Batnae. He had done this despite Abraham's failure to present any defence of his conduct. Ibas was nonetheless frustrated in the endeavour by an archdeacon from Batnae and in his annoyance now appointed the magician who was under sentence of death to be the bishop of the city. The archdeacon, who had reported to him the uproar in the city over the appointment, he excommunicated. He pressed on, however, but, since mat-ters had not gone according to plan, he now made Abraham a guest-master (*xenodochos*) in his church. The authors of the charge conclude their case by observing sarcastically that their most scrupulous bishop now had in his pos-session a text containing magical incantations and that if the letter of the law was to be followed, he ought to hand over a completely abandoned man to the governor of the province.[59]

It goes without saying that we have to take with a pinch of salt accusations of magic-working made against a man charged with promulgating a heresy. The failure of the Synod to pay any further attention in its deliberations to these particular charges is a good sign that they are not to be taken seriously. However tempting it may be, we are not justified in drawing conclusions of the same order about the charges brought against the nephew of Ibas. The two cases are significantly different. Sophronius is only incidentally, and very much as an afterthought, accused of being a Nestorian. No serious attempt is made to document that accusation. The real gravamen of the case against Sophronius is his magic-working, about which detailed testimony is pro-vided. The charges against Sophronius were contained in a written petition submitted to the Synod by a presbyter, and two deacons from Constantia.[60] On the motion of Juvenalius, Bishop of Jerusalem, they were read aloud and entered into the proceedings of the Synod. The petition began with a gen-eral preamble that summarized the case against Sophronius: he was a nephew of Ibas, Bishop of Edessa, and had disgraced his priestly office; far from fulfilling the duties of his office, he had engaged in dealings with demons, made astrological calculations and practised various forms of pagan divination and soothsaying; he had, furthermore, absorbed the wicked teach-ings of Nestorius from his kinsman Ibas and, not content with that, he had also launched himself into the pursuit of the wicked practices mentioned.

Sophronius' case is dealt with quite differently from that of the bishops charged only with subscribing to the teachings of Nestor: they are deposed without further ado by the Synod. The appropriate authority to investigate and pass judgment on the case of Sophronius in the eyes of the Synod was the senior bishop of the See of Osrhoene, namely, the Bishop of Edessa, sitting with his fellow-bishops from the same see. Local synods, accordingly, were held to have jurisdiction over bishops charged with practising magic.

There is no suggestion at any point of having the civil authorities deal with the case of Sophronius. That is not surprising. The Church from the time of Constantine the Great had by and large been conceded the right to discipline its own. That right was re-asserted in the Canons of a number of Church Councils. Magic-working of the kind that Sophronius was accused of having pursued was, nonetheless, a serious civil offence and was potentially an area in which there could be a conflict between ecclesiastical and civil jurisdictions. There are two known instances of churchmen being brought before civil courts and convicted of magic-working. The better known of these is the case of the Spanish bishop, Priscillian of Avila, who in AD 386 was condemned to death in Trier for having practised sorcery.[61] At Burdigala (Bordeaux) in Aquitaine he had refused to submit to the authority of a synod specially set up to hear his case and that of some of his associates and had appealed to Maximus, who had just overthrown the Emperor Gratian. This was probably a miscalculation, since Maximus' authority was shaky, extending only to Britain and Gaul, and Maximus himself was eager to be seen as a defender of Christian orthodoxy. Maximus was not, therefore, necessarily going to be well-disposed towards a fellow-Spaniard whose consecration as a bishop was questionable and who had been engaging in distinctly unorthodox religious practices.

A rump-synod of Spanish and Aquitanian bishops, meeting at Saragossa, had already in AD 380 pronounced against some of the practices followed by the Priscillianists. Two of the practices condemned may be singled out for special mention: women going to the houses of men to whom they were not related to read the Bible (Canon 1); going barefoot (Canon 6). One of the complaints against the Priscillianists continued to be that they kept company with women, while the charge of walking with feet unshod carried with it the suggestion of pagan sacrifice and magical rites.[62] What was merely hinted at in Saragossa became a formal charge in the synod that took place in Bordeaux: Ithacius, Bishop of Ossonuba, Priscillian's principal opponent amongst the Spanish bishops, seems to have accused Priscillian of having practised incantations over the first fruit of the crops and of having taught how to make a magical unguent effective and how to negate its effects.[63] When one of Priscillian's allies, Instantius, was deprived of his position as bishop by the Synod of Bordeaux, Priscillian decided to appeal to Maximus rather than have his case heard by this convocation of bishops. He was followed to Trier by his main accusers, Ithacius and Hydatius. Maximus, despite the protests of Martin of Tours, who was present in Trier, decided that the case should be heard in front of his praetorian prefect, Euodius, a man with a reputation for severity. The prosecutor was Ithacius. Priscillian was tried and convicted of sorcery (*maleficium*). He did not deny that he had studied vile doctrines, that during the hours of darkness he had held gatherings of depraved women and that he had prayed in a state of nakedness. It rather looks as if these admissions had been extracted under judicial torture. Priscillian was kept in custody until the case could be referred to Maximus. His verdict was that Priscillian and his associates ought to be executed. At this point, Ithacius, realizing that as a bishop he had put himself in an invidious position by acting as a prosecutor in a capital case, withdrew. Maximus replaced him as prosecutor with an official from the Treasury who insisted on the death sentence, which was duly carried out.[64]

In AD 388, Maximus was overthrown and one of the consequences of his removal was that at a Spanish synod shortly after he was deposed Ithacius and his associate Hydatius were not only stripped of their positions but excommunicated and driven into exile, because they had been responsible for the execution of Priscillian.[65] Either before this event or during his subsequent exile Ithacius composed an apologia in which he set out his version of the doctrines taught by Priscillian and described the magical arts employed by Priscillian and the licentious practices he had followed; the source of Priscillian's expertise in sorcery he ascribed to a certain Marcus from Memphis, who was extraordinarily well versed in magic and was a pupil of the founder of the heresy of Manichaeism, Mani.[66]

The circumstances of Priscillian's trial are so extraordinary that it would be unwise to draw any general conclusions from it. The case of the presbyter from a village near the capital of Cyprus, Constantia, is rather different. His fate suggests that clergymen could be and were prosecuted for witchcraft by the civil authorities. The story of his trial is one of a series of edifying tales ascribed to a monk from Sinai called Anastasius.[67] There is no reason to doubt the essential authenticity of the tale, although details in it have clearly been embellished to demonstrate the power of God. The events recounted are said to have taken place some ten years before what is called the capture of Cyprus when Arcadius was archbishop of the island. This must be a reference to the first Arab attack on the island in AD 648/49 or that four years later in AD 653, although strictly speaking there was no conquest of the island.[68] It was not Arcadius, the archbishop, who tried the presbyter, but the governor of the province, to whom the presbyter had been denounced as a magician. Since the author of the story expresses no surprise at a churchman's being tried by the civil rather than the ecclesiastical authorities, this may have been what would normally have happened at least at that date. When the trial took place, the governor occupied a seat in front with his assessors sitting on a bench beside him. The most intelligent and literate of the assessors had proceeded to ask the defendant if he was not afraid that God would visit an immediate punishment on him for serving and participating in communion when he was a servant of the Devil and utterly defiled. The man had replied that he had not in fact served communion to anyone, since immediately on becoming a magician (*pharmakos*) an angel of God had bound his hands behind his back to a pillar when he entered the church and had himself served communion. The assembled crowd on hearing this were moved to praise God, shouting out: 'Great is the God of the Christians! Great is the faith of the Christians! Let us not judge the priests. The angels consecrate the mysteries of Christ and bestow them on us'. The presbyter, condemned out of his own mouth, was then burned at the stake in the presence of all. The story of the trial of the presbyter is by no means a transcript of its proceedings, but its author does at least succeed in evoking what must have been the highly-charged atmosphere of such a trial and of the part played in it not only by the assessors but by the crowd who had assembled to watch it.

# 10

## SORCERERS AND SORCERESSES FROM CONSTANTINE TO THE END OF THE SEVENTH CENTURY AD

### Introduction

Much more is known about magic-working in the first three Christian centuries than in any period of Classical Antiquity. This is probably a function of the nature and richness of the sources for the period and not of any great upswing in the incidence of occult practices. Presenting a balanced picture of magic-working and magic-workers in a world in which Christianity enjoyed a degree of power and prestige that it had hitherto not known is not a simple task. It is all too easy to ignore the continuities and to overemphasize the discontinuities. Changes did take place in the way in which men looked at the world that affected the practice of magic and who it was who practised it, but at the same time inevitably much remained the same.

Very much the same types of person continue to practise magic under a Christian Empire as before. Prostitutes and procuresses still actively engage in magic. Mendicant magicians are very much a presence. There are indications that long before Constantine magic-working was endemic amongst wrestlers and charioteers. Our later sources show unequivocally that magicians emerged from the ranks of wrestlers, charioteers, musicians and in general entertainers. The old woman who is summoned to the house to heal the sick with amulets and incantations now comes much more clearly into focus. New forms of magician do appear. The most conspicuous of these are Christian clergymen. Many clergymen were no doubt unfairly denounced as magicians by their opponents, but there can be no question that some members of the clergy did exploit the authority their position gave them to claim expertise in certain forms of magic and to make a living from its practice. In sum, although changes do occur, it was very much the same sort of person to whom people turned for help when they wanted magic performed on their behalf. Continuities are far more conspicuous than discontinuities.

The Christian view of magic in this period is not a consistent one: sometimes it is maintained that there is a reality to what magic seems to accomplish and on other occasions that reality is denied and we are told that it is just an illusion engineered either by sleight of hand or by demons. There is,

273

nonetheless, general agreement that the effects of magic, whether illusion or reality, are the work of the Devil and the demons of whom he is the leader. The early Christian apologist Tatian, writing around the middle of the second century AD perhaps in Rome, in his only surviving work, the *Oration to the Greeks*, argues that the herbs and roots, sinews and bones used by sorcerers (*goetes*) are not effective in themselves, but are the elements that demons make into potent forces and then use for their wickedness; what actually happens is that whenever they see men using the devices, they take the opportunity to enslave the users to themselves.[1] Tatian gives the Devil no explicit part to play, but Justin Martyr, Tatian's teacher, who takes exactly the same position as his pupil on demons and magic, credits the 'so-called Devil' with having empowered the Egyptian magicians at the time of the Exodus.[2] The Devil may then have played a part in Christian demonology from a very early period.

## Christian clerics and priests as magicians

There is no evidence that any pre-Constantinian Christian priest or cleric exploited the illegality of his faith and the suspicion of practising illicit human sacrifices that attached to Christians to present himself as an expert in magic. There is, on the other hand, a good deal of evidence that magic-working on the part of priests and clerics in post-Constantinian Christianity was not an unusual occurrence. Canons of the Church forbid and lay down penalties for those who practise it, councils of the Church have to deal with bishops accused of engaging in magic-working or of tolerating that activity amongst their clergy, there are episodes in the lives of saints in which the saint confronts a cleric who practises magic or in which he himself is accused by jealous fellow-clerics or laymen of having used magic in effecting miraculous cures and finally, a bishop has to warn his flock against accepting amulets intended to protect against illness from clerics.

That priests and clerics behaved in very much the same way as those around them is hardly occasion for surprise. It is necessary, nonetheless, to look a little more closely at who it is in the clergy who practise magic and what kind of magic it is in which they engage. It is also proper to ask whether there is any necessary relationship between the clerical office the magician holds and his being a magician or whether it is just a coincidence that some clerics are magicians.

The most difficult cases to deal with are the bishops who are accused of practising magic. There is first of all the problem of deciding how much credibility is to be given to the accusations that are brought against them. It is undoubtedly the case that doctrinal differences and professional jealousies led to some of these accusations, which is not to say that those who brought the accusations did not sincerely believe them. The late sixth or early seventh century author of the *Life of Symeon Stylites the Younger* records two episodes in which Symeon's ability to effect miraculous cures was put down to his being a sorcerer, while the writer who a little later wrote a *Life* of the mother of the saint tells of a third incident.[3] A stylite with miraculous powers is not a bishop. The stories about Symeon do nonetheless show in a general way how readily accusations of magic-working could arise, if a man was a powerful and charismatic figure.

Even if an accusation does seem to have substance to it, the magic-working of the bishop has still to be made sense of and placed in some larger context. Four bishops are known to have been charged in one way or another with engaging in sorcery. There are also the two men, one a convicted magician, the other one of his associates, whom Ibas, the Nestorian Bishop of Edessa, tried, in the latter case unsuccessfully and in the former successfully, to impose as bishop on the city of Batnae. Of the four bishops accused of magic-working three were formally charged in the Councils of the Church with practising magic. In one case, the charge resulted in the bishop's being deposed; in another, the bishop was able to confute his accusers; the outcome of the third case is not recorded. There is, in addition, a bishop appointed to a see and kept initially from taking up the position because he was accused of having practised astrology. It is significant that these charges tend to come to the surface during synods devoted to settling issues of doctrine or to rooting out heretics. There are two ways of looking at the tendency: one is to dismiss charges of sorcery made in such a context as the almost inevitable byproduct of doctrinal difference; the other is to acknowledge that in periods of internal turmoil unpleasant truths, which would otherwise have been suppressed, might emerge. Prudence suggests that both possibilities should be weighed and a decision taken on the merits of the case.

The earliest known instance of a bishop being charged with magic is that of Athanasius, the Patriarch of Alexandria. It looks to our eyes as if this was a deliberate and cynical attempt at framing Athanasius, but the version of events on which modern scholars have to rely is one told from Athanasius' point of view. Athanasius' enemies may very well have been convinced that he was a sorcerer in league with the Devil and that he owed his success to the black arts. Athanasius himself or his supporters may have unwittingly contributed to that reputation by promoting his fame as a clairvoyant. Sozomen, the ecclesiastical historian, who has a digression on Athanasius' ability to see into the future, indeed says that pagans and the heterodox attributed it to sorcery.[4]

Although Athanasius was formally acquitted of the charge of sorcery, the suspicion that he was a sorcerer continued to haunt him and he never really succeeded in ridding himself of it. In fact, some twenty years after he had managed to overturn the charge of sorcery, two ecclesiastical councils, dominated by his Arian opponents, had him removed from office on the ground that he had, because of his expertise in divining from lots and from birds, been able to predict the future.[5] The sentence was confirmed by the Emperor Constantius, who was of the Arian persuasion, despite the opposition of Leontius, the Bishop of Rome. Leontius had argued that a man should not be condemned in his absence, unseen and unheard.[6] It goes without saying that it is difficult to separate fact from fiction in disputes over questions of doctrine, but Athanasius probably did lay himself open to the charge of being a sorcerer and of having acquired knowledge of the future by illegitimate means by playing the part of a divinely-inspired holy man.

There is little room for doubt there was nothing to the charge that Athanasius was a sorcerer. At the same time we need to recognize that his opponents will have found it easy to persuade themselves of Athanasius' powers as a magician and will have been quick to find evidence of sorcery in what happened around him. It is also possible to see in the case of Ibas of Edessa how those hostile to him came to conclude that he was a sorcerer.

Ibas is in the chants of the people and clergy a magician and a second Simon Magus. Then there were chants in which charges of magic-working and charioteering alternate with each other. The series begins with the chant asking that no one should accept the magician; it is followed by the demand that no one should accept the charioteer and then, by way of amplification, the charioteer-bishop, on the heels of which comes the charge that Ibas had worn linen-garments in a certain church, which is followed in its turn by the charge that concludes the series: Abraham had organized races in the circus for him. The Abraham in question is Abraham the guest-master for whose exile the crowd is about to ask.[7] He is to be identified with the deacon Abraham, a confessed associate of the convicted sorcerer, John, and the man Ibas makes a guest-master when he is unable to secure his appointment as a bishop. The linen garments Ibas is said to have worn in church are the linen garments that magicians were said to wear to perform their rites.[8] Whether or not he had worn such garments, the rumour that he had done so must have been taken as confirmation by the hostile that Ibas was indeed a sorcerer. Ibas' interest in and sponsorship of chariot-racing with the help of the guest-master Abraham, a man presumably by now notorious in the eyes of the Monophysite opposition as a magician, will also have contributed to his reputation as a magician. Charioteers were after all notorious for practising sorcery both on their own behalf and on behalf of others. Ibas' interest in chariot-racing, his known support for Abraham and his having worn linen garments in church will have been proof positive in the eyes of his critics that he was guilty of sorcery.

Whatever their theological opponents may have believed, Athanasius and Ibas were almost certainly not guilty of having engaged in sorcery. There are, however, a pair of bishops who may very well have been practising magicians. First of all there is the bishop accused of magic and deposed on that score. His name was Paulinus. His removal from office is undoubtedly to be connected with the Arian controversy, but in his case there may have been something to the crime with which he was charged. We learn about his existence from an encyclical emanating from the Oriental Council of Serdica (Sofia) of AD 343, justifying the excommunication of the main Western anti-Arian representatives at the Council. The encyclical is to be found in a collection of documents relating to the Arian controversy put together by Hilary of Poitiers. It accuses Ossius of Cordova, one of the leaders of the Western delegation, of having consorted when he was in the East with wicked and depraved men and, in particular, of having enjoyed a close friendship with Paulinus, a bishop who had been accused of witchcraft and on that account driven out of the Church and who was at the time of the encyclical living in a state of apostasy, publicly fornicating with concubines and prostitutes; his magical books had been burned by Macedonius, Bishop and Confessor of Mopsuetia.[9] Two things are certain about Paulinus: he was accused of sorcery and removed from his bishopric; and books containing magical recipes said to belong to him were burned by a fellow-bishop. Since in all likelihood religious differences played a part in Paulinus' removal, we cannot be absolutely sure that he was not framed. Nonetheless, it does look on balance as though we have in Paulinus an example of a learned magician who was also a bishop.

In the synod in which Ibas was deposed Sophronius, Bishop of Constantia, was accused of magic-working and details were given of what he had done. The charges against Sophronius were contained in a written petition submitted to the synod by a presbyter, and two deacons from Constantia.[10] On the motion of Juvenalius, Bishop of Jerusalem, they were read aloud and entered into the proceedings of the synod. The petition began with a general preamble that summarized the case against Sophronius. The particulars of the accusation against Sophronius are that, after losing on a journey a certain sum of money, he had made those he suspected swear on the Gospel.[11] Not satisfied with doing that, he had compelled them to submit to the pagan ordeal of eating bread and cheese. This will have been a form of the ordeal prescribed by a magical papyrus as a way of bringing a thief to book.[12] The thief, when given the cheese to eat, was supposed to have been unable to swallow it, thus revealing his guilt. In this case the ordeal had revealed nothing because, we may imagine, all of those tested had been able to consume the bread and cheese without difficulty. Sophronius now had recourse to *phialomanteia* or *lekanomanteia*. We are not told how Sophronius did this, but we are almost certainly meant to understand that he had got a boy over whom incantations had been uttered to gaze into the bowl. The demon obligingly revealed the identity of the thief to him, his name and the way in which he was clothed, not because, the petition tells us, the demon was interested in having the thief convicted, but because he wanted the Bishop to sink into the deepest perdition.

The petition proceeds to describe some further divinatory procedures in which Sophronius had engaged in the episcopal residence. Their purpose was, though the petition does not say so, to find out when the son of the

Bishop would return from a visit to Constantinople. The petitioners say that they owed their knowledge of what had taken place to a servant of the Bishop, Simon by name, whose son had played the part of the medium in the second session. Sophronius had made the boy and one of his own relatives, the deacon, Abraham, enter his bedchamber. In the middle of the room stood a table; below the table lay a censer for the demons; on the table there was a bowl containing oil and water. Sophronius set the boy, who was naked, beside the table. He and the deacon were completely clad in clean linens. The deacon began to whisper the words that the Bishop had in his evil expertise in divination formulated. The pair then asked the boy what he saw in the bowl, to which he replied that he saw lightning coming out of the bowl. After a pause of a few minutes he was questioned again and answered that he saw a man clad in crimson sitting on a golden throne and wearing a crown on his head. Their next move was to make a deep hole behind the door, which they filled with oil and water, and they placed the boy beside it. The boy was now asked what he saw in the hole. His response was that he saw Habib, the son of the Bishop, who happened to have gone to Constantinople, riding on a black female mule, blinded in the eyes and followed by two men who were on foot. Then the boy was brought an egg and, when it had been opened and the white poured off, he was asked what he saw in the yoke. This time he saw Habib riding on a horse wearing a necklace about his neck and with two men going ahead of him. On the following day the son of the Bishop did indeed return from Constantinople, just as his father had foreseen. The petition reports that the boy employed in the procedures had in the presence of his mother and father and in front of witnesses sworn on the Gospels that what he had seen had come to pass. In addition, the boy testified that for the next eight months whenever he went walking, seven men clad in white were wont to go ahead of him. For these eight months the boy was out of his mind and was only brought back to his senses with some difficulty by being brought to holy places and anointed with oil.

The petition now turns from magical divination to Sophronius' involvement with astrology. A sub-deacon of Constantia and two deaconesses were known to have copied out astrological texts and the chief doctor of the city was known to have read them. A deacon had seen Sophronius going through the episcopal residence carrying a copper ball representing the heavens and had then reported the matter to all of his fellow-deacons.

In Sophronius we almost certainly do have a bishop with a learned interest in magic. It is difficult to believe that the charges brought against him are unfounded. Had his enemies wanted to accuse him of magic-working, it seems unlikely that they would have settled on so tame a charge as using magical divination to recover stolen property and the use of the same technique to learn when someone would return from a journey. That we have in Sophronius not just a man with a passing interest in magic, but someone with an almost academic interest in the subject is suggested by the number of different techniques he employs to reveal what is hidden.

Finally, there is Eusebius, the Arian-leaning Bishop of Emesa in Syria. Born in Edessa around AD 300 of an old and aristocratic family he was said from an early age to have devoted himself to sacred writings, which suggests that he belonged to a Christian family. In Edessa he also received an education in Greek literature and rhetoric before taking instruction in biblical interpretation in Caesarea Maritima and Scythopolis in Palestine. He next settled in Antioch and moved from there to Alexandria to study philosophy and to avoid ordination. He returned to Antioch and while there resisted the attempt of his teacher in Caesarea, Eusebius, to have him appointed Bishop of Alexandria to replace Athanasius, who had been deposed. Eusebius of Caesarea now tried to make him Bishop of Emesa, but the city was split over his appointment. It was at this point that the accusation of practising astrology surfaced. The new Bishop retreated to Laodicea, where he was supported by the man to whom we owe our knowledge of his career, George of Laodicea. From Laodicea he went to Antioch before being re-established in his diocese, but not without having had to endure the charge of subscribing to the heresy called Sabellianism.[13] George of Laodicea, the source of this account, was a man well-disposed to Eusebius of Emesa and will have presented Eusebius' career in the most favourable light possible. Even so, there is an interlude in Eusebius' *curriculum vitae* that must have aroused concern and that was open to interpretation: his departure for Alexandria to study philosophy and his refusal to be ordained. Philosophy in Alexandria at this time means Neoplatonism. So inevitably at this stage in his career Eusebius will have associated with committed Neoplatonists concerned to preserve what they understood to be the Hellenic tradition. That was bad enough, but there was also the theurgy that some of the Neoplatonists, whether professors or students, will have practised. Eusebius was, in sum, vulnerable to attack. Whatever the rights of the matter may have been, there was a sufficiently strong case mounted against him to cause him to retreat.

Of the lower clergy a fairly large number are known either to have been accused of being magicians, to have been convicted while in office or at an earlier stage in their lives of practising sorcery or to have been exposed as sorcerers. There are from Edessa the deacon Abraham, called before an ecclesiastical court to explain his associations with a convicted magician, and the magician John, caught red-handed at sorcery, who is then appointed to an episcopal see. It is to be presumed that the latter had held some minor office in the Church before his elevation to a bishopric. Constantia also has a deacon called Abraham, the man who participated in a magical ceremony with Sophronius. In Ancyra, a man said to have been convicted of sorcery was baptized and made a deacon by the Bishop, while in Cyzicus the Bishop appointed to a diaconate a fugitive from justice who had been indicted for sorcery.[14] In Cyprus in the first half of the seventh century there is the presbyter who is burned at the stake as a sorcerer, after having been tried and convicted by a tribunal presided over by the governor.[15] These are the members of the lower clergy known to have been accused of sorcery. Those who were never brought to book were almost certainly more numerous. Little is heard about them, but that the cleric who practised sorcery was a recognized figure is suggested by a story told in the *Life of Theodore of Syceon*. It is that when Theodore, a man renowned for his sanctity, was in Bithynia at a place called Optatianae, which lay just outside the western wall of the city of Nicomedeia, a cleric who practised sorcery and who was known as the Goat of Bithynia had come rushing up to him seeking his help, as a wolf had made off with one of his sons and the other had disappeared; Theodore told him that he would find the second son dead in the River Psilis and that he should reform himself and repent.[16] The Goat of Bithynia was not just a recognized type, but was also presumably a real person.

The existence of persons who use their priestly office to confer authority on their magic-working is to be inferred primarily from the Canon emanating from the Council in Laodicea that forbids those holding a priestly or clerical office to be magicians, utterers of incantations, astrologers or manufacturers of phylacteries.[17] It is not certain that any of the presbyters and deacons either accused or convicted of magic-working whom we have encountered in fact used their priestly position to enhance their authority as magicians, but there can be no doubt of the existence of men who exploited their position within the Church to trade in amulets or phylacteries that might contain sacred material and readings from Scripture. The Canon from Laodicea specifically forbids those holding a priestly or clerical office to make phylacteries. In addition, Caesarius of Arles in a sermon directed against those Christians who in sickness go to various forms of soothsayer, employ singers of incantations and attach diabolical phylacteries and magical symbols to themselves, says that some of the persons with whom he is concerned sometimes even get amulets from those holding clerical office and from those who have the status of priests (*clericis ac religiosis*). He warns that such amulets should not be accepted; they contain no remedy from Christ but the Devil's poison; no faith should be placed in their ability to heal, even if it is said that the phylacteries contain holy material and divine readings.[18] The persons of whom Caesarius speaks evidently traded on the authority of their religious calling in dispensing amulets, but they also, it is to be surmised, made use of their knowledge of Scripture and their ability to write to produce the sacred texts that they enclosed within the phylacteries they sold.

In the very different circumstances of Upper Egypt a century and more earlier there is evidence of men using the authority given them not by their ecclesiastical office but by their religious vocation dealing in amulets. In a sermon directed against the followers of Origen Shenoute rehearses the theme, not perhaps so well worn in his day as it was to become later, of the wise man who gives thanks to God in the moment of his suffering in contrast to those who forget God and run to enchanters and to sanctuaries where they carry out rituals of a deceptive nature. Still pursuing the same theme, the preacher declares that he has seen with his own eyes the head of a snake tied to someone's hand, the tooth of a crocodile attached to the arm of another and yet a further person with the claws of a fox bound to his foot. The man in question was a high official (*archon*). Shenoute had reproved him by inquiring whether he imagined the claws of the fox would cure him, to which the man, hoping presumably to deflect further criticism, had replied that he had been given the amulet by an old monk who had told him to wear it if he wished to receive relief.[19]

Finally, there are the scribes employed in churches or within the ecclesiastical establishment who use their scribal expertise to copy out books of magic or astrological handbooks. Zacariah in his *Life of Severus* tells of a scribe and lector of a church in Beirut called Martyrius who was asked by a law student to copy out a magical book for him.[20] Then there are the sub-deacon and deaconesses in Constantia who copied out astrological texts, presumably for their bishop, Sophronius, to peruse.[21]

## The drunken old sorceress Christianized

In the eyes of Caesarius of Arles it does not mitigate the offence that, enclosed in a healing-amulet procured from a priest, there may be sacred material and readings from Scripture.[22] The device is for him in essence no different from a pagan amulet with magical symbols on it. John Chrysostom takes very much the same line as Caesarius with those who bring old women into houses to cure sickness, even though the old women are devoted Christians and invoke the name of God in their incantations. For Chrysostom they are a trap laid by the Devil and sweetened by honey, but what they do is not what a Christian ought to do when confronted by sickness. The existence of such women is interesting from our point of view, since it shows that the institution of the old woman who healed through incantations and the application of amulets was in Antioch in the late fourth century AD still a force, but one that had taken on a Christian colouring. It is not to be assumed, however, that everywhere by this date all such elderly wise women were Christians and that all of them had given their healing rituals a Christian tone. In the late fourth century, the Christianized wise woman may have been a phenomenon peculiar to a few large cities with substantial Christian communities.

However that may be, the drunken old woman summoned to houses to heal the sick is something of a worry for Chrysostom as a presbyter in Antioch. That is to be inferred from his going out of his way in a homily on a topic far removed from sorcery to warn his congregation against bringing such old women into their houses. The homily, one of a series based on Paul's Epistle to the Colossians, is on the subject of gratitude to God, which is on the face of it a far cry from old women healing the sick. Chrysostom none-theless contrives to bring the homily around to that subject.

Chrysostom begins the homily on giving thanks to God by observing that, while it is easy enough to express our gratitude to God when our fortunes are good, it is much less easy in adversity. He then conjures up the example of a mother who gives thanks to God if her child falls sick. She does the same if the child dies, and declares it to be the daughter of Abraham. If another child falls sick at a later date, she does not apply amulets to it, for she (like Abraham) has already mentally sacrificed her son. She would rather see her son dead than be guilty of idolatry. The woman who does make use of amu-lets is guilty of idolatry. However many clever arguments those who deal in amulets devise, using them is still idolatry. Such persons may say that they call on God and do no more than that and present other such arguments and they may even declare that the old woman is a Christian and a faithful one moreover. Chrysostom tells the mother to say to the old woman that if she is indeed a faithful Christian, she should use the sign of the Cross, since this is the only weapon and the only remedy she knows. Continuing in this vein he makes the point that a doctor who performed incantations would not be called a doctor; these are not the remedies a doctor uses; by parity of reason-ing neither are they the remedies of a Christian; other women yet again apply the names of rivers as amulets and in their effrontery perform many such acts.

Chrysostom is now in full flow on the real subject of the homily and makes no further mention of giving thanks to God until he reaches the end of the sermon. He turns to his flock and warns all of them that if any of them are found using amulets or incantations or any other such devices, he will not spare them. In answer to the mother who asks if the child is to be allowed to die, he replies that the child who has been saved by such devices has lost its soul, while the child who dies lives. Chrysostom moves on to deal with another way in which the Devil in the form of a person who urges that amu-lets be used burrows under the defences of a Christian mother: someone could not persuade such a woman to perform a sacrifice to save a child, since the idolatrousness of that course would be obvious, but if the tempter says it is not idolatry, only an incantation, his congregation should be aware that that is the ploy of the Devil to hide the sin and sweeten the poison with honey; the tempter knows he cannot persuade the mother to follow the route to sacrifice, so the course of action he urges is to have recourse to amu-lets and old wives' tales; yet when someone follows that route, the Cross is dis-honoured and magical letters are preferred to it; Christ is cast out and in his place a drivelling, drunken old woman is brought in. Chrysostom brings this line of reasoning to a close by observing that even an intelligent Hellene would not tolerate the use of amulets; there is after all the story of the Athe-nian demagogue who put on amulets, only to be mocked and excoriated by a philosopher who was a teacher of his.[23]

The homily ends with Chrysostom answering another objection that one of his congregation might raise: why are there not now those who raise corpses from the dead and accomplish healings? His answer is that such signs were necessary when the faith was weak and when it still needed to take root; now that it is strong, the eyes of men should be turned to the hereafter, not to this life; since that is so, there is no reason to commit idolatry to remain in this life. The homily closes with a final rhetorical question: what of the rest of the ridiculous nonsense: the ashes, the embers and the salt; and the old woman brought into the house? The answer that the preacher gives is that it is all ludicrous and shameful, not to speak of what the old woman says, which is that the Evil Eye has stolen the child and taken it away.[24]

In the sermon addressed to catechumens Chrysostom's larger topic is the renunciation on the part of the Christian of the pomp of the Devil. The preacher does not inveigh against the better-known manifestations of the worldliness of the Devil, such as the theatre and horse racing, but only against a Christian's allowing his behaviour to be governed by portents. From the topic of portents Chrysostom passes to those who make use of amulets and incantations and who tie bronze coins of Alexander of Macedon to the head and to the feet. He reminds the catechumens that Christ died on the Cross for them and put an end to death; will they then place their hopes in the image of a king of the Hellenes? Warming to his theme, he adds that it is not only amulets that the catechumen carries around on his person, but also incantations, and then there are the drunken old women who cannot walk straight whom he introduces into the house. Chrysostom points out that when he takes issue with such practices and proposes doing away with them, people, who imagine that they are putting up some sort of defence, declare that the woman uttering the incantations is a Christian and that she voices no other word than the name of God. That she should use the name of God in vain, say she is a Christian, yet act as a Hellene Chrysostom finds abhorrent.[25]

Old women who were summoned to houses to heal the sick by means of incantations and amulets are obviously no novelty in the Greek and Roman world. What is new about the old women of whom Chrysostom complains is that they introduce Christian rigmarole into their incantations and that they profess to be Christians. Otherwise they employ the same magical devices that their pagan counterparts employ: they use the letters of the alphabet in certain combinations; they employ the names of rivers in their incantations; and salt, ashes and embers play a part in the rituals they perform to nullify the effects of the Evil Eye.

At least a generation before Chrysostom, Athanasius in Alexandria felt it necessary to address the same concerns. In a fragment of a homily he advises Christians, if they should succumb to a sickness that is hard to heal, to sing psalms and pray to God for help; amulets and sorceries give empty succour; the person who uses them shows himself faithless and not one of the faithful: a pagan and not a Christian and a fool and not intelligent. To show the folly of having resort to amulets and sorcery to cure illness, Athanasius evokes what is evidently meant to be a ludicrous image, that of an old woman, costing eleven obols or a quarter-measure of wine, pouring out an incantation that would more properly be employed to charm a snake over a patient, who for his part gapes like a donkey and has around his neck the filth coming from some four-legged beast rather than a Cross, despite the fact that the Cross has the power not only to scare illnesses off but even the serried ranks of demons; whence it is that no sorcerer ever wears a Cross.[26]

Athanasius says nothing about the old woman's introducing Christian elements into her ritual and maintaining that she was one of the faithful. It may be that such women did not yet exist in Alexandria. What he does say about the woman is that she cost eleven obols or a quarter of wine. Chrysostom provides us with no information on how the old women who were summoned to houses to perform incantations were paid, but he does mention their drunkenness and their unsteady gait.[27] Drunkenness and being paid off in a large quantity of wine are the only identifying features that these women are given. It goes without saying that Chrysostom and Athanasius will use any stick they can to beat those who resort to incantations and amulets and that they are happy to employ the stereotype of the drunken old woman who performs sorcery. It does not follow that because the image is a stereotyped one, the old women summoned to cure sickness or take off the Evil Eye were not very often impoverished old women who fought off the horrors of their existence with wine.

## Haruspices

In the Roman West, there is evidence that a number of the diviners who inspected the entrails of sacrificed animals, the *haruspices*, extended the scope of their activities into the summoning up of spirits for magic. The factors that effected the transformation are obscure. It is just possible that the demonization of *haruspices* by Christians, conscious of the place that blood-sacrifice played in the lives of these men, was a contributory factor. It would after all make perfect sense for Christians to conclude that *haruspices* had dealings with the demons who clustered around the altars at which they performed their sacrifices. The trouble is that the evidence such as it is suggests that *haruspices* may even before Constantine have extended the scope of their activities into the summoning up of spirits. Firmicus Maternus in the preamble to his astrological compendium, *Mathesis*, which was completed in the period between AD 334–37 while its author was still a pagan, assumes that the summoning of supernatural powers was one of the functions of a *haruspex*.[28] The extreme penalties that Constantine in his legislation of AD 319 imposed on *haruspices* and pagan priests who cross the threshold of a private dwelling and those who summon them, in the former case death at the stake, in the latter exile to an island, lends force to the suspicion that Constantine's aim was as much that of suppressing the practice of magic as making the performance of pagan rites more difficult.[29] That would suggest that the magic-working of *haruspices* was a problem long before a Christian emperor came to the throne.

Augustine in his *Confessions* tells of a man whom he calls a *haruspex* coming to him and offering for a fee to help him win a competition in the composition of verse to be held in the theatre in Carthage. This was during the time in which Augustine lived in that city and taught rhetoric there. What the *haruspex* proposed to do was to sacrifice living creatures on Augustine's behalf and through the sacrifice win the support of demonic forces that would help Augustine's cause.[30] Augustine does not say how the demons whom the *haruspex* was to summon were to help him win the competition, but there is a fair likelihood that what the *haruspex* was essentially promising to do was to send demons to impede the efforts of Augustine's rivals. That would mean that *haruspices* claimed to be able through blood-sacrifice to perform binding-spells.

Paulinus in his biography of Ambrose has a story about a *haruspex* called Innocentius who had performed sacrifices to arouse demons against Ambrose, though to no avail, since the demons were terrified of the saint. The story told by Paulinus was that Innocentius had, while being tortured in a trial concerning magic-working, begun to confess to matters quite other than those about which he was being interrogated. His confession was that he had sacrificed at dead of night to stir up hatred against Ambrose, but the more he exercised his evil arts, so much the more did the people come to love the Catholic faith and their bishop; he had even sent demons to kill Ambrose, but they had not been able to get near him nor his residence, since an insuperable wall of fire surrounded it that burned them when they got close.[31] The *haruspex* in this case performs his blood-sacrifice at dead of night as though it were a magical act, and he uses the blood-sacrifice to summon demons to perform two very different forms of magic, first to make Ambrose hated and then, when that fails, to kill him.

Finally, there is the magic that Ammianus Marcellinus relates that a *haruspex* called Amantius had performed. Amantius' magic-working became known in the course of an inquiry conducted in Rome in AD 370 by Maximinus, the *praefectus annonae*, that is, the official in Rome who was in charge of the corn supply.[32] Amantius emerged into the light of day when information was laid against a former proconsul of Africa called Hymetius, who was already in trouble with Valentinian. Hymetius was said to have employed Amantius, the best known of the *haruspices* of that time, to perform sacrifices, so that certain base goals might be accomplished.[33] Amantius steadfastly denied the charge under torture, but then a letter written in Hymetius' own hand was produced from amongst Amantius' secret papers in which Hymetius asked the *haruspex* to perform certain sacred rites to persuade the divine to soften the wrath of the Emperors.[34] Frontinus, a member of Hymetius' Council as proconsul, was accused of having helped with the prayer to the gods. He was scourged and sent into exile in Britain. Amantius the *haruspex* was condemned to death and executed. As for Hymetius, he was brought before the *praefectus urbi* and Maximinus, but appealed to Valentinian for his protection, which he got. Valentinian referred the matter to the Senate, who sentenced Hymetius, much to the annoyance of the Emperor, to exile in Dalmatia.[35] Amantius is accused then of carrying out a sacrifice to accomplish the same goal that the kind of spell called a *thymokatochos*, which is to say a spell intended to check the wrath of another, was meant to achieve.[36] There is even a recipe in a magical formulary for a spell specifically designed to check the wrath of emperors.[37]

What the unnamed *haruspices* mentioned by Augustine, Innocentius and presumably Amantius have in common is that they perform the normal blood sacrifices of *haruspices,* but then use the sacrifice to summon up spirits to accomplish goals that were normally attained by other forms of magic. The *haruspex*, in short, presents himself as an all-purpose magician able through his specialized knowledge of sacrifice to work many different kinds of magic. It is precisely the prejudice that *haruspices* such as Amantius will have aroused against all *haruspices* that Valentinian will in AD 371 have tried to dissipate when he told the Roman Senate that in his judgment haruspicy had nothing in common with magic and that it and other religious activity sanctified by ancestral usage were no crime; haruspicy itself had nothing reprehensible about it; what he banned was haruspicy's being exercised to a harmful end.[38]

Neither Augustine nor Paulinus have anything to say about who the *haruspices* whom they mention were. Ammianus Marcellinus, on the other hand, does provide some clues to the identity of magic-working *haruspices*. Amantius is not the only *haruspex* engaged in sorcery to emerge from Maximinus' investigations in AD 370. There is also a Campanian *haruspex*. Maximinus' inquiries had begun when Chilo, a former deputy of the praetorian prefect, and his wife had complained to the *praefectus urbi* that an attempt was being made on their lives with spells and asked that those whom they suspected should be arrested. The suspects were an instrumental musician (*organarius*) called Sericus, a wrestler (*palaestrita*) by the name of Asbolius and a *haruspex* from Campania, whose name Ammianus does not give.[39] The wrestler or *palaestrita* is not one of the well-to-do young men who frequented the gymnasium, but a member or former member of one of the troupes of wrestlers who performed in the arena as part of the entertainment provided there. The instrumental musician (*organarius*) Sericus also belongs to the world of entertainment and so to the lowest and most despised levels of society.[40] The indications are then that *haruspices* who practise magic come from the lowest strata of society. That is not to say that some of them were not more prosperous than others. Amantius was the best-known *haruspex* of his time and clearly had a distinct identity, whereas the Campanian *haruspex* remains anonymous.[41] A sign of Amantius' standing is Hymetius' communicating with him directly in writing and not through an intermediary. Not only is a communication from Hymetius found in his house, other documents are discovered there also. Amantius could clearly read and write. He also has a permanent place of residence. Amantius may have been somewhat unusual; other *haruspices* may have been barely literate vagrants. Whatever the circumstances of their lives may have been, they are very much the descendants of the private *haruspices* who from at least the Middle Republic presented a problem to the Roman authorities.

## Jewish magicians

Long before Christianity established its dominance Jews were famed for their skill in magic. Under the new Christian dispensation men continued to look to Jews for help in magic-working. Whether the gradual Christianization of the Empire increased the notoriety that Jews enjoyed as sorcerers or had little or no effect is difficult to say. Legally the new dispensation made little difference.[42] The same cannot be said of the measures taken by the institutional Church. Its forbidding contact between Christians and Jews will have done little to help relations between the two groups and will have contributed to the feeling that there was something sinister to Jewish practices. Jews are certainly treated as a race apart in a way that pagans are not. Contact with them brings taint. A sense of the prejudice surrounding Jews within the Church is to be gained from some of the canons that emerged from a synod of Spanish bishops which met at some time before AD 314 at Elvira: one of them forbids giving communion to a member of the clergy or a practising Christian, if he has eaten with a Jew, until the fault is corrected;[43] another commands landowners not to let Jews bless their crops, lest that nullify the Christian blessing; the penalty here is excommunication.[44] Such canons were taken quite seriously to judge from some of the accusations that the opponents of Sophronius, the Bishop of Constantia in Syria, made against him: he was charged with having eaten with a Jew in the episcopal residence and then with having brought the Jew into the Church of the Apostoles while a service was taking place, an action that resulted in the congregation rising up against the Jew and driving him out.[45]

In an earlier chapter a number of the factors that contributed to Jews taking on the rôle of magic-worker were analysed. Some of them were probably still operative, but there is at least one additional factor at work. There emerges within Judaism a mystical strand that has an interest in the occult and that is influenced by Gentile magic. It will have given magic-working a certain respectability and at the same time made it more popular. The formulae that it taught for effecting changes in the natural order do not differ greatly from the promises made in magical recipes in Greek and Coptic magical papyri. A manuscript discovered some thirty years ago known as the *Sefer*

*Ha-Razim* or *Book of the Mysteries*, which is unquestionably the work of a believing Jew who could write Hebrew of some elegance, contains, for example, a series of magical recipes that tell how to achieve success in chariot-racing, win the favour of a beautiful woman, get into the good graces of a ruler and cure sickness. There is dispute over the provenance of the text, although it is generally agreed that it is to be dated to the third or fourth century AD.[46] Then there are the magical recipes found in the genizah or treasure-house of the synagogue in Cairo; they belong in their present form to a much later date, specifically to the eleventh century, but they too almost certainly have their origins in Late Antiquity, since they bear an unmistakable resemblance to the recipes contained in the Greek magical papyri. Their presence in the genizah is hard to explain, but it does suggest that the synagogue in Cairo may at some stage have been a centre of magic-working.

Whatever went on in the synagogue in Cairo, there is not much room for dispute that people made their way to synagogues in Antioch to seek help when confronted with illness. They did so in the conviction that Jewish magic was peculiarly powerful and was able to defeat sickness. Whether they looked to Jews associated with the synagogue for other forms of magical help is not recorded. The ability of Jews from the synagogue to cure the sick was just one of the many attractions that Judaism held for a considerable number of Christians in Antioch. So immediate was the danger in John Chrysostom's eyes that he felt obliged on first being ordained as a presbyter in Antioch in 386 to ignore the threat that the Arians presented. As he saw it, his first duty was to mount a sustained attack on the Christians in Antioch who were drawn to Judaism or who had dealings with Jews.[47] He did so in a series of sermons delivered in 386 and 387 just before major Jewish festivals were to take place. The situation with which he was confronted was that a significant number of Judaizing Christians were to be found attending the synagogue on the Sabbath and were to be seen on the high holy days joining in celebrating Jewish festivals.[48] It was not only men who were drawn to the synagogue; women seem to have gone there without their husbands.[49] In Chrysostom's view, those Christians who found their way to the synagogue risked demonic assault, since demons dwelt in the souls of Jews and in the places in which they gathered.[50]

In the last in the series of sermons Chrysostom dilates on the subject of Christians going to the synagogue seeking to be cured of illness. He has nothing to say about Christians approaching Jews to have the more spectacular forms of sorcery performed for them, nor does he make any reference to the help that the Jewish magicians might afford in matters of love. The recipes in the *Sefer Ha-Razim* and in the recipe-books in the genizah of the synagogue in Cairo do not confine themselves to curing disease, but cover the whole gamut of ancient magic. Chrysostom's failure to mention anything other than medicinal magic, accordingly, cries out for explanation. The need for explanation is made the more acute by the lurid picture that the preacher paints of life in the synagogue and of the vices to which Jews were prone. They knew, on Chrysostom's account, only one kind of behaviour: gluttony, drunkenness, getting cut up in fights over pantomimes and wounded in battles about charioteers.[51] The synagogue for its part drew in effeminate perverts, whores and whoever made a living from the stage or theatre, which is to say, pantomimes.[52] This is exactly the milieu in which erotic magic and binding-spells might have been expected to flourish. Yet Chrysostom has nothing to say about them. A possible explanation is that Chrysostom does not himself really believe what he has to say about the synagogue's attracting the more disreputable elements in Antiochean society to itself. That these are figments of his overheated imagination does not, on the other hand, seem very likely. Some other explanation must be sought for Chrysostom's failure to take account of the more serious forms of magic-working. It may be part of a wider pattern: no Christian preacher in this period addresses the threat presented to a Christian by the temptation to practise black magic, despite the fact that the temptation was very clearly there; the only topic addressed is the performance of magical ceremonies to heal sickness. The existence of a well-established topic almost certainly partly explains Chrysostom's developing the theme of the danger of Jewish medicinal magic and his ignoring other kinds of magic. There may be another factor at work: there was a much greater danger of a Christian apostatizing to Judaism if Jewish magic succeeded in curing his illness than there was if a Jewish magician successfully nobbled the horses and charioteers of an opposing team.

The synagogue is only the source of the help that Christians who are sick seek, not the place where they are helped. The cure is effected in their own houses and takes the form not of an old woman performing incantations and attaching amulets but of a number of men carrying out the same action. The Christian who has these men thrown ignominiously out of his house will, according to Chrysostom, win the praise of men.[53] If Chrysostom is to be trusted, the Jewish healers boasted of demons who could cure sickness, a boast which Chrysostom says makes no sense, since demons as the servants of the Devil, who is the slayer of mankind, could hardly be expected to heal.[54] What Chrysostom must mean is that Jewish experts in incantations said that they knew how to invoke demons who cured sickness. Who these Jewish performers of incantations and adepts with amulets were we are not told. They were certainly men, they worked in groups and they were to be found in or through the synagogue. They were not then magicians who happened to be Jews and who traded on their Jewishness to impress their clientele, but men who had some recognized rôle in the synagogue or connection with it. They were not summoned to the house of the sick person by an underling sent to knock at a door in a back-alley, but the sick man had to go to the synagogue himself to get help. It is hard to tell whether women also went to the synagogue seeking help in the face of illness, since Chrysostom uses only the masculine gender in speaking of those who had recourse to the help afforded by the synagogue. Chrysostom makes much of the lack of shame such a man must show in going to the synagogue and being prepared to expose himself to the mockery and contempt that he will find there.[55] That men had to present themselves in person and implicitly or explicitly acknowledge the inability of the Christian god to help them is surely part of the price that the Jews in the synagogue exacted for their services.

How these Jewish performers of incantations represented themselves Chrysostom does not say. Did they present themselves as healers or as conjurors of demons and sorcerers? Chrysostom is in no doubt about what they are: magicians (*pharmakoi*) and sorcerers (*goetes*).[56] There is, however, a passage in the sermon that encourages the idea that the parties to the transaction may, while aware of what was going on, have concealed the reality behind polite talk of the sick being helped: Chrysostom, exhorting his congregation to confront those fellow-Christians who had been attracted to the synagogue, suggests that if one of the backsliders defends his going to the Jews by bringing up their promise to cure sickness, their healing techniques should be exposed for what they were, acts of magic (*manganeiai*), incantations (*epodai*), amulets (*periammata*) and spells (*pharmakeiai*).[57]

A slightly more sinister view of Jewish magic than that of Chrysostom, but from the first half of the sixth century, is visible in a homily for the mid-Pentecost preached by Leontius of Byzantium, presumably in Byzantium: it emphasizes the Jew's magical manipulation of demons, but still places a heavy emphasis on the Jew as expert in the use of amulets. In the homily Leontius conducts an imaginary debate with Jewish opponents over whether Christ or Solomon exerts a greater control over demons. The Jews, who are referred to as lovers of demons (*philodaimones*), protest that Solomon is lord of the demons, that he shut them all up one by one and that he bound them down by using Jewish magical symbols (*characteres*), to which the preacher replies, addressing his opponents as 'Jews, who tie on amulets (*petaloraptai*) and who manipulate demons by magic (*manganodaimones*)', that Solomon, far from lording it over demons, fell prey to demons himself.[58] Later in the homily the preacher dwells on the time at which the festival takes place, which is just when Herod laid his hands on members of the Church intending to do them harm,[59] to ask a series of questions about what happened at that time to which a corresponding series of answers is given, amongst them that at that time ventriloquists (*engastrimythoi*) were muzzled and the magic of amulets (*periapton manganeiai*) was cast away.[60] Since the answers by and large celebrate the triumph of Christian practices over Jewish ones, the presumption must be that the preacher associates ventriloquism and the use of amulets with Jews. The image of Solomon to which Leontius' Jews subscribe looks very like the Solomon of the sub-magical text from Late Antiquity known as the *Testament of Solomon*: it portrays a Solomon who binds and fetters demons and makes them contribute to the construction of his temple in Jerusalem. Leontius' view of Jewish magic may well be shaped by a text that is partly Christian in inspiration, but it is evidently one that he assumed his hearers shared. Reservations may be in order about Leontius' evocation of a Jewish vision of Solomon, but there is no reason to doubt that in Byzantium in the first half of the sixth century Christians still procured magical amulets from Jews.

Chrysostom may have nothing to say about the darker aspects of Jewish magic-working, but the Jews were undoubtedly suspected of practising the most malign forms of magic. A story that Epiphanius, Bishop of Constantia in Cyprus at the end of the fourth century, tells about a Jewish convert to Christianity called Josephus reflects some of the suspicions that Christians harboured about magic-working on the part of Jews. He says he had heard it from Josephus himself when he encountered him, by now an old man, in Scythopolis in Palestine. Josephus, who was a real person of some prominence in late fourth-century Palestine, was a native of Tiberias whom Constantine had advanced to the rank of count. Although the story is told in an apparently artless way with Epiphanius expressing hesitation over details on which his memory is shaky, it is in reality an extremely skilfully-articulated account of Josephus' conversion to Christianity and of one incident in his career after being converted.

Josephus was, by Epiphanius' account, a man of the highest rank in the Jewish community in Tiberias, before his conversion to Christianity. What the stages were in Josephus' career between his conversion and Constantine's advancing him to the rank of count Epiphanius does not say. Constantine, at any rate, is said to have told Josephus that he would grant him any request he should make, to which Josephus' response was that he should like to be allowed to build Christian churches amongst the Jews in Tiberias, Diocaesarea, Sepouris, Nazareth and Capernaum. The request was granted. He began his work in Tiberias, where the foundations already lay of what was the greatest temple in the city, which Epiphanius thinks, if his memory serves him aright, was called the Hadrianeum. The walls on all four sides already stood some height above the ground. Josephus' pretext for building a church in the structure was that an attempt had been made to convert it to a bath. Since lime was needed for the work of building, Josephus had many lime-kilns constructed outside the town. It was at this point that the well-born (*gennadai*) Jews began to employ binding-spells (*katadeseis*) to prevent the fuel in the kilns from catching properly alight. Epiphanius introduces his account of the interruption by saying that the Jews, a people who are ready to turn to every form of audacity, did not on this occasion refrain from the magic-working endemic amongst them. Josephus, stung by this turn of events, got a container of water and, before a large crowd of Jews who had assembled to see what would happen, made the Sign of the Cross with his finger on the vessel and, calling upon Jesus by name, said: 'In the name of Jesus of Nazareth whom my fathers and the fathers of all those here crucified, let this vessel have the power in it to annul the magic and sorcery that these men here have worked and let it have the power to bring to life the fire needed for the completion of the house of the Lord'. He then sprinkled the kilns with the water and the spells on them were broken and the fire burst forth. The crowd who were present cried out: 'There is one god who helps the Christians'.[61]

Jews who practised magic continue to be intermittently attested well into the seventh century. Two of them have an identity. The *Life of Symeon Stylites the Younger* tells of a Jewish doctor-cum-magician who attended the Emperor Justinian II in his last illness. The story begins with Ioannes Scholasticus, the Patriarch of Constantinople, writing to Symeon begging him to solicit God's help in curing the Emperor. Symeon writes back to say that nothing unpleasing to God should be done to cure the illness and that, if forbidden practices were avoided, the illness would be cured. The Emperor ignores the advice and surrenders himself to men who are described as soul-destroyers and not of the party of God. It is they who bring in Timotheos, a practising Jew who professed to be a doctor, but who was in reality an enemy of God because he worshipped demons and was a devotee of sorcery (*goeteia*). When the Patriarch learned what had happened, he wrote warning against following such measures, but was ignored. Timotheos then went ahead and applied his wonted *pharmaka*. Symeon, for his part, had a vision of what was happening and wrote to the Patriarch warning him of God's anger, a message which the patriarch conveyed to the Emperor and his consort, only to be ignored again. Worse was to follow: a female ventriloquist (*engastrimythos*) was brought in by the Empress to divine the nature of the illness. Symeon had a further vision portending the inauguration of a new Emperor, which was duly proved to have been true.[62] Disentangling what actually happened in Constantinople is difficult, but there is little room for doubt that a Jewish doctor was employed, even though the Church did not allow Christians to employ such doctors, and that he was suspected of practising magic. That the Emperor and his Empress had in their desperation recourse to such a man is possible and is made the more likely if the Empress did indeed turn to an *engastrimythos* for help. It may be that she was also imagined to be Jewish because of the association of ventriloquism with Jews.

Jewish magicians are also recorded in Cyprus in the seventh century. There is nothing to suggest any connection on their part with the synagogue. It is also probably just a matter of chance that two Jewish magicians are attested in Cyprus in the first century AD and that two more are mentioned in the seventh. There is no reason to believe that there was a school of magicians, let alone of Jewish magicians, in Cyprus that lasted from the first until the seventh century. In Constantia, at about the time of the trial of the presbyter for magic-working, a Jew called Daniel was burned to death as a magician.[63] He was reputed to have said as he was being thrown into the fire that his magic had had no effect on Christians who took part in communion; the power of his spells had been completely nullified.[64] Daniel was certainly a real person. It would be unwise to place such confidence in the existence of the Jewish magician of whom Sophronius of Jerusalem tells. Sophronius' story is that a well-known Cypriot doctor called Theodorus had been left paralysed by sorcery. When Theodorus was unable to find a cure, the healing saints, Cyrus and John, appeared to him in a dream and both told him how to cure himself and revealed the source of his troubles: he was first to anoint the parts of his body that were affected with an ointment made from the roasted lungs of a pig dissolved in wine, and to dig under the threshold of his bedroom where he would find the magical instrument that was affecting him. Theodore followed the instructions and, once the object buried at the door of his bedroom was exposed, the magician who had buried it disappeared from the face of the earth. He turned out to have been a Jew.[65] The story can hardly be used as testimony to the presence on Cyprus in the seventh century of a second Jewish magician, but it is evidence that the Jewish magician was a recognized figure and that there were known techniques for counteracting his magic by using a salve made from an animal abhorrent to the Jews.

## Charioteers

There are indications that chariot-racing was at least from the second century AD the focus of a good deal of magic-working. That binding-spells inscribed on sheets of lead and directed against the charioteers who belonged to the teams which competed against each other in the circus or hippodrome were regularly deposited in these places and in other locations is well attested. It is impossible to give a precise date to the tablets, but some of them will certainly go back to the second century AD. The explanation that Pausanias attributes to an Egyptian for horses panicking at a certain point on the racecourse at Olympia is relevant here, for unless the practice of burying curse-tablets in hippodromes and circuses was well known, it would not have made much sense to have an Egyptian speak of Pelops receiving an unspecified object from a magician and of his having buried it to upset the horses of Oenomaus.[66] The general assumption is that such tablets were written at the behest of a fan hostile to a charioteer or charioteers from a team other than the one the fan favoured or for a gambler who had put his money on another charioteer. It is to be suspected that the charioteers themselves were actively engaged in putting spells on each other.[67] What can confidently be asserted is that long before Christian emperors ruled the Roman world, chariot-racing encouraged sorcery.

In the eyes of Christian authors the greatest and in some ways most characteristic of the evils associated with chariot-racing was sorcery. For John Chrysostom chariot-racing is almost a byword for sorcery. In one homily, after berating his congregation for going to the theatre, he turns his attention to the other forms of entertainment that they frequent by asking rhetorically what he is to say of the magic-working of the horse races along with that of the contests with wild beasts.[68] In another homily, he complains that men are quite ignorant of well-known characters in Scripture and cannot say, if asked, how many Apostles there were, but nonetheless have a profound intimacy with the world of the racecourse in the form of its horses and their charioteers; their lives are quite consumed by chariot-racing; instead of spending their life on prayer, they spend it on shouting and disturbances, vile language, battles, pleasures that have no proper place and deeds performed through magic.[69] Another Christian author of the fourth century AD, Amphilochus of Iconium, in a poem written in iambs, describes chariot-racing in the hippodrome as a contest in sorcery (*goeteia*), not speed.[70] The sorcery that Amphilochus has in mind is that practised by the sorcerers to whom the maddened fans hasten in their insane desire for victory. The sorcerers, for their part, according to Amphilochus, summon up evil demons to help them bring about spills, collisions and deaths.[71]

It would be unwise to discount what John Chrysostom and Amphilochus have to say about sorcery in the hippodrome as Christian propaganda. Their testimony is confirmed by other forms of evidence. Jerome in his *Life of Hilarion the Hermit* tells of two encounters that Hilarion, a Syro-Palestinian saint, had with the sorcery of the hippodrome.[72] Both episodes are set in Gaza. In one of them a charioteer of that city became so rigid while driving his chariot that he was unable to move his hands or bend his neck to look back. This had happened to him because a demon had struck him. He was brought to his bed, where he lay, able only to move his tongue in prayer. Hilarion told him that he could not be cured until he expressed belief in Jesus and renounced his craft. The charioteer did both of these things and was healed.[73] The story is of interest more for what Jerome takes for granted than for what he explicitly tells us. He does not have to inform his readers that the demon who causes the charioteer to seize up in the middle of the race has been conjured up by someone who does not want the charioteer to win, nor that the inability of the man to move any part of his body was precisely the condition that many binding-spells were expressly intended to bring about. As for the man's having to renounce his craft before he can be saved, that was hardly an idiosyncratic move on Hilarion's part, but represents the policy of the Church. One of the Canons of the Council of Elvira requires charioteers and dancers to renounce their crafts before they can be treated as believers.[74]

The other story is not about a charioteer, but about a citizen of Gaza and a Christian called Italicus, who raised horses to race them in the hippodrome. He had as his rival a magistrate (*duumvir*) who was a devotee of the Syro-Palestinian god, Marnas. Because his rival had at his beck and call a magician who was able by the incantations that he addressed to demons both to hold back the horses of his opponents and speed on his own, Italicus approached Hilarion and begged him for help: he did not want to harm his rival, only to defend himself against the man. Hilarion at first thought that the request was beneath his dignity and suggested that Italicus should save his soul by giving the money which he devoted to his chariot-teams to the poor. Italicus replied that it was not a matter of his actually wanting to race horses, but that his position required him to do so; furthermore, as a Christian, he was unable to use magic; he sought help against the adversaries of God amongst the people of Gaza not for his own sake, but for the Church of Christ which they were mocking. Hilarion's fellow-monks now pleaded with him to help. He acceded to their request and gave instructions that the clay cup from which he drank should be filled with water and handed over to Italicus. The latter took the vessel and with it besprinkled his stable, his horses, his charioteers, the chariot and the starting-gates.[75] Great expectation filled the crowd. When the signal for the start was given, Italicus' horses flew ahead, while those of his rival were left far behind. Some of the pagans even joined in the applause on Italicus' side, since Marnas had been defeated by Christ. Italicus' rivals were furious and demanded that Italicus be punished as a Christian magician.[76]

The lesson to be drawn from the tales that Jerome tells is that magic-working was not only practised by charioteers and the urban masses, but that the rich men who sponsored chariot-teams might engage in it also. A little more of the world in which these patrons of the games lived emerges from a speech in which Libanius denounces young men who are sent to a great city to study rhetoric, but who because of lack of application never bring their studies to fruition. He brings up the part the races played in distracting the young men from their studies: in contrast to diligent students to whom the races were nothing, the only concern of these young men was how such-and-such a charioteer would defeat a rival; a sorcerer (*goes*), in consequence, who promised the desired result had in their eyes a status higher than a god.[77] He goes on to speak of the continuing fascination that some of the young men had with chariot-racing and with the company of charioteers, even after they had sold the horses that they had bought as a civic liturgy for the chariot-races: they became so absorbed in the races that they judged a day good or bad by the victories or defeats of their favourite charioteers.[78]

Libanius and Jerome not only give us a glimpse of men from the upper class actively engaged in the magic-working of the hippodrome they also conjure up the behaviour of a crowd fully aware that sorcerers were at work and all too ready to come to the conclusion that upset victories represented the triumph of a magician. Behind Jerome's reference to the call that Italicus' defeated rivals put up for his punishment as a magician will be orchestrated chants decrying the victorious owner as a magician. Libanius, for his part, makes a telling comparison between the lassitude of the citizen-body when confronted by his complaints about the sorcery that had been directed against him and what happened when a horse or charioteer was thought to have been impeded by sorcery: it was as though the city itself had perished.[79]

The suspicion of sorcery in the hippodrome could, accordingly, cause convulsions in the city.

It is not only in the Greek East in the late fourth century that the assumption that sorcery was ever-present in the hippodrome is encountered. Evidence exists that the same phenomenon was visible in Italy one hundred years later. There is from the year AD 507 an extraordinary letter written under the name of the Emperor in the West, Theoderic, by Cassiodorus, a high imperial functionary, to Faustus, the praetorian prefect in Rome in which the writer dwells on the case of a certain charioteer called Thomas, who had come from the East to Italy and whom the Emperor had chosen to reward with a monthly largess to secure his continued presence in Italy. The number of victories Thomas had won was so great that he was called a wizard (*maleficus*), a charge which we are told charioteers welcomed as a compliment. The writer then comments that where the victory cannot be attributed to the quality of the horses, it needs must be assigned to the wickedness of magic.[80] Successful charioteers are then imagined as a matter of course to have practised magic, a charge which the charioteers, far from rejecting, took a positive delight in, since it added to their fame. The crowd in the Greek East drew the same conclusions to judge from a Byzantine astrological manuscript that contains an excerpt from an astrological writer of the High or Late Empire who had devised a special system for divining winners in chariot-racing. The author, an otherwise unknown figure called Theodorus of Alexandria, says that because of a failure to understand the true cause of the victory many or rather almost all judge the winning charioteer to be a magician.[81]

Cassiodorus's letter and Theodorus refer to the common assumption that it is the charioteers themselves who perform magic. Not all charioteers will have practised on their own behalf. There will have been charioteers who looked to others to perform their magic for them in the conviction that such persons were more effective and powerful magicians than they themselves could ever be. Ammianus records the conviction of a charioteer who falls into this category. The conviction was the result of an investigation in Rome in AD 364 into witchcraft instituted by Apronianus, the *praefectus urbi*. The charioteer was called Hilarinus and he was convicted of having sent his son, a boy who was just entering adolescence, to a sorcerer (*veneficus*) to have him taught certain of the more arcane and forbidden portions of the craft of the sorcerer. Hilarinus confessed to his having made the arrangement to ensure that the aid he sought should come from within his own household and so that no one else should be privy to it. He was sentenced to death, but escaped from the rather lax custody of the executioner to a Christian shrine, whence he was dragged forth to be executed on the spot.[82] That it was quite normal for charioteers to have magic performed for them by others is also suggested by the explanation given by Procopius of Caesarea for the facility in sorcery that Antonina, the wife of Belisarius, Justinian's great general, possessed, which was that both her father and grandfather were charioteers who had plied their trade in Byzantium and Thessalonica and that she had consorted with the sorcerers associated with the paternal side of her family and from them had learned the key elements of their craft.[83] Whatever reservations the reader may feel about the reliability of this information, the notion that charioteers retained their own favourite sorcerers will hardly be Procopius' invention.

Since charioteers lived in a world in which magic-working was endemic, it is hardly surprising that some of them became adepts themselves. Most of the sorcery they practised will have been directed at other charioteers. The popular charioteer called Athanasius, who was burned to death in Rome under Valentinian after having been caught engaging in sorcery, presumably falls into this category.[84] But the reputation of charioteers as magic-workers also brought them contracts from men who needed sorcery that had no connection with the hippodrome performed for them. In the revelations about magic-working in Rome that followed the arrest of the Campanian *haruspex* and his allies Ammianus says that three men of the highest rank (*clarissimi*) were accused of having participated in the sorcery in which the Campanian *haruspex* and his associates were implicated and of having supported a charioteer called Auchenius for that purpose.[85] They were acquitted and we hear no more of Auchenius. They provided Auchenius with funds, surely not because they were interested in his engaging in sorcery on their behalf against other charioteers and their horses, but because they wished him to employ his craft against their enemies.

Ammianus' own view of the character of charioteers and their propensity for magic is to be seen in a digression, strongly reminiscent of Juvenal's denunciation of Roman degeneracy, on the decline in moral standards that had taken place under Valentinian. Ammianus cites as an instance of the decline the readiness of some men, when a creditor pressed them too hard, to have recourse to a charioteer capable of acts of unlicensed audacity, who would make sure that the creditor was charged with being a magician. The unfortunate creditor was then only able to buy his way out of the accusations at heavy expense, after having given an undertaking that he was owed nothing.[86] The passage tells us something about the reputation of charioteers: they were men who felt no moral or legal scruples and lent their hand readily to acts of audacious criminality. That is straightforward enough. What requires interpretation is the embarrassed debtor's going to a charioteer to get him to charge the creditor who is causing trouble with being a sorcerer. The explanation must lie in the widespread assumption that charioteers were mixed up with sorcery and associated with sorcerers, if they were not sorcerers themselves. They were the sort of men to whom people went if they wanted someone who could plausibly claim to know who was practising magic.

So close was the association in the minds of men between charioteers and magic-working that it even found expression in official edicts. In an edict issued in Rome on August 16th AD 389 under the Emperors Valentinian, Theodosius and Arcadius dealing with the arrest of magicians, charioteers are singled out as those most likely to contravene the edict and as those most likely to murder by clandestine means persons accused of magic under the edict. The punishment to be visited on those who contravene the edict in the latter way is to be death, because the presumption exists that persons who have killed someone accused of murder have done so either to prevent the accused revealing their complicity in his crime or as a pretext for exacting personal vengeance.[87]

Charioteers appear to have been a race apart: their sons tended to become charioteers and they took as their wives women with associations with the theatre.[88] The father and grandfather of Antonina, the wife of Belisarius, are instances of the pattern: a son following in the footsteps of his father and becoming a charioteer.[89] It would in fact be surprising should a high proportion of the sons of charioteers not have been brought up to follow the calling of their fathers. Boys from such a background are not likely to have had too many other opportunities for employment and they will have had the immeasurable advantage over other boys of having been brought up amongst horses and of having learned how to handle them.

Antonina's mother was a prostitute from the stage.[90] There is nothing in Procopius' description of the mother as a woman who had prostituted herself from the stage that would have shocked or surprised an ancient reader. In the ancient world, women who appeared on the stage were assumed to be available for prostitution. There would in fact have been considerable surprise had that expectation been belied.[91] Most of them were dancers or women who mimed rôles rather than actresses in our sense. It is women of this sort whom charioteers appear to have married. One degraded and socially isolated calling was of necessity thrown into the arms of another. To find instances besides that of Antonina's mother and father of actresses marrying charioteers requires inspired guesswork, since direct evidence is just not available. There are, however, from late fourth- and early fifth-century Rome a series of curse-tablets directed against charioteers that not only identify the charioteer by his nickname but also as the son of such-and-such a mother. The mothers have such names as Dionysia, Fortuna, Paschasia and Veneria, names that are reminiscent of the stage-names taken by panto-mimes.[92]

## Wrestlers

The same competitive pressures that led charioteers to practise magic will almost certainly have led the wrestler (*palaestrita*), Asbolius, who was accused along with the instrumental musician, Sericus, and the Campanian *haruspex* to engage in sorcery.[93] There is one other reference in the literature of Late

Antiquity to the association of wrestling and magic. Libanius in his autobiographical *apologia*, in dealing with the wrongs done him by the *consulares* of Syria, Festus and Aetherius, speaks of Festus' having schemed to encompass his downfall by using a certain Pisidian called Martyrius; in Libanius' view, Martyrius' only real failing was the enthusiasm that athletes aroused in him; his passion for wrestlers did, however, make Festus imagine that he was a sorcerer (*goes*). The details of how Festus tried to use Martyrius against Libanius are unclear, since Libanius chooses to give less than a full and coherent account of the trial in which Martyrius was apparently meant to implicate him. What he does say is that the trial collapsed because Festus had left in a hurry to take up the governorship of Asia and the judges were unable to comprehend why Martyrius had been brought before them.[94] What has to be explained here is why an enthusiasm for wrestlers, not wrestling, should create the presumption that the enthusiast is a sorcerer. Libanius clearly does not feel he has to explain why Festus should have conceived of such an idea: the connection in thought must have seemed obvious to him. Our reconstruction of what has to be understood has to proceed from what we know about the association of chariot-racing with sorcery. If what went on there has any bearing on the inference drawn by Festus from the interest Martyrius took in wrestlers, it rather looks as if wrestlers aroused the same partisan feelings as charioteers and such feelings in their turn led to magic-working. If wrestling gave rise to magic-working amongst its aficionados, it is reasonable to assume that those who wrestled also resorted to sorcery.

The callings of the persons in whose company Asbolius is found suggest very strongly that he was not one of the athletes who took part in the major athletic festivals, but a member of a troupe of professional athletes. As for the wrestlers whose ardent follower Martyrius was, it is hard to see how Martyrius' enthusiasms could have been fuelled by the wrestling contests that took place every four years at the Olympic Games in the suburb of Antioch called Daphne. It is possible that he travelled from city to city following the athletes as they competed in different sets of games, but it seems on the whole more likely that he became obsessed with wrestlers who competed or rather performed in Antioch on a more regular basis.

One of the venues at which the troupes of professional athletes to which Asbolius and the wrestlers in Antioch belonged were to be seen was the amphitheatre. Their performances came to replace gladiatorial combats. They also provided entertainment in the circus and hippodrome and on other occasions. From the sixth century AD there is from Oxyrrynchus on the Nile a programme for races in the hippodrome. After each race entertainments of various kinds are offered. When the fifth race is over, the audience are to be diverted by a troupe of athletes (*xystos*).[95] Singing rope-dancers, mimes, dogs and gazelles make up the rest of the entertainment. Given the setting in which these athletes are found it is inconceivable that they are amateur athletes from a gymnasium, although the term employed to refer to them, *xystos*, was used to denote a conclave of amateur athletes. They must be a troupe of professional athletes. From the other end of the now fragmented Roman Empire Sidonius Apollinaris, in celebrating the entertainments provided by a notable from Narbonne in the middle of the fifth century AD, mentions wrestling as one of the turns that the lyre-players, performers on reed-pipes, mimes, rope-walkers and clowns provided.[96]

## Entertainers from the theatre

The factors that turned the instrumental musician, Sericus, into an expert magician may have not been quite so straightforward as those that made magicians out of charioteers and wrestlers. The theatre in general was certainly notorious for its magic-working; magicians, charioteers and pantomimes tended to be associated as a single group in men's minds. Thus, Palladius in the account he gives of the life of John Chrysostom, asserts that it was the ambition of one of Chrysostom's opponents, Porphyrius, who became in AD 404 Bishop of Antioch, to stand at the head of the magicians (*goetes*), charioteers and pantomimes and to dine with them and that, furthermore, he joined in contests with the magicians and was on friendly terms with them, a fact that was noted in the records of several magistrates.[97] Chrysostom himself in a list of the ills which the theatre inflicted on society speaks of it as the birthplace of sorcerers (*goetes*).[98]

From the lurid account that Procopius in his *Secret History* gives of the career of the Empress Theodora, before she met and married Justinian, it is possible to see how the theatre and the hippodrome could come together to form one world. The story presents severe problems for those anxious to separate the true from the false, but for the purposes of social history it hardly matters what is embroidery and what is not, since what it illustrates is how the worlds of the theatre, amphitheatre and hippodrome overlapped and how someone growing up in that environment was exposed to magicians and sorcerers.[99] Procopius maintains that Theodora as Empress was fond of magicians and sorcerers, since she had consorted with them from her childhood and because the practices they followed had brought her to her present eminence. He goes on to say that her hold over Justinian was attributed by some to the demons she invoked to make him pliant to her will.[100] The milieu in which Theodora had associated with magicians and sorcerers was the world of the amphitheatre, hippodrome and theatre. Her father, Akakios, who died when she and her two sisters were young, had looked after the animals to be used in beast hunts in Constantinople, in which capacity he was given the title or sobriquet of Bear-keeper. He belonged to the organization built around the chariot-team known as the Greens.[101] The tentacles of the organizations dependent on the Greens and their principal rivals, the Blues, had spread in Constantinople not only into activities traditionally associated with the amphitheatre, but also into the theatre: there were troupes of actors and actresses that belonged to the two groups. Constantinople's lack of either a theatre or an amphitheatre may have contributed to the extension of the domain occupied by the chariot-teams into other fields of entertainment, since the hippodrome there had to house not only chariot-racing, but animal hunts and theatrical shows. Akakios' widow took up with another man, whom she hoped would support her orphaned children and would step into the job that her late husband had held. Unfortunately, the dancer of the Greens, Asterius, who controlled the position, was persuaded by a bribe to give the job to someone else.[102] Theodora's mother now took her children, arrayed as suppliants, to the beast hunt and there supplicated the assembled crowd. The Greens rejected her plea, but the Blues, who were also necessarily present, made her new partner their animal-keeper, since the incumbent had just died.[103] When Theodora reached puberty, she was put on to the stage by her mother as a mime and thereafter followed that calling along with that of a prostitute, until she met Justinian.[104]

One of the reasons for the association of sorcery with the theatre was the prostitution that the women who appeared on stage practised. John Chrysostom brings up, as an example of someone who had repented of her former ways, a prostitute (*porne*) of his own day who had occupied the most prominent position on the stage in Antioch and had won a name for herself as far afield as Cilicia and Cappadocia; the success of the woman in emptying men's pockets and in capturing orphans some people put down not just to her looks, but to the sorcery and the spells she cast. She had, says Chrysostom, captured even the brother of the Empress.[105]

The sorcerers whom John Chrysostom complains emerged from the theatre excited the idle populace and helped the dancers enjoy greater applause.[106] It is well known that there was a certain amount of rivalry amongst the followers of different dancers and that passions could run high and lead to violence and rioting.[107] Dancers also competed, although not formally, to capture the favour of the crowd. The magic worked in connection with the theatre was, accordingly, not restricted to helping female mimes and pantomimes capture rich clients it was used to stir up the populace and to win dancers favour in the eyes of the audience. Chrysostom speaks here in the masculine gender of dancers, but this may well be one of those generic masculines that takes in women also.

In sum, the young women who used the exposure that they gained by dancing or acting to win rich lovers for themselves come from an environment in which magic-working was very much at home. They themselves are likely to have been familiar with the sorcerers whom the world of entertainment attracted and will have made use of them and then will perhaps have begun to practise magic on their own behalf. It is not surprising, accordingly, that actresses-cum-prostitutes should be found practising sorcery.

## Prostitutes as sorceresses

The presbyter who was burned to death as a magician in Constantia in Cyprus around AD 625 was said to have eaten and drunk with prostitutes and sorcerers, using communion plates and other sacred vessels for the purpose.[108] The story testifies to the persistent association in men's minds of prostitution and sorcery. That prostitutes of a less exalted form than the actresses and dancers we have just looked at continued to resort to magic-working should not be in doubt. The sermons of John Chrysostom are again our main source of information on this topic. He paints a deliberately alarming picture of the magic-working of prostitutes and of the other dangers attendant on having an affair with such a woman. His purpose in doing so is largely to discourage married men from having relationships with such women, which, in his eyes, though probably not in those of his flock and certainly not in the eyes of the law, constituted adultery. He seems to be a good deal less exercised by the relationship envisaged in love-elegy, that between a young unmarried man and a prostitute, although he is fully aware of its existence.

The prostitutes whom Chrysostom has in mind are not common prostitutes who work in a brothel. They are women who have their own houses or establishments, who have some sort of independence and who compete to win or retain the attentions of as rich a lover as possible. They may choose to eject one man in favour of a successful rival and to bar the rejected lover from their premises thereafter. Chrysostom knows perfectly well that there are gradations within the world of prostitution and that at the bottom of the heap are the women found in brothels who are so ugly and shameless that gladiators, those who fight with wild beasts and runaway slaves, would hardly accept their services.[109]

Chrysostom takes it for granted that prostitutes will resort to love-philtres and drugs to draw men to themselves. Some girls, he complains, compete with prostitutes in trying to attract men by their unseemly and coquettish behaviour and by doing exactly what prostitutes do: grinding down the same drugs, mixing the same drinks and preparing the same hemlock; they only stop short of saying: 'Come here and let us roll together in love; I have sprinkled the bed with saffron and the couch with cinnamon'.[110] In a denunciation of men who desert their wives for prostitutes, Chrysostom holds such men responsible not only for the prostitutes murdering their unborn children, but also for their idolatry, which takes the form of incantations, libations, love-philtres and the many other such contrivances that the prostitutes devise to make themselves attractive to men. He adds that there are, besides the drugs they employ against the unborn child in their womb, those that they direct against the wronged wife and the myriad plots that they mount, their summoning up of demons and consultations of the spirits of the dead.[111] In another sermon on the wrongfulness of resorting to prostitutes, Chrysostom takes a somewhat different tack in trying to dissuade married men from visiting such women, pointing out that they face the danger of perishing by a miserable death brought on by the love-philtres and other kinds of sorcery employed by the women in their efforts to separate them from their lawfully wedded wives and bind them to themselves in unqualified love. Chrysostom proceeds to explain why the magic-working of prostitutes is effective against such men: men who resort to licentious behaviour strip themselves of the protection of God, so that the prostitute is free to mount an assault that has the assurance of an easy victory; to that end she will summon up her personal demons, tie on thin sheets of metal and carry out her machinations.[112] Prostitutes will also have tried to usurp the place of the wife by making her distasteful to her husband.[113]

Who were the prostitutes of whom Chrysostom is speaking? It goes without saying that poverty or slavery was what led women into prostitution. Very often they will have in effect been sold by their parents to the procurer or procuress. A papyrus from Hermopoulis in Egypt from the latter part of the fourth century AD records the trial of a man who had killed the common prostitute with whom each evening he ate; her mother, described as a poor old woman, says that she had handed her daughter over to a pimp so that she could get the wherewithal to live, and asks the court that she be recompensed for her loss.[114] Procurers will also have picked up girls who for one reason or another lived on their own and put them to work. A decree of Justinian speaks of procurers searching out pitiable young women, entrapping them with gifts of clothing and shoes and then keeping them imprisoned in their establishments.[115] A passage in a series of explications of Isaiah, clearly intended for public delivery and commonly attributed to Basil the Great, who was the Bishop of Caesarea in Cappadocia in the second half of the fourth century AD, describes another less predictable way in which girls might come into contact with procuresses and be led into a life of prostitution: a man acquires some wretched woman, and instead of having her taught weaving, hands her over because she is a slave and can do nothing about it, to be taught the lyre, perhaps paying a fee, to a woman who may be a procuress and who, after having exhausted her own body in all forms of licentiousness, instructs young women in vice.[116] The procuress may then be a worn-out old prostitute who takes slave-girls from their masters to instruct them in the lyre and at the same time introduces them to prostitution. The men who have their slave-girls taught the lyre are not men who live on the margins of society but men who are listening to the preacher's sermon and whom the preacher evidently feels to be amenable to moral suasion. The sermon does not, unfortunately for our purposes, pursue further the careers of the girls who are taught to play the lyre and explain how they can practise prostitution while being the slaves of respectable members of society.

## Amulet-makers, amulet-dealers and utterers of incantations

### *The Eastern Empire*

The type of magic-worker over whom the Fathers of the Church, both in the Greek-speaking East and the Latin West, are most greatly exercised are the persons promising to cure illness by incantations and amulets or claiming to be able to discover its cause by divinatory procedures. They were reasonably enough thought to be a special threat to the integrity of Christians, since they preyed on people at their weakest and most vulnerable. The very large number of protective amulets that survive from the Late Roman Period afford some idea of the size of the problem that confronted the Church.

The general term for a protective or curative amulet is in the Greek of this period a *periamma* or a *periapton* and in the Latin a *ligatura* – literally something that is tied on – or sometimes *phylacterium* – a Greek term that is not much used in the Greek texts we possess. Most amulets will have been worn about the neck, but this was not invariably so. John Chrysostom inveighs against bronze coins of Alexander the Great that were tied to the head or the feet.[117] Coins that were pierced, presumably to be worn as amulets, are attested. Earrings also functioned as amulets, if worn on one ear by men. They were, according to Augustine, worn in the service of demons and not as a decoration.[118] The most common form of amulet worn about the person, and probably generally about the neck, will have been a piece of material on which magical symbols were inscribed or that contained some protective incantation. The devices that had magical symbols on them took their name from the symbols and were called in Latin *characteres*.[119] Chrysostom speaks of women protecting their children by attaching amulets with the names of rivers written on them and of other similar acts of effrontery.[120] What sort of protection the names of rivers were supposed to afford eludes us. Finally, there was the more straightforward form of amulet with an incantation on it. Caesarius speaks of their being tied around the neck.[121] Examples of such amulets survive.

Many of these amulets will have been written on perishable materials. There are some examples from Egypt of amulets in the form of incantations written on papyrus, but most of what survives consists of thin sheets of precious metal (*lamellae*) on which are inscribed magical symbols or apotropaic incantations. The sheets of metal were then rolled up and placed in small cylindrical containers. It may be just such objects to which Chrysostom refers when he adduces Job and Lazarus as men of exemplary piety for their choosing to perish amongst the ills that surrounded them rather than running to seers, going to those who practised incantations, the tying on of leaves (*petala*) and the stirring up of magic.[122] Besides amulets on which writing or symbols were inscribed, there were amulets made of natural substances that were supposed to have magical properties. Augustine and Caesarius both tell of amulets consisting of plants (*herbae*) worn around the neck.[123] In the same breath that he mentions plant-amulets Caesarius speaks of amulets of amber.[124] The latter form of amulet may well have had writing on it or a magical symbol. Finally, there are the amulets made of animal excrement to which Athanasius alludes.[125]

The sheer number of amulets that survive from the Late Roman Period in the East imply the existence of a host of persons actively involved in the creation, sale and application of the devices. John Chrysostom mentions three categories of person who exploited this market: persons who made their living from amulets and who defended themselves as Christians; old women, nominally Christians, who uttered incantations over the sick in which they invoked the name of God; and Jewish healers from the synagogue. It is unlikely that these were the only sorts of paramedical healers of whose services the Christian community in Antioch availed itself, but they are the only ones who engage Chrysostom's interest. He makes no mention of Christians having recourse to unabashedly pagan forms of medicinal magic and he naturally enough has nothing to say about the persons to whom pagans turned when sick.

It is likely, for instance, that the female magic-worker and healer whose defeat at the hands of Hypatius, the superior of the monastery of the Rufinianae in the vicinity of Chalcedon, recorded in his *Life* by Callinicus is to be imagined as a pagan sorceress who invokes demons to aid her in her healing.[126] Hypatius became aware of her existence when he tried to cure a man of a wound that had suppurated badly and refused to heal. When his efforts at healing at first proved of no avail, Hypatius became suspicious and asked the man whether he had committed some wrong. The man confessed that before he had come to the monastery, a woman carrying a knife had uttered incantations over the wound. Hypatius then related to the man a dream that he had experienced the night before in which he had seen a woman sitting outside the gate of the monastery and at a little distance from her the Devil enthroned on a dais and attended by many demons. The monks had issued out of the monastery to drive the woman off. The demons had fought back, until Hypatius had himself appeared. At that point the Devil had told his underlings to give ground, since they would be able to accomplish nothing against Hypatius. They had all then vanished. As for the man with the suppurating wound, he had recovered in a few days. The implication of the dream is undoubtedly that the woman who intoned the incantation was in league with the Devil and was helped by demons. That does not of itself make her a practitioner of pagan magic, but the chances are that she was supposed to be just that.

The same may be true of the makers of phylacteries whom Athanasius' fellow-bishops encountered in the towns and villages of Egypt. They had found themselves in these places when they were driven out of Alexandria because of their allegiance to Athanasius. The sermon in Coptic ascribed to

Athanasius is an invaluable source of information on the apotropaic and magico-medical practices of the towns and villages beyond Alexandria.[127] What Athanasius' fellow-bishops saw in the towns and villages of their exile were persons engaging in abominable practices, which consisted in plunging infant children into dirty water and into water from the games or perhaps the arena of the theatre; they also poured water over the children upon which incantations had been uttered; broke pots, while saying: 'We drive out the Evil Eye'; attached phylacteries to their children made by those whose bodies were the dwelling-house of demons. The bishops reported yet others who anointed their children with an evil oil and they told of amulets and other objects that were attached to the heads and necks of the children.[128] Is Athanasius referring to magicians performing pagan magic, does he have pagan priests in mind or does he mean that anyone who manufactures amulets is doing the work of demons? None of these possibilities can be excluded, but the vehemence of the expression tips the balance slightly in favour of pagan priests or paganizing magicians. The passage is certainly evidence of the existence in the smaller towns and villages of mid-fourth century Egypt of persons who specialized in the manufacture of amulets and whom Christians should have known better than to have had anything to do with.

It is even more difficult to tell whether a female seer (*mantissa*) and maker of amulets in a text that belongs to seventh-century Cyprus is to be seen as essentially a pagan figure who leads Christians astray or as something quite different. The story of her defeat is told in the *Life of Symeon Salos*, a Syrian holy man of the second half of the sixth century AD. His exploits are set in Emesa. The *Life* was written by Leontius of Neapolis in Cyprus and belongs to the seventh century. It has been argued that it is more likely to reflect conditions in the seventh century than the one in which it is set.[129] Symeon is certainly largely the creation of Leontius himself. The female seer (*mantissa*) who made phylacteries and incantations will have been a woman who manufactured phylacteries and wrote incantations on them or uttered incantations over them to make them effective. Symeon, who was a holy fool, a *salos*, contrived to make the woman his friend by handing over to her the gifts, whether of small change, of bread or of clothing, that he had collected. One day he had asked her whether she would like him to make a phylactery for her that would afford her protection against the Evil Eye. She replied that indeed she would, reckoning that although he was a fool, he might still be successful. Symeon went off and wrote in Syriac – presumably a language she could not understand – on a tablet: 'Let God render you ineffective and let him stop you turning men away from himself to yourself'. He then gave it to the woman, who wore it and who as a result was no longer able to prophesy nor to make phylacteries.[130]

Some of the apotropaic amulets that survive from Late Antiquity as well as the recipes that exist for them promise to ward off ills of all kinds. Other recipes and amulets are much more specific and are only designed to deal with certain dangers or diseases. Since the incantations and magical characters in these custom-designed amulets have a specific aim, it would not be altogether surprising that there should have been some specialization in the incantations actually intoned over different kinds of illness. That in its turn would suggest that some paramedical healers will have made much of their expertise in certain areas. Ammianus Marcellinus tells of a simple old woman, executed in AD 371 as a criminal by the proconsul of Asia, Festinus Tridentinus, who cured with soothing incantations the kinds of fevers that recur periodically, by which he probably means bouts of malaria.[131]

It is also almost certain that persons existed who proclaimed themselves expert in nullifying the effect of spells cast by magicians. That they were a presence is to be inferred from a story told in the *Life of Symeon Stylites the Younger* about a presbyter from a village called Kassa, who out of envy had accused Symeon of practising magic and had even anathematized him. That had led to his having had a vision in which he saw a number of demons tying his hands behind his back and to his being unable to read from the Gospels or to raise the Host. He had set out to look for help and had been unsuccessful, although he had encountered some people who had made rather a mockery of him by telling him that sorcery (*goeteia*) of some sort was responsible for his suffering and had taken what little money he had without in any way helping him; they had in fact made him rather worse.[132]

### Paramedical healers in the West

Most of our information about paramedical healers in the Latin West comes from North Africa from the beginning of the fifth century AD and from Southern Gaul a generation or so later. It would clearly be imprudent to extrapolate from what Augustine of Hippo and Caesarius of Arles have to say to what was true of other communities throughout the Latin West in this period. But since both Augustine and Caesarius living in quite distant and quite different societies know of specialists in divining the cause of an illness and in curing it of very much the same kind, it is reasonable to suppose that such persons were to be found elsewhere in the West. It will not, furthermore, do to dismiss the testimony of Caesarius here because it echoes Augustine, as indeed it does. It may be that Augustine has imposed some of his preoccupations on Caesarius or Caesarius may have found in Augustine a voice that spoke to issues dear to Caesarius' heart. Whatever the true relationship is between the pair, it remains the case that Caesarius' sermons are not literary exercises but reflect his pastoral concerns as a bishop.

The pages of Augustine and Caesarius produce a bewildering variety of specialists in divining and healing by occult means. The precise job performed by some of them is veiled in obscurity. Amongst those who are consulted about the cause of an illness there are astrologers (*mathematici*), diviners from entrails (*haruspices*), those whose divinations are based on drawing lots (*sortilegi*), diviners (*divinatores*) who employ magical arts and who may be the same persons as the diviners called simply *divini*, inspired seers (*arrepticii*) and finally, a form of diviner called a *caraius* or *caragius*. One of the things done by the person called the *divinus* was to acquire a belt or an undergarment from one who was sick, so that he might measure and examine it and then pronounce on the course of action to be taken for the sick man and whether there was any prospect of his escaping from the illness.[133]

Those are the persons who are consulted about the cause of illness. Those who do something about it are almost as varied a group. There are the men who perform incantations (*incantatores* or *praecantatores*) and the women who do the same thing (*praecantatrices*); they seem to differ from the men who make or tie on amulets (*alligatores*), who may or may not be distinguishable from those versed in what are rather misleadingly called remedies (*remediatores*). Finally, there is the man who carries out fumigations to cure illness.[134] The only female experts besides the women who perform incantations or *praecantatrices* who are explicitly mentioned are the women known as *erbariae* and *dematriculae*. The former are evidently women versed in the magical qualities of the plants that are worn as amulets. The identity of the *dematricula* presents more of a problem. Other persons who have no special expertise may appear to offer their help. They may take the form of a friend, a neighbour and a neighbouring maidservant.

Such hints as we have from the pages of Augustine and Caesarius would suggest that since incantations were performed over amulets, the division between the intoners of incantations and those who were concerned with amulets cannot have been a very sharp one. Augustine, for example, forbids the use of the *remedia* of *incantatores*.[135] In such a context, *remedium* has quite a concrete sense and is basically an amulet.[136] Caesarius, for his part, speaks of attaching incantations (*praecantationes*) to the neck.[137] As for the *remediator* and the *alligator*, they are probably one and the same man; the *alligator* ties on or makes diabolical or sacrilegious remedies, while the *remediator* has his sacrilegious amulets (*ligaturae*).[138]

The *alligator* and the *remediator* performed a function similar to but probably not exactly the same as the drunken old women of whose presence at the bedsides of sick children John Chrysostom complains. *Alligatores* and *remediatores* attached amulets to the sick; they may also have uttered an incantation as they did so. Augustine speaks in two sermons of persons who come to the bedside of the sick to press amulets on them, but does not identify the parties concerned, although he does provide a clue to who they are. In one of these sermons Augustine says that one of the temptations sent by Satan to a man lying ill in bed is the appearance of some female creature (*muliercula*), or a man, if he can be called that, who suggests that the sick man should attach an amulet to himself if he wishes to be well, or should employ an incantation for the same purpose.[139] Augustine expresses himself in an ambiguous fashion, but it is likely his meaning is that the woman or the man is encouraging the sick man to allow them to attach the amulet to him. In another sermon containing a version of the same scene of temptation, there is no ambiguity about what the visitors to the sickbed do: they tie on amulets and make use of certain signs (*characteres*).[140] Since magical signs or *characteres* are regularly inscribed on apotropaic amulets, this must be what Augustine imagines the visitors are doing.[141] He himself distinguishes between the *ligaturae* and *remedia* that consist of incantations and those that are made up of the marks known as *characteres*.[142] Both Augustine and Caesarius speak of attaching or tying *characteres* to the neck, by which they will mean the practice of tying amulets with magical signs on them to the neck.[143] As those who come to the bed of sickness know what magical signs to inscribe, the presumption must be that they are professionals and are *remediatores* or *alligatores*.

Augustine employs the masculine demonstrative to refer to the visitors to the bedside, which means that some at least of them are male. Now if the persons of whom Augustine in the other sermon speaks so disparagingly, the *mulercula* and the man who is barely a man, follow the same calling as those who attach amulets and use magical signs, then it follows that not all *alligatores* or *remediatores* were men. It is difficult to decide what the exact intent of the disparaging way in which Augustine refers to the male and female visitor is, but in the case of the woman the diminutive that he employs in speaking of her carries connotations of a humble and despicable social status. That in its turn is an indication that the woman is not the social equal of the sick man, but is an inferior who is only present in his bedchamber for a very special reason, either because she has *ligaturae* or *remedia* to attach to the neck of the man or because she knows how to intone incantations.

It is not only professionals who find their way to the bedsides of the sick to press amulets on them. Friends and neighbours may also come, but it is those they bring in their train who are especially interesting. Augustine has another sermon on how it is possible for a man while lying sick in bed to become a holy martyr by fighting the good fight and not succumbing to the promise of bodily salvation but spiritual death that various tempters offer him. The tempters at the bedside of the sick man are the friend who suggests amulets, the muttering neighbour, his maidservant and sometimes her *dematricula*, a figure to whom we shall return shortly.[144] The *dematricula*, if she turns up, carries wax or an egg in her hands. The tempters say to the sick man: 'Do this and you will be saved. Why do you lengthen your sickness? Put on this amulet. I have heard someone invoking the name of God and the Angels over it'.[145] It is hardly surprising that a friend and a neighbour should visit the bed of a sick man and suggest remedies to him, but that the neighbour should bring his maidservant and she perhaps her *dematricula* is strange, unless the maidservant and the *dematricula* have some special rôle to play in the proceedings.

Identifying the *dematricula* presents difficulties, but what is fairly clear is that she comes to the scene equipped to perform a purificatory ceremony. What she brings the wax for is a puzzle, although its use in various magical rituals is well attested. There is no cause for hesitation over the meaning of the egg. From the Greek-speaking world we have the testimony of Lucian and Clement of Alexandria and from Rome that of Ovid, Juvenal, Martial and Apuleius to the use of eggs in ceremonies of purification.[146] In Rome, the person who employs the egg is characteristically an old woman.[147]

Who is the *dematricula*? She belongs in some way to the world of the neighbouring maidservant.[148] The word is a diminutive in form, which in a context such as this normally signifies social disdain on the part of the speaker. The woman is then a humble and insignificant woman. The root of the word may be either the word for a mother, *mater*, in which case the prefix *de* presents a problem, or the word for a womb or a vein in the neck, *matrex*. The verb *dematricare* is to be found in a veterinary work of Vegetius, an author of the late fourth century AD, and is used of the process of drawing blood from a vein in the neck of equines called the *matrex*.[149] A *dematricula* would, if the root is *matrex*, be a woman whose concern was the womb. She might then be a midwife or someone who induced abortions. If the root is *mater*, she is an old woman of some kind.

The precise identity of the *dematricula* must remain unclear, but what can confidently be said about her is that socially she is part of the nexus of relationships surrounding the neighbouring maidservant. The presence of the maidservant of the neighbour is not explained, but it is a fair guess that she is there because she is expert either in applying amulets or in intoning incantations. She is likely to have been brought to the scene because of her skills, not because she was or could have been a friend of the sick man, nor because neighbours were in the habit of bringing their maidservants with them on when they went to call on the sick. She and the *muliercula* of the other sermon will have belonged to the same world. None of this takes us very far along the road towards learning who the male *alligatores* and *remediatores* were, but it does tell us something about where some of the female experts in amulets and incantations came from and what company they kept. It is frustrating not to be able to pin down who the *dematricula* was exactly, but we are probably not too far off the mark if we think of her as a woman whose concern was female problems and one with whom maidservants would have had dealings.

Caesarius, for his part, complains that there are some women whose immediate response when a child falls sick is not to anoint the child with oil blessed by a presbyter and place all of their hope in God, but to consider consulting a diviner or interpreter of lots or a woman expert in herbal magic or in sacrificing and measuring the clothing of the child and attaching *characteres* and incantations to it; other women yet again – and these are women who pass for wise Christian women – when the Devil uses nursemaids or other women to suggest the use of such devices reply that they do not get involved in such matters, since they have been told in church that they cannot both drink from the cup of the Lord and that of demons, but then, as if having said that excused them from any further responsibility, tell the women to go and do what they know how to do and to avail themselves of whatever is needed from the cellar.[150] The implication of what these apparently scrupulous Christian women say to the nursemaids and the other women who suggest having recourse to the occult to cure the child is that the servant-women themselves know what to do and will do it.

What a Christian who fell seriously ill in Hippo or Southern Gaul experienced was probably not very different from what happened to someone in Rome in the Late Republic or Early Empire who became sick: older women of humble origins appeared to perform purificatory ceremonies, attach amulets and utter incantations. The one concession to Christian sensibilities that they or those who brought them made was to assert that the name of God and his Angels had been invoked over the amulet. The women who were expert in applying amulets and in healing the sick by magic were as likely as not to be maidservants and their associates. There were no doubt other types of women who were adepts in paramedical healing, but they have left no trace of their existence.

The problem of who the male *incantatores* and *praecantatores* and *alligatores* and *remediatores* were remains. There is not much doubt about part of the activities of *alligatores* and *remediatores*: they tied amulets to the sick. But did they make the amulets themselves or, if not, where did they get them? The *incantatores* are an equally intriguing group. Very little is heard about men intoning incantations at the bedsides of the sick, until they are encountered doing so in the pages of Augustine, but neither he nor Caesarius thinks it worthwhile to say who they are. They must have been very much part of the fabric of society.

## Wandering magicians in the Greek East

The mendicant holy men (*agyrtai*) who in the pagan period were to be encountered at the crossroads of a town, in its marketplace or in the vicinity of the temples of the Mother Goddess or Isis did not disappear with the Christianization of the Roman Empire. What happened to the begging-priests of the Mother Goddess is not known, but it is to be surmised that they lingered on in some form or another. There is some evidence for their continued existence in John Chrysostom's assertion that once Julian the Apostate came to supreme power in AD 361, various forms of magician, including the mendicant priests of the Mother Goddess, were to be seen flocking to the royal palace.[151] That Chrysostom exaggerates is hardly in doubt, but his accusation does suggest that such priests were still to be found.

The Fathers of the Church certainly still continue to speak of *agyrtai*. John

311

Chrysostom associates them with the market place or the crossroads, as do speakers in the Church Council held at Ephesus in AD 431.[152] Epiphanius invariably refers to the founders of the various heresies that he catalogues as *agyrtai*, because of the similarity they bear in his eyes at any rate to wandering mendicants. From the warning that Chrysostom issues against giving heed to diviners (*manteis*), oracle-mongers (*chresmologoi*) and finally, *agyrtai* it is apparent that mendicant holy men were still present in Antioch at the end of the fourth century.[153] Epiphanius is not then using a term of abuse that in his own day had little application.

Not much information is to be gleaned from John Chrysostom on what these people did and who they were, although he does say that ambiguous prophetic utterances of the kind given Croesus by the Pythia at Delphi were characteristic of the forecasts made by *agyrtai* at crossroads.[154] While Epiphanius' traduction of the various heresiarchs as *agyrtai* may do these persons less than justice, it does throw a good deal of light on who the *agyrtai* of his time were, where they came from in the world and how they behaved. His description of the life and career of Mani or Cubricus, the founder of Manichaeism, may not be of much help to those who wish to reconstruct the origins of Manichaeism, but it does provide an insight into the *agyrtai* of Late Antiquity and their social circumstances.

Mani, according to Epiphanius, was the slave of a childless Persian widow. He had inherited from her the books of doctrine and magical texts into whose possession she had come when her lodger, an Egyptian called Terbinthus, had been killed in attempting to fly from the roof of a house. Terbinthus had been driven to resort to the magical feat of flying to re-establish his credibility, after having been confuted on a point of doctrine by the priests of Mithras. Terbinthus, who had himself changed his name to the Assyrian word Buddha, was both the slave and follower of a certain Scythianus, a man born in the area where Palestine meets Arabia. Scythianus had received a Greek education and had shown some signs of ability, before going off to India to seek his fortune there in trade. It was in Jerusalem that Scythianus had finally met his fate, which was the same fate as his pupil Terbinthus or Buddha was to meet later: he too was defeated in debate, and, since he was a sorcerer (*goes*), he had had recourse to the magical texts that he had collected in the course of his sojourn amongst the Indians and then amongst the Egyptians and had attempted to fly, with predictable consequences. To Terbinthus his slave and follower he had entrusted all of his possessions. The pupil had run off with them to Persia and had not returned them to Scythianus' widow in the Egyptian Thebaid. She was a former prostitute of great beauty whom Scythianus had married after purchasing her and setting her free. Scythianus had met the prostitute when he arrived in Egypt from India laden with the goods that he had acquired in that land. To promote the life of luxury he had fallen into in Egypt he composed four books of doctrine in which he drew freely on Pythagoras.

It was these four books of wisdom along with the magical texts that Cubricus or Mani, as he now came to call himself, inherited from the Persian widow. He was no more successful than his predecessors in trying to persuade others of the truth of the doctrines contained in the four books. But when he heard that the son of the Persian king lay seriously ill in bed, he thought that this was his opportunity and that he would find in the books he had inherited some cure for the boy. He set out for the Persian capital, where he sought to publicize his philosophy and announced that he could save the boy. The boy unfortunately died in the midst of Mani's ministrations and he was thrown into gaol to await a suitably unpleasant fate. Before his incarceration he had sent some of his followers to Jerusalem to purchase the Christian Gospels. They returned with the books, which they showed him in his prison cell. He did not, however, stay there long, but escaped by bribing a guard. To avoid the arm of the Persian king, Mani now made his way into Roman territory to Mesopotamia. As for the Christian Gospels, he incorporated elements of them into his teaching.[155]

Epiphanius speaks disparagingly of Mani as a sorcerer (*goes*) and a mendicant (*agyrtes*) in recounting Mani's unsuccessful attempt to cure the son of the Persian king. His account of Mani's career and character is designed to persuade his readers that Mani, despite his pretensions and the claims of his followers, conformed to a pattern with which they were all familiar: he was a mendicant holy man, charlatan and opportunist who turned his hand to magic when needed and who made his way from place to place trying to exploit the gullibility of the public at each new stop in his wanderings. To make Mani into a typical mendicant holy man-cum-sorcerer Epiphanius endows him with what may be inferred was the appropriate background for such a man: he is a slave who has inherited his line of business or bag of tricks from a set of predecessors who are almost as disreputable as himself, although the ultimate source of the wisdom that he purveys, Scythianus, had enjoyed a good education and was able to put together four books that constituted a religious and philosophical system. The mendicant holy man-cum-sorcerer is, accordingly, for Epiphanius a man of obscure origins who appears out of the East and who has somehow or other inherited some sacred texts on which he bases his claims to superior wisdom. The pattern here is much the same as it was in the High Roman Empire or indeed in the fifth and fourth centuries BC. Lucian casts Alexander of Abunoteichos in very much the same mould: a boy of obscure origins apprenticed to an older magician from whom he learns his trade; after the death of his mentor the young man pursues a travelling career as a sorcerer throughout Asia Minor and Macedonia, before he eventually sets up a fraudulent oracle in an obscure town in Paphlagonia.

In sum, the evidence that we have tells very strongly in favour of the continued existence of mendicant holy men-cum-sorcerers. Some of the varied cast of prophets, seers, fortune-tellers, experts in incantations and amulets of which Augustine and Caesarius speak may have belonged to this category of person. Whether they continued in the latter part of the fourth century AD to make the remaining pagan shrines the centre of their activities we are not told. The story told by Zacariah about vagabond-magicians descending on Beirut at the end of the 480s to prey on the gullible by putting it about that they had learned from the *magoi* and the Persians of treasure that Dareius had buried there suggests that by that date wandering sorcerers had adapted their techniques to the new conditions and used churches and the tombs in and around them as a suitable location for their magic-working and necromancy.[156]

## Learned magicians

There is evidence that in the Christianized Roman Empire fairly large numbers of highly-educated men took an interest in magic, at least to the point of owning magical formularies, even if they did not actually put the recipes in the formularies into practice. According to Ammianus, one of the measures that the authorities took in Antioch in AD 371 was to collect and burn many piles of magical handbooks under the eyes of judges. This was done, the historian says, to lessen the ill-will that the persecutions for magic-working in Antioch had created, even though the titles of many of the codices burned showed them to be works about the liberal arts and the law.[157] Ammianus goes on to say that magical spells were surreptitiously deposited in the furniture of the accused and were then as it were discovered, so that they might be read out in court. This led to a panic in the eastern provinces that resulted in everybody burning every book they possessed.[158] A good deal of allowance has to be made for exaggeration on Ammianus' part, but he does seem to assume that educated men might well have magical texts in their possession. Then there is the case in Rome in AD 368 of a boy in his early youth, the son of a prefect, who was convicted in an investigation conducted by Maximinus himself of having copied out a codex containing magical material and executed, after he and his father had made the miscalculation of appealing to the Emperor.[159]

The students of Roman Law in Beirut belonging to the circle of John Foulon whose magic-working came to light in the 490s, after they had attempted to sacrifice an Ethiopian slave, are all said to have possessed magical texts.[160] One of the striking features of the story is how important a part handbooks on magic played in the aspirations of these well-to-do young men to perform magic. There was no question of men of this sort serving an apprenticeship with a professional magician, although they might very well have had contacts with such persons. Their knowledge of magic had to come mostly from books, which no doubt assumed a significance in their lives that they would not have had for a man who needed to make his living from magic-working. If Zacariah's description of the contents of John Foulon's book is accurate, the book pretended to be based on learned authorities: Zoroaster, Ostanes and Manetho. It is natural to suspect that the magical texts in the possession of the educated took a somewhat different form from the handbooks belonging to working magicians and were written in a more pretentious style. Now the persons whom Zacariah names come from the ruling class in their native cities and might be expected to attain high office in the imperial administration. They were evidently young men of independent means. Chrysaorius of Tralles, one of those who practised magic, has sufficient means to hire a ship to take his children, their mother, who was his concubine, his furniture, books and silver back from Beirut to Tralles.[161] Zacariah's *Life of Severus* does, however, give the impression that there was something unusual in finding so many educated young men actively engaged in magic-working.[162] The possession of a magical text was then perhaps no very good indication that its owner would put the material in it to any practical application.

It should not be assumed that in the fourth and fifth centuries the form in which magical lore circulated amongst educated was the codex. Magical spells circulated in other ways. A letter from the second half of the fourth century AD discovered recently in a house in Kellis, (modern Ismant el-Kharab), one of several settlements in the Dakleh Oasis in the Western Desert of Egypt, shows that recipes for individual spells existed and might be written out and sent as part of a letter. The village was deserted by about AD 400. The document in question was found in a sector of the village in which Manichaeans had settled by about AD 300. It is reasonable to assume from other documents found beside it and from internal evidence that it was part of the detritus of the Manichaean community. The letter itself was sent by one Manichaean living in a community other than Kellis to a Manichaean in Kellis. The presence of two Coptic–Syriac glossaries of Manichaean terms written on wooden boards and a text in both Greek and Syriac written on vellum points to the community's being engaged in missionary activity and perhaps to its involvement in the translation of Manichaean texts from Syriac into Coptic.[163] It also looks as if the house in which the magical texts were found, which is known as House 3, was the dwelling-place of a complex family group, a fairly common pattern in Roman Egypt. Texts that properly belonged to other houses and families may have been deposited in House 3 when the settlement was being abandoned, but it is on the whole likely that most of the texts found in the house had belonged to members of the family group who had inhabited it.[164]

The writer of the letter, Valens, has copied out for the benefit of the recipient, his fellow Manichaean, Psais, a spell designed to effect a separation between a man and a woman.[165] He apologizes for its not being quite the spell for which Psais had asked him; the piece of papyrus on which the correct spell was written had been mislaid. The spell that Psais has been sent is what is labelled in the magical papyri either a *diakopos*, a spell intended to drive asunder, or a *misethron,* a spell designed to engender hatred. It is not a work-ing spell, but a pattern that Psais can follow, substituting for the expressions 'so and so, the offspring of so and so' the names of the parties whom he wishes to divide and cause to quarrel.[166] The letter then constitutes evidence that one man might write to another asking whether the other had at hand a spell that would achieve a certain end and get in return a pattern for the spell requested. What is sent is conspicuously not a formulary, but a template copied out apparently from another template written on a single piece of papyrus. Such pieces of papyrus were evidently easily mislaid.

Our knowledge of the contents and intellectual tone of magical formular-ies in Late Antiquity is based above all on formularies copied out in Egypt in the fourth century AD that were perhaps part of a single collection, but that are now dispersed in libraries in Paris, Berlin, Leiden and London. Whether the contents of the formularies from Egypt bear any likeness to the formular-ies that were in circulation in Antioch during the persecutions there is impossible to tell, but they do give some indication of what in Late Antiquity educated men with some intellectual pretensions may have looked for in magic. It has already been noted that the formularies, especially the most extensive of them, that are now in Paris, contain not only recipes for run-of-the-mill magical procedures, but also instructions for transcending the limi-tations of the body to commune with the divine. Extrapolating from the con-tents of the formularies to the interests and pretensions of their owner or owners is risky, but the peculiar combination of the high-minded and tran-scendental with the profane in the form of erotic spells that aim at nothing more than bringing a partner to bed in a state of sexual arousal does suggest a man who harbours the hope that magic will at the same time provide him with an instrument for satisfying his sexual lusts and fantasies, but also with a procedure for attaining union with the divine. His intellectual aspirations reflect the Platonism of his day.

We can get some idea of what that Platonism might mean for those with a disposition towards magic by looking at Proclus as a theurgist. Proclus, who was born in AD 410 or 412 and died in his bed in AD 484/5, succeeded his own teacher Syrianus as head of the Platonic school in Athens. The voluminous surviving commentaries of Proclus on Platonic dialogues put Proclus' philo-sophical ability beyond question. We are confronted, accordingly, with what to modern ways of thinking is something of a paradox: a philosopher of the highest order with a taste not only for the mystical, but for the magical, although he would not have chosen to see the matter in that way. Now if as austere and as intellectual a figure as Proclus practised magic, it is fair to ask what did those who were less gifted but at the same time less restrained in their appetites and passions do. The example of Proclus suggests an intellec-tual climate favourable to magical experiment.

Proclus was born in Constantinople, where his father was a lawyer in the imperial service. Both his parents came from Xanthos in Lycia and it was there that they brought the boy at an early age. He received his primary education in Lycia, before being sent to Alexandria to further his studies in literature and rhetoric. While there he studied Latin, since he was destined for the same career as his father. One of his teachers, Leonas the Isaurian, must have been struck by the promise that the young man displayed, since he took him with him to Constantinople, but the youth was drawn back to Alexandria and to the study of philosophy. Rhetoric and his other earlier studies were abandoned and he devoted himself to the study of Aristotle under Olympiodorus. After he had got as much from Olympiodorus as he could, he sailed for Athens, where the teachers of rhetoric vied for his favours. Rhetoric no longer held any interest for him and it was then that he fell in with Syrianus, who was shortly to succeed his own teacher, Plutarch, as head of the Platonic School in Athens.[167] Proclus studied under the aged Plutarch for two years and read with him Aristotle's *De anima* and the *Phaedo* of Plato.[168]

According to his biographer Marinus, Proclus received his instruction in theurgy from Asclepigeneia, the daughter of Plutarch. Asclepigeneia was the repository of all of the theurgic wisdom that had been accumulated by her great-grandfather, Nestorius, and passed on to her by her father.[169] The explanation for Asclepigeneia's being Proclus' teacher and not her father lies presumably in Proclus' not being ready for theurgic instruction in the two years in which Plutarch was his teacher. It is interesting, however, that it was not Syrianus who instructed Proclus, but Asclepigeneia. In passing on theurgic lore only within the family, the theurgist is taking a leaf out of the book of the magician, since magicians also maintained the fiction that theirs was an esoteric branch of knowledge, only to be handed on to trusted intimates. About Asclepigeneia herself nothing further is known. Her name, however, is an appropriate one for the daughter of a man whose life was bound up with a form of Platonism in which Pythagoreanism and the cult of Asclepius played a large part.

Quite a lot is known about Nestorius, the grandfather of Plutarch, and the source of the theurgic lore that resided in his descendants. Proclus in his commentary on Plato's *Republic* himself twice refers to Nestorius: once as a truly holy man and then later as the mighty *hieratikos*.[170] A *hieratikos* is in Proclus' terminology a theurgist, although it is to be doubted whether he would have thought all theurgists worthy of so honorific an appellation. It is in any case clear from the way in which Proclus speaks of Nestorius that he was a holy man of extraordinary prominence. On the earlier of the two occasion on which Proclus has occasion to mention him it is to bring up the secret of the right-angled triangle that Nestorius had unveiled, after having been taught it by persons referred to by Proclus as his betters. Proclus rather remarkably calls it a spell or conjuration (*agoge*). It is a device to ensure by a combination of geometry and astrology successful births. It makes use of the principle of a sympathetic relationship between the seven vowels and the seven planets and the seventeen consonants of the Greek alphabet and the twelve signs of the zodiac.[171] Where the vowels represent a planet that does good, no aspiration is to be employed in their utterance (*ekphonesis*) and when the opposite holds good, aspiration is to be used.[172] Proclus raises the matter, in commenting on the discussion in the *Republic* of the best time for marriage and procreation, not as a point of academic interest, but to give his wholehearted endorsement to it. Later in the commentary, to illustrate the transmigration of souls from one species of brute beast to another, Proclus relates an experience that Nestorius had had in Rome: he had encountered a nobly-born woman who was scarcely able to speak because of her unhappiness over the memory of her previous lives; she had remembered that in a previous cycle of existence she had been the maidservant of hawkers in Athens, but was distressed that she could not remember what they had ordered her to do; she had then met an apparition who had told her of her previous existences as a dog, a snake, a bear, then a human being again. Nestorius not only cured her of these distressing memories but implanted in her hope for the future. To do so, he had employed gods to help him.[173]

Proclus, as Marinus tells the story, had no inhibitions about using his theurgic skills to influence the natural order. In the paragraph that he devotes to Proclus' theurgic exercises Marinus says that his teacher employed Chaldaean unions with the divine, entreaties and wordless wheels and that he was inducted into their use along with that of utterances (*ekphoneseis*) by Asclepigeneia; even before that, after undergoing Chaldaean rites of purification, he had had concourse with apparitions of Hecate that were filled with light and appeared of their own accord; the last-named apparitions he had written about in a monograph devoted to them. His main theurgic feat had been to use the wheel called the *iynx* to promote rain and free Attica from a drought; finally, he had experimented with the prophetic powers of the tripod and had produced verses that predicted what his lot in life would be.[174]

Proclus seems to have had the good sense to stay out of public life and keep his head down. If ambition had moved him to exert his influence in public, any enemies he made would have had an easy target for their accusations. They could, for instance, have brought up what he had written about bringing a statue of a god to life by theurgic means. A person, whom Proclus calls the performer of initiations, which is to say the theurgist, attached symbols to statues of the gods to make them receptive to receiving higher powers.[175] The symbols used were the magical signs known as *characteres*, which were employed in conjunction with life-giving words to bring the statue to life and make it move.[176] As for the theurgic initiatory rites performed on statues to give them life and empower them to predict the future, Proclus speaks about the procedure in commentaries on Platonic dialogues and on Euclid. These commentaries reflect the lectures that Proclus gave on Plato and Euclid. The interpretations he presents are not necessarily his own original work, but belong to a tradition of Neoplatonist exegesis, which he will have absorbed principally from the lectures of his predecessor Syrianus.

That lectures endorsing rituals deriving ultimately from the practices of magicians and designed to bring statues alive should have been delivered in Athens to however select an audience and then should have been worked up as commentaries to be circulated is salutary for those used to the intellectual witch-hunts that have been conducted in recent times. It reminds us how careful we must be about bringing our own presuppositions to bear in interpreting Late Antiquity. Proclus did not think of himself as a magician, but he almost certainly knew that those not sympathetic to his position would have seen him as a sorcerer. That knowledge did not keep him from recommending theurgic practices and from pursuing them himself. Nor did it keep his pupil and biographer, Marinus, from admiringly recording the practical applications to which Proclus put his theurgical learning.

## In-house magicians

No trace is to be found in this period of the well-educated Greek taken up by a rich Roman who turns his hand to magic on behalf of his patron. The phenomenon, however, of the in-house magician is not entirely unknown. Maximinus, the prefect in charge of the Roman corn supply, who had at an earlier stage in his career governed both Corsica and Sardinia, is said by Ammianus Marcellinus to have acquired a Sardinian who was an adept at summoning up harmful spirits and at predicting the future through necromancy. Ammianus adds that so long as the man was alive, Maximinus was afraid to begin proceedings against others, lest he be betrayed, but rumour had it that Maximinus had employed some devious means to bring about the death of the man.[177] It is unlikely that Ammianus actually had evidence of the Sardinian's having practised magic on Maximinus' behalf, but the story is consistent with the portrait of Maximinus that Ammianus wishes to create: an unscrupulous and blood-thirsty monster who did not hesitate to execute persons for offences of which he himself was guilty.[178] The same pattern is observable in Ammianus' account of Festus Tridentinus' conduct as governor of Asia: he was a man who tried to emulate Maximinus' blood-stained rise to power and influence; amongst those guilty of trivial forms of magic whom he executed, despite having employed her to cure his daughter, was a simple-minded old woman expert in soothing incantations.[179] Ammianus is, in short, not necessarily a wholly reliable witness in the matter of the Sardinian magician employed by Maximinus, but his story is at least an indication that people were prepared to entertain the idea of a great man having a personal magician at his beck and call.

Another putative example of an in-house magician is the slave whom a Roman senator is supposed to have sent to a man learned in the evil art of magic. A formal agreement of apprenticeship on behalf of the slave is said to have been all but signed specifying that the slave should be taught some arcane expiatory techniques. The senator is said by Ammianus to have done

319

this in imitation of Hilarinus the charioteer, who had sent his son to a magician to learn the magician's craft. The story is told to illustrate the licence that came to pervade Rome, once magic-working was no longer actively prosecuted.[180]

## Conclusions

It should be fairly clear by now that in this period those who made a living from magic-working or who asked for a fee for their services were at best persons of obscure birth, and were more likely than not to be slaves, former slaves or persons whose status was a dishonourable one because of the calling they pursued. In the great cities magic-workers were to be found in the ranks of the actresses, charioteers, prostitutes, ex-prostitutes and in general amongst those persons who entertained the public. These were the persons to whom people turned to have serious magic-working performed for them. When sickness fell on a house, poor old women were called in to apply amulets to the invalid and perform incantations. No precise information is available about who they were, other than that some of them invoked God in their incantations and were ostensibly Christian. Their identity is bound up with the larger problem of the identity of the urban poor in Late Antiquity. In addition to the persons actually practising magic there were also those engaged in the important and significant ancillary service of manufacturing amulets. Some of them were persons who capitalized on their special expertise in matters divine. Clerics who traded in amulets fall into this category as does the female seer tricked by Symeon Salos. There were no doubt fluctuations from city to city and time to time in the numbers of those who performed magic in return for a fee, but such persons were a fixed feature of the great cities of the Late Roman Empire.

The charioteers, actresses and prostitutes who offered their services as magicians were more or less permanently domiciled in the cities in which they worked. Not all magicians were, so to say, of fixed abode. Wandering holy men were still a feature of the Late Roman world. They will have been the sorts of person who put on conjuring shows and told fortunes at street-corners and in the marketplace. Who they were is cloaked in obscurity. They were certainly persons who had no standing in society and who had to live by their wits. They were very likely to be slaves and ex-slaves who had received some education and who were eager to better themselves.

The well-educated man who is attracted to magic had been a feature of the Greek world since the Hellenistic Period and the Roman world from the Late Republic. Men with an interest in philosophy seem even before that date to have been drawn to magic and the occult. This was no less the case in Late Antiquity and, if anything, was even more true. Neoplatonism gave added intellectual respectability to the pursuit of the occult. Philosophers had always dabbled in magic under the guise of Pythagoreanism, but the incorporation of the magical techniques described in the *Chaldaean Oracles* into a philosophical system enabled those who were predisposed towards the occult to persuade themselves that what they did was sanctioned by the gods and was a natural development of what Plato had taught. It would be a grave mistake to imagine that it was the feeblest minds of the age who actively practised theurgical magic. The truth of the matter is that some of the most intelligent men of the time were the vigorous proponents of theurgy. Such inhibitions as they may have had about making their interests public were not because they thought they might be laughed at, but because they feared that the Christian authorities might perversely misconstrue what they were doing and take action against them.

The wider influence of theurgy on the practice of magic in this period is difficult to calculate. It is impossible, for example, to say whether the rituals prescribed in some of the magical papyri for elevating the soul to union with the divine derive from theurgy or whether the rituals of theurgy have their origins in the practices of magicians. Cross-fertilization is not unlikely. It is also hard to assess the effect that the example of the theurgists had on the wider educated public: did it make magic-working respectable and encourage it or did it have no effect? The sorcery performed by educated men of which we do hear shows little sign of the influence of theurgy. So far as can be judged, it had a severely practical bent and did not have a mystical side to it, but there may well have been those who were attracted to magic as much by the hope of receiving revelations into the higher mysteries as they were by the more tangible benefits that magic promised. What the sources mention again and again are educated men practising magic either to seduce a woman or to find out about what was hidden from human eyes. For the most part the educated men who resorted to magic were fairly young and tended to be part of a larger group. Despite its pretensions to secrecy magic was very often an activity practised by a group and often enough in groups. That there were in all of the major cities of the Roman Empire covens of well-to-do, educated young men engaged in the practice of magic seems unlikely. Such groups seem to have sprung up in certain places at certain times. Magic-working is for the members of the group an excitingly illicit activity that gives them a certain cachet and makes them feel more adventurous than their fellows.

# NOTES

## INTRODUCTION

1 The focus of Bernand 1991 is, despite its title, *Sorciers grecs*, not so much the sorcerer as magic-working. The same is true of Luck 1962, whose title *Hexen und Zauberei in der römischen Dichtung* belies the content of the work.

2 A conspicuous exception is the discussion of prostitutes practising sorcery in Modena at the end of the sixteenth century in the essay by O'Neil 1987.

3 Briggs 1996: 169–86 has a fascinating chapter on the part played by cunning folk in the prosecution of witches.

4 A version of this theory is to be encountered in Luck 1985: 'The roots of magic are no doubt prehistoric. There is reason to believe that some fundamental magical beliefs and rituals go back into the cult of the great earth goddess'.

5 Murray 1921.

6 Cohn 1975: 99–125.

7 Ginzburg 1991: 207–25.

8 Ginzburg 1991: 2–4.

9 Ginzburg 1980 and 1983.

10 The exception is an inscription from the Umbrian town of Tuder (modern Todi) of the second century AD thanking Iuppiter Optimus Maximus for having revealed the presence of a hidden curse-table directed at the town-councillors (*decuriones*) and recording the punishment of a public slave for the crime (*CIL* 11.3639).

11 25–7.

12 Cf. Wallace-Hadrill 1994: 118–42.

13 So Winkler 1990: 71–98; Winkler 1991: 214–43.

14 Bremmer 1985: 289–93.

15 So Henderson 1987: 126.

16 Burkert 1962: 43–5.

17 Chantraine 1933: 267.

18 The thesis that the seventh-century Greek colonists of the Black Sea had come into contact with Scythian shamans and that such figures as Aristeas of Proconnesus and Hermotimus of Clazomenae were shamans goes back to an article of Meuli 1935. Dodds 1951: 121–76 gave the thesis a wider diffusion. Despite the damaging criticisms of Bremmer 1983: 25–48 the thesis still has its adherents.

19 Chantraine 1968: s.v. *goao* takes *goes* to designate a magician who specialized in cries and incantations.

20 So Johnston 1999: 103, a position already taken by Jebb 1893: 62, also on the basis of the Suda.
21 s.v. *goeteia* The proximate source of the entry in the Suda is a commentary of the sixth century AD on four sermons by Gregory Nazianzus (*Pseudo-Nonniani in IV Orationes Gregorii Nazianzeni Commentarii* ed. Nimmo Smith, *Comm.* IV.70.9–10). The distinctions can hardly be the invention of the commentator, Pseudo-Nonnus, who will have found them most likely in a lexicographer.
22 Potter 1994: 12.
23 Nock 1972.
24 West 1971 240–1; endorsed by Burkert 1992: 41–6, esp. 178 n.3 in his discussion of wandering charismatics in the Archaic Period.
25 *Praeparatio sophistica* p. 56.8 de Borries.
26 Chantraine 1968 s.v. *manganon.*
27 It is the thesis of Faraone 1999 that *philtron* is the name for the magical techniques used by women to secure or retain the *philia* or affections of men as against the spells that men out of lust use to draw women to them, which are called *agogai* or *philtrokatadesmoi.* The thesis cannot be sustained; men also use *philtra* or *amatoria* with quite predatory sexual purposes in mind as indeed do women; and *philtrokatadesmoi* are in any case just a form of *philtron.*
28 For a summary-account of the tablets from Selinus, see Jameson et al. 1993: 125–31.
29 Cf. Pl. *Resp.* 364c2–5, *Leg.* 933a2–b5.
30 *SEG.* 43.434.

## 1 THE FORMATION AND NATURE OF THE GREEK CONCEPT OF MAGIC

1 For a brief but fairly comprehensive summary of the anthropological literature on the subject of religion and magic, see Cunningham 1999.
2 For a recent assertion of the universality of magic, see Luck 1999: 218: 'The magic of all periods and cultures has much in common, but there are striking local variations of universal practices and beliefs'.
3 Leach 1982: 133.
4 For references to the literature on this controversy, see Versnel 1991: 193 n.8.
5 Versnel 1991: 184–5 with 195 n.25.
6 A position advocated by Versnel 1991: 185, who quotes with approval the assertion of Snoek 1987: 7 (*non vidi*): 'It should be clear then, that an emic scholarly approach is a *contradictio in terminis.* Scholarly discourse is always etic and should therefore be conducted in etic terms'. Versnel is followed by Faraone 1999: 17 n.75. Versnel maintains that it is impossible to understand the ancient concept of magic as an ancient would have understood it and that we must in consequence use the concept of magic with which we moderns operate in writing about the ancient world. It is obviously true in a not very interesting sense that we do not see the world in the same way that ancient man did, but that does not mean that his ways of thinking remain utterly closed to us. Most of us, for instance, do not have the same moral outlook as an Athenian juryman of the fourth century BC, but it does not follow that his way of thinking is a closed book to us. If Versnel is correct, we might as well abandon any hope of understanding ancient man.
7 This is the situation that leads Hopkins 1965: 125 to make the following categoric statement, quoted with approval by Versnel 1991: 185: 'Yet as moderns and as historians we have no alternative but to use our own concepts

and categories to explain other societies'. Hopkins, nonetheless, does go on to acknowledge that there are difficulties when our own 'conceptualization of the external world' and that of the society under study are at odds.

8  Graf's views on the topic will be cited from Graf 1996, which is essentially a new edition in German of Graf 1994, a work originally published in French. Graf 1998 is an English translation from the original French edition and lacks the corrections and additions of the German edition. Graf was to some extent anticipated by Lloyd 1990: 43 in his discussion of applying categories across cultures when there is no counterpart to the category in the culture to which it is applied. Magic, Lloyd concludes, does not present that problem, since not only do the Greek have a word for it, 'they might even be said to have invented that category'.

9  Graf 1996: 31–6.

10 Graf 1996: 36.

11 The discussion of magic in the Hebrew Bible by Schäfer 1997b: 27–33 does not exercise itself over the question of the existence of a concept of magic, but seems to assume that such a concept existed, since practices that would in the eyes of modern Western man be thought magical are abominated.

12 So Ritner 1993: 1 and Ritner 1995: 43–60.

13 Ritner 1993: 14–15.

14 Ritner 1993: 20: 'There can thus be no question of the legitimacy of magic in pharaonic Egypt.'

15 11.24–37.

16 4.227–30.

17 4.231–2. The first evidence of Polydamna thought of as a sorceress appears at the end of the third century BC in a poem by Euphorion (fr. 14 *CA*).

18 *Od.* 10.230–43; 281–306.

19 11.739–41.

20 Passages such as the Circe-episode have led Gordon 1999: 178 to speak of 'a magic before magic.'

21 Ar. *Plut.* 303–10.

22 Theocr. 2.14–15.

23 *Hom. Hymn Dem.* 227–30.

24 So Richardson 1974: 229 citing Maas 1944: 36–7, who compared the lines to the verses at the end of an incantation belonging to the fourth century BC inscribed on a lead tablet found at Phalasarna on Crete (Jordan 1992) that offer protection against various forms of sorcery. Two further examples of the incantation, also from the fourth century and also inscribed on lead, from Selinus and Epizephyrian Locri, have now emerged (Costabile 1999: 29–42).

25 Pfister 1924: 330.

26 19.455–7.

27 Cf. Soph. *Aj.* 581–2.

28 289e4–90a3.

29 *Chrm.* 155e5–8.

30 *Pyth.* 3.47–53.

31 426b1–2.

32 Alex. Trall. 2.475 Puschmann.

33 The Chorus at *Ag.* 1019–24 asks who can by incantation call back up again blood that has been spilled on the ground and immediately answers its own question with the example of Orpheus whom Zeus prevented not without inflicting hurt on him from summoning up the dead. Teaching of the same order is to be found in a speech of Apollo at *Eum.* 644–51 in which a distinction

is made between forms of harm that can be cured and the irreparable damage that killing does: Zeus has created no incantations (*epodai*) to cure the latter, although he is prepared to reverse everything else.

34 Hippoc. *Morb. sac.* 1.27–31 Grensemann. Further examples in Abt 1908: 50–56.

35 Faraone 1991: 6; Graf 1991: 188–213.

36 DK 22 B 14 = Clem. Alex. *Protr.* 2.22.2–3.

37 DK 22 F 15.

38 Lloyd 1979: 12–13 is inclined to suspect that Clement may have doctored the list and added the word *magoi* to it. Graf 1995: 31 and Graf 1998: 21 argues that Heraclitus did indeed speak of *magoi*.

39 On itinerant priests and charismatics from the East in the Archaic Greek world, see Burkert 1983: 115–19.

40 So also Graf 1998: 21.

41 609–21.

42 686–8.

43 686–8, 697.

44 628–80.

45 Johnston 1999: 117–18 says of the *gooi* that they 'are certainly more than *gooi* in the old-fashioned sense, for they literally compel Darius to appear'. There does appear to be more to the *gooi* than ritualized cries of lamentation, but there is nothing in Aeschylus' Greek to suggest that Darius feels compelled by them to leave the Underworld for the land of the living.

46 *Praep. soph.* 127 de Borries.

47 A remark made by Hercules in Euripides' *Alcestis* of 438 BC (1127–8) provides reason for thinking that *psychagogia* was by then a distinct speciality and, furthermore, that a degree of contempt attached to it. What Hercules, who has in fact literally wrested Alcestis, the wife of Admetus, from the grip of Hades, says, after Admetus has raised the possibility that the woman he sees in front of him may be an apparition from the dead, is that Admetus is making a *psychagogos* out of a man who is his guest-friend (*xenos*). The point of the remark would seem to be either that it is a little strange for Admetus, a king, to admit to enjoying a relationship of guest-friendship with anything as lowly as a professional summoner up of the souls of the dead or more likely that it is insulting of him to call his friend a *psychagogos* and to suggest that he can do no better than bring back a ghost. A scholiast on the line says that certain *goetes* who by purificatory rites (*katharmoi*) and acts of sorcery (*goeteia*) summoned up the dead to haunt (*epagein*) and who removed such hauntings were called *psychagogoi* in Thessaly and that such persons had, according to Plutarch (fr. 126 Sandbach), been summoned by the Laconians when the ghost of Pausanias disturbed those who visited the temple of Athena Chalkiokos. The idea that *psychagogos* is what a *goes* who specializes in handling the ghosts of the dead is called in Thessaly is the invention of a scholiast discussing a play set in Thessaly, which he knows is a centre of sorcery. The extent of the scholiast's dependence on Plutarch does not extend beyond the story of the Laconians summoning *psychagogoi* to deal with the restless spirit of Pausanias. Plutarch cannot then be taken to have said that the Spartans hired *psychagogoi* who were *goetes* skilled in summoning and sending away the dead, nor can the scholiast's invention safely be combined with the story at Thuc. 1.134.4 of the instructions given by the Delphic Oracle about the burial of Pausanias as evidence that the Oracle ordered the employment of such experts and as an indication that 'the *goes* was anything but an outcast, feared by the average Greek of the classical period' (Johnston 1999: 108–9).

48 1553–64. On the antecedents of the ode, see Dunbar 1995: 711.

49 The other is 1470–93.

50 Frs. 273, 273a.1–2, 276 Radt.

51 Fr. 275 Radt.

52 Fr. 2 Bernabé.

53 *FGrH* 70 F 104.

54 *FGrH* 3 F 47 = *sch. in* Ap. Rhod. 1.1129. Carl Wendel, the editor of the *scholia* to Apollonius Rhodius emended *analyontes* to a participle meaning 'miners of metals', *metalleuontes*. Burkert 1962: 39 n.14, followed by Johnston 1999: 105 n.54, points out that the unemended Greek makes good sense in the context.

55 DK 31 B 111.

56 8.59. On Satyrus' procedures in composing his biographies with particular reference to his *Lives* of poets, see Lefkowitz 1991.

57 Diog. Laert. 8.58–9.

58 Burnett 1930: 201 n.2, followed by Guthrie 1965: 135, places more trust in the tradition than I would and maintains that Satyrus' information comes from Alcidamas, a rhetorician, who is said to have been a pupil of Gorgias.

59 Ar. *Nub.* 749–57.

60 Eur. *Suppl.* 1110–11.

61 Hippoc. *Morb. sacr.* 1.10–12, 26 Grensemann.

62 Eur. *IT* 1337–8.

63 Eur. *Ba.* 233–8, 258–62.

64 Eur. *Or.* 1494–8.

65 *Morb. sacr.* 1.29–31 Grensemann.

66 1.132.3.

67 These white horses will be the inspiration for the white Nysaean horse that the *magoi* of Babylon sacrifice to the sun when Apollonius of Tyana comes to visit them (Philostr. *VA* 1.31).

68 7.113.2–114.1.

69 7.191.2.

70 The evidence for its date is inconclusive. For discussion, see Guthrie 1969: 192 n.2, who himself favours a date before Euripides' *Troades*.

71 *Hel.* 11.

72 *Hel.* 14.

73 For Hecate as the goddess *par excellence* of the magician, see Johnston 1999: 203–4, who holds that it was in virtue of the control the goddess exercised over the unquiet dead she had this power.

74 395–8.

75 375–85.

76 716–19.

77 1048–57.

78 387–90.

79 233–8.

80 555–77.

81 There is, however, now a lead tablet from Pella in Macedonia belonging to the third quarter of the fourth century BC in which a woman seeks to prevent a man from marrying another woman and tries to keep him entirely for herself (Voutiras 1996).

82 582–7.

83 9.312–13.

84 *Misein: Ant.* 495–96, fr. 737 Radt; *stygein: Aj.* 133, *Ant.* 571.

85 *Phil.* 86–7.

86  *Aj.* 46, 1004, *OR* 125, 533, *Ant.* 915, *OC* 716, *Phil.* 984.

87  477–9.

88  499, 503, 505.

89  500–2.

90  503–6.

91  507–12.

92  Plut. *Luc.* 43.2; Ach. Tat. 4.15.3; Ov. *Ars am.*; Plin. *HN* 25.25; Juv. 6.610–20; Suet. *Cal.* 50, *Poet.* 16 Rostagni = Hieron. *Chron..* See also Hopfner 1927: 206–7.

93  509–15.

94  *Morb. sacr.* 1.27–31 Grensemann.

95  Soph. *Trach.* 689.

96  1330–8.

97  [Eur.] *Rhes.* 943; Lys. 6.53; Isoc. *Loch.* 3.

98  *In Ioh. tract.* 97.2–3 *CCSL* 36: *ipsa quippe occultatione condiunt quodammodo nefarii doctores sua uenena curiosis; ut ideo se existiment aliquid discere magnum, quia meruit habere secretum, et suauius hauriant insipientiam, quam putant scientiam, cuius prohibitam quodammodo furantur audientiam.*

99  Heraclitus DK 22 F 14.

100  232–8.

101  The evidence is assembled by Johnston 1999: 88.

102  See Johnston 1999: 89 with n.11. Graf 1996: 156–7 denies that black magic was actually practised in Mesopotamia, on the ground that we only hear of it in exorcistic texts; it is, accordingly, to be treated as the fantasizing of the exorcist.

103  Reiner 1995: 98 with n. 417.

104  28.7–25.

105  Auld 1994: 29.

106  Ar. *Vesp.* 1019–20.

107  1330–8.

108  Eur. *Andr.* 157–60.

109  DK 22 F 14.

110  932e1–33b5.

111  933d7–e4.

112  933a2–5.

113  *Soph.* 234c2–7, 235a1, 241b6–7, *Pol.* 303c1–5.

114  *Euthydem.* 288b7–8, *Resp.* 380d1–6, 383a2–5.

115  *Phileb.* 44c8.

116  *Grg.* 483e5–6.

117  *Legg.* 649a2–6.

118  *Men.* 80a1–8.

119  *Leg.* 909b3–5.

120  *Resp.* 572e4–73a2 speaks of *magoi* inducing longing in a man, which must mean that *magoi* were known or reputed to perform attraction-spells. The other reference is at *Plt.* 280d7–e5 to the *alexipharmaka* against forces human and divine that is the concern of *mageutike* (sc. *techne*), which means that *mageia* was already by Plato's day thought of as a *techne* or art.

121  *Leg.* 933d7–e5.

122  *Leg.* 933a2–3.

123  Temple-robbers (853e5–6); those entering sacred space still tainted by homicide (866a5–6); those who intentionally kill members of their own immediate family (873a5–6); those over forty who get into a fight (880a3–6); those who strike men substantially older than themselves (880b7); those violently manhandling members of their immediate family (880e6–8); those

striking members of their immediate family (881a7–8); those who strike their mother or father or grandparents (881b3–4); those convicted of bearing false witness on three separate occasions (937c4).

## 2 SORCERERS IN THE FIFTH AND FOURTH CENTURIES BC

1 For a description of the tablets, see Christidis et al. 1999: 67–8.
2 Voutiras 1998: 1 n.1 gives a list of the known curse-tablets from Macedonia.
3 The Sicilian curse-tablets with the exception of those found very recently are conveniently assembled by López 1991.
4 The text of the incantation from Phalasarna is most conveniently found in Jordan 1992; that from Epizephyrian Locris is in Costabile 1999: 29–42, though its identity was not wholly recognized there and will be demonstrated by Jordan in a forthcoming article; the incantation from Selinus, which is now in the Getty Museum, will be published shortly by Jordan and Roy Kotansky.
5 *FGrH* 3 F 47.
6 Graf 1996: 36, esp.: '*Dass die Magiediskussion also erst einmal ausserhalb der Polisgemeinschaft geführt wurde, erklärt das oben bemerkte Paradox, dass Platon die Magie bekämpft, seine Standesgenossen sie anwenden*'. Johnston 1999: 122 with n.100 speaks of there being virtually no constraints on the activities of *goetes* during the Classical Period and takes the legislation proposed by Plato in the *Laws* to imply that in Athens there was no legislation against sorcery; she interprets Plato's failure to cite instances of laws against sorcery in other cities to mean that they too lacked such legislation. The same arguments could be used to show that Plato only proposes legislation in the *Laws* when it is lacking in Athens and other cities, which is manifestly false.
7 MacDowell 1978: 197; Saunders 1991: 303 n.9 and 322 with n.126, where puzzlement is expressed about how magic in light of the assumptions of Greek religion could constitute impiety.
8 Derenne 1930: 232–3; Reverdin 1945: 215–16; Dodds 1951: 204–5 with n.98; Versnel 1990: 115–18, who with Derenne argues that it is specifically the seemingly innovatory character of magical ritual that led to prosecution under the law of impiety.
9 *FGrH* 328 F 60.
10 [Dem.] 25.79.
11 14.6. See further, Ziehen 1934: 2237–9.
12 Harrison 1968: 171; MacDowell 1978: 181–3; Todd 1993: 187; Hunter 1994: 70.
13 The fear expressed at Pl. *Leg.* 910b1–6 that allowing *asebeis* to perform religious rites in private may draw the anger of the gods on the whole city will reflect Athenian thinking about *asebeia*.
14 Roughly the suggestion of MacDowell 1978: 197.
15 56 Hausrath = 56 Perry. On the *recensiones Augustana* and *Accursiana* of Aesop's fables, see Perry 1936: 71–208.
16 Diog. Laert. 5.5.80, on which see Perry 1936.
17 Keller 1861–67: 369–70.
18 On the paraphrasing of fables as school rhetorical exercises, see Morgan 1998: 221–3. The redoing of the sorceress-fable as such an exercise is attested in a papyrus of the second century AD (*P.Haun.* 46).
19 There are at least three grounds for discounting the possibility that the fable was a later invention on the part of someone conversant with the passage in Plato's *Republic* in which Adeimantus describes the actions of those who profess to be able to heal people of the crimes they or their forebears have committed:

there is nothing in the *Republic* about prosecution for *asebeia*; the fable contains a word used in an otherwise unattested sense; the fable really only has a point in a fourth-century Athenian context.

20 Versnel 1990: 117 and Johnston 1999: 113 put a different construction on what the woman was doing: they assume on the basis only of the *recensio Augustana* that the woman used the incantations to appease the dead. That is not what the Greek says and it makes the taunt largely meaningless.

21 The conclusion drawn by Derenne 1930: 230 from the fable that magical practices were vulnerable to prosecution for *asebeia* on the ground that they constituted innovations in cult goes rather beyond what may legitimately be inferred from the fable.

22 19.281.

23 *Sch. in* Dem. 19.281.

24 2.267.

25 2.262–8.

26 40.9.

27 Dion. Hal. *Din.* 11.

28 The source used by Josephus, who must have been someone who had an interest in the history of prosecutions for impiety in Athens, is not beyond reproach. Dover 1988: 145–6 has hypothesized a tract by Demetrius of Phalerum on the prosecutions for impiety undergone by intellectuals in Athens, written to draw attention to the tension that had always existed between the Athenian people and philosophers. That there was a work on roughly that topic seems likely, but it must have had a rather wider compass than just intellectuals, if Ninos was included in it. Nor can absolute confidence be placed in the reliability of the ancient commentator: the story that there was an oracular utterance authorizing Glaucothea to conduct private initiations has certainly been made up to explain why Glaucothea was not prosecuted for the same offence as Ninos (Parker 1996: 194–5 n.152). It does not follow that because one element in a story is patently a fabrication, what remains must also be rejected. That said, it has to be observed that it would take no great ingenuity to make up the story of Ninos' having been charged with mocking the official mysteries.

29 *SIG³* 985 (Philadelphia in Lydia); Philostr. *VA* 4.18, 8.19, 30.

30 1188b31–37. For the Areopagus as the court that took cognizance of homicides caused by poison: Arist. *Ath. Pol.* 57.3.

31 [Arist.] *Ath. Pol.* 57.3.

32 2.181.2–4.

33 157–60, 205–7, 355–6.

34 355–60.

35 MacDowell 1978:149–53.

36 80a2–b7.

37 Hansen 1976; MacDowell 1978: 148–9; Todd 1993: 117–18; Hunter 1994: 135–6.

38 [Arist.] *Ath. Pol.* 52.1.

39 Graf 1986: 27.

40 233, 352–7, 434–42, 497, 509.

41 2.19. At [Arist.] *Probl.* 917a6–7 *thaumatopoiia*, being a mime and playing the pipes are given as instances of the kinds of calling persons of base character choose.

42 1321b4–23.

43 763c3–64c4.

44 *Leg.* 764b1–c4.

45 907d4–910e3.

46 909b6–d2.

47 933d7–e4.

48 932e2–4, 933d1–e4.

49 385–96.

50 Rigsby 1976: 109–14 sees in *magos* a reference to the reputation that the *magoi* of the east had as kingmakers. The basis for the assertion are the words *deinoi magoi te kai tyrannopoioi*, 'clever *magoi* and tyrant-makers', at Pl. *Resp.* 572e4. But it is not clear that the expression means that the persons referred to are eastern *magoi* and not magicians able to implant *eros* in a man and so able to turn him into a tyrant. The translation 'impostor', 'charlatan' (Kamerbeek 1967: 98; Dawe 1982: 132) is unsatisfactory, since it does not capture the denotation of the term but only and somewhat misleadingly one connotation. *Goetes* very often use special effects to make themselves seem to be able to do or to know what either they do not know how to do or do not know. Someone who pretends to knowledge or a skill that he does not possess without taking steps to create the illusion of expertise would not be called a *goes*. Lloyd-Jones' rendering 'wizard' in the new Loeb *Sophocles* hits the nail on the head.

51 1.10 Grensemann.

52 1.29–31 Grensemann.

53 1.33–8 Grensemann.

54 1.32 Grensemann.

55 364b5–c5.

56 The lines from Homer (*Il.* 9.497–501) are part of the speech in which Phoenix tries to persuade Achilles to give up his wrath by arguing that even the gods can be assuaged by prayer and sacrifice. Linforth 1941: 75–85 argues that the *agyrtai* and *manteis* are not to be identified with the persons who provide the hubbub of books. The run of sense strongly suggests that the same group are still the subject and in both parts of the passage the purificatory and healing sacrifices are to be performed in a convivial atmosphere filled with good cheer. Reverdin 1945: 225–6 and Graf 1996: 26 assume that the *agyrtai* and *manteis* are the subject of the passage throughout.

57 910a7–b3.

58 910b5.

59 909a8–b6.

60 910b3–6.

61 908d1–7.

62 932e1–33e4.

63 933a2–b5.

64 *FGrH* 328 F 60.

65 They are sometimes called *Orpheotelestai* and assumed to be the same kind of person as the *Orpheotelestai* whom Theophrastus, writing towards the close of the fourth century, mentions (*Char.* 16.11). These were the persons to whom the man who is excessively afraid of the divine (*deisidaemon*) made an expedition once a month to be initiated, taking with him his wife, if she did not have other obligations, and in her absence the wet-nurse, and in any case the children. But these *Orpheotelestai* exist in a fixed location and perhaps cater to a rather humbler clientele. Boyancé 1937: 9–31; Reverdin 1945: 226–7 maintain that they are not humble *Orpheotelestai* from the crossroads; Plato's target is officially sanctioned mystery-cults such as those at Eleusis, while the seers whom he has in mind are major figures such as Abaris, Mopsus, Epimenides and Onomacritus. What Plato's feelings were about the Eleusinian Mysteries is an

interesting question, but it is not directly at issue in the passages from the *Republic* and the *Laws*. The mystery-ceremonies in them do not take place in the public arena, but in private dwellings; as for the *manteis*, they would seem to belong to the world that Plato knew and not to the legendary or semi-legendary past.

66 Besides *Resp.* 364b6–c2 and *Leg.* 909b2–4 there is a further passage in which Plato speaks of persons of a beastly and greedy cast of mind falling upon guard-dogs, shepherds and their ultimate masters to persuade them that by fawning words and incantatory prayers it is possible to take unfair advantage and suffer no adverse consequence amongst men (*Leg.* 906b3–c2). The female *magos* in the Aesopic fable (56 Hausrath = 56 Perry) who announced that she was an expert in incantations and in laying to rest divine wrath is probably to be imagined doing roughly the same sort of thing that Plato's *agyrtai* and *manteis* did and to have employed her incantations in carrying out that task. For whom she performed the service the fable does not exactly say, although the considerable living she made from her activities suggests that her clients were persons of substance.

67 Cf. [Eur.] *Rhes.* 503, 715.

68 *Agyrtai* who are *manteis*: Soph. *OT* 387–90; Pl. *Resp.* 364b5; Plut. *Lyc.* 9.5 (*agyrtikos mantis*). The rôles of seer and priest were not necessarily exclusive: in some cults the votaries of the deity were also seers.

69 1195.

70 1273–4.

71 Cybele is first attested in the Greek world around 600 BC. On the appearance of her cult, see Burkert 1979: 102–4; Graf 1985: 107–15; Parker 1996: 191 with n.140; Roller 1999: 119–85.

72 Pi. *Dith.* 2.8–10 (fr. 70b Snell).

73 fr. 66 K.-A. Hesychius s.v. *agersikybelis* takes Cratinus to be saying that Lampon was both an axe-wielder (*kybelistes*) and an *agyrtes*. There is no doubt a play on the word *kybelis*, 'axe', and on its part in sacrifice, but the real point of the insult lies in the comparison of Lampon to a *Gallos*. Cratinus makes the point by using the feminine termination in -*is*. Hesychius s.v. *kybebis*, in fact, says that the by-form of *kybelis kybebis* was a name for a *Gallos*. In Cat. 63 feminine terminations are used in describing and referring to Attis, once he has castrated himself. A variation on the insult is to be found at Verg. *Aen.* 9.617–20, where the Trojans are ordered as Phrygian females, not Phrygian men (*o vere Phrygiae neque enim Phryges*), to pursue their worship of the *Magna Mater* with flute, drum and castanet. Ultimately insults of this form go back to *Il.* 2.235. Burkert 1979: 104 implies that one of the evil omens which on Plutarch's account of the event preceded the departure of the Sicilian Expedition, namely, the man who standing astride the altar of the Twelve Gods castrated himself with a stone (*Nic.* 13.3–4), is the first reference we have to *Galloi* in the cult of Cybele. The allusion in Cratinus is probably earlier.

74 Lysippus fr. 6 K.-A., a contemporary of Aristophanes and Cratinus, called him an *agyrtes*.

75 Arist. *Rhet.* 1405a19–22. Demosthenes with what was clearly an insult of the same form refers to the mother of Aeschines as a female drum-player (*tympanistria*).

76 fr 47 Wehrli; cf. Ael. *VH* 9.8.

77 Antiphan. fr. 159 *CAF* II.

78 Cf. Parker 1996: 159: 'A cult such as that of the Great Mother probably came to Athens not direct from Phrygia but via Ionia, where it had long been

naturalized. In such a case, were the Athenians receiving a Greek or an oriental cult?'

79  *Lyc.* 9.5; cf. Plut. *Apophth. Lac.* 226d; Porph. *Abst.* 4.3.34.
80  The anachronisms in the passage taken in conjunction with the known tendency of later times to attribute to Lycurgus legislation that cannot possibly have been his make it certain that the passage has no evidentiary value for conditions in Archaic Sparta.
81  Diog. Laert. 10.4
82  *Apophth. Lacon.* 224e.
83  On such men, see Latte 1939: 851–2; Nilsson 1951: 130–42; Fontenrose 1978: 145–58; Garland 1990: 82–5.
84  19.5–9.
85  61.
86  109–30.
87  *IG* 2².1708.5.
88  1045–95.
89  1115–6.
90  970–89.
91  2.8.2.
92  2.21.3.
93  8.1.1.
94  *Pax* 1045, 1120, 1121, *Av.* 983.
95  See MacDowell 1990: 287–92.
96  7.6.3–4.
97  *Pax* 1047.
98  Xen. *Hell.* 3.3.3.
99  He is Evenius, a seer from Apollonia (9.93–4).
100  An unnamed *mantis* present at the court of Polycrates of Samos (3.132.2); Callias (5.44–5); Tellias (8.27.3); Teisamenus (9.33–6); Hegesistratus (9.37).
101  Callias and Teisamenus.
102  Hdt. 9.93–4.
103  9.95.
104  *Resp.* 364e3–5.
105  [Dem.] 25.80.
106  Green 1994: 2.
107  Harris 1989: 98–106.
108  233–38.
109  Strabo (10.3.22) says that some make the Dactyls native to Cretan Mount Ida and others make them incomers, but all suppose that they were sorcerers (*goetes*) and that they had dwelt in the vicinity of the Mother of the Gods on Phrygian Mount Ida.
110  *FGrH* 70 F 104. This is the extent of the fragment of Ephorus in F. Jacoby, *FGrH*.
111  18.259–60.
112  Diog. Laert. 10.4.
113  18.129–30. Empousa was a female apparition (*phasma*) of great beauty, capable of transforming herself into many forms. Hence the nickname bestowed on the woman.
114  Blümner 1918: 8.
115  Changing forms: *Euthyd.* 288b7–8; *Resp.* 380d1–6, 381e8–10, 382a2–5; *goeteia* and *thaumatopoia*: *Resp.* 584a7–10, 602d1–4, *Soph.* 234c2–35b6.
116  1493–9.
117  233–4, 273–313.

118 434–52.
119 4.105.2.
120 *Sch. in* Dem. 19.281. The *neoi* for whom she provides the philtres are, if the word is being used in its normal acceptance, post-ephebic young men who have yet to marry, and not as Versnel 1990: 116 has it, young people.
121 Soph. *Trach.* 1138–40.
122 [Arist.] *Ath. Pol.* 50.
123 Christidis et al. 1999: no. 1.
124 Christidis et al. 1999: no. 4.
125 Christidis et al. 1999: no. 1.
126 Christidis et al. 1999: no. 4; Evangelidis 1935: 257 (n. 23).


## 3 SORCERESSES IN FIFTH AND FOURTH CENTURY ATHENS

1 Plin. *HN* 25.10; Quint. *Inst.* 5.10.25.
2 478–81.
3 1269–74.
4 Pl. *Resp.* 381d4–7.
5 Dem. 19.281.
6 [Dem.] 25.79–80.
7 [Dem.] 25.79–80.
8 [Dem.] 25.80.
9 *FGrH* 328 F 60.
10 For a highly readable account of prostitution in its various forms in Athens in the fifth and fourth centuries BC, see Davidson 1997: 73–136.
11 [Dem.] 59.18–21, 26–31, 108.
12 *FGrH* 115 F 253.
13 *FGrH* 115 F 254.
14 6.19–22.
15 *Mem.* 3.11.1–5.
16 6.21.
17 Xen. *Mem.* 3.11.16–18.
18 303–10 with 179.
19 *DTAud* 70–73.
20 *DTWü* 870.5; *DTAud* 70.3.
21 *DTAud* 70.1–2.
22 *DTAud* 71.
23 *DTAud* 72.
24 *DTWü* 87.
25 5.
26 Theophilus, *Philautos* fr. 11 K.-A.
27 *DTWü* 68.
28 *DTWü* 84a.
29 *DTWü* 84b.
30 *DTAud* 68.
31 122–30, 373.
32 478–82, 509–15.
33 *In noverc.* 14–16.
34 17–19.
35 On the low social standing of the sorceresses of Comedy, see Oeri 1948: 21–45, 48–50.
36 Oeri 1948: 13–18, 39–46; Henderson 1987: 119–20.

37 Bremmer 1985: 289–90; Henderson 1987: 119.
38 Cf. Theopomp. *Pamphile* frs. 41–2 K.-A.; Curt. 5.7.3.
39 *Lys.* 463–6, *Thesm.* 347–8, 730–7, *Plut.* 435–6.
40 Fr. 73–6, 81 K.-A.
41 Fr. 3.1–2 K.-A.
42 Fr. 186 K.-A.
43 20.41.5. Schwartz 1905b: 1855 argues that Diodorus is here drawing on Douris of Samos.
44 fr. 11 *CAF* II.
45 fr. 192 Körte[3] = Plin. *HN* 30.7: *fabulam complexam ambages feminarum detrahentium lunam.*
46 So Oeri 1948: 49; Gomme and Sandbach 1973: 368 incline to think it is a woman.
47 56 Hausrath = 56 Perry.
48 *Resp.* 364b5–c2, *Leg.* 906b3–c2, 909a8–b6.
49 *Char.* 16.13. The squill will be the so-called Epimenidean squill that takes its name from the legendary purifier of that name (Theophr. *Hist. pl.* 7.12.1). So Parker 1983: 231.
50 *De superst.* 166a. The larger context of the passage suggests that the old woman daubs mud about the person of the party purified, which is also what Demosthenes (18.259) says Aeschines did to purify would-be initiates and what the Babylonian magician does to purify Menippus before his descent to the Underworld (Lucian, *Necyom.* 7).
51 1.26 Grensemann.
52 1.39–40 Grensemann.
53 [Dem.] 25.8o.
54 Winkler 1991: 227–8.
55 Fr. 146 Wimmer = Plut. *Per.* 38.2.
56 Much the same story, though to a very different end, is told about the Cynic philosopher Bion of Borysthenes, who had fiercely denounced old women hanging amulets on everything (F 30 Kindstrand), but who, when confronted with the possibility of his own demise, willingly held out his neck to an old woman to put an amulet containing a spell around it, had leather phylacteries bound about his arms and had a branch of laurel placed above his door (Cougny, *App. Anth.* 5.37.14–23; Diog. Laert. 4.54).
57 Women making amulets: Diod. Sic. 5.64.7; old women hanging amulets: Bion Borysth. F 30 Kindstrand = Plut. *De superstit.* 168a; Bas. *Schol. inedit. ad* Greg. Naz. cited by Bast in Koen et al. 1811: 874; Ioh. Chrys. *hom in 1 Cor. PG* 61.105–6.
58 789.
59 384–5 and 395–8. For Hecate as Medea's teacher in magic, cf. Ap. Rhod. *Argon.* 3.529–30.
60 Fr. 534 Radt.
61 *Sat.* 5.19.10: *Medeam describit maleficas herbas secantem, sed aversam, ne vi noxii odoris ipsa interficeretur.*
62 1048–57.
63 843–5.
64 999–1015.

## 4 SORCERERS IN THE GREEK WORLD OF THE HELLENISTIC PERIOD

1 An account not too dissimilar from this is to be found in Green 1990: 52–64, 586–681.
2 The phrase is that of Brown 1970: 17–45 taking issue with MacMullen 1966: 95–127, who argued for a decline in rationality on the part of the Roman élite in the second and third centuries BC as a consequence of their succumbing to the superstitious and magical beliefs of the masses.
3 *Argumentum* a.
4 *Sch. in* Theocr.2.69/70.
5 So Delorme 1960: 120; Sherwin-White 1973: 291.
6 On proprietary palaestrae, see Delorme 1960: 261.
7 Theocr. 2.8, 96–7.
8 Theocr. 2.29, 96.
9 Bean 1980: 92–5.
10 Sherwin-White 1973: 90–110.
11 *IG* 12.3 Suppl. 1389. Cf. Fraser 1972: I 66–7.
12 Theocr. 2.114–15.
13 Paus. 6.17.2.
14 *Metam.* 15. So Sherwin-White 1973: 291.
15 Sherwin-White 1973: 247–8.
16 Sherwin-White 1973: 246–7.
17 9.6.2: *primusque Berosus in insula et civitate consedit, ibique aperuit disciplinam, postea studens Antipater, iterumque Achinapolus, qui etiam non e nascentia sed ex conceptione genethlialogiae rationes explicatas reliquit.*
18 Tatian *Or. ad Graec.* 36.
19 Kuhrt 1987: 43–4, developing the suggestion of Momigliano 1975: 148, advances the hypothesis that Berosus as astrologer and founder of an astrological school on Cos was a figure invented by Greeks in the later Hellenistic Period to give authority to certain predictions. But that hardly explains why Berosus should have been credited with having established a school specifically on Cos and with having been given a statue in a gymnasium in Athens.
20 Schwartz 1899: 316. Answered by Schnabel 1923: 10–13.
21 *SEG* 31.576. Cf. Bowersock 1983: 491; Millar 1987: 126.
22 For decisive reasons against an Alexandrian setting, see Fraser 1972: II 876–8 n.30; and for a Coan setting, see Sherwin-White 1973: 106 n.122.
23 1–16.
24 27–33.
25 51–5.
26 67–90.
27 So Gow 1952: II 33. Faraone 1999: 153–4 holds that Simaetha is a courtesan.
28 40–1.
29 Cf. Theodoret HE 3.86.
30 70–4, 145–54.
31 90–1, 94–101.
32 139.
33 163–4.
34 *DTAud* 5, 10.
35 *DTAud* 13.
36 *DTAud* 1A.1–18.
37 *DTAud* 1A.30–3.

38 *DTAud* 4A.
39 *DTAud* 8.14–16.
40 Ptolem. *FGrH* 161 F4; Plut. *Alex.* 77.7–8; Just. *Epit.* 9.8.2, 13.2.11.
41 *A.P.* 5.205.
42 Niko the Samian: Athen. 5.220f; Niko of Asclepiades: *A.P.* 5.150, 164, 209.
43 15.29.8–9.
44 Ap. Rhod. *Argon.* 4.1668–69; Ov. *Metam.* 7.190–1.
45 On the circumstances in which the Greeks fell to their knees to worship the gods and the types of divinity to which such obeisance was made, see Bolkestein 1929: 23–39; van Straten 1974: 159–89.
46 Nilsson 1967: 159; Burkert 1977: 128.
47 54–6.
48 Theophr. fr. 146 Wimmer = Plut. *Per.* 38.2.
49 1–2.
50 18–21.
51 59–62.
52 F 30 Kindstrand = Plut. *De superstit.* 178d.
53 5.64.6–7.
54 Robert 1965: 265–6.
55 Bruneau 1970.
56 Cf. Diod. Sic. 31.43.1.
57 6.39–40.
58 7.126–7.
59 *Sch.*(a & b) *in* Theocr. 7.127.
60 Winkler 1991: 227 with 240. n.73, where the Assyrian stranger is cited as one of the male ritual experts who in literature are sought out by women in preference to women; Simaetha has gone to him, because 'the local old ladies who knew spells were unable to help'. This misrepresents what we are told in Theocr. 2, where there is no suggestion that Simaetha has gone to the Assyrian after being let down by the old women.
61 Hdt. 7.63.
62 The fundamental discussion of the topic is Nöldeke 1871: 443–68. See also Millar 1993: 227, 454–5 and Millar 1997: 247.
63 *A.P.* 7.417 = Gow-Page, *HE* 3984–93.
64 *Sch. in* 161/62. The same point of view is reflected at a later date in a dialogue of Lucian in which Menippus of Gadara tells of going to Babylon to ask for the help of one of the *magoi*, who are for him the pupils and successors of Zoroaster. His reason for going to them is that they are reputed to know how to gain entrance to Hades through incantations and rituals. When he does get to Babylon, the man whom he finds to help him is a Chaldaean with the splendidly Persian name of Mithrobarzanes (*Men.* 6). Lucan declares that Thessalian witches can trump anything Persian Babylon and Memphis may attempt (6.449–51).
65 Schwartz 1905a: 672 for the case for dependence on Posidonius.
66 2.29.2.
67 *De agric.* 5.4: *haruspicem, augurem, hariolum, chaldaeum ne quem consuluisse velit.*
68 Val. Max. 1.3.3; Liv. *Oxy. Per.* 54.
69 Polyaen. 4.20.1. Cf. Strab. 16.1.6.
70 9.6.2.
71 See Millar 1993: 242–6.
72 *FGrH* 139 F 30 = Arr. *Anab.* 4.13.5–6; Curt. 8.6.16.
73 Plut. *Mar.* 17.1–5; Val. Max. 1.3.4; Frontin. *Strat.* 1.11.12.

74 Plut. *Crass.* 8.4.

75 *Cleom.* 12.4.

76 *FGrH* 87 F 108.

77 Verbrugghe 1975: 193–4 believes that Posidonius visited Sicily after 90 BC and collected information from local families about the two Sicilian Slave Wars.

78 Bar Kokhba, the leader of the Jewish uprising in the time of Hadrian, is credited with having breathed flames from his mouth. He was supposed to have performed the trick by blowing on smouldering straw that he had in his mouth (*stipulam in ore succensam anhelitu, ut flammas evomere putaretur* Hier. *Adv. Ruf.* 3 *PL* 23.502).

79 Diod. Sic. 34/35.2.5–15; Flor. 2.7.4–6.

80 7.3.11.

81 *FGrH* 715 F 33 = Strab. 15.1.60.

82 15.1.70.

83 Diod. Sic. 5.64.7.

84 7 fr. 18.

85 10.3.23.

86 Egyptian: Columella *Rust.* 7.5.17, 11.3.53 with Fraser 1972: I. 440; education in Greek of temple-scribes: Thompson 1994: 75.

87 Fraser 1972: I. 440.

88 *HN* 30.3–4.

89 1. *praef.* 8.

90 On all of this, see Momigliano 1975: 7–8.

91 Suid. s.v. Pases.

92 Plin. *HN* 24.156: *in promisso herbarum mirabilium ocurrit aliqua dicere et de magicis. quae enim mirabiliores? Primi eas in nostro orbe celebravere Pythagoras atque Democritus, consectati Magos.*

93 *HN* 24.159: *nec me fallit hoc volumen eius a quibusdam Cleemporo medico adscribi, verum Pythagorae pertinax fama antiquitasque vindicant, et id ipsum auctoritatem voluminum adfert, si quis alius curae suae opus illo viro dignum iudicavit, quod fecisse Cleemporum, cum alia suo et nomine ederet, quis credat?*

94 *Agr. Orig.* 157 with Plin. *HN* 20.78, 24.158.

95 7.5.17: *sed Aegyptiae gentis auctor memorabilis Bolus Mendesius, cuius commenta, quae appellantur Graece* Χειρόμηκτα, *sub nomine Democriti falso produntur.*

96 *HN* 24.160: *Democriti certe chiromecta esse constat; HN* 30.10: *in tantum fides istis fasque omne deest, adeo ut qui cetera in viro probant, haec opera eius esse infitientur.*

97 24.160–6, 26.18–19.

98 *HN* 24.162.

99 *KAR* 61.22–25. A translation of the tablet with commentary is to be found in Biggs 1967: 70–1.

100 *PGM* VII.411–16. The relevance of this procedure to the Babylonian spell was noted by Reiner 1990: 421–4.

101 *PGM* LXIII.10–14.

102 For the requirement for this procedure that the organ be taken from a living creature: Damogeron-Evax LXVIII.6 Halleux-Schamp; for the requirement in general that the part removed be taken from a living creature: Plin. *HN* 8.83, 28.114 (*bis*),220, 30.20,51,98,100, 32.139; for the further requirement that the creature from which the part has been taken be released alive: *PMG* VII.187–90; Plin. *HN* 29.101,131, 30.99,100, 32.102,133.

103 (1) *Cod.* 1265 of National Library of Athens and *Cod.* 115 of the Historical Society of Athens published in Delatte 1927: 88.5–8; (2) *Cod. Parisin. Gr* 2316 published in *CCAG* VII.3.32.

104 *HN* 29.81 *nec omittam in hac quoque alite exemplum magicae vanitatis, quippe praeter reliqua portentosa mendacia cor eius inpositum mammae mulieris dormientis sinistrae tradunt efficere, ut omnia secreta pronuntiet.*

105 Astrological texts in Palestinian Aramaic that derive from Babylonian exemplars have now been found. See Greenfield and Solokoff 1989: 201–14.

106 *HN* 29.82.

107 *PGM* VII.168–86.

108 *Pap. Holm.* 12 p. 3 Lagercrantz.

109 Cf. Plin. *HN* 19.20, 28.181, 32.141, 35.175.

110 Plin. *HN* 37.169.

111 So Ziegler 1967: 2210.


## 5 MAGIC AS A DISTINCTIVE CATEGORY IN ROMAN THOUGHT

1 For a succinct and trenchant discussion of some of the unexamined assumptions that have affected the interpretation of Roman literature and religion, see Feeney 1998: 1–11.

2 See Kaimio 1979: 21–5.

3 Cf. Plaut. *Pseud.* 712.

4 *Agric.* 5.4.

5 *CIL* 10.104.

6 Graf 1996: 54–7 gives a very different account of the development of the concept of magic in Rome than that given here. He divides the development into two stages: an earlier phase under the Republic in which there existed two groups of ritual practices, taking very much the same form, the one intended to benefit others and the other to harm them and their possessions; neither *veneficia* and *mala carmina* nor ritual techniques for healing were referred to in popular parlance as *magia*, nor again were they associated with what was foreign; a later phase that came into being under the Julio-Claudians and that saw a hellenized Roman élite appropriating the Greek notion of *magia*, applying it to *veneficium* as it had traditionally been conceived and to ritual healing techniques and adding to it astrology to form a new amalgam, which was viewed as Persian and foreign. Such a treatment of the naturalization of the Greek concept of magic in Rome places a great deal of weight on when and in what circumstances the word *magia* first appears and accords much importance to the self-conscious reflections of the educated on the nature of magic.

7 *DTAud* 138.

8 *DTAud* 124–6.

9 *DTAud* 128.

10 *DTAud* 192–3.

11 Poccetti 1979: no. 189.

12 Franciscis and Parlangèli 1960: 28–9 no. 13.

13 Lazzarini 1994: 162–9.

14 Diod. Sic. 16.15.1–2.

15 Corell 1993: 261–8.

16 Varr. *Ling.* 7.107.

17 Varr. *Ling.* 7.97,107; Macrob. *Sat.* 1.6.9–10.

18 Naev. com. fr. 71 Ribbeck = Varr. *Ling.* 7.107.

19 *Mil.* 1398–9.

20 Gratt. *Cyneget.* 399–407.

21 399–400: *quid, priscas artes inventaque simplicis aevi / si referam?*

22 Aymard 1951: 43–63.

23  2.5.6: *in eaque* (sc. *templa*) *remedia, quae corporibus aegrorum adnexa fuerant, deferebantur.*

24  405: *et magnis adiutas cantibus herbas.*

25  *Aul.* 85–6, *Amph.* 1041–4, *Bacch.* 812–13, *Epid.* 221, *Most.* 218–19, *Pseud.* 868–72.

26  *Apol.* 30 = Laev. fr. 27 Courtney. For sorceresses gathering roots, cf. Ap. Rhod. *Argon.* 4.51–3.

27  *Laevius* is Lipsius' conjecture for the manuscripts *Laelium.*

28  fr. 271 Marx: *aetatem et faciem ut saga et bona conciliatrix.*

29  *Boethuntibus* fr. VI Rychlewska: *non ago per sagam pretio conductam, ut vulgo solent.*

30  Non. 23: *Sagae mulieres dicuntur feminae ad lubidinem virorum indagatrices; unde et sagaces canes dicuntur, ferarum vel animalium quaesitores.*

31  Herod. 1.37–47. Cf. Lucian *Dial. meretr.* 7.2.

32  fr. XX (378–82) R³.

33  fr. 646 Kock.

34  Fraenkel 1960: 133–4 argues that the passage is a Plautine invention and does not derive from a Greek model.

35  692–4: *da quod dem quinquatrubus / praecantrici, coniectrici, hariolae atque haruspicae; / flagitiumst si nihil mittetur quae supercilio spicit.*

36  fr. 15 Riese: *ut faciunt pleraeque, ut adhibeant praecantrices nec medico ostendant.*

37  fr. 63 Marx.

38  Petronius (*Sat.* 131.5: *hoc peracto carmine ter me iussit expuere terque lapillos conicere in sinum, quos ipsa praecantatos purpura involverat.*) has a scene in which he uses the verb *praecantare* of the incantation an old woman utters over pebbles that are to be employed in curing the hero of the story, Encolpius, of the impotence from which he suffers. What Encolpius is required to do is to spit thrice into the breast of his garment and to cast into the same spot the pebbles that the old woman had wrapped in crimson thread and uttered her incantations over. It is difficult to say what the force of *praecantare* is in this instance: whether it means no more than intone an incantation over or whether it means intone an incantation that will heal.

39  *In* Hor. *Carm.* 1.27.21: *sagae sunt praecantatrices, quae vel arcessere carminibus mala hominibus possunt vel expellere.*

40  On Gnaeus Gellius, see Münzer 1912: 998–1000.

41  fr. 9 *HRR* = Solin. 2.28; Sil. 8.498–501; for the tradition that the Marsi were the descendants of a son of Circe: Plin. *HN* 7.15, 25.11; Aul. Gell. 16.11.1.

42  Strab. 5.3.6; Cic. *ND* 3.48; Verg. *Aen.* 7.10–22.

43  Dench 1995: 159–66.

44  7.750–60.

45  fr. 575–6 Marx.

46  Cf. Hor. *Epod.* 17.29, *Sat.* 1.9.29; Juv. 3.169, 14.180; Plin. *HN* 21.78, 25.11, 28.19,30; Sil. Ital. 8.495.

47  On the threatening foreignness of the peoples of the Central Apennines, the Marsi, Paeligni and Sabelli, and their association with witchcraft, see Dench 1995: 154–74.

48  *Leg.* 2.26, *Fin.* 5.87, *Tusc.* 1.108, *ND* 1.43, *Div.* 1.46–7, 90–1.

49  *Div.* 1.43: *cum poetarum autem errore coniungere licet portenta magorum Aegyptiorumque in eodem genere dementiam, tum etiam vulgi opiniones.*

50  *HN* 29.81, 30.8, 32.34, 37.155.

51  *HN* 29.81.

52  *HN* 32.34, 37.155.

53  *Carm.* 88–91. The *magus*-epigram is 90.

54  Graf 1996: 37–8 takes it for granted that the Romans should think of Persian

religious practices as impious. The poem is in his view a somewhat frigid exercise in ethnographic learning.

55  Xanthus *FGrH* 765 F 59.
56  217: *subito totam causam oblitus est idque veneficiis et cantionibus Titiniae factum esse dicebat.*
57  Plut. *Lucull.* 43.1–2; Plin. *HN* 25.25; *De vir. illustr.* 74.8.
58  Pliny (*HN* 25.25) says Lucullus died of the effect of the philtre: *ego nec abortiva dico ac ne amatoria quidem, memor Lucullum imperatorem clarissimum amatorio perisse.*
59  For Nepos' *De viris illustribus* as the source of the anecdote, see Wissowa 1901: 1412.
60  *Vat.* 14: *quae te tanta pravitas mentis tenuerit, qui tantus furor ut, cum inaudita ac nefaria sacra susceperis, cum inferorum animas elicere, cum puerorum extis deos manis mactare soleas, auspicia quibus haec urbs condita est, quibus omnis res publica atque imperium tenetur, contempseris, initioque tribunatus tui senatui denuntiaris tuis actionibus augurum responsa atque eius conlegi adrogantiam impedimento non futura?*
61  Hor. *Epod.* 1.5.32–40.
62  Philostr. *VA* 7.11, 8.7; Dio Cass. 74.16.5; 79.11.3; Justin. Mart. *Apol.* 18.3; Euseb. *h.e.* 7.10.4; Greg. Naz. *Contra Iul.* 1 *PG* 35.624; Luc. 6.710; Juv. 6.550–2; *SHA* 17.8.2; *CIL* 6.3.19747. Sacrifice of adults for magical purposes: Theodoret. *h.e.* 3.26 *GCS* 44.205; Socrat. *h.e.* 3.2; Plin. *HN* 30.12.
63  4.493–4: *testor, cara, deos et te, germana, tuumque / dulce caput, magicas invitam accingier artis.*
64  4.480–91.
65  1–10.
66  8: *per inprobaturum haec Iovem.*
67  29: *abacta nulla Veia conscientia.*
68  49–54.
69  51–2: *quae silentium regis, / arcana cum fiunt sacra.*
70  4.1020.
71  79: *per triplicis vultus arcanaque sacra Dianae.* For *sacra arcana* used of the mysteries of Demeter, cf. Ov. *Metam.* 10.436.
72  83–6.
73  87–8: *venena magnum fas nefasque, non valent / convertere humanam vicem.*
74  1.11 Grensemann.
75  99–107.
76  400–1: *non illa metus solacia falsi / tam longam traxere fidem.*
77  405–7: *et magnis adiutas cantibus herbas / an sic offectus oculique venena maligni / vicit tutela pax impetrata deorum.*

## 6 CONSTRAINTS ON MAGICIANS IN ROME

1  *HN* 30.12.
2  Cic. *De rep.* 2.61.
3  For a general account of the circumstances and the intent of the codification, see Heurgon 1973: 169–77; Cornell 1995: 272–80.
4  3.31.8. For discussion, see Ogilvie 1965: 449–50.
5  *HN* 28.17–18: *non et legum ipsarum in duodecim tabulis verba sunt: qui fruges excantassit, et alibi: qui malum carmen incantassit* (cf. *Tab.* VIII.8a: *qui fruges excantassit*, 8b: *neve alienam segetem pellexeris.*
6  Verg. *Ecl.* 8.96–9; Tib. 1.8.19–21; Prop. 4.5.5–20; Ov. *Rem. amor.* 255–60. This accomplishment is to be distinguished from getting trees to leave their place,

which is also something magicians are regularly said to do; cf. Verg. *Aen.* 4.491; Ov. *Am.* 3.7.31, *Her.* 6.88, *Met.* 7.204, 14.406; Val. Flacc. 6.443; Sil. Ital. 8.501; Claud. *In Rufin.* 1.158.

7 For discussion of the two main dates in which the episode is likely to have occurred, see Forsythe 1994: 377–8.

8 *HRR* fr. 33 = Plin. *HN* 18.41–2.

9 *Ceu fruges alienas perliceret veneficiis.*

10 *Veneficia mea, Quirites, haec sunt. nec possum vobis ostendere aut in forum adducere lucubrationes meas vigiliasque et sudores.*

11 So Graf 1997: 107–9.

12 For doubts about the authenticity of the whole story, see Latte 1960: 6–7 = Latte 1968: 840, who in the view of Forsythe 1994: 376–7 fails to take account of details that tend to corroborate the reality of the trial.

13 Beckmann 1923: 8–15 reviewed instances of the use of the verb *excantare* and concluded that it means 'to move by words or song into one's own possession', a conclusion that Fraenkel 1925: 184–5 argued needed modification, since there were instances of the verb that meant no more than 'make to go away'.

14 For discussion, see Gordon 1999: 255–8.

15 *Inst.* 7.3.7: *diversum est genus cum controversia consistit in nomine quod pendet ex scripto, nec versatur in iudiciis nisi propter verba quae litem faciunt: ... an carmina magorum veneficium. res enim manifesta est sciturque non idem esse ... non idem carmina ac mortiferam potionem, quaeritur tamen an eodem nomine appellanda sint.*

16 Quint. *Inst.* 7.3.10: *interim quaeritur in rebus specie diversis, an et hoc et hoc eodem modo sit appellandum, cum res utraque habet suum nomen, ut amatorium, venenum.*

17 *HN* 9.79: *est parvus admodum piscis adsuetus petris, echeneis appellatus. hoc carinis adhaerente naves tardius ire creduntur, inde nomine inposito. quam ob causam amatoriis veneficiis infamis est et iudiciorum ac litium mora, quae crimina una laude pensat fluxus gravidarum utero sistens partusque continens ad puerperium.*

18 Tac. *Ann.* 4.22: *mox Numantina, prior uxor eius, accusata iniecisse carminibus et veneficiis vaecordiam marito, insons iudicatur.*

19 Tac. *Ann.* 4.22.

20 Cf. *Apol.* 25: *aggredior enim iam ad ipsum crimen magiae,* 27: *ceterum ea quae ab illis ad ostendendum crimen obiecta sunt vana et inepta simpliciter vereor.*

21 *Apol.* 90: *missa haec facio. venio nunc ad ipsum stirpem accusationis, ad ipsam causam maleficii.*

22 *Apol.* 90: *respondeat Aemilianus et Rufinus, ob quod emolumentum, etsi maxime magus forem, Pundentillam carminibus et venenis ad matrimonium pellexissem.*

23 Aelius Marcianus, a lawyer of the third century, seems to say that love-philtres (*amatoria venena*) were not punished under the *Lex Cornelia* (*Dig.* 48.8.3), but only *venena* intended to kill a man. But since his discussion is concerned solely with the fifth chapter in the law, that dealing with the making, selling or possession of *venena* intended to kill a man, it may be that all he means is that the *Lex Cornelia* makes no provision for cases in which death results from the use of a love-philtre. The sentence which follows, which is that there is a *senatus consultum* relegating to exile a woman who not out of malice but in an inadmirable fashion causes the death of a woman to whom she has given a drug intended to cause conception, does suggest that his interest is in drugs that cause death.

24 *Dig.* 48.8.12: *idem* (sc. *Modestinus*) *libro duodecimo pandectarum. ex senatus consulto eius legis poena damnatur iubetur, qui mala sacrificia fecerit habuerit.*

25 So Gordon 1999: 258.

26 Paulus, *Sent.* 5.23.15: *qui sacra impia nocturnave, ut quem obcantarent defigerent*

*obligarent, fecerint faciendave curaverint, aut cruci suffiguntur aut bestiis obiciuntur.*
Liebs 1989: 210–47 argues that the *Sententiae* are the product of late third-
century Africa.

27  5.23.14, 17.

28  5.23.17: *magicae artis conscios summo supplicio adfici placuit, id est bestiis obici aut
cruci suffigi. ipsi autem magi vivi exuruntur.*

29  *Inv.* 3.10.42 Rabbe.

30  Garnsey 1970: 110–11 argues on the basis of the exile imposed on the eunuch
Sempronius Rufus by Septimius Severus because he was a magician (Dio Cass.
78.17.2) that the stiffer penalties exacted for *veneficium* mentioned in the
*Sententiae Pauli* are post-Severan.

31  *Polemo* 44–5 Hinck.

32  590.

33  For discussion, see Gordon 1999: 259.

34  There is no hint in either of the two references in Cicero to the necromancy of
Appius Claudius Pulcher that there was anything illegal about it (*Tusc.* 1.37,
*Div.* 1.132).

35  *Apol.* 47: *alterum horum fatearis necesse est, aut illicitum non fuisse in quo tot conscios
non timuerim, aut si illicitum fuit, scire tot conscios non debuisse.*

36  *Apol.* 47: *magia ista, quantum ego audio, res est legibus delegata, iam inde antiquitus
XII tabulis propter incredundas frugum illecebras interdicta.*

37  8.7.

38  *VA* 7.39.

39  *VA* 5.12.

40  *Math.* 3.11.1.

41  *Math.* 7.23.25.

42  *Math.* 4.19.27.

43  *Math.* 6.17.3.

44  *Math.* 7.23.6.

45  *Math.* 3.11.5: *erunt etiam fideiussores et ex hac re maximis periculis conquassantur et ad
humilitatem paupertatemque deveniunt; quod cum illis contigerit, inlicitarum
quarundam artium auctores erunt vel sequestres, vel conscii in quibusdam comprehensi
maximis periculorum laqueis implicantur, ut damnationis animadversione plectuntur.*

46  *Math.* 1.28.18, 3.12.6, 4.9.8, 12.4, 7.23.25.

47  Cf. *Math.* 4.12.4: *aut absconsarum aut inlicitarum litterarum actibus inhaerescunt.*

48  MacMullen 1966: 124–5; Graf 1996: 45–6.

49  Fögen 1993. For further criticism, see Gordon 1999: 259–66.

50  *Coll. Mosaic. et Roman. legg.* 15.3.

51  39.16.8: *quotiens hoc patrum avorumque aetate magistratibus negotium est datum uti
sacra externa fieri vetarent, sacrificulos vatesque foro circo urbe prohiberent, vaticinos
libros conquirerent comburentque, omnem disciplinam sacrificandi praeterquam more
Romano abolerent.*

52  25.1.8–12.

53  The disparaging tone of the expression is guaranteed by the insulting
comparison of Flamininus' sacrificing on the battlefield to such a priest
(*auspicantem immolantemque et vota nuncupantem sacrificuli vatis modo* Liv.
35.48.13). It is not as Liebeschuetz 1979: 4 would have it an instance of the
failure of a Greek to comprehend the niceties of Roman ritual.

54  Tac. *Ann.* 2.32: *facta et de mathematicis magisque Italia pellendis senatus consulta.*

55  57.15.8–9.

56  56.25.5.

57  *Chron. ann. cccliv MGH* IX p. 145: *hoc. imp.* (sc. *Tiberio Claudio*) *primum venenarii*

*et malefici comprehensi sunt; homines XLV, mulieres LXXXV ad supplicium ducti sunt.* I am indebted to Peter Brown for the reference.

58 Dio Cass. 49.43.5.

59 On the power of the aedile, see Nippel 1995: 16–19. Günther 1964: 254 asserts without adducing any evidence that Agrippa expelled the magicians and astrologers because they were on Antony's side and not Octavian's.

60 Liv. *Per. Oxy.* 54.192; Val. Max. 1.3.3: *Cn. Cornelius Hispalus praetor peregrinus M. Popilio Laenate L. Calpurnio coss. edicto Chaldaeos citra decimum diem abire ex urbe atque Italia iussit, levibus et ineptis ingeniis fallaci siderum interpretatione quaestuosam mendaciis suis caliginem iniecientes.*

61 Val. Max. 1.3.3: *idem Iudaeos, qui Sabazi Iovis cultu Romanos inficere mores conati, repetere domos suas coegit.* This is Iulius Paris' epitome of Valerius Maximus. Nepotianus, the other epitomator tells essentially the same story (*pace* Schäfer 1997a: 106–7) with one addition, Hispalis' destruction of private Jewish altars in public places (*Iudaeos quoque, qui Romanis sacra tradere sua conati erant, idem Hispalus urbe exterminavit arasque privatas e publicis locis abiecit*). Behind Jupiter Sabazius is likely to lie Iao Sabaoth rather than a syncretism of the Phrygian god Sabazius and the Jewish God (Schäfer 1997a: 51).

62 Liv. 4.30.9, 25.1.8, 39.8.4.

63 So Beard et al. 1998: 113.

64 Cic. *Div.* 1.92: *senatus decrevit ...ut de principum filiis sex singulis Etruriae populis in disciplinam traderentur, ne ars tanta propter tenuitatem hominum a religionis auctoritate abduceretur ad mercedem atque quaestum*; cf. Val. Max. 1.1.3.

65 Plaut. *Mil.* 692–4; Cato *Agric.* 5.4.

66 Plut. *Sull.* 5.9–11, 37.1–2.

67 2.24.3: *et in iis quidam magi ex notis corporis respondissent caelestem eius vitam et memoriam futuram.*

68 Jer. *Chron.*: *Anaxilaus Larisaeus Pythagoricus et magus ab Augusto urbe Italiaque pellitur.*

69 *P.Yale* Inv. 299. Originally published by Parássoglou 1976 and substantially improved by Rea 1977.

70 Frankfurter 1998: 147–61.

71 Vv. 4–9.

72 V.7.

73 Parássoglou 1976: 265–7.

74 Vett. Val. 4.15.4.

75 Hephaest. 2.23.7.

76 19.23–41.

77 1.10.

78 *VA* 6.41.

79 *VA* 4.18.

80 *VA* 8.19.

81 *VA* 8.30.

82 *SIG*[3] 985 = *LSAM* 20. Sokolowski 1955: 56–7 suggests that the interest the founder of the cult in Philadelphia takes in the moral probity of those who are to be admitted to the shrine is unusual and makes him more of a mystic and philosopher than someone concerned only to promote a cult. He is followed in this by Betz 1994: 253. Parker 1983: 74 n.4 also views the regulations as exceptional, but because of their severity in permanently excluding those who have committed sexual offences. It is not quite fair to say that Dionysus is concerned to prevent those who are guilty of moral failings from participating in the cult; his concern is really with those who are implicated in magic-working

or who are sexually tainted in some way. That the regulations are exceptionally rigorous is not to be gainsaid. They may nonetheless represent a fairly widespread feeling that the gods were deeply offended by certain sexual offences. The young Apollonius, for instance, forbids the priest of Asclepius at Aegeae to grant entry to the sanctuary to a rich Cilician who had had sexual relations with his stepdaughter, because he was impure (Philostr. *VA* 1.11).

83  1–14.
84  15–18.
85  20.
86  25–46.
87  25–41.
88  *VA* 4.18.
89  910c6–d1.
90  Pl. *Leg.* 910a7–b6.


## 7  SORCERERS AND SORCERESSES UNTIL THE EARLY EMPIRE

1  692–4.
2  *Telamo* 319–23 Vahlen.
3  *Harioli* or *hariolae*: *Amph.* 1132–3, *Poen.* 791–3; *superstitiosi* or *superstitiosae*: *Amph.* 323, *Curc.* 397, *Rud.* 1139–40.
4  *Agr.* 5.4.
5  Cic. *Div.* 1.4: *ex quo genere saepe hariolorum etiam et vatum furibundas praedictiones, ut Octaviano bello Corneli Culleoli, audiendas putaverunt.*
6  *Div.* 1.132.
7  *Agr.* 5.4.
8  Liv. *Per. Oxy.* 54.192; Val. Max. 1.3.2.
9  *Div.* 2.99.
10  *Div.* 1.132.
11  Cf. Hor. *Sat.* 1.6.113–14: *fallacem circum propter vespertinumque pererro / saepe forum; adsisto divinis*; Liv. 39.16.8; Juv. 6.582–4.
12  Cic. *Div.* 1.132.
13  *Curc.* 483, *Mil.* 692–4.
14  Plaut *Mil.* 692–4; Cat. *Agr.* 5.4.
15  483–84: *in Velabro vel pistorem vel lanium vel haruspicem / vel qui ipsi vortant vel qui aliis ubi vorsentur praebeant.*
16  *Curc.* 253, *Mil.* 693, *Poen.* 444.
17  Cic. *Div.* 1.132.
18  *Div.* 1.132.
19  Cic. *Div.* 1.132.
20  39.16.8.
21  39.8.3–4: *Graecus ignobilis in Etruriam primum venit … sacrificulus et vates, nec is qui aperta religione propalam quaestum et disciplinam profitendo, animis errore imbueret, sed occultorum et nocturnorum antistes sacrorum initia erant.*
22  Asc. *in Mil.* 45: *Licinium quendam de plebe sacrificulum qui solitus esset familias purgare. Sacrificulum* is Manutius' correction for the *sacrificorum* of the manuscripts.
23  *Mar.* 42.7; cf. App. *B Civ.* 1.326. The source of the story is probably Posidonius (Scardigli 1977: 64). In Plutarch and Appian *haruspices* are rendered by *thytai*, 'sacrificers', which is one of the ways in which *haruspices* is put into Greek (Mason 1974: 54).
24  218–19.

25 221.

26 Turpilius, *Boethuntibus* fr. VI Rychlewska; Lucilius fr. 271 Marx.

27 *In* Hor. *Carm.* 1.27.21.

28 692–4.

29 *Catus vel de liberis educandis* fr. 15 Riese: *ut faciunt pleraeque, ut adhibeant praecantrices nec medico ostendant.*

30 So Münzer 1930: 2001; Scardigli 1977: 28–9.

31 Münzer 1930: 2001 goes too far in suggesting that Posidonius saw the woman as a compatriot.

32 On the sources for Plutarch's *Marius* and for differing views on the reliability of the work, see Weynand 1935: 1365.

33 Plut. *Mar.* 17.1–5; Val. Max. 1.3.4 (Nepot.); Frontin. *Strat.* 1.11.12.

34 Plut. *Mar.* 17.1–5.

35 *Strat.* 1.11.12: *C. Marius sagam quandam ex Syria habuit, a qua se dimicationum eventus praediscere simulabat.*

36 Plut. *Crass.* 8.4.

37 Scardigli 1977: 213.

38 App. *Hisp.* 366–7.

39 Porphyrion *in* Hor. *Sat.* 1.8.25: *memini me legere apud Helenium Acronem Saganam nomine fuisse Horati temporibus Pompei sagam senatoris qui a triumviris proscriptus est.*

40 Wessner 1912: 2840–1.

41 Luc. 6.430–4.

42 3.58–62.

43 *Div.* 1.132: *nunc illa testabor non me sortilegos neque eos qui quaestus causa hariolentur, ne psychomantia quidem, quibus Appius, amicus tuus, uti solebat, agnoscere.*

44 Tib. 1.2.45–6; Ov. *Am.* 1.8.28–30; Hor. *Sat.* 1.8.28–30.

45 Cic. *De div.* 1.105: *quem inridebant collegae eumque tum Pisidam, tum Soranum augurem esse dicebant.*

46 Cf. Cic. *Div.* 1.2, 25, 92, 2.80.

47 2.70: *sed primum auspicia videamus. difficilis auguri locus ad contra dicendum. Marso fortasse, sed Romano facillimus. non enim sumus ei nos augures, qui avium reliquorumve signorum observatione futura dicamus.*

48 On all of this, see Rawson 1985: 302.

49 Cic. *Fam.* 4.13.3.

50 *Schol. Bob. in Vat.* 14 (p. 146 St.): *fuit autem illis temporibus Nigidius quidam, vir doctrina et eruditione studiorum praestantissimus, ad quem plurimi conveniebant. haec ab obtrectatoribus velut factio minus probabilis iactitabatur, quamvis ipsi Pythagorae sectatores existimari vellent.*

51 14: *volo ut mihi respondeas tu, qui te Pythagoreum soles dicere et hominis doctissimi nomen tuis immanibus et barbaris moribus praetendere.*

52 *Schol. Bob. in Vat.* 14 (p. 146 St.): *hoc ipsum plenissime purgavit atque defendit et non sine laude protulit in ea oratione quam pro ipso Vatinio scribere adgressus est.*

53 30–2.

54 *Schol. Bob. in Vat.* 14 (p. 146 St.).

55 Cardauns 1960: 47 n.83 suggests that the rumour of child sacrifice arose out of the practice of employing boy-mediums for divination.

56 *Tim.* 1: *denique sic iudico, post illos nobiles Pythagoreos, quorum disciplina extincta est quodam modo, cum aliquot saecla in Italia Siciliaque viguisset, hunc existisse, qui illam renovaret.*

57 *Tim.* 1: *fuit enim vir ille cum ceteris artibus, quae quidem dignae libero essent, ornatus*

*omnibus, tum acer investigator et diligens earum rerum, quae a natura involutae videntur.*

58  1.35: *non reperio causam. latet fortasse obscuritate involuta naturae; non enim me deus ista scire sed his tantum modo uti voluit.*

59  *Chron.* 156 H.: *Pythagoricus et magus.*

60  *Schol. Bob. in Vat.* 14 (p. 146 St.).

61  *Apol.* 42.

62  Noted by Rawson 1985: 182.

63  *HN* 29.138: *magnam auctoritatem huic animali perhibet Nigidius, maiorem Magi, quoniam retro ambulet terramque terebret, stridat noctibus.*

64  *HN* 30.84: *Nigidius fugere toto die canes conspectum eius, qui e sue id animal evellerit, scriptum reliquit.*

65  29.69: *reverti autem ad percussum serpentem necessitate naturae Nigidius auctor est.*

66  Serv. *in Ecl.* 4.10: *Nigidius de diis lib.: quidam deos et eorum genera temporibus et aetatibus dispescunt, inter quos et Orpheus primum regnum Saturni, deinde Iovis, tum Neptuni, inde Plutonis; nonnulli etiam, ut magi, aiunt, Apollinis fore regnum: in quo videndum est, ne ardorem, sive illa ecpyrosis appellanda est, dicant.*

67  *Chron.: Anaxilaus Larisaeus Pythagoricus et magus ab Augusto urbe Italiaque pellitur.*

68  *haer.* 1.7.1–2.

69  Ps. Cypr. *De rebapt.* 16 (III.89–90 Hartel).

70  *HN* 19.20, 28.180, 32.141, 35.175.

71  *HN* 19.19; Sext. Emp. *Pyrrh. hyp.* 1.46.

72  *HN* 28.180.

73  35.175.

74  *lusit et Anaxilaus.*

75  25.154: *Anaxilaus auctor est mammas a virginitate inlitas semper staturas.*

76  6.425–34.

77  6.812–15.

78  *Inst.* 5.10.25: *sexus, ut latrocinium facilius in viro, veneficium in femina credas.*

79  *HN* 25.10: *durat tamen tradita persuasio in magna parte vulgi, veneficiis et herbis id cogi eamque unam feminarum scientiam praevalere.*

80  *Chron. ann. cccliv MGH* IX p. 145.

81  1.1.19–24.

82  *Am.* 3.7.27–35.

83  *Am.* 1.14.39–40.

84  2.99–107.

85  1.2.41–56.

86  55–64.

87  Griffin 1985: 1–31.

88  Winterbottom 1984: XIII.

89  Winterbottom 1984: XIV–XVI.

90  [Quint.] *Decl. min.* 385.

91  [Quint.] *Decl. maior.* 14 and 15.

92  *Veneficium, iudices, tota vita meretricis est.*

93  [Quint.] *Decl. maior.* 14.5.

94  14.6: *excogitasti, per quod maritos a coniugum caritate diducas, per quod iuvenum mentes abiungas ab aliis fortasse meretricibus.*

95  *Epod.* 3.7–8, *Sat.* 2.1.48, 8.94–5.

96  61–6.

97  64–9.

98  Hor. *Epod.* 5.69–70.

99  *Epod.* 5.69–70: *indormit unctis omnium cubilibus / oblivione paelicum.*

100  49–60.

101  20–3.

102  Porph. *in Epod.* 3.7: *sub hoc Canidiae nomine Gratidiam Neapolitanam unguentariam intellegi vult.*

103  59–60: *nardo perunctum, quale non perfectius / meae laborarint manus.*

104  41–3.

105  *Epod.* 17.46: *o nec paternis obsoleta sordibus.*

106  *Epod.* 17.4–5: *per atque libros carminum valentium / refixa caelo devocare sidera.*

107  25–8. Cf. *Sat.* 1.8.23–5; Ov. *Metam.* 7.182–3.

108  29–40.

109  41–7.

110  58: *et Esquilini pontifex venefici.*

111  *Epod.* 5.71–2: *solutus ambulat veneficae / scientioris carmine.*

112  7–8: *an malas / Canidia tractavit dapes?*

113  [Quint.] *Decl. min.* 385.

114  [Quint.] *Decl. min.* 385.6.

115  *Ars am.* 2.99–107.

116  105–6: *nec data profuerint pallentia philtra puellis; / philtra nocent animis vimque furoris habent.*

117  75–159.

118  504–44.

119  1, 36–44.

120  38–41: *quia nos libertinae sumus, et ego et tua mater, ambae meretrices fuimus: illa te, ego hanc mihi educavi ex patribus conventiciis, neque ego hanc superbiai caussa pepuli ad meretricium quaestum, nisi ut ne essurirem.*

121  530–1.

122  199–202.

123  192–3: *di deaeque omnes me pessumis exemplis interficiant / nisi ego illam anum interfecero siti fameque atque algu.*

124  139–42.

125  Ov. *Am.* 1.8.5–18; Prop. 4.5.11–18; Tib. 1.5.49–56.

126  Tib. 1.5.49–50: *sanguineas edat illa dapes atque ore cruento / tristia cum multo pocula felle bibat.*

127  Ov. *Am.* 1.8.29–30.

128  So McKeown 1989: 215.

129  9.29.

130  Ov. *Am.* 1.8.2; Prop. 4.5.64, 67–8.

131  Ov. *Am.* 1.8.3–4, 111–12, 114; Tib. 1.5.50; Prop. 4.5.2, 75.

132  Gow and Page, *HE* 2385–90, 356–61 = *A.P.* 7.455, 353; cf. Gow and Page, *HE* 786–93 (Ariston) = *A.P.* 7.457; *HE* 1647–50 (Dioscorides) = *A.P.* 7.229; *A.P.* 7.329 (anon.); Plaut. *Curc.* 139–40.

133  77 (*multibiba atque merobiba*), 79–110b.

134  799–801.

135  18.

136  120–3: *Idem mihist quod magnae parti vitium mulierum quae hunc quaestum facimus: quae ubi saburratae sumus, largiloquae extemplo sumu', plus loquimur quam sat est.*

137  149: *et multiloqua et multibiba, est anus.*

138  541–2.

139  106–8.

140  Cf. Ov. *Fast.* 3.765–6: *cur anus hoc faciat, quaeris? vinosior aetas / haec erat et gravidae munera vitis amat.*

141  6.291, 7.353, 455, 456, 457, 11.409.

142 *PGM* VII.174.

143 *Fast.* 2.571–83.

144 Fr. 27 *HRR.*

145 Fr. 221 *ORR*<sup>e</sup>.

146 6.11a.4.

147 *Rep.* 4.6: *ita magnam habet vim disciplina verecundiae: carent temeto omnes mulieres.*

148 2.1.5: *vini usus olim Romanis feminis ignotus fuit, ne scilicet in aliquod dedecus prolaberentur, quia proximus a Libero patre intemperantiae gradus ad inconcessam venerem consuevit*, 6.3.9: *et sane quaecumque femina vini usum immoderate appetit, omnibus et virtutibus ianuam claudit et delictis aperit.*

149 Dion. Hal. *AR* 2.25.6; Cic. *Rep.* 4.6.

150 3.761: *aptius est deceatque magis potare puellas.*

151 3.759–66.

152 *Am.* 1.8.113–14.

153 4.5.67–70.

154 3.329–38.

155 3.339–48.

156 Luck 1999: 219 is inclined to deny that the rites performed are straightforwardly magical, although he concedes they may be apotropaic. He supposes the old woman not to be part of the family to which the girls belong and to have been summoned from outside to conduct a rite to protect the family against an 'evil tongue'. But the 'Evil Tongue' or *mala lingua*, which to judge from Catull. 7.12 and Verg. *Ecl.* 7.25–8 consists in praising someone to draw a *fascinatio* on them, is not mentioned here, but only the tongues and mouths of enemies (*hostiles linguas inimicaque vinximus ora* 581).

157 2.571–72: *ecce anus in mediis residens annosa puellis / sacra facit Tacitae (vix tamen ipsa tacet).*

158 2.573–82.

159 For a detailed discussion of the ritual, see Tupet 1976: 408–414, who, however, introduces an element that has no warrant in the text, that the girls will each deposit a lead figurine in the vicinity of a member of their family who has died recently (409–10).

160 Causing a woman to fall in love with a man: Prop. 1.1.19–26; Ov. *Ars. am.* 2.99–107; impotence: Ov. *Am.* 3.7.27–35; destruction of hair: Ov. *Am.* 1.14.39–40; blinding a partner: Tib. 1.2.41–50; freeing from love: Tib. 1.2.59–62.

161 Tib. 1.2.53: *haec mihi composuit cantus, quis fallere posses.*

162 2.229–31.

163 1.5.9–16.

164 2.328–31.

165 7.54, 11.49.

166 4.4.

167 126–38.5.

168 1.8.5–6: *sacrificia, nisi ex praecepto domini, ne fecerit. haruspices sagasque, quae utraque genera vana superstitione rudes animos ad impensas ac deinceps ad flagitia compellunt, ne admiserit.*

169 *Agr. Orig.* 5.4.

170 542–7.

171 544–5: *interpres legum Solymarum et magna sacerdos / arboris ac summi fida internuntia caeli.*

172 Dio Cass. 49.43.5.

173 Tac. *Ann.* 2.32; Dio. Cass. 57.15.8–9.

174 *Chron. ann. cccliv MGH* IX p. 145.

175 *denique exstat senatus consultum Pomponio et Rufo coss. factum quo cavetur, ut mathematicis, Chaldaeis, ariolis et ceteris, qui simile inceptum fecerint, aqua et igni interdicatur, omniaque bona eorum publicarentur: et si externarum gentium quis id fecerint, aqua et igni interdicatur, ut in eum animadvertatur 233* Rudorff.

176 57.15.8.

177 Plin. *HN* 30.1–2; Tertull. *De idol.* 39.

178 69–72.

179 75–6.

180 *De merc. conduct.* 40.

181 For a judicious discussion of the problem, see Jones 1986: 78–82.

182 On Lucian's views on philosophers, see Jones 1986: 24–32.

183 Similarly Jones 1986: 80.

184 *CIL* 3.7107.

185 Porph. *Vit. Plotin.* 20.

186 Albin. *Eisag.* 6; Diog. Laert. 3.56, 9.45.

187 9.45.

188 Diog. Laert. 9.41.

189 Diog. Laert. 9.38.

190 The characterization is that of Gundel 1938: 582–3.

191 57.15.7.

192 Tac. *Ann.* 6.21; Suet. *Tib.* 14.4.

193 On the date, see Vouaux 1922: 203–7.

194 For the place of composition, see Vouaux 1922: 207–13, who believes that it was written somewhere in the Greek East and that the topography of Rome and Italy were well known to Christians at this time. Lampe 1989: 99 n.299 argues for Asia Minor, because the work makes no mention of data well known to Christians living in Rome. Bremmer 1998: 13–16 also argues for composition in Asia Minor.

195 4: *videbitis me crastina die, hora circiter septima, supra portam urbis volantem in eo habitu in quo nunc me videtis loquentem nobiscum.*

196 31–2.

197 1 *Apol.* 26.1–2; cf. Iren. *haer.* 1.23.1.

198 *Ann.* 2.27.

199 On the rhetorical element in Tacitus' historical writing, see Woodman 1988: 160–96.

200 2.27: *Firmius Catus senator, ex intima Libonis amicitia, iuvenem improvidum et facilem inanibus ad Chaldaeorum promissa, magorum sacra, somniorum etiam interpretes impulit.*

201 2.28: *donec Iunius quidam temptatus ut infernas umbras carminibus eliceret.*

202 2.30.

203 2.31.

204 2.33.

205 There is a certain Percennius, once a leader of theatrical troupes and now a common soldier, who foments sedition amongst the Pannonian legions when Augustus dies (*Ann.* 1.16: *erat in castris Percennius quidam, dux olim theatralium operarum, dein gregarius miles.*); in the same disturbances a certain Vibulenus, another common soldier, addresses the soldiers from the shoulders of his comrades in inflammatory tones (*Ann.* 2.22: *et Vibulenus quidam gregarius miles.*); a Roman knight called Falanius was charged with having enlisted amongst the priests of the cult of Augustus a certain Cassius, an actor in mimes, who had prostituted his body (*Ann.* 1.73: *Cassium quendam mimum corpore infamem.*); the man responsible for the jerry-built wooden amphitheatre at Fidena which

collapsed with a great loss of life is a certain Atilius of freedman-birth (*Ann.* 4.62: *Atilius quidam libertini generis.*).

206 Cf. *Hist.* 2.61, 78; *Ann.* 2.55.
207 57.15.9.
208 App. *B.C.* 3.9; Cic. *Att.* 14.15.2.
209 Dio Cass. 58.15.3; Tac. *Ann.* 4.29, 6.19.
210 Tac. *Ann.* 4.30, 14.48.
211 Suet. *Ner.* 49.2.
212 Cf. Dio Cass. 62.26.3.
213 *Ann.* 16.30.
214 16.31: *tum interrogante accusatore an cultus dotalis, an detractum cervici monile venum dedisset, quo pecuniam faciendis magicis sacris contraheret.*
215 16.31.

## 8 WITCHES AND MAGICIANS IN THE PROVINCES OF THE ROMAN EMPIRE

1 Fowden 1993: 168–72.
2 MacMullen 1966: 121–4 is ready to dismiss the particular charges made against Apuleius, but prepared to acknowledge that Apuleius' philosophical tastes bring him dangerously close to theurgy; Graf 1996: 61–82 is inclined to believe that it was Apuleius' status as a successful outsider in Oea that led to the main charge against him, while the ancillary charges are the product of misunderstandings.
3 29.
4 Lucian, *Vit. auct.* 2; Apul. *Apol.* 4.
5 Porph. *Vit. Pyth.* 4 records a tradition that Pythagoras had a daughter called Arignote. Arignotus would then be a suitable name for a Pythagorean philosopher.
6 29–31.
7 33–4.
8 Porphyry's doubts are expressed in the *De regressu animae* F288 and F289 Smith (= Augustin. *De civ. D.* 10.9).
9 Suid. s.v. Ioulianos Chaldaios; Claud. *De VI Cons. Honor.* 348–50. SHA *Heliogab.* 9.1 has it that Marcus Aurelius through the spells and consecration performed by Chaldaeans and magicians succeeded in making the Marcomanni the friends of the Roman people (*dictum est a quibusdam per Chaldaeos et magos Antoninum Marcum id egisse, ut Marcomanni p. R. semper devoti essent atque amici, idque factum carminibus et consecratione*).
10 Dio. Cass. 72.8.2–4; Suid. s.v. Arnouphis.
11 246d6–49d3.
12 *De civ. D.* 10.9.
13 *De regressu animae* F289 Smith = Augustin. *De civ. D.* 10.9: *ut videas eum inter vitium sacrilegae curiositatis et philosophiae professionem sententiis alternantibus fluctuare. nunc enim hanc artem tamquam fallacem et in ipsa actione periculosam et legibus prohibitam cavendam monet.*
14 For a judicious account of the relationship of magic to theurgy and a discussion of the elements drawn from magic that have been taken into the *Chaldaean Oracles*, see Johnston 1990: 77–148.
15 Proclus' biographer and pupil, Marinus, says that Proclus employed *iynges* to induce rain when Attica was suffering from a drought (*Vit. Procl.* 28). Michael Psellus (*Opusc. min.* II.133–4 O'Meara) provides a description of the form taken

by the *iynx* used by theurgists, which he says was known as Hecate's wheel
(*Hekatikos strophalos*).

16  Eunap. *VS* 5.1.7–10.
17  Eunap. *VS* 5.1.12–15.
18  Eunap. *VS* 5.2.2–9.
19  For a characterization of the basic nature of Gnosticism, see Rudolph 1983: 55.
20  Acts 8.9–25; Justin. *Apol.* 1.26.2–4; Iren. *haer.* 1.16.3.
21  *haer.* 1.7.2.
22  2.9.14.1–8.
23  See Dieterich 1921: 40–1; Hopfner 1983: I.780.
24  *PGM* IV.562–3.
25  *Mus. script. Gr.* p. 277 Jan.
26  21, 26.
27  *Alex.* 5.
28  *VA* 1.2.
29  *VA* 1.4–13.
30  *VA* 1.13.
31  *VA* 1.14–17.
32  Philostr. *VA* 4.10.
33  *PGM* IV.26–53, 161–221, 261–86, 475–829.
34  *PGM* IV.2441–56.
35  15.677d-f.
36  XV.1–4 Heitsch.
37  The most recent discussion of the poem and of the identity of its author is by
    Bowie 1990: 80–3.
38  The *testimonia* for his life are to be found at *FGrH* 616.
39  *FGrH* 616 T 4 = Joseph. *Ap.* 2.28.
40  *FGrH* 616 T 10a = Gell. *NA* 5.14.
41  *FGrH* 616 T 13 = Plin. *HN praef.* 25.
42  *FGrH* 616 T 10a = *NA* 5.14.
43  *FGrH* 616 F 5 = Gell. *NA* 5.14.5.
44  The inscription is perhaps the earliest incised on the Colossus. It was above all
    Hadrian who contributed to the popularity of paying a visit to the monument
    (Bernand and Bernand 1960: 165).
45  Bernand and Bernand 1960: no. 71.
46  *HN* 30.18.
47  *HN* 24.167.
48  *HN* 30.18: *seque evocasse umbras ad percunctandum Homerum, quanam patria
    quibusque parentibus genitus esset, non tamen ausus profiteri, quid sibi respondisse
    diceret.*
49  Suid. s.v. Pases.
50  34–6.
51  [*Clem. Hom.*] 2.30.2.
52  [*Clem. Hom.*] 4.6.
53  [*Clem. Hom.*] 5.2–19.
54  *Philopseud.* 34.
55  The Greek version is printed in *CCAG* VIII.III.134–65; the Latin in *CCAG*
    VIII.IV.253–62. Both versions have also been edited and printed in parallel
    columns by Friedrich 1968. There is an account of the work in English by Smith
    1978: 172–85.
56  *CCAG* VIII.III.164–5.
57  1–28 Friedrich.

58 Lucian, *Philopseud.* 31.
59 *VA* 7.39.
60 *VA* 6.10.
61 *haer.* 4.32.1, 39.1.
62 *haer.* 4.32.2, 35.4, 36.1, 37.2,3.
63 *De merc. conduct.* 27, 40.
64 *Alex.* 11.
65 3–4.
66 5.
67 *VA* 1.2.
68 Orig. *Cels.* 1.38.
69 40.
70 6–7.
71 Luc. *Alex.* 4; Philostr. *VA* 1.7.
72 13.5–12.
73 On the identity of Sergius Paullus and on his influence on Paul, see Mitchell 1993: II.5–8 and more briefly Mitchell and Waelkens 1998: 11–12.
74 *HN* 30.11: *est et alia magices factio a Mose et Janne et Lotape ac Iudaeis pendens, sed multis milibus annorum post Zoroastrem. tanto recentior est Cypria.*
75 *AJ* 20.142.
76 Lucian, *Alex.* 6. The Greek term used, *pacheis*, which means literally 'thick', or 'fat', carries connotations of both wealth and stupidity when used metaphorically of persons.
77 On *planos* as the equivalent of *goes*, see Samain 1938: 457–64.
78 Just. *dial.* 69.6–7; Pall. *v.Chrys.* 49 Coleman-Norton.
79 13.3.
80 Vett. Val. 1.3.29, 2.17.57.
81 Vett. Val. 1.3.29, 2.17.57.
82 Vett. Val. 2.17.57.
83 16. The *Traditio*, originally written in Greek, exists only in Coptic, Arabic and Ethiopic versions and in part in Latin (Schwartz 1963: 270–1; Botte 1984: 18–19; Bradshaw 1992: 89–91).
84 Funk 1905: 537 translates the word by '*captator carminum magicorum*', that is, 'one who seeks out spells'; Lampe, *Greek Patristic Lexicon* s.v. more correctly gives 'a charmer of wild beasts', but the parallel he cites from Thdt. *Ps.* 57.6 makes 'snake-charmer' virtually certain. Metzger 1987: III.289 avoids the issue with '*enchanteur*'.
85 8.32.11.
86 1.4.1–5.
87 1.3.1.
88 Cels. 5.27.3c; *Dig.* 47.11.10.
89 Lucian, *Alex.* 6.
90 47.9: *ego putabam petauristarios intrasse et porcos, sicut in circulis mos est, portenta aliqua facturos.*
91 Plin. *Ep.* 4.7.6; Quint. 2.4.15, 10.1.8.
92 Petr. *Sat.* 68.4–7.
93 *Apol.* 23, *Idol.* 9, *Praescript. haer.* 43, *Carn. Christ.* 5.
94 Philostr. *VA* 4.39.
95 Philostr. *VA* 5.9.
96 *VA* 5.42.
97 *VA* 8.7.
98 Orig. *Cels.* 4.33; cf. 4.34–5.

99 Orig. *Cels.* 7.36; cf. 7.40.
100 7.9.
101 On the name, see Hopfner 1990: II.2.351.
102 2.28–30.9.
103 3.16.1–2, 17.1–5.
104 3.16.2–4.
105 6.20.18–19.
106 So also Howie 1991: 79 n.95 citing Fehling 1989: 49–57 and his analysis of invented authorities in Herodotus.
107 *Vit. Plot.* 10. The significance of the incident has been much debated by those interested in the history of theurgy within Neoplatonism and Plotinus' part, if any, in it. Cf. Hopfner 1990: II.1.125; Eitrem 1942: 62–5; Dodds 1946: 60–9 = Dodds 1951: 286–91; Sodano, 1958: XXVIII–XXX.
108 19.11–20.
109 M. Ant. *Med.* 1.6; Lucian, *Philops.* 15–16.
110 *haer.* 1.23.4.
111 19.19.
112 *AJ* 8.45.
113 *AJ* 8.45–48.
114 *AJ* 8.49.
115 16.
116 173.
117 Orig. *Cels.* 7.9. Cf. 1.50.
118 32.9.
119 Apul. *Metam.* 8.27–28; [Lucian] *Asin.* 38.
120 Apul. *Metam.* 8.24.2: *unum de triviali popularium faece, qui per plateas et oppida cymbalis et crotalis personantes deamque Syriam circumferentes mendicare compellunt.*
121 Apul. *Metam.* 9.9.3–10.3; [Lucian] *Asin.* 41.
122 Prop. 2.19.9–10; Ov. *A.A.* 1.67–88, 3.387–93; *Tr.* 2.287–301; Tertull. *Apol.* 15.7.
123 Ov. *Ars am.* 77–8, 3.393; *Tr.* 2.297–8; Juv. 6.489, 9.22.24; Mart. 11.47.4.
124 Orig. *Cels.* 7.9.
125 *De Pyth. or.* 407c. Heintz 1997: 61–9 treats this passage and similar passages in which false prophets are attacked and accused of practising magic as a stereotypical invective learned in the schools of rhetoric and regularly used by those who wished to discredit the prophetic and thaumaturgical practices of their religious rivals and opponents. It can hardly be denied that men traduced religious rivals in such terms, but it will not do, as Heintz tends to do, to explain away every passage in which a man is said to be a magician as mere invective with no substance to it. Magicians were a feature of ancient life and were to be found in certain places acting in a certain way. It was precisely the existence of such a reality that people like Polemon, as Heintz 1997: 42 himself seems to recognize, drew on in constructing insulting pictures of their opponents.
126 *De spec. leg.* 3.101.
127 *De spec. leg.* 3.100.
128 *Paed.* 3.4.28.3 SC.
129 Winkler 1991: 228 speaks of the picture Clement paints as though it were a product of Clement's imagination and did not correspond to a reality. He has to dismiss such passages out of his commitment to the view that the old women who offer help in erotic magic and the women who avail themselves of the help are no more than projections on the part of men of their own behaviour onto women.
130 Orig. *Cels.* 1.68.

131 Orig. *Cels.* 3.50.
132 32.9.
133 *VA* 8.7.
134 *VA* 3.17.
135 *VA* 3.17.
136 *VA* 6.10.
137 *VA* 6.11.
138 Orig. *Cels.* 1.68.
139 Hopfner 1974: I.58–60.
140 *PGM* IV.2734–5.
141 *Physiogn.* I.162–63 Förster. Gleason 1995: 8 takes the attack to be a backhanded compliment and testimony to Favorinus' spellbinding powers of oratory. That rather misses the point of an invective that exploits the similarities between a sophist on tour and a vagabond magician and the public performances both put on (Heintz 1997: 42). Holford-Strevens 1988: 74 n.12 suggests, comparing the cases of Apuleius and the sophist Hadrian (Philostr. *VS* 690), that it was Favorinus' all too great a familiarity with magic that had led to the charge.
142 28.
143 *Carn. Christ.* 5.
144 Lucian, *Philopseud.* 13; *Alex.* 24; *PGM* XIII.278–82.
145 Heliod. *Aeth.* 6.14; Luc. 6.615–23; Apul. *Metam.* 2.28.
146 The key passages are Ar. *Vesp.* 1018–20; Pl. *Soph.* 252c6–9; Hippocr. *Epid.* 5.63; Plut. *De Def. Or.* 414e, for whose interpretation, see Dodds 1951: 71–2; MacDowell 1978: 264. Clem. Alex. *Protrep.* 2.11.2 speaks of the continuing popularity amongst the masses of *engastrimythoi* in his own day. Hopfner 1990: II.2.276 remains the standard discussion. By the end of the first century AD, if not earlier, those who specialized in ventriloquistic prophetic utterance were called Pythones, if male, and Pythonissae, if female, a practice that continued into Late Antiquity and held good for the Greek East and the Latin West (Plut. *De defect. or.* 414c; Euseb. *Comm. in Isaiah.* 1.53 *GCS*).
147 Greg. Nyss. *De Python.* Klostermann.
148 1 *praef.*
149 2.69.
150 Orig. *Cels.* 1.68.
151 *Alex.* 11–26.
152 *haer.* 4.34.
153 *haer.* 28.8–9, 41.
154 *VA* 7.39; Lucian *Alex.* 21.
155 Orig. *Cels.* 7.9. Cf. 1.50.
156 Jordan 1985.
157 Jordan 1985: nos. 7.10–11, 9.10.
158 Jordan 1985: no. 4.
159 Jordan 1985: no. 6.
160 Jordan 1985: nos. 1–4.
161 *VA* 7.39.
162 Arnob. *Adv. nat.* 1.43: *quis enim hos nesciat … aut in curriculis debilitare incitare tardare.*
163 Jordan 1985: nos. 1–3, 5.
164 Jordan 1985: nos. 1.17–18, 3.2.
165 Jordan 1985: no. 5.6.
166 Jordan 1985: no. 2.2–3.
167 Jordan 1985: nos. 1.4, 2.5, 3.4–5, 5.4.

168 *Math.* 3.7.7, 9; 5.5.6; 7.26.3; 8.20.4, 23.2.

169 *De superst.* 166a.

170 9.

171 166a.

172 *De spec. leg.* 3.101.

173 4.5.2–3.

174 3.11.1.

175 Wachsmuth 1864: 60–1 cites a spell from Crete quoted by Chourmouzis 1842: 26 n.3; Herzfeld 1986: 110 cites a similar spell currently used that he had got from one expert in taking off the eye. See also Stewart 1991: 233–4.

176 16.16

177 Jordan 1985: no. 8.

178 Jordan 1985: no. 9.

179 1.2, 8.3.

180 4.

181 Lucian's motive in making Athens the setting of the *Dialogues* is a literary one and not the nostalgia to be found in so many Greek writers of the High Roman Empire that looks back longingly to the halcyon period in which Greece was free and her cultural achievements were unmatched. On the tendency to view of most Greek authors of the Roman Empire to view the Greek past in this way, see Bowie 1970: 3–41 = Bowie 1974: 166–209.

182 *Apotelesm.* 4.309–16.

183 *Apotelesm.* 1.256–61.

184 3.44.

185 6.11.

186 For a collection of references to the practice, see Hopfner 1990: II.2.309.

187 2.69.

## 9 CONSTRAINTS ON MAGICIANS UNDER A CHRISTIAN EMPIRE

1 *CTh* 8.16.4, 5, 6.

2 *CTh* 9.16.1, 2.

3 *CTh* 9.16.1.

4 *CTh* 9.16.1: *superstitioni enim suae servire cupientes poterunt publice ritum proprium exercere.*

5 *CTh* 9.16.3: *eorum est scientia punienda et severissimis merito legibus vindicanda, qui magicis adcincti artibus aut contra hominum moliti salutem aut pudicos ad libidinem deflexisse animos detegentur. nullis vero criminationibus inplicanda sunt remedia humanis quaesita corporibus aut in agrestibus locis, ne maturis vindemiis metuerentur imbres aut ruentis grandinis lapidatione quaterentur, innocenter adhibita suffragia, quibus non cuiusque salus aut existimatio laederetur, sed quorum proficerent actus, ne divina munera et labores sternerentur.*

6 See Rike 1987: 8–36; Barnes 1998: 166–7.

7 Barnes 1998: 82–4 presents reasons for thinking that Ammianus had once been a Christian.

8 Barnes 1998: 15, 187–95.

9 So Barnes 1998: 15.

10 On the place of rhetoric in Tacitus' *Histories* and *Annals*, see Woodman 1988: 160–96. Matthews 1989: 8–9 argues that a letter of Libanius (*Ep.* 1138) of the year AD 392 addressed to a Marcellinus from Antioch who was making a name for himself in Rome by giving readings from sections of his writings is the historian. If the identification is correct, there is all the more reason to think that Ammianus may

356

have written his work in a consciously declamatory style. The identification has been contested by Fornara 1992: 328–44, who argued that Marcellinus was not the historian, but a rhetorician from Antioch. Barnes 1998: 54–7 follows him and adds as a supporting argument that the letter is addressed to someone who has recently come to Rome and not a man who has been there for a decade. The strongest reason for thinking Marcellinus is the historian is that the work of the man in question is divided up into many sections for performance (*epideixis*). It is hard to see what other kind of continuous prose composition than a history could have been divided up into sections suitable for declamation.

11  *Ep.* 1063.2.

12  16.8.2: *nam siquis super occentu soricis vel occursu mustelae vel similis signi gratia consuluisset quemquam peritum, aut anile incantamentum ad leniendum adhibuisset – quod medicinae quoque admittit auctoritas – reus, unde non poterat opinari, delatus raptusque in iudicium poenaliter interibat.*

13  19.12.3–6.

14  19.12.9–14.

15  19.12.14: *nam siqui remedia quartanae vel doloris alterius collo gestaret, sive per monumentum transisse vesperum malivolorum argueretur indiciis, ut veneficus sepulchrorumque horrores et errantium ibidem animarum ludibria colligens vana pronuntiatus reus capitis interibat.*

16  Cf. Ioh. Chrys. *hom. 8 in Col. PG* 62.358; Augustin. *Doct. christ.* 2.20.

17  16.8.2: *nam si quis ... adhibuisset*; 19.12.14: *nam si qui ... gestaret.*

18  Cf. Syme 1968: 32: 'No names, he is portentously vague, and he seems to exaggerate grossly when he goes on to denounce the triviality of the charges: a man might be condemned to death for wearing amulets against ailments or for passing among graveyards at night'.

19  29.2.20–3. Maximinus had become *vicarius urbis* in AD 370/71 and was then summoned to Gaul to become the praetorian prefect there. Festus was to go on to become proconsul of Asia, in which capacity in AD 372 he had the philosopher Maximus executed.

20  29.2.24.

21  29.2.25–8.

22  26.12.24: *et quamquam sint multa et varia, quae, ut levius interpretemur, egit asperrime: pauca tamen dici sufficiet, quae sunt nota ac pervulgata.*

23  *CTh* 9.16.4: *Chaldaei ac magi et ceteri, quos maleficos ob facinorum magnitudinem vulgus apellat, nec ad hanc partem aliquid moliantur.*

24  *CTh* 9.16.6: *si quis magus vel magicis contaminibus adsuetus, qui maleficus vulgi consuetudine nuncupatur.*

25  *CTh* 9.16.5: *multi magicis artibus ausi elementa turbare vitas insontium non dubitant et manibus accitis audent ventilare, ut quisque suos conficiat malis artibus inimicos. hos, quoniam naturae peregrini sunt, feralis pestis absumat.*

26  *CTh* 9.16.7: *ne quis deinceps nocturnis temporibus aut nefarias preces aut magicos apparatus aut sacrifica funesta celebrare conetur.*

27  4.3.2–3.

28  *CTh* 9.16.9: *haruspicinam ego nullum cum maleficiorum causis habere consortium iudico neque ipsam aut aliquam praeterea concessam a maioribus religionem genus esse arbitror criminis. testes sunt leges a me in exordio imperii mei datae, quibus unicuique, quod animo inbibisset, colendi libera facultas tributa est. nec haruspicinam reprehendimus, sed nocenter exerceri vetamus.*

29  8.32.11.

30  *LSAM* 20; Philostr. *VA* 4.18, 8.19, 30.

31  Philostr. *VA* 4.18.

32 *Canon* 8 (Rhalles-Potles IV.114).
33 *Canons* 65 and 72 (Rhalles-Potles IV.221 and 232).
34 *Canon* 93 (Rhalles-Potles IV.250).
35 *Canon* 3 (Rhalles-Potles IV.306–7).
36 For discussion, see Riedel in Riedel and Crum 1904: X–XXVI.
37 Haas 1997: 150 goes a little too far in maintaining on the evidence of the Canons that magicians and diviners were ubiquitous in Alexandria.
38 *Canon* 25.
39 *Canon* 71.
40 *Canon* 72.
41 *Canon* 41.
42 *Canon* 36 = Lauchert 76.
43 *Brev. Can.* 110 (*CCSL* 149.296): *ut diaconus aut clericus magus et incantator non sit neque phylacteria faciat.*
44 *Con. Trull. Canon* 61 (Lauchert 125–6).
45 *CTh* 9.16.12: *mathematicos, nisi parati sint codicibus erroris proprii sub oculis episcoporum incendio concrematis catholicae religionis cultui fidem tradere numquam ad errorem praeteritum redituri, non solum urbe Roma, sed etiam omnibus civitatibus pelli decernimus.*
46 On the date of the trial of Priscillian, see Chadwick 1976: 132–8.
47 63 *PO* 2.
48 62–63 *PO* 2.
49 57–70 *PO* 2.
50 70–75 *PO* 2.
51 Trombley 1994: II.40.
52 *Cod. Iust.* 1.11.9. *prooem.*
53 Flemming 1917.
54 Labourt 1904: 131–7.
55 On Constantia's place in the administrative structure of the Late Roman Empire, see Dillemann 1962: 107–9.
56 Flemming 1917: 19.1–2.
57 Flemming 1917: 27.24–9.
58 Flemming 1917: 27.34–6.
59 *Act. Chalc.* 11.73.4; (*ACO* II.i.383).
60 Flemming 1917: 80–5.
61 On the events leading up to the trial and on the trial itself, see Chadwick 1976.
62 Cf. Hor. *Serm.* 1.8.24; Ov. *Metam.* 7.183.
63 Prisc. *Tract.* 1.28 *CSEL* 18.
64 Sulp. Sev. *Chron.* 2.49–51 *CSEL* 1.
65 Prosper. *Chron. ad ann.* 389 (*Chron. min.* 1.462); Isid. Sev. *Vir. inl.* 15 *PL* 83.1092.
66 Isid. Hispal. *Vir. inl.* 15 *PL* 83.1092: *scripsit quemdam librum sub apologetici specie, in quo detestanda Priscilliani dogmata et maleficiorum eius artes libidinumque eius probra demonstrat, ostendens Marcum quemdam Memphiticum magicae artis scientissimum discipulum Manis et Priscilliani magistrum.*
67 Anast. S. *relat.* 49 Nau.
68 See Browning 1977–79: 101–16 and Kyrris 1984: 149–75.

## 10 SORCERERS AND SORCERESSES FROM CONSTANTINE

1 17.
2 1 *apol.* 14.1, 2 *apol.* 5.4, *dial.* 69.1. For full discussion of early Christian views of magic, see Thee 1984: 329–40.

3 *v. Sym. Styl. J.* 130, 234 van den Ven; *v. Martha* 54–55 van den Ven. On the dating of the two lives, see van den Ven 1962: I.77–8, 102–3.

4 *h.e.* 4.10.5.

5 Amm. Marc. 15.7.8: *dicebatur enim fatidicarum sortium fidem, quaeve augurales portenderent alites scientissime callens, aliquotiens praedixisse futura.*

6 Amm. Marc. 15.7.7–10.

7 Flemming 1917: 19.1–2, 27.24–9, 34–6.

8 Cf. Philostr. *VA* 8.7.

9 *Collect. Antiar. Paris.* Ser. A 4.27.6 *CSEL* 65: *turpiter namque Paulino quondam episcopo Daciae individuus amicus, homini qui primo maleficus fuerit accusatus et de ecclesia pulsus usque in hodiernum diem in apostasia permanens cum concubinis publice atque meretricibus fornicetur, cuius maleficiorum libros Macedonius episcopus atque confessor a Mobso combussit.*

10 Flemming 1917: 80–5.

11 For a detailed commentary on the magical techniques employed by Sophronius, see Peterson 1948: 95–102 = Peterson 1959: 333–45.

12 *PGM* V.173–212.

13 Socr. *h.e.* 2.9.

14 Sozom. *h.e.* 4.24.7,10.

15 Anast. S. *relat.* 49 Nau.

16 *v. Theodor.* 159 Festugière.

17 Can. 36 = Lauchert 76.

18 *Serm.* 50.1.

19 *Contra Origenist.* 0209–0258 Orlandi.

20 65–6 *PO* 2.

21 *Akten* 83.

22 *Serm.* 50.1.

23 The demagogue is Pericles and the story, somewhat misremembered and perhaps distorted to meet the needs of the homily, is that found in Plutarch's *Pericles*, where Pericles as evidence of the straits that he is now in shows to a friend visiting him on his sickbed the amulets put around his neck by women (38.2).

24 *hom. 8 in Col. PG* 62.357–9.

25 *catech. 2 PG* 49.239–40.

26 *Fr. de amul. PG* 26.1320.

27 *catech. 2 PG* 49.240; *hom. 8 in Col. PG* 62.357–9.

28 2.30.4–6.

29 *CTh* 9.16.1–2.

30 *Conf.* 4.2: *recolo etiam, cum mihi theatrici carminis certamen inire placuisset, mandasse mihi nescio quem haruspicem, quid ei dare uellem mercedis, ut uincerem, me autem foeda illa sacramenta detestatum et abominatum respondisse, nec si corona illa esset immortaliter aurea, muscam pro uictoria mea necari sinere. necaturus enim erat ille in sacrificiis suis animantia et illis honoribus inuitaturus mihi suffragatura daemonia uidebatur.*

31 *Vit. Ambros.* 20 *PL* 14.36.

32 On the date of the inquiry, see Barnes 1998: 241–6.

33 28.1.19: *Amantius haruspex, ea tempestate prae ceteris notus, occultiore indicio proditus, quod ob prava quaedam implenda, ad sacrificandum ab eodem esset adscitus Hymetio.*

34 28.1.20: *commonitorium repertum est, manu scriptum Hymetii, petentis ut obsecrato ritu sacrorum sollemnium numine, erga se imperatores delenirentur.*

35 28.1.17–23.

36  *PGM* X.24, XXXVI.36.

37  *PGM* XXXVI.37.

38  *CTh* 8.16.9: *haruspicinam ego nullum cum maleficiorum causis habere consortium iudico ... nec haruspicinam reprehendimus, sed nocenter exerceri vetamus.*

39  28.1.8.

40  Sericus was not an organist, but played an instrument. See Löschhorn 1971: 225–6.

41  28.1.19.

42  Wilkens 1983: 49–55 reviews the evidence and comes to the conclusion that in post-Constantinian imperial legislation there is no sign of a worsening in the legal position of Jews.

43  *Conc. Elv.* Canon 50 Lauchert.

44  *Conc. Elv.* Canon 49 Lauchert.

45  Flemming 1917: 80–5.

46  I depend on the account given by Wilkens 1983: 86–7.

47  On Chrysostom's sermons against the Judaizers, see Wilken 1983: 66–8.

48  *Jud.* 1.1 *PG* 48.844.

49  *Jud.* 2.3 *PG* 48.861.

50  *Jud.* 2.3 *PG* 48.861.

51  *Jud.* 1.4 *PG* 48.848.

52  *Jud.* 1.2 *PG* 48.846, 2.3 *PG* 48.861.

53  *Jud.* 8.7 *PG* 48.937–8.

54  *Jud.* 8.8 *PG* 48.940.

55  *Jud.* 8.8 *PG* 48.940.

56  *Jud.* 8.7 *PG* 48.937.

57  *Jud.* 8.5 *PG* 48.935.

58  *mesopent.* (*hom.* X) 97–110 *CCSG* 17.

59  Acts 12.1–4.

60  430–32 *CCSG* 17.

61  *haer.* 30.12.1–8 *GCS* 25.347–8.

62  *v. Sym. Styl. J.* 208–11 van den Ven.

63  Anast. S. *relat.* 50 Nau.

64  For communion as a prophylactic against magic, see Pall. *h. Laus.* 17.9; Cyr. S. *v. Euthym.* 57 *TU* 49.2.

65  *v. Cyr. et Jo. PG* 87(3):3625.

66  6.20.18–19.

67  The suggestion has been made by Rea 1972–73: 92–7 that a lead tablet from the circus in Lepcis Magna, written in Greek and directed at a charioteer and his horses, was the work of a fellow-charioteer anxious to put a rival out of commission. The reasoning behind the hypothesis is that since Lepcis Magna, to judge by its inscriptions, was a predominantly Latin-speaking community, the tablet is unlikely to have been written by or for a native of that community. The party responsible is most likely, accordingly, to have been a charioteer whose home was somewhere in the Greek East and who had come to Lepcis to compete in the circus there.

68  *hom. 12 in 1 Cor. PG* 61.103.

69  *hom. 48 in Jo. PG* 59.321.

70  *Seleuc.* 179.

71  *Seleuc.* 158–65.

72  *Vit. Hilar. PL* 23.36–9.

73  *Vit. Hilar. PL* 23.36.

74  *Conc. Elv.* Canon 62 Lauchert.

75  A similar tale is told by Epiphanius about Josephus the converted Jew (*haer.*

30.12.1–8) and about Symeon Stylites the Younger, who gave water and earth that he had blessed to an old man whose family, cattle and wine had been bewitched by a magician. The old man then sprinkled the water on everyone and everything affected, causing the demons who were persecuting him to vanish and the persons, beasts and wine that had been affected to recover immediately (*v. Sym. Styl. J.* 49 van den Ven).

76 *Vit. Hilar. PL* 23.38–9.
77 *Or.* 35.13.
78 *Or.* 35.14.
79 *Or.* 36.15.
80 *Var.* 3.51.1–2: *frequentia palmarum eum faciebat dici maleficum, inter quos magnum praeconium videtur esse ad talia crimina pervenire. necesse est enim ad perversitatem magicam referri, quando victoria equorum meritis non potest applicari.*
81 *CCAG* 8.198 (*Cod. Par. Gr.* 2423 F. 17).
82 26.3.3.
83 *Anecd.* 1.11–12.
84 Amm. Marc. 29.3.5.
85 28.1.27: *omnes clarissimi, arcessiti in crimen, quod eiusdem conscii veneficii aurigam fovere dicebantur Auchenium.*
86 28.4.25.
87 *CTh* 9.16.11: *quod si quisquam ex agitatoribus seu ex quolibet alio genere hominum contra hoc interdictum venire temptaverit aut clandestinis suppliciis etiam manifestum reum maleficae artis suppresserit, ultimum supplicium non evadat geminae suspicionis obnoxius, quod aut publicum reum, ne facinoris socios publicaret, severitati legum et debitae subtraxerit quaestioni aut proprium fortassis inimicum sub huius vindictae nomine consilio atrociore confecerit.*
88 See Cameron 1973: 156–7.
89 Procop. *Anecd.* 1.11.
90 Procop. *Anecd.* 1.11.
91 Herter 1960: 99–100.
92 So Cameron 1973: 157–8.
93 Amm. Marc. 28.1.8.
94 *Or.* 1.150–1.
95 *POxy.* 2707. See Cameron 1976: 213–14.
96 *Carm.* 23.300–3.
97 *v. Chrys.* 94 Coleman-Norton.
98 *hom. 37 in Mt. PG* 57.427.
99 On the nature of the bias in Procopius' account, see Cameron 1985: 49–83.
100 *Anecd.* 22.27–8.
101 *Anecd.* 9.2.
102 Cf. Cameron 1985: 11.
103 Proc. *Anecd.* 9.4–7.
104 Proc. *Anecd.* 9.8.
105 *hom. 67 in Mt. PG* 58.636.
106 *hom. 37 in Mt. PG* 57.427.
107 Ioh. Chrys. *Jud.* 1.8 *PG* 48.848.
108 Anast. S. *relat.* 49 Nau.
109 *Thdr. 2* 14.2 *SC* 117.
110 *fem. reg.* 1 Dumortier. For the use of hemlock in love-philtres, cf. Ioh. Chrys. *hom. 37 in Mt. PG* 57.257.
111 *hom. 24 in Rom. PG* 60.626–27. For wives being killed by the sorcery of prostitutes, cf. *virg.* 52 *SC* 125.

112 *hom. in 1 Cor.* 7:2 *PG* 51.217.

113 Thdt. *h. rel.* 3.8 SC 234.

114 *BGU* IV.1024.7.9–18. Further discussion in Bagnall 1993: 196–8.

115 Iust. *Nov.* 14 *prooem.*

116 *Is.* 5.158 Trevisan.

117 *catech.* 2 *PG* 49.240.

118 *Ep.* 245.2 *CSEL* 57.582: *execranda autem superstitio ligaturarum, in quibus etiam inaures uirorum in summis ex una parte auriculis suspensae deputantur: non ad placendum hominibus sed ad seruiendum daemonibus adhibentur,* cf. *Doc. christ.* 2.20 *CSEL* 32.

119 Augustin. *Doc. christ.* 2.20 *CSEL* 32, *Serm.* 328 *Rev. Ben.* 51.19, *Serm.* 260D *MiAg* 1.500; Caes. Arel. *Serm.* 1.12, 13.5, 14.4, 50.1, 52.5, 184.4, 204.3.

120 *hom. 7 in Col. PG* 62.358.

121 *Serm.* 52.5.

122 *Jud.* 8.6 *PG* 48.936. For *petalon* used on the lead-sheet of which binding-spells were written: Audollent 155 B 22–3.

123 Augustin. *Doc. christ.* 2.29; Caes. Arel. *Serm.* 13.5, 14.4.

124 *Serm.* 13.5, 14.4.

125 *Fr. de amul. PG* 26.1320.

126 *v. Hypat.* 28.1–4 *SC* 177.

127 Lefort 1958: 5–50, 209–39.

128 Pp. 94–6 in the text printed by Lefort 1958. Van der Vliet 1991: 225–28 identifies the 'water from the theatre' with the oil scraped off athletes by strigils prescribed in various medico-magical recipes. This seems far-fetched.

129 So Krueger 1998: 21–2, who argues that the *Life* reflects conditions in the Cyprus of Leontius' own day, but presents no very convincing instances of anachronisms.

130 *v. Sym. Sal.* 162–3 Rydén.

131 29.2.26: *anum quandam simplicem, interuallatis febribus mederi leni carmine consuetam, occidit ut noxiam, postquam filiam suam ipso conscio curauit accita.*

132 *v. Sym. Styl. J.* 239 van den Ven.

133 Caes. Arel. *Serm.* 184.4.

134 Caes. Arel. *Serm.* 184.4.

135 *Serm.* 56 *Rev. Ben.* 68.34.

136 August. *Serm.* 335D *PLS* 2.778: *remedia inlicita collo suo suspendunt.*

137 *Serm.* 52.5: *aliquas praecantationes adpendamus ad collum.*

138 August. *Serm.* 15A *SL* 41: *remediorum diabolicorum alligator,* De catech. rud. 7: *remediorum sacrilegiorum alligatoribus; Serm.* 335F *Rev. Ben.* 51.21: *remediatorem sacrilegis ligaturis.*

139 *Serm.* 286 *PL* 38.1300: *ergo cum torquetur doloribus, uenit linguae tentatio, accedit ad lectum aut muliercula aliqua, aut uir, si uir dicendus est; et dicit aegroto, fac illam ligaturam, et sanus eris: adhibeatur illa praecantatio, et sanus eris.*

140 *Serm.* 328 *Rev. Ben.* 51.19: *et ueniunt ad illum qui in lecto iacet et dicunt illi uel faciunt ligaturas uel characteres nescio quos, et tentatur et dicitur illi.*

141 On *characteres,* see Hopfner 1983: I.819–20.

142 *Doct. Christ.* 2.20.

143 August. *Serm.* 260D *Miscellanea Agostiniana* (Rome 1930) I.500; Caes. Arel. *Serm.* 1.12, 13.5, 14.4, 50.1, 184.4, 204.3.

144 *Serm.* 335D *PLS* 2.778: *suggerente amico, et mussitante uicino aut uicina ancilla, aliquando et dematricula eius.*

145 *Serm.* 335D *PLS* 2.780: *sed ecce adstat uicinus et amicus et ancilla, etiam dixi, forte dematricula, ceram uel ouum manibus ferens et dicit: fac hoc et saluus eris. quid*

*prolongas tuam aegritudinem? fac hanc ligaturam. ego audivi qui nomen dei et angelorum ibi invocat.*

146  Lucian *Catapl.* 7, *Dial. mort.* 1.1; Clem. Alex. *Strom.* 7.4.26; Ov. *Ars. am.* 2.329–30; Juv. 6.517–18; Mart. 7.54; Apul. *Metam.* 11.16. On the egg in magic: Haussleiter 1959: 737–8 (Greco-Egyptian), 740 (Roman), and 743–4 (Christian); on the egg in this incident: Dölger 1940/41: 59–60.

147  Ov. *Ars am.* 2.329–30; Mart. 7.54.

148  Cf. *Serm.* 335D *PLS* 2.778: *suggerente amico, et mussitante uicino aut uicina ancilla, aliquando et dematricula eius.*

149  *Mulom.* 3.7.3.

150  *Serm.* 52.5: *et cum haec quasi excusans se dixerit: ite, et facite vos quomodo scitis; expensa vobis de cellario non negatur. quasi vero per haec verba possit tam detestabili crimine innoxia deteneri.*

151  *pan. Bab.* 2 77 Schatkin.

152  *subintr.* 11 Dumortier; *pan. Bab.* 2 88 Schatkin; *ACO* 1.1.3.21, 1.1.6.79 Schwartz.

153  *hom. 8 in 2 Tim. PG* 62.650.

154  *pan. Bab.* 2 88 Schatkin.

155  *haer.* 66.1.4–5.2 *GCS* 37.14–22.

156  71 *PO* 2.

157  29.1.41.

158  29.2.2–4.

159  28.1.26.

160  Zacariah, *Vita Severi* 57–70 *PO* 2.

161  75 *PO* 2.

162  57–70 *PO* 2.

163  *T. Kell. Syr./Copt.* 1, *T. Kell. Syr./Copt.* 2, *P. Kell. Syr./Gr.* 1.

164  Worp 1995: 50–4.

165  *P. Kell.* Copt. 35 published by Mirecki et al. 1997: 1–32.

166  Given that the spell is essentially a model to be followed, the layout of the spell within the letter can hardly be designed to enable Valens to tear it off and use it as a 'ready-made amulet' as Mirecki et al. 1997: 3 suggest.

167  Marin. *Vit. Procl.* 6–11.

168  Marin. *Vit. Procl.* 12.

169  *Vit. Procl.* 28.

170  *In rem publ.* 2.64, 324.

171  On the use of vowels and consonants in magic and as symbols for the planets and signs of the zodiac, see Reitzenstein 1904: 288–91; Hopfner 1984: I.150, 775; Dornseiff 1922: 82–4.

172  *In rem publ.* 2.64–5.

173  *In rem publ.* 2.324–25.

174  *Vit. Procl.* 28.

175  *In Tim.* 1.51. For the identification of the performer of initiations with the theurgist, cf. Procl. *In Eucl.* 138.

176  *In Tim.* 3.6.

177  28.1.7: *nanctus hominem Sardum ... eliciendi animulas noxias et praesagia sollicitare larvarum perquam gnarum.*

178  On the unfairness of the characterization of Maximinus, see Barnes 1998: 101.

179  29.2.6.

180  26.2.4–5.

# BIBLIOGRAPHY

Abt, A. (1908) *Die Apologie des Apuleius von Madaura und die antike Zauberei*, RGVV 5.2, Giessen: Verlag von Alfred Töpelman.

Auld, A.G. (1994) *Kings without Privilege: David and Moses in the Story of the Bible's Kings*, Edinburgh: T. and T. Clark.

Aymard, J. (1951) *Les chasses romaines des origines à la fin du siècle des Antonins*, Paris: de Boccard.

Bagnall, R. (1993) *Egypt in Late Antiquity*, Princeton: Princeton University Press.

Barnes, T.D. (1976) 'Sossianus, Hierocles and the antecedents of the Great Persecution', *HSCP* 80: 239–52.

—— (1998) *Ammianus Marcellinus and the Representation of Historical Reality*, Ithaca and London: Cornell University Press.

Bean, G.E. (1980) *Turkey beyond the Maeander*, 2nd edn, London: Ernest Benn.

Beard, M., North, J. and Price, S. (1998) *Religions of Rome I: A History*, Cambridge: Cambridge University Press.

Beckmann, F. (1923) *Zauberei und Recht in Röms Frühzeit. Ein Beitrag zur Geschichte und Interpretation des Zwölftafelrechtes*, Diss. Münster, Osnabrück: von Nolte.

Bernand, A. (1991) *Sorciers grecs*, Paris: Fayard.

Bernand, A. and Bernand, É. (1960) *Les inscriptions grecques et latines du Colosse de Memnon*, Cairo: Institut Français d'Archéologie Orientale.

Betz, H.D. (1991) 'Magic and mystery in the Greek magical papyri', in C.A. Faraone and D. Obbink (eds) *Magika Hiera: Ancient Greek Magic and Religion*, New York: Oxford University Press: 249–59.

—— (1994) 'Transferring a ritual: Paul's interpretation of baptism in Rome', in *Paulinische Studien: Gesammelte Aufsätze* III, Tübingen: J.C.B. Mohr: 240–71.

Biggs, R.D. (1967) *ŠÀ.ZI.GA: Ancient Mesopotamian Potency Incantations*, Texts from Cuneiform Sources 2, Locust Valley NY: J.J. Augustin.

Blümner, H. (1918) 'Fahrendes Volk im Altertum', *Sitzungsberichte der philsophisch-philologischen und der historischen Klasse der Bayerischen Akademie der Wissenschaften zu München, Abhandlung* 6.

Bolkestein, H. (1929) *Theophrastos' Charakter der Deisidaimonia als religionsgeschichtliche Urkunde*, RGVV 21.2, Giessen: Verlag von Adolf Töpelmann.

Botte, B. (1984) *Hippolyte de Rome, La tradition apostolique d'après les anciennes versions*, 2nd edn, Sources chrétiennes 11, Paris: Les Éditions du Cerf.

Bowersock, G. (1983) '*Antipater Chaldaeus*', *CQ* n.s. 33: 491.

Bowie, E.L. (1970) 'Greeks and their past in the Second Sophistic', *Past and Present* 46: 3–41 = M.I. Finley (ed.) *Studies in Ancient Society*, London 1974: Routledge and Kegan Paul: 166–209.

—— (1990) 'Greek poetry in the Antonine Age', in D.A. Russell (ed.) *Antonine Literature*, Oxford: Oxford University Press: 53–90.

Boyancé, P. (1937) *Le culte des Muses chez les philosophes grecs*, BEFAR 141, Paris: de Boccard.

Bradshaw, P.F. (1992) *The Search for the Origins of Christian Worship: Sources and Methods of Study for the Early Liturgy*, New York: Oxford University Press.

Bremmer, J. (1983) *The Early Greek Concept of the Soul*, Princeton: Princeton University Press.

—— (1985) 'La donna anziana: libertà e indipendenza', in G. Arrigoni (ed.) *Le donne in Grecia*, Bari and Rome: Laterza: 289–93.

—— (1998) 'Aspects of the *Acts of Peter*: women, magic, place and date', in J.N. Bremmer (ed.) *The Apocryphal Acts of Peter: Magic, Miracles and Gnosticism*, Leuven: Peeters: 1–20.

Briggs, R. (1996) *Witches and Neighbours: The Social and Cultural Context of European Witchcraft*, London: HarperCollins.

Brown, P. (1970) 'Sorcery, demons and the rise of Christianity: from late antiquity into the Middle Ages', in M. Douglas (ed.) *Witchcraft Confessions and Accusations*, London: Tavistock Publications: 17–45.

Browning, R. (1977–79) 'Byzantium and Islam in Cyprus in the Early Middle Ages', *Epeteris tou Kentrou Epistemonikon Ereunon* 9: 101–16.

Bruneau, P. (1970) *Recherches sur les cultes de Délos à l'époque héllenistique à l'époque impériale*, BEFAR 217, Paris: de Boccard.

Burkert, W. (1962) 'ΓΟΗΣ. Zum griechischen "Shamanismus"', *RhM* 150: 136–55.

—— 1977. *Griechische Religion der archaischen und klassischen Epoche*, Stuttgart: W. Kohlhammer.

—— (1979) *Structure and History in Greek Mythology and Ritual*, Berkeley, Los Angeles and London: University of California Press.

—— (1983) 'Itinerant diviners and magicians: a neglected element in cultural contacts', in R. Hägg and N. Marinatos (eds), *The Greek Renaissance of the Eighth Century* BC: Tradition and Innovation, Skrifter utgivna av Svenska Institutet i Athen, Series 4o, 30, Stockholm: Svenski Institutet i Athen: 115–19.

—— (1992) *The Orientalizing Revolution: Near Eastern Influence on Greek Culture in the Early Archaic Age*, Cambridge, Mass.: Harvard University Press.

Burnett, J. (1930) *Early Greek Philosophy*, 4th edn, London: Adam and Charles Black.

Cameron, Alan (1973) *Porphyrius the Charioteer*, Oxford: Oxford University Press.

—— (1976) *Circus Factions*, Oxford: Oxford University Press.

Cameron, Averil (1985) *Procopius*, London: Duckworth.

Cardauns, B. (1960) *Varros Logistoricus über die Götterverehrung*, Würzburg: K. Triltsch.

Chadwick, H. (1958) 'Ossius and the Council of Antioch', *JThS* n.s. 9: 292–304.

—— (1976) *Priscillian of Avila: The Occult and the Charismatic in the Early Church*, Oxford: Oxford University Press.

Chantraine, P. (1933) *La formation des noms en grec ancien*, Paris: C. Klincksieck.

—— (1968–80) *Dictionnaire étymologique de la langue grecque* I-IV, Paris: C. Klincksieck.

Chourmouzis, M. (1842) Κρητικά, Athens: Elias Christophides.

Christidis, A.-Ph., Dakaris, S., Vokotopoulou, I. (1999) 'Magic in the oracular tablets from Dodona', in D.R. Jordan, H. Montgomery and E. Thomassen (eds) *The World of Ancient Magic: Papers from the first International Samsen Eitrem Seminar at the Norwegian Institute at Athens 4–8 May 1997*, Bergen: The Norwegian Institute at Athens: 67–72.

Cohn, N. (1975) *Europe's Inner Demons*, London: Chatto-Heinemann for Sussex University Press.

Corell, J. (1993) '*Defixionis tabella* aus Carmona (Sevilla)', *ZPE* 95: 261–68.

Cornell, T.J. (1995) *The Beginnings of Rome: Italy and Rome from the Bronze Age to the Punic Wars (c. 1000–264 BC)*, London: Routledge.

Costabile, F. (1999) '*Defixiones* da Locri Epizefiri: nuovi dati sui culti, sulla storia e sulle istituzioni', *Minima epigraphica et Papyrologica* 2: 23–77.

Cunningham, G. (1999) *Religion and Magic: Approaches and Theories*, Edinburgh: Edinburgh University Press.

Davidson, J. (1997) *Courtesans and Fishcakes: The Consuming Passions of Classical Athens*, London: HarperCollins.

Dawe, R.D. (ed.) (1982) *Sophocles, Oedipus Rex*, Cambridge: Cambridge University Press.

Delatte, A. (1927) *Anecdota Atheniensia* I, Bibliothèque de la Faculté de Philosophie et Lettres de l'Université de Liège, Fasc. XXXVI, Liège and Paris: H. Vaillant-Carmanne and É. Champion.

Delorme, J. (1960) *Gymnasion: Étude sur les monuments consacrés à l'éducations en Grèce*, BEFAR 426, Paris: de Boccard.

Dench, E. (1995) *From Barbarians to New Men: Greek, Roman and Modern Perceptions of People from the Central Appennines*, Oxford: Oxford University Press.

Derenne, E. (1930) *Les procès d'impiété intentés aux philosophes à Athènes au $v^{me}$ et au $iv^{me}$ siècles avant J.-C.*, Liège and Paris: H. Vaillant-Carmanne.

Dieterich, A. (1921) *Eine Mithrasliturgie*, 3rd edn, Leipzig and Berlin: Teubner.

Dillemann, L. (1962) *Haute Mésopotamie orientale et pays adjacents*, Bibliothèque archéologique et historique 72, Paris: P. Geuthner.

Dodds, E.R. (1946) 'Theurgy and its relation to Neoplatonism', *JRS* 36: 60–69 = Dodds, E.R. (1951): 286–91.

Dodds, E.R. (1951) *The Greeks and the Irrational*, Berkeley and Los Angeles: University of California Press.

Dölger, F.J. (1940/41) 'Das Ei im Heilzauber nach einer Predigt des hl. Augustinus', *Antike und Christentum* 6: 57–60.

Dornseiff, Franz (1922) *Das Alphabet in Mystik und Magie*, Leipzig and Berlin: B.G. Teubner.

Dover, K.J. (1988) 'The freedom of the intellectual in Greek society', in *The Greeks and their Legacy*, Oxford: Blackwell: 134–58.

Dunbar, Nan (1995) *Aristophanes, Birds edited with introduction and commentary*, Oxford: Oxford University Press.

Eitrem, S. (1942) 'La Théurgie chez les Néo-Platoniciens et dans les papyrus magiques', *Symb. Oslo.* 22: 49–79.

Evangelidis, D. (1935) "Ηπειρωτικαὶ ἔρευναι? I. Ἡ ἀνασκαφὴ τῆς Δωδώνης (1935)', 'Ηπειρωτικὰ Χρονικά 10: 193–260.

Evans-Pritchard, E.E. (1937) *Witchcraft, Oracles and Magic amongst the Azande*, Oxford: Oxford University Press.

Faraone, C.A. (1991) 'The agonistic context of early Greek binding spells', in C.A.

Faraone and D. Obbink (eds) *Magika Hiera: Ancient Greek Magic and Religion*, New York: Oxford University Press: 3–32.

—— (1999) *Ancient Greek Love Magic*, Cambridge, Mass.: Harvard University Press.

Feeney, D. (1998) *Literature and Religion at Rome*, Cambridge: Cambridge University Press.

Fehling, D. (1989) *Herodotus and his Sources* tr. J.G. Howie, Leeds: Francis Cairns.

Flemming, J. (1917) *Akten der ephesinischen Synode vom Jahre 449, Abh. königl. Gesell. Wissen. zu Göttingen*, Phil.-Hist. Kl. n.s. 15.

Fögen, M.T. (1993) *Die Enteignung der Wahrsager: Studien zur kaiserlichen Wissensmonopol in der Spätantike*, Frankfurt-am-Main: Suhrkamp.

Fontenrose, J. (1978) *The Delphic Oracle*, Berkeley, Los Angeles and London: University of California Press.

Fornara, C. (1992) 'Studies in Ammianus Marcellinus I: the letter of Libanius and Ammianus' connection with Antioch', *Historia* 41: 328–44.

Forsythe, G. (1994) *L. Calpurnius Piso Frugi and the Roman Annalistic Tradition*, Lanham, Maryland: University Press of America.

Fowden, G. (1993) *Egyptian Hermes: A Historical Approach to the Late Pagan Mind*, 2nd edn, Princeton: Princeton University Press.

Franciscis, A. de and Parlangèli, O. (1960) *Gli Italici del Bruzio nei documenti epigrafici*, Naples: L'Arte tipografica.

Fraenkel, E. (1925) Review of Beckmann (1923), *Gnomon* 1: 184–85.

—— (1960) *Elementi Plautino in Plauto*, Florence: La Nuova Italia.

Frankfurter, D. (1998) *Religion in Roman Egypt: Assimilation and Resistance*, Princeton: Princeton University Press.

Fraser, P.M. (1972) *Ptolemaic Alexandria* I-III, Oxford: Oxford University Press.

Friedrich, H.-V. (1968) *Thessalos von Tralles*, Beiträge zur klassischen Philologie 28, Meisenheim am Glan: Verlag Anton Hain K.G.

Funk, F.X. (1905) *Didascalia et constitutiones apostolorum* I, Paderborn: F. Schoeningh.

Garland, R. (1990) 'Priests and power in Classical Athens', in M. Beard and J. North (eds) *Pagan Priests*, London: Duckworth: 73–91.

Garnsey, P. (1970) *Social Status and Legal Privilege in the Roman Empire*, Oxford: Oxford University Press.

Ginzburg, C. (1980) *The Cheese and the Worms: The Cosmos of a Sixteenth-Century Miller*, trs. J. and A. Tedeschi, Baltimore: The Johns Hopkins University Press.

—— (1983) *The Night Battles: Witchcraft and Agrarian Cults in the Sixteenth and Seventeenth Centuries*, trs. J. and A. Tedeschi, Baltimore: The Johns Hopkins University Press.

—— (1991) *Ecstasies: The Deciphering of the Witches' Sabbath*, tr. R. Rosenthal, New York: Penguin Books.

Gleason, M. (1995) *Making Men: Sophists and Self-Presentation in Ancient Rome*, Princeton: Princeton University Press.

Gomme, A.W. and Sandbach, F.H. (1973) *Menander: A Commentary*, Oxford: Oxford University Press.

Gordon, R. (1999) 'Imagining Greek and Roman magic', in *The Athlone History of Witchcraft and Magic in Europe* II: *Ancient Greece and Rome*, London: The Athlone Press: 159–275.

Gow, A.S.F. (1952) *Theocritus* I-II, 2nd edn, Cambridge: Cambridge University Press.

Graf, F. (1985) *Nordionische Kulte: Religionsgeschichtliche und epigrapische Untersuchungen zu den Kulten von Chios, Erythrai, Klazomenai und Phokaia*, Bibliotheca Helvetica Romana 21, Rome: Schweizerisches Institut in Rom.

—— (1991) 'Prayer in magical and religious ritual', in C.A. Faraone and D. Obbink (eds), *Magika Hiera: Ancient Greek Magic and Religion*, New York and Oxford: Oxford University Press.

—— (1994) *La magie dans l'antiquité gréco-romaine*, Paris: Les Belles Lettres.

—— (1995) 'Excluding the charming: the development of the Greek concept of magic', in M. Meyer and P. Mirecki (eds) *Ancient Magic and Ritual Power*, Religions in the Graeco-Roman World 129, Leiden: E.J. Brill: 43–62.

—— (1996) *Gottesnähe und Schadenzauber: die Magie in der griechisch-römischen Antike*, Munich: C.H. Beck.

—— (1997) 'How to cope with a difficult life: a view of ancient magic', in P. Schäfer and H.G. Kippenberg (eds) *Envisioning Magic: A Princeton Seminar and Symposium*, Leiden: E.J. Brill: 93–114.

—— (1998) *Magic in the Ancient World*, tr. Franklin Philipp, Cambridge, Mass.: Harvard University Press.

Green, J.R. (1994) *Theatre in Ancient Greek Society*, London: Routledge.

Green, P. (1990) *From Alexander to Actium: the Hellenistic Age*, Berkeley, Los Angeles and London: University of California Press.

Greenfield J.C. and Solokoff, M. (1989) 'Astrological and related omen texts in Jewish Palestinian Aramaic', *JNES* 48: 201–14.

Griffin, J. (1985) *Latin Poets and Roman Life*, London: Duckworth.

Gundel, W. (1937) 'Thrasyllos (7)', *RE* 6A: 581–84.

Günther, Rigobert (1964) 'Der politisch-ideologisch Kampf in der römischen Religion in den letzten Zwei Jahrhunderten v. u. Z.', *Klio* 42: 209–97.

Guthrie, W.K.C. (1965) *A History of Greek Philosophy* II: *The Presocratic Tradition from Parmenides to Democritus*, Cambridge: Cambridge University Press.

—— (1969) *A History of Greek Philosophy* III: *The Fifth-Century Enlightenment*, Cambridge: Cambridge University Press.

Haas, C. (1997) *Alexandria in Late Antiquity: Topography and Social Conflict*, Baltimore: The Johns Hopkins University Press.

Hansen, M.H. (1976) *Apagoge, Endeixis, and Ephegesis against Kakourgoi, Atimoi and Pheugontes: A Study in the Administration of Justice in the Fourth Century BC*, Odense University Classical Studies 8, Odense: Odense University Press.

Harris, W.V. (1989) *Ancient Literacy*, Cambridge, Mass.: Harvard University Press.

Harrison, A.R.W. (1968) *The Law of Athens: The Family and Property*, Oxford: Oxford University Press.

Haussleiter, J. (1959) 'Ei', *RAC* 4: 737–38.

Heintz, F. (1997) *Simon "Le Magicien": Actes 8, 5–25 et l'accusation de magie contre les prophètes thaumaturges dans l'antiquité*, Cahiers de la Revue Biblique 39, Paris: J. Gabalda.

Henderson, J. (1987) 'Older women in Attic Old Comedy', *TAPA* 117: 105–30.

Herter, H. (1960) 'Die Soziologie der antiken Prostitution im Lichte des heidnischen und christlichen Schriftum', *JAC* 3: 70–111.

Herzfeld, M. (1986) 'Closure as cure: tropes in the exploration of bodily and social disorder', *Current Anthropology* 27: 107–20.

Heurgon, J. (1973) *The Rise of Rome to 264 BC*, Berkeley and Los Angeles: University of California Press.

Holford-Strevens, L. (1988) *Aulus Gellius*, London: Duckworth.

Hopfner, T. (1927) 'Philtron', *RE* 20: 203–08.

—— (1974–90) *Griechisch-ägyptischer Offenbarungszauber: Seine methoden* I-II, repr. Amsterdam: Verlag Adolf M. Hakkert.

Hopkins, K. (1965) 'Contraception in the Roman Empire', *Comparative Studies in Society and History* 8: 124–57.

Howie, J.G. (1991) 'Pindar's account of Pelops' contest with Oenomaus', *Nikephoros* 4: 55–120.

Hunter, V.J. (1994) *Policing Athens: Social Control in the Attic Lawsuits, 420–320 BC*, Princeton: Princeton University Press.

Jameson, M., Jordan, D.R. and Kotansky, R.D. (1993) *A Lex Sacra from Selinous*, Greek, Roman, and Byzantine Monographs 11, Durham NC.

Jebb, R.C. (ed.) (1893) *Sophocles, The Oedipus Tyrannus*, Cambridge: Cambridge University Press.

Johnston, S.I. (1990) *Hekate Soteira: A Study of Hekate's Roles in the Chaldean Oracles and Related Literature*, American Classical Studies, Atlanta: Scholars Press.

—— (1999) *Restless Dead: Encounters between the Living and the Dead in Ancient Greece*, Berkeley, Los Angeles and London: University of California Press.

Jones, C.P. (1986) *Culture and Society in Lucian*, Cambridge, Mass.: Harvard University Press.

Jordan, D.R. (1985) 'Defixiones from a well near the southwest corner of the Athenian Agora', *Hesperia* 54: 205–55.

—— 1992: 'The inscribed lead tablet from Phalasarna', *ZPE* 94: 191–94.

Kamerbeek, J.C. (ed.) (1967) *The Plays of Sophocles: Commentaries IV: Oedipus Tyrannus*, Leiden: E.J. Brill.

Kaimio, J. (1979) *The Romans and the Greek Language*, Commentationes Humanarum Litterarum 64, Helsinki: Finnish Society for Sciences and Letters.

Keller, O. (1861–67) *Untersuchungen über die Geschichte der griechischen Fabel*, N. Jahrb. für Phil. und Paed. Supplementband 4.

Koen, G., Bast, F.I., Boissonade, I.F. and Schafer, G.H. (1811) *Gregorius Corinthius et alii grammatici, De dialectis linguae graecae*, Leipzig: A.G. Weigel.

Krueger, D. (1998) *Symeon the Holy Fool: Leontius' Life and the Late Antique City*, Berkeley, Los Angeles and London: University of California Press.

Kuhrt, A. (1987) 'Berossus' *Babyloniaka* and Seleucid rule in Babylonia', in A. Kuhrt and S. Sherwin-White (eds) *Hellenism in the East*, London: Duckworth.

Kyrris, C. (1984) 'The nature of the Arab-Byzantine relations in Cyprus from the middle of the 7th to the middle of the 10th century AD', *Graeco-arabica* 3: 149–75.

Labourt, J. (1904) *Le christianisme dans l'empire Perse sous la dynastie Sassanide*, Paris: V. Lecoffre.

Lampe, P. (1989) *Die stadtrömischen Christen in der ersten beiden Jahrhunderten*, 2nd edn, Tübingen: J.C.B. Mohr.

Latte, K. (1939) 'Orakel', in *RE* 18: 851.

—— (1960) 'Der Historiker L. Calpurnius Piso Frugi', *SDAW, Kl. für Sprach. Lit. und Kunst* nr. 7: 6–7 = *Kleine Schriften zu Religion, Recht, Literatur und Sprache der Griechen und Römer*, Munich (1968): C.H. Beck: 840.

Lazzarini, M.L. (1994) 'Una nuova *defixio* greca da Tiriolo', *A.I.O.N.* fil. 16: 162–69.

Leach, E. (1982) *Social Anthropology*, Oxford: Oxford University Press.

Lefkowitz, M.R. (1981) *The Lives of the Greek Poets*, London: Duckworth.

—— (1958) 'L'homélie de S. Athanase de papyrus de Turin', *Le Muséon* 71: 5–50, 209–39.

Lefort, L.-TH. (1935) 'Athanase, Ambroise et Chenoute', *Le Muséon* 48: 55–73.

Liebeschuetz, J.W.H.G. (1979) *Continuity and Change in Roman Religion*, Oxford: Oxford University Press.

Liebs, D. (1989) 'Römische Jurisprudenz in Afrika', *ZSS RA* 160: 210–47.

Linforth, I. (1941) *The Arts of Orpheus*, Berkeley and Los Angeles: University of California Press.

Lloyd, G.E.R. (1979) *Magic, Reason and Experience: Studies in the Origins and Development of Greek Science*, Cambridge: Cambridge University Press.

—— (1990) *Demystifying Mentalities*, Cambridge: Cambridge University Press.

López Jimeno, Maria del Amor (1991) *Las tabellae defixionis de la Sicilia griega*, Amsterdam: A.M. Hakkert.

Löschhorn, B. (1971) 'Die Bedeutungsentwicklung von lat. *organum* bis Isidor von Sevilla', *MH* 28: 193–226.

Luck, G. (1962) *Hexen und Zauberei in der römischen Dichtung*, Zurich: Artemis.

—— (1985) *Arcana Mundi: Magic and the Occult in the Greek and Roman Worlds*, Baltimore and London: The Johns Hopkins University Press.

—— (1999) *Ancient Pathways and Hidden Pursuits: Religion, Morals and Magic in the Ancient World*, Ann Arbor: University of Michigan Press.

Maas, P. (1944) 'ΕΠΕΝΙΚΤΟΣ', *Hesperia* 13: 36–37.

MacDowell, D. (1978) *The Law in Classical Athens*, London: Thames and Hudson.

—— (1990) 'The Meaning of ἀλαζών', in E. Craik (ed.) '*Owls to Athens': Essays on Classical Subjects for Sir Kenneth Dover*, Oxford: Oxford University Press: 287–92.

McKeown, J.C. (1989) *Ovid, Amores* II, Arca 22, Leeds: Francis Cairns.

MacMullen, R. (1966) *Enemies of the Roman Order: Treason, Unrest, and Alienation in the Empire*, Cambridge, Mass.: Harvard University Press.

Mason, H. (1974) *Greek Terms for Roman Institutions: A Lexicon and Analysis*, American Studies in Papyrology 13, Toronto: Hakkert.

Matthews, J. (1989) *The Roman Empire of Ammianus Marcellinus*, London: Duckworth.

Metzger, M. (1985–87) *Les Constitutions Apostoliques* I-III, Sources chrétiennes 320,329,336, Paris: Les Éditions du Cerf.

Meuli, K. (1935) 'Scythica', *Hermes* 70: 121–76 = *Gesammelte Schriften* II, Basel and Stuttgart (1975): Schwabe: 817–89.

Millar, F. (1987) 'The problem of Hellenistic Syria', in A. Kuhrt and S. Sherwin-White (eds) *Hellenism in the East*, London: Duckworth: 110–33.

—— (1993) *The Roman Near East 31* BC – AD *337*, Cambridge, Mass.: Harvard University Press.

—— (1997) 'Porphyry: ethnicity, language, and alien wisdom', in J. Barnes and M. Griffin (eds) *Philosophia Togata* II, Oxford: Oxford University Press: 241–62.

Mirecki, P., Gardiner, I. and Alcock, A. (1997) 'Magical spell, Manichaean letter', in P. Mirecki and J. BeDuhn (eds) *Emerging from Darkness: Studies in the Recovery of Manichaean Sources*, Leiden, New York and Cologne: E.J. Brill: 1–32.

Mitchell, S. (1993) *Anatolia: Land, Men, and Gods in Asia Minor* I-II, Oxford: Oxford University Press.

Mitchell, S. and Waelkens, M. (1998) *Pisidian Antioch: The Site and its Monuments*, London: Duckworth with The Classical Press of Wales.

Momigliano, A. (1975) *Alien Wisdom: The Limits of Hellenization*, Cambridge: Cambridge University Press.

Morgan, T. (1998) *Literate education in the Hellenistic and Roman worlds*, Cambridge: Cambridge University Press.

Münzer, F. (1912) 'Gn. Gellius (4)', *RE* 7: 998–1000.

—— (1930) 'Martha (2)', *RE* 14: 2001.

Murray, M.A (1921) *The Witch-Cult in Western Europe*, Oxford: Oxford University Press.

Nilsson, M. (1951) *Cults, Myths, Oracles and Politics in Ancient Greece*, Lund: C.W.K Gleerup.

—— (1967) *Geschichte der griechischen Religion* I, 3rd edn, Munich: C.H. Beck.

Nippel, W. (1995) *Public Order in Ancient Rome*, Cambridge: Cambridge University Press.

Nock, A.D. (1972) 'Paul and the Magus', in Z. Stewart (ed.) *Essays on Religion and the Ancient World* I, Oxford: Oxford University Press: 308–30.

Nöldeke, T. (1871) 'ΆΣΣΥΡΙΟΣ, ΣΥΡΙΟΣ, ΣΥΡΟΣ', *Hermes* 4: 443–68.

Oeri, H.G. (1948) *Der Typ der komischen Alten in der griechischen Komödie*, Diss. Basel: B. Schwabe.

Ogilvie, R. (1965) *A Commentary on Livy: Books 1–5*, Oxford: Oxford University Press.

O'Neil, M. (1987) 'Magical healing, love magic and the Inquisition in late sixteenth-century Modena', in S. Haliczer (ed.) *Inquisition and Society in Early Modern Europe*, Beckenham: 88–114.

Orlandi, T. (1985) *Shenute, Contra Origenistas*, Rome: C.I.M.

Parássoglou, G.M. (1976) 'Circular from a Prefect: *Sileat omnibus perpetuo divinandi curiositas*', in A. Hanson (ed.) *Collectanea Papyrologica: Texts Published in Honor of H.C. Youtie*, Papyrologische Texte und Abhandlungen 19, Bonn: Habelt: I.261–74.

Parker, R. (1983) *Miasma: Pollution and Purification in Early Greek Religion*, Oxford: Oxford University Press.

—— (1996) *Athenian Religion: A History*, Oxford: Oxford University Press.

Perry, B.E. (1936) *Studies in the Text History of the Life and Fables of Aesop*, Philological Monographs of the American Philological Association 7, Haverford: The American Philological Association.

Peterson, E. (1948) 'Die Zauber-Praktiken eines syrischen Bischofs', *Lateranum* n.s. 14: 95–102 = *Frühkirche, Judentum und Gnosis*, 1959, Rome: Herder: 333–45.

Pfister, F. (1924) '*Epode*', *RE* Supplementband 4: 323–44.

Poccetti, P. (1979) *Nuovi documenti italici: A complemento del Manuale di E. Vetter*, Pisa: Giardini.

Potter, D. (1994) *Prophets and Emperors: Human and Divine Authority from Augustus to Theodosius*, Cambridge, Mass.: Harvard University Press.

Rawson, E. (1985) *Intellectual Life in the Late Roman Republic*, London: Duckworth.

Rea, J. (1972–73) in J.H. Humphrey, F.B. Sear and M. Vickers (eds) 'Aspects of the Circus at Lepcis Magna', *Libya Antiqua* 9–10: 92–97.

—— (1977) 'A New Version of P.Yale Inv. 299', *ZPE* 27: 15–56.

Reiner, E. (1990) 'Nocturnal talk', in T. Abusch, J. Huehnergard and P. Steinkeller (eds) *Lingering over Words: Studies in Ancient Near Eastern Literature in Honor of William L. Moran*, Harvard Semitic Studies 37, Atlanta: Scholars Press: 421–24.

—— (1995) *Astral Magic in Babylonia*, Transactions of the American Philosophical Society 85(4), Philadelphia: The American Philosophical Society.

Reitzenstein, R. (1904) *Poimandres: Studien zur griechisch-ägyptischen und frühchristlichen Literatur*, Leipzig: B.G. Teubner.

Reverdin, O. (1945) *La religion de la cité platonicienne*, Paris: de Boccard.

Richardson, N.J. (1974) *The Homeric Hymn to Demeter*, Oxford: Oxford University Press.

Riedel, W. and Crum, W.E. (1904) *The Canons of Athanasius of Alexandria*, London and Oxford: Williams and Norgate.

Rigsby, K.G. (1976) 'Teiresias as Magus in *Oedipus Rex*', *GRBS* 17: 109–14.

Rike, R.L. (1987) *Apex omnium: Religion in the Res Gestae of Ammianus*, Berkeley, Los Angeles and London: University of California Press.

Ritner, R. (1993) *The Mechanics of Egyptian Magical Practice*, Studies in Ancient Oriental Civilization 54, Chicago: University of Chicago Press.

—— (1995) 'The religious, social and legal parameters of traditional Egyptian magic', in M. Meyer and P. Mirecki (eds) *Ancient Magic and Ritual Power*, Religions in the Graeco-Roman World 129, Leiden: E.J. Brill: 43–62.

Robert, L. (1965) *Hellenica: Recueil d'épigraphie de numismatique et d'antiquités grecques* 13, Paris: Librairie d'Amérique et d'Orient: 265–66.

Roller, L. (1999) *In Search of God the Mother: The Cult of Anatolian Cybele*, Berkeley, Los Angeles and London: University of California Press.

Rudolph, K. (1983) *Gnosis*, tr. R.M. Wilson and others, Edinburgh: T. and T. Clark.

Samain, P. (1938) 'L'accusation de magie contre le Christ dans les Évangiles', *Ephemerides Theologicae Lovanienses* 15: 449–90.

Saunders, T.J. (1991) *Plato's Penal Code: Tradition, Controversy, and Reform in Greek Penology*, Oxford: Oxford University Press.

Scardigli, B. (1977) 'Echi di atteggiamenti pro e contro Mario in Plutarco', *Critica Storica* 14: 185–253.

Schäfer, P. (1997a) *Judeophobia: Attitudes towards the Jews in the Ancient World*, Cambridge Mass.: Harvard University Press.

—— (1997b) 'Magic and religion in ancient Judaism', in P. Schäfer and H.G. Kippenberg (eds) *Envisioning Magic: A Princeton Seminar and Symposium*, Leiden: E.J. Brill: 19–44.

Schnabel, P. (1923) *Berossos und die babylonisch-hellenistische Literatur*, Leipzig: Teubner.

Schwartz, E. (1899) 'Berossos (4)', *RE* 3: 309–16.

—— (1905a) 'Diodoros (38)', *RE* 5: 66–704.

—— (1905b) 'Duris (2)', *RE* 5: 1853–56.

—— (1963) 'Über die pseudapostolischen Kirchenordnungen', in *Gesammelte Schriften* V, Berlin: de Gruyter: 192–273.

Sherwin-White, S.M. (1973) *Ancient Cos*, Hypomnema 51, Göttingen: Vandenhoeck und Ruprecht.

Smith, J.Z. (1978) *Map is not Territory*, Leiden: E.J. Brill.

Snoek, J.A.M. (1987) *Initiations: A Methodological Approach to the Application of Classification and Definition Theory in the Study of Religions*, Diss. Leiden, Pijnaker: Dutch Efficiency Bureau.

Sodano, A.R. (1958) *Porfirio, Lettera ad Anebo*, Naples: L'Arte tipografica.

Sokolowski, F. (1955) *Lois sacrées de l'Asie Mineure*, Paris: de Boccard.

Stewart, C. (1991) *Demons and the Devil*, Princeton: Princeton University Press.

Syme, R. (1968) *Ammianus and the Historia Augusta*, Oxford: Oxford University Press.

Thee, F.C.R. (1984) *Julius Africanus and the Early Christian View of Magic*, Tübingen: J.C.B. Mohr.

Thompson, D.J. (1994) 'Literacy and power in Ptolemaic Egypt', in A.K. Bowman and G. Woolf (eds) *Literacy and Power in the Ancient World*, Cambridge: Cambridge University Press: 67–83.

Todd, S.C. (1993) *The Shape of Athenian Law*, Oxford: Oxford University Press.

Trombley, F.R. (1994) *Hellenic Religion and Christianization C. 370–529* I-II, Leiden: E.J. Brill.

Tupet, A.-M. (1976) *La magie dans la poèsie latine* I, Paris: Les Belles Lettres.

van den Ven, P. (1962–70) *La vie ancienne de S. Syméon Stylite le Jeune (521–592)* I & II, Subsidia hagiographica 32, Brussels: Société des Bollandistes.

van der Vliet, J. (1991) 'Varia Magica Coptica', *Aegyptus* 71: 217–42.

van Straten, F. (1974) 'Did the Greeks kneel before their gods?', *BABesch* 49: 159–89.

Verbrugghe, G.P. (1975) 'Narrative patterns in Posidonius' *History*', *Historia* 24: 189–204.

Versnel, H.S. (1990) *Inconsistencies in Greek and Roman Religion* I: *Ter Unus, Isis, Dionysos, Hermes: Three Studies in Henotheism*, Studies in Greek and Roman Religion 6, Leiden: E.J. Brill.

—— (1991) 'Some reflections on the relationship magic-religion', *Numen* 38: 177–97.

Vouaux, L. (1922) *Les actes de Pierre*, Paris: Letouzey et Ané.

Voutiras, E. (1996) 'À propos d'une tablette de malédiction de Pella', *REG* 109: 678–82.

—— (1998) ΔΙΟΝΥΣΟΦΩΝΤΟΣ ΓΑΜΟΙ: *Marital Life and Magic in Fourth Century Pella*, Amsterdam: Gieben.

Wachsmuth, C. (1864) *Das alte Griechenland im Neuen*, Bonn: M. Cohen.

Wallace-Hadrill, A. (1994) *Houses and Society in Pompeii and Herculaneum*, Princeton: Princeton University Press.

Wessner, P. (1912) 'Helenius Acron', *RE* 7: 2840–44.

West, M.L. (1971) *Early Greek Philosophy and the Orient*, Oxford: Oxford University Press.

Weynand, R. (1935) 'Marius (14)', *RE* Supplementband 6: 1363–1425.

Wilkens, R.L. (1983) *John Chrysostom and the Jews: Rhetoric and Reality in the Late 4th Century*, Berkeley, Los Angeles and London: University of California Press.

Winkler, J.J. (1990) *The Constraints of Desire: The Anthropology of Sex and Gender in Ancient Greece*, New York: Oxford University Press.

—— (1991) 'The constraints of Eros', in C.A. Faraone and D. Obbink (eds) *Magika Hiera*, New York: Oxford University Press: 214–43.

Winterbottom, M. (1984) *The Minor Declamations ascribed to Quintilian*, Berlin and New York: de Gruyter.

Wissowa, G. (1901) 'Cornelius Nepos', *RE* 4: 1407–17.

Woodman, A.J. (1988) *Rhetoric in Classical Historiography*, London: Croom Helm.

Worp, K.A. (ed.) (1995) *Greek Papyri from Kellis* I, Oxbow Monographs 54, Oxford: Oxbow Books.

Ziegler, K. (1967) 'Zachalias', *RE* 9A: 2210.

Ziehen, L. (1934) 'θεωρίς', *RE* 5A: 2237–39.

# INDEX

Abraham, deacon in Edessa 268–9, 279
Acron, Helenius, commentator on
  Horace 167, 180
*Acts of the Apostles* 158–9, 208, 223, 231,
  247
*Acts of Peter* 196–8, 238
Acusilaus of Argos, mythographer 31
aedile, police powers of 153
Aeschylus, *Agamemnon* 65, 80; *Persians*
  29–30; *Psychagogoi* 30–1; *Xantriai* 80
Aesop, *Fables* 51–2, 91
Afranius, Lucius, *Vopiscus* 132
*ageirontes, see agyrtai*
*agoranomoi* 59, 77
Agrippa, Marcus 155, 192
*agyrtai* (*ageirontes, ochlagogoi, circulatores*)
  61–74, 80, 94, 115–17, 224–43,
  249–50, 265–6, 311–14
*alazon* 70
Alexander of Abonuteichos 209, 220–4,
  240–2
Alexandria 203, 216, 235, 259–60, 279
*alligatores, see* amulets, application of
*amatoria, see* love-philtres
Ammianus Marcellinus 251–4, 285–7,
  296–7, 307, 314
Amphilochus of Iconium 294
amulets (*periammata, periapta, petala,
  ligaturae, remedia*); 24–5, 129–30, 252,
  254, 261, 280–81, 304–11; application
  of 93, 108–9 282–3, 289–90, 308–11;
  dealers 280–8; makers of 261, 280,
  306;
Anastasius of Sinai 271–2
Anaxilaus of Larissa 123, 156, 172–4,
  208
Antioch 288–90

Antiphon 88–9
Antonina, wife of Belisarius 296–8
*apagoge* 57
Apion 213–16
Apollonius of Tyana 159–61, 209–24
Appius Claudius Pulcher 168–9
Apuleius of Madaura 147, 204; *Apologia*
  149, 171; *Metamorphoses* 159, 192, 226,
  229, 233
Arignotus 204–5, 212, 216
Aristophanes, *Birds* 31, 68–9; *Clouds* 42;
  *Knights* 68; *Peace* 68–9, 71; *Plutus* 84
Aristotle, *Magna Moralia* 54–5; *Politics* 59
Arnobius 244
Arnouphis, Egyptian magician 206
*Art of Thrasymedes* 219, 242
Artemidorus 239, 249
Assyria, viewed as part of Persia 109–10
*astynomoi* 59, 76–7
Athanasius, Patriarch of Alexandria
  259, 275–6, 283–4, 305–6; *Canons of*
  259–60
Athenaeus, *Deipnosophistae* 212–13
Atomus, Cypriot Jewish magician 224
Augustine, Bishop of Hippo 40, 206,
  307–11; *Confessions* 285

Babylonia, *see* Persia
Bar-Jesus, Cypriot Jewish magician
  223–4
Basil 258–9, 261, 303
*baskania, see* Evil Eye
Beirut 263–7
Berosus 101–2
binding-spell (*katadesis, katadesmos,
  defixio, devotio*) 17–18, 32, 48, 99, 259,
  291–2

CPSIA information can be obtained
at www.ICGtesting.com
Printed in the USA
ISOW03n1124051116
5995FS